LETS GO RPG & R

The IBM i & AS/400

RPG & RPGIV

Programmer's
Guide

AS/400 and IBM i RPG & RPG IV Concepts, Coding Examples & Exercises

– A Comprehensive Book of updated Information and RPG examples for the new and experienced AS/400 and IBM i on Power Systems Application Developer –

BRIAN W. KELLY

Referenced Material : *The information in this book has been obtained through personal and third party observations, interviews, and copious research and analysis. Where unique information has been provided or extracted from other sources, those sources are acknowledged within the text of the book itself. Thus, there are no formal footnotes nor is there a bibliography section. Any picture that does not have a source was taken from various sites on the Internet with no credit attached. If any picture owner would like credit in the next printing, please email the publisher.*

Published by: LETS GO PUBLISH!
Brian P. Kelly, Publisher
P.O Box 621
Wilkes-Barre, PA 18703
info@letsgopublish.com
www.letsgopublish.com
Library of Congress Copyright Information Pending

Book Cover Design by Michele Thomas; Editing by Brian P. Kelly

ISBN Information: The International Standard Book Number (ISBN) is a unique machine-readable identification number, which marks any book unmistakably. The ISBN is the clear standard in the book industry. 159 countries and territories are officially ISBN members. The Official ISBN for this book is:

978-0-9982683-1-6

The price for this work is : $29.99 USD

10	9	8	7	6	5	4	3	2	1

Release Date: October 2006, October 2016

Table of Contents

Preface:

This book was origianlly built to be a textbook for university, college, and community college level courses for both the RPG/400 and RPGIV programming languages. The finished product is much more than that. It is also a tutorial, a by-example guide, as well as a complete reference for all IBM i on Power SystemsRPG based application development

Finally, there is one book—a Developer's Guide for IBM i on Power Systems. Both RPG & RPGIV programming are fully covered in this text. The book was originally developed in pocket-book form but in its latest revision at pocket size, it was literally too big toprint. It is far too extensive in this version to use the smaller book size. It may not be in big pocket guide form any more but it is still tutorial in nature and all the goodies are in one books. Take a look at the Table of Contents.

Along with the tutorials to help you learn the language, this guide is also packed with reference material so you do not have to switch to a new book once you learn the language. For example, there is all the reference help you need to be able to use every op-code in RPG/400 and RPGIV as well as mostly all of the built-in functions BIF that you may ever need to use. If you are looking for how to use the new RPGIV keywords and the exclusive 'D' Spec, it's got that too!

There are lots of RPG books but there has never been an RPG book like this. Instead of arguing about the merits of RPG/400, the cycle, and the modern feel of ILE RPG, this book teaches it all. You'll be pleased with all the valuable explanations and examples. You won't want to put down this comprehensive guide to learning all forms of AS/400 and IBM i RPG programming now that you've got your hands on it. This book is almost 50 years overdue.

In today's IT landscape, most AS/400 and IBM i shops support both RPG and ILE RPG. Besides its down-home writing style, the major benefit of this book is that it is built as an essential text for anyone charged with the responsibility of maintaining and extending RPG code at all levels. And that means a new approach to the historical cycle, RPG/400, basic and advanced RPGIV, Eval and extended Factor 2 operations, prototypes and procedures, free form RPG and, of course embedded SQL. It's all in there – from the simple to the sublime. This Guide has an example for nearly every type of RPG operation you can imagine from interactive workstation code to subfiles, to database and device operations.

Author Brian Kelly designed this book to show you how to use RPG by working with rich examples that you'll use over and over again. Additionally, for each example, there is the exact explanation you need to get a head start on being an RPG guru. This is the first RPG book to hand to your new developers and veterans alike. More importantly, it is the right size text for any relevant modern business programming course at your nearby university or community college.

Both entry level and existing programmers will enjoy the easy to read, down home style of this pocket guide. The book gives a general notion of how programming systems work and it shows how to begin developing and maintaining code to help get you started in learning RPG. Even if you are new to AS/400 and IBM i, and you want to understand how to use RPG for programs that you now code in other languages, you can learn all you need to get the job done right from this pocket book. It is written in a way that assumes very little prior RPG or even generic programming knowledge.

Go ahead and leaf through this book now. You'll see it is chocked full of examples. Many screen shots are included so you can code the RPG examples in the book right along with your AS/400 or IBM i on Power Systemsserver.

Who Should Read this book?

New programmers, existing programmers, supervisors, operation personnel, or any other person in your organization who need to know how to program in basic or advanced RPG/400 or RPGIV. Many IT managers today are looking for ways to educate other staff in IBM i RPG. Look no further. If you plan to train operations people or PC people as AS/400 developers, or you want to help your staff better understand the marvels of IBM i RPG business-oriented programming, this is the right book.

With all of the smart PC technicians in every business and institution today, there are many who would appreciate the opportunity to learn the major IBM i on Power Systemsbusiness programming language – RPG/400 and/or RPGIV. Many of these would do very well as programmers if redeployed. This book can be all you need to move them off the mark.

If you've always wanted to be able to tell your team what you know about RPG, ILE, RPGIV, and embedded SQL programming on the AS/400 and IBM i on Power Systems, but you did not have the time, rest assured that Brian Kelly has done it for you with this book. He's said what you would have said if you had the time to say it. Moreover, the folks at LETS GO PUBLISH think you'll like what you would have said.

Consider creating a home-made RPG programmer with a minimal start-up investment. It may be a good deal for you and for your company.

Though rich in content, none of IBM's RPG reference and user manuals are built to teach you the language. They are for reference. There is way too much in IBM's manuals to learn it all but they are great detail references for specific topics. This Pocket Guide for RPG uses a different approach. It is your teaching / learning vehicle to RPG. It is your new tool to help you solve programming problems efficiently with RPG coding. Once you have learned how to program in RPG, the completeness of this book permits it to also serve you as a handy "pocket" reference and as a guide for using new techniques.

There is no doubt that RPG and RPGIV together represent the finest business programming language ever developed. I wish you well in your RPG business programming endeavors, and I hope to see you again reading another Lets Go Publish Pocket Guide in the future.

Feel free to shop for the original version of this book and other LET'S GO PUBLISH! Books at BookHawkers (www.bookhawkers.com). This version of the book is available only at Amazon, Kindle and the fine booksellers to whom they distribute.

Brian P. Kelly, Publisher
Wilkes-Barre, Pennsylvania

About the Author

Brian W. Kelly retired as a 30-year IBM Midrange Systems Engineer in 1999. While with IBM, he was also a Certified Instructor and a Mid-Atlantic Area Designated Specialist. When IBM began to move its sales and support to Business Partners, he formed Kelly Consulting in 1992 as an IT education and consulting firm. Kelly developed numerous AS/400 professional courses over the years that range from soup to nuts.

He has written 88 books with better tha half of them on advanced IT topics. He has also written hundreds of articles with many about current IT topics. These include articles for The Four Hundred, Midrange Computing, Showcase, News/400, AS/400 Systems Management, AS/400 Internet Expert, Computer Business News, Search400, and others. Kelly has also developed and taught a number of college courses and recently retired as a member of the Business / IT faculty at Marywood University in Scranton, Pennsylvania, where he also served as IBM I technical advisor to the IT faculty.

Chapter 1 Introduction to the RPG Language

What is RPG?

RPG is one of the few languages that was originally created for punch card machines that is still in common use today. Today's most modern RPG version is known both as RPGIV and as ILE RPG. Though RPGIV can run many of the programs designed in the 1960's, this new RPG language is with little doubt the most functionally complete programming language of all time. Originally developed by IBM in 1960 to run on the very popular IBM 1401 business computer, IBM has continued to extend the RPG standard so that it stands well ahead of all other modern languages.

RPG began as an acronym for **Report Program Generator**, which was descriptive of the original purpose of the language: *generation of reports* from data files, including matching record and sub-total reports. IBM engineers took pains to make the 1950's 1401 computer system easy to program by those trained to work with the punched card equipment that was prevalent in those days. This simple language called RPG made it easy to automate routine processes, and to print results on standard tabular forms.

RPG was not created to be a general-purpose programming language. Many consider this the basis for its power. Underlying every early RPG program was the 407 Accounting Machine sequencing algorithm, hardwired into the software, relieving the programmer of the burden of controlling the input process procedurally. Early textbooks called RPG a problem oriented language because it was designed to solve simple business problems – especially reporting. These texts compared RPG to COBOL, which was characterized as a procedural language in which the programmer used input output commands inside of the program to perform the functions that were inherent automatically in the RPG language. Thus, early COBOL programs were always substantially longer than early RPG programs.

The RPG programming language initially used fixed-format cards. When the cards had been used within the context of the 407 Accounting Machine, the control panel would pick up the data from various card columns, perhaps add the data to accumulators and then print a line on a report. By mimicking this electromechanical machine, original RPG programming was little more than a fill-in-the-blanks operation. For example, if columns 47-53 of a transaction card held a part number, which was used as a control field, a two character designation in RPG was all you had to provide to make it happen.

Early RPG purists believe that versions of RPG after the first version (RPG II to RPG IV) were corrupted by the pressure to turn RPG into a general-purpose programming language. Many who worked with the early versions were able to use and to study its sheer simplicity and elegance before this aspect was diminished with the many enhancements over the years. For the purists, the enhancements came at the expense of the simplicity that had been originally built into the language from its origins as a software replacement for IBM's big tabulating accounting machines.

In many ways, the design of the original RPG language had many similarities to what are called fourth generation languages or 4GL languages. In fact, just as most if not all 4GL's, the original RPG met with its greatest resistance from those programmers who wanted to control all aspects of the programs they wrote. Understanding what a language was going to do for them and merely filling in the blanks was not something to which the experienced programmers of the day were ready to adapt.

Creating New RPG Programmers

In the 1960's the supply of programmers was not very deep so IBM and other companies trying to gain a computer sale would often have to sell the business prospect on the idea of creating its own programmer(s). Sometimes it was the shipping clerk; sometimes it was the head order taker; sometimes it was a bookkeeper, and sometimes it was a woman or man picking or packing items in the warehouse. Once the "programmer" was selected, his or her life changed substantially.

Instead of their former position responsibilities, they were now on the forefront of the computer revolution. As a trusted employee of the organization, they were trained to understand the business computer of the day and the computer language that best fit the computer. This selection often overwhelmed the individual selected but soon, they knew that something good had just happened to them.

In small businesses in which IBM's "Marketing Representatives" had convinced the business executives that they too could benefit from automation, the programming language most often selected was none other than RPG. This language was better accepted by those just learning about computers as a means to create grassroots solutions for the businesses that had given them this phenomenal opportunity to learn about computers. Once introduced to RPG, the neophytes knew they could master its intricacies and they could use its simplicity to help their organization. They were not computer professionals by design but by destiny they were soon to be.

From their humble beginnings, however, they were not concerned about the latest and greatest in programming facility or function. They did, however, want to know how they could best help the organization become successful using the computer system that had been selected. Those programmers selected in this fashion, and there are many, embraced the RPG language as a means of making their respective organizations successful because they could readily understand what it would take to make it happen. RPG was the intuitive business language that helped many of these initial pioneers believe that they could become professional business programmers. And, they did!

Non-RPG Programmers

During this same time, there were also many engineers and scientists who had begun to tinker with computer technology. These professionals did not necessarily understand a debit from a credit or a pick list from a payroll stub. Moreover, they were hoping that nobody would come by any time soon with an explanation of these that made sense. They simply were not tuned into the business of business.

Being math or science oriented, they flocked to the notion of assembly language (almost as primitive as computer machine language). They also fell in love with the FORTRAN language. FORTRAN comes from the two words *Formula* and *Translation* and this language was created by engineers for engineers. With these tools, they were able to solve problems using simultaneous linear equations and other complex mathematical notations that would have taken days in the past. These soon-to-be computer science types had no inclination to program business applications, nor were they attracted to anything that the business oriented RPG language had to offer.

IBM Leads the RPG Way

IBM quickly became the leader in business application programming. Not only did Big Blue create the RPG language for small businesses but it also perfected COBOL (Common Business Oriented Language) for its mainframe computers. Though Big Blue did offer RPG for mainframes and it eventually offered COBOL for smaller business machines, RPG became the dominant business language for small to medium sized businesses and COBOL became the dominant business language for larger businesses. First RPG was built for the 1401, then the System/360 model 20 and then the System/3.

The Minicomputer Revolution

While IBM was perfecting the notion of business computing on its small business line headed by the System/3 and then its mainframe line with the System/370, a new breed of computer systems became very popular without any help from IBM. Companies such as DEC, Hewlett-Packard, Wang, and Data General sprang up and took the engineering / scientific world by storm. These machines cost one third or less of the price of an IBM System/370 and unlike IBM's processing power-challenged System/3 line, they ran engineering and scientific programs quite well.

Moreover, because these minicomputers were in the price range of s System/3 and even much less, businesses began to use these machines to perform routine business applications. The hardware vendors helped this trend by building their own version of RPG and they added all of IBM's System 3 and later small business machine customers to their prospect list. During these days, I can remember IBM using the term, "They're eating our lunch," to describe how well the minicomputer vendors were doing in traditional IBM business computer territory.

Though many of the machines provided RPG, it was not the favorite language of the engineers and scientists who often ran the computer departments or the departments in which minicomputer class machines were installed. To be frank, it was not even on the list. Instead of RPG, they advocated such lower level computer science type languages as C, Pascal, and BASIC. These came into being and soon became pervasive on the minicomputers of the day.

IBM Not Popular in Higher Education

Nobody can say for sure what came first, the chicken or the egg. However, over the last thirty or more years -- perhaps dating back even thirty-years sooner to Harvard's snub of Thomas Watson Sr. re: the Harvard / IBM Mark I Computer in the 1940's, colleges and universities have not held IBM or its products in especially high regard. Do academics dislike IBM because the company has traditionally made its living using languages such as RPG or COBOL; or do the academics dislike RPG and COBOL, especially the IBM-defined RPG, because they are made by IBM. These questions are at the center of the debate.

Regardless of the reason, there has been little love between IBM and the computer science community in academia for quite some time. Overall, this has hurt IBM to a degree but it has also hurt IT students expecting to be able to be employed in a mostly IBM-oriented business world without having been given the proper business programming credentials.

It is no wonder that the minicomputer quickly became the best friend of the computer-oriented academic community. Colleges and Universities began to stock their new Computer Science programs with the minicomputers of the 1970's rather than IBM System/370s or System/3s that were available at the time. The apparent bias for these new minicomputers was so strong that IBM was often not even invited to propose its solutions to higher learning institutions. Thus, more and more computer specialists emerged from colleges and universities without ever having been introduced to RPG business programming. Yet record computer purchases from companies across the world kept making IBM's RPG-driven business computers the leaders in the industry.

RPG Kills the Minicomputer Revolution

Though RPG has proven itself well over the years, providing the production data processing for many successful companies, using IBM's small-business computer lines, the unwarranted bias from academia and from the computer science community continues. RPG and now RPGIV is the last language to be considered in computer science departments.

Despite this fact, until the mid 1990's, IBM's new account marketing engine with the RPG-oriented AS/400 as its major tool, absolutely defeated all of the minicomputers that ever existed: DEC, Data General, Wang, and others. One must ask how wrong the academicians must have been to embrace technology that was so easily defeated by IBM in the business world, where the computing rubber actually meets the road.

Did the rigidity of the academic computer science community against IBM's unique business computing approach help or hurt students in these institutions? Clearly it hurt students looking for a well-paying computer position in industry. For IBM to overcome the disadvantage of graduating students not being familiar with its best-selling products, the company developed its own courses and its own education centers and companies trained non-degreed personnel to fill the jobs that would have been easily gained by knowledgeable students. In many academic computer programs today, this anti-IBM scenario persists and students continue to be short-changed on higher-paying job prospects than those available in the entry Windows market.

IBM's victory over all minicomputer vendors was so complete that even the mighty Hewlett Packard had to give up on its own proprietary line of computers. Even before its merger with COMPAQ, who had bought-out DEC several years earlier, HP had become mostly known as a small printer company. IBM's System/36, System/38, and finally its 1988-introduced AS/400 lines and today's IBM i on Power Systemswon the day for Big Blue and the business oriented RPG language was the major weapon to help make that happen.

Chapter Summary

RPG is one of the few languages that was originally created for punch card machines that is still in common use today. First christened **Report Program Generator**, and then plain old RPG, the original purpsose was *generation of reports* from data files

The original RPG programming language used only a fixed processing cycle it was designed to process cards. In many ways, the design of the original RPG language had many similarities to what are called fourth generation languages or 4GL languages.

Many early RPG programmers were taken from other areas of the business and trained. This placed these computer neophytes into the forefront of the computer revolution – right alongside the computer scientists in some cases. The latter were not so fond of the RPG language

IBM used RPG to win the minicomputer revolution putting all but HP out of business. Though it was popular in business because of its ease of use characteristics, RPG was not well loved by the academic world and many of these same sentiments exist in academia today.

Key Chapter Terms

407 Accounting Machine	Electromechanical	RPG II
4GL	FORTRAN	RPG standard
Academia	Hewlett Packard	Small business, 4, 5
AS/400	Higher Education	System/3
Business computing	IBM 140	System/360
Business language	Mark	System/370
COBOL	Minicomputer revolution	System/38
COMPAQ	purists, RPG	Thomas Watson
Computer science	Report Pgm Generator	Universities
DEC		

Review Questions:

1. RPG was originally built for what type of machines?

2. What attribute of the RPG language separates it from all other languages and why?

3. RPG stands for.

4. Is / Was RPG a general purpose programming language? Why? / Why not?

5. Why do some suggest that RPG is a fourth generation programming language?

6. Were early RPG programmers trained by colleges and Universities?

7. How did the computer science community feel about RPG?

8. Why was RPG successful?

Chapter 2   The History of the RPG Language

Filling in the Blanks

In describing RPG, I touched on a few of the historical aspects of the language. In this section, it's time to fill in the blanks to better present the origins of a language known as much for its strong business capabilities and success as it is for the legions of computer science types and hackers who refuse to touch it.

In the Beginning

The beginning of data processing as we know it in the modern era actually began back in the 1890s, some 25 years before Tom Watson Sr.'s, coming as an outsider from NCR Corporation to become General Manager of IBM. Watson would waste no time taking over the IBM Company as its CEO. While toiling in the 1890's trying to solve a major dilemma of the US Census department in getting its once a decade census tabulated in less than ten years. Herman Hollerith found a solution that would keep the IBM company going for over sixty years. While working for the Computing Tabulating and Recording Company (CTR) one of the predecessor companies of which IBM was founded, he devised a machine to tabulate punched cards to help complete the 1890 census and save the day for the Census Department.

His invention led to many similar and complimentary products by IBM over the next sixty or more years until the company launched its first computer in the 1950's. But, way before the 1950's, IBM was content making a killing selling what the company called tabulating equipment and which the industry simply referred to as "Tab" machines. In 1934, for example, IBM introduced its 405 Alphabetical Accounting Machine. This was IBM's high-end Tab offering, and by the way, it was the first one to be called an "Accounting Machine."

Fixed Cycle Accounting Machines

The 405 was "programmed" by a removable plug board with over 1600 functionally significant "hubs," with access to up to 16 accumulators. This high end mechanical monster could tabulate at a rate of 150 cards per minute (cpm), or tabulate and print at 80 cpm. The print unit contained 88 type bars, the leftmost 43 for alphanumeric characters and the other 45 on the right for digits only. The 405 was IBM's flagship product until after World War II. In fact, during the war, retrofitted 405s were used not only as tabulators but also as the print device for top-secret relay calculators built by IBM for the US Army Signal Corps. They were used for decrypting German and Japanese coded messages. Eventually, IBM introduced a model 402, model 403, and a more advanced model 407 for businesses in the 1950's. All of these models were big revenue producers for the IBM Company and they helped many business operations become more efficient.

In the late 1950's to the early part of the 1970's while IBM was beginning to focus on its emerging computer lines, the company was still renting these behemoths to smaller and smaller companies. It was not until 1969 that IBM formally replaced its Tab line with its diskless all-card System/3 and its miniature 96-column card. For a number of years thereafter, IBM's new account sales personnel sold first time computer users on the IBM Tab line since these old war horses rented for about half of what a System/3 cost. After all, IBM only permitted its customers to rent its machines back then so the longer one of those electromechanical marvels was doing its job, the more profitable the experience was for IBM.

Because of its similarity to a 405 machine cycle, the RPG cycle was the key to making the language an initial success. The cycle enabled processes during which an RPG program automatically read a record and performed certain routines. This fixed cycle was at the heart of file processing. Unlike other high-level languages, RPG didn't require a lot of work with file declarations for opening and closing files, and working with files, nor did it require a complex list of instructions to simply print data. The infamous RPG cycle took care of all that for the programmer. Those who learned how to work with the cycle were far more productive than those programmers who worked with other languages.

The Four RPGs

So, with the IBM 1130 and the disk enhancements to the System/3, the RPG language compiler as originally announced for the 1401 was enhanced and re-announced as RPG II. From the very early RPG I language introduced to mimic the electromechanical machines, IBM has been continually improving the language. Historically, these improvements have brought four different RPG languages to market.

RPG I

Prior to RPG II of course, with RPG I and the 1401, the programmer used the many statement types defined by the RPG language to interface with what we now refer to as a "fixed logic cycle." With the fixed logic cycle and the RPG code as "written" by the programmer, the 1401 computer could pretend that it really was a 407-style accounting machine and that the program as devised by the programmer provided the variables and logic in much the same fashion as the removable wired circuit panel of its electromechanical predecessor.

RPG II Adds More Capabilities

RPG appeared first on the 1130 in 1965 and soon after it was available for the System/360 Model 20 through the end of the 1960s. As the third system to pack RPG in its arsenal, IBM's 1969 introduction of its Ssytem/3, the new RPG II programming language something that had to be noticed.

Though the 1130 had a fine RPGII compiler, the machine was marketed by IBM as a scientific computer, having superseded IBM's long standing 1620 unit. When the 1130 was equipped with an RPG II compiler, however, it became a very capable business machine. The IBM plan did not think it had any business-only customers looking for success by installing an IBM 1130 unit. However, the orders came and IBM did not refuse these orders. With RPG II as a business mainstay, the 1130 became far more popular than it would have ever been with just FORTRAN as its guiding light.

In 1977 the WORKSTN device was a real phenomenon. IBM defined the notion of a display screen. The displays screen was defined externally to the program and was manipulated within the program using normal RPG operations against screen names. An extension was added to the RPG File description specification to permit what was called a format member to be compiled along with the program. From this member, the programmer could select screen names for output / input to interact with a user.

Prior to the native WORKSTN device support for the System/34, display terminals were not ever integrated into compilers. In fact, terminals were supported only via special add-on support in the form of the Communication Control Program (System/3 CCP) or the Customer Information Control System (System/370 CICS). Both CCP and CICS had their own system generation process and specialized operation codes such as Get and Put. Moreover, these tools required skills above and beyond that of a normal programmer. The WORKSTN file was so easy to use that many who had become adept at CCP or CICS could not believe that it could possibly work. It worked, and it made the RPG language the easiest to use for business full screen at a time interactive processing.

RPG III

In 1978, IBM announced a machine that was so elegant architecturally that it would take the company almost another two years to deliver its first customer's shipment. It was called the IBM System/38 and it was a minicomputer class machine but IBM liked to call it a small business computer. The System was built to be the replacement box for the IBM System/3. It was clearly the most advanced general-purpose computer of its day, complete with a built-in relational-like database management system and natural workstation facilities that were far better than even the System/34.

With the System/38, IBM introduced the RPG III language which brought a host of new functions to the language, among these, a nearly complete set of structured programming operations (e.g., IF-THEN-ELSE, DO). With these new features, programmers were able to define RPG programs which did not require understanding a hint of the RPG cycle. IBM did not eliminate the RPG cycle with the System/38 and in fact, along with all file input/output facilities, the cycle was enhanced to use externally described files.

The System/38 permitted the input and output of files to be described externally such as in a workstation file object or a database file object. At compile time, the programmer merely added a switch in the File Description Specification to tell the compiler that the input and output specs for a file were to be obtained from an external object (the file itself). The compiler would then dutifully go to the object and bring the specs into the program, provide them in the compiler listing and make them available for use within the program. This saved the programmer massive amounts of time.

In 1988, IBM introduced the AS/400 and the company provided another new compiler called RPG/400. Because of the many flavors of RPG that were currently being used, IBM packaged all of its exiting compilers into this new edition. Thus, on the new IBM AS/400, the RPG compilers that were available included the following:

1. RPG38 System/38-compatible RPG III.
2. RPG36 System/36-compatible RPG II.
3. RPG AS/400-compatible RPG III. Known as RPG/400
There was and still is little discernable difference between the System/38 RPGIII and the AS/400 RPG III. (RPG/400)

RPG IV – Best Language on any Platform

In 1994, IBM introduced the first significant update to the RPG language in more than 15 years—ILE RPG a.k.a. RPG IV. The introduction of RPG IV marked the first time ever that the RPG specifications had been significantly revamped. A new data definition specification was added and the long suffering File Extension specification form was eliminated from the new language.

With RPG IV, IBM also eliminated virtually all of the perceived limitations of previous versions of RPG. With RPG IV, for example, there are natural expressions in the language. Mathematics and conditioning capabilities were enhanced and leading edge DATE and TIME arithmetic operations have been made available. .

This latest version of RPG is, by far, the richest language in existence. Though it is more capable and therefore more complex that the RPG of the 1960's, it is still easy to learn and it offers a ton of functions for day-to-day, general-purpose business applications. With its reasonably new free form facilities and its many built in functions, and its effective use of subprocedures for modular programming, RPGIV also has an affinity to the block structured languages used within the computer science community. As such, it makes it easier for IBM i on Power Systemsprogramming shops to train today's college graduates for a career as a IBM i on Power Systems IT professional. Moreover, with RPGIV, the concepts learned are applicable to other programming languages.

So, in 1994 with version 3 Release 1 for CISC and in 1995 with Version 3 Release 6 for RISC architecture, IBM brought forth its fourth major release of RPG. Dubbed RPG IV by those who use, the official name is ILE RPG, recognizing its dependence on the more advanced Integrated Language Environment in which it prospers.

RPGIV Improvements

In addition to the enhancements made in i6.1 through i7.2 and since, which are included in the last chapter of this book, some of the improvements to RPG with RPG IV include the following:

1. New 'D' Specification: In addition to the specifications for RPG/400, IBM introduced a new specification form called the Definition 'D' spec. All non-external data definitions can now be coded using the new 'D' spec that is new to ILE RPG. In addition you can define "named constants" that greatly simplify coding these in the C-spec's. Also C-spec formats have changed slightly to provide for variable names of up to 10 characters (up from 6 in RPG/400) and longer operation codes.

2. New Operations: Several new operations have been added. One that provided the ability to code math in a formula-like fashion is the EVAL operation. In essence it permits you to evaluate a mathematical expression similar to COBOL and other mathematical programming languages such as Basic, FORTRAN, PL/1, etc.

3. Modularity: With ILE, you can now write modules (non-executable) in several languages and bind them together into a single ILE program. This program can be an RPG IV program. You can also use RPG modules in other language programs. Thus you can use the best language (ILE C, ILE COBOL, ILE RPG, ILE CLP) for a process or you can use existing modules to write a program.

4. Larger size fields: With RPGIV, the RPG spec has been widened to 100 characters to accommodate up to ten character field names and larger operation codes.

5. Date fields / operations: One of the first major differentiations between RPG/400 and RPGIV is the new compiler's ability to deal with the date data type. For example operations exist to subtract a duration from a date and get a duration or to subtract two dates and have the result presented as a duration.

6. Procedures: IBM has also built into the language the notion of callable procedures – implemented with subprocedures and functions.

7. Built-In Functions (BIFs): Many built-in functions or BIFS have been added to the RPGIV language including *%date, % days, %months, %years, %diff, %abs, %editc, %subdt, %DEC, %INT, %UNS, %FLOAT, %error.*

8. Free format RPG specifications: We may joke that this is not your father's RPG because it isn't. In fact, with RPG FREE form, IBM has given the RPG programmer the opportunity to code without the typical columnar boundaries of RPG/400. As an added benefit, IBM has also provided the ability to add free-form SQL statements within the RPG language to make RPG an even friendlier language for those who choose to use embedded SQL for database access.

The Once and Future RPG

IBM continues to enhance RPGIV for IBM i on Power Systems. Yet, the enhanced language is not available on any other platform. Industry consultants have suggested to IBM that it make this very powerful business language available on all of its platforms. Consultants have also suggested to IBM that since RPGIV is more than ten years old, it is time fro IBM to rename RPG. The natural next name, of course would be RPG V but some have suggested that IBM give the language a name that releases it from its "legacy" status.

From its name, the computer science community has pegged RPG as an old language and it is tough for RPG developers to get from under that label. Thus, an all-out assault by IBM is being requested in which three major changes need to occur with the language.

1. New name that includes both business and power connotations – such as The All-Business language.

2. Availability on all other platforms from PC servers to UNIX, Linux, and mainframe boxes. After all, it is IBM's best business language.

3. Natural Web operations within the language specification in the form of a browser device file and op codes to send and receive Web pages of any form – HTML, XML, JSP, JSF, etc.

IBM, are you listening?

Chapter Summary

The data processing era formally began when Herman Hollerith, an IBM scientist found a solution for the 1890 census using punched cards. The cycle based accounting machines that printed the tabulated card data were the precursors to the RPG I language and its fixed cycle style of processing.

IBM systems from the 1401 on, such as the 1130, System/3, System/34, and System/ 36 were all equipped with RPG as standard fare. Even IBM mainframes had a version of RPG

From its beginnings as a problem oriented language, RPG has evolved into a full-featured procedural language with numerous enhancements over the almost 50 years of its existence. Some of the most noteworthy enhancements to the language over the years include the following:

- ✓ Operations outside the cycle
- ✓ WORKSTN file
- ✓ Integrated database Operations
- ✓ Device files such as Display Files
- ✓ Structured operations
- ✓ Date and time Operations
- ✓ Subprocedures
- ✓ Built-In Functions
- ✓ Free-format RPG

Key Chapter Terms

%FLOAT	DEC	Named constants
%INT	Device	Natural expressions
%UNS	Disk processing	NCR Corporation
1890 census	Display devices	Old language
3340 disk drives	Display file	Purists
407 Accounting Machine	Display screen	Random
5444 disk drives	DO	Real pgm language
5445 disk drives	EVAL	Release, 10
5496 Data Recorder	EXCPT	RPG fixed logic cycle
96-column cards	External data definitions	RPG II

All-Business language	Externally described data	RPG III
BIFs	Field names	RPGIV
Block struct. languages	Fixed cycle	RPG-only machine
Built-in functions	FORTRAN	Screen name
Business language	FREE operation	SET
Card hoppers	Free format RPG	Small business
Card reader	Hackers	Structured operations
CCP	Herman Hollerith	Subprocedures
CHAIN	IBM 1130	System/3
CICS	IBM 1401	System/34
CISC	IF-THEN-ELSE	System/370
Compile	ILE	System/38
Computer science	Interpreting	TAB equipment
CTR	Keypunch	Transistor
'D' spec	Marywood University	Unit-record system
Database file	Mercy Hospital	Variables
Database Mgt.	MFCU	WORKSTN
DATE and TIME	Model	

Review Questions

1. What major event in history signaled the beginning of the data processing era.

2. What major event in history signaled the beginning of IBM as a formidable data processing power.

3. What is a fixed cycle accounting machine?

4. What was the first IBM machine to use RPG?

5. Which IBM machine had no disk when it was introduced and its only language was RPG II?

6. Which scientific machine was used for business purposes because of the RPGII language?

7. What are the four RPGs?

8. Why is RPGII better than RPG?

9. Which system first was able to use terminals in a program as a real device?

10. Why was the RPG WORKSTN device looked upon as revolutionary for its day?

11. What major difference is there between RPGII and RPGIII?

12. What is the difference between a display file and a System/34 screen format member?

13. What differentiates RPGIV from RPGIII (RPG/400)?

14. Why do many believe that RPGIV is the best language ever created?

15. Are there things that today do not exist in RPG that would be very helpful to the RPG programming community?

Chapter 3   Understanding the RPG Fixed Logic Cycle

Cycle Operations Are OK!

When RPG got its first face lift in the mid 1960's with RPG II demand (out-of-cycle) operations, the RPG language purists were those who wanted the cycle to be fully preserved at all costs. They were not happy that RPG had lost its innocence and was on its way to becoming a real programming language.

Ironically, those who would be called RPG purists today are those who want to keep RPG on the bleeding edge of compiler functionality. Prior to V5R4, for example, there had been clamor in these ranks for more built-in functions, such as those available in Java and there was insistence that IBM provide a move corresponding type operation in much the same fashion as that available in COBOL. In response, IBM added these features to RPGIV. This group is driving the RPG language in a similar way to PL/1 from the 1970's. PL/1 was to be the language of languages with the best features from all other languages. RPG may very well become that one language that offers the full gamut of compiler innovations.

In the latest enhancements, the language draws new facility from both Java and COBOL, two completely different languages. With all of the new facilities being placed with the RPGIV language, perhaps the ultimate destiny for RPG is even more than the All-Business Language moniker that many of us would like. The Once and Future RPG may very well become the All-Everything Language just as the **IBM i on Power Systems** itself has become the All-Everything machine.

I mention the new purists because they would not approve of me first presenting the RPG cycle in this book or even presenting it at all. These modern purists have wrestled RPG away from its roots so far that many would be pleased that its roots disappear. They would not approve of 4GL or 5GL languages either since their world needs to include pointers and heavy duty built in functions that rival the most complex languages of today.

Despite the purists, I begin this technical work with the RPG cycle because (1) it affords me the opportunity to examine the meaning of the specifications in the RPG/400 language right along with the RPG cycle; (2) Many RPG/400 cycle programs in RPG shops continue to be used and continue to need maintenance; (3) Even those shops that have converted to RPGIV for new development still use the RPG IV cycle for those programs that were migrated since RPGIV fully supports the RPG cycle; and (4) For applications that must produce printed reports, the RPG cycle still provides the most efficient means of report writing short of using 4GL tools. For report-writing in fact, RPG with the fixed logic cycle in use is very much a 4GL unto itself.

A Quick Look at the RPG Cycle

Long before programmers learn their first language, they are introduced to computer concepts. Within the notion of basic computer concepts is the notion of INPUT > PROCESS >OUTPUT as shown in Figure 3-1

Figure 3-1 Input Process & Output

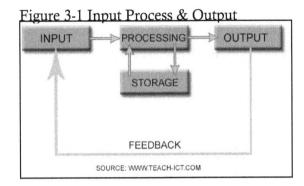

SOURCE: WWW.TEACH-ICT.COM

Just about any computer program that you will ever write accepts input, processes the input, and produces a report of some kind. The report may be a line on a screen or a full display panel or a real business report. Moreover, as you can see in Figure 3-1, in addition to producing output in the form of a report or display, a program also can store data in database files (storage) for future use.

So, whether you write the cycle yourself in every program or you choose to use the IBM RPG fixed logic cycle, which by the way is excellent for report-writing, your code will behave as if it is in a big INPUT> PROCESS> OUTPUT cycle for in fact, it is.

So, it is no wonder that the very first data processing machines, the electromechanical behemoths from the 1930's were hard wired to this cycle. It is also no wonder why the first RPG compiler, written to emulate these machines was soft-wired to this cycle. And, because it eliminates coding if you know what you are doing, it is no wonder that RPG programmers for years had no problem using the RPG cycle for their most complex reporting functions.

Report Headings

So, now let's take a look at the RPG cycle so we can understand just what it is all about. Before we do that, however, I would like you to think of what the first thing that a report writing program might do – even before it reads or processes any data. If you guessed that it may put out report titles for the first page of the report since they do not depend on any data being read, you are correct. And, if you carried this notion one step further and suggested that they also prepare the titles so that they can be put out on top of every other page in the report, you would be correct again.

The RPG cycle is built so that report titles are a natural part of the language and they occur first. Thus as difficult as it may be to realize at first, output happens before input at the beginning of each RPG cycle from the first through the end of the program. Rather than start with input, it starts with output thereby giving the program the opportunity to get those titles on the report before the first data is read.

With that as a backdrop, and without further ado, let's take a look at the RPG cycle first shown in Figure 3-2.

Figure 3-2 The 7 Major Steps of the RPG Fixed Logic Cycle

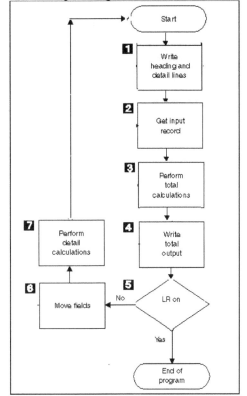

The various work components of the RPG cycle as shown in Figure 3-2 are as follows:

Step 1 – Write Heading and Detail Lines

1A. For reports, first page headings that you specify are printed.

1B. For reports, overflow headings that you specify are printed. Overflow headings are those headings that are repeated on each page after the prior page hits a bottom of the page overflow

1C. Detail output is printed. On the first cycle, since no data has been read, there is no detail data to print. Detail output consists of any output line that can be written or updated to any device – printer, disk, tape, etc. Data fields that are read during the input part of the cycle in Step 2 are held in memory as variables and are not made available to the program until Step 6. These variables may be operated upon in calculations and their contents can be modified. New variables can be defined within calculations and these can store the result of operations. The newly defined variables as well as the input variables or the modified input variables as well as constants can be placed in the output record that is written.

It helps to repeat that since no input data is available during the output part of the first fixed cycle the program produce no output during the first output time of the cycle. If you follow this logic, it also says that any input that is read that must be printed will not print until the next output time in the cycle. Thus, data read on the first cycle in step 2 is not available for output until at the beginning of the second RPG cycle at step 1.

Step 2-- Get Input Data

2. The first record is read from the primary file. Though the record has been read, however, RPG does not make the data available to the program until Step 6 of the cycle. When coding with the cycle this needs to be considered since in cycle 3 for example, the record read in this step of the cycle is not the record whose fields are available to the program. The prior record's data is still in the program fields until Step 6.

This may not make sense right now but it will as you study the next parts of the cycle which include total calculations and total output. When RPG is finishing up the totals for a group of data, this event has been triggered by the cycle knowing that the record about to be read into the fields for processing is the first record of a new group. In Step 2, RPG learns that the next record is from a different group. When writing reports, this means it is time to perform any special calculations that must be done at this time of the cycle (step 3) and then it is time to write out the totals (step4).

In many ways, in addition to bringing the record into a buffer in memory, Step 2 is RPG peeking ahead in that buffer to see what the next record is. In this way, it "knows if" whether it should take totals or if it should keep reading records from the current group. This facility also comes in handy when doing matching records so that RPG can look ahead to see the sequence of the matches so that it knows which record to move in for processing.

Step 3 – Perform Total Calculations

3. Total calculations are then performed. Total calculations are totals that occur after major, intermediate, or minor control field breaks. Since during the first cycle, no data has been read at this point in the cycle, there will be no control level breaks and therefore, no control level calculations will be performed. However, there will be calculations whenever control fields change in subsequent cycles.

To understand how control level calculations work, consider the following example. Let's say the program is written to total gross sales by city, when the "city" control field changes. In this example the first city record is Kingston and the second is Plymouth. After the second record is read, at the start of the second cycle at step 2, this would cause a minor (least important) control break. This is also called Level 1. During the period in which the cycle provides some time for total calculations (step 3), it starts by enabling Level 1 total calculations followed by Level 2; then Level 3 until finally it reaches Level 9, the maximum number of levels as can be defined in an RPG program. In the city example, during this opportunity to take totals, the programmer would tell the RPG compiler to add the city total of gross sales to the state total of gross sales and store it for the level 2 total on state.

If we decided that we would also like state totals in this report, since the state is a higher level organization than the city, we could use the next highest control break level or L2. Then when the state changes from say Alabama (AL) to Alaska (AK), during the L1 cycle, the programmer would tell the RPG compiler to add the city totals to the state totals and during the L2 cycle, the programmer would tell the RPG compiler to add the state totals to the final total accumulator.

Step 4 -- Write Total Output

4. Total output is printed. Total output includes totals that have been accumulated, such as the field in which we store the city total and the field in which we store the state total. When the city total changes, for example, we probably want to print the total on the report with the City name next to it. This type of output would occur during the L1 output cycle. If there were no control breaks during this cycle, then no output triggered by a control indicator (L1 or L2) would be produced.

If the L2 control field changes (state in this case) that automatically means that an L1 break also occurs. (If the state changes, by definition, you can bet the city changes). So for an L2 break, L2 totals are produced as well as L1 totals. Likewise if an L9 break occurs, all other total levels from L8 to L1, in addition to L9, are prepared to produce output. Likewise if a final total occurred, it would automatically create a level break at the highest level defined in the program – L9 at the highest but just L2 in our case with State and City.

Step 5 – LR On?

5. The program checks to see if it should end by checking the LR indicator. A special "indicator" called LR causes the program to end if it is set on when all of the files that are being processed are out of records or if this indicator "LR" it is set on in detail calculations from the last cycle. When the program sees that LR is on at this point of the cycle, it ends the program gracefully and closes all of the files.

Step 6 -- Move Data from Input Area to Fields

6. Input is processed by moving input area buffer contents to the RPG fields that you defined to hold them. When RPG has completed performing level (control break) output (This can be disk, tape, card, printer or any output conditioned by a level indicator at total level time), the cycle moves to input processing time and it populates the fields in the file read in Step 2 with the data that is stored in the input buffer.

Step 6 works hand in glove with Step 2 but they occur at different times in the cycle. The following (step 7) refers to Step 2 and Step 6 as if they are one input routine. This is not how it really happens but it will help in understanding the interrelationship.

Step 7 -- Perform Detail Calculations

7. Detail calculations are performed. What are detail calculations? They are calculations that get performed when records are processed. Detail calculations are permitted to occur for each record that passes through Step 6 of the RPG cycle as shown in Figure 3-2. If, for example, each record contains the order quantity and the price, each RPG cycle as coded in the C specifications, the programmer can write code to multiply the quantity ordered by the price and

create a result field called the extended price. Since basic RPG/400 permits just names of six characters, the result field name might be called XPRICE or something else to properly reflect its meaning and the limit of six characters.

Since RPG calculations have what are called conditioning indicators, calculations are not necessarily performed each time that the program passes through the detail calculations part of the RPG fixed logic cycle. If, for example, the master and the time card records for payroll are being processed through one file, then, assuming that masters are sequenced before corresponding time card records, the programmer may wish to take action only when a time card record is read. In that way, the information from the master such as the pay rate can stored until the time card is read. Then the rate can be used when the time record is read and the program can multiply the two numbers to get the gross pay amount. To set this up, the programmer would assign a switch called an indicator to the master and an indicator to the transaction file and those RPG cycles, in which a master record is read, based on its indicator, calculations can be conditioned not to occur. Likewise, for those RPG cycles in which a time card is read, based on its indicator, calculations can be conditioned to occur.

Additional INPUT Processing Information

For example, if there is one card reader / hopper defined to the program, after RPG reads a record the cycle would keep repeating Steps 2 and 6 in turn and would in essence keep going back to read another card or disk record. If there are two card readers as in the old System/3 and both are defined in the program, or there are two disk files defined, RPG will keep going back to the first hopper or first file until it is empty or the disk file is at end of file. At this time, RPG would begin reading data from the other hopper or the second disk file until it is empty. When both hoppers are empty or the disk files are at end of file indication, RPG automatically turns on a switch called the last record indicator or LR and it declares that the program can end and then it ends the program as described in Step 5 above.

It is unusual to have two files that need to be processed and the job is such that one can be processed fully before the other is even begun. Yet, with no special coding in RPG, that is what occurs. In real business processing situations, however, the program requirements most often dictate that the records from one file be interspersed with the records from the second file.

RPG Matching Records Processing

For example, you may have master payroll records specified as *File 1*. You may have time cards specified as *File 2*.   To prepare for this computer run, which depends on both files being in sequence by say, employee number or a field called EMPNO, you would sort the both files by employee number so they are in the same sequence. Your program logic would want to be able to read the master payroll record for employee 1 and then the time card for employee1 and then it would want to read employee 2's master and then employee 2's time card and so on until all employees were processed. Once the program reads the master and the time card for each employee, it has enough information to calculate the payroll.

During the input part of the cycle in Step 2, RPG provides for a period in which two or more files of records that are all in sequence by the fields specified for the match can be read and be declared a match. In this scenario, the time cards and the employee master file would be in different card hoppers in old systems or they would be in different disk files in more modern IBM i on Power Systems units. This notion is referred to in RPG as "matching records" and it is a big plus for using the RPG cycle for report writing functions when two or more files are needed for processing. It is also handy when updating master files from transaction files.

To use the matching records facility within the RPG cycle, the programmer must have a very good understanding of the detailed RPG cycle since the needs of the program are more involved than when using just one input file. In addition to telling the compiler which file should be read first (primary file – pay master) and which should be read second (secondary file – time card), the programmer must also designate the name(s) of the field(s) that must match. In this example, the one field name is EMPNO in both files.

Designating Record Types

RPG provides a designator that can be placed next to the field names in both files within the RPG Input Specifications. In other words, the programmer must place a designator in a field from each of the files to be matched. This can be referred to as a matching designator. If there is just one field to match, then the only matching designator required is known to RPG as "M1." However, unlike the present example, which needs just one field (EMPNO), if there is more than one field that must be matched (and up to nine fields), then RPG makes available other matching designators --- M2 through M9. When more than one matching designator (M2 to M9) is specified, all match fields that are specified must be matched from each file before the special "indicator" known as "MR" for match indicator is as we say, "turned on."

So, let's say in our simple example that we have two files. We mark the employee number fields (EMPNO) in both files in the RPG program input specs with the M1 designator. From here on, when this program runs, RPG itself makes sure that both files are in sequence and when there is a match, it turns on a special matching switch called the matching record indicator or MR. The programmer can then use the status of this switch (on or off) to cause desired events to occur in the program that otherwise would be difficult to achieve. Additionally, if by any chance the files are found by RPG to not be in sequence by the matching designators, the program will halt with an error condition.

Record Identifying Indicator Processing

There is another phenomenon in the RPG fixed cycle called the record identifying indicator. Each time RPG reads a master record with the cycle, for example, it tells the programmer from which file it read the record by turning on an indicator that the programmer associates with the file. If RPG turns indicator 01 on for example, that may mean a master record has been read and if RPG turns on indicator 02 that may mean that a time card record has been read. This powerful, yet simple communication gives RPG a simple way of telling programs what is happening so that the program can take the proper action.

What is an indicator?

The RPG language provides a programmer with a tool box of 99 indications to use for their own purposes. The indication that a particular record type has been read can be stored in a special type of "field" called an indicator. To make it easy to remember, most programmers use various indications to change the value of the indicator fields from 0 to 1. Moreover, because these are special fields that exist in no other programming language, RPG also permits just two values in the field – either a "0" or a "1." When the value is "0," RPG programmers say the indicator (numbered 1 through 99) is "off." Just like a light switch, when the value is one, RPG programmers say that the indicator is "on." So all 99 indicators in RPG can be tested to see if they contain values of "0" or "1" as well as being tested for "on" or "off."

With the notion of indicators and the RPG cycle, the compiler provides some additional facility. If, next to the input record on the RPG Input Specification, you choose to specify an indicator to turn on if a particular record ID is read, RPG will gladly turn on that indicator if it reads a record meeting the criteria you have specified. In the time card file and master file example, since we would only have one time card for one master, it would suffice to do no testing for record contents since it is reading the data from two different files. In this scenario, we already know that if a record is read from the primary it is a master and if it is read from the secondary, it is a time card. Thus, in this two-file example, there is no further need to define markings inside the records to identify them.

So, for the record that defines the master file on the RPG Input specifications in the RPG program, the programmer assigns an indicator. Let's say the programmer choose indicator 01. Now, for the record that defines the time card in the RPG program, let's say the programmer chooses 02.

Once the programmer has done this, independent of the matching status or the reading sequence of the program, whenever the program reads a master record, regardless of its EMPNO value, record identifying indicator "01" will be turned on and record identifying indicator "02" (time card) will be off. That is because only one record identifying indicator can be on at one time. RPG processes just one record each cycle. Likewise, whenever the program reads a record from the time card file, independent of the matching status or the reading sequence of the program, and regardless of its EMPNO value, record identifying indicator "02" will be turned on and record ID indicator 01 will be turned off.

Primary and Secondary Files

The second last phenomenon that we will discuss regarding matching records is the notion of primary and secondary files. The 407 Accounting Machine had just one hopper so it did not need anything on a wiring board to signal a match from two card readers. RPG is more sophisticated. It says that one file can be designated as primary and a second file can be designated as secondary for processing purposes within a program. If there are three card readers and/or many tape and many disk devices (files) in play, then theoretically, there can be as many – even twenty or more files defined in just one program. If these files are not defined as random or keyed-access files – in other words, they are to be processed sequentially, the programmer would need to designate all but one as secondary files in terms of matching records processing. Just one file in all cases can be defined as the primary file.

Internally, based on the order of specification (Line 1 vs. Line 2) defined in the program, RPG would designate these files as tertiary, quaternary, quinary, senary, septenary, octonary, nonary etc. based upon the order in which the programmer specified them in the File Description

Specification section in RPG. In today's processing, I rarely if ever see a tertiary sequential file. Multiple files other than the primary and the designated secondary are most often defined to RPG as something other than secondary – such as keyed index files or random files. However, you may run into someone else's code in which they have chosen to use more than one secondary file for matching records purposes.

The MR Indicator

The last phenomenon in understanding the RPG cycle with matching records is that the MR indicator comes on at a certain times in the cycle as do the record identifying indicators. They are turned off by RPG at a designated time in the cycle. For the novice RPG programmer, this is really a big pain to understand. "Real programmers" and RPG purists like to be in control of the program. Great programmers however can take a powerful tool like "Matching Records," learn it inside and out, and be substantially more real and more productive than a "real programmer." More importantly, by understanding the cycle, as noted earlier in this book, programmers can get much more done in report programs than by having to write the code themselves. To be good at the cycle, however, you have to understand the cycle. You have to know when RPG does what it does. You have to understand when RPG turns on record IDs and matching indicators and when it turns them off.

For example, if the pay rate is in the master record, we know that when it is read, indicator 01, the designated master record identifying indicator, is turned on. If the next master record has the same EMPNO field value as the record just read, RPG will read another record from the master file (primary). Since we have a one to one relationship of master to time card, in this example this cannot happen – but if it does, it is an error condition.

In this example, we know that the next record that RPG will read will come from the time card file (secondary) one input cycle after the matching master was read. Right before RPG reads the record for the time card record; it cleans up its act and turns off the indicator (01) that recognized that a master had been read in the last cycle. Prior to the time card record being read then, there are no record identifying indicators in the "on" condition. When RPG goes ahead and reads the time card record from the secondary file, it turns on indicator 02.

It helps to know that RPG can actually peek ahead (Step 2 of the cycle) at the cards or sequential disk records or tape records to see what they contain even if it is not going to read them on this particular input cycle. No, I am not kidding. RPG knows for example when it reads the master record from file 1 for EMPNO # 1 that there is a matching time card record for employee 1. It already knows that because it has peeked ahead. So, even though it is processing the payroll master record from the primary file with indicator 01, it is smart enough to turn on this special indicator called "MR" to indicate that the next time card record what will be read from the secondary file will match this master that is now being processed. The fact is that when the master is read, RPG "sees" the matching time card record sitting over there in the other file's input buffer, even though it has yet to read it. Yes, that is neat!

If the pay rate is in the master and the hours are in the time card record, when the master is read and indicator 01 comes on, the hours are still not yet available for employee # 1. So, we cannot calculate gross pay at that time in the cycle. So a condition that we might call "MR" and "01," means that we have a master read and being processed and its *matching* time card has not yet been read. Notice the word matching in the prior sentence. When we eventually read the time card, RPG has already turned off the master indicator (01) and then it turns on indicator 02. So, if you are keeping score at home, you might say that when the record identifying indicator "02" and the "MR" indicator is on, the primary record just read matches the secondary record that is now being processed. That is great information for a programmer to gain without having to write the code for it. All you must do is be conversant with the RPG cycle.

Multiple Output Records per Cycle.

As an additional plus, for those systems such as the 1130 and the System/360 that were equipped with disk drives, as well as the later System/3 machines and every machine since, when the RPG language read an input record, it could also write a record in the same cycle while it was also producing a print line as what we call the detail output part of the cycle.

Actually, RPG could outdo its electromechanical predecessor by punching out many more cards in one cycle than it could read. Each of these card records, however, would have to be described in detail in the RPG output area. Each record described would be written as long as the conditioning indicators were satisfied. No, we have not described conditioning indicators in any degree of detail yet. Let's just say that they make output occur conditionally based on whether certain indicators are on or off. When all output is done, the program with its fixed logic cycle always goes back to read another record. When there are no more records to read, as noted in Step 5 of the Cycle above, RPG sets on its infamous *last record* indicator called "LR" and the program ends and is removed from memory.

RPG Fixed Logic Cycle Summary

If we go back to Step 6 and Step 7 of the cycle, once a given input record is read, the next step is that it is time again for detail calculations. This is the classic processing part of the RPG cycle that we have just described. The next step, of course is output at Step 1 and thus we have a complete cycle:

INPUT >> Processing >> OUTPUT

We learned that detail calculations occur in that part of the RPG cycle after the detail input has been read. The word "detail" describes what happens in each normal RPG cycle as an individual record is processed (not counting total calculations or total output time). As noted above in the matching example, a detail record ID indicator of 02 means we have read in a time card. If we also have an MR match with the master record, then we know that the master record for that time card is also in memory.

If we are trying to assure that our output occurs after all of the information for one employee has been read, RPG helps again. We know that the detail time card record turns on indicator 02. We know that because this record matches a master, RPG is keeping indicator MR on for us. So, if indicator 02 is on and indicator MR is on, we know that RPG is processing a time card record and the time card record matches the master record that RPG read in the prior cycle. Thus, it is a logical time to condition some calculations that should occur when the time card is being processed for a matched master.

In other words, it would be quite appropriate to condition detail calculations to occur when both indicators 02 and MR are both on. In this case, we specify a calculation to multiply the rate times the hours to produce the first gross amount for the employee. Since the first gross amount per employee would not be an input field, the program would use RPG calculations to create this field for us within the detail calculation specifications.

So, as we wrap up this example in summary form, RPG will have read all of the data and performed the calculations and more than likely, because we have told it so, it will print an output line on a piece of paper that is in the printer. Once this happens, it is time to recycle – run the cycle again and again and again – until we run out of input.

So, the next generic cycle step is to skip back to the beginning of the RPG cycle to that spot that we designated above as the first step (1) in the cycle. Of course, we ignore the headings now since we are not on the 1st page headings since they occur just once in a program – to be able to print the first page information. They were done in cycle 1. Since RPG at this point is continuing to processing its first input record, it is highly unlikely that we printed enough detail records that the first page is full. Therefore, there will be no overflow processing on the second cycle and the next record can be brought in at Step 2 of the cycle. Then, we finish up total calculations from the prior input record in Step 3 in the cycle and the cycle keeps moving. In step 1, it helps to remember that RPG will print anything it can such as the contents of the last record read– not just headings as long as the output lines are either not conditioned or are conditioned with indicators that are on.

That actually about does it for our treatment of the generic RPG cycle in this book. To strengthen your knowledge of the RPG cycle, however, we provide a living example of the processing we have just explained in words. We defer this example to Chapter 5 in which we show the code to achieve what we have discussed regarding the cycle and as we fill them out, we describe the RPG specification forms so that you can get a better appreciate the form of this phenomenal language.

Since we are moving to code a program in Chapter 5, we take a short RPG break in Chapter 4 and we describe the Program Development Manager and the Source Entry Utility as the two tools that you will need in a green screen environment to be able to type in your RPG code, compile it, and run it on your IBM i on Power Systems.

Chapter Summary

In this chapter we introduced the RPG cycle, a very powerful tool for report writing programs. The cycle begins by providing an opportunity to print headings, then it reads a data record, provides total calculations and total output, checks for end of job, makes fields available from the record just read, performs detail calculations and detail out put and gets ready for another round of output on the second cycle. The cycle cycles and cycles until all the input is processed.

RPG has a notion called an indicator that can be assigned to records in files. When particular records are read, RPG turns on indicators associated with them and turns off all of the other record identifying indicators. RPG also has a means of taking summary totals using various control levels from 1 to 9. Total calculations and total output occur when there is a change in a control record.

Matching records is another very powerful tool in RPG, especially when there are just two sequenced files in a program, though many files can be matched. By designating various fields in records to match with up to 9 designators (M1 to M9), when all of the matched fields in one file match those in another, RPG turns on the special MR indicator.

Because you can define multiple detail records for each input cycle, RPG has the ability of printing (outputting) multiple lines or records during one cycle or every cycle based on output record conditioning by using indicators to determine what gets output in what cycle.

Key Chapter Terms

Built-in functions	Keyed-access files	LR indicator
Business processing	L1 cycle	M1 - M9
Communication	L2 cycle	Maintenance
Compile	Last record indicator	Peek ahead
Computer concepts	Level 1	Pointers
Conditioning indicators	Level 2	Primary file
Control breaks	Level 3	Program Dev Mgr
Control field	Level 9	Purists, RPG
Control level	LR indicator	Record ID Indicator
Data fields	M1 - M9	Record types
Data proc machines	Maintenance	Report headings
Detail calcs	Master record	Report titles
Detail lines	Matched fields	Reporting functions
Detail output	Matching records	RPG fixed logic cycle
Detailed RPG cycle	Matching status	RPG II
Field name	MR indicator	RPG output area
Final total	Multiple output records	RPGIV language
First cycle	New group	Secondary files
First page	Output line	Sequence
First record	Overflow headings	Sequential file
Get input data	Overflow processing	Source Entry Utility
Indicators	L2 cycle	State totals
Input area buffer	Last record indicator	System/3
Input cycle	Level 1	Total calculations
Input routine	Level 2	Total calculations
Input variables	Level 3	Total output
Keyed index files	Level 9	

Review Questions

1. What was the first enhancement to the RPG language that caused it to lose its "innocence?"

2. What is the most basic processing cycle?

3. What are the major steps in the RPG cycle?

4. Why do report headings occur in Step 1 of the cycle?

5. What other headings are performed in Step 1?

6. In Step 2 of the cycle when RPG reads a record into memory, how does the data get into your RPG fields?

7. What are total calculations?

8. What is meant by total output?

9. Why are the total parts of the RPG cycle sometimes referred to as in-between time?

10. How many levels of totals does the RPG cycle support?

11. What is an indicator?

12. What is the purpose of the LR indicator?

13. Why is Step 6 of the RPG cycle necessary?

14. What is meant by detail time?

15. What happens during detail calculations?

16. Is there something called Detail Output? If yes, explain?

17. What is matching records processing?

18. If only one record at a time gets read by the RPG cycle, how can it know there is a match?

19. Why does a record identification indicator help with matching records?

20. What are primary, secondary, and tertiary files?

21. Why are M1 through M9 different from the MR indicator?

22. What is the maximum number of records that RPG can input in one cycle – if using only the cycle for input?

23. What is the maximum number of output records that RPG can put out in one cycle?

Chapter 4 Developing RPG Applications

Writing Your Programs

It is a far cry from conceptualizing a program and a way of processing as we did last Chapter to writing RPG programs. Yet, in Chapter 5, we demonstrate how to write the RPG program that we conceptualized just a few pages ago. If we were to look at every line of the RPG program from Chapter 5 right now, what would we do with them? How would we get them into the IBM i on Power Systems, and how would we transform the RPG source into object code that we could run.

Thirty years ago this discussion would have been unnecessary. Programmers would simply get out their RPG coding pads and a few well-sharpened pencils and they would write the whole program on these sheets. Then, they would give the sheets to a keypunch operator who would type each line on the sheet into a diskette record or a card record. The programmer would then submit the card deck or the diskette to a computer operator who would run it through the machine for compilation and give the programmer back the compile listing complete with its error listing. From then on the programmer would type up the changes on diskette or cards and represent the program for recompilation until it gave a clean compile at which the programmer would begin testing to assure the program would work.

Well, today there are no keypunches or key to diskette machines and operators are typically uninvolved in a programming process. Yet, the program still must be keyed, the program still must be compiled, and the programs till needs a clean compile and it needs to be tested. So how does that get done?

That's why this chapter is in the book. It has little to do with RPG itself but it is essential for RPG programmers to develop, code, compile, and test their programs. The tool that is typically used in an IBM i shop is the aging Program Development Manager or PDM that was introduced in 1988 with the AS/400. IBM is pushing a nice Windows based tool called WebSphere Development Studio Client (WDSC) that has not been adopted by most of the IBM i on Power Systems community for one reason or another. This chapter then is about PDM since it is more widespread and it does a nice job of aiding the development process, though it is green screen based.

Programming Development Manager (PDM)

PDM is part of the Application Development Tool Set (ADTS) which had been a staple for application development on the AS/400 since 1988, when they were announced. In early 2000, the whole ADTS was repackaged and it became part of the WebSphere Development Studio for IBM i product set. PDM is, therefore, not an island. It works with all of the other tools in the tool set including the following:

1.   Source Entry Utility (SEU)
2.   Screen Design Aid (SDA)
3.   Data File Utility (DFU)
4.   Advanced Printer Function (APF)
5.   Report Layout Utility (RLU)

PDM Features

In order to enter a program into a IBM i on Power Systems source file, besides the WDSc Editor which we look at briefly in Chapter 20, the major tool used is called the Source Edit Utility or SEU. This is # 1 in the above list and it is a very important tool. PDM is a menu driven productivity tool for programmers. SEU is launched from the PDM panels. To the extent that PDM has play with SEU, it is covered in this book. For a more detailed explanation of the development environment on the IBM i on Power Systems, you may want to read a book I wrote called the IBM i Pocket Developer's Guide, available at both IT Jungle and MC Press.

PDM provides a focal point and an integrated environment for using the development tools available to the programmer on the AS/400. It works with lists of items to be developed or maintained. Virtually all types of objects can be accessed using PDM interfaces, though it is most commonly used for programs, display files (or screens), and data base objects (or files).

The IBM i on Power Systems is an object based system and so you will hear the term used in this book quite often. In its natural state, the IBM i on Power Systems operating IBM i/OS manages objects through a directory structure known as a library. So, we say that objects such as files, output queues, and programs are "stored" in libraries. Just as nothing is stored "in" a directory, we really mean that the library is a means of locating the objects.

A special type of file called a source file is used with IBM i/OS and PDM to store your source programs. A file on IBM i on Power Systems has some of the characteristics of a subdirectory in that a source file can contain many source members. If you write fifty source programs (program before it is compiled and translated into machine code), each source program is identified by its own name within the source file.

The structure of a file in IBM i/OS permits what are called members (individually identified files with the same shape as the major file definition) to reside inside of a file structure. A source file then is a normal IBM i/OS database file that is shaped so that it is a natural for storing source. Each source program that you write in RPG/400 for example would be stored in a sub-object called a member which is a component of a file. The file is stored in a library.

PDM then is a list manager that can work with lists of libraries, objects including file, and members and it can help you create objects and run programs on the system. To be a programmer on IBM i on Power Systems, you must understand PDM and the source editor, SEU.

PDM: the List Manager

Libraries, objects, and members can be selected easily from lists provided by PDM. Option numbers are provided for the most commonly used programming functions, to save you keystrokes. PDM is smart enough, that if you have not filled in required parameters, it automatically invokes a prompting facility to get that done. Additionally, developers can build their own options that can be used in standard PDM panels and they can change PDM's default values.

For example, on development-only machines, the "Compile in batch?" option of PDM invoked via the Change Defaults option (F18) may be set to "N," so the developer can more productively work with PDM members. This can also be done on production machines, but the users or the programming manager may very well complain about its impact on system performance. Overall, the major benefit of this PDM option is that it makes programmers more productive.

What Does PDM Do?

There are three main functions as displayed on the PDM main menu. These are as follows:

1. Work with libraries
2. Work with objects in libraries
3. Work with members in a source file

Whether you are working with libraries, objects, or members, from the list provided, PDM enables you to place an option number next to the library, object, or member. The option number corresponds to a function such as copy, move, rename, delete, view, change, execute, compile, save, or restore. Based on the option number, and the type of object being operated upon, PDM will ask you for additional information to complete the operation, and then it will go ahead and apply the function to the library, object, or member as requested.

Starting PDM

Let's start PDM so that we know what it looks like. Ask your program administrator if your shop has its own way of beginning the programming environment and follow their instructions. If there are no specific instructions, you can simply type STRPDM at a command line on your IBM i on Power Systems and press ENTER. The panel in Figure 4-1 appears.

From this panel in Figure 4-1, we will first select work with libraries, option 1. Before you press ENTER here, there's a little more to know.

Figure 4-1 The PDM Main Menu

```
                    PDM MAIN Menu
                    HELLO
        AS/400 Programming Development Manager (PDM)

  Select one of the following:

        1. Work with libraries
        2. Work with objects
        3. Work with members

        9. Work with user-defined options
  Selection or command
  ===> 1


  F3=Exit     F4=Prompt  F9=Retrieve  F10=Command Entry
  F12=Cancel  F18=Change defaults
```

Figure 4-2 Specify Libraries to Work With

```
              Specify Libraries to Work With

  Type choice, press Enter.

    Library . . . . . . . . .   *ALL   *LIBL, name, *generic*, *ALL,
                                       *ALLUSR, *USRLIBL, *CURLIB


  F3=Exit     F5=Refresh     F12=Cancel
```

Work with Libraries Using PDM

The panel in Figure 4-3 below, is an example of a typical list of libraries that would appear if one took option 1 from the menu "Work with Libraries," shown in Figure 4-1. On the way you will see the panel in Figure 4-2. For this example, type *ALL and press ENTER.

Notice the layout of the PDM screens. Figure 4-3 is representative of PDM's list screens. They all follow this same list panel standard format. Information concerning what list you are looking at is at the top. Next is a list of options that can be entered in any of the option fields next to the items listed. The list of items (in this case, libraries) is in the middle of the screen. Near the bottom of the screen is a command line on which AS/400 commands or parameters for the option specified above for a library can be entered.

Notice in Figure 4-3, that we have marked two libraries for rename. If we hit ENTER with the 7's in place, we will be prompted to enter the name to which we would like to change them.

Figure 4-3, Work with Libraries Using PDM

```
            Work with Libraries Using PDM           HELLO

  List type . . . . . . .    *LIBL_____

  Type options, press Enter.
    2=Change              3=Copy     5=Display    7=Rename
    8=Display description 9=Save     10=Restore   12=Work with ...

  Opt  Library    Type     Text
  __   FROMDEBS   *PROD
  __   GENERAL    *PROD    General Query Library for Helpdesk
  __   GL02       *PROD    GL02 REL. 9.9
  __   GRIMEDEN   *PROD    COLLECTION - created by SQL
  __   GUEST      *PROD
  __   GUITEST    *PROD    Test Lib for Web GUI
  __   HAWKEYE    *PROD    PATHFINDER - CALL HAWKEYE/HAWKEYE
  7    HELLO      *PROD
  7    HELLOA     *PROD
                                                 More...
  Parameters or command
  ===> _____
  F3=Exit      F4=Prompt        F5=Refresh        F6=Add to list
  F9=Retrieve  F10=Command Entry F23=More options F24=More keys
```

Work With Objects

Instead of working with libraries, this time, let's pick option 2 from the panel in Figure 4-1, *Work with objects*. For this PDM exercise, there should be a small library called HELLO prebuilt, so that when you get the *Specify Objects to Work With* Panel, as shown in Figure 4-4, you would choose the HELLO library and let the rest default to *ALL. Before you press ENTER on the *Specify Objects to Work with* Panel, take a look at the other options.

Figure 4-4 Specify Objects to Work with Panel

```
                        Specify Objects to Work With
Type choices, press Enter.

    Library  . . . . . . .     HELLO       *CURLIB, name
    Object:
      Name . . . . . . . .     *ALL        *ALL, name, *generic*
      Type . . . . . . . .     *ALL        *ALL, *type
      Attribute  . . . . .     *ALL        *ALL, attribute, *generic*,
                                                 *BLANK
                                                          F3=Exit      F5=Refresh
F12=Cancel
```

Typically, the only option that is filled in is the *library name* (contains the objects to be worked with). However, the PDM user could also fill in *Object Type* (e.g., PGM, USRPRF, FILE, etc.), and *Object Attribute* (e.g., CLP, CBL, PF-SRC, etc.). This limits (subsets) the resulting list of objects to those types/attributes.

A user could also enter a name or a generic name (BURGE*, SA*, *SA*, *SA) which also limits the list to those beginning with, containing, or ending with certain characters. As your development efforts produce fruits, the number of objects to maintain grows quickly, and these filtering techniques help you in finding the items you want posthaste.

The default library for this option is always the job's current library. For your information, the current library can be specified in the user profile, can be overridden at sign-on, or can be changed using the *CHGCURLIB* command. You can, of course type in the library name in Figure 4-4 as is shown.

After you go through the selection process described above, and you press ENTER with just the library HELLO typed in, you would see the *"Work with Objects Using PDM"* panel such as that in Figure 4-5.

Figure 4-5 *Work with Objects Using PDM*

```
              Work with Objects Using PDM                      HELLO

Library . . . . .   HELLO_____       Position to . . . . . . . .
                                      Position to type . . . . .
Type options, press Enter.
  2=Change      3=Copy         4=Delete    5=Display      7=Rename
  8=Display description         9=Save    10=Restore    11=Move ...
Opt  Object      Type       Attribute   Text
     HELLOAC001  *PGM        CBL         Advanced Hello World,
 __  HELLOAR001  *PGM        RPG         Advanced Hello World,
 __  LANGUAGE    *FILE       PF-DTA      LANGUAGE File Hello Wld
 __  PANEL       *FILE       DSPF        Display File Panel For
 __  QCBLLESRC   *FILE       PF-SRC      FILE FOR ILE COBOL SOURCE
 __  QCLSRC      *FILE       PF-SRC      CL Source File
 12  QDDSSRC     *FILE       PF-SRC      dds source
 __  QRPGLESRC   *FILE       PF-SRC      RPGIV Source File
                                                         More...
Parameters or command
===>
F3=Exit         F4=Prompt        F5=Refresh        F6=Create
F9=Retrieve     F10=Command entry  F23=More options  F24=More keys
```

Work with Other Options

Option 12, as shown in Figure E9, and visible when you hit F23, is used frequently to work with a selected object. This can come in really handily if you are working with objects and then, for example you want to work with members of the QDDSSRC source file. If the QDDSSRC source file is on your screen as in Figure 4-5, just take option 12 on that line and you will be taken to a *Work with Members* panel for the members in QDDSSRC. It's a handy trick!

If you want to perform an action, such as option 12, but you cannot see it, it helps to remember that there are a number of command keys and options that are not visible from all views. To change your view, press F23 or F24. As you can see from the prompts and function key definitions in Figure 4-5, there are a lot of things that can be done with PDM objects.

Work With Members

Now let's pick PDM Main menu option 3, *Work with Members.* This is very important for SEU work since it is the entrée to source files where RPG source programs are stored. If you take the option from the main menu to Work with Members, you would then get a screen requesting which source file to use. For this example, pick QDDSSRC in library RPGBOOK. QDDSSRC is the source file name that IBM has chosen for DDS. Thus, most programmers use this source file (can exist in many libraries) to store display file and database file objects.

On this same panel, after selecting option 3, you could request a sub-setting of the member list by generic name and/or source type (e.g., PF, CBL, RPG38, etc.) This helps filter the list to meaningful items. To get to the member list panel, you have to fill in the panel answering the requests. Then press ENTER to get to the *"Work with Members using PDM"* screen, as shown in Figure 4-6.

Hitting F23 and F24 gives you even more options and more command keys as shown in Figures 4-7 through 4-9.

Figure 4-6 Work with Members

```
Work with Members Using PDM              HELLO

File  . . . . . .    QDDSSRC
  Library . . . .    HELLO              Position to  . . . . .
Type options, press Enter.
 2=Edit 3=Copy  4=Delete 5=Display  6=Print    7=Rename
 8=Display desc 9=Save 13=Change text 14=Compile 15=Create module...
Opt  Member     Type         Text
  2  JOBINFO    PF           Job Information File For SBMJOB
  _  LANGUAGE   PF           LANGUAGE File For Hello World
  _  LOGICINF   PF           Job Information File For
  _  MASTER     PF           Master Payroll File
  _  PANEL      DSPF         Display File Panel For Adv
  _  TESTFILE   PF           Testing File
  _  UIINF      PF           Job Information File For
                                                Bottom
Parameters or command
===>
F3=Exit      F4=Prompt      F5=Refresh      F6=Create
F9=Retrieve  F10=Command entry F23=More options  F24=More keys
```

Figure 4-7   Additional Options (F23)
```
14=Compile   16=Run procedure    17=Change using SDA
19=Change using RLU     25=Find string ...
```

Figure 4-8 Additional keys (F24)
```
F11=Display names and types F12=Cancel   F13=Repeat
F14=Display date     F15=Sort date
F23=More options     F24=More keys
```

Figure 4-9 Additional keys (F24)
```
F16=User options F17=Subset  F18=Change defaults   F21=Print list F23=More options
F24=More keys
```

As you can see, the *"Work with Members Using PDM"* panel looks like the other PDM "work with" screens. However, there are more options than the libraries and objects panels. For example, there are a number of functions that apply only to members only, such as those in the list shown in Figure 4-10.

Figure 4-10 Functions that Can Be Applied to Source Members

Function	Description
Edit (SEU)	Edit any type of source code-RPG, COBOL, database)
Compile	Compile any type of program - RPG, COBOL, database.
Change using SDA	This option works only if the type is a display file.
Change using RLU	This option works only if the type is a printer file

Editing Source Members

When a developer places an option 2 for Edit with *SEU* next to a member, such as JOBINFO, as shown in the example in Figure 4-6, the *SEU* brings a syntax checker with its editor to match the *Type* parameter. If the Type is *RPG*, the *RPG* syntax checker examines every statement that is keyed and forces you to correct those in error during your editing session. If the *C* language type is used, then *C* is what checks the member syntax during the *SEU* keying process. The same syntax examines the source during editing as during the compilation process.

Compiling (Creating Objects from Members)

By placing a 14 next to the object you want to be compiled, *PDM* invokes the proper compiler based on the "type" parameter. If, for example, you coded an *RPG* program as a *CBL* type, then *PDM* would invoke the *COBOL* compiler to compile your RPG source. If you want the *RPG* compiler, just make sure that the "Type" says *RPG or ILERPG*, or key over whatever it says, and make it *RPG*. Then invoke option 14 again. If you do as prescribed in this example, the *RPG* compiler will be invoked to compile your source into an *RPG *PGM* object.

Member Source Types

A sampling of valid source types which you can use is shown in Figure 4-11. The "type" column as shown in Figure 4-6 is where a developer can key in a valid source type, to identify the specific type of source which is what the member should contain.

Not only does PDM invoke the editor or the compiler quite well, it enables common functions such as COPY and DELETE to be performed almost as quickly as the click of a mouse. Let's use the panel in Figure 4-6 as a basis to perform a copy. Let's copy a member to another member, thereby creating a new member.

Figure 4-11 Sampling of Source Types

Type	Description
BAS	Basic
C	C Language
CBL	COBOL
CBLLE	ILE COBOL for AS/400
CBL36	COBOL System/36
CBL38	COBOL System/38
CLLE	ILE Control Language
CLP	Control Language
CLP38	System/38 Control Language
CMD	Command
DSPF	Display File
DSPF36	Display File System/36
etc.	

COPY Members with PDM

In fact, let's copy 3 members. To do this, enter a "3" for COPY next to 3 members in the list in 4-6 and press ENTER. The panel in Figure 4-12 appears.

Figure 4-12 Copy Members using PDM

```
                        Copy Members  From file . . . . . . . :    QDDSSRC
    From library . . . . :     HELLO

 Type the file name and library name to receive the copied members.

    To file . . . . . . . .    QDDSSRC___  Name, F4 for list
       To library . . . . .    QGPL_____

 To rename copied member, type New Name, press Enter.

  Member         New Name
  JOBINFO        JOB2INF
  MASTER         MASTERP
  PANEL          PANELA                                              Bottom
 F3=Exit        F4=Prompt       F5=Refresh       F12=Cancel
 F19=Submit to batch
```

The PDM gives lots of prompting opportunities such as those in Figure 4-12. This panel is prompting the user to input more information about the members that we asked to copy from the previous screen. The three members that you asked to copy are shown with the COPY option given. To make this work, you fill in the file and library to which you want to copy these members. You can add a new name for each new member as you see fit.

As you can see in Figure 4-12, we have already filled in the new names for our to-be-copied members. Since you are copying them to a different QDDSSRC source file in a different library (QGPL), you could have let the names remain the same since this would not have created any duplicates in the originating library.

When you hit the ENTER key on this panel, the three members are copied to QDDSSRC in QGPL as fast as a cat swoops down on a nice piece of chicken.

Source Entry Utility (SEU)

Every machine has an editor which is recognized as the tool by which programmers get their source programs keyed into the system. On mainframes, for example, a favorite tool is called ISPF. On Microsoft PCs, there is the old standby DOS EDIT. On IBM PCs, after the breakup of the Microsoft and IBM friendship, the editor provided simply "e." It is similar to DOS EDIT. On the IBM i on Power Systems, the newest editors are packaged with the WebSphere Development Studio client (WDSC), which is slowly being accepted by the user community, but the most widely used editor continues to be the Source Entry Utility or simply, SEU.

SEU Features Overview

SEU is packed with editing power. Most SEU users have little idea as to just how powerful this editor actually is. Full screen editing with prompts and formats, syntax checks, as well as move, copy and delete commands, are about all you typically need to be a proficient SEU user. Yet, there is a lot more! AND I MEAN A LOT!

Compiling and Executing your Program

Once you have finished with SEU, take option 3 to save your work in the RPGSRC file for program new or the QDDSSRC source file if you are working with the database code for file VENDORP. You will return to PDM as seen in Figure 4-24

Figure 4-24 shows option 14 being selected next to the NEW member which is our RPG source program that we just finished editing. It has been saved in the QRPGSRC file in the RPGBOOK library on the HELLO IBM i on Power Systems.

Figure 4-24 Compiling the RPG Program

```
             Work with Members Using PDM                    HELLO

File  . . . . . . .   QRPGSRC
  Library . . . .     RPGBOOK        Position to  . . . . .

Type options, press Enter.
 2=Edit  3=Copy  4=Delete 5=Display     6=Print      7=Rename
 8=Display desc  9=Save 13=Change text 14=Compile 15=Create mod

Opt  Member      Type    Text
14   NEW         RPG     RPG/400, Interactive
__   OLDCALL03   RPG     Advanced Hello World, RPG/400 w/Call
__   SUBFILARRY  RPG
__   SUBFILE     RPG
__   UI03        RPG     Advanced Hello World, RPG/400, Submit
__   UI04        RPG     Data queue Calling Program
__   UI05        RPG     EOFDLY      Interactive Program
__   UI05A       RPG     EOFDLY      Interactive Program
                                                      More...
Parameters or command
===> _____
F3=Exit     F4=Prompt          F5=Refresh        F6=Create
F9=Retrieve F10=Command entry  F23=More options  F24=More keys
```

You can type 14 and hit enter and the program will compile in batch using some configuration information stored in a job description object known as QDFTJOBD on the IBM i on Power Systems. You can also pick option 13 on PDM and change the defaults to compile interactively if you are permitted to do so. Once you place the 14 next to the source that you want to use to create the IBM i on Power Systems object of the same name, you can also press F4 (the prompter) to see just what the command is that actually does the compilation. This is shown in Figure 4-25.

Figure 4-25 RPG Compiler Options – Launched from PDM.

```
                 Create RPG/400 Program (CRTRPGPGM)

Type choices, press Enter.

Program . . . . . . . . . . . . > NEW          Name, *CTLSPEC
  Library . . . . . . . . . . > RPGBOOK        Name, *CURLIB
Source file . . . . . . . . . > QRPGSRC        Name, QRPGSRC
  Library . . . . . . . . . . > RPGBOOK        Name, *LIBL, *CURLIB
Source member . . . . . . . . > NEW            Name, *PGM
Generation severity level . . . 9              0-99
Text 'description' . . . . . . . *SRCMBRTXT
                        Additional Parameters

Replace program . . . . . . . . > *NO          *YES, *NO
                                                    Bottom
F3=Exit F4=Prompt F5=Refresh  F10=Additional parms   F12=Cancel
F13=How to use this display   F24=More keys
```

When you press Enter after filling in the compile parameters as shown in Figure Compile 2, the RPG program is compiled and it is placed in the RPGBOOK library. In order to get a clean compile, you must assure that the display file and the database file are in your library list or the list used by the default job description QDFTJOBD. See your system administrator to assure this.

If you get a compilation unsuccessful message or you want to see the compiler printout for any reason there are a number of ways to get your printout. One is to bring up SEU again and the program which you want to examine. Press F15 for the Browse / Copy options and go down mid way until you see the last of the following lines:

```
Selection  . .  . . .    2              1=Member
                                        2=Spool file
                                        3=Output queue
Browse/copy spool file  .     NEW
```

Pick option 3 and press Enter and you will see a panel like that shown in Figure 4-26.

Figure 4-26 RPG Compiler Options – Display OutQ

```
                      Work with Output Queue

Queue:   QPRINT         Library:  RPGBOOK        Status:  RLS

Type options, press Enter.
 1=Send 2=Change 3=Hold 4=Delete 5=Display 6=Release   7=Messages
 8=Attributes           9=Work with printing status

Opt  File    User    User Data  Sts  Pages  Copies Form Type  Pty
5    NEW     BKELLY              RDY      7       1 *STD           5

                                                   Bottom
Parameters for options 1, 2, 3 or command
===>  _____
F3=Exit   F11=View 2   F12=Cancel   F20=Writers   F22=Printers
F24=More keys
```

Pick option 5 next to the output queue entry and press Enter. You will see the compiler listing as shown in Figure 4-27.

Figure 4-27 RPG Compiler Listing with Errors

```
                      Display Spooled File
File . . . . . :   NEW                 Page/Line   1/1
Control . . . .                        Columns    1 - 78
Find . . . . .
*...+....1....+....2....+....3....+....4....+....5....+....6.....
 5722WDS V5R3M0  030905        IBM RPG/400              HELL
 Compiler . . . . . . . . . . IBM RPG/400
 Command Options:
   Program  . . . . . . . . . RPGBOOKNEW
   Source file  . . . . . . . RPGBOOKQRPGSRC
   Source member  . . . . . . NEW
   Source listing options . . *SOURCE  *XREF    *GEN     *N
   Generation options . . . . *NOLIST  *NOXREF  *NOATR   *N
   Source listing indentation . *NONE
   Type conversion options  . . *NONE
   Sort sequence  . . . . . . . *HEX
   Language identifier  . . . . *JOBRUN
   Etc.
...
5722WDS V5R3M0  030905        IBM RPG/400              HELL
SEQUENCE
NUMBER    *...1....+....2....+....3....+....4....+....5....
                S o u r c e   L i s t i n g
     H
100  FNEW    CF  E                  WORKSTN
200  F* LOGICAL FILE VENDMST BUILT OVER VENDORP WITH KEY
* 2120      300   DATA DESCRIPTIONS FOR FILE NEW NOT FOUND.
300  FVENDMST IF  E        K        DISK
* 2120      300   DATA DESCRIPTIONS FOR FILE VENDMST NOT FOUND.
400  I             'VENDOR NOT FOUND   'C          ERRMSG
A000000 INPUT FIELDS FOR RECORD VENDFMT FILE NEW FORMAT VENDFMT.
500  C             *IN03    DOWEQ*OFF
600  C                      EXFMTVENDFMT
```

```
Program Source Totals:
   Records . . . . . . . . . :   12
   Specifications  . . . . . :   11
   Table Records . . . . . . :    0
   Comments  . . . . . . . . :    1
Compile stopped. Severity level 40 errors found in file.
       * * * * *  E N D   O F   C O M P I L A T I O N   * * * *
```

Most programmers debug their programs looking at the error listing on their workstations, though some like to have the paper printed to be able to see all the machinations of the compiler listing all at once. Typically, the first thing a programmer would do is go to the bottom of the listing to see what the errors are. Near the bottom of the listing, is an error message flagged as the following

```
* QRG2120 Severity:   40    Number:    1
 Message . . . . :   External description not found for file specified
as externally described. File ignored.
```

This tells you that the externally described files that you expected the compiler to find have not been found. NEW is a small program and the error types seem to have to do with the fact that the fields and indicators (*7030 messages) were not defined because the database file and the workstation file were not found. These are easy to correct. In fact, the best way to debug compile listing issues is one error at a time so you can see what makes the program compile. So, if we added the RPGBOOK library to the library list in our case, this would solve the problems and the next compile would be clean.

Running the NEW Program

Once the program compiles, that does not mean it will work. The next step is to run it. A simple way of testing programs when in PDM is to hit F3 to get out of the Work with members panel and return to the main PDF panel. Select option 2 to Work with objects. Look for object type *PGM in the alphabetical list until you find program NEW. This is the compiled object program. To run this, place a 16 next to the object and press Enter. The program will then run and run fine, hopefully if you have coded your logic properly and all of the underlying objects in the program are located by the library list.

To run a program without PDM, assure that the underlying objects are in your library list and then on a IBM i on Power Systemsi command line type the following:

CALL NEW

That's about it. Your program will run just as if you had typed option 16 in PDM.

Summary and Conclusions:

In this chapter, we studied the IBM green screen development environment known as Program Development Manager (PDM) and the powerful Source Entry Utility (SEU), the editor used by almost all developers on the IBM i on Power Systems. In Chapter 20 in an introduction to Screen Design AID, we also introduce the newer WDSC environment and its editor and show how it can be used to edit your source code and how WDSC can be used to compile your programs.

Since a developer uses SEU as a tool to enter the source for objects such as programs and data files, in this chapter, we chose a simple RPG and database example. With these examples, we presented the facts first in lecture format, and then we followed this with a look at how the function behaved with a live-looking IBM i on Power Systems panel to solidify and augment the learning. In this process, you created source, learned how to change defaults, copied and moved lines, created database source and RPG program source code, entered data, displayed data, and then, again using SEU, you saved it all into the source file repository (QRPGSRC or QDDSSRC).

Hopefully, you were able to use a IBM i on Power Systems machine to give you a hands-on approach and an effective learning tool. But, either way, this chapter gave you the opportunity to understand how to edit and save code on the AS/400 and then use PDM to compile and execute it.

Now that you have completed this chapter, you are armed with the green-screen development tool of the champions, PDM & SEU. The concepts you learned here will also help you if you choose to take IBM's advice and move to the WDSC editor. Regardless of your tool choice in the future, PDM & SEU can provide you with immediate benefit today.

Congratulations and best wishes in all of your future editing projects.

Key Chapter Terms

*BLANK	DFU	Record format
*FILE	Diskette	Repeat lines
*IN	Display file	Rpt Layout Utility
*OFF	DOS Edit	RPG source
*ON	Edit	RPGBOOK library
*PGM object.	Error listing	SAVE
5250	Error message	SDA
5250 emulation	Exclude	SELECT
Advanced Prt Function	Executing	SET
BOTTOM	Factor	SEU
Browse/Copy	Field attributes	SEU command line
CALL	FIND	SEU commands
CANCEL	Format line	SEU line commands
CBL	IFxx	SEU Window Line
CC	Insert lines	Shift left
CHANGE	Insert with prompt	Shift right
Change Session	Keypunch	SEU target
Defaults		
Clean compile	Line Commands	Show
COBOL	Library	Skeleton
Columns scale	Member	Source file
Compile listing	MM	Source program
Compiling	Module	Source types
Computer operator	Move lines	Split session editing
Copy lines	Object based	STRPDM
CRTRPGPGM	Object type	STRSEU
Current library	PDM,	Syntax Checking
Data File Utility	PDM Source Types	System administrator
Data markers	PDM Features	Tabs line
Database file	PDM -Starting	TN5250
DD	PF	TOP5
DDS	Printer file	WDSC
Default library	Prompt command	Window command
DELETE	QDDSSRC	Work with libraries,
Delete lines	QDFTJOBD	Work with members
Destinations	QGPL	Work with objects
Development process	QRPGSRC	
Device	QRPGLESRC	

Review Questions

1. What was the typical method thirty years ago for a programmer to get their program into machine readable form?

2. What is the name of the greens screen program used to manage the development process on the IBM i on Power Systems today?

3. What functions does PDM provide?

4. What is the name of the GUI equivalent to PDM and why is it important to your future development needs?

5. The tool that can be launched from PDM that enables you to enter RPG source statements into the IBM i on Power Systems known as?

6. PDM works with what three object types?

7. The Work with ? facility shows lists of source programs that can be edited.

8. How do you select a source program for editing from a PDM list?

9. How do you create a new source program in PDM?

10. What is a member?

11. What bearing on development does the member source type play?

12. What would you do if you were asked to write a program that would be more than 80% identical to a program that you had previously written?

13. How would you copy, and how would you delete a source member?

14. How do you start the Source Entry Utility (SEU)?

15. List the salient features of the SEU program?

16. What are prompt lines?

17. Is the compiler the first IBM i on Power Systems tool that examines your source for syntactical accuracy? If so, how does it perform this task. If not, what does and how?

18. What type of functions might you perform with SEU line commands? Do these make SEU stilted or productive?

19. What is the difference between formatting and prompting?

20. At the top of the SEU edit panel, there is an area for commands. How are these commands that you would use here different from line commands?

21. What is the major difference between the single character line commands and their double character equivalents?

22. What line command would you use to Copy? Delete? Insert?

23. What is the difference between a Move and a Copy line command?

24. What is the target area? How do you specify this?

25. What command key is used to end SEU and save your program?

26. What PDM option do you use for a straight RPG compile?

27. Is there a way to bring up your compile listing in the middle of your SEU session so you can correct compile errors without a printout? How?

28. When you get a clean compile, what is the next step?

29. How do you execute an RPG program that has just been compiled?

Chapter 5 Your First RPG Program

The Specs for Your First Program

Now that you have been introduced to the original notion of RPG programming using the RPG fixed logic cycle, let's use this knowledge to solve a simple business reporting problem. Suppose we have two files from which we would like to gain information – a payroll master and a time card file; and we would like to print a report in a very understandable fashion including totals and subtotals.

For this program, let's say we have the two files above – the very same files that we used to describe the RPG cycle, level breaks, matching records, and record identifying indicators above. Our objective, in the form that a programmer often receives a request for a program from as systems analyst is to print a report that looks like the report shown in Figure 5-1. The input for the report comes from two database files, the descriptions of which are shown in Figures 5-2 and 5-3.

Figure 5-1 Program Output from Running Sample Learning Program

```
      THE DOWALLOBY COMPANY GROSS PAY REGISTER BY STATE           2/21/06
ST     CITY          EMP#      EMPLOYEE NAME        RATE    HOURS      CHECK

PA     Wilkes-Barre  001       Bizz Nizwonger       7.80    35.00     273.00
PA     Wilkes-Barre  002       Warbler Jacoby       7.90    40.00     316.00

                               TOTAL CITY  PAY FOR Wilkes-Barre      589.00

PA     Scranton      003       Bing Crossley        8.55    65.00     555.75

                               TOTAL CITY  PAY FOR Scranton          555.75

                               TOTAL STATE PAY FOR PA             1,144.75

AK     Fairbanks     004       Uptake N. Hibiter    7.80    25.00     195.00
AK     Fairbanks     005       Fenworth Gront       9.30    33.00     306.90
                     006 NO MATCHING MASTER                 40.00
AK     Fairbanks     007       Bi Nomial            8.80    39.00     343.20

                               TOTAL CITY  PAY FOR Fairbanks        845.10

AK     Juneau        008       Milly Dewith         6.50    40.00     260.00
AK     Juneau        009       Sarah Bayou         10.45    40.00     418.00

                               TOTAL CITY  PAY FOR Juneau           678.00

                               TOTAL STATE PAY FOR AK            1,523.10

NJ     Newark        010       Dirt McPug           6.45    35.00     225.75

                               TOTAL CITY  PAY FOR Newark          225.75

                               TOTAL STATE PAY FOR NJ             225.75

                               FINAL TOTAL PAY                 2,893.60
```

To be able to print this report, you must be able to define the two files to RPG with the master as primary and the time card file as secondary. During first page or overflow time on the report, you want the report heading as well as the one line of column headings printed. For each master, there is just one time card. Print an error message if there is a time card and no master. If there is a master and no time card, let's just let that alone. When the time card record is read and there is a match with a master record, calculate gross pay and print a detail line on the report. Each time the city changes, total the columns shown on the sample by city. Each time the state changes, total the city and then total the state. As shown on the report. Each time the program ends – when the LR indicator turns on (only once in a program) print out the city totals, followed by the state totals, followed by the final totals.

This constitutes a summary of the written specs for the program you are about to write. Systems analysts are often more formal in their communications with programmers, but at a basic level, that about does it in informal shops. To know how to write the program, it will help to review the information I presented on the RPG cycle but, other than that, you're ready to go.

So, in the next chapter, we show you line for line how to write the RPG fixed cycle program that accomplishes the mission as defined. Well, not exactly! The fact is that I have not even offered you one thought on the various and many specification sheets that are the blood and guts of this powerful language. So, maybe you can't begin just yet. First, it seems that you must find out about those infamous RPG form types in which all you have to do is fill-in the blanks.

Well, not exactly! Sure, I could start there, but then this would be like every other book that has attempted to overwhelm the learner with every option on every RPG form – the easy and the difficult; the often used, the less-often used and the hardly ever used. I am not going to do that to you. You bought this book so that you could take a quick course to very simply learn the basics of the RPG/400 and RPGIV languages. From what you learn in this book, you can grow into a more knowledgeable RPG programmer but when you leave this book, you will already know how to get a lot done with the language.

So, I will explain the option that you need to choose on the RPG specification sheet to perform the functions that you need to do in this program for it to meet the specs as given and to produce the report as shown. While we are on the form, I will also explain some of the other options on the form that you might use in other programs.

By the way (BTW), systems analysts most often provide mock-ups of printer output, often in the form of a printer spacing chart (like graph paper) that shows where each constant and each field on the report is to appear. So, with Figure 5-1, we have actually given a little more in this instance to show you how your output is to look.

Now is the time, if you are extremely adventurous to feel free to go out to IBM's Web site or another to learn as much as you can about the components of this program as coded on RPG sheets. You may even want to try to code the program with what you pick up on your Web trip. This will not hurt even if you mess it up badly. Even if you try to code the program in pseudo code before you move on to the following mini-tutorial for this program, it would help you learn this topic more precisely. You'll learn why all of your documented assumptions are wrong – and that will help you learn RPG.

But, even if you choose to take the less difficult way out, which is also OK in this book, and in fact, which this book enables, after you sit back and relax and you read-on, soon you will have coded your first RPG program, and you will understand it. How about that for a challenge?

A Description of the Data

As those who have become acquainted with the iterations of AS/400 to the IBM i over the years will attest, the platform has a nice, proprietary, even snappy database language of its own in support of the relational database. So, instead of showing the data descriptions for these two files in a CREATE TABLE format, I have chosen to show it in the DDS format, which is the native database language of the AS/400.

Since most of the data defined in these two layouts are self descriptive (even without column headings and text), let me take a brief opportunity to describe the data in Figures 5-2 and 5-3.

Figure 5-2 DDS Layout of EMPMAST Record

```
           *************** Beginning of data ******
FMT PF   .....A..........T.Name++++++RLen++TDpB..
0001.00      A           R PAYR
0002.00      A             EMPNO        3S 0
0003.00      A             EMPNAM      20
0004.00      A             EMPRAT       5S 2
0005.00      A             EMPCTY      20
0006.00      A             EMPSTA       2
0007.00      A             EMPZIP       5S 0
           ***************** End of data *********
```

Figure 5-3 DDS Layout of TIMCRD Record

```
FMT PF   .....A..........T.Name++++++RLen++TDpB.
0001.00      A           R TIMR
0002.00      A             EMPNO        3S 0
0003.00      A             EMPHRS       4S 2
           ***************** End of data ********
```

DDS provides a means of defining a field name and a length and an attribute (alphabetic, numeric, etc.). If the field is numeric, then DDS demands that you specify the number of decimal places. These fields are described below in more detail.

Besides fields, in the two DDS descriptions above, you also must name the record formats. In this example, we named them PAYR and TIMR respectively as you can see in the figures. A record format is a way of naming the format of the file (all the fields). It permits all of the fields in that format to be referenced in any program by this one name.

Following the record format name for a physical file, as shown in the DDS in Figures 5-2 and Figure 5-3, the database designer gets to describe all of the fields that make up the format of the record in the file – ie – the record format. EMPMAST (employee master file) has six fields defined for it and TIMCRD (time card file) has just two. In all cases in the DDS shown in these two figures, the data being described is self evident. Let's use the numeric field description below as a one line example.

```
0004.00 A...    EMPRAT  5S 2
```

The first number shown after the field name in the figures is the length of the field. If the field is numeric, more information is given. If it is character, such as a name, no more needs to be described. The length is all DDS needs and it will determine the start and finish positions in the records for alphabetic data. The 'S' shown in these examples stands for decimal data (regular numeric) that has no strange IT format. In other words it is not packed data or binary or floating point or fixed point. It is merely numeric data – one number for storage position. You can say what it is without being a computer scientist and that is one of RPG's strengths.

Then in all cases, you see a number or a zero after the 'S' in these field definitions. It appears only when there is an 'S' specified. This is where the database designer tells the DDS compiler the number of decimal places that the database must remember about the numeric value when it is stored. For example, the number 2, as you would expect, signifies that two positions of the length are reserved for the decimal positions. If a value with three or more decimal position is stored in the EMPRAT field above, the value would be truncated to two decimal positions. And, that's about all there is to defining homes for data field values in the natural database for the IBM i – a.k.a. DDS.

The Data Itself

When you program in RPG or any other language, it is easy to make assumptions about how the data will look. As many times as not, when programmers are trying to figure out why the code of which they labored and labored does not work, it is not the logic, it is bad data. The data doesn't always arrive in the program as expected. Sometimes it is shaped improperly and sometimes it is not correctly sequenced. Programmers struggle for answers when their logic really is sound and yet the program does not work.

Beginning programmers almost always blame the compiler or the system for messing them up when a program does not work. Yet, in almost all cases, the beginning programmer is wrong and they find that there was something not quite right with their logic. Then, as the programmers gets more experienced and they no longer are amused at blaming the compiler and being wrong, they rightfully check and double check their code to make sure they have not made a mistake that a peer would recognize immediately. In this stage, programmers become programmers. In fact, most who adopt the rule that the compiler is never wrong find that this helps them in their quest for excellence.

However, when they do become excellent programmers from this rigid discipline to which they subject themselves, ironically, they continue to blame themselves when they hit a problem they absolutely cannot solve. They continue to look for a solution without seeking help or crying foul.

The irony is that as a programmer actually becomes excellent, they do not always realize it. Eventually they realize that compiler writers are not perfect. In fact, many compiler writers at IBM or Microsoft or wherever are just out of college. And, though IBM and others have checks and balances to prevent bad code from entering the compiler or OS realm, sometimes it happens. Otherwise, there would be no fixes or IBM PTFs. When an experienced RPG programmer relearns that sometimes the compiler is actually may be wrong, they become even better at their trade.

But, to become good at what they do, they first must subsume their initial arrogance and they must discipline themselves into assuring that nothing is wrong with their code. It is very embarrassing to rant about the failings of others when the failings are actually your own.

Most RPG programmers are amazed at their first taste of understanding their own excellence. Being trained to "blame me first," there is an initial shock in learning that the compiler or the OS may be bad, and not their RPG code. Along this path to excellence, great programmers also learn that if it is not the compiler and it is not the logic, it must be the data.

No matter how foolproof the logic, if the data appears in what a programmer would offer is an "illogical sequence," the most meticulous code will not perform correctly. So, along the way to excellence, after really understanding the language, programmers learn to explain most of the inexplicable by taking a hard look at the input data during the debugging cycle.

It is in this vein that we offer Figure 5-4 and Figure 5-5 for your reading and digestion pleasure. These are pictures of the actual data that are in these samples. Since this is a sample world in which we are forced to live -- in learning a programming language, the data used to produce the results is the key to solving any issues that are not caused by logic flaws., When you get the work of the systems analyst as your input for a project, sometimes it is necessarily incomplete or it is overly complete as the phenomenon of analysis paralysis (over analysis) subverts the project. Only through major testing with real data can anybody – even the best programmers -- actually determine that bad data has entered the system.

Figures 5-4 and Figures 5-5 show the data, in query form to help understand the real flow when you apply your own desk-check logic to the data.

Figure 5-4 Query Listing of EMPMAST File Data

```
                              Display Report
                                      Report width
Position to line  . . . . .              Shift to column
Line      ....+....1....+....2....+....3....+....4....+....
          EMP EMPNAM          EMP EMPCTY      EMP    EMP
          #                   RAT             STA    ZIP
000001     1 Bizz Nizwonger   7.80 Wilkes-Barre PA   18702
000002     2 Warbler Jacoby   7.90 Wilkes-Barre PA   18702
000003     3 Bing Crossley    8.55 Scranton    PA    18702
000004     4 Uptake N. Hibiter 7.80 Fairbanks  AK    99701
000005     5 Fenworth Gront   9.30 Fairbanks   AK    99701
000006     7 Bi Nomial        8.80 Fairbanks   AK    99701
000007     8 Milly Dewith     6.50 Juneau      AK    99801
000008     9 Sarah Bayou     10.45 Juneau      AK    99801
000009    10 Dirt McPug       6.45 Newark      NJ    07101
****** ******** End of report ********
```

Figure 5-5 Query Listing of TIMCRD File Data

```
                        Display Report

Position to line  . . . . .              Shift
Line    ....+....1....
        EMPNO  EMPHRS
000001    1     35.00
000002    2     40.00
000003    3     65.00
000004    4     25.00
000005    5     33.00
000006    6     40.00
000007    7     39.00
000008    8     40.00
000009    9     40.00
000010   10     35.00
****** ********  End of report  ********
```

Chapter Summary

Before a programmer begins to code a program, the program needs to be defined by a systems analyst or a programmer operating as a Programmer / Analyst. The programmer receives a set of specifications for the project. The specifications include the input file descriptions, the output definitions, and the logic instructions to code so that the input can make the transition to output.

The better the communication is between and analyst and a programmer the fewer struggles the programmer will have in capturing the intended logic and coding it into the program. Despite everybody's best efforts, however, sometimes after clean compile, the program does not work and will not work. If the analyst's specifications are correct and the program is written in full conformance with those specifications, it could be a program bug. New programmers are more inclined to blame the design or the compiler for errors. Most often such errors are caused because the programmer is not as familiar with communications conventions as they could be or because the wrong language tool is used or because there is a programming logic flaw. The sooner a new programmer accepts this, the better at the trade they will become.

Sometimes, the compiler is in error but very rarely. As you become a better programmer, you may discover compiler bugs but they come few and far between errors. When you encounter a stubborn problem in making your code work, always verify that the test data is constructed properly for the test results you are expecting.

Key Chapter Terms

Analysis paralysis	Desk-check	Matching records
Bad data	Error message	Packed data
Clean compile	Fixed point	Query
Communication	Floating point	Record format
Create table	IBM PTFs	RPG logic cycle
Decimal data	Master record	

Review Questions

1. What are programming specifications?

2. Why is it that this program can work even though the states are not in sequence?

3. At what point in the cycle will you print the headings in the report noted in this chapter?

4. CREATE TABLE is an SQL command to create database file definitions. What is the native language on IBM i on Power Systems that is used to do the same thing?

5. Once you type in the DDS for the database into the QDDSSRC source file, the next step is to load data into the file? Why or why not?

6. Do DDS source programs get compiled with PDM option 14 in the same manner as RPG programs? Why or why not?

7. How do you suppose the data shown in the Query reports in this chapter actually got into the files?

Chapter 6 The Specifics of RPG Coding –Control Specification – by Example

From Coding to Decoding

Though the Systems Analysis and Design textbooks would show otherwise, the fact is that most programmers today do not get their programming requirements from a systems analyst who is designing a new application system. In fact, most programmers get little to no documentation at all from the requester. In most cases, no systems analyst exists in an RPG shop. Thus, the programmers in the mid-sized to small shops are referred to as programmer / analysts. The requester of a program change is typically a user whose change application has been approved by a steering committee or perhaps the IT Director.

Most small shops do not believe they have the time to deal with the formality of the natural change process as documented in the Systems Design and Analysis text books. Therefore, the information that comes from the requester or the IT manager in most cases is much lighter than the specs outlined in Chapter 5 under the heading, "the specs for your first program." The burden rests on the programmer /analyst to find the program(s) that must be changed and then, go ahead and make the change, test the change to make sure it works, and then put the change into production.

Once the program is found, the process of decoding must begin. Decoding an existing program is actually as important a skill as coding a program originally. Trying to appreciate the art that a brother or sister programmer deployed when making the code work the first time is most often more difficult than making the change itself.

In today's IT environment RPG detractors with computer science backgrounds will quickly point out their opinions that RPG is irrelevant as a language. Others will tell you that the RPG cycle is irrelevant in a modern programming language. The fact is, once you get out of college, unless you work for the most rigid and the most precise shops, in your role as a programmer, the only thing that matters is that you can read code and that you can fix code. Being able to write code from scratch, though a valuable skill, is simply not as important. .

Once you begin a career in RPG programming, you will find code written in each and all of the techniques available in a computer programming language. For RPG programmers, this includes the RPG fixed logic cycle, RPG II type code, RPG III style, as well as RPG IV. Additionally, there are externally described and internally described variants. Though many would tell the neophyte to stay clear of the cycle, it not only has its place in new development, but it also is an extremely valuable skill in being able to decode the many applications that once in a while come up for air and need to be fixed or adjusted to meet a new need.

So, we begin our description of the coding necessary to deal with the specs of our payroll sample by decoding the program from scratch.

Check the page count. I have almost passed page 100 and I have not shown many lines of RPG code. I'm setting you up, of course for learning RPG a little at a time rather than by being introduced to it a big blob at a time. By now, you have the flavor of early RPG and you have a notion that it may be very good to solve business problems that you have not even begun to discuss.

So, before we move into the mundane of describing the program solution to Chapter 5, let's consider that all RPG coders who use any form of the language believe they are RPG coders. That means that you do not have to be at the bleeding edge of RPG IV to be serving your company well.

In this book, of course, we assume nothing. Many original RPG programs exist (cycle and otherwise) in the code inventories and packages within long-standing RPG shops today. The inventories include cycle programs that were coded in RPG, RPG II, RPG III or RPG IV. Since it is extremely important to be able to update such code, RPG *"decoding"* of cycle programs and other older RPG forms is a necessary skill for an RPG programmer. Therefore, in this book, to help you become a guru in RPG decoding techniques, we show several methods of achieving the same end in the programming examples.

Well Not Exactly!

Once you learn RPG itself via RPG/400, it will be easy to relate to the same facilities as delivered within RPGIV. This book will show you how to do that all along the way to learning RPG. For the RPGIV specific advanced language features, since they are almost as different as COBOL is different from RPG, we have included several chapters at the end of the book that specifically address the new facilities such as ILE., sub procedures, and Free-Format RPG. All along we show the specific coding examples in RPGIV.

How different is RPGII from RPG/400? In its basic form, RPGIV and RPG/400 are very similar. Therefore, from a teaching/learning perspective, this book focuses on RPG/400 in our early examples and then shows the same code in RPGIV. When it is appropriate to explain a feature of RPGIV that is substantially different from the RPG/400 model, we will take the time in place to make the explanation.

RPG is a wonderful language and you will soon see why. The fact is that Java and C programmers and even old-time procedural COBOL programmers have not typically liked RPG. Likewise, RPG purists of all genres do not like Java, C, or COBOL. Old-time RPG programmers do not have that warm of a feeling either for free format RPG and those features that make the language look more like Java and C. And, as would be expected, those who have adopted the RPG IV language as their first language or who like the types of constructs that have been added to RPG IV that make the language more universally appealing are in conflict with the old-line RPG crowd. Something less than half of the RPG programmers out there have wholesale adopted RPGIV and a lesser percentage use the newest bells and whistles.

Figure 6-1 RPG Cycle Program PAREG with State Totals and Matching Records

```
*************** Beginning of data **********************
          67891123456789212345678931234567894123456789512345678961234567889
0001.00 H* RPG HEADER (CONTROL) SPECIFICATION FORMS
0002.00 H
0003.00 F*
0004.00 F* RPG FILE DESCRIPTION SPECIFICATION FORMS
0005.00 F*
0006.00 FEMPMAST IPEAE                      DISK
0007.00 FTIMCRD  ISEAE                      DISK
0008.00 FQPRINT  O  F        77     OF      PRINTER
0009.00 I*
0010.00 I* RPG INPUT SPECIFICATION FORMS
0011.00 I*
0012.00 IPAYR          01
0013.00 I             EMPNO                      EMPNO   M1
0014.00 I                                        EMPCTYL1
0015.00 I             EMPSTA                      EMPSTAL2
0016.00 ITIMR          02
0017.00 I             EMPNO                      EMPNO   M1
0018.00 C*
0019.00 C* RPG CALCULATION SPECIFICATION FORMS
0020.00 C*
0021.00 C   02 MR    EMPRAT   MULT EMPHRS   EMPPAY 72
0022.00 C   02 MR    EMPPAY   ADD  CTYPAY   CTYPAY 92
0023.00 CL1          CTYPAY   ADD  STAPAY   STAPAY 92
0024.00 CL2          STAPAY   ADD  TOTPAY   TOTPAY 92
0025.00 O*
0026.00 O* RPG OUTPUT SPECIFICATION FORMS
0027.00 O*
0028.00 OQPRINT  H 206      1P
0029.00 O        OR 206      OF
0030.00 O                                    32 'THE DOWALLOBY COMPANY'
0031.00 O                                    55 'GROSS PAY REGISTER BY '
0032.00 O                                    60 'STATE'
0033.00 O                          UDATE Y   77
0034.00 OQPRINT  H 3        1P
0035.00 O        OR 3        OF
0036.00 O                                     4 'ST'
0037.00 O                                    13 'CITY'
0038.00 O                                    27 'EMP#'
0039.00 O                                    45 'EMPLOYEE NAME'
0040.00 O                                    57 'RATE'
0041.00 O                                    67 'HOURS'
0042.00 O                                    77 'CHECK'
0043.00 O        D 1       02NMR
0044.00 O                                    46 'NO MATCHING MASTER'
0045.00 O                          EMPNO   27
0046.00 O                          EMPHRS1  67
0047.00 O        D 1       02 MR
0048.00 O                          EMPSTA    4
0049.00 O                          EMPCTY   29
0050.00 O                          EMPNO   27
0051.00 O                          EMPNAM   52
0052.00 O                          EMPRAT1  57
0053.00 O                          EMPHRS1  67
0054.00 O                          EMPPAY1  77
0055.00 O        T 22      L1
0056.00 O                                    51 'TOTAL CITY  PAY FOR'
0057.00 O                          EMPCTY   72
0058.00 O                          CTYPAY1B 77
0059.00 O        T 02      L2
0060.00 O                                    51 'TOTAL STATE PAY FOR'
0061.00 O                          EMPSTA   54
0062.00 O                          STAPAY1B 77
0063.00 O        T 2       LR
0064.00 O                          TOTPAY1  77
0065.00 O                                    50 'FINAL TOTAL PAY'
***************** End of data *****************************
```

Figure 6-2 RPG Cycle Program PAREG – Internally Described Data

```
0001.00 F* RPG HEADER SPECIFICATION FORMS
0002.00 H
0003.00 F*
0004.00 F* RPG FILE DESCRIPTION SPECIFICATION FORMS
0005.00 F*
0006.00 FEMPMAST IPEAF       55              DISK
0007.00 FTIMCRD   ISEAF       7              DISK
0008.00 FQPRINT  O  F        77        OF    PRINTER
0009.00 I*
0010.00 I* RPG INPUT SPECIFICATION FORMS
0011.00 I*
0012.00 IEMPMAST AA  01
0013.00 I                                    1   30EMPNO   M1
0013.01 I                                    4  23 EMPNAM
0013.02 I                                   24  282EMPRAT
0014.00 I                                   29  48 EMPCTYL1
0015.00 I                                   49  50 EMPSTAL2
0015.01 I                                   51  550EMPZIP
0016.00 ITIMCRD   AB  02
0017.00 I                                    1   30EMPNO   M1
0017.01 I                                    4   72EMPHRS
0018.00 C*
0019.00 C* RPG CALCULATION SPECIFICATION FORMS
0020.00 C*
0021.00 C    02 MR    EMPRAT    MULT EMPHRS     EMPPAY  72
0022.00 C    02 MR    EMPPAY    ADD  CTYPAY     CTYPAY  92
0023.00 CL1           CTYPAY    ADD  STAPAY     STAPAY  92
0024.00 CL2           STAPAY    ADD  TOTPAY     TOTPAY  92
0025.00 O*
0026.00 O* RPG OUTPUT SPECIFICATION FORMS
0027.00 O*
0028.00 OQPRINT  H 206      1P
0029.00 O        OR 206      OF
0030.00 O                               32 'THE DOWALLOBY COMPANY'
0031.00 O                               55 'GROSS PAY REGISTER BY '
0032.00 O                               60 'STATE'
0033.00 O                     UDATE Y    77
0034.00 OQPRINT  H 3        1P
0035.00 O        OR 3        OF
0036.00 O                                4 'ST'
0037.00 O                               13 'CITY'
0038.00 O                               27 'EMP#'
0039.00 O                               45 'EMPLOYEE NAME'
0040.00 O                               57 'RATE'
0041.00 O                               67 'HOURS'
0042.00 O                               77 'CHECK'
0043.00 O        D 1       02NMR
0044.00 O                               46 'NO MATCHING MASTER'
0045.00 O                     EMPNO     27
0046.00 O                     EMPHRS1   67
0047.00 O        D 1       02 MR
0048.00 O                     EMPSTA     4
0049.00 O                     EMPCTY    29
0050.00 O                     EMPNO     27
0051.00 O                     EMPNAM    52
0052.00 O                     EMPRAT1   57
0053.00 O                     EMPHRS1   67
0054.00 O                     EMPPAY1   77
0055.00 O        T 22      L1
0056.00 O                               51 'TOTAL CITY  PAY FOR'
0057.00 O                     EMPCTY    72
0058.00 O                     CTYPAY1B  77
0059.00 O        T 02      L2
0060.00 O                               51 'TOTAL STATE PAY FOR'
0061.00 O                     EMPSTA    54
0062.00 O                     STAPAY1B  77
0063.00 O        T 2       LR
0064.00 O                     TOTPAY1   77
0065.00 O                               50 'FINAL TOTAL PAY'
```

Rather than suggest that one faction in the RPG fight is correct and another is off-base, since decoding for maintenance purposes is an absolute necessity, we will start with the basics of all RPG and move on from there. It would be inappropriate to teach just free-format RPG with the built-in block language structures since the code libraries that you will find in practice do not have much of this. So, we have chosen to help you learn to be a real RPG programmer first. You can then stretch those skills to be an advanced RPGIV programmer after you gain knowledge of RPG as practiced in most IT shops.

Decoding the PAYREG RPG Program

The PAREG program that we will be decoding in this chapter and the next several chapters is shown first in Figure 6-1. The RPGIV version of the same program as converted using IBM's CVTRPGSRC facility is shown in Figure 13-2.

Still, another version of this program is necessary in order to cover the notion of externally described data files and internally described files in RPG. Figure 6-1 shows the program as it would be written today using externally described data. Figure 6-2 shows the same program using internally described data, which is often called program described data.

You will notice that the only difference between the two programs is in the Input (I) specifications. Program described data use two coding formats for input known as the I and the J. The I part captures the record identification information. The J part captures the input field information. For externally described files, the SEU formats are called IX and JX respectively. The X designation is for eXternal. Overall there is not much difference between the I and IX and the J and JX formats.

Internally & Externally Described Data

Internally described RPG data means that the data is described within the program. The field names and attributes are assigned within the program. The length is specified within the program. That is the big difference functionally between external and internal descriptions. When a program that uses internal descriptions is compiled, the compiler gets the exact record layout from the program itself. When a program that uses external descriptions is compiled, the compiler fetches the data descriptions from the database and manufactures the input and output specifications in the compiled program to save the programmer the work of all that coding.

Besides the input area, there are also changes in the PAREG program in the File Description area. Column 19 of the File Description specification asks if the input and output descriptions from the file should be fetched from the data base (coded as E) or whether they should use the fixed format within the program (coded as F). Based on this switch the compiler knows how to do its job. Additionally, since using the "F" switch means the compiler does not visit the external file description to get the data definitions, it has no means of knowing the record length. So, you can see by examining Figure 6-1 and Figure 6-2 that the PAREG program in Figure 6-2, which uses internally described data definitions has a record length of 55 specified for the EMPMAST file and a record length of 7 for the TIMCRD file. This coding is unnecessary for the File when using external descriptions.

Let's begin our decoding by describing the form types used in the all RPG programs including the PAREG program.

Looking at the code in Figure 6-1, you can see that there are numbers in columns 1-7, then there is a space, and then there is a letter. Walking down the program line by line, in the column that holds the letter, you can see that there are 2 H's, 6 F's, 9 I's, 7 C's, and 41 O's. The program described version in Figure 6-2 uses the same sequence numbers with suffixes to distinguish new lines. It has 13 input lines. When present, the forms are always presented to the RPG compiler in the following sequence.

The names for these specifications are as follows:

H	Header (Control) Specification Form
F	File Description Specification Form
I	Input Specification Form
D	Definition Specification – RPGIV only
C	Calculation Specification Form
O	Output Specification Form

Three other RPG/400 forms not used in this program are as follows:

E	File Extension Specification Form (after F)
L	Line Counter Specification (after E or F if no E)
P	Subprocedure Specification form-- RPGIV only –> used where needed

The Extension spec is used to describe arrays and tables and the Line Counter form is used to specify the length and overflow lines of forms suing special sized (not 8.5 X 11) paper. The Extension form is covered in Chapter 16 and the Line Counter is covered in Chapter 7. The definition specification picks up a lot of the work of the overworked RPGIV input specification as well a most of the work of the Extension RPG/400 Extension specification, which is not supported in RPGIV.

The vision of the programs in Figure 6-1 and 6-2 is deceiving in that the column shown that has the specification type is presented as column 8 in the figure. However, this is not the case. To create the figure, I used the Source Entry Utility, described in Chapter 4. I positioned column 6 using a Window command so that it would be the first column of the program shown. SEU provides the numbers on the left side as a guide for editing. Those numbers do not exist in the RPG statement. So, even though it looks like column 8, please make the mental adjustment so that just as the format line above shows, the RPG form spec ID is in column 6.

Columns 1 through 5 of all RPG statements are no longer used. In the past when each line in a program was typed on a punch card, it was important to number the cards in case they fell on the floor and needed to be machine sorted back in sequence. RPG/400 defines 80 columns of each form for your use. Since we do not have to deal with the first five columns at all, you can see we are making terrific progress.   All of the form types that we are about to study below are typed in column 6 of the forms in Figure 6-1.

H-- Header (Control) Specification Form

Only one control specification is permitted in a program. Yet, as shown in statement 1 and statement 2 of the PAREG program, we clearly have two H forms in this program. Whenever an * is placed in column 7 of any RPG form type, the source line becomes a comment line. It does not matter whether column 6 contains a valid form type. Whenever there is an asterisk (*) in column 7 the line is a comment line. Thus, in our example there are not two H specifications. The first one is a comment line in which we have placed a comment. The second is the control statement which has no entries in this case.

The control (Header – H) specification provides the RPG/400 compiler with information about your program and your system. This includes the following information:

- ✓ Name of the program
- ✓ Date format used in the program
- ✓ Alternative collating sequence or file translation if used
- ✓ Debug Mode (1 in column 15)

The control (H) specification is optional and thus in program *PAYREG*, since it has no entries, it was not necessary to specify it at all..

The detailed format of the RPG/400 Header specification is as follows:

H Columns 7-14 (Reserved)

H Column 15 (Debug)

Place a 1 in column 15 to turn on Debug.

H Columns 16-17 (Reserved)

H Column 18 (Currency Symbol)

Any character except zero (0), asterisk (*), comma (,), period (.), ampersand (&), minus sign (-), the letter C, or the letter R may be specified as the currency symbol.

H Column 19 (Date Format)

Specify the format of the RPG/400 user dates. The allowable entries are as follows:

Blank Defaults to month/day/year if position 21 is blank. Defaults to
day/month/year if position 21 contains a D, I, or J.
M   Month/day/year.
D   Day/month/year.
Y   Year/month/day.

H Column 20 (Date Edit)

The entry in this position specifies the separator character to be used with the Y (date) edit code – typically slash (/), period (.), or dash (-).

H Column 21 (Decimal Notation)

Specify the notation to be used for the user date. This entry also specifies the decimal notation and the separator used for numeric literals and edit codes. The term decimal notation refers to the character that separates whole numbers from decimal fractions.

H Columns 22-25 (Reserved)

H Column 26 (Alternate Collating Sequence)

The allowable entries are as follows: Blank= Normal collating sequence is used. S=Alternate collating sequence is used.

H Columns 27-39 (Reserved)

H Column 40 (Sign Handling)

A blank entry is required. The sign is always forced on input and output of zoned numeric fields.

H Column 41 (Forms Alignment)

Should forms be aligned on first page printing? The allowable entries are as follows:

Blank First line is printed only once.
1   First line can be printed repeatedly allowing the operator to adjust the printer forms.

If the program contains more than one printer file, the entry in position 41 applies to each printer file that has 1P (first-page) output. This function may also be specified by the CL command OVRPRTF (Override to Print File) or in the printer device file and can be affected by the ALIGN option on the STRPRTWTR command.   Use column 41 only when the first output line is written to a printer file.

H Column 42 (Reserved)

H Column 43 (File Translation)

A blank entry says no translation occurs. An entry of F indicates that a file translation table is to be used to translate all data in specified files.

H Columns 44-56 (Reserved)

H Column 57 (Transparency Check)

Sometimes data composition messes up the best coding. There are few instances but they exist in which the transparency of characters needs to be checked. The allowable entries are as follows:

Blank No check for transparency.
1   Check for transparency.

If you specify 1 in position 57 of the control specification, the RPG/400 compiler scans literals and constants for DBCS characters. It does not check hexadecimal literals.

H Columns 58-74 (Reserved)

H Columns 76-80 (Program Identification)

Considering that most RPG programs are written today with No H specification whatsoever, the typical way of naming an RPG program is the default of taking the name of the source member and making it the name of the program object.

The symbolic name entered in these positions is the name of the program that can be run after compilation. You can override this name with the PGM parameter in the CL command CRTRPGPGM (Create RPG Program) which is used to create an object from your source RPG program.

If you do not specify a name in positions 75 through 80 of the control specification or on the CRTRPGPGM command, but the source is from a database file, the member name is used as the program name. If the source is not from a database file, the program name defaults to RPGOBJ.

If you specify the program name on the control specification, its maximum length is 6 characters. If you specify the program name in the CRTRPGPGM command, its maximum length is 10 characters.

RPGIV Header (H) Specification

The Header specification is also called the CONTROL specification. It is seldom used in RPG/400 programs written today. Just as in RPG/400, the H spec in RPGIV provides information about generating and running programs. However, with RPGIV, there are three different ways in which this information can be provided to the compiler and the compiler searches for this information in the following order:

1. A control specification included in your source with an H in column 6
2. A data area named RPGLEHSPEC in *LIBL
3. A data area named DFTLEHSPEC in QRPGLE

Once one of these sources is found, the values are assigned and RPGIV H keywords that are not specified are assigned their default values.

Header option 1 is similar to RPG/400 in that you specify the options in the program. With option 2, you get to include a prewritten H spec called RPGLEHSPEC in a data area object in your program merely by permitting the compiler to find the object in your library list. Header option 3 is similar to option 2 and option 1 with nothing specified. In other words, RPG finds the default H spec data area object that it stores under the name of DFTLEHSPEC in the QRPGLE library from which the compiler itself gets launched.

The fact that there is an option 1 is where the similarities end between the standard H spec and the new RPGIV H spec.

As an introductory book to RPG, it is not the author's intention to provide all of the information that exists in IBM manuals on a given topical area. Some of the keywords are self-explanatory and thus will be helpful immediately. However, some of them are not self explanatory and demand that the reader be well versed in other topics that are not given extensive treatment in this book. For example, there are a number of keywords that require a high level of understanding of the Integrated Language Environment as well as the notion of sub procedures in RPGIV. Though these topics are touched on adequately in the latter chapters of this book, we do deal with advanced features in this book. The good news as with most of RPG is that the defaults do a fine job of covering the options that a beginner programmer needs to get a quick start in programming RPGIV as well as ILE and subprocedures – but they come later..

The format of the new RPGIV H spec is very simple"

Column 6   H
Columns 7-80   Area for header spec keywords
Columns 81 – 100   Comments

The RPGIV Header spec is keyword driven in much the same way as other IBM i on Power Systems artifacts, such as physical files, logical files, and display files are specified to their respective compilers.

The keyword format is simply as follows:

Keyword(value)

Figure 6-2 shows each of the RPGIV keywords that can be used in the H specification with a brief explanation. The table also shows one option specified as a sample and other options in a separate column.

Figure 6-2 Header Keywords and Options

Keyword / Sample	Other Options	Meaning
ACTGRP(*NEW)	*CALLER; 'activation-group-name'	Type of activation group
ALTSEQ{*NONE)	*SRC; *EXT	Alternate sequence?
ALWNULL(*NO)	*INPUTONLY; *USRCTL)	Nulls allowed?
AUT(*LIBRCRTAUT)	*ALL; *CHANGE; *USE; *EXCLUDE	Authority given to users for use of program
BNDDIR('BINDER')	:'binding-directory-name'...	List of binding directories
CCSID(*GRAPH: Ignore)	*SRC; number	Set default graphic
CCSID(*UCS2: 13488)	Number	Set default UCS-2 CCSID
COPYNEST(32)	Number	Maximum nesting depth for COPY directives (1 – 2048)
COPYRIGHT('Kelly Consulting')	'copyright string'	Set copyright info
CVTOPT(*DATETIME)	*{NO}DATETIME *{NO}GRAPHIC *{NO}VARCHAR *{NO}VARGRAPHIC	How compiler handles dates, etc.
DATEDIT(*DMY)	*MDY, or *YMD	Format for Y edit code
DATFMT(*ISO)	Valid date formats	Internal date format
DEBUG{*YES)	*NO	Debug on or off
DECEDIT(*JOBRUN)	Value	Char used for dec. pt.
DECPREC(30)	31	Decimal precision
DFTACTGRP(*YES)	*NO	Default activation
DFTNAME(MYPROG)	RPG Name	Specify pgm name

ENBPFRCOL(*PEP)	ENTRYEXIT; *FULL	Is full performance collection enabled?
EXPROPTS (*MAXDIGITS)	*RESDECPOS	Precision rules
EXTBININT{(*NO)	*YES	Internal or external binary format is used.
FIXNBR(*ZONED)	*{NO}ZONED; *{NO}INPUTPACKED)	Should decimal data errors be auto-fixed?
FLTDIV{(*NO)	*YES	Use floating divide
FORMSALIGN{(*NO)	*YES	Repeat 1p output for forms alignment
FTRANS{(*NONE)	*SRC	File translation?
GENLVL(10)	Number 1 – 20	Errors > this value will stop compile
INDENT(*NONE)	character value	Should structured operations be indented?
INTPREC(10)	20 (10 or 20)	Intermediate precision
LANGID(*JOBRUN)	*JOB; language-identifier	Language ID
NOMAIN	For module	No main proc
OPENOPT (*NOINZOFL)	*INZOFL	Set OF indicator to off when file opened
OPTIMIZE(*NONE)	*BASIC	*FULL)	Level of optimization
OPTION(*XREF)	*{NO}XREF; NO}GEN; *{NO}SECLVL; *{NO}SHOWCPY; *{NO}EXPDDS; *{NO}EXT; *{NO}SHOWSKP); *{NO}SRCSTMT); *{NO}DEBUGIO)	Specifies compiler options
PRFDTA(*NOCOL)	*COL	Collect profile data?
SRTSEQ(*HEX)	*JOB; *JOBRUN; *LANGIDUNQ; *LANGIDSHR; 'sort-table-name'	Sort sequence table
TEXT(*SRCMBRTXT	*BLANK; 'description'	Descriptive text
THREAD(*SERIALIZE)	Not specified	Serialize thread?
TIMFMT(*ISO)	Time format options	Time format
TRUNCNBR(*YES)	*NO	Use truncated value or produce an errormsg.
USRPRF(*USER)	*OWNER	Which authority?

Chapter Summary

The PAREG example program series is introduced in this chapter in both an external and an internal format. Internal format means that the fields are defined in the program and external format means that the field definitions are brought in from the objects at compile time.

The specifications for the RPG/400 and RPGIV compiler are as follows:

H	Header (Control) Specification Form
F	File Description Specification Form
E	File Extension Specification Form -- RPG/400 only
L	Line Counter Specification (after E or F if no E)
I	Input Specification Form

P   Subprocedure RPGIV – used where needed
D   Definition Specification – RPGIV only
C   Calculation Specification Form
O   Output Specification Form

RPG/400 and RPGIV programs are formed by using the specifications above and combining them into programs or modules.

The CONTROL specification which is housed in the RPG H (header) spec controls the execution of the program. In RPG/400, this is a fill-in the blanks facility whereas in RPGIV, it is all keyword oriented. Each RPG/400 H column is examined in this chapter to give a full flavor for what can be accomplished. The reader should take a few minutes to examine these but should be aware that other than the DEBUG option, these entries are seldom used. In fact, with all of the other ways to debug RPG programs, even the DEBUG option sees little action nowadays.

With RPGIV, programming convenience has been enhanced with a number of CONTROL keywords providing directives to the compiler. The full list of all H spec keywords is provided in this chapter and it would serve the reader well to take a look at these to get an appreciation for the additional power of the RPGIV language.

Key Chapter Terms

*BLANK	DFTNAME	Output Spec
*DMY	ENBPFRCOL	OVRPRTF
*ISO	EXPROPTS	PRFDTA
*MDY	EXTBININT	Pgm described data
*YMD	Extension spec	Program ID
ACTGRP	Externally described data	Purists, RPG
ALIGN	Field	Record length
ALTSEQ	Attributes	RPG coders
ALWNULL	File Description spec	RPG fixed logic cycle
AUT	File translation	RPGII
Block Language	First page	RPGIII
BNDDIR	FIXNBR	RPGIV
Calculation spec	FLTDIV	RPGLEHSPEC
CCSID	FORMSALIGN	RPGOBJ
CHANGE	FTRANS	Sequence
CHECK	GENLVL	Source Entry Utility
COBOL	Header Spec	SRTSEQ
Code inventories	INDENT	Steering committee
Comment line	Input Spec	STRPRTWTR
Control spec	Internally described data	Structured operations
COPYNEST	INTPREC	Prrocedure Spec
COPYRIGHT	IT Director	Subprocedures
CRTRPGPGM	Keywords	Systems Analysis
CVTOPT	LANGID	Test
DATFMT	Line Counter spec	TEXT
DEBUG	Maintenance	THREAD
DECEDIT	Module	Time
Decimal data	NOMAIN	TIMFMT
Decimal notation	Objects	Transparency Check
Decoding	OF indicator	TRUNCNBR
DECPREC	OPENOPT	UDATE
Definition Spec	OPTIMIZE	USRPRF
DFTACTGRP	OPTION	Window command
DFTLEHSPEC		

Review Questions

1. What is the difference between coding a program and decoding a program?

2. What is the programmer's job after receiving program specifications?

3. What is internally described Data?

4. What is externally described data?

5. What are the form types that are found in the various flavors of RPG?

6. What is the header specification used for in RPG/400?

7. What is the major difference separating the RPG & RPGIV headers specifications.

8. What are the three different ways the Control specification values can be included in RPGIV programs?

9. Using the chart in this chapter as a guide, as well as Internet research, what is the purpose of the following H spec keywords for RPGIV and when should they be used? ALTSEQ ALWNULL AUT BNDDIR CCSID COPYNEST

10. Using the chart in this chapter as a guide, as well as Internet research, what is the purpose of the following H spec keywords for RPGIV and when should they be used? CVTOPT DATEDIT DATFMT DEBUG DECEDIT DECPREC

11. Using the chart in this chapter as a guide, as well as Internet research, what is the purpose of the following H spec keywords for RPGIV and when should they be used? DFTACTGRP DFTNAME ENBPFRCOL EXPROPTS EXTBININT FIXNBR

12. Using the chart in this chapter as a guide, as well as Internet research, what is the purpose of the following H spec keywords for RPGIV and when should they be used? FLTDIV FORMSALIGN FTRANS GENLVL INDENT INTPREC

13. Using the chart in this chapter as a guide, as well as Internet research, what is the purpose of the following H spec keywords for RPGIV and when should they be used? LANGID NOMAIN OPENOPT OPTIMIZE OPTION PRFDTA

14. Using the chart in this chapter as a guide, as well as Internet research, what is the purpose of the following H spec keywords for RPGIV and when should they be used? SRTSEQ TEXT THREAD TIMFMT TRUNCNBR USRPRF

Chapter 7 The Specifics of RPG Coding –File Description & Line Counter Specifications – by Example

Talking to the Outside World

As in all programs that use files, the language must provide a means of linking from the program to the outside world. The File Description Specification, a.k.a. the 'F' spec is the way this communication is achieved in RPG.

F-- File Description Specification Form

We continue our decoding adventure for File Descriptions and Line Counters in this Chapter. A sample filled-in RPG/400 File description coding sheet is shown in Figure 7-1. Notice that column 66 of the line in which the CUSMSTF file is defined has an A in it. For viewing purposes we moved that column two columns away from the end of the form so it could be seen.

Figure 7-1 Sample File Description form (amalgamated & truncated)

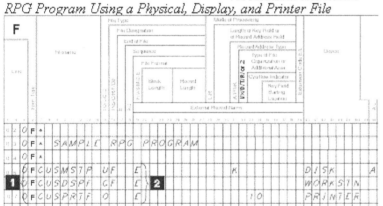

* Note – The A in column 66 next to "DISK" has been moved for viewing.

Before SEU (See Chapter 4), programmers painstakingly coded their RPG programs on coding sheets that were 8 ½ X 11" in size. Figure 7-1 reflects a hand-written coding sheet.

Notice in the area marked as 2 that column 19 contains an E for all of these files. That means that the files are externally described and no record length is required on the File Description statement for these three files. Notice also that there is no primary and no secondary file defined as in our PAREG standard example. That means that this program does not depend on the RPG cycle.

The customer master file CUSMSTF and the customer display file CUSDSPF each use an F designator in column 16 rather than the P or S that we have used in the PAREG program. This means that the file is fully procedural. Fully procedural (F) files can be processed by the many RPG operations such as read (READ), read equal (READE), chain (CHAIN) etc. that we will be covering in Chapters 14 (RPG) & 15 (RPGIV). The fully procedural file gives the RPG & RPGIV programmer great latitude in the calculations specification to determine which operations occur at what times.

In the PAREG program, column 15 is coded with either an 'I' for input or an 'O' for output. The sample lines for the first two files in Figure 7-1 are coded with a 'U' and a 'C' respectively. The 'U' indicates that this file can be used for input and that the records read will be locked for update. The program can then update the data in the record in memory and then with an update (RPG/400- UPDAT, RPGIV- UPDATE) operation write the changed data back to disk. The record gets unlocked when the update is complete or when the program reads another record in the same file.

The 'C' (combined) designation is very similar to the 'U' (update) operation but it is reserved for device files such as terminals. For the program to be able to write the screen and then read the data back, the display file must be coded with a C in column 15 to designate that combined operations of output and input are available.

Notice on the right of the form that the device type is coded as WORKSTN. PAREG uses only two DISK devices and one PRINTER device. So now you know how to define a simple workstation device in your RPG programs. Workstation (WORKSTN) files can be designated as input (I) or output (O) also but most programmers prefer to use the 'C' designator regardless of the type of operations that they will use against the file.

The CUSMSTF file also has a 'K' designation in column 31. This is to tell the compiler that the file will be processed by a key, such as customer number. It also says that the file has an index associated with it. The file can be a keyed logical or physical file. Looking out on the right to column 66, you will notice an A designation. This tells the RPG compiler that this file can not only be used for input and update operations but it can be used for WRITE operations which add records to the file.

That's a lot to know about file description specifications and it should give you a head start in decoding and understanding the File description specifications used in the PAREG example.

Why File Descriptions?

File description specifications describe all the files that your program uses. The information for each file includes the following:

- ✓ Name of the file
- ✓ How the file is used
- ✓ Size of records in the file
- ✓ Input or output device used for the file
- ✓ If the file is conditioned by an external indicator.

For your convenience we have collected the six 'F' specs from the external and internal versions of PAREG and have listed them again in Figure 7-2 and 7-3 respectively. It may help to recall that the only difference between the external and internal versions in this program is the record length and the F instead of an E in column 19.

Figure 7-2 PAREG RPG/400 External File Descriptions
```
         678911234567892123456789312345678941234567895123
0003.00 F*
0004.00 F* RPG FILE DESCRIPTION SPECIFICATION FORMS
0005.00 F*
0006.00 FEMPMAST IPEAE                     DISK
0007.00 FTIMCRD  ISEAE                     DISK
0008.00 FQPRINT  O    F        77     OF   PRINTER
```

Figure 7-3 PAREG – File Descriptions Internally Described Data
```
         678911234567892123456789312345678941234567895123
0003.00 F*
0004.00 F* RPG FILE DESCRIPTION SPECIFICATION FORMS
0005.00 F*
0006.00 FPAYMAST IPEAF      55            DISK
0007.00 FEMPTIM  ISEAF       7            DISK
0008.00 FQPRINT  O    F      77      OF   PRINTER
```

Statements 3 through 5 contain asterisks in column 7, therefore, they are comments used for documenting the program. Statements 6 through 8 are very important to the functioning of this program as they define both the two input files and the printer file.

F Column 7-14 File Name

Columns 7-14 of the F spec are where you make the link to the outside world in RPG. Every file must have a unique file name that is defined to the IBM i/OS system. The file name can be from 1 to 8 characters long, and must begin with an alphabetic character. As you can see in Figures 7-2 and 7-3, the three file names we define in the PAREG program are EMPMAST, TIMCRD, and QPRINT.

Using the DDS that we described in Figures 5-2 and 5-3, we created two database files named EMPMAST and TIMCRD respectively. See Chapter 4 for the instructions on how to enter database DDS into the system with SEU. In statement 8, we see the name QPRINT, which is the name of a reserved printer file in IBM i/OS that IBM makes available for your use in RPG. So, each time you create a program that prints a report, you may use the print file QPRINT to permit this to happen. You may also create your own print file. This is shown in Chapter 23. When you create your own print file, you would use the name of that file in place of QPRINT.

In RPGIV, the file name can be ten characters and it occupies columns 7 to 16.

F Column 15 File Type – I, O, Etc.

Column 15 is where you define the file type. The question you ask in order to know how to fill in this column is: "How will I use this file – input or output?" The choices of entries for Column 15 are as follows:

I   Input file.
O   Output file.
U   Update file.
C   Combined (input/output) file.

In our example program, we defined EMPMAST and TIMCRD as I for input. These two database files will provide the input for our program. We defined QPRINT as O for output since we will produce an output report from the input data read from the database files. If we were going to write records back to the EMPMAST or TIMCRD databases, we would have coded it as U for update. We have no use for the C for combined in this program since there is no interactive display device. Later when we work with display files in which we write a program to interact with a terminal user, we will use the C designation to indicate that we both write to the display and read from the display using the same file description specification.

In RPGIV, the File Type is specified in position 17.

F Column 16 File Designation – Primary, Secondary, etc.

Column 16 is used to designate that a file will use the RPG cycle or not and it is used to provide a means for special files to be loaded into the system to control processing. It also provides for files to be processed outside the RPG cycle

The entries that can be used in column 16 and their meaning are presented below:

Blank Output file
P   Primary file
S   Secondary file
R   Record address file
T   Array or table file
F   Full procedural file

Blank, P, S-- Output, Primary, and Secondary

The QPRINT file defined in the File Description specifications of the PAREG RPG program is output-only and thus, we describe it in column 16 with a blank entry. The EMPMAST file is designated as primary. This means that it will be the first file read and it will be the first file read when there is a matching time card record (secondary.) The TIMCRD file is designated as secondary since it is not read until *all* of the matching primaries are read for an employee. Since in our example, there will be just one payroll master for each time card, the actuality is that after a matched master, the matching time card record, designated as secondary will be read next. More than one secondary file can be specified but this is not necessary in the PAREG standard example.

Though the PAREG program does not include any other entry types, the other possible choices are explained below for completeness.

R-- Record Address File

A record-address file (RA) is a sequentially organized file used to select records from another file. Only one file in a program can be specified as a record-address file. One of the frequent uses for an RA file is to process the results of what is called and address sort. In other words, you can run the FMTDTA AS/400 command to sort a file and instead of writing out a big file with a big record length, you can ask the sort to create a file of record addresses that are in the sequence in which you wish to process the data. If your program were working with the output of such a sort, you would designate it with an R in column 16 of the F specification. In this book, since logical files have mostly replaced the need for RA files in RPG, we do not offer any examples of using RA files.

T-- Array or Table File

Array and table files are specified by placing a T in position 16. Arrays and tables are small files, often consisting of codes. In processing data elements are often checked against these codes to assure that the input is valid or to find a matching explanation for a code. A table for lookups might be used for payroll codes as an example. The code M in the table might have a matching explanation called Married and the code F might have a matching explanation called Female. RPG provides a means of compiling these codes at the back of the program (Compile time) and this is very convenient when the codes are not expected to change frequently.

For codes that change frequently, such as the tax tables in a payroll program, it is not wise to compile these with the program since each time the government makes a change, you must alter the program contents and you must recompile (retranslate into machine language) the program. For situations such as this, RPG provides this nice facility (T option) in which the table or array can be pulled in from disk right before the program is executed. In this way, the changes can be made to the table or array on disk without the program having to be modified or recompiled.

F-- Full Procedural File

As the name implies, full procedural files are those that give the programmer full procedural control of happenings in a program. This is a very important entry and will be explored with examples further in this book in far greater detail. This entry is used when the input, output and update functions are controlled by calculation operations. File operation codes such as CHAIN or READ or UPDAT or WRITE are used to do input, output, or input/output, or record add functions.

In RPGIV, the File Designation is specified in position 18.

F Column 17 (End of File)

This entry is used with primary and secondary files to instruct the program about how it can end naturally. For RPG programs to end, the LR indicator must be turned on. When just one file is used for input, the entries are moot since LR will naturally be turned on when all records from the file have been read. If a primary and a secondary file were defined for input such as in our example, we would not want the LR indicator to turn on and end the program after all the primaries are read because we may still have a matching time card record to be processed.

The entries for this column are as follows:

E   All records from the file must be processed before end

Blank This file does not have to be fully processed to end

However, if position 17 is blank for all files, then RPG defaults that all records from all files must be processed before end of program (LR) can occur. If position 17 is not blank for all files, all records from this file may or may not be processed before end of program occurs in multi-file processing. In PAREG, both input files must finish being read before the program can end.

In RPGIV, the End of File is specified in position 19. The Add records column of RPG/400 (column 66) is specified in RPGIV in position 20.

F Column 18 (Sequence)

You use this handy facility to sequence check your input, combined our update files when they are being read as primary and/or secondary files.

The possible entries for this column are as follows:

A   Match fields are in ascending sequence.
Blank   Same as A
D   Match fields are in descending sequence.

This column works hand in glove with the match field indication on the Input Specification form that is used to assure a match between two files such as the EMPMAST and TIMCRD files. Both input files defined in PAREG in Figure 7-2 have an A designation meaning that the match fields (EMPNO) must be in ascending sequence. Jumping ahead just a little, to show you exactly what I mean by match fields, I have duplicated the Input lines in Figure 7-4 for your reading convenience:

Figure 7-4 PAREG Match Field Input Specifications
```
          67891123456789212345678931234567894123456789512345678961234567 8
0009.00 I*
0010.00 I* RPG INPUT SPECIFICATION FORMS
0011.00 I*
0012.00 IPAYR          01
0013.00 I              EMPNO                              EMPNO   M1
0014.00 I                                                 EMPCTYL1
0015.00 I              EMPSTA                             EMPSTAL2
0016.00 ITIMR          02
0017.00 I              EMPNO                              EMPNO   M1
```

On line 12, the record format name PAYR from the primary file called EMPMAST is specified. Following this on line 13 the EMPNO field from EMPMAST is referenced. The M1 in column 61 next to the EMPNO tells the compiler that this field is a match field and it tells the compiler that if there is an 'A' or 'D' entry in column 18 of the File description, the file EMPMAST must be in sequence – either ascending or descending. In PAREG of course it is ascending. If the file records as they are read by the program are not in sequence, the RPG program will halt with an error condition. The M1 in line 17 does the same thing for the TIMCRD file.

In RPGIV, the Sequence works the same but is specified in position 21.

F Column 19 (File Format)

This column is used to tell the compiler from what source the input and output descriptions will come for each file in the program. The input / output definitions may come from within the program on input and output specification sheets. When defied in the program, these file formats are referred to as program described or internally described files. The definitions may also come externally from within a database, workstation, printer or other file object that is referenced within in the program. These file formats are referred to as externally described files.

The possible entries for File Format are as follows:

F   Program described file
E   Externally described file

An F in position 19 indicates that the records for the file are described within the RPG/400 program on input/output specifications. An E in position 19 indicates that the record descriptions for the file are external to the RPG/400 source program. The compiler obtains these descriptions when the program is compiled and it then includes them in the source program and in the accompanying source listing.

As you can see in line 8 of PAREG, the QPRINT print file is described with an 'F' entry in column 19. This means that the record length will be provided by file description and the format of the output records will be provided within the program as you can see in lines 25 through 65 of Figure 6-1.

As you can also see in lines 6 and 7 of the external version of the program, Figure 7-2, both the EMPMAST and the TIMCRD files have an 'E' entry in file description column 19 and thus they are externally described. The internally described PAREG shown in Figure 7-3 has an F in column 19 for internal fixed format. The external definitions will be brought into the program at compilation time. A snapshot of a compile listing showing the full inclusion of the data definitions brought in from the external database file defined in the RPG program is shown in Figure 7-5.

Figure 7-5 Compile Listing of External Input Expanded

```
     1000   I* RPG INPUT SPECIFICATION FORMS
     1100   I*
     1200   IPAYR          01
     1300   I                   EMPNO                               EMPNO    M1
     1400   I                                                       EMPCTYL1
     1500   I                   EMPSTA                              EMPSTAL2
     1500    INPUT  FIELDS FOR RECORD PAYR FILE EMPMAST FORMAT PAYR.
    A000001                     EMPNO                   1    30EMPNO    M1
    A000002                                             4    23 EMPNAM
    A000003                                            24    282EMPRAT
    A000004                                            29    48 EMPCTYL1
    A000005                     EMPSTA                 49    50 EMPSTAL2
    A000006                                            51    550EMPZIP
     1600   ITIMR          02
     1700   I                   EMPNO                               EMPNO    M1
     1700    INPUT  FIELDS FOR RECORD TIMR FILE TIMCRD FORMAT TIMR.
    B000001                     EMPNO                   1    30EMPNO    M1
    B000002                                             4    72EMPHRS
```

The sequence designators in Figure 7-5 that begin with 'A' are the specifications that were brought in from the EMPMAST file from record format name PAYR. The sequence designators that begin with B were brought in from the TIMR record format from the TIMCRD file.

As a point of note, when external files are used with fully procedural files, no input specifications need to be presented to the RPG program at all so this can be a great saving in coding. However, when a program uses level breaks or match fields as the PAREG program does, the program uses the input form in order to tell the compiler what the match fields are and what fields should be used for various level totals. Notice in Figures 5-1 and 5-4 that just the lines of input with the M1, L1, and L2 designated input fields needed to be specified. The other input field definitions were brought in from the external file definitions.

In RPGIV, the File Format is specified in position 22.

F Columns 20-23 (Reserved)

As you can see in the program, there are no entries in positions 20 through 23. In fact, these must be blank. In older RPG's these positions were available to specify a block length. Since the database itself is used to determine blocking during execution, there is no need for this in RPG. When a block length is allowed, for example, there are parameters in the CL command OVRDBF that permit a blocking factor to be specified. Our simple program, PAREG uses not such facility.

F Columns 24-27 (Record Length)

Programmers use positions 24 through 27 to indicate the length of the logical records contained in a program-described file. The maximum record size that can be specified is 9999; however, record-size constraints of any device may override this value.

Notice that the QPRINT file has a 77 as its record length. That is because the longest print line ends printing in column 77. The EMPMAST and the TIMCRD files are both externally described in Figure 7-2, therefore, their record lengths are provided by the external object and this entry must be blank for externally described files. For the internally described version, as shown in Figure 7-3, the record length for EMPMAST is specified as 55 and for TIMCRD as 7.

In RPGIV, the record length can be longer by one column and is specified in positions 23 to 27.

F Columns 28-39 (Other Entries)

Positions 28-39 are not needed for the PAREG program. We show the other entries here, however, so that this book can also be used for you as a reminder guide. We will revisit File Descriptions in examples in later chapters when this information is germane to a problem we are solving.

F Column 28 Limits Processing

The entries for column 28 are as follows:

L   Sequential-within-limits processing by a record-address file
Blank   Sequential or random processing

You specify an L in column 28 to indicate limits processing otherwise let the column blank. The default then is no limits processing. The limits file is a file of limits in which each record contains a set of limits that consists of the lowest record key and the highest record key from that particular section of the indexed file to be processed. You may have multiple limits records in the file. When a limits record is read, the corresponding record with the key value in the file is processed.

The record address file with the limits record would require its own File Description statement. The L in 28 is for the keyed file that will be processed via the limits file.

In RPGIV, Limits processing is also specified in position 28.

F Column 29-30 Length of Key or Record Address

The entries specified in columns 29 to 30 pertain to program described keyed (indexed) database files. If you are not coding a program described file or the file is not keyed, then leave these positions blank. Otherwise, place the total length of the key field(s) in 29-30.

In RPGIV, the length of key or RAF is specified in position 29 – 33.

F Column 31 Record Address File Type

A record address file is a file used to process another file. See limits file explanation for column 28 above. Whereas the file that would have an L specified in column 28 is the keyed master file, the entries in column 31 describe the RAF file that will control the processing of that file.

The FMTDTA command (a.k.a. the IBM i on Power Systems sort) has the ability to produce a record address file of relative record numbers (also called an address-out or ADDROUT file or record address file [RAF]). ADDROUT sorts were very prevalent when disk was very expensive. Instead of a fully sorted file that included all of the records in the file that were part of the sort output, the ADDROUT file contained the addresses of the records such that if the records were brought into the program in the sequence of the ADDROUT records, the file data would appear to be sorted in the program. In addition to being very clever, this saved much disk space. CL programs using ADDROUT sorts continue to run in IBM i on Power Systems shops today.

The entries for RAF include the following:

Blank Relative record numbers are used to process the file.
Records are read consecutively.
Record address file contains relative-record numbers
Keys in record-address-limits file are in the same format as keys
in the file being processed.

A   Character keys (valid only for program-described files
specified as indexed files or as a record-address-limits file).

P   Packed keys (valid only for program-described files specified as
indexed files or as a record-address-limits file).

K   Key values are used to process the file. This entry is valid only
for externally described files.

Figure 7-1 shows the K entry for the CUSTMSTF designating that a key would be used and that the file was indexed.

In RPGIV, the RAF type is specified in position 34.

F Column 32 File Organization

Column 32 is used for Internally Described Files only.

Other than the blank entry which is for both program described and externally described files, the two entries that may be specified in this column are for program described files only. The possible entries are as follows:

Blank The file is processed without keys, or the file is externally described.
I   The file is an Indexed file. (program-described files).
T   The file is a Record address file that contains relative-record
Numbers (valid only for program-described files).

In RPGIV, the File Organization is specified in position 35.

F Columns 33-34 Overflow Indicator

When a printed form passes the last line of print on a form, RPG can sense that the overflow has occurred and it can communicate that fact to the programmer through a number of indicator choices OA-OG, and OF. By habit, I use OF because it reminds me of the word overflow. However, with some programmers writing programs that produce two or more reports on different printers, it is good that RPG permits eight different overflow indicators to be used – one for each of up to eight printer files. This is the place in the program in which you tell RPG what the overflow indicator is going to be for a particular printer file.

The entries for overflow are as follows:

Blank   No overflow indicator is used.
OA-OG,   Specified overflow indicator conditions the lines to be
OV   printed when overflow occurs.

01-99   Set on when a line is printed on the overflow line, or
                the overflow line is reached or passed during a space or
                skip operation.

Indicators OA through OG, and OV are not valid for externally described printer files. Use positions 33 and 34 to specify an overflow indicator to condition which lines in each PRINTER file will be printed when overflow occurs. This entry is valid only for a PRINTER device. Overflow only occurs if defined.

Only one overflow indicator can be assigned to a file. If more than one PRINTER file in a program is assigned an overflow indicator, that indicator must be unique for each file.

F Columns 35-38 (Key Field Starting Location)

This entry is for internally described files only. The possible entries for these RPG/400 columns are as follows:

Blank Key fields are not used for this program-described file, or
           the file is externally described.
1-9999 Record position in a program described indexed file in which
           the key field begins.

This area is not used for externally described files. For program described index database files, use positions 35 through 38 to identify the record position in which the key field for the indexed file begins. An entry must be made in these positions for a program described indexed file. The key field of a record contains the information that identifies the record. The key field must be in the same location in all records in the file. The entry in these positions must be right-adjusted. Leading zeros can be omitted.

In RPGIV, the information for the key field starting location for program described files is now in a keyword with this format:

`KEYLOC(number)`

F Column 39 (Extension Code)

As RPG was developed, the File Description specification could no longer hold all of the information that was needed to handle the requirements of the language. Since much of the information that needed to be added had to do with data, IBM created what was originally called the File Description Extension form. It was an extension to File Description. We cover this form in detail in Chapter 16. Over time, since the File Description Extension itself grew in size, and some of the material did not relate at all to files, IBM reduced the size of the File Description Extension moniker to just Extension. Without a historical perspective, the word Extension has no real meaning.

As internal line control facilities began to take over in printers from the old carriage control tapes, the line counter specification was also devised as another file extension. However, since the word extension had already been taken, IBM fashioned the L spec or Line Counter specification to help with printer files.

To link the file with the extension or line counter, the compiler writers included a column in File Descriptions that alerted the compiler that there was an extension specification expected for the file being defined. The entries for the Extension Code therefore are as follows:

Blank No extension or line-counter specifications are used.
E   Extension specifications further describe the file.
L   Line counter specifications further describe the file.

Use position 39 to indicate whether the program-described file is further described on the extension specifications or on the line counter specifications (printers). An E in position 39 applies only to array or table files or to record-address files; an L in position 39 applies to files assigned to the PRINTER device.

Extension and Line Counter specifications in RPGIV have been replaced by a combination of keywords and the new 'D' specification. This entry is therefore moot in RPGIV.

F Columns 40-46 (Device)

Positions 40-46 of file description is where you specify the name of the generic device type that will be used in the program. In essence this is where the file name is linked with the specific device type that the file name references.

The possible entries for the device in RPG programs are as follows:

PRINTER   File can have control characters for printers
DISK   File is a database file on a disk device
WORKSTN   File is a workstation file – terminal I/O
SPECIAL   User supplies special routine for device

In the PAREG program, we used positions 40 through 46 to specify the RPG/400 device name to be associated the three files in the program. The file names EMPMAST, TIMCRD, and QPRINT were specified in positions 7 through 14. EMPMAST and TIMCRD are designated as DISK files and QPRINT is designated as a PRINTER files.

Since the AS/400 has natural print spooling. The RPG program will not ever have to communicate directly with a printer. However, it will send the appropriate control characters for printing through the device file in play (QPRINT in this case). The output will be in an output queue associated with the user's job and it can be printed by using the operating system facility known as spooling by starting a "writer" against an output queue. If this presents an issue for you in your shop, see your system administrator since each shop may have different printers and different printer standards.

The **WORKSTN** device in RPG (Figure 7-1) permits files that are created using a tool called SDA (Described in Chapter 20) to be linked with the RPG program. Using this facility, RPG programmers can use the WRITE or READ operations to WRITE or READ full screen panels of data to terminal or PC emulated displays. RPG also has an operation that we will discuss that performs both a WRITE to a Display and a READ from a display in just one operation. The RPG operation code for this is EXFMT. Since there are no interactive devices in the PAREG program we defer this discussion until Chapter 20..

We have completed all we need to know about the very valuable File Description Specification for our PAREG problem. There are some more entries that can be made on file descriptions so, for completeness these are examined below.

In RPGIV, the Device is specified in positions 37-42.

F Column(s) 47-52 (Reserved)

Positions 47 through 52 are not used in PAREG and for all programs, these positions must be blank.

F Column 53 (Continuation Lines)

RPG supports the ability to have special things defined in File Descriptions for which there is no room on the F spec. So, a continuation of the F spec is permitted by placing a K in position 53. This indicates a continuation line. We need no continuation lines in the PAREG program.

The functions implemented via File Description continuation line entries are covered after column 80 of File Descriptions. Most of the facilities provided via continuation entries are provided in RPGIV via keywords.

F Column(s) 54-59 (Routine)

When you must use SPECIAL as the device entry (positions 40 through 46), you also must name a routine in positions 54 through 59 to handle the support for the special device. The routine name must be left-adjusted within these columns. This entry is used by the compiler to produce the linkage to the routine. The PAREG program used no special routines and therefore these entries were not needed.

F Column(s) 60-65 (Reserved)

Positions 60-65 are not used in PAYREG and for all programs, these positions must be blank.

F Column 66 (File Addition)

Sine the PAREG program is database input-only, there was no need to specify to the compiler that the file described in positions 7-14 might have records added to it during processing. However, in future programs in this book, we will be adding records to files, and when we do, this entry will be needed.

The allowable entries for column 66 are as follows:

A   Records will be added to the file
Blank   Records will not be added to the file

An 'A' in position 66 indicates whether records are to be added to a DISK file during processing. A blank means records will not be added
For an output file (O in position 15), however, a blank is equivalent to an A since by definition output means added records.

The File Addition keyword exists in RPGIV but has been moved to column 20 from 66.

F Column(s) 67-70 (Reserved)

Positions 67-70 are not used in PAREG and for all programs, these positions must be blank.

F Column(s) 71-72 (File Condition)

Programmers sometimes try to get all they can into one program and they will often use the same program to provide two functions that are similar, rather than write a second program. Sometimes, the difference in program is the input or output form that the job requires. To help programmers in their efforts to be efficient, RPG provides the ability to include or exclude certain files at execution time with a facility called an external program switch. The PAREG program does not use an external switch nor do any other programs examples in this book. However, since you may find it a handy tool, we are providing a description of the function and how to make it work for you.

The entries that can be used in 71-72 are as follows:

Blank The file is used by the program, if input file, it is opened.
U1-U8 The file is used by the program only when the indicator is on.
UC   The programmer controls the first open of the file

When switches 1 to 8, also known as U1 to U8 (U for user switch) are used, the effect on the file description is ignored when the indicator is off. Thus it is like a blank being specified. When UC is sued, RPG does not automatically open the file for use as it usually does. Instead, the programmer controls the first open using the OPEN operation in calculations.

F Column(s) 73-74 (Reserved)

Positions 73-74 are not used in PAREG and for all programs, these positions must be blank.

F Column(s) 75-80 (Comments)

Since most of the file description form is used with real, live potential entries, there is not much left for comments. Positions 75 to 80 can be used for comments, or left blank.

FC File Description Continuation Lines

Even with the File Description Extension specification as well as the Line Counter specification (column 39), both of which extend or continue the File Description specification, there still is not enough room in the File Description area to provide for all of the options that must be specified. Therefore, IBM has defined a continuation column (53) by which the entries for File Description can be "extended even further."

A continuation line can be specified on the main file-description specification line if the functions use positions 54 through 65 for their definition. However, the use of certain keywords defined below, such as SFILE, RENAME, IGNORE, and PLIST cannot be defined on the same spec with the main file description line. For these and for situations in which multiple keywords need to be used, additional lines cane be used to continue the File Description form. Any number of continuation lines can be specified. A continuation line is indicated by a K in position 53 of the F spec. The format description of the F continuation specification follows:

FC Columns 7 – 18 Unused

These positions must be blank for a separate continuation line.

FC Columns 19 – 28 External Name of Record Format

These columns positions are used to specify the external name of the record format that is to be renamed (RENAME) or ignored (IGNORE).

FC Columns 29 – 46 Unused

These positions must be blank for a separate continuation line.

FC Columns 47 – 52 Record # Field for Subfile

When programming to use interactive workstation capabilities in RPG/400, there is a facility known as a subfile that can be appended to the display file through the use of DDS and specific RPG entries to support the use of the subfile. See Chapter 21. A subfile in essence is a memory file of repeating lines (records) that would appear on a display. The memory file can be accessed within a program by record number. In columns 47 – 52, you specify the name of the numeric field that will contain the relative record # associated with the subfile.

This field name gets specified on a subfile options keyword (SFILE). For the SFILE options, these positions must specify the name of a Relative Record Number (RECNO) field. For other continuation line options, these positions (47 – 52) must be blank.

FC Column 53 Continuation Character (K)

A 'K' indicates a continuation line.

FC Columns 44 – 59 & 60 – 67; 'K' Options

These positions are used together. Positions 54 through 59 specify the option, while positions 60 through 67 provide further explanation of the option. See "Continuation Line Options Summary Chart" in   Figure 7-6 for a look at the available continuation options and coding requirements.

FC Columns 68 – 74 Unused

These positions must be blank for a separate continuation line.

FC Columns 75 – 80 Optional Comments

This space is available for comments

FC Options and Entries for Continuation

Many of the entries in Table 7-6 have to do with device files used for data communications or for WORKSTN files. Though there is a place for these options and entries, this is not a beginner's topic so if this stuff is as clear as mud as you look at the table, that's OK for now. One day, when you need a tool, such as those described in the table, you will know they exist, and you will know where to find them. The function and purpose of the tools below are provided in very brief terms with the intention of providing a light familiarity. When the reader chooses to use this material, what is provided below will help you but for a complete explanation, you will need to consult the IBM manuals to get the grit and detail. The valid entries for positions 54 through 67 are shown in the chart in Figure 7-6.

Figure 7-6 Continuation Line Options Summary Chart

Option (54-59)	Entry (60-67)	Function & Purpose
COMIT	Blank	This entry is specified to indicate that the file is opened for commitment control. This enables the COMIT and ROLBK operation codes in RPG/400.
ID	Field Name	Provide the name of a 10 character field to capture the name of the device providing the record to the program.
IGNORE	Blank	Permits you to selectively ignore specific record formats from files. The record format name would be specified in positions 19 to 28 of the continuation line

IND	Indicator	General indicators from 01 to the indicator specified in 60-67 are saved and restored for each device that is attached to this program.
INFDS	DS Name	Provide the name of a data structure that RPG can use to contain the exception / error information associated with device operations. The DS name is entered in columns 60-65 and left justified. If multiple INFDS are used in a program, each must be given a unique name in this area.
INFSR	Subroutine Name	The file exception/error subroutine named (left justified) in positions 60 through 65 may receive control following file exception/errors. The subroutine name may be *PSSR, which indicates that the user defined program exception/error subroutine is to be given control for errors on this file.
NUM	Maximum	Workstation programs can acquire workstation. In most programs, just one device, the requester of the program, is used with a program. However, some programs are written to acquire devices and begin communication with them for a program purpose.
PASS	*NOIND	This facility exists mostly to accommodate programs coming from other systems such as System/3 or System/36. If you were to write a program fresh today, you would not use program described workstation input and this keyword would be moot. However, to use this facility, you would specify PASS *NOIND on the file description specification continuation line for a program described WORKSTN file if you are taking responsibility for passing indicators on input and output. With PASS *NOIND, the RPG/400 language does not pass indicators to data management on output and does not receive them. In this scenario, you would pass indicators by describing them as fields (in the form *INxx, *IN, or *IN,xx) in the input or output record.
PLIST	Parameter List Name	This entry is valid only when the device name specified in positions 40 through 46 of the main file-description line is SPECIAL. Positions 60 through 65 give the left-justified name of the parameter list to be passed to the special routine. The parameters identified by this entry are added to the end of the parameter list passed by the program.
PRTCTL	Data Structure Name	There is a facility for program described printer files called dynamic printer control. If this keyword is used, the option is being used
RECNO	Field Name	This entry is optional for disk files to be processed by relative-record number. A RECNO field must be specified for output files processed by relative-record number, output files that are referenced by a random WRITE calculation operation, or output files that are used with ADD on the output specification.
RENAME	Rec. Format Name	This entry, which is optional, allows you to rename record formats in an externally described file. Positions 19 through 28 of the continuation line specify the external name of the record format that is to be renamed. Positions 60 through 67 specify the left-justified name of the record as it is renamed for use in the program.
SAVDS	Data Structure Name	Positions 60-65 contain the left-justified name of the data structure saved and restored for each device. Before an input operation, the data structure for the device operation is saved. After the input operation, the data structure for the device associated with this current input operation is restored.
SFILE	Record Fmt Name	If the main file-description line contains E in position 19 and WORKSTN in positions 40 through 46, this option must be used to define any subfiles to be used in the file. Positions 60 through 67 must specify, left justified the RPG/400 name of the record format to be processed as a subfile.

Positions 47 through 52 must specify the name of the relative-record number field for this subfile. The relative-record number of any record retrieved by a READC or CHAIN operation is placed into the field named in positions 47 through 52. This field is also used to specify the record number that RPG/400 uses for a |

		WRITE operation to the subfile (memory file) or for output operations that use ADD.
SLN	Field Name	Positions 60-65 contain the left-justified name of a start line number (SLN) field. The SLN field determines where (which line #) a record format is written to a display file. The main file-description line must contain WORKSTN in positions 40 through 46 and a C or O in positions 15. The data description specifications for the file must specify the keyword SLNO(*VAR) for one or more record formats.

RPGIV File Description Keywords

Just like with the Header Specification, RPGIV handles many of the items that were required to be specified with columns in RPG/400 File Descriptions using keywords or options as in Figure 7-6. There is no continuation line needed in RPGIV as these functions are coded with keywords. In Figure 7-7, you can see six lines of RPGIV code with File Description keywords shown.

Figure 7-7 Sample RPGIV File Descriptions with Keywords

```
FFILE1P    O    E              DISK      EXTMBR('FILE1ALL')
F                                        RENAME(FILE1PR:ALLPR)
FFILE2P    O    E              DISK      EXTMBR('FILE2LST')
F                                        RENAME(FILE2PR:LSTPR)
FFILE3P    O    E              DISK      EXTMBR('FILE3OTH')
F                                        RENAME(FILE3PR:OTHPR)
```

Table 7-8 shows the keywords, samples in action, options, and the meaning of File Description keywords. RPGIV provides positions 44 to 80 of the F specification for stringing out keywords. Multiple keywords can be placed on each line and multiple lines can be used to accommodate necessary keywords.

Table 7-8 RPGIV File Description Keywords

Keyword / Sample	Other Options	Meaning
BLOCK(*YES)	*NO	Should records fro this file be processed in a block?
COMMIT(YESORNO)	RPG_name	Enable commit with a "1" value
DATFMT(*ISO)	Format{separator}	Specifies the date format
DEVID(devname)	Field name	Field contains the name for the device supplying the last record processed.
EXTFILE(RPGBOOK/TIMECD)	Filename; libname/filename *LIBL/filename	Specify external file name
EXTIND(*INU1)	(*INUx)	Open file if external indicator is on.
EXTMBR(MEMBER2)	*First; *All, member name	Specify specific member name in file to be opened
FORMLEN(50)	number	Specify forms length in lines for line counter function
FORMOFL(44)	number	Specify line # which turns the overflow indicator on.
IGNORE(RFMT01: RFMT02)	(recformat{:recformat... })	Ignore one or many record formats from this file.
INCLUDE(RFMT01: RFMT02)	(recformat{:recformat... })	Include one or many record formats from this file.
INDDS(INDICATORS)	DS_Name	Load workstation indicators into this structure during execution
INFDS(FEEDBACK)	DS-Name	Name the info DS that will be associated with this file
INFSR(SUBNAME)	*PSSR; (SUBRname)	Name subroutine to get control if error.
KEYLOC(45)	Number	Specify the location of the key in an program described file.
MAXDEV(*ONLY)	*FILE	Restricts # of acquired devices such as workstations

OFLIND(OF)	OA-OG, OF	Specify the overflow indicator for a printer device file
PASS(*NOIND)	No other option	Do programmers control indicator passage?
PGMNAME(SPECDEV)	program_name	Provide name of program to handle a special device.
PLIST(BIGPARMS)	(Plist_name)	Provide the name for a parameter list to be used with called or calling programs.
PREFIX('GRP1.')	(prefix{:nbr_of_char_replaced})	Prefix is appended to the beginning of each field in this file to avoid duplicate names when used with other files.
PRTCTL(FRMCTLDS)	(data_struct{:*COMPAT})	Provide name of forms control data structure
RAFDATA(RAFFILE)	Filename	Specify the name of the RAFFILE to control record processing for this file
RECNO(RRN)	(Fieldname)	Specify the field name to contain the record # to write output records to a direct file
RENAME(FM1:FM2)	(Ext_format:Int_format)	Rename the external record format for program use to avoid conflicts
SAVEDS(SAVEFIELDS)	DS Name	Provide a DS name so that RPG will save fields for each device before each input operation.
SAVEIND(55)	Number	Similar to SAVEDS. Specify how many indicators you want saved.
SFILE(SFL3:RRN3)	(recformat:rrnfield)	Specify name of subfile format and the field name to be used for subfile record processing.
SLN(15)	Number (1 to 24)	Starting line # to place record formats for this workstn file. At least one screen panel must use SLNO(*VAR)
TIMFMT(*ISO)	format{separator}	Specify time format
USROPN	No other values	This file will be opened in the program – RPG will not automatically open it.

L -- Line Counter Specification Form

The Line Counter specification was designed as an extension to File Description for printer files. Its purpose is to provide the programmer with a means of defining necessary things such as the forms length and overflow position of special forms such as invoices, statements or checks. The form is quite simple, and though we did not need a line counter in the PAREG program, the entries in the example shown below reflect the default line counter used in PAREG.

When you line up all the forms for an RPG program, you place the Line Counter specifications right after File Description specifications unless there are Extension specifications. If there are Extension specifications, then Line Counter follows Extension. Figure 7-9 shows the Line Counter specification default that was used in the PAREG program.

Figure 7-9 Default Line Counter Specification
```
FMT *     ..... *. 1 ...+... 2 ...+
0004.00      L*
FMT L    .....LFilename066F1060O1.
0005.00      LQSYSPRT 066FL060OL
```

L Column 7-14 File Name

In columns 7-14, specify the file name of the PRINTER file as previously specified on file description specification form.

L Column 15-17 Lines per Page

In Columns 15 – 17, specify the number of printing lines on the form. The available entries are 2 through 112.

L Column 18-19 Form Length

Specify the letters "FL" in columns 18 – 19 to indicate that the entry in positions 15 through 17 is the form length. Positions 18 and 19 must contain FL if positions 15 through 17 contain an entry.

L Column 20-22 Overflow Line Number

The line number you specify in columns 20-22 is the overflow line number. When printing hits this point on a page, the RPG program turns on the overflow indicator OA-OG, OF to inform the program that the last print line on the form has been reached..

L Column 23-24 Overflow Line Indicator

Specify the letters "OL" in columns 23 – 24 to indicate that the entry in positions 20 through 22 is the overflow line. Positions 23 and 24 must contain OL if positions 20 through 22 contain an entry.

L Column 25 - 74 Blank

L Column 75 - 80 Optional Comments

RPG IV Line Counter Information

In RPGIV, the columns of the Line Counter specification are handled by the FORMLEN and FORMOFL keywords. They are specified in File Description for the printer file. The File Description RPGIV keywords are described in Table 7-8.

Chapter Summary

The File Description Specification, a.k.a. the 'F' spec is the way this communication is achieved to outside devices in RPG.

The File description specification is the place in which the programmer provides a name for the file being used in the program. If the input output descriptions for the file are to be fetched automatically the programmer places an E in column 19. If the programmer is going to build them in the program, column 19 will have an F for fixed. Column 19 therefore is the determinant as to whether the files used in the program are externally described o internally described.

Column15 is also very important as the programmer specifies the purpose of the file – input, output, or both. The compiler brings in the appropriate routines to handle those types of operations. Column 16 is where the programmer specifies whether the RPG cycle is going to be actively used in the program. A P or S designation means that RPG will control the cycle of input for the program and provide a means for the file to be modified.

For internally described database file, among other things, the programmer specifies the record length, the key location and the key length. For externally described files, these entries are not required unless the program is using the key to the file in program operations.

In summary, File Description specifications describe all the files that your program uses. The information for each file includes the following:

- ✓ Name of the file
- ✓ How the file is used
- ✓ Size of records in the file
- ✓ Input or output device used for the file
- ✓ If the file is conditioned by an external indicator.

For specific functions that require additional entries that are not found on the File Description specification itself, RPG provides a Continuation specification.

The RPGIV File Description specification looks very much like the RPG/400 version other than some repositioning of columns. Additionally, RPGIV uses keywords to specify a number of items that were required to be specified with columns in RPG/400 File.

The Line Counter specification was designed as an extension to File Description for printer files. Its purpose is to provide the programmer with a means of defining necessary things such as the forms length and overflow position of special forms such as invoices, statements or checks.

In RPGIV, there is no Line Counter specification. The columns of the Line Counter specification are handled by the FORMLEN and FORMOFL keywords. They are specified in File Description for the printer file. The File Description specification and the RPGIV keywords are described in the next section.

Key Chapter Terms

*FILE	Form Length	QPRINT
*IN	Format	RAFDATA
*IN	FORMLEN	Random
*ISO	FORMOFL	READ
*PSSR	Full procedural file	READC
Array or table file	IGNORE	READE
Arrays	INCLUDE	RECNO
BLOCK	INDDS	Record #
CHAIN	INFDS	Record address file
COMIT	INFSR	Record format
COMMIT	Key Field	Record length
Continuation lines	KEYLOC	RENAME
Data elements	Keywords	ROLBK
Data Structure	Length	Routine
Database file	Limits Processing	SAVEDS
DATFMT	Line Counter spec	SAVEIND
DEVID	Lines per page	SFILE
End of File	MAXDEV	SLN
EXFMT	OFLIND	SPECIAL
Extension Code	OPEN	Subfile
External indicator	Overflow indicator	System administrator
EXTFILE	Overflow line Number	U1 to U8
EXTIND	OVRDBF	UPDAT
EXTMBR	PASS	UPDATE
File Addition	PGMNAME	USROPN
File Description Spec	PLIST	WORKSTN
File Designation	PREFIX	WRITE
File Name	PRTCTL	
File Organization		

Review Questions

1. How does an RPG program speak to devices and databases not contained within the program itself?

2. What does the A mean that gets coded in Column 66 of RPG or in column 20 of RPGIV mean the same thing? What does it mean in both cases?

3. What determines whether the RPG cycle is used?

4. Why is a fully procedural file in RPG needed?

5. What is the difference between the C entry and the U entry in column 15 of the RPG/400 specification? Does it mean the same in RPGIV?

6. What does the K (column 31 of RPG/400) designator mean for database files and why is it needed? Is it always needed?

7. Give five purposes for the file description specification?

8. What does the EA entries mean in the PAREG program?

9. What is the difference in the File Description specification between the external and internal PAREG versions? Why?

10. What is an overflow indicator and what purpose does it serve for a database file?

11. Can tape files be specified in RPG/400 or RPGIV?

12. When a WORKSTN file is used, does the programmer first have to create the file or is it created by the RPG compiler – explain?

13. What is the meaning of the extension code in column 39 of the RPG/400 specification? In what column is this in RPGIV and how is the File Description Extension function implemented in RPGIV?

14. Provide three purposes for the File Description Continuation specification? How is this done in RPGIV?

15. What is the purpose of the line counter specification in RPG/400 and RPGIV? Is anything else required in RPGIV for line counter facility?

Chapter 8 The Specifics of RPG Coding – Input – by Example

The Many Faces of RPG Input

RPG is an evolving language. At the time of its introduction in 1988, for example the base RPG in RPG/400 was well over 30 years old. Each year as the specifications for RPG got better and better, the challenge for the designers was how to fit the new function in the same number of specifications and columns while adhering to the 30-year old 80 column limitation.

From reading Chapter 7, you now know that File Descriptions were expanded in three different ways. Line Counter specs (L) were built to better describe more modern printers. Extension (E) specifications were built to handle arrays and tables (– covered in Chapter 16), and the File continuation was introduced to deal with the nuances of workstation and telecommunications files. In fact, for a brief period, File Description actually spawned a third spec called the Telecommunications (T) specification which was used to talk to batch terminals in the 1970's before the System/38 was introduced.

So, you will not be surprised that the Input specification is also overloaded with baggage. First of all, input specifications always had two purposes: (1) identify records as they are read and (2) define the data fields. So, there were always two formats to the Input specification. In 1978 with the introduction of the System/38, IBM introduced RPGIII. This flavor of RPG permitted the RPG input specifications to be fetched and formatted from the database itself by the compiler at compile time.

This saved tremendous amounts of coding but it added a new wrinkle to input specs. When input needed to be defined or changed for one reason or another, such as reducing the size of a database field from 10 characters to 6 for the RPG limitation, a means on the INPUT coding sheet needed to be created. Since database files do not like more than one record type, the old way of identifying records needed to be replaced in such a way that RPG could create a place in input for each different screen format or each format in a logical file. Additionally, Input needed to be provided for Control Fields and for Match Fields even when the rest of the data descriptors were fetched from the database.

IBM answered the call with two more forms of the RPG Input specification, both to handle what is called externally described data. Since the new formats handled externally described data, the old formats were then said to use internally described data or program described data – synonyms for the notion that the data elements used in the program were the ones described in the program – regardless of what was in the database. Just as with the program described data, one format handled record IDs and the other handled field definitions.

The System/38 also introduced new uses for the Input specification: Data structures and named constants were introduced and assigned Input columns. Unlike COBOL which has a Data Division that does not care about whether a data element is used for input or output, RPG had only input and output specs for major data definitions and operations. Since it did not make sense to define data in output, the named constant took on a new format of the Input spec as did the Data Structures. Named Constants are covered in Chapter 9 and Data structures are covered both in Chapter 9 and in Chapter 17.

Though named constants and structures are important, we would be getting ahead of ourselves at this point by describing them fully since the PAREG standard program, which is still our simple guiding example, gets along fine without either.

Internally & Externally Described Input

Externally described input files are far more efficient to code than program described (internally described) input files. However, because there are still many RPG programs that use program described data, especially in shops that have migrated from System/36 machines; we cover program described data for completeness. Since PAREG uses externally described data, this chapter first defines the structure of the external form for input and then goes back for completeness and fills in the blanks for the internal / programmed described format of Input.

I – Input Specification Form

For an externally described file, input specifications are optional. Yet, they have value in instances in which the programmer would like to add RPG/400 functions to the external description – such as matching records and level breaks. The PAREG program is an example. So we use Input specifications as we did in the PAYREG program, even though its input is externally described. This enabled us to describe the matching fields as well as the control fields needed in this program to create the report.

To make it easier for you to follow along with the role and the format of the input specification, we show the input portion of the compile listing of the PAREG program in Figure 8-1. This is important in understanding internal and external data descriptions in RPG, since as you can see in the Input specifications and the expanded source.

We have already learned that any statement with an asterisk in column 7 is a comment and thus, statements 10 and 11 are comments. Statement 12 is a record format identifier, whereas statements 13 through 15 are the field definitions for the payroll master. As you may be able to tell by looking at Figure 6-1, the format of the record identifier and the format of the field definitions are substantially different. So, unlike the File Description Specification (F- spec), which has just one format, for externally supplied input, there are two very different types of input specifications.

Figure 8-1 Compile Listing of External Input Expanded

```
   1000    I* RPG INPUT SPECIFICATION FORMS
   1100    I*
   1200    IPAYR          01
   1300    I                   EMPNO                        EMPNO    M1
   1400    I                                                EMPCTYL1
   1500    I                   EMPSTA                       EMPSTAL2
   1500     INPUT   FIELDS FOR RECORD PAYR FILE EMPMAST FORMAT PAYR.
  A000001                      EMPNO                1    30EMPNO    M1
  A000002                                           4    23 EMPNAM
  A000003                                          24    282EMPRAT
  A000004                                          29    48 EMPCTYL1
  A000005                      EMPSTA              49    50 EMPSTAL2
  A000006                                          51    550EMPZIP
   1600    ITIMR          02
   1700    I                   EMPNO                        EMPNO    M1
   1700     INPUT   FIELDS FOR RECORD TIMR FILE TIMCRD FORMAT TIMR.
  B000001                      EMPNO                1    30EMPNO    M1
  B000002                                           4    72EMPHRS
```

For the externally described files such as the two we have coded in the PAREG program, entries on the input specifications are divided into the following categories:

1. Record identification entries
   (positions 7 through 14, and 19 and 20)
   These identify the record (the externally described record format) to which RPG/400 functions are to be added.

2. Field description entries
(positions 21 through 30, 53 through 62,and 65 through 70)
These describe the RPG/400 functions to be added to
the fields in the record.

Field description entries are always written on the lines following the corresponding record identification entries. For data structures, which are fully described in Chapters 9 and 17, the entries on input specifications are divided into the following categories:

1. Data structure statements
(positions 7 through 12, 17 through 30, and 44 through 51)
These entries define data structures to RPG.

2. Data structure subfield specifications
(positions 8, and 21 through 58)
These entries describe subfields of the data structures.

Just as the field descriptors for input, data structure subfield specifications are written on the lines following the data structure statements.

Input Specification Quick Summary

As a quick summary on the externally described versions of the record and field oriented input specification, it is clear to see that the I spec is a real workhorse for RPG. Ironically, its overuse for non-input functions is one of the major reasons why IBM created the data specification ('D' spec) for RPG IV. This 'D' spec resembles the Data Division in COBOL. For RPG/400, however, since there is no 'D' spec, you will find machinations of the good old input spec helping you with the coding for all of the following RPG facilities:

✓ Entries for program described files
✓ Entries for externally described files
✓ Entries for data structures
✓ Entries for named constants

RPG Input Form Types

To help you gain a better appreciation for the many combinations of input specification formats, a picture is worth a thousand words. Years ago, RPG programmers would code their programs on paper sheets such as the one in Figure 8-2. As you can see by examining Figure 8-2, there are many different formats for RPG for both program described and externally described formats

Figure 8-2 RPG Input Specification Form – Entry Choices

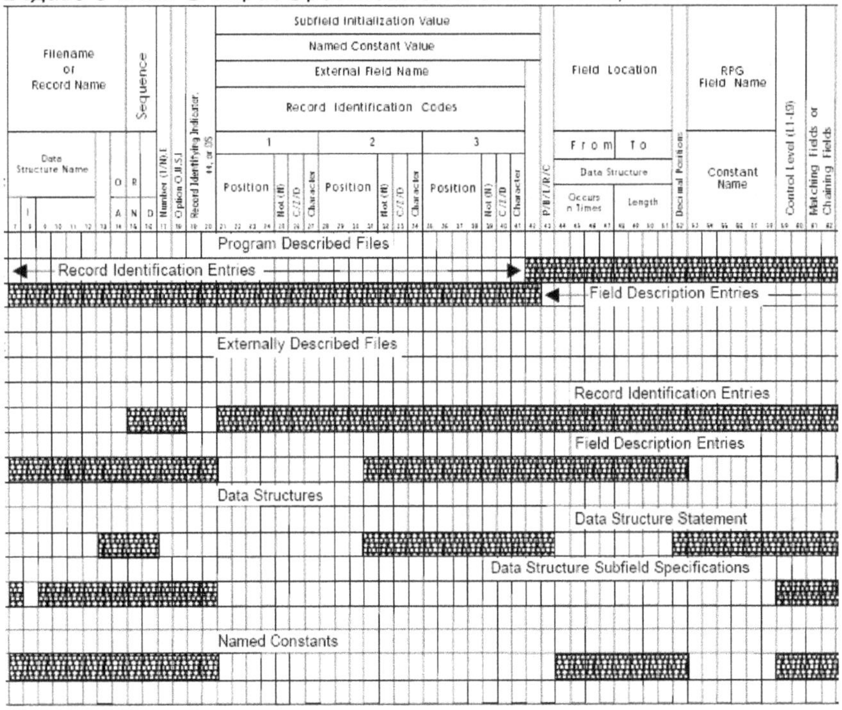

PAREG Record and Field Statements

The PAREG program needs the external form for both the Record ID Entries and the Field Description Entries. As we examine the PAREG coding in light of these forms, you will see how the Record ID part helped us identify the primary and secondary files with record identifying indicators. You will also see how the Field part provided space for the entries necessary both match fields and control levels and you will see that the match fields help assure that there is an in-sequence time card record for each payroll master record. So, there is no doubt they both halves of the external input format are necessary in RPG and no doubt that both are absolutely necessary for the success of the PAREG program. Let's first look at the record ID part of input and then we'll move to the field description part.

I Externally Described Record ID Entries

Externally described file input specifications provide additional coding for records to be processed in an RPG program. Since their typically is no Record ID character in database files with multiple record types, input specs are used to differentiate records. Additionally, the record format can be renamed as needed using input specifications specifically designed for externally described files. On the field side, of course input specs permit fields to be referenced so that level indicators and matching fields indicators can be specified.

The following section describes in reasonable detail the entries for the Record ID part of the External Input form. Since RPGIV in many cases uses a different column for the same function, immediately after the description of the RPG/400 entry, the RPGIV function location is provided. The designator **IEDRI** is used to begin each header so it is easy to spot the entries that belong with Input, Externally Described, Record Identification.

IEDRI Columns 8-14 Record Name

For the record name specified in columns 8-14 of the Input specification, the allowable entries include the following:

1. The external name of the record format. The file name cannot be used or an externally described file.

2. The RPG/400 name specified by the RENAME option on the file description specifications continuation line if the external record format was renamed. A record format name can appear only once in positions 7 through 14 of the input specifications for an RPG program.

In RPGIV, the Record name is specified columns 7 – 16.

IEDRI Columns 16 – 18 Reserved

Columns 15-18 of the externally described input form are reserved for future use. No entries should be placed in these columns.

IEDRI Columns 19 – 20 Record Identifying Indicator

When an optional record identifying indicator is specified in columns 19-20, it will be turned on if the record format name in 8-14 is the one read by the program.

In RPGIV, the Record ID Indicator is specified in columns 21 – 22.

IEDRI Columns 21 – 41 Unused

Columns 21 to 41 are unused for externally described input specifications. They must be coded as blank.

IEDRI Columns 42 – 74 Reserved

Columns 42-74 are reserved for future use for externally described input specifications. They must be coded as blank.

IEDRI Columns 75 – 80 Reserved

Positions 75-80 of the externally described record ID input form can be used for comments, or left blank.

Applying Input Record IDs to PAREG

Now, let's take a look at the input records coming in from the EMPMAST and the TIMCRD files. In Chapter 3, we showed the DDS in Figure 3-2 for EMPMAST. You may recall that the first line of the DDS described the record format. This line looked like this:

```
0001.00        A              R PAYR
```

DDS specs have their own spec type 'A' in column 6. The R in column 17 says this is a record format line. In DDS, you place an R in this column to identify the record format by name. The name PAYR in column 19 is the name we gave to the record format of the PAYMAST file. Look at the similarities of this with the following RPG Input spec as originally typed in the PAREG program (Figure 5-1)

```
0012.00    IPAYR      01
```

The notion of a record format name is very similar to the record id notion within the RPG language as shown immediately above in the blown up input specification from line 12.   In most cases, the coding is that simple.

There is a notion in IBM i's DB2 native database coding called Logical files or views. These logical views can be built over one or several database files and can present data from multiple database files. All relational databases can present a JOIN view in which pieces of multiple records in multiple files make up one record in the joined logical view.

IBM i's DB2 is the only database that can provide a hierarchical view of physical files with different formats in much the same way file systems handled multiple record types years ago. When a multiple format logical view is created over a number of physical files, the format name in the physical file, such as EMPMAST's, PAYR, and TIMECRD's TIMR becomes the format name used to differentiate the records in input specs when processed through the logical file. Instead of two files being defined to the program as in PAREG, for example, just the Logical File would be coded and it would presents both record types with their differing formats to the program in a pre-designated sequence such as by the EMPNO field..

So, if PAYR and TIMR record formats were in a logical view sequenced by EMPNO, the 55 character PAYR format would come in and then the 7 character TIMR format would come in through the one file description spec. The programmer would identify each of these with the IEDRI form – one for each record format and then would specify each of the format names in IEDRI exactly the same way as they are specified in the PAREG program. When PAYR is read, indicator 01 would be turned on as identification and when record TIMR is read, indicator 02 would be turned on.

Therefore, both logical files with multiple formats as well as primary and secondary files with one format each can be read by the fixed logic cycle of an RPG program such as PAREG. Therefore it is incumbent on RPG to have a vehicle to differentiate one record format from another. The record format input specification IEDRI provides this vehicle.

To help us remember what the Input Specs are like in PAREG, we present Figure 8-3. We have seen this Figure before as Figure 7-5 in Chapter 7. You may recall it is the compiled input specs. Therefore it includes external fields from the database that are not described in the program code. The program code has regular statement #s to the left whereas the code fetched from the database has long numbers such as A000001 beginning with a vowel to the left.

Figure 8-3 Compile Listing of External Input Expanded

```
1000  I* RPG INPUT SPECIFICATION FORMS
1100  I*
1200  IPAYR          01
1300  I              EMPNO                        EMPNO   M1
1400  I                                           EMPCTYL1
1500  I              EMPSTA                        EMPSTAL2
1500   INPUT  FIELDS FOR RECORD PAYR FILE EMPMAST FORMAT PAYR.
A000001               EMPNO               1    30EMPNO   M1
A000002                                   4    23 EMPNAM
A000003                                  24    282EMPRAT
A000004                                  29    48 EMPCTYL1
A000005               EMPSTA             49    50 EMPSTAL2
A000006                                  51    550EMPZIP
1600  ITIMR          02
1700  I              EMPNO                        EMPNO   M1
1700   INPUT  FIELDS FOR RECORD TIMR FILE TIMCRD FORMAT TIMR.
B000001               EMPNO               1    30EMPNO   M1
B000002                                   4    72EMPHRS
```

When an RPG programmer decides that matching or control fields must be specified, the language requires that for an externally described file, a record format must precede the field specs. After the 'I' in column 6, (columns 7 through 14) the programmer specifies the name of the format that matches the name of the format in DDS, which to be more exact is the format name in the physical database file itself.

After the format name, if you keep moving right along the RPG form, you will come to an '01" starting in position 19. This is very important for this program. The "01" is the record identifying indicator for the EMPMAST file. Just what does this mean? It means that whenever a record is read during the fixed logic cycle, RPG will check to see if it is a record from the PAYR record format. in the database. If it is, then RPG will turn on indicator "01" so it can be used within the program.

In older RPG's, and for program described data, 7 – 14 would contain the name of the File (EMPMAST) as defined in the File Descriptions this the. For externally defined files, however, RPG demands that the programmer specifies the same format name as the name used to build the database.

Once we know how to describe an input record format for one RPG file, we can describe it for any. Let's take a shot at decoding the record format for the TIMCRD file which is found on the PAREG program at statement 16.

```
0016.00 ITIMR          02
```

Other than the sequence number and the I in column 16, again the programmer needs just two entries to make this external record ID work in the PAREG program The DDS for the TIMCRD database file were originally shown back in Figure 3-3. Just as PAYR is the record name specified in DDS in Figure 3-2 for the EMPMAST database file, TIMR is the record format name specified in DDS for the TIMCRD database file. Thus in the input statement defined at statement 16 in the PAYREG RPG program, TIMR is the record format specified. Additionally, the programmer has told RPG to turn on indicator "02" as a record identifying indicator whenever a time card record is read.

That's' the essence of the record format input specification. For the PAREG program, by turning on indicator 01, it tells RPG that an EMPMAST record was read and it is available for processing in this detail cycle. By turning on indicator 02, it tells RPG that a TIMCRD record was read and that it is available fro processing this detail cycle. As you may recall from Chapter 1, right before RPG reads from the file last processed, it does housekeeping by turning off all of the matching and record identifying indicators so that when it turns on indicator "01" or indicator "02" there is no residue left from other detail cycles. If the status of Indicator 01 in the PAREG program is "ON," then the Master has just been read. On the other hand, if the status of indicator "02," is on, then the time card record has just been read.

I Externally Described Field Description Entries

Unlike the program described record ID and field description portions of the RPG input specification, which is really an 80 column form cut just about in half, the externally described versions each start at position 7 of the input specification. In this section, we examine the field description entries for externally described files.

The designator **IEDFD** is used to begin each header so it is easy to spot the entries that belong with Input, Externally Described, and Record Identification.

Field Specifications in RPG/400

There are more entries in the field specification form in RPG/400 than we need for PAREG so while we are examining the entries in PAREG, we will also explain any other entries on the form type. The field entries from the EMPMAST are listed below followed by blank line and the fields from the TIMCRD file.

Figure 8-4 Field Entries as Coded in PAREG

```
0013.00 I...       EMPNO   ...         EMPNO    M1
0014.00 I...                           EMPCTYL1
0015.00 I...       EMPSTA ...          EMPSTAL2

0017.00 I...       EMPNO   ...         EMPNO
```

IEDFD Columns 7 – 20 Reserved

Columns 7 – 20 of the externally described field description form of the input specification has reserved positions for future use, thus none of these positions were coded for PAREG

IEDFD Columns 21 – 30 External Field Name

For the PAREG program, no entries need to be made in this area. Yet, if you look at the four field entries specified in this program, you will see that three are entries for three of the four input fields. This area needs to be used only when you have chosen to rename a field from the database. Say, you want to reference the field called EMPNO, for example as EMP# in the program. By specifying EMPNO in this area and then specifying EMP# in the program field area (53-58) the field name will be EMP# when referenced in this program

A big reason for renaming fields is that sometimes database administrators use all ten positions of the field name in DDS. Since RPG/400 field names can be just 6 characters in length, a rename would be necessary to use the field in the program.

There are no such examples in the PAREG program. However, we did add an entry for all fields but EMPCTY of the EMPMAST file in this external name for rename area. This was unnecessary. It was done merely to show you how a rename of a field could readily be accomplished.

In RPGIV, the External Field Name is also specified in columns 21 – 30.

IEDFD Columns 31 – 52 Reserved

Columns 31 – 52 of the externally described field description form of the input specification have reserved positions for future use.

IEDFD Columns 53 – 58 Field Name

For files that are externally described, no input specifications are required unless the programmer uses special RPG functions that depend on input lines being marked appropriately. In other words, the field name entry is made only when it is required for the RPG/400 function (such as control levels or matched fields or renamed fields) that must be added to the external description.

The four field name entries (lines 13 to 15 from the EMPMAST database and line 17 from the EMPTIN database) ***** ????as defined in PAYREG are easy to spot in Figure 8-4. The field name entry can be specified with one of the following:

The name of the field as defined in the external record description (if 6 characters or less).

The name specified to be used in the program that replaced the external name specified in positions 21 through 30.

In RPGIV, the Field Name is specified in columns 49 – 62.

IEDFD Columns 59 – 60 Control Level

The entry in position 59 and 60 indicates whether the field is to be used as a control field in the program.

The allowable entries for positions 59 and 60 are as follows:

Blank This field is not a control field.
L1-L9 This field is a control field.

The input specifications for the fields in the EMPMAST file used to define control level totals are shown below:

```
0014.00 I...                    EMPCTYL1
0015.00 I...    EMPSTA          EMPSTAL2
```

The code above tells the RPG compiler that the State field (EMPSTA) is a second level control field and any change in this field as primary (Payroll Master) records are being read will trigger a control break from which second level (L2) control level calculations and second level control level output can be created during the RPG cycle. If the City (EMPCTY) field changes while master records are being read, a first level break is triggered and those calculations and output designated to occur during an L1 break can then occur. A higher level break always triggers a lower level break. Thus in this example, if the state field changes, the city calculations (L1) will occur, followed by city total output (l1), followed by state total calculations (L2) followed by state total output (L2).

In RPGIV, the Control Level is specified in columns 63 – 64.

IEDFD Columns 60 – 61 Match Fields

This entry indicates whether the field is to be used as a match field. The allowable entries in columns 60 – 61 are as follows:

Blank   This field is not a match field.
M1-M9   This field is a match field.

Match fields are the key to making this PAREG program work. The two lines that specify the match fields in the PAREG program follow this paragraph. The data records in both files are in sequence by EMPNO in order for this to work. They get in sequence using the IBM fort known as Format Data or FMTDTA. When the records match, RPG turns on a special indicator called MR to help control the operations of the program. Knowing a match has occurred is an extremely valuable piece of information as you will see in the rest of this program. When the "MR" indicator is turned on by RPG detecting a match between the primary and secondary files, it can be used to further condition operations in the program.

```
0013.00 I...     EMPNO...        EMPNO     M1
0017.00 I...     EMPNO...        EMPNO     M1
```

The two fields above are shown in context in Figure 8-3 within their specific record formats (from the EMPMAST and TIMCRD database files respectively). Statement 13 belongs with EMPMAST and statement 17 belongs with TIMCRD.

As you can see on line 12 in Figure 8-3, the EMPNO field from the EMPMAST file (format PAYR) is matched on line 17 with the EMPNO field from the TIMCRD file (format TIMR from line 16) By placing M1 on each field, this entry is used to match the records of the one file with those of the other.

Sometimes the names for fill-in items in RPG do not make sense in a broad context. For example, the designator M1 can also be used to sequence check match fields within one file. Obviously with just one file specified, there could be no match and thus the designation of matched fields does not really work in that case. Nonetheless, columns 61-62 would be where the programmer would specify matching for just one file if the programmer would like the RPG compiler to sequence check the incoming data (ascending or descending – depending on the code in the file description specification). For PAREG, which has two input files, we get sequence checking of both files as well as matching.

What about M2 through M9?

M1 is the lowest order field that can be specified in a multi-field match. If, for example the EMPNO field were duplicated in departments in an organization, then the only way to assure a real match on employee would be to include the department number as a match field. Assuming that both databases were populated with a field called EMPDNO for employee department number (**Note lines 12.01 and 16.01**) the code would look like that shown in Figure 8-5.

Match field designators M3 to M9 work in the same fashion. Thus, in RPG you can have up to nine match fields involved in a sequence check or a match. If they are in match relationship, all fields specified, M1 through M9 must match in order for the MR indicator to be turned on.

One more point on this example. To keep matters simple we chose to use the same field names in both databases for the EMPNO and EMPDNO fields. This is not necessarily a good idea in practice but it helps in teaching and learning. For the EMPMAST file, for example, it may be appropriate in our shop standards to begin each field with the three letters, EMP. However, for the TIMCRD file, using EMP for each field can create confusion when both files are used in the same program. Therefore, it would probably be more appropriate to use a prefix of TIM, rather than EMP for the fields in the TIMCRD file. This is fine with RPG. The field names do not have to be the same. In fact, the input specifications to accommodate this are shown in Figure 8-6..

Figure 8-5 Duplicate Employee # within Department #

```
0009.00 I*
0010.00 I* RPG INPUT SPECIFICATION FORMS
0011.00 I*
0012.00 IPAYR          01
0012.01 I              EMPDNO...      EMPDNO  M2
0013.00 I              EMPNO...       EMPNO   M1
0014.00 I                             EMPCTYL1
0015.00 I              EMPSTA...      EMPSTAL2
0016.00 ITIMR          02
0016.01 I              EMPDNO...      EMPDNO  M2
0017.00 I              EMPNO...       EMPNO   M1
```

Figure 8-6 Input Specs shown with Better Naming Conventions

```
0009.00 I*
0010.00 I* RPG INPUT SPECIFICATION FORMS
0011.00 I*
0012.00 IPAYR          01
0012.01 I              EMPDNO...      EMPDNO  M2
0013.00 I              EMPNO...       EMPNO   M1
0014.00 I                             EMPCTYL1
0015.00 I              EMPSTA...      EMPSTAL2
0016.00 ITIMR          02
0016.01 I              TIMDNO...      TIMDNO  M2
0017.00 I              TIMNO...       TIMNO   M1
```

Some other helpful rules are as follows:

- ✓ Match fields can be specified only for fields in pri /secondary files.
- ✓ Match fields within a record are designated by an M1 through M9 code entered in positions 61 and 62 of the appropriate field description specification line.
- ✓ A maximum of nine match fields can be specified.
- ✓ The match field codes M1 through M9 can be assigned in any sequence.
- ✓ When more than one match field code is used for a record, all fields can be considered as one large field. M1 or the lowest code used is the rightmost or low-order position of the field. M9 or the highest code used is the leftmost or high-order position of the field.

In RPGIV, the Match Fields are specified in columns 65 – 66. .

IEDFD Columns 63 – 64 Reserved

Columns 63 – 64 of the externally described field description form of the input specification have reserved positions for future use.

IEDFD Columns 65 – 70 Field Indicators

Though the program PAREG does not have a use for field indicators, columns 65 to 70 of the I specification field spec is where they are specified.
The entries for this area are as follows:

Blank	No indicator specified
01-99	General indicators for programmer use
H1-H9	Halt indicators – cause the machine to halt
U1-U8	External indicators – externally supplied
RT	Return indicator. – causes return to calling program

When you choose to supply entries in positions 65 through 70, you can test the status of a field or of an array element as it is read into the program during the input phase of the RPG cycle. The field indicators are specified on the same line as the field to be tested. Depending on the status of the field (65-66 - plus, 68-68 minus, 69-70 "zero, or blank"), the appropriate indicator is set on and can be

In RPGIV, the Field Indicators are specified in columns 69 – 74.

IEDFD Columns 71- 74 Reserved

Columns 71-74 of the externally described field description form of the input specification has reserved positions for future use

IEDFD Columns 75 – 80 Comments

Columns 75 through 80 can be used for comments, or left blank.

Now, to put the whole INPUT specification, let's start with the Record ID area of program described files, work our way to the filed area of program described files, then let's look at record IDs in externally described files and field entries for externally described files. Following this, we'll examine the Data Structure and the data structure subfield formats of the input specification. In many ways, you can easily conclude that there are in fact six different formats for the input specification and some for them have nothing to do with input. If you have come to that conclusion, you are correct.

I Program Described Record Identification Entries

In the rest of this chapter, we examine the Record ID area of program described files, and work our way to the field area of program described files. Following this, in Chapter 9, we examine the data structure and the data structure subfield formats of the input specification. From what we've done so far and where we are heading, you can easily conclude that there are in fact six different formats for the input specification and some of these have nothing at all to do with input. If you have come to that conclusion, you are mostly correct. There is actually one more variant of input that we cover in Chapter 8. This is the named constant and clearly a constant is something that does not get read in as input from an external device. But, it makes more sense on an Input spec tan an Output spec.

Program described input specifications describe everything about the types of records within the file, the sequence of the types of records, the fields within a record, the data within the field, the indicators based on the contents of the fields, control fields, fields used for matching records, and fields used for sequence checking.

In Chapter 6, we showed both the externally described version and the internally described version of the PAREG program. Figure 8-7 shows the input specifications for the internally described version of PAREG.

The designator **IPDRI** is used to begin each header so it is easy to spot the entries that belong with Input, Program Described, Record Identification.

Figure 8-7 Internally (Program) Described Input for PAREG

```
0009.00 I*
0010.00 I* RPG INPUT SPECIFICATION FORMS
0011.00 I*
0012.00 IEMPMAST AA  01
0013.00 I...              1   30EMPNO   M1
0013.01 I...              4 23 EMPNAM
0013.02 I...             24 282EMPRAT
0014.00 I...             29 48 EMPCTYL1
0015.00 I...             49 50 EMPSTAL2
0015.01 I...             51 550EMPZIP
0016.00 ITIMCRD  AB  02
0017.00 I...              1   30EMPNO   M1
0017.01 I...              4 72EMPHRS
```

IPDRI Columns 8-14 File Name

For **program described files**, you specify the File name of the input file in 8-14 – EMPMAST and TIMCRD in PAREG. It must be the same file name that you already described in the File Description area. In File Descriptions, this file must have been described as an input file, an update file, or a combined file. The file name must be entered on the first record identification line for each file and it can be entered on subsequent record identification lines for that file (lines 12 & 16 in Figure 8-7) but the file name can be skipped if the record id being defined is from the same file (such as in a multi-format logical file or a display file). All entries describing one input file must appear together (12 – 15.01 and 16-17.01); they cannot be mixed with entries for other files.

In RPGIV, the File name is in positions 8-16.

IPDRI Columns 14-16 (Logical Relationship)

For program described input, multiple tests can be performed on input data to determine which record has been read. The logical relationship is either coded in an RPG statement following a statement that has the file name in 8-14 or it follows a subsequent record definition. The logical relationship links multiple input tests together. The entries are as follows:

AND   More than three identification codes are used.
OR   Two or more record types have common fields.

PAREG has no logical relationships defined. If there were, the code might look as shown in Figure 8-8 for EMPMAST.

Figure 8-8 Logical Relationship – One Record

```
        45678921234567893123456789 41
IEMPMAST AA  01  56 CA  57 CB  58 CC
I        AND      59 CD
Field Definitions here...
```

In this case, we are looking for real codes in the record (ABCD in 56 – 59) since that's how internally described programs are most often designed. If there were a second master record format in the file, say with a record code of ABCE, the two program described record IDs would be coded as in Figure 8-9.

Figure 8-9 Logical Relationship – Multiple Records

```
          45678921234567893123456789 41
IEMPMAST AA  01  56 CA  57 CB  58 CC
I        AND     59 CD
Field Definitions here...
I        BB  03  56 CA  57 CB  58 CC
I        AND     59 CE
Field Definitions here...
```

In this example, indicator 01 would turn on for an "ABCD" master format and indicator 03 would turn on for an "ABCE" master format. The field from and to positions of each format with internally described data can be substantially different. The other parts of the specifications are about to be explained.

In RPGIV, the Logical Relationship is in positions 16-18.

IPDRI Columns 15-16 (Sequence)

The entries for Sequence are as follows:

AA-ZZ The program does not check for special sequence.
01-99 The program checks for special sequence within the group.

The Internally described PAREG program uses AA and AB for Sequence (Figure 8-7). An alphabetic sequence entry tells RPG to not check the record sequence of the input data. A numeric sequence entry does a lot of work for the programmer if sequencing of records is important to the application. Most often, especially with single record format disk files, the alpha sequence is used.

The numeric sequence entry works in combination with the number (position 17) and option (position 18) entries. It causes the program to check the sequence of input records within a file. If the sequence is not correct, control passes to the RPG/400 exception/error handling routine. If AND or OR lines are specified, the sequence check is performed on the main record line of the group, not on the AND or OR lines.

Let's suppose that our data is coming from a program described file with multiple record types – payroll master file, time card file, and deduction file. In this scenario, each record is the same length since each is in the same file. Shorter record designs are merely padded with blanks at the end of the record. But the fields in the records do not have to line up and in fact will not. Each has its won layout though it exists in the same file. Many former System/36 applications are built like this. Let's look at the abbreviated record layouts in Figure 8-10. As you can see, besides a record identification field, we defined fields for each of these files. This figure shows how the format of each record is different

Figure 8-10 Three Record Types from Same File

Emp Master	From / To	Time Card	From / To	Deduction	From / To
RECID	1 / 1 / A	RECID	1 / 1 / B	RECID	1 / 1 / C
EMPNO	2 / 5	EMPNO	2 / 5	EMPNO	2 / 5
EMPNAM	6 / 35	HOURS	6 / 8	DEDNO	6 / 7
EMPAD1	36 / 65	NA	9	DEDAMT	8 / 12
# per EMPNO		1		Up to 4	

In addition to the length of the RECID field, we also show the constant contents. In this case, the master record has an A, the time card has a B, and the deduction record(s) has a C. Thus, each of the record types in the file are uniquely identified so that RPG can differentiate them on input and be able to turn on the appropriate record identification indicator.

Each of the files also has an EMPNO (employee number) field which permits the data to be presorted in record id within EMPNO sequence prior to running the program. After the EMPNO field the records begin to take different shapes. EMPNAM (employee name) for example is 30 positions in length, HOURS (hours) is 3 positions and DEDNO (deduction number) is two positions. The next field defined in each record starts in a different position – 36, 9, and 8 respectively. In fact, there is not a third field defined for time card in this design since there is already enough information in the record.

The preprocessing sort is integral to understanding sequencing. All records are sorted within EMPNO sequence. If we have 100 employees and 3 records are processed for each employee for each payroll, then 300 records are processed. In groups of three each – one group of A, B, and C record types for each. In other words, one master, one time card, and one deduction record for each employee. The sequencing capabilities of RPG are very powerful in that for every group of records, A, B, and C, you get to say with a numeric value, whether the A should be first, the B, or the C.

In this example we defined our records in the sequence A,B, C that we would like them processed in each group. Since pay rate is typically in the master, we would have the master record (A record type) read 1st, then the time card record (B record type). Once the time card is read, we can calculate gross pay and "net pay before deductions." The deductions, (C record type) such as United Way and Savings bonds can then be processed (deducted) from the net pay before deductions to get the payroll check amount.

So, for RPG to assure that our records are in sequence, we can use the sequence entry and we would assign a 1 sequence to master, a 2 sequence to time card, and a 3 sequence to deductions. If ever the record types were not in this sequence for each employee, RPG would halt the program with an error message.

In RPGIV, Sequence is in positions 17 – 18.

IPDRI Column 17 (Number)

For PAREG, since an alphabetic sequence # was used, no number entry is required for column 17. The allowable entries for the number position (column 17) are as follows:

Blank	The program does not check record types for a special Sequence (positions 15 and 16 have alphabetic entries).
1	Only one record of this type can be present in the sequenced group.
N	One or more records of this type can be present in the sequenced group.

This entry must be used when a numeric entry is made in positions 15 and 16. If an alphabetic entry is made in positions 15 and 16, this entry must be blank.

To code for the example shown in Figure 8-10, the programmer would place a 1 in column 17 for the A record (sequence 01) since there is to be just one master; a 1 in column 17 for the B record (sequence 02) for the time card since there is to be just one time card; and an N in column 17 for the deduction record since there can be one or many of them. In other words, for each payroll group, we are asking RPG to check for one and only one master as the first record (A) type of the group as well as one and only one time card as the second record type (B) of the group.

 It gets trickier for the deduction record as we are saying that there can be multiples of the third record type. As your own experience with payroll indicates, employees can have many deductions – loans, United Way, Savings bonds etc.

In RPGIV, Number is in positions 19.

IPDRI Column(s) 18 (Option)

For PAREG, since an alphabetic sequence # was used, no Option entry is required for column 18. The possible entries for column 18 are as follows:

Blank	The record type must be present if sequence checking is specified.
O	The record type is optional (that is, it may or may not be present) if sequence checking is specified.

This entry must be blank if positions 15 and 16 contain an alphabetic entry. Sequence checking of record types has no real meaning when all record types within a file are specified as optional (alphabetic entry in positions 15 and 16 or O entry in position 18).

Going back to the three record type samples in our payroll example from Figure 8-10, we know that if there is a group of records for a particular employee (EMPNO), there must be at least a master and a time card record. The programmer would code column 18 as blank meaning that these records are required in each group. If it is possible, such as with part-time workers, that an employee (even just one) would not have any deductions, then this column must be coded as O for optional so that RPG will not generate an error for these employees. So, if we code the deduction record as optional, if it (C record type) is not there, it is OK but of it is there, it must follow the B record type.

In RPGIV, Option is in position 20.

IPDRI Column(s) 19-20 (Record Identifying Indicators)

Both forms of the PAREG program use record identifying indicator 01 for the EMPMAST and record identifying indicator 02 for the TIMCRD file. The possible entries for positions 19-20 (Record Identifying Indicator, or **) are as follows:

Blank	No indicator is used.
01-99	General indicator
L1-L9 or LR	Control level indicator used for a record identifying indicator or LR indicator.
H1-H9	Halt indicator.
U1-U8	External indicator.
RT	Return indicator.
**	Look-ahead field (not an indicator). Look-ahead can be used only with a primary or secondary file.

The whole purpose of these columns and the record identification codes in positions 21 through 41 are to be able to inform the program as to which record has been read so it can be processed uniquely compared to all other record types. For example, the program would code to test for an A in the payroll example records first shown in Figure 8-10 and if the record code is an A, the programmer would code an indictor in 19-20 so the program would turn it on to indicate that an A record was read – So also for a B and a C record.

The indicators specified in these positions are used in conjunction with the record identification codes (positions 21 through 41).

When ** is used with a primary and secondary file, RPG is able to peek ahead in the file at the next record to be processed in a file.

In RPGIV, Record identifying Indicator is in position 21 – 22.

IPDRI Column(s) 21-41 (Record Identification Codes)

The entries a programmer makes in positions 21 through 41 provide a means for the program to identify each record type in an input file consisting of multiple types of records. Up to three test sets can be included on one statement and the tests can be extended by using the AND/OR logical relationship column described above (columns 14-16). The best example for this for a PAREG variant is shown in Figure 8-9.

If the file contains only one record type, which is the case with most files used with IBM i on Power Systems, the identification codes can be left blank. However, a record identifying indicator entry (positions 19 and 20) and a sequence entry (positions 15 and 16) must be made. It is OK for the sequence entry to be alphabetic meaning no sequence.

Three sets of entries to be tested can be made in positions 21 through 41: Set 1 is 21 through 27; set 2 is 28 through 34; and set 3 is 35 through 41. Each set is shaped the same and each is divided into four groups. For want of better names, we will call these parts: (1) position, (2) not, (3) code part, and (4) character.

It helps to remember that we are coding at this point to test input record types so that RPG will turn on an indicator that we can use in our program to process a particular record type. We are not defining anything here. We are merely testing conditions to see if they meet a particular record type's criteria.

(1) Position refers to the specific position in a data record that we will be testing for its contents. If a record is 100 characters long, we can test in any of 100 places for a record code that differentiates this record from others. If we use the three record types defined in Figure 6-3, we can see that there is just one record code that differentiates each record and it is located in position 1 of the record.

There are applications that build standard messages so that data can be passed from program to program and depending on the code in the message, the data with the message is formatted specifically for that message and it differentiates that message from all other messages. If an organization chose a four digit code for example for that message ID, the ID itself could be examined in this input area provided there were fewer than 99 different combinations of codes that were deployed in the application. To test for four codes, all three groups on one input statement would need to be used and the AND relationship would need to be used to examine the fourth position.

(2) Not refers to the negative of the test. If the test, for example is looking for an A in column 1, and the N was specified in the record ID group, if there was **NOT** an A in column 1, the indicator specified in columns 19 and 20 would turn on to ID the record.

(3) Code part refers to the part of the one character that is being tested. You can choose the whole character, the zone of the character or just the digit portion.

(4) Character refers to what you are looking for in that particular area of the record. In our example, if we were looking for an A record code we would test position 1 of the record with not being blank and a C in the Code part and an A in the character part so that an indicator – let's say indicator 1 in 19 and 20 would get turned on each time the program read a master record.

Table 8-11 shows which input test sets use which positions in each set.

Table 8-11 Test Set Positions

Test Set	21-27	38-34	35-41
Position	21-24	28-31	35-38
Not	25	32	39
Code Part	26	33	40
Character	27	34	41

Entries in these sets need not be in any particular sequence. For example, the programmer can make an entry in positions 28 through 34 without requiring an entry in positions 21 through 27. Entries for record identification codes are not necessary if input records within a file are of the same type.

A catch-all can be coded as an input specification containing no record identification code. This defines the last record type for the file, thus allowing the handling of any record types that may be in the file but have not specifically been coded in the program.

If no record identification codes are satisfied during the input cycle, control passes to the RPG/400 exception/error handling routine.

In RPGIV, Record Identification codes are in positions 23 – 46.

I Program Described Field Description Entries

Column 42 is reserved for future activity in RPG/400 but since there is no future development of the RPG/400 compiler in RPG, it is s safe bet we do not have to learn about whatever column 42 is about. From column 43 over to the right for program described data, RPG provides space to describe the fields and their attributes as they are to be read in from files.

The data description part of RPG begins with column 43 of the input specification as described below. Just as the record identification entries were all prefixed with IPDRI, field entries for the **I**nput **P**rogram **D**escribed **F**ield **D**escriptions shall be prefixed with IPDFD:

Figure 8-7 is repeated here as Figure 8-12 for your convenience Take another look at the field definitions before you continue.

Figure 8-12 Internally (Program) Described Input for PAREG
```
0009.00 I*
0010.00 I* RPG INPUT SPECIFICATION FORMS
0011.00 I*
0012.00 IEMPMAST AA   01
FMT                    PFromTo++DField+L1M1FrPlMnZr
0013.00 I...                  1    30EMPNO      M1
0013.01 I...                  4  23 EMPNAM
0013.02 I...                 24  282EMPRAT
0014.00 I...                 29  48 EMPCTYL1
0015.00 I...                 49  50 EMPSTAL2
0015.01 I...                 51  550EMPZIP
0016.00 ITIMCRD   AB   02
0017.00 I...                  1    30EMPNO      M1
0017.01 I...                  4    72EMPHRS
```

IPDFD Position 43 (Data Format)

The PAREG program uses two files which have two data types – character and signed decimal. Neither of these types needs to be coded in column 44 and therefore, PAREG has no entries. The allowable entries for the data format area in position 43 are as follows:

Blank   The input field is in zoned decimal format or is a character field.
P   The input field is in packed decimal format.
B   The input field is in binary format.
L   The numeric input field has a preceding (left) plus or minus sign.
R   The number input field has a following (right) plus or minus sign.

The RPG programmer uses position 43 of program described input to specify the format of the data in the records in the file that are to be read. This entry has no effect on the format used for internal processing of the input field in the program. For example, a nun-packed numeric entry will be read from disk and converted to internal packed decimal form for processing since that is how the IBM i on Power Systems likes to do its math.

In RPGIV, Data Format is in position 36.

IPDFD Position 44-51 From / To Record Positons

The PAREG program described input is shown in Figure 8-12. As you can see, it is best to think of this 8 position as two four position areas. The programmer specified the beginning position of the record in the first half and the ending position of the record in the second half. The allowable entries in these two "half areas" are as follows:
From:
Columns 44-47
1-9999   Specify a 1- to 4-digit number. This entry is for the beginning of a field
                    (from position)

To:
Columns 48-51
1-9999   Specify a 1- to 4-digit number. This entry is for the end of a field
1-10000   (to position).

The from and to location entry describes the location and size of each field in the input record. Most other programming languages require a beginning position and length or just a length in describing input. RPG is much easier to deal with for the novice since the field specifications also serve as a nice and neat record layout.

In positions 44 through 47 the programmer specifies the location of the field's beginning position in the record being read; and in positions 48 through 51 the programmer specifies the location of the field's end position in the record being read. To define a single-position field, just enter the same number in positions 44 through 47 as in positions 48 through 51. Numeric entries must be right-adjusted; leading zeros can and most often be omitted.

Additional Information re: from / to length

The maximum number of positions in the input record for each type of field is as follows:

# Pos.	Type of Field
30	Zoned decimal numeric (30 digits)
16	Packed numeric (30 digits)
4	Binary (9 digits)
256	Character (256 characters)
31	Numeric with leading or trailing sign (30 digits)
9999	Data structure.

In RPGIV, the From / To positions are 37 to 46.

IPDFD Column(s) 52 Decimal Positions

The PAREG program has three different entries for the # of decimal positions. For EMPNO and EMPZIP, for example the entries are zero. This means that the field is numeric (signed decimal format) but it has no decimal places. For EMPNAM, EMPCTY, and EMPSTA, the entries are blank. This means that these fields are of character type. For EMPHRS and EMPRAT, the entries are both 2. This means that the fields are numeric (signed decimal) and that two positions of the field length is reserved for decimal positions. The allowable entries for column 52 are as follows:

Blank   Character field
0-9   Number of decimal positions in numeric field.

In combination with the data format entry in position 43, this entry describes the full format of the field. This entry indicates whether the field described on this line is a character field or a numeric field. If the field is numeric, an entry must be made (0 to 9). This entry represents the number of decimal positions to be carried for the field coming in. For a numeric field, obviously the number is limited by and cannot exceed the length of the field.

In RPGIV, Decimal positions are in positions 47 – 48.

IPDFD Column 53-58 Field Name

The Field names for the files defined in PAREG are clearly shown in Figure 8-12. The allowable entries for field name in positions 53 to 58 are as follows:

Symbolic name   Field name, data structure name, data structure
Subfield name, array name, array element,
PAGE, PAGE1-PAGE7, *IN, *INxx, or
*IN,xx.

These positions name the fields of an input record that are used in an RPG/400 program. This name must
follow the rules for RPG symbolic names.

In RPGIV, Field Name is in positions 49 – 62.

IPDFD Column(s) 59 – 60 Control Level

The following entries in EMPMAST have control level indication specified.

```
29  48  EMPCTYL1
49  50  EMPSTAL2
```

City has an L1 indicator and State has an L2 indicator. The allowable entries in columns 59-60 for control
level are as follows:

Blank   This field is not a control field. Control level indicators
cannot be used with full procedural files.
L1-L9   This field is a control field.

Specify the control level indication in positions 59 and 60 to indicate the fields that are used as control
fields. A change in the contents of a control field causes all operations conditioned by that control level
indicator and by all lower level indicators to be processed.

Sometimes it is appropriate to use two or more fields for the same control field. This is called a split control
field. It is a control field that is made up of more than one field, each having the same control level
indicator. The first field specified with that control level indicator is placed in the high-order position of the
split control field, and the last field specified with the same control level indicator is placed in the low-order
position of the split control field.

In RPGIV, Control Level indicators are specified in positions 63 – 64.

IPDFD Column(s) 61 - 62 Matching Fields

The following asterisked entries in EMPMAST have matching fields specified.

```
0012.00 IEMPMAST AA   01
FMT                           PFromTo++DField+L1M1
**13.00 I...          1    30EMPNO    M1
0016.00 ITIMCRD   AB   02
**17.00 I...          1    30EMPNO    M1
```

This shows that the EMPNO field in EMPMAST file is set up to match the EMPNO field in the TIMCRD
file. Just one field is sued for the PAREG match definition.

The allowable entries for positions 61-62, matching fields are as follows:

Blank   This field is not a match field.
M1-M9   This field is a match field.

This entry is used to match the records of one file with those of another or to sequence check match fields
within one file. Match fields can be specified only for fields in primary and secondary files.

To specify that you are using matching records or match fields, place an M1 through M9 code in positions 61 and 62 of the appropriate field description specification line. A maximum of nine match fields can be specified.

The match field codes M1 through M9 can be assigned in any sequence. For example, M3 can be defined on the line before M1, or M1 need not be defined at all.

When more than one match field code is used for a record, all fields can be considered as one large field. M1 or the lowest code used is the rightmost or low-order position of the field. M9 or the highest code used is the leftmost or high-order position of the field.

If match fields are specified for only a single sequential file (input, update, or combined), match fields within the file are sequence checked to assure they are in ascending or descending sequence. In this case, the MR indicator is not set on (just one file) and cannot be used in the program. An out-of-sequence record causes the RPG/400 exception/error handling routine to be given control.

In addition to sequence checking, match fields are used to match records from the primary file with those from secondary files. When all the specified match indicators in the primary match those specified for the secondary, a special indicator called MR is turned on by RPG.

In RPGIV, Matching Fields are specified in positions 65 – 66.

IPDFD Column(s) 63 - 64 Field Record Relation

The PAREG program does not use field record relation.

The possible entries for field record relation include blank which means that the field is common for all record types. The entries can be any of the various indicators that are available in RPG/400 from 01 to 99, l1 to l9, MR, U1 to U8, H1 to H9, to RT.

Field record relation is a means of reducing the coding required when the same field exists in multiple record formats of the same file. Indicators are used to associate fields within a particular record type when that record type is one of several in an OR relationship. This entry reduces the number of lines that must be coded. The field with the same indicator specified in 63 - 64 as an ORed record identifying indicator gets used if the corresponding record is read.

It is a simple concept. The field described on a line is extracted (included in the input fields) from the record by the RPG/400 program only when the indicator coded in positions 63 and 64 is on or when positions 63 and 64 are blank. When positions 63 and 64 are blank, the field is common to all record types defined by the OR relationship.

In RPGIV, Field Record Relation is specified in positions 67 – 68.

IPDFD Column(s) 65-70 Field Indicators

The PAREG program does not use Field Indicators.

The entry can also be any of the various indicators that are available in RPG/400 from 01 to 99, MR, U1 to U8, H1 to H9, to RT. Level indicators and MR are not allowed..

Entries in positions 65 through 70 save coding in calculations for field values. By specifying an indicator in the +, -, Or 0 area of 65 – 70, each entry is examined for positive, negative or zero as it is read into the program. Field indicators are specified on the same line as the field to be tested. Depending on the status of the field (plus, minus, zero, or blank), the appropriate indicator is set on and can be used to condition later specifications.

Positions 65 and 66 (plus) and positions 67 and 68 (minus) are valid for numeric fields only. Positions 69 and 70 can be used to test a numeric field for zeros or a character field for blanks.

In RPGIV, Field Indicators are specified in positions 69 – 74.

IPDFD Column(s) 71 – 74 Unused

The area in the input spec from columns 71-74 is unused for program described files.

IPDFD Column(s) 76 – 80 Comments

Positions 75 through 80 can be used for comments, or left blank. These positions are not printed contiguously with positions 6-74 on the compiler listing.

RPGIV Program Described Files

RPGIV has several input field specifications that do not exist in RPG/400. These are captured in the section below with the header IPIV.

IPIV Columns 31-34 Data Attributes

Positions 31-34 specify the external format for a date, time, or variable-length character, graphic, or UCS-2 field. If this entry is blank for a date or time field, then the format/separator specified for the file (with either DATFMT or TIMFMT or both) is used. If there is no external date or time format specified for the file, then an error message is issued.
For character, graphic, or UCS-2 data, the *VAR data attribute is used to specify variable-length input fields. If this entry is blank for character, graphic, or UCS-2 data, then the external format must be fixed length.

IPIV Column 35 Date/Time Separator

Position 35 specifies a separator character to be used for date/time fields. The & (ampersand) can be used to specify a blank separator. For an entry to be made in this field, an entry must also be made in RPGIV input positions 31-34 (date/time external format).

Chapter Summary

There is no better indication that the many function patches on the RPG language were coming apart and in need of a permanent fix than the highly versatile input specification. There are literally many faces of input as columns have had to be defined and redefined over the years to squeeze in all of the new language function without adding a new specification type.

It can be argued that the Input Specification is overloaded with baggage. In addition to its primary two purposes of uniquely identifying records and defining internal data fields, the language actually has two versions of each of these – one for external and one for internally described data.

So, there were always two formats to the Input specification. In 1978 with the introduction of the System/38, IBM introduced RPGIII. This flavor of RPG permitted the RPG input specifications to be fetched and formatted from the database itself by the compiler at compile time.

Additionally, data structures were added to the language. Since RPG/400 had no data specification for working storage as in COBOL, the Input spec got the calla gain f or data structure identification as well as data structure subfields. So far, as you can see there are six functions for input and there are more. Finally, the language was enhanced with named constants and again, the only place that made any sense was to cut up the input spec again and redefine its columns.

Even when the input specifications are provided externally, when a program uses the cycle to define match fields and level breaks, the input specification is how it is done. Additionally, since the database permits ten character and even larger names, and RPG/400 permits just 6 character names, the input specification is also used as a bridge for externally described input data when the input data field names are longer than 6 characters. The rename facility accommodates this but again using an old workhorse of a tired RPG specification.

In addition to the Definition 'D' specification which are used for structures and constants and the like in RPGIV, the language has several input field column specifications that do not exist in RPG/400.

Key Chapter Terms

AND/OR	Input field entries	RECID
Decimal Positions	Input speci	Record format
Decoding	Logical Relationship	Record ID indicators
Digit portion	M1 - M9	Record ID codes
Display file	Master record	Record name
DS subfield spec	Match field codes	Record types
Expanded source	MR indicator	RENAME
External field name	Multiple record types	Renaming fields
External format	Named constants	Subfields
Field indicators	Naming Conventions	TIMFMT
Field record relation	Out-of-sequence	To record
File name	PAGE1-PAGE7	Total calculations
First record	Peek ahead	Total output
H1 to H9	Primary file	U1 to U8
Indicators	Pgm Desc Rec. ID	Zoned decimal
Input cycle		

Review Questions

1. Give seven different forms of the RPG/400 input specification?

2. Why does RPGIV not need as many forms for input definition as RPG/400?

3. What is the purpose of the record ID form of RPG?

4. When multi-format external logical files without unique record ID contents are used in RPG programs, how are the records identified and how can an indicator be turned on to identify a specific record?

5. Is there a substantive difference between the RPG/400 record ID formats (external and internal) from the RPGIV record formats? Explain?

6. Is there a substantive difference between the RPG/400 field definition formats (external and internal) from the RPGIV field definition formats? Explain?

7. In your own words, what is the difference in Input for externally defined data and internally described data in RPGIV and RPG/400?

8. Discuss the similarity between the compile listing of the external PAREG version and the internal version of the program?

9. What is the difference between L1 and LR9?

10. What is the difference between M1 and MR?

11. What is field record relation and would it increase or decrease code if it were used?

Chapter 9 The Specifics of RPG Coding – Input Structures & Constants – by Example

What is a Data Structure?

A data structure is simply a packaging of data elements as in a record. In fact, a record is a data structure. In programming for computer science applications and business alike, a data structure is a way of storing data in a computer so that it can be used efficiently. In computer science, a carefully chosen data structure will allow a more efficient algorithm to be used. In business programming careful design of data structures can provide an ease of understanding and application standardization. A well-designed data structure allows a variety of critical operations to be performed using as little resources, including programmer coding time, as well as both execution time and memory space, as possible.

In this chapter we show how to code both program-described and externally described data structures. A program described data structure is identified by a blank in position 17 of the data structure statement. The subfield specifications for a program-described data structure must immediately follow the data structure statement. An externally described data structure is identified by an E in position 17 of the data structure statement. The subfield descriptions for this are contained in an externally described file with one record format. The file merely serves as a means of grabbing the data definition.

The data contents of the file are irrelevant to the data structure. To bring the data structure definition from the external file into the program, at compile time, the RPG/400 program uses the external name to locate and extract the external description of the data structure subfields. An external subfield name can be renamed in the program, and additional subfields can be added to an externally described data structure in the program.

In RPG, Data structures are very powerful data configurations that have a number of purposes. For example, a data structure can be used to:

1. Allow the division of a field into subfields without using the MOVE or MOVEL operations.
2. Operate on a subfield and change the contents of a subfield.
3. Redefine the same internal area more than once using different data formats.

Data Structure Record ID Entries

Data structures are defined on the input specifications in RPG/400 and in the 'D' spec in RPGIV. In RPG/400, they are defined the same way records are defined. The record specification line contains the data structure statement (DS in positions 19 and 20) and the data structure name is optional. The field specification lines contain the subfield specifications for the data structure.

Though Data Structures (DS) use the Input specification, programmers must use care when arranging the structures so that they appear in the program after the normal input specifications for records. All entries describing a data structure and its subfields must appear together

In RPGIV, the data structure is defined on the new 'D' type specification which is covered in Chapter 13, 23, and 24 along with any additional detail and sample code using RPG/400 Data Structures. The PAREG program that we have been working with uses no data structures. Therefore, the examples we choose will not be completely reflective of code that is found in the sample program to this point. However, they will be similar. The designator **IDSRI** is used to begin each header so it is easy to spot the entries that belong with Input, Data Structure, Record Identification.

Let's start our examination of data structures with a hypothetical example shown in Figure 9-1 that has some basis in our EMPMAST file, but as you can see this data structure has a different format than the EMPMAST file and it has more fields defined. Thus, it makes a better example for us for this topic.

Figure 9-1 Sample Employee Data Structure

```
IEMPDS1      DS...    100
I...                    1    50EMPNO
I...                    6    30 EMPNAM
I...                   31    60 EMPAD1
I...                   61    90 EMPAD2
I...                   91   110 EMPCTY
I...                  111   112 EMPSTA
I...                  113  1170EMPZIP
I...                  118  1252EMPPAY
I...                  126  1310EMPHIR hiredate
I...                  126  1270EMPYR
I...                  128  1290EMPMO
I...                  130  1310EMPDA
```

This data structure is internal. It is named EMPDS1. It has 100 occurrences of a record layout that has 12 fields. One field, EMPHIR (Employee date of hire) is subdivided by the structure into separate YEAR, MONTH and DAY fields. See how convenient it is to redefine a structure within RPG/400.

IDSRI Column(s) 7-12 Data Structure Name

Positions 7 through 12 of the DS format of the Input Spec can contain the name of the data structure being defined. The name in the example in Figure 9-1 is **EMPDS1**. The data structure name is optional, and is limited to the 6 character spaces provided. A data structure name can be specified anywhere a character field can be specified. If the data structure is externally described and positions 21-30 are blank, this entry must contain the name of an externally described file.

IDSRI Column(s) 13-16 Reserved

Columns 13-16 of the data structure record format form of the input specification has reserved positions for future use

IDSRI Column(s) 17 External Description

The example in Figure 9-1 is internal so this column is blank. The External Description area in column 17 can have the following entries:

Blank   Subfield definitions for this data structure follow this
             specification.
E   Subfield definitions are described externally. Positions 7 through 12 must
             contain the name of an externally described file if positions 21 through 30 are
             blank.
             The file name must be limited   to 6 characters.

IDSRI Column(s) 18 Option

The example in Figure 9-1 uses no Option entry.

The Option field has just a few entries but it enables a number of very powerful facilities of data structures – initialization, program status, and data area data structure. Initialization involves the filling of subfields with zeros or blanks; program status provides information about program operations in a handy special purpose data structure. A data area is akin to a one record disk file that is external to the program and brought in during program startup or during data area operations. Adding a data structure to a data area provides the one record with a layout of fields and field names that are available to the program.

The allowable entries include the following:

✓ **Blank**   This data structure is not a program status or data area data structure, and this data structure is not globally initialized.
✓ **I** Data structure initialization. All subfields in the data structure are initialized; characters to blank, numeric to zero, in the order in which they are defined, during program initialization.
✓ **S** This data structure is the program status data structure. Only one data structure can be specified as the program status data structure.
✓ **U** This is a data area data structure. The external data area (named in positions 7 through 12) is retrieved when the program starts and rewritten when the program ends. If you put blanks in positions 7 through 12, the local data area is used. It is important to note that the data area specified by the data structure is locked for the duration of the program.

IDSRI Columns 19–20 Record ID Indicator

Since the example in Figure 9-1 reflects a real data structure, positions 19-20 contain the letters "DS." In the position typically reserved for an input record identifying indicator to be specified, for a data structure record ID, the letters "DS" must be provided in columns 19 – 20.

IDSRI Columns 21 – 30 External File Name

The example in Figure 9-1 is internal so this column is blank. The external name of the database file from which the data structure definitions are pulled is specified in columns 21 – 30. Using External structures accommodates standardization and it reduces the amount of coding – especially for long data structures. The allowable entries are as follows:

Blank   The data structure subfields are defined in the program.
File name   This is the name of the file whose first record format
            contains the field descriptions used as the subfield
            descriptions for this data structure.

IDSRI Column(s) 31 – 43 Reserved

Columns 31 – 43 of the data structure record format form of the input specification has reserved positions for future use

IDSRI Column(s) 44-47 Data Structure Occurrences

The example in Figure 9-1 is set up to contain 100 records (occurrences) in memory. A simple data structure is similar to a one record memory file. Data structures however can have multiple memory records called occurrences. In columns 44-47, you specify the number of occurrences that this particular data structure should have. The allowable entries are as follows:

Blank This is not a multiple-occurrence data structure.
1-9999 The number (right-adjusted) indicating the number of occurrences of a multiple-occurrence data structure.

These positions must be blank if the data structure is the program status data structure (indicated by an S in position 18), a file information data structure (INFDS), or a data area data structure.

IDSRI Column(s) 48 – 51 DS Length

In the example in Figure 9-1, the length of the data structure is 131 but the compiler must calculate that by adding up the subfields. The length of a data structure can either be specified in positions 49-51 of the Data Structure Record Format or it can be calculated by the compiler. It is optional. The possible entries are as follows:

Blank Length of the data structure is either the length specified on the input field specifications if the data structure is an input field or the highest To position specified for a subfield within the data structure if the data structure is not an input field.
1-9999   Length of the data structure.

If the length is specified, it must be right-adjusted. If this entry is not made, the length of the data structure is one of the following:

A. The length specified on the input field specifications if the data
structure name is an input field.

B. The highest To position specified for a subfield within the data structure if the data structure name is not an input field.

IDSRI Column(s) 52 – 74 Reserved

Columns 52 – 74 of the data structure record format form of the input specification has reserved positions for future use

IDSRI Columns 75 – 80 Comments

Columns 75 through 80 can be used for comments, or left blank. These positions are not printed contiguously with positions 6-74 on the compiler listing.

I Data Structure Subfield Entries

In this section, the subfield entries required for data structures are examined in detail. See the I Data Structure Record Format header above for more information on data structures as well as Chapter 17. The designator **IDSSF** is used to begin each header so it is easy to spot the entries that belong with Input, Data Structure, Subfield..

IDSSF Column 7 Reserved

Column 7 of the data structure subfield form of the input specification has reserved this position for future use

IDSSF Column 8 Initialization Option

The example in Figure 9-1 is basic and it uses no initialization options.

That which the record format giveth the subfield can taketh more, so to speak. Position 18 of the DS record format provides an I option to initialize the subfields to either zeroes or blanks. This option trumps that option by permitting the subfield to be initialized with a real value, rather than a zero or blank. The allowable entries for this option include the following:

Blank No subfield initialization other than that specified in record format.
I   Subfield is initialized to value specified in positions 21 to 42 of this statement.

IDSSF Columns 9 – 20 Reserved

Columns 9 – 20 of the data structure subfield form of the input specification has reserved these positions for future use

IDSSF Columns 21 – 30 External Field Name

The example in Figure 9-1 is internal so this column is blank.

When an externally described data structure is coded in a program, sometimes there is a field name conflict and the subfield in the external structure must be renamed to be able to be used properly in the program. To rename a subfield in an externally described data structure, specify the external name in positions 21 through 30, and specify the name to be used in the program in positions 53 through 58. The remaining positions of the DS subfield form must be blank.

IDSSF Columns 21 – 42 (Initialize Value)

The example in Figure 9-1 uses no initialization. When a subfield is to be initialize with a specific value, specify a literal value or a named constant in these positions. If no value is specified and position 8 contains I, the subfield is initialized to zero or blanks, depending on the field type. The value may be continued on the next line. Obviously the initialization value cannot be sued with an externally described DS since the fields are mutually exclusive.

IDSSF Columns 31 – 42 Reserved

Columns 31 through 42 of the data structure subfield form of the input specification must be blank, if an external field name is specified in positions 21 to 30.

IDSSF Column 43 Internal Data Format

The subfields in the example in Figure 9-1 use only character or zoned decimal format and therefore, for all subfields described , this column is blank.

Since data fields can be defined with the DS subfield form, the programmer must specify what type of data is to be stored in each subfield of a data structure. Unlike the external data format field, the entry determines the internal format of the data. The allowable entries include:

Blank Subfield is in zoned decimal format or is character data if position
52 (decimal positions) is blank.
P Subfield is in packed decimal format.
B Subfield is in binary format.

IDSSF Column 44 – 51 Field Location

The subfields in the example in Figure 9-1 use these columns to specify the from and to positions of each subfield. The EMPHIR field uses the same are of the structure as does the EMPYR, EMPMO, and EMPDA fields combined.

In columns 44-47 you specify the "From" position and in columns 49-51 you specify the "To" position of the subfield. Both the "From" and the "To" values must be right-justified, and leading zeroes may be omitted. The allowable entries are as follows:

From:
Columns 44-47
1-9999 Specify a 1- to 4-digit number. This entry is for the
                beginning of a field (from position)

To:
Columns 49-51
1-9999 Specify a 1- to 4-digit number This entry is for the end of
                a field (to position).

IDSSF Column 52 Decimal Positions

The subfields in the example in Figure 9-1 use this position for the number of decimal places. The only field with more than zero decimal places is EMPPAY with two places defined out of the length of the field. Those subfield entries with 0 decimals are by default numeric zoned decimal format and those with no entry for decimal places are character format.

The allowable entries for column 52 are as follows:

Blank   Character field
0-9   Number of decimal positions in numeric field.

In combination with the data format entry in position 43, this entry describes the full format of the field. This entry indicates whether the field described on this line is a character field or a numeric field. If the field is numeric, an entry must be made (0 to 9). This entry represents the number of decimal positions to be carried for the field coming in. For a numeric field, obviously the number is limited by and cannot exceed the length of the field.

IDSSF Column 53-58 Field Name

In positions 53 through 58, enter the name of the subfield that is being defined. The name can be an array name, but cannot be an array element name. Twelve meaningful subfield names are provided for your inspection if Figure 9-1.

IDSSF Columns 59 – 74 Reserved

Columns 59 through 74 of the data structure subfield form of the input specification must be blank. This space is reserved for future use.

IDSSF Columns 75 – 80 Comments

Columns 75 through 80 can be used for comments, or left blank. These positions are not printed contiguously with positions 6-74 on the compiler listing.

I Named Constant Entries

The input specification in RPG/400 is definitely overworked. It is the major utility player for a language that evolved past the logical means of supporting it without change. The major changes to the RPGIV language have addressed all of these concerns. In RPGIV, the Named Constant is defined on the new 'D' type specification which is covered in Chapter 13 along with some additional detail and sample code.

But, before we get to RPGIV we need to take a look at how to define constants in RPG/400 and provide them with a name. That is what this section is about. The designator **INC** is used to begin each header so it is easy to spot the entries that belong with Input, Named Constant.

The example to keep in mind as we examine the structure of the named constant variant of the INPUT specification is shown in Figure 9-2.

Figure 9-2 Continued Named Constant
```
I...    'Press Enter to con-  C...      CONTNU
I...    'tinue operation.'
```

The name of this constant is CONTNU and it is continues so that it can fit in all of the words, "Press Enter to continue operation." The text on the first line continues to the second. The first line contains a C in position 43 and the second line is blank in position 43 meaning it is continued.

INC Columns 7 – 20 Reserved

Columns 7 through 20 of the named constant form of the input specification must be blank. This space is reserved for future use.

INC Columns 21 – 42 Constant

Columns 21-42 are reserved in the named constant form of the input specification for the contents of the named constant field which may hold a real constant or an edit word. The constant may be continued on subsequent lines by coding a hyphen as the last character. For character named constants the hyphen replaces the ending quote. A continued numeric constant must result in a valid decimal number with at most 30 digits, a maximum of 9 being to the right of the decimal point. Named constants can be declared anywhere in the input specifications.

INC Columns 43 Type / Continuation

Just as a DS entry differentiates a data structure from an input spec, a C in column 43 tells the compiler that this is a named constant. If one or more lines above this entry contain a C, then this line may be a blank meaning it if only other blanks for comments separate this from the C entry then this is a continuation of a named constant.

The allowable entries are as follows:

C   Type of name is constant
Blank Constant continuation line

INC Columns 44 – 52 Reserved

Columns 44 – 52   of the named constant form of the input specification must be blank. This space is reserved for future use.

INC Columns 53 – 58 Constant Name

Place the name of the constant in columns 53 – 58. Normal RPG field naming rules apply

INC Columns 59 – 74 Reserved

Columns 59 – 74 of the named constant form of the input specification must be blank. This space is reserved for future use.

INC Columns 75 – 80 Comments

Columns 75 through 80 can be used for comments, or left blank. These positions are not printed contiguously with positions 6-74 on the compiler listing.

Chapter Summary

A data structure is a packaging of data elements in the form of a record. Data structures are used in RPG to define groups of related fields and for RPG internal operations using the UPDAT and WRITE operations, a data structure is needed to define the shape of the data that is being sent out.

In RPG, Data structures are very powerful data configurations that have a number of purposes. For example, a data structure can be used to:

4. Allow the division of a field into subfields without using the MOVE or MOVEL operations.
5. Operate on a subfield and change the contents of a subfield.
6. Redefine the same internal area more than once using different data formats.

Data structures are defined on the input specifications in RPG/400 and in the 'D' spec in RPGIV. The RPG/400 record specification line contains the data structure statement (DS in positions 19 and the field specification lines contain the subfield specifications for the data structure.

Though Data Structures (DS) use the Input specification, programmers must use care when arranging the structures so that they appear in the program after the normal input specifications for records. All entries describing a data structure and its subfields must appear together

The input specification in RPG/400 is also used to define "named constants." The D specification is used for these in RPGIV.

Key Chapter Terms

'D' spec	DS occurrences	Input Structures
Constant, named	Duration	Local data area
Data area DS	External description	Memory file
Data elements	External field name	Named Constant
Data Structure	Format	Record format
Data structure def.	INFDS	Subfield entries
DS length	Initialization	

Review Questions

1. What is a data structure?

2. What are the two pieces of a data structure?

3. Why are data structures needed some times for calculation operations against internally described files?

4. In RPG, Data structures are very powerful data configurations that have a number of purposes. Name three purposes for a data structure?

5. How is a data structure defined in RPG/400? RPGIV?

6. What is a multiple occurrence data structure?

7. How can the definition of a data structure be provided to the compiler without the programmer having to type all of it?

8. What is a data area object?

9. What is meant by data structure initialization?

10. What is a local data area?

11. What is a program status data structure? How many data areas can be specified as the program status data structure? What makes a data area a program status data structure?

12. What is a data area data structure? How is it coded?

13. What is subfield initialization?

14. What is a named constant?

15. How is a named constant continued?

16. How are named constants handled in RPGIV?

Chapter 10   The Specifics of RPG Coding – Calculations – by Example

Mathematics and Logic

The Calculation form is where most of the action takes place in RPG programs. All programming languages provide a vehicle for arithmetic and logical operations and RPG programmers use the calc form to get these functions accomplished. Of course, when the RPG cycle is used as in the PAREG program, the calculation form does not get the input/output action since that is handled by the cycle itself.

The calculation specifications for the external PAREG program (Figure 6-1) and internal PAREG program (Figure 6-2) that we have been decoding over the last few chapters are repeated below for your convenience as we examine them in detail in this chapter. You will first notice that in column 6, there is the 'C' official specification designator to differentiate the CALC format of this RPG form from all others. The statements coded on this spec form are executed in the RPG cycle during either detail time calculations (Step 7) or total time calculations (Step 3). This is the place in RPG in which the bulk of the decision making as well as the computations take place. One can expect lots of action with a stop at the 'C' spec during the fixed logic cycle.

As you examine the calculation specification shown in Figure 10-1, you will notice that each statement is divided into three parts that specify the following:

1. The conditions under which the calculations are to be done: The conditioning indicators specified in positions 7 through 17 determine when and under what conditions the calculations are to be done.

2. The type of calculations to be done: The entries specified in positions 18 through 53 determine the kind of calculations to be done, specify the data (such as fields or files) upon which the operation is to be done, and they specify the field that is to contain the results of the calculation.

3. The type of tests that are to be made on the results of the operation: Indicators may be specified in positions 54 through 59 of RPG/400 specs. These are used to test the results of the calculations and the indicators that are turned on or off can affect subsequent calculations or output operations. The resulting indicator positions (54 to 59 in RPG/400) have various uses, depending on the specific operation code. For a perspective on the uses of these positions for various operations, see the individual operation codes in Chapter 14, RPG (/400) Operations and Chapter 15, RPGIV Operations and Built-In Finctions.

All detail operations that are unconditioned are performed each cycle. All unconditioned operations that are specified at a total level will be executed unconditionally when RPG passes through that particular total cycle. Any arithmetic operation that is performed, including the compare operations, which internally subtract Factor 2 from Factor1, sets the status of the indicators specified on the right side of the calculation spec. This section is known as the resulting indicator area.

Three indicators can be specified in this area and RPG will turn one of them on during a calculation operation depending on the result. The three conditions that can be specified in RPG/400 are (1) columns 54 & 55 [greater than zero – non-blank and positive], or (2) columns 56 & 57 [less than zero --negative or minus], or (3) columns 58 & 59 [equal to each other -- or equal to zero]. Only one of these conditions will occur after an arithmetic or logic operation and thus if indictors 01, 02, and 03 are selected respectively as resulting indicators, If the results are positive, 01 is turned on; if the results are negative, 02 is turned on, and if the results are equal or zero, 03 is turned on.

The positive, negative or equal status is determined when the field in Factor 1 is compared, added, subtracted, multiplied, or divided to/by the field in Factor 2 as B. When this happens as part of RPG's magic, the other two indicators specified that are not true (not set on) for this operation are actually set off. Hence, just one of the three conditions will be reflected by the status of the indicators.

The process works exactly the same in RPGIV. However, since the RPG IV calculation specification is shaped differently than the RPG/400 statement, the three resulting indicators in an RPGIV calculation are reflected in columns 71-72, 73-74, and 75-76 respectively. Figure 10-1 shows how indicators 01, 02, and 03 would be specified in statement 21 of the PAREG program if we had a reason to test the results of the multiplication operation. Indicator 01 would turn on if the result was positive. If negative or zero, 01 would be turned off. Indicator 02 would turn on if the result was negative. If positive or zero, 02 would be turned off. Indicator 03 would turn on if the result was zero. If positive or negative, 03 would be turned off.

Figure 10-1 Resulting Indicators Specified in Multiply

```
678911234567892123456789312345678941234567895123456789
C*
C* RPG CALCULATION SPECIFICATION FORMS
C*
C   02 MR    EMPRAT     MULT EMPHRS     EMPPAY  72 010203
```

The RPG Calculation Specification

To give you a head start to decoding the PAREG calculations, lets' take a shot at decoding the filled in entries in Figure 10-2. Of course, we have no real idea of what this program is, where it came from, who wrote it, what it does, etc. But isn't that what you will experience when you get to look at your first program written by somebody in the "shop." So, let's take a shot at decoding this program one line at a time. Let's first see what it would look like in Figure 10-3 if we typed it up nice with a source editor such as SEU.

Figure 10-2 Old-Time Filled-In Calc Spec

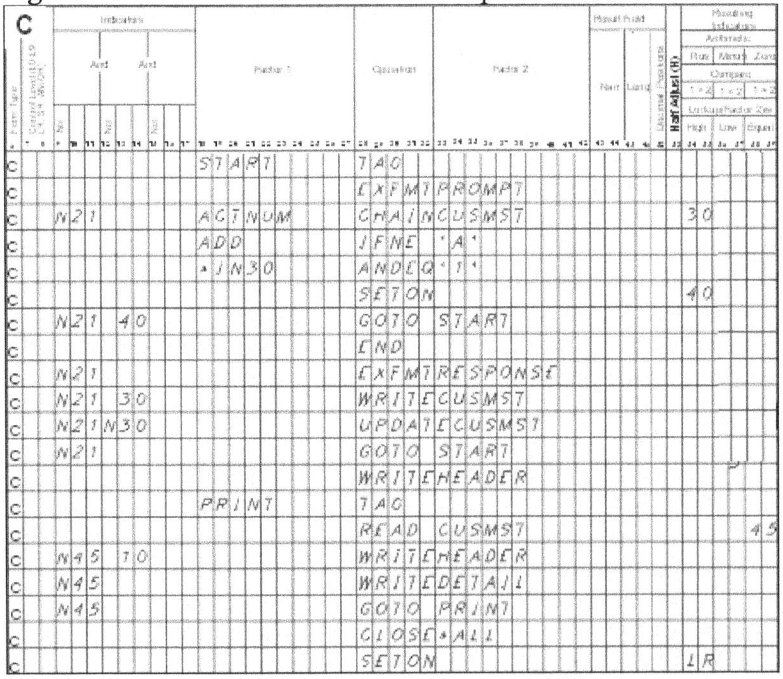

Form Type	Indicators	Factor 1	Operation	Factor 2	Resulting Indicators
C		START	TAG		
C			EXFMT	PROMPT	
C	N21	ACTNUM	CHAIN	CUSMST	30
C		ADD	IFNE	'A'	
C		*IN30	ANDEQ	'1'	
C			SETON		40
C	N21 40		GOTO	START	
C			END		
C	N21		EXFMT	RESPONSE	
C	N21 30		WRITE	CUSMST	
C	N21 N30		UPDAT	CUSMST	
C	N21		GOTO	START	
C			WRITE	HEADER	
C		PRINT	TAG		
C			READ	CUSMST	45
C	N45 70		WRITE	HEADER	
C	N45		WRITE	DETAIL	
C	N45		GOTO	PRINT	
C			CLOSE	*ALL	
C			SETON		LR

Now, let's examine each of these specifications in detail and decode them as best we can. After you have done your best with the limited operations knowledge that we have covered at this point, come back and look at the results in Table 10-4.

Figure 10-3 Typed Version of Written Code

```
FMT C   CL0N01N02N03Factor1+++OpcdeFactor2+++ResultLenDHHiLoEq
0026.00 C             START    TAG
0027.00 C                      EXFMTPROMPT
0028.00 C   N21       ACTNUM   CHAINCUSMST                  30
0029.00 C             ADD      IFNE 'A'
0030.00 C             *IN30    ANDEQ'1'
0031.00 C                      SETON                        40
0032.00 C   N21 40             GOTO START
0033.00 C                      END
0034.00 C   N21                EXFMTRESPONSE
0035.00 C   N21 30             WRITECUSMST
0036.00 C   N21N30             UPDATCUSMST
0037.00 C   N21                GOTO START
0038.00 C                      WRITEHEADER
0039.00 C             PRINT    TAG
0040.00 C                      READ CUSMST                      45
0041.00 C   N45 10             WRITEHEADER
0042.00 C   N45                WRITEDETAIL
0043.00 C   N45                GOTO PRINT
0044.00 C                      CLOSE*ALL
0045.00 C                      SETON                            LR
```

Table 10-4 Decoding CUSTMST Program

St#	What does it do?
26	Provides a spot in the program to which a GOTO can branch. Sine this is in the beginning, it is probably a return point for processing or for errors.
27	The EXFMT sends out a screen panel named in Factor 2 as PROMPT from a display file described in file descriptions. When this operation starts it sends out the PROMPT panel. Then it waits for the user to enter something into the prompt screen. Then, the operation reads the data into the program and fills up the input fields defined for that particular display format.
28	It looks like indicator 21 means that the user selected an option in the program (possibly an indicator on the PROMPT panel) to print a report and if indicator 21 is not on the CUSMST file will be updated. The ACTNUM field which came in from the prompt panel is used to chain to (random read) the customer master file to pull up that account record. More than likely indicator 21 turns on as a result of some action on the screen, such as a user hitting F21 and the indicator is passed to the program along with the screen panel. Set indicator 30 on If the record does not exist in the customer master file. If the account is found, load the fields with the CUSMSTcusmst account information
29	The "ADD" field which was read in from the PROMPT panel is tested for the negative of a value 'A' (anything but A is true) It looks like they are testing to see if the user wants to add a record if it is not found in the customer master.
30	Indicator 30, (meaning the CUSMST record was not found on the CHAIN operation) is tested to see if it was turned on. If this condition is true (record not found) and the prior condition is true (not A), then the if statement evaluates as true. If either are false, the If statement is false.
31	If both are true, indicator 40 is turned on to record this status meaning that no record was found and the use does not want to create a record.
32	If both are true which sets indicator 40 on, and if indicator 21 is not on, the GOTO will be executed and the program will go back to start. If 40 is not on or 21 is on, the next statement (34) will be executed. So, if the record is not found and the user did not say to add the record, then go back to start. If the user said to add the record, proceed. with the program. If indicator 21 is on, the program passes on and goes to the PRINT routine after writing headings.
33	This ends the action for the IF group 30-33
	What does it mean to have arrived here in the program. Indicator 40 is not on and 21 is or is not on not on. If 21 is not on, this means that either the terminal operator typed an A to say it was OK to create a new record or there was no A but the record was found. – therefore the record from CUSTMAST is OK to update. That's what we know at this point. So we write a new record if no 40 and the A was keyed or we update the record read if no 40 and the record was found (30 not on) If 21 is on, we are heading to the print routine but first we will print headings.
34	If indicator 21 is not on, 40 is not on, so Send out the response display with the EXFMT operation to get the information to update or create a data record in the customer file, then wait for a response from the screen user to get the customer fields from the panel, then load the input fields and indicator fields from the RESPONSE panel to the CUSTMST record format for update or output.
35	If indicator 21 is not on, and indicator 30 is on (customer master does not exist) write out a customer master record

36	If indicator 21 is not on, and indicator 30 is not on (customer master was found and in memory, go ahead and update the customer master with the information that was received in the RESPONSE display panel.
37	If 21 is not on, go to start (26) to get more data. If 21 is on, proceed to next statement in program (38) to start the print routine
38	Write the headings from an externally defined print file to a printer (spooled).
39	Provides a spot in the program to which a GOTO can branch. Since this is in the beginning of a routine loop called PRINT, this is where the CUSMST file gets read and printed..
40	Read the CUSMST file from the beginning to create a report. Turn on Indicator 45 if all the records have been read from the CUSMST file.
41	If 45 is not on (not the end of the CUSMST file yet) and 10 is on because of an overflow condition on the printer, print the headings again
42	If 45 is not on (not the end of the CUSMST file yet) print out a detail line to the externally described print file record format named detail.
43	If 45 is not on (not the end of the CUSMST file yet) go to PRINT at line 39 to read another record and go through the print cycle again.
44	When the report is printed, close all the files
45	Set on LR so the program can end

Now, wasn't that fun? If you stay with that little menagerie of operations as in Figure 10-2 and 10-3, until you know it cold or are fairly clued in, you will already have a jump start on learning what RPG is all about. Now, let's examine each of the calculation statements in the PAREG program starting with the four functional lines of code in Figure 10-5.

Figure 10-5 RPG Calculations for PAREG

```
        67891123456789212345678931234567894123456789512
0018.00 C*
0019.00 C* RPG CALCULATION SPECIFICATION FORMS
0020.00 C*
0021.00 C    02 MR    EMPRAT    MULT EMPHRS    EMPPAY    72
0022.00 C    02 MR    EMPPAY    ADD  CTYPAY    CTYPAY    92
0023.00 CL1          CTYPAY    ADD  STAPAY    STAPAY    92
0024.00 CL2          STAPAY    ADD  TOTPAY    TOTPAY    92
```

Statement numbers 18, 19 and 20 are comments (* in column 7) so they have no bearing on the logic of the program whatsoever. Following the comments are the detail calculations. These are the calculations without an * in column 7 and without an "L1 or L2 " in columns 7 and 8. They are shown in statement 21 and 22 in Figure 7-2. As you have learned, each time a record is read from the primary or the secondary file(s) (Steps 2 and 6) the next step in the cycle (Step 7) is for RPG to execute these detail calculations.

The first detail calculation specified in statement 21 occurs when the 02 record (TIMCRD) is read and there is a match with the payroll master record for that employee.

Statement 23 and 24 demonstrate total calculations. You may recall that in the RPG cycle at Step 3, whenever there is a change in the value of the control field that is marked by L1, those calculations with an L1 such as statement 23 above are performed. This processing occurs after the last record read from the prior group of records with the same control field value (EMPCTY -city) and before the first record of a group with a new control field value is processed. In the RPG cycle, we might say that all level calculations occur "in-between time." For the PAREG program, the level 1 break occurs when the City value in the group of pay records change from say, Scranton to Wilkes-Barre.

L2 calculations work the same as L1. In this case, a change in the EMPSTA field -- state, creates an L2 control break and L2 calculations occur In the PAREG program, the only L2 calculation line is shown as statement 24 above. For the PAREG program, the level 2 break occurs when the State value in the group of pay records change from say, Alaska to Pennsylvania. Of course whenever there is a higher level such as when the state changes forcing a Level 2 break, there is also a corresponding Level 1 break forced by the L2 change. This makes lots of sense logically for if we were processing Anchorage Alaska and the next record were Anchorage, Pennsylvania, the two of these are definitely different cities.

Calculation Specification Statement Format

Now that we have examined the calculations specification in light of the CUSTMST program snippet in 10-2 and 10-3 and the PAREG calculations in Figure 10-5, let's look at the full calculation specification in much the same way as we examined the Header, File Description, Line Counter, and the many Input variants. As you know by now, the specification form begins with the requisite 'C' that must appear in position 6 to identify this line as a calculation specifications. In addition to column, 6, the calc spec has many other options that we can specify. Let's review them now. For the calculation specification we use the header designation of C to easily differentiate this form from all others.

C Columns 7-8 (Control Level)

The possible entries for the control level are as follows:

Blank A. Operation is performed at detail calculation time for each program if conditions are met
B. Operation is performed within a subroutine

L0 The operation is done at total calculation time for each program cycle – independent of control fields

L1-L9 The operation is done when the appropriate control break occurs at total calculation time, or when the indicator is set on.

LR The operation is done after the last record has been processed or after the LR indicator has been set on.

SR The calculation operation is part of an RPG/400 subroutine. A blank entry is also valid for subroutines

AN, "And" and "Or" Indicators are used to group calculations
OR to have more than one line condition the calculation.

The RPGIV CALC specification also uses columns 7 & 8 for the control level information

PAREG and Control Levels

There are only two calculation specifications in PAREG that occur at total time. They are listed in Figure 10-6.

Figure 10-6 Total Calculations – Occur After Control Break
```
0023.00 CL1        CTYPAY     ADD  STAPAY     STAPAY  92
0024.00 CL2        STAPAY     ADD  TOTPAY     TOTPAY  92
```

Notice in the PAREG program calculations specifications shown completely in Figure 10-5 that the Control Level calculations are specified after the detail calculations. This is not by happenchance. Detail calculations (no L indication in column 7) come before L1 come before L2 come before L3 etc. come before LR calculations.

We must relate this to the RPG cycle since in order to have level calculations; you must be using the RPG cycle. Control level calculations occur in Step 3 of the RPG cycle that we described in Chapter 3. Though they are specified in the program after detail calculations, in fact, they occur in the cycle at step 3 whereas detail calculations occur in Step 7 right before the cycle goes back to the top for detail output..

Let's spend just a little time to refresh your memory. Figure 10-6 is shown to help jog your RPG cycle learning from Chapter 3. The cycle starts with 1P output to provide a means to get headings on reports prior to records ever being read. PAREG dutifully produces its 1P output in accordance with the cycle. This first cycle of course, there is no detail output from data since no data has been read. So, RPG goes ahead starts the next input process in step 2 to get the next record for processing.

RPG however, does not make the information from the fields it just read available to the cycle until step 6, so it still has the stuff from the last record read by the time it hits step 3 in the cycle. To get the gist of total calculations, let's move away from the RPG first cycle. Let's say instead that RPG has just read in a record in which the state field EMPSTA in PAREG is different from the last state field that was read. Using the data from Figure 5-1 as an example, suppose Pennsylvania (PA) changed to Alaska (AK).

Figure 10-6 The 7 Major Steps to the RPG Fixed Logic Cycle

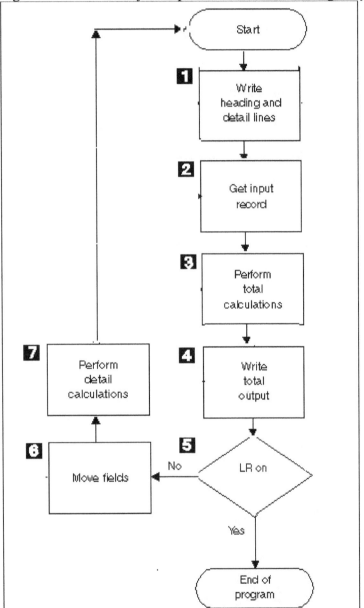

This means that the totals for Pennsylvania can be accumulated and printed. The state creates a level 2 break which always forces a Level 1 break. The L1 break is processed first. So, when the state changes, the city by definition is also different and it changes also. During this time in which the data from the last record is available though the next record is read, RPG learns of the control field change and starts the L1 calculations and then the L2 calculations as specified in Figure 10-6.

Thus, by the time the L2 calc in line 24 of Figure 10-6 is executed, the pay total for the last city processed for PA is added to the state total (STAPAY) at L1 total time. Then the L2 calc is executed which takes the STAPAY (state total for PA) and adds it to the total pay for all states (TOTPAY). After level calculations, PAREG moves to step 4 of the cycle which is total output which is covered in Chapter 11.

As a sneak peak into total output, consider that we have the city and state totals prepared to print at the end of Pennsylvania and before the record from Alaska that has been read actually has its fields available for processing. So, if we were to print a State by the state total, it would be PA, not AK because the data from the record has not yet been moved to the fields at this point of the cycle.

C -- Columns 10-17 (Indicators)

Logic type decisions are what separate computers from calculators. A logic decision in all cases begins with a test of one value against another and that test can provide three different results

1.   Is Value 1 greater than Value 2 (+, HI,>)
2.   Is Value 1 less than Value 2 (-, LO, <)
3.   Is Value 1 equal to Value 2 (0, EQ, =)

Logic tests in typical programming are followed by branch operations. A branch operation after a logic test can alter the address of the next program instruction to be someplace in the program other than the next sequential instruction. If you have three different routines that you would like to fire up, based on the results of the value test (HI, LO, EQ), then there would be three different branches that could be taken by the program. Each branch could take the program to a different routine based on the result of the test. That's program logic.

RPG calculations can be set to execute each detail cycle or they can be set to execute under certain "conditions." In most programming language, a form of an "IF" operation provides a means for the bulk of the logic decisions in a program.

RPG/400 and RPGIV have many variations of the IF statement available but there is also a mechanism that is unique to RPG called conditioning indicators. Three ANDed sets of these can be specified in RPG/400 in columns 10-17. In RPGIV, one set can be specified in columns 10-11.

Pseudo Code

In our PAREG program, we know that whenever we have just read a TIMCRD record and it matches the EMPMAST record that was just read, we would like to calculate the gross pay by multiplying the hours by the hourly pay rate. The pseudo-code logic to perform this function using an "IF" operation is shown in Figure 10-6.

Figure 10-6 Pseudo Code for PAREG
```
IF (Time Card Record is in process and If Time Card Record Field EMPNO = EMPNO in
PAYMAST) then GROSS PAY (SIZE 7,2) EQUALS PAYRATE TIMES HOURS WORKED  ELSE READ NEXT
RECORD.
```

That's pretty verbose pseudo code if I don't say so myself. Let's see if we can't get that pseudo code down to a more manageable size by using some things that we already know about this RPG program. We know that if there is a match between the M1 specified fields that an indicator MR is turned on for us. That means that the value of indicator MR is equal to 1.

We also know that if the time card record is in process, then RPG will turn on its record identifying indicator, which we have told the compiler is Indicator 02 So if Indicator 02 is equal to 1, we are processing the correct record. We also have database fields for the rate and hours from their respective files and we know that RPG would like any field we create on the fly to have no more than 6 characters in its name. The size for the result field of GROSS PAY must be given to the compiler since the field is being created on the fly. It is not a database field. So, now our pseudo code can look as teeny as the code shown in Figure 10-7.

Figure 10-7 Reduced Pseudo Code for PAREG
```
If (INMR = "1" and IN02 = "1") THEN EMPPAY (SIZE 7,2) = EMPRAT  MULT EMPHRS
```

This can read in English as follows: "if indicators MR and 02 are both on then create the field EMPPAY seven positions in length with two decimal places and store in it the results of the multiplication of the EMPPRAT and EMPHRS fields."   The EMPRAT in the EMPMAST file is set up with two decimal places. There is also an implied else and that is if the condition is not true, go to the next statement.

The pseudo "IF" statement provides the means of specifying that we want the operation to take place only if two conditions are true. This means that the conditions are logically "ANDed" and linked since both need to be true for the operation to take place. Moving away from pseudo code to RPG, it is in columns 9 through 17 of the CALC spec that these conditions cane be specified in straight, unstructured RPG. Let's look more closely at the first calculation from statement 21 to see how this logic fits.

Figure 10-8 Detail Calculations from PAREG
```
          67891123456789212345678931234567894123456789
0021.00 C    02 MR    EMPRAT    MULT EMPHRS    EMPPAY
```

Yes, all of that pseudo code and all of that reduced pseudo code is accomplished in this simple statement. You can see that there is an 02 and an MR indicator specified in 9 through 17. Any indicator specified here is a conditioning indicator and all of the indicator sets that are specified for the multiplication operation to take place.

This example shows there is room for a third indicator in positions 16 and 17 so three indicators can be ANDed on the same statement to condition just one calculation. The RPGIV spec has reduced this to just one indicator space. You may also have noticed that three positions are reserved for each indicator. MR, for example is in columns 12 to 14 and it appears right justified. So, you may be wondering what can be placed in position 12? The answer includes the option of *blank,* which means that we are conditioning with a positive of the indicator value. If, on the other hand, we placed an 'N' for *not* in position 12, then we would be testing for the negative of the indicator or an *off* condition.

Moving away from PAREG for just a minute, let's show how this operation would look if we were to look for the Not condition (N) of three indicators, 02, MR, and 01.

Figure 10-9 Not Condition in Play for Calculations Spec
```
          67891123456789212345678931234567894123456789
00xx.00 C  N02NMRN01EMPRAT    MULT EMPHRS    EMPPAY
```

The RPG calculation spec example in Figure 10-9 tests for the negative of 02, MR, and 01 respectively. The negative must be true in the example, meaning that all of the indicator must be off for the condition to be true. All three sets are ANDed and therefore all need to be true for the condition to be true and for the multiplication operation to take place.

When three indicator tests are not enough for one calculation there is the option to place the AN operation in positions 8 and 9 as explained above.
Also, if we would like to make these conditions OR's instead of AND's, the letters "OR" can be placed in positions 7 and 8 of a new line. The code in Figure 10-10 demonstrates this.

Figure 10-10 ANDing and ORing CALC specs
```
          67891123456789212345678931234567894123456789
00xx.00 C  N02NMRN01
00xx.00 COR 06 07 08
00xx.00 CAN 67        EMPRAT    MULT EMPHRS    EMPPAY
```

A maximum of seven AND/OR lines can be specified in one group. This reads that if 02 is not on and MR is not on and 01 is not on perform the operation, or if 06 is on and 07 is on and 08 is on and 67 is on, perform the operation. If either side of the OR condition is true, the operation is performed.

 The entry in positions 7 and 8 of the line immediately preceding an AND/OR line or a group of AND/OR lines determines when the calculation is to be processed (detail or total time). The entry in positions 7 and 8 on the first line of a group applies to all AND/OR lines in the group. Since the control level indicator (L1 through L9, L0, or LR) is entered for total calculations or an SR or blanks for subroutines, or a blank for detail calculations, the subsequent AN/OR line knows whether it is part of detail calculations, subroutine calculations, or total calculations and it behaves accordingly.

You can see how efficient traditional RPG is in its use of space for calculation statements. As we go through the rest of the calc statement columns, you will see that it is even more efficient than the examples that we have shown..

Taking Totals

Since we have already shown just one detail calc which calculates the gross pay, let's now examine the next three statements in PAREG since we have already discussed the notion of detail calculations and level calculations.

Figure 10-11 PAREG Total Accumulation Calculations
```
0022.00 C    02 MR    EMPPAY    ADD  CTYPAY    CTYPAY  92
0023.00 CL1           CTYPAY    ADD  STAPAY    STAPAY  92
0024.00 CL2           STAPAY    ADD  TOTPAY    TOTPAY  92
```

In statements 22 to 24 in Figure 10-11, the program is preparing totals for printing during the creation of the report. The City total is first and each time a gross pay value is calculated, it is added to the total in City Pay. When City Pay is printed on the report after a city changes, the CTYPAY field is cleared so it can accumulate again. Each time the city changes (L1), an L1 break occurs. During L1 calculations, you can see that the state total is accumulated (added to). The city total is added to the state total for later printing. When the state total is printed, so also is the city total and both are cleared and reset.. Whenever the state changes (L2) , an L2 break occurs and the state total (STAPAY) is added to TOTPAY to create a final total for the report.

Yes, it is probable that all of these defined totals and totals of all kinds (including the STAPAY and TOTPAY totals in Figure 10-11) could be created by detail time additions to the collection buckets. Instead we use an approach that uses less resources. Rather than first filling a city total collection bucket and then a state total collection bucket and dumping each bucket at each level of collection, we could have added EMPPAY to all totals at detail time.

And, yes, RPG might be far easier to understand in this case if we chose to do that. However, totaling items at level time instead of detail time takes less machine instructions --- and that is a fact. If there are six records for example worth of totals in the CTYPAY bucket when it gets added in statement 23, then that would be five ADD calculations that we saved by doing it that way. So, the RPG cycle does offer IT RPG shops opportunities to conserve precious processor cycles.

Every chance we get, we try to help the learner understand that RPG is very understandable. It does so much that even pseudo-code appears complex when real RPG is exposed. Yet, we have advanced no more than column 17 of the calc spec. It's almost time to move on.

Before we move on, since the conditioning section of each calculation specification can be triggered by so many unusual options, it's time we explained how they might gain influence:

The least understood of all RPG notions is that of the "indicator." However, that is not where the conundrum is finished. In all other languages, especially COBOL, conditions, such as those specified in columns 10-17 of the calc spec, that are detected at a logic point in the program that need to be remembered later in the program are stored in things that are colloquially described as "switches." If you understand the notion of a COBOL switch, you know that the purpose and meaning of an RPG indicator is the same as that of a switch.

One of the major revisions to calculations in RPGIV is the elimination of second two indicator blocks in columns 12-17. RPGIV has room for just one indicator block from positions 9 to 11.

C – Columns 18-52 Factors and Operators

The inventors of RPG considered that in every calculation there are at least two factors, an operation, and a result, so they named the two areas in which the factors are placed "Factor 1" and "Factor 2" respectively and they aptly named the operation area as "Operation," and the area for the result of the calculations as the Result Field.

The optional field length comes next followed quickly by the number of decimal positions. Within this vast area of 45 columns in RPG/400 and 59 columns in RPGIV, the meat of the calculation operations takes place. The collective format of the sub areas for both RPG/400 and RPGIV are shown in Table 10-12.

Table 10-12 Meat of the Calculation Spec – RPG/400 and RPGIV

Function	RPG/400	RPGIV
Factor 1	18- 27	12-25
Operation (plus op extender)	28-32 (none)	26-35 (extender)
Factor2	33-42	36-49
Extended Factor 2	NA	36-80
Result Field	43-48	50-63
Length	410-51	64-68
Decimal places	52	610-70
Operation Extender	53	NA (26-35)

C -- Columns 18 – 27 Factor 1

In Factor 1 you specify the name of a field or you can provide actual data (literals) or RPG/400 special words such as (*NAMVAR DEFN) on which an operation is to be done. The entry must begin in position 18. The entries that are valid for factor 1 depend on the specific operation specified in positions 28 through 32.

C -- Columns 28 – 32 Operation

Columns 28 through 32 specify the type of operation to be done using other elements on the calc form - Factor 1, Factor 2, and the Result Field entries. The operation code must begin in position 28. The program processes the operations in the order specified on the calculation specifications form. The RPG operations are examined in detail in Chapters 14 (RPG) & 15 (RPGIV).

C -- Columns 33 – 42 Factor 2

You specify the name in Factor 2 of a field or you give the actual data (literals) on which you want a particular calculation is to be done. For the file operation codes, factor 2 names a file or record format to be used in the operation. The entry must begin in position 33. Just as for Factor 1, the entries that are valid for Factor 2 depend on the specific operation code used on the CALC spec. in n positions 28 through 32.

C -- Columns 43 – 48 Result Field

You specify a result field to catch the result of operations. After an arithmetic operation for example, the result field contains the result of the calculation operation specified in positions 28 through 32

C -- Columns 49 – 51 Length

In columns 49 through 51 specify the length of the result field. This entry is optional, but can be used to define a field that is not defined elsewhere in the program or in an external database. The below entries for the length are allowed if the result field contains a field name.

1-30   Numeric field length.
1-256 Character field length.
Blank The result field is defined elsewhere.

The length entry specifies the number of positions to be reserved for the result field. The entry must be right-adjusted. The unpacked length (number of digits) must be specified for numeric fields.

If the result field is defined elsewhere in the program, no entry is required for the length. However, if the length is specified, and if the result field is defined elsewhere, the length must be the same as the previously defined length.

If half-adjustment is specified in position 53 of the calculation specifications, the entries for field length (positions 49 through 51) and decimal positions (position 52) refer to the length of the result field after half-adjustment.

C -- Columns 49 – 51 Decimal Positions

In column 52 indicate the number of positions to the right of the decimal in a numeric result field that is defined in columns 49 – 51. The allowable entries are:

Blank The result field is character data or has been defined elsewhere in
           the program.
0-9   Number of decimal positions in a numeric result field.

If the defined result field is numeric and it contains no decimal positions, enter a '0' (zero). For character data, this position must be blank. This position can also be left blank if the result field is numeric but was described by input or calculation specifications or in an external description. In this case, field length (positions 49 through 51) must also be left blank. Obviously, the number of decimal positions specified cannot exceed the length of the field.

C- Column 53 (Operation Extender)

Various operations use this extender operation for different purposes. We have not examined the use of input output operation codes, such as READ as of yet, but when we do, the Operation Extender will take on even more meaning.

The possible entries for the extender field are as follows:

Blank No operation extension supplied.
H   Half adjust.
N   Record is read but not locked (Update files).
P   Pad the result field with blanks.

An H indicates whether the contents of the result field are to be half adjusted (rounded). Half-adjusting is done by adding 5 (-5 if the field is negative) one position to the right of the last specified decimal position in the result field. The half adjust entry is allowed only with arithmetic operations.

The 'P' operation will also make sense after we study the various operations that can be used in RPG. For example, the 'P' entry indicates that, for CAT, SUBST, MOVEA, MOVEL, or XLATE operations, the result field is padded on the right after executing the instruction if the result field is longer than the result of the operation. Padding is done from the left for MOVE. This will make more sense in Chapters 14 & 15 as we explore operations in greater detail.

RPGIV does not have a column corresponding to the operation extender. Instead in the expanded operation area, each op code that has an extender adds the extender or extenders by adding a set of parentheses to the operation and the extenders are placed in between the parentheses right next to the operation code. RPGIV operations are covered in Chapter 15.

C – Columns 54-59 (Resulting Indicators)

These six positions used to hold up to three indicators can be used, for example, to test the value of a result field after the completion of an operation, or to indicate an end-of-file, error, or provide an indication that a record was not found. Depending on the operation, the three areas that are often associated with a +, =, or – or grater, equal, or less than arithmetic result conditions can be used for other purposes. Each operation that is studied may have its own specific use for these three indicator areas.

The resulting indicator positions have different uses, depending on the operation code specified. See the individual operation codes in Chapters 14 & 15 for a description of the associated resulting indicators.

Remember the following points when specifying resulting indicators:
When the calculation operation is finished, before the resulting indicator conditions are set, any resulting indicators that are on are set off. Then the new resulting indicators are set.

Our program PAREG is so simple, there are no resulting indicators in play. Figure 7-1 shows an RPG/400 program with the resulting indicators specified. RPGIV resulting indicators are specified in positions 71 to 76.

C- Columns 60-80 (Comments)

Positions 60 through 80 of each RPG/400 calculation specification line can be used for comments to document the purpose of that calculation. That's 15 more positions than the File Description and Input specifications and it comes in handy often to identify the purpose of the resulting indicators that are turned on during calculations. RPGIV provides the same number of comment lines in positions 81 to 100.

Another Look at PAREG Example CALCS

Let's take another look in Figure 10-13 at the four calculation operations from PAREG to see how the factors and operations that we just examined in detail look in practice.

Figure 10-13 Closer Look at PAREG CALCS

```
   Factor 1   OP    Factor2     ResultLGTD
   89212345678931234567894123456789512
1  EMPRAT     MULT  EMPHRS      EMPPAY   72
2  EMPPAY     ADD   CTYPAY      CTYPAY   92
3  CTYPAY     ADD   STAPAY      STAPAY   92
4  STAPAY     ADD   TOTPAY      TOTPAY   92
```

Depending on the type of operation, calculation oriented or input/output oriented, the types of values placed in Factor 1 and Factor 2 will vary. In the multiply operation (MULT) in the line labeled 1 above, the field or value placed in Factor 1 (EMPRAT) is multiplied by the field or value placed in Factor 2 (EMPHRS) to produce a value that gets loaded into the result field (EMPPAY). The three ADD operation lines labeled 2 through 4 above are fairly readable and self explanatory. The value in the field specified in Factor 1 in all cases is added to the value in the field specified in Factor 2 to produce the result that is stored in the Result field.

Notice the length of 7 for EMPPAY and the length of 9 for all the other values. RPG/400 has no single area in which field declarations are made and there is no working storage section as in COBOL in which to define independent variables. This may sound like a disadvantage of the language until you see that you can actually define new fields on the fly in calculations. When you want to take a total, for example, you invent a field name such as EMPPAY that does not exist in any database used in the program.

Since EMPPAY is not defined within a database or an input specification, it can be defined in calculations with a length and a decimal designation. If there is a number placed in the Decimals column from 0 to 9, the field is numeric. If no decimal is specified then the field is alphabetic. The largest numeric field is 32 bytes and the largest alphabetic field that can be defined on the fly is 256 bytes. In the PAREG program section above, each of the fields were defined as numeric with 2 decimal places.

Factor 1 and / or factor two, depending on the operation used can contain a field, a numeric value or an alphabetic constant. For numeric operations, the factors both must be numeric as they are in the sample program.

There is a more simple way, a short cut form of CALCS, to specify the three calculation lines labeled 2 through 4 above. This is shown in Figure 10-14.

Figure 10-14 Short Form of CALC Operations

```
  Factor 1   OP    Factor2    ResultLGTD
  89212345678931234567894123456789512
2              ADD   EMPPAY     CTYPAY  92
3              ADD   CTYPAY     STAPAY  92
4              ADD   STAPAY     TOTPAY  92
```

In this shorter form of the ADD statement, for example, the compiler assumes that Factor 1 is the same named field as the result field.

The various operations and combinations of formats with Factor 1 and Factor 2 to support those operations are described in Chapters 14 & 15.

As you could see in describing all of the coding columns, the RPGIV format for calculations is very similar to the RPG/400 version. Significantly more space is provided for the factors. The operations are 'a' and the result field.

Moreover, as RPG is being rethought to make it more like other languages, the notion of using indicators is being minimized. RPGIV provided only one set of conditioning indicators in columns 9 to 11. If more are needed, the And and Or functions can be used.

Chapter Summary

The Calculation form is where most of the work is done in RPG programs. This is the place in RPG in which the bulk of the decision making as well as the computations take place.

A calculation form consists of three areas

1. The conditions under which the calculations are to be done:

2. The entries for the calculations

3. The type of tests that are to be made on the results of the operation: HI, LO, EQ

All detail operations that are unconditioned are performed each cycle. All unconditioned operations that are specified at a total level will be executed unconditionally when RPG passes through that particular total cycle. Any arithmetic operation that is performed, including the compare operations, which internally subtract Factor 2 from Factor1, sets the status of the indicators specified on the right side of the calculation spec. The process works exactly the same in RPGIV.

Calculations that occur at level time in both RPG and RPGIV are coded with a level indication of L0 to L1 in columns 7 & 8. This area is also used for ANDed and ORed calculations. There are two level calculations in the PAREG program chapter example.

There are almost always two factors in every calculation in addition to an operation, and a result field to hold the answer. Unlike most other languages, RPG calculations can define fields on the fly, though this is not recommended if the data can be defined in input or in the definition spec in RPGIV.

There is an operation extender for a number of RPG/400 and RPGIV operations. In RPG/400 column 53 is used to specify half adjust (H), don't lock record (N), or pad result (P). In RPGIV, the extended is specified in parentheses right next to the operation code. Other than the shortened indicator area, and the lengthened factors, result field and operations area, RPGIV calculations look like RPG/400

Key Chapter Terms

*NAMVAR	Field name	READ
1P output	Final total	Record format
AN operation	First cycle	Result Field
CALC spec	First record	Resulting indicator
calc statement	Format	SETON
CAT	GOTO	SETOFF
CHAIN	Half adjust	Special words
CLOSE	Indicators	State totals
Conditioning indicator	Length	Subroutine calcs
Control field	Level 1	SUBST
Control level	Level 2	TAG
Decimal positions	LR indicator	Time
Decoding	MOVEA	Total calcs
DEFN	MOVEL	Total output
Detail calculations	MULT	Total time
Detail calculations	NEXT	Turned off
Display file	OP-code	Turned on
ELSE	OP-extender	Type of tests
EXFMT	Pad	Variables
Factor 1	Pseudo Code	XLATE
Factor 2		

Review Questions

1. Which specification form does most of the work in most RPG programs? Why?

2. What is a conditioning indicator?

3. What is a resulting indicator?

4. What is meant by Factor 1 and Facorr2?

5. Why is there an area referred to as the Result Field in RPG/400 and RPGIV?

6. What happens in a cycle program if no conditioning indicators are on any of the detail calculations?

7. How many conditioning indicators are permitted in RPG/400 and RPGIV? How are they specified?

8. What does HI, LO, EQ mean in the resulting indicator area?

9. Describe the following calculation in your own words?

```
6789112345678921234567893123456789412345678951234567 89
C*
C* RPG CALCULATION SPECIFICATION FORMS
C*
C   02 MR  EMPRAT   MULT EMPHRS   EMPPAY  72 010203
```

10. Describe the following print routine in your own words?

```
0039.00 C              PRINT      TAG
0040.00 C                         READ CUSMST                   45
0041.00 C  N45 10                 WRITEHEADER
0042.00 C  N45                    WRITEDETAIL
0043.00 C  N45                    GOTO PRINT
0044.00 C                         CLOSE*ALL
0045.00 C                         SETON                      LR
```

11. In the following calculations, why would you choose not to collect the final total at L1 time?

```
0023.00 CL1    CTYPAY   ADD STAPAY   STAPAY 92
0024.00 CL2    STAPAY   ADD TOTPAY   TOTPAY 92
```

12. Describe the following calculations in your own words?

```
00xx.00 C  N02NMRN01
00xx.00 CAN 06 07 08
00xx.00 COR 67    EMPRAT   MULT EMPHRS   EMPPAY
```

Chapter 11 The Specifics of RPG Coding – Output – by Example

Showing the Results

For all the good describing files, reading input, and computing results does for programming, it provides no value to regular human beings unless the results are communicated in the form of a printed report, a display, or an updated file. In RPG, the output specification is used to provide a means of coding this communication.

O-- Output Specification Form

The Output Specification Form is where most of the coding takes place in the PAREG program, which we have been decoding for the last set of chapters. Since PAREG is a report-writing style fixed cycle program, it is understandable that the bulk of the programming is done with the output form. All of the output specifications for the PAREG program originally shown in Figure 6-1 that we are about to decode are repeated below for your convenience. The output for the PAREG program is all program described and since there is so little externally described printed output in RPG, this topic is not covered in this book. Therefore, the output for Figure 6-1 and Figure 6-2 is repeated below since it is the same. Notice that in column 6, there is the 'O' designator to differentiate the format of this RPG form from all others.

Figure 11-1 RPG/400 Output Specs for PAREG

```
          6789112345678921234567893123456789412345678951234567896123456
0026.00 O* RPG OUTPUT SPECIFICATION FORMS
0027.00 O*
0028.00 OQPRINT  H  206   1P
0029.00 O        OR 206   OF
0030.00 O                            32 'THE DOWALLOBY COMPANY'
0031.00 O                            55 'GROSS PAY REGISTER BY '
0032.00 O                            60 'STATE'
0033.00 O                   UDATE Y  77
0034.00 OQPRINT  H  3     1P
0035.00 O        OR 3     OF
0036.00 O                             4 'ST'
0037.00 O                            13 'CITY'
0038.00 O                            27 'EMP#'
0039.00 O                            45 'EMPLOYEE NAME'
0040.00 O                            57 'RATE'
0041.00 O                            67 'HOURS'
0042.00 O                            77 'CHECK'
0043.00 O        D  1     02NMR
0044.00 O                            46 'NO MATCHING MASTER'
0045.00 O                   EMPNO    27
0046.00 O                   EMPHRS1  67
0047.00 O        D  1     02 MR
0048.00 O                   EMPSTA    4
0049.00 O                   EMPCTY   29
0050.00 O                   EMPNO    27
0051.00 O                   EMPNAM   52
0052.00 O                   EMPRAT1  57
0053.00 O                   EMPHRS1  67
```

```
0054.00 O                          EMPPAY1     77
0055.00 O         T 22     L1
0056.00 O                                      51 'TOTAL CITY   PAY FOR'
0057.00 O                          EMPCTY      72
0058.00 O                          CTYPAY1B    77
0059.00 O         T 02     L2
0060.00 O                                      51 'TOTAL STATE PAY FOR'
0061.00 O                          EMPSTA      54
0062.00 O                          STAPAY1B    77
0063.00 O         T 2      LR
0064.00 O                          TOTPAY1     77
0065.00 O                                      50 'FINAL TOTAL PAY'
```

The first two statements (26, 27) in calculations are comments as they each have an asterisk in column 7.

Output Record ID and Control Entries

Just like the Input Specification which have two major formats for both externally described and internally described files, so also does the Output form. The first format of the Input form is called the Record Identification and Control Entries. Whereas in input, we place indicators in this area to test which record format was read, in out put we use indicators to tell the RPG compiler which record it should write.

Just as RPG permits record IDs to be tested on input using the left half of the Input form, so also does it condition and control output using the left half of the RPG output form. For the PAREG program, the left half of the RPG/400 form ends in position 31 while for those programs that use a more modern form of exception (calculation-driven) output, the area from 32 to 37 is used for what is referred to as an exception name. The notion of an exception name will be examined in Chapter 23 in program set PAREG2. So for now, we end the Record Intentification and Control Entries for the PAREG program at column 31 for RPG/400. For RPGIV, the area ends in column 51

The output section of PAREG is shown in its entirety in Figure 11-1 above. For our analysis on how output is controlled let's take all of the record ID code from Figure 11-1 and place it in a separate figure (Figure 8-2) so we can get a closer look at it. To do this, we will just eliminate the right half of the output form in which control is not included. Take a look at Figure 8-1 now and see if you can spot all of the record conditioning and control statements that should be in Figure 11-2.

Hopefully you spotted them all. There are nine of them and they are presented below in Figure 11-2 for your immediate and close-up examination. The original line numbers have been included to make it easier for you to compare back to the full output form in Figure 11-1.

Figure 11-2 Record Conditioning and Control Output for PAREG
```
0028.00 OQPRINT   H   206    1P
0029.00 O         OR  206    OF
0034.00 OQPRINT   H   3      1P
0035.00 O         OR  3      OF
0043.00 O         D   1      02NMR
0047.00 O         D   1      02 MR
0055.00 O         T   22     L1
0059.00 O         T   02     L2
0063.00 O         T   2      LR
```

OPDRI -- Specification Columns 7-14

Immediately following the O, since we have designated the printer file to be a program described output file, we get to do lots more describing column by column. The first thing you notice is that in statement 28 above, the file name (7-14) is QPRINT. This is the same name as defined in File Descriptions. Because this is a program described file for the printer, we use the file name as described in File Descriptions instead of the record format name as we did for input.

Though RPG programmers sometimes define their own print files to the IBM i to provide special formatting for certain reports such as invoices and statements, many continue to use any of the IBM default printer files such as QPRINT. (See Chapter 23 to see how to create your own printer file). The key thing in output is that when you begin to code the Record Identification and Control format of the output specification, if you have just one print file to which to refer, you must use the same name to reference the print file you have defined in the F specification. In this case the name is QPRINT.

Printing to Multiple Printers

Of course, RPG/400 programs can have multiple printers defined for output. For this, additional F specs would be used with different file names. To assure that the correct output goes to the correct printer, when there are multiple printers, the programmer uses the File Name area from 7 to 14 of the O spec to designate the file that is related to the printer to which output is to be directed.

In RPGIV, the File name is expanded to 10 positions from 7 to 16.

OPDRI Columns 14-16 (Logical Relationship)

Statements 29 and 35 in the output specifications of program PAREG make use of this logical relationship area. Looking above just a bit, you may recall that the File Name was within positions 7 and 14 of the O spec. Yet, the logical relationship is taking up one of those columns. The only reason that is OK is that the File Name does not get repeated on a logical relationship continuance line.

You must decode the Logical Relationship column in statements 29 and 35 and recognize that this continues the conditional testing as to whether the output record will be written. If either set of conditions exist (indicators 1P or OF as specified on lines 28 and 29) for example, that means that the output line will be printed.

We will be examining the specific conditions (1P or OF or other indicators) under which lines print below, but for this lesson it is important to gain that the logical relationship column of a second and possibly even a third line of Record ID and Control Entries broadens the conditions under which a line will print or a record will be written. If instead of the "OR" relationship which we show, the actual relationship were AND, the logical relationship column again can serve to expand the conditions under which an output record will be written. For the AND condition, you would place the letters AND on the second and subsequent Record ID and Control Entries. A modified sample of lines 28 and 29, using an "AND" linkage is shown below:

```
0028.00 OQPRINT   H   206     1P
0029.00 O         AND 206     OF
```

Now that you know how to "AND" out put conditions together, it is helpful to know that RPG provides a natural way to provide "ANDing." Without any words you can see the "ANDed" conditions below:

```
0028.00 OQPRINT   H   206     1P OF
```

This line is conditioned by the 1P indicator and the OF indicator, meaning it should print in the first output cycle before input and it should print whenever the OF indicator is turned on as printing fills up the prior page. We will be examining those columns very shortly… and by the way, don't run away yet, because the coding we did above for AND, though syntactically correct, is illogical.

For RPGIV, the logical relationship is specified in columns 16-19.

OPDRI — Column 15 (Type)

Though seemingly innocuous, the infamous Output Type column has created as much frustration for procedural programmers as the notion of L1 and L2. The idea of conditioning indicators for output lines is very logical. In the big picture, however, it takes a good knowledge of the RPG cycle in order to know just when those conditioning indicators might be on or off. Since we have made it through the CALC spec, it may help to know that the notion of total time output is really not much different than the notion of level calculations (columns 7 and 8) that are used for calculations to occur in between control breaks.

In fact a look at the cycle would reveal that as soon as Control Level calculations are performed, the RPG cycle moves on a mythical journey to something called total output time so that it can print what it has accumulated. For those watching at home, total output time is another of these in-between time cycle notions that occur in between control break changes.

To be specific, the RPG cycle saga continues right here from calculations since this "in between time" is really the part of the cycle from step 2 in which a record gets read until step 6 in which RPG makes the data from that record available. During this time totals for the prior group can be taken in Cycle step 3 and then in Cycle step 4, the totals that were accumulated can be printed with the heading information from the prior record, not the record just read. See Figure 4-1 for verification. Thus, the total for Pennsylvania that prints right before the detail record for Alaska gets processed can actually print PA next to the total since PA has not yet been replaced by AK – even though the AK record is in. AK does not replace PA in memory until step 6 of the RPG cycle.

The coding for column 15 is self revealing and is as follows:

H   Heading records in a printed report (occur only when the first Report page is to be printed or when the printer has passed the last line on the prior page – a condition called "overflow" or printer overflow. This is relevant only with printers. Heading records usually contain constant identifying information for reports such as titles, column headings, page numbers, and date. What typically differentiates these records from pure detail records is that they require no variable input. The data is typically coded as constants or reserved words. RPG can print headings even before it has gone its first input cycle. Heading records are printed during the detail print cycle.
There is no structural difference in RPG between H and D specifications other than the intention of the programmer.

D   Detail records usually contain data that comes directly from the input record or that is the result of calculations processed at detail time in the RPG cycle. For example, the field in our program named EMPPAY is created at detail calculation time within the RPG cycle.

T   Total records usually contain data that is the end result of specific calculations on several detail records. In the PAREG program, the City, State and Final totals fir this mold

E   Exception records are not needed for the PAREG program. These are lines of output that will print when triggered by a specific calculation operation for output known as EXCPT. EXCPT is described in detail in Chapter 23.

The type specification in RPGIV is located in column 17.

OPDRI – Column 16 (Fetch Overflow / Release)

PAREG does not use the Fetch Overflow / Release facility. There are a number of mythical notions that many who have toiled learning the RPG cycle have wrestled with. Fetch Overflow is one of them. In a nutshell, because RPG records can be written at detail, total or exception output time, sometimes the wrong cycle is in play to print the overflow headings. Fetch overflow (F) option is a way around this problem. It has enough of its own issues that if you learn that you need Fetch overflow in one of your programs, you will already be in graduate level RPG. We do not need Fetch overflow in the PAREG program.

We do not need the RELEASE facility or the 'R' code in column 16 in this PAREG program either. The 'R' for release comes about in programs that control their own access to databases (non cycle programs) and after they have made a request for input and a record is inside the RPG program staged for update, circumstances in the program may alter the requirement to actually update the database record. So, for those using the RPG cycle, the R code in column 16 will release the exclusive update lock on the record and make that particular record available to other programs.

Fetch Overflow and Release options are provided in RPG IV column 18.

OPDRI – Columns 17-22 (Space and Skip)

Figure 11-2 is repeated below so that we can examine the Space and Skip entries used in PAREG

Figure 11-2 Record Conditioning and Control Output for PAREG

```
0028.00 OQPRINT  H  206    1P
0029.00 O        OR 206    OF
0034.00 OQPRINT  H  3      1P
0035.00 O        OR 3      OF
0043.00 O        D  1      02NMR
0047.00 O        D  1      02 MR
0055.00 O        T  22     L1
0059.00 O        T  02     L2
0063.00 O        T  2      LR
```

Line 28 & 29 skips to line 6 of the form and prints the (1P) 1st line of headings or overflow, which in PAREG is the report title. It then spaces 2 lines after printing the report title. Lines 34 and 35 print the report column headings and then space three lines to begin printing the detail lines. The detail lines (43 and 47) print when data is read after each line the printer spaces one to the next line and awaits printing. In line 55, the City total spaces 2 lines and then prints the City total. It hen spaces two lines. In line 59, the printer spaces 0 lines (city already moved it down two lines) and then it prints the State total followed spacing of two lines. In line 63, for the final total, the printer spaces another two lines for big separation between the final total and the last state total and then the line prints the final total information.

Powerful Report Writing

Only a programmer who has never tried to perfect the look of a spiffy aged trial balance report or a sales report with five dimensions of totals or a properly formatted GL financial statement would even consider pooh-poohing the raw power in RPG that intrinsically enables report formatting. Yet, they are out there and some would choose to double or triple the number of statements in a program rather than use RPG's (Report Program Generator) innate reporting facilities. If I were to correct myself on this statement, I would change the word "use" to learn. Hey, you are struggling through the cycle and soon you will understand that the cycle is remarkable once you have made that "4GL" reporting investment in your career.

Spacing & Skipping

Let's envision a physical printer. In other words, a physical printer would be one that actually is forced to print on paper and not to PDF. Spooling has separated most of us in the tech community from the care and feeding of printers. Yet, they have their needs. Let's not look at HP's or Xerox's big lasers now or we won't get the right picture and we will miss the learning opportunity. Let's envision a line printer of any name. It can print one line at a time. Coincidentally, the RPG cycle prints one detail line at a time.

Now, let's go back even ten years from this. You can't get the notion of spacing and skipping without this. The big behemoth printers were capable of printing upwards o 4,000 lines per minute mechanically by impact. Such printers still exist today and their owners do not want to get rid of them though maintenance is now quite prohibitive.

These printers were equipped with a paper tape which controlled a skipping carriage. When a program sent out a skip command it was to one of 12 channels in the paper tape. So, a high speed skip to channel 6 might bypass 30 lines or more on a preprinted form and go ahead and print the needed total at the bottom of the form on the correct line every time. These little carriage tapes were Mickey-Mouse to computer operations so printer companies such as IBM made the little tape electronic and then gave the programs the control to send the printer to an exact line on a page – no matter how many lines had to be skipped.

Almost instantaneously a printer could go from line 5 to line 35 and print the next line of the form. It worked just as well as the carriage control printers but now, instead of skipping to a channel, the programs were able to skip to a specific line number. It was a great advancement in technology and the RPG language matched the ability of the system by providing skip to line facilities instead of carriage control slots.

Yet, sometime, no matter where you were on a form or a report printout, you would need to skip one more line to print a total or such. Thus, the notion of line spacing persisted even after the skipping technology advancement. Whether the following is true or not does not matter sine it is a constraint regardless. RPG was devised so that the compiler would support no more than three lines of spacing before or after a print line. IBMers told me over the years that this was a printer issue, not an RPG issue. I think it was neither.

I think now that it was IBM believing that a programmer ought to be using skipping if they have to leave three blank lines on a report. So, IBM would not permit more than 3 lines to be spaced before and 3 lines to be spaced after each of those Record Identification and Control Entries. For printer control, "them" are still the rules in RPG today.

The column specifications in RPG and RPGIV today that provide spacing and skipping before and after are shown in Table 11-3.

Table 11-3 Printer Spacing and Skipping

Printer Function	RPG/400	RPGIV
Spaces before	17	40-42
Spaces after	18	43-45
Skip to line before	19, 20	46-48
Skip to line after	21, 22	49-51

If a space/skip entry is left blank, the particular function with the blank entry (such as space before or space after) does not occur. If entries are made in position 17 (space before) or in positions 19 through 22 (skip before and skip after) and no entry is made in position 18 (space after), no space occurs after printing.

OPDRI – Columns 23-31 (Output Indicators)

The same notion of conditioning indicators applies to output as it does to calculations. In calculations, for example, we learned that there were three distinct slots on one calculation specification in which the programmer could specify three indicators to condition operations and all of those indicators were automatically involved in an "AND" condition. They all had to be on for the line to be executed.

Positions 23 to 31 of output represent the same notion. Three indicators are permitted – that's two positions each or six positions of the nine. Just like CALCS, each one of the indicators can be negated with the "not" modifier by simply placing an N in position 23, 26, or 29 as long as an indicator was specified in the two right adjacent columns.

To show you what this looks like let's take a peek at statements 43 and 47 of PAREG in Figure 11-4.

Figure 11-4 Detail Record Conditioning
```
0043.00 O          D 1      02NMR
0047.00 O          D 1      02 MR
```

These two Record Identification and Control Entries each use two of the natural "ANDed" slots for indicators to condition the output. Both use indicator 02 and indicator MR, meaning a time card record was read and there is a match. Well, at least that is what statement 47 does. Statement 43 tests to see if the time card just read does not have a matching master (PAYMAST). Of course that means that the 02NMR is clearly an error condition. It is fair to ask, as we decode this section, what are we asking the program to do when this condition occurs?

To know the answer to this, we must also look at the field codes (which we have not yet explained). However, we can rough up an explanation with what is obvious. The print line and the error conditioning (02 NMR) are shown immediately below:

Figure 11-5 Error Conditioned Output

```
0043.00 O...    D 1... 02NMR
0044.00 O...                         46 'NO MATCHING MASTER'
0045.00 O...            EMPNO        27
0046.00 O...            EMPHRS1      67
```

Right after the detail (D) indicator there is a blank and then in position 17 of Line 43, there is a "1." This tells the printer to space one before printing an error message if indicator 02 (a time card) is on and indicator MR is not on (NMR). If both are true then this is a non match with PAYMAST. So, after executing a one space before, this code tells the RPG compiler to go ahead and print the employee number and the number of hours next to an error message of "NO MATCHING MASTER," that ends in printer position 46 of the report.

Thus, the RPG cycle MR technique as coded in this program with 02 and NMR permits the program to identify a condition in which we have a time card with a missing master. We could do the same type of check if we have a PAYMAST record with a missing time card. This condition would be made known by an indicator 01 on condition along with the NMR. However, we have not coded that in this example.

The output field conditioning indicators for RPGIV have the same meaning and they live in columns 21 to 29 of the RPGIV calc spec respectively.

Field Description and Control Entries

Using the Record Identification and Control Entries as we have above, the objective is to specify the conditions under which a print line is produced by the program. Via the conditioning indicators that we have used in this program, 1P, OF, 01, 02, and MR, we have conditioned lines to print in a sequence that can produce the output report that we defined first in Figure 4-1.

Before we discuss the Field description part of the Field Description and Control Entries form, let us first look at the control entries. Just as we conditioned print lines at the record level, the Control entries portion of this form permits us to condition specific fields to print when and if a line is printed. Theoretically a line can be enabled to print at the record level and because no fields are conditioned to print, a blank line may be produced

OPDFD- Columns 7 through 22 Reserved

No entries permitted in the RPG/400 Field Description Form from column 7 to column 22.

OPDFD- Columns 23–31 Output Indicators

The conditioning output indicators occupy the same relative space in this Field Form as they do in the Record Form – 23 to 31 and they work the same way. If all of the indicator statuses that are tested on a field line create a true condition, then the field will be printed. Of course, there are no such controls needed in the PAREG program since no fields need to be conditioned for printing. Each line that is conditioned in the PAREG program prints all fields and literals that are defined for the print line in the end positions noted on this form.

RPGIV's output indicators are provided for in columns 21 to 29.

The variable output fields printed on the report defined in Figure 5-1 are shown in Figure 11-6 twice with their original line numbers. There are lots of lines missing in this example. As you may recall from the full PAREG program in Figure 5-1, the end positions on the print line to print these fields are often the same because they in fact print on different lines – Heading, detail, Level 1, Level 2, and LR.

Figure 11-6 Output Fields for PAREG

```
          67891123456789212345678931234567894123
0033.00 O                         UDATE Y    77
0046.00 O                         EMPHRS1    67
0052.00 O                         EMPRAT1    57
0053.00 O                         EMPHRS1    67
0054.00 O                         EMPPAY1    77
0058.00 O                         CTYPAY1B   77
0062.00 O                         STAPAY1B   77
0064.00 O                         TOTPAY1    77
        O*************************************************************
0033.00 O                  45 46N47UDATE Y    77
0046.00 O                  NMRN1PNOFEMPHRS1    67
0052.00 O                     31 EMPRAT1    57
0053.00 O                    n29 EMPHRS1    67
0054.00 O                  01    EMPPAY1    77
0058.00 O                       36CTYPAY1B   77
0062.00 O                       N56STAPAY1B   77
0064.00 O               N83      TOTPAY1    77
```

There is one difference as you can see. Some of the fields in the repeated group have numbers next to them to the left. These numbers are in columns 23 to 31 and are field conditioning indicators. For the PAREG program, they are absolutely meaningless but they sure give you an idea of how to code field indicators.

The UDATE field for example only prints in position 77 if indicator 45 and 46 are on and 47 is off. EMPHRS only prints in 67 if MR, 1P, and OF are all off. TOTPAY prints in 77 only if 83 is off.. As you can surmise, field indicators can create holes in output lines for information that should not be printed. You can also specify two different fields to print in the same position on the same line and before printing assure that just one of the printing conditions is true.

OPDFD-- Columns 32-37 Field Name

When coding output for PAREG, we placed the names of the fields that we wanted to print in positions 32 through 37. In Figure 11-6, you can see not only the field names and the end positions but also the editing codes which will soon be discussed. Because other elements besides fields are also specified in columns 32-37, let's a get a full appreciation for all the entries and their meanings:

   ✓ Field name
   ✓ **Blanks** if a constant is specified in positions 45 through 70
   ✓ **Table name**, array name, or array element
   ✓ Named constant

✓ **RPG/400** reserved words such as PAGE, PAGE1 through PAGE7, \PLACE, UDATE, \DATE, UDAY, \DAY, UMONTH, \MONTH, UYEAR, \YEAR, \IN, \INxx, or \IN,xx
✓ **Data structure name** or data structure subfield name.

Field Names, Blanks, Tables and Arrays

Tables and Arrays are described in Chapter *****. To be used for output, the field names used must be defined in the program, either explicitly or implicitly from being within an externally described file.

You should not enter a field name if a constant or edit word is used in positions 45 through 70. The end positions represent an either / or scenario. If a field name is entered in positions 32 through 37, positions 7 through 22 must be also be blank.

The RPGIV field name is coded in positions 30 – 33 and the field name can be indented (leading blanks).

OPDFD Column 38 Edit Codes

The PAREG program takes advantage of another very powerful facility in RPG known as Edit Codes. These codes get specified on a field line in column 38 of the output specification. A snippet from the PAREG program showing all of the lines that have edit codes is shown in Figure 11-7.

Figure 11-7 Output Fields for PAREG

```
        67891123456789212345678931234567894123
0033.00 O                    UDATE Y   77
0046.00 O                    EMPHRS1   67
0052.00 O                    EMPRAT1   57
0053.00 O                    EMPHRS1   67
0054.00 O                    EMPPAY1   77
0058.00 O                    CTYPAY1B  77
0062.00 O                    STAPAY1B  77
0064.00 O                    TOTPAY1   77
```

As you can see by walking down column 38, we were not very picky in our use of edit codes. In line 33, for example, we use the reserve word UDATE to print the system data along with a special Y edit code that makes sure the slashes are placed properly. The rest of the fields above from PAREG use the "1" edit code.

Table 11-7 shows some of the fields from the report in Figure 4-1 and how the edit code has made the printed data look much better

Table 11-7 Output Editing of PAREG Fields

Field Represents	**No Edit**	With Edit
UDATE	022106	2/21/06
RATE	780	7.80
HOURS	3500	35.00
CHECK	27300	273.00
TOTAL CITY PAY FOR WILKES-BARRE	58900	589.00
TOTAL CITY PAY FOR SCRANTON	114475	1,144.75
FINAL TOTAL PAY	289360	2,893.60

We picked these two (Y and 1) edit codes for PAREG because that's all we needed. But, they came from a very wide and diverse barrel. Let's take a look at all of the edit codes in the barrel in Figure 11-8 as well as what they actually mean. Edit codes do so much work with so little work involved that it is best to best explain it all with combinations of minus signs and CR signs and slashes and dashes.

So we borrowed the table from IBM's AS/400 Reference Manual and it is shown in Figure 11-8 just to show you how much can really be stashed in this one column.

In RPGIV, the Edit Code place is column 44.

OPDFD —Column 39 Blank After

PAREG uses the notion of blank after for two output fields as follows:

```
0058.00 O...        CTYPAY1B 77
0062.00 O...        STAPAY1B 77
```

The total for city pay is collected by adding the individual's gross pay to the city pay total for each time card record read that also has a match (02 MR). When the city total is printed, the next logical step would be to clear out the total accumulator so that the prior city's total does not get mixed in with the new city's total. So also for the state total when it is printed. In typical programming languages, a separate operation or small routine would be invoked to reset the city accumulator. In RPG it can be done with one column called blank. This very handy tool shows the power of RPG for report writing. And it certainly saves programmer coding. Immediately after RPG prints CTYPAY and STAPAY fields, it clears them (blanks them out) to prepare the fields for collecting the next city or state's total pay.

Figure 11-8 Complete RPG Edit Code Table and Meanings

Edit Code	Commas	Decimal Point	Sign for Negative Balance	Entry in Column 21 of Control Specification			Zero Suppress
				D or Blank	I	J	
1	Yes	Yes	No Sign	.00 or 0	.00 or 0	0.00 or 0	Yes
2	Yes	Yes	No Sign	Blanks	Blanks	Blanks	Yes
3		Yes	No Sign	.00 or 0	.00 or 0	0.00 or 0	Yes
4		Yes	No Sign	Blanks	Blanks	Blanks	Yes
5-9[1]							
A	Yes	Yes	CR	.00 or 0	.00 or 0	0.00 or 0	Yes
B	Yes	Yes	CR	Blanks	Blanks	Blanks	Yes
C		Yes	CR	.00 or 0	.00 or 0	0.00 or 0	Yes
D		Yes	CR	Blanks	Blanks	Blanks	Yes
J	Yes	Yes	- (minus)	.00 or 0	.00 or 0	0.00 or 0	Yes
K	Yes	Yes	- (minus)	Blanks	Blanks	Blanks	Yes
L		Yes	- (minus)	.00 or 0	.00 or 0	0.00 or 0	Yes
M		Yes	- (minus)	Blanks	Blanks	Blanks	Yes
N	Yes	Yes	- (floating minus)	.00 or 0	.00 or 0	0.00 or 0	Yes
O	Yes	Yes	- (floating minus)	Blanks	Blanks	Blanks	Yes
P		Yes	- (floating minus)	.00 or 0	.00 or 0	0.00 or 0	Yes
Q		Yes	- (floating minus)	Blanks	Blanks	Blanks	Yes
X[2]							Yes
Y[3]							Yes
Z[4]							Yes

[1] These are the user-defined edit codes.

The entries for column 39 are as follows:

Blank The field is not cleared (reset).
B   The field is reset to blank or zero after the output operation

In RPGIV, the Blank after code is placed in column 45.

OPDFD - Columns 40-43 End Position

Figure 11-1 shows all the output and Figure 11-9 sets up a learning sample from PAREG to show the end positions in header (literal) output from the beginning of the output section in Figure 11-1. In Figure 11-1, both literals and variables for the PAREG program are coded along with their end positions, which do not overlap in the PAREG program..

Fields in output can be specified in any order because the sequence in which they appear on the output records is determined by the end position entry in columns 40 through 43. If fields overlap, the last field specified is the only field completely written. In other words, RPG moves all the fields you specify into the output record prior to printing it. As it moves them in, it builds the print line in the sequence that the fields are specified taking care to end each field as it is placed in the print buffer in the position defined in 40-43 as the end position. The last field specified may very well overlap another field.

In this case, RPG dutifully places the full contents of that field in the buffer and overlays whatever value may have been there from a field specified in a lower numbered statement.

The PAREG program has no fields that overlap so this is not an issue in our sample program. When edit codes are used, the programmer must leave room to the left on the print line to assure that the fully edited field can fit without creating an overlay issue with the low order positions of the field to the left.

The entries that can be specified in the END position area from 40 – 43 are as follows:

1-n   Numeric value for print line end position
K1-K8   Length of format name for WORKSTN file
                  RPG provides a facility to program describe format
                  names in the RPG II style.
+nnn   Number of spaces to leave between last field specified
                  Sometimes programmers do not want to precisely
                  calculate the exact end position for a printed field or
                  constant. RPG provides the "+" option to leave a certain
                  amount of space in between fields saving the
                  programmer the work of figuring out specifically where
                  everything ends The sign must be in position 40.
-nnn   Negative of above
  nnn   Same position as last

Let's take a look at the first section of output in the PAREG program shown in Figure 11-9 for a real example:

Figure 11-9 End Positions
```
          67891123456789212345678931234567894123456789512345678961234567 8
0028.00 OQPRINT  H  206    1P
0029.00 O       OR  206    OF
0030.00 O                                      32 'THE DOWALLOBY COMPANY'
0031.00 O                                      55 'GROSS PAY REGISTER BY '
0032.00 O                                      60 'STATE'
0033.00 O                          UDATE Y     77
```

Positions 40 through 43 define the end position of a field or constant on the output. Lines 30 to 32 specifies constants and their end positions on the print line while line 33 specifies the reserved word UDATE which tells the RPG compiler to access the system date and print it ending in position 77.

Valid entries for end positions are blanks, +nnn, -nnn, and nnnn. All entries in these positions must end in position 43. Enter the position of the rightmost character of the field or constant. The end position must not exceed the record length for the file.

The plus (+) and minus (-) additions are a tool to help programmers design simple forms without having to use detailed printer spacing charts. The +nnn or -nnn entry specifies the placement of the field or constant relative to the end position of the previous field. The sign must be in position 40. The number (nnn) must be right-adjusted, but leading zeros are not required. To calculate the end position, use these formulas:

```
EP = PEP +nnn + FL
EP = PEP -nnn + FL
```

EP is the calculated end position. PEP is the previous end position. For the first field specification in the record, PEP is equal to zero. FL is the length of the field after editing, or the length of the constant specified in this specification. The use of +nnn is equivalent to placing nnn positions between the fields. A -nnn causes an overlap of the fields by nnn positions.

For example, if the previous end position (PEP) is 6, the number of positions to be placed between the fields (nnn) is 5, and the field length (FL) is 10, the end position (EP) equals 21.

In RPGIV, the end position is specified in columns 47-51.

OPDFD - Column 44 (Data Format)

The PAREG program does not need this column to get its job done. This area is not needed for printed reports. The entries are for disk files and are as follows:

Blank The field is written as zoned decimal numeric or character or a constant.
P The field is written in packed decimal format.
B The field is written in binary format.
L The numeric output field is written with a preceding (left) plus or minus sign.
R The numeric output field is written with a following (right) plus or minus sign.

This position must be blank if editing is specified. In RPGIV, the data format code is specified in columns 52.

OPDFD - Columns 45-70 Constant or Edit Word

Let's look at Figure 11-10 for some of the constant (literal) data from PAREG and two edit word examples in statement 99.03 and 100 that are not in PAREG. The extra code shows a seven position field being edited with an edit word. In 99.03, the zeroes are replaced by a floating dollar sign that prints to the left of the high order non-zero digit. In 100, the same field is edited with a fixed place dollar sign.

Figure 11-10 Constant & Edit Word Examples from PAREG etc.

```
          6789112345678921234567893123456789412345678951234567 89
0034.00 OQPRINT   H   3       1P
0035.00 O           OR  3       OF
0036.00 O                                     4  'ST'
0037.00 O                                    13  'CITY'
0038.00 O                                    27  'EMP#'
0039.00 O                                    45  'EMPLOYEE NAME'
0040.00 O                                    57  'RATE'
0041.00 O                                    67  'HOURS'
0042.00 O                                    77  'CHECK'
0099.00 O*
0099.01 O*  Floating dollar sign followed by fixed dollar sign
0099.02 O+
0099.03 O                        NUM7        90  '    $0.  '
0100.00 O                        NUM7        90  '$    0.  '
```

As we decode the PAREG output specifications, we quickly see that the only use that the PAREG program makes of columns Positions 45 through 70 is for program literals which are also called constants since they do not change. Statements 36 to 42 of the program as shown above represents the headings for the columns of the report and this "line" or record is formatted by its end positions as specified in 40 to 43. In position 45 in the referenced PAREG statements, there is a required quote and immediately following the literal is a second single quote to signify the end of the literal. When the line prints each of the described literals will print ending in the positions specified next to them in positions 40 to 43.

Coding literals is one of the easiest things in RPG and it makes the language very powerful in being able to provide descriptive report titles and column headings as noted above.

Figure 11-11 Literals Used for Totals

```
          6789112345678921234567893123456789412345678951234567 89
0055.00 O           T  22      L1
0056.00 O                                    51  'TOTAL CITY   PAY FOR'
0057.00 O                        EMPCTY       72
0058.00 O                        CTYPAY1B     77
0059.00 O           T  02      L2
0060.00 O                                    51  'TOTAL STATE PAY FOR'
0061.00 O                        EMPSTA       54
0062.00 O                        STAPAY1B     77
0063.00 O           T   2      LR
0064.00 O                        TOTPAY1      77
0065.00 O                                    50  'FINAL TOTAL PAY'
```

Literals are not always used for headings, however. As you can see in the output snippet from PAREG in Figure 11-11, literals are marked at the appropriate spot of output to provide a caption for the intermediate (city and state) and the final totals. The literal prints to the left of the fields in this case as shown in Figure 11-12 below:

Figure 11-12 Literals Used to Mark Totals

```
    TOTAL CITY  PAY FOR Newark          225.75

    TOTAL STATE PAY FOR NJ              225.75

    FINAL TOTAL PAY                   2,893.60
```

Columns 45 to 70 can be used for other functions, though our sample program PAREG does not deploy any of those functions. For example it can be used to specify an RPG II style screen format name or an edit word as shown in Figure 11-10 w. See Chapter 20 for a discussion of screen formats.

RPG/400 Edit Words

Though PAREG does not used Edit words, there is no better place to describe this facility than right here. If you have editing requirements that cannot be met by using the edit codes described above, you can use an edit word or named constant. An edit word allows you to directly specify:

- ✓ Blank spaces
- ✓ Commas and decimal points, and their position
- ✓ Suppression of unwanted zeros
- ✓ Leading asterisks
- ✓ currency symbol, and its position
- ✓ Constant characters
- ✓ Negative sign, or CR, as a negative indicator.

Describing Edit words can make up lengthy book chapter in itself. Yet, a whole chapter on edit words simply is not worth your time. So, we will explain the notion and then show you some examples. As many things in RPG, it is good to know they are there in case you ever need them for coding or decoding but when you move from learning to having reference needs, IBM's free RPG manuals will be your best tool.

As you can see in the 26 spaces space provided on the output spec, RPG edit words can be up to 24 characters long and must be enclosed by apostrophes, unless of course it is a named constant which is covered in Chapter 9.

What are the parts of an edit word?

An edit word consists of three parts: the body, the status, and the expansion. The following shows the three parts of an edit word:

Figure 11-13 Make Up of an Edit Word

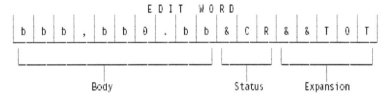

Body - Status - Expansion

The body is the space for the digits transferred from the source data field to the output record. The body begins at the leftmost position of the edit word. The number of blanks (plus one zero or an asterisk) in the edit word body must be equal to or greater than the number of digits of the source data field to be edited. The body ends with the rightmost character that can be replaced by a digit.

The status defines a space to allow for a negative indicator, either the two letters CR or a minus sign (-). The negative indicator specified is output only if the source data is negative. All characters in the edit word between the last replaceable character (blank, zero suppression character) and the negative indicator are also output with the negative indicator only if the source data is negative; if the source data is positive, these status positions are replaced by blanks. Edit words without the CR or - indicators have no status positions.

The status must be entered after the last blank in the edit word. If more than one CR follows the last blank, only the first CR is treated as a status; the remaining CRs are treated as constants. For the minus sign to be considered as a status, it must be the last character in the edit word.

The expansion is a series of ampersands and constant characters entered after the status. Ampersands are replaced by blank spaces in the output; constants are output as is. If status is not specified, the expansion follows the body.

Since a picture is worth a thousand words, the following examples, taken from IBM's reference manual should help in bringing home the notion of edit codes and how useful their use can be in your report creation.

Figure 11-14 Zero Suppression

Edit Word	Source Data	Appears in Output Record as:
'bbb0bbbbbb'	00000004	bbbb000004
'bbb0bbbbbb'	012345	bbbb012345
'bbb0bbbbbb'	012345678	bb12345678

Figure 11-15 More Zero Suppressions

Edit Word	Source Data	Appears in Output Record as:
'0bbb'	0156	b156
'0bbbb'	0156	b0156

Figure 11-16 Zero Suppression with Two Decimals

Edit Word	Source Data	Appears in Output Record as:
'bbbbbb0.bb'	000000001	bbbbbbb.01
'bbbbbb0.bb'	000000000	bbbbbbb.00
'bbb,b0b.bb'	00000012	bbbbbb0.12
'bbb,b0b.bb'	00000123	bbbbbb1.23
'b0b,bbb.bb'	00000123	bb0,001.23

Figure 11-17 Zero Suppression, Two Decimals, Asterisk Front Fill

Edit Word	Source Data	Appears in Output Record as:
'*bbbbbb.bb'	000000123	*bbbbb1.23
'bbbbb*b.bb'	000000000	******0.00

Figure 11-18 Zero Suppression, Two Decimals, Asterisk Front & Back Fill

Edit Word	Source Data	Appears in Output Record as:
'bbbbb*b.bb**'	000056342	****563.42**

Figure 11-19 Zero Suppression, Two Decimals, Floating Dollar Sign

Edit Word	Source Data	Appears in Output Record as:
'bb,bbb,b$0.bb'	000000012	bbbbbbbbb$.12
'bb,bbb,b$0.bb'	000123456	bbbb$1,234.56

Figure 11-20 Miscellaneous Edit Words / Results

Input	Edit Word	Edited Result
0042	"0_HRS.__MINS.&0""CLOCK"	_0HRS.42MIN._0"CLOCK
000000	"_,___.0_"	_____.00
000000	"_,___.0_"	| _____0
000000	"_,_0_DOLLARS__CENTS&CR"	___0DOLLARS00CENTS___
+000002	"__0LBS.&__OZ.TARE&-"	____0DOLLARS00CENTS___
013579	"&_,*_0,___"	***130,579
100199	"__/__/__"	10/01/99
00123456	"_,__$,0__.__"	___1$,234.56
-0000000000	"_____*&CR"	*********___
0000135678	"__,___,___DOLLARS__CENTS"	_____1,356DOLLARS78CENTS
-0034567890	"___,___,_&0.__CR**"	___$345,678.90CR**

Besides the fancy edit word tricks shown in Figure 11-20, there are plenty more than those that we have the opportunity to show in this book. But, now you know how powerful the edit word facility is in RPG/400 and you have seen a number of interesting uses for this tool. If you can't find an edit code to do the formatting that you are looking for, it helps to know that there is not much you can't do with an edit word. Again, if it is taking you time to get your edit word working, and you still have issues, all of the rules are well explained in IBM's RPG/400 Reference Manual for the latest release.

The Constant Edit Word area in RPGIV is in columns 53-80.

OPDFD -- Columns 71-74 Reserved

For a field definition, positions 71 through 74 must be blank.

OPDFD -- Columns 75-80 Comments

For output, there is a paucity of space provided for comments as there is overall in RPG. Positions 75 through 80 can be used for comments, or left blank. Most programmers, who make meaningful and formatted comments in RPG, use multiple statements with the "*" in column 7 for their verbiage.

Comments in RPGIV are in columns 81 – 100. The output form in RPG as you have seen is very similar to that in RPG/400.

Chapter Summary

Output is the reason companies buy computers. In RPG, the output specification form is used to provide the user with a look at the work that the program has accomplished. There are plenty of output lines in PAREG compared to most of the other sections of the program.

Just like the Input Specification form, output has two sections also. The one section described the records to be outputted and the other describes the fields. Both records and indicators can be conditioned.

One of the key areas of in output is column 15. Here the programmer specifies whether there should be an H for heading, D for detail, T for total or E for exception output. The first three have to do with the RPG cycle and when it is read t print and the last has to do with exception output which is controlled in calculations by the programmer.

For printer formatting, there are opportunities in the record definition for spacing lines or skipping to lines before or after printing the current line. There is a handy column for edit codes and if this doesn't help you dress your output enough, there is another area in which you can define specific edit words to create just about any pattern that you may need.

Key Chapter Terms

1P indicator	Logical relationship	Record length
4GL	NMR	Report titles
Blank after	OF indicator	Skip after
decoding	Output field desc	Skip before
Edit	Output indicators	Space after
End position	Output line	Space before
Error message	Output record ID	Tables
EXCPT	Output spec	Total output
Fetch overflow	Output type	Total time
Field control entries	PAGE	UDATE
Field name	Printer file	Variable output fields
Final total		

Review Questions

1. Why is output an essential part of programs?

2. In which sequence are the codes in column 15 specified? What do they mean?

3. What does 1P mean?

4. Can OA be substituted for OF in this program? Why? Why not? If so, how?

5. How many potential lines of output are there below? Describe each of the lines of output as to when the line will be printed?

Figure 11-2 Record Conditioning and Control Output for PAREG

```
0028.00 OQPRINT   H  206      1P
0029.00 O         OR 206      OF
0034.00 OQPRINT   H  3        1P
0035.00 O         OR 3        OF
0043.00 O         D  1        02NMR
0047.00 O         D  1        02 MR
0055.00 O         T  22       L1
0059.00 O         T  02       L2
0063.00 O         T  2        LR
```

6. What is the best way to print to multiple printers in one program?

7. What is an exception name? How could exception output be printed if there were no EXPCEPT name used?

8. Why would Fetch Overflow be used?

9. Assuming the line is set to print this cycle, describe the conditions under which each of the columns will print and where will they print?

```
0033.00 O              45 46N47UDATE  Y     77
0046.00 O          NMRN1PNOFEMPHRS1         67
0052.00 O              31    EMPRAT1         57
0053.00 O             n29    EMPHRS1         67
0054.00 O          01        EMPPAY1         77
0058.00 O                  36CTYPAY1B        77
0062.00 O                 N56STAPAY1B        77
0064.00 O          N83       TOTPAY1         77
```

10. In the above example, what is UDATE?

11. What does the B following these two field names mean?

```
0058.00 O...        CTYPAY1B 77
0062.00 O...        STAPAY1B 77
```

12. What is a literal?

Chapter 12 Decoding and Debugging RPG Programs

The PAREG Program Decoded

Now that we have been fully introduced to RPG/400 specifications and many of the options on each of the various coding forms, it's time to examine the PAREG program one more time to assure that we can decode it (read it with understanding) in anticipation of a potential maintenance change.

That is the other half of the development cycle in which you write and implement and then fix or enhance and implement. The enhancement that we will be making after we do the once through on the PAREG program is the introduction of the DEBUG operation to the program. In my personal experience and as I witnessed others learning RPG for the first time, a key factor in understanding the RPG cycle is to watch what is happening through the eyes of a debug listing.

This is not "Source Level Debugging" but it is an innovative operation code called DEBUG which opens up the RPG cycle for viewing while a report is being printed. For the RPG craftsman needing that special look in a report or a form, the DEBUG operation is priceless.

To get the decoding process moving, let's repeat the objects that are involved in our study. Figure 12-1 is the report; Figure 12-2 and 12-3 are the data and Figure 12-4 is the compile listing of the program.

Figure 12-1 Program Output from Running Sample Learning Program

```
        THE DOWALLOBY COMPANY GROSS PAY REGISTER BY STATE          2/21/06

ST      CITY          EMP#    EMPLOYEE NAME        RATE    HOURS     CHECK

PA      Wilkes-Barre  001     Bizz Nizwonger       7.80    35.00    273.00
PA      Wilkes-Barre  002     Warbler Jacoby       7.90    40.00    316.00

                              TOTAL CITY PAY FOR Wilkes-Barre      589.00

PA      Scranton      003     Bing Crossley        8.55    65.00    555.75

                              TOTAL CITY PAY FOR Scranton          555.75

                              TOTAL STATE PAY FOR PA             1,144.75

AK      Fairbanks     004     Uptake N. Hibiter    7.80    25.00    195.00
AK      Fairbanks     005     Fenworth Gront       9.30    33.00    306.90
                      006 NO  MATCHING MASTER               40.00
AK      Fairbanks     007     Bi Nomial            8.80    39.00    343.20

                              TOTAL CITY PAY FOR Fairbanks        845.10

AK      Juneau        008     Milly Dewith         6.50    40.00    260.00
AK      Juneau        009     Sarah Bayou         10.45    40.00    418.00

                              TOTAL CITY PAY FOR Juneau           678.00

                              TOTAL STATE PAY FOR AK            1,523.10

NJ      Newark        010     Dirt McPug           6.45    35.00    225.75

                              TOTAL CITY PAY FOR Newark           225.75

                              TOTAL STATE PAY FOR NJ              225.75

                              FINAL TOTAL PAY                   2,893.60
```

Figure 12-2 Query Listing of EMPMAST File Data

EMP #	EMPNAM	EMP RAT	EMPCTY	EMP STA	EMP ZIP
000001	1 Bizz Nizwonger	7.80	Wilkes-Barre	PA	18702
000002	2 Warbler Jacoby	7.90	Wilkes-Barre	PA	18702
000003	3 Bing Crossley	8.55	Scranton	PA	18702
000004	4 Uptake N. Hibiter	7.80	Fairbanks	AK	99701
000005	5 Fenworth Gront	9.30	Fairbanks	AK	99701
000006	7 Bi Nomial	8.80	Fairbanks	AK	99701
000007	8 Milly Dewith	6.50	Juneau	AK	99801
000008	9 Sarah Bayou	10.45	Juneau	AK	99801
000009	10 Dirt McPug	6.45	Newark	NJ	07101

```
****** ********  End of report  ********
```

Figure 12-3 Query Listing of TIMCRD File Data

EMPNO		EMPHRS
000001	1	35.00
000002	2	40.00
000003	3	65.00
000004	4	25.00
000005	5	33.00
000006	6	40.00
000007	7	39.00
000008	8	40.00
000009	9	40.00
000010	10	35.00

```
****** ********  End of report  ********
```

Figure 12-4 Expanded Fields Compile Listing PAREG

```
                        S o u r c e   L i s t i n g
   100  H* RPG HEADER SPECIFICATION FORMS
   200  H
   300  F*
   400  F* RPG FILE DESCRIPTION SPECIFICATION FORMS
   500  F*
   600  FPAYMAST IPEAE                    DISK
         RECORD FORMAT(S):  LIBRARY RPGBOOK FILE PAYMAST.
                     EXTERNAL FORMAT PAYR RPG NAME PAYR
   700  FEMPTIM  ISEAE                    DISK
         RECORD FORMAT(S):  LIBRARY RPGBOOK FILE EMPTIM.
                     EXTERNAL FORMAT TIMR RPG NAME TIMR
   800  FQPRINT  O  F    77     OF    PRINTER
   900  I*
  1000  I* RPG INPUT SPECIFICATION FORMS
  1100  I*
  1200  IPAYR          01
  1300  I                                        EMPNO   M1
  1400  I              EMPCTY                     EMPCTYL1
  1500  I              EMPSTA                     EMPSTAL2
  1500   INPUT   FIELDS FOR RECORD PAYR FILE PAYMAST FORMAT PAYR.
A000001                                    1    30EMPNO   M1
A000002                                    4    23 EMPNAM
A000003                                   24    282EMPRAT
A000004              EMPCTY               29    48 EMPCTYL1
A000005              EMPSTA               49    50 EMPSTAL2
A000006                                   51    550EMPZIP
  1600  ITIMR          02
  1700  I              EMPNO                      EMPNO   M1
  1800  C*
  1900  C* RPG CALCULATION SPECIFICATION FORMS
  2000  C*
```

```
1700      INPUT  FIELDS FOR RECORD TIMR FILE EMPTIM FORMAT TIMR.
B000001                        EMPNO                    1    30EMPNO   M1
B000002                                                 4    72EMPHRS
2100  C    02 MR    EMPRAT     MULT EMPHRS    EMPPAY   72
2200  C    02 MR    EMPPAY     ADD  CTYPAY    CTYPAY   92
2300  CL1            CTYPAY    ADD  STAPAY    STAPAY   92
2400  CL2            STAPAY    ADD  TOTPAY    TOTPAY   92
2500  O*
2600  O* RPG OUTPUT SPECIFICATION FORMS
2700  O*
2800  OQPRINT  H  206      1P
2900  O         OR 206      OF
3000  O                                       32 'THE DOWALLOBY COMPANY
3100  O                                       55 'GROSS PAY REGISTERBY'
3200  O                                       60 'STATE'
3300  O                            UDATE Y    77
3400  OQPRINT  H  3        1P
3500  O         OR 3        OF
3600  O                                        4 'ST'
3700  O                                       13 'CITY'
3800  O                                       27 'EMP#'
3900  O                                       45 'EMPLOYEE NAME'
4000  O                                       57 'RATE'
4100  O                                       67 'HOURS'
4200  O                                       77 'CHECK'
4300  O         D 1        02NMR
4400  O                                       46 'NO MATCHING MASTER'
4500  O                            EMPNO      27
4600  O                            EMPHRS1    67
4700  O         D 1        02 MR
4800  O                            EMPSTA      4
4900  O                            EMPCTY     29
5000  O                            EMPNO      27
5100  O                            EMPNAM     52
5200  O                            EMPRAT1    57
5300  O                            EMPHRS1    67
5400  O                            EMPPAY1    77
5500  O         T 22       L1
5600  O                                       51 'TOTAL CITY  PAY FOR'
5700  O                            EMPCTY     72
5800  O                            CTYPAY1B   77
5900  O         T 02       L2
6000  O                                       51 'TOTAL STATE PAY FOR'
6100  O                            EMPSTA     54
6200  O                            STAPAY1B   77
6300  O         T 2        LR
6400  O                            TOTPAY1    77
6500  O                                       50 'FINAL TOTAL PAY'
      * * * * *  E N D   O F   S O U R C E  * * * * *
```

The Decoding Process

You start the full decoding process from top to bottom. There are no entries in the Headers specification so it is moot to decode for this run. Then as you examine the File Descriptions in the PAREG program the world of the logic in this RPG program begins to unfold before you.

There is a primary database file for master records, a secondary database file for time card records and a printer file for a report. A quick look at the output specs and you can verify that this program's mission is to print a report.   From file description, you also know that the data will be in ascending sequence and a drop down look at Input tells you that there is just a sequenced field designated as M1 and its name is EMPNO.

While in the Input area, as you look down to statement 17, you can see that there is a second M1 specified for the time card file. This tells you that the reading of the primary and secondary files will be controlled by the matching records logic of the RPG fixed cycle. You have learned a lot about the program already.

Looking a little closer at the INPUT specs, you will see that there is an L1 indicator specified on City and an L2 indicator on State. That typically means that the program will be performing some intermediate (in-between detail time) calculations and intermediate output probably for totaling functions when a state and/or city control break occurs.

If you take a quick look at calculations, at statements 23 and 24 respectively, you can see that this hypothesis (speculation) is true as there is a total calculation for city and one for state.

Now, looking down to output, you can see that the L1 and L2 totals are defined on total cycle 'T' lines at statements 55 to 65. You can see an L1 printout for a city break, an L2 printout for a state break, and a final total when the last record (LR) is processed.

You have covered a big part of the logic already in trying to get a handle on what this program does (decoding).

Going back to the input record area at statements 12 and 16, you can see that a payroll master record is identified with indicator 01 when it is read and a time card record is identified by indicator 02 when it is read. Below each of these records, you can see the input specifications that you typed in the program so as to provide the matching and control level selections and since this is a compile listing, you can also see the other fields that automatically come into the program from the externally described databases.

 Looking into the fields printed in the output lines, you can see that the names are the same as the input fields. RPG does not make a programmer move input to output records for printing. Just by specifying the name on output, RPG will provide the move from the input files to the print line for you.

We have looked at just about everything so far other than what happens at detail time in the cycle. The two detail calculations shown in statements 21 and 22 are executed only when a time card record (indicator 02) is read. The two detail output lines at statements 43 and 47, are printed only when a time card record (indicator 02) is on.

Though the payroll master (PAYMAST) as processed in the primary file has its own indicator (01), the indicator is not used at all in this program. In fact, if I showed you the bottom of the compile listing, you would see that indicator 01 is unused and the compiler is complaining about it. It conditions nothing.

That means that each time a master is read, nothing happens in the detail cycle. And we know that RPG intersperses the reading of the masters and the time cards through its matching records logic based on the ENPNO match fields (M1).

Of course you would also see that it is not just the 02 indicator that causes calculations to occur and lines to be printed. It has a partner in crime. In this case, the partner is the MR indicator which comes on when there is a match between the primary and secondary file. When indicator 01 and MR are on however, this means that the program has read a master record and it matches the time card about to be processed. We do nothing in this program with this information.

The fact is that we need the time card information in order to have a complete unit of information for an employee. So when the condition of 02 on and MR on is true, we know that the last master read was the master for the time card being processed so the master fields and the time card fields represent the fields for the same employee. Thus, a look at lines 21, 22, and 47, shows the calculation of pay taking and the accumulation of the city total and then the printing of the line with the master, time card and the just calculated gross pay field.

There is one more condition for which this program tests and it causes output to be produced if the condition is true. The program tests to see if there is a time card record (indicator 02 is on) has been read without a corresponding matching master (indicator MR is off). In other words, if 02 and NMR are both true, then an error message gets printed by the output record at statement 43.

And that's that for simple decoding of the PAREG program. Once you have decoded a program, you then can maintain it. The next logical step for you to learn this stuff cold would be to walk through the RPG cycle with the data and see what happens. I'll get you started on that right now.

RPG Cycle and PAREG Decoding

We learned that the very first ting that happens in an RPG program that uses the cycle is that output is produced. We call this type of output "heading output," though in fact the 'H' and 'D' for heading and detail occur at almost the same exact spot in the detailed RPG cycle. In other words, though there is a separate heading cycle and detail cycle, in many ways they appear to be the same and not many programs need to know that they are not the same. So, now walking through this program from the start, what would happen the first cycle?

Looking at the output specifications we see some good documentation for headings in that we used the 'H' designator rather than the D in lines 28 and 34. So, during the first cycle, RPG is willing to print whatever we specify in an unconditioned state or if any of the conditions are met in any of our detail or heading output lines.

So, while RPG is hoping to print something at the beginning of the program, we have both of these lines conditioned with an indicator called 1P and another called OF. These are both special indicators. RPG makes the 1P indicator available every time it passes through this very first cycle. The second time around, it will not be on. RPG turns on the OF indicator if you specify it in the 'F' spec for the print file whenever the last print line of a defined print page is passed.

Since our report is just one page with the data provided, OF will never come on. But, we are staged for more employees. If we have more employees and the number of print lines increases, the OF indicator will cause the print headings to print on every subsequent page in the report.

1P stands for 1st Page indicator and it is most often ORed with the OF indicator to assure that headings are printed on each page. So, in our sample printout in Figure 12-1, the headings were created by the 1P indicator being on the first cycle of the program. Here's a question for you. If we chose to not put a 1p indicator there at all but left it blank, would any heading printing have occurred on the 1st page?

In essence we are saying to RPG that the line is to print unconditionally during the detail cycle in which heading output is produced. So, yes, we would have headings? Now, what happens on the second cycle if we have removed 1P as a conditioning indicator? Now, you've got to start looking at the data in Figures 12-2 and 12-3, because when we hit output in the second cycle, we have read our first 01 record (PAYMAST).

Well, we know that we do nothing in the cycles in which a 01 record is read and RPG very nicely takes the data from the database and moves it into the PAYMAST fields, replacing the blanks and zeroes that were there from the beginning of the program. What about heading output when a 01 record is read?

If our heading lines are unconditioned, then they will print every cycle. The 1p and the OF not only tells RPG to print when 1P and OF are on, it also tells RPG to "not print" when they are not on. So, by using these indicators, we are spared from having headings on top of each detail line. In fact, if we got a heading for 01 and then got another the next cycle for 01, we would have two sets of headings for each one detail line.

Let's go back to having the 1P there and we have just read an 01 record. When RPG takes us to detail calculations, do we have anything to calculate or print? No! Nothing is unconditioned and nothing is conditioned for 01. So, we pass through the cycle and read the next record. It comes from the secondary because matching records logic says intersperse the reading from both files based on the match field (EMPNO). The 02 record is read and MR is on.

We perform the two CALCS conditioned on 02 and MR and now RPG takes us to the detail output cycle. We print the 02 MR line at statement 47 and that's it for detail output. Now, RPG takes us to total output. Do we have a control break?

Yes, the state for employee 001 is PA and the city is Wilkes-Barre. At the beginning of the program L1 and L2 fields compare against blank fields since this is the first employee for the city. Therefore, L2 and L1 calculations and L2 and L1 output should occur when we go to the total output cycle. But it doesn't. RPG effectively knows that this is the first control break of the first cycle so it foregoes doing the total calculations and total output until the next set of data arrives.

When the two records, 01 and 02 are read for employee 2, the same thing happens as for employee 1. However, RPG looks up when it is finished with the employee 02 detail stuff and it says hey, there is a change here for the city but not the state for employee 003. So, before employee 03 is processed, at in-between time in total calculations and total output, RPG first calculates based on L1 conditioning and then it prints the L1 totals before it goes back to read another record.

When the matching records for employee 3 are processed, RPG again looks ahead and it sees that with the next record for employee 004, there is both a state and a city change coming so it turns on indicators L1 and L2 and the L1 and L2 calculations are executed and the L1 and L2 totals for both city and state are printed.

Now, if you move to the bottom of the report in Figure 9-2, you see three totals. When there are no more records to be read, RPG turns on LR which automatically turns on L2 and L1 and so the total calculations are performed and the total output is produced for city and state and also for the grand total.

Now, you might want to pick up with record 4 and walk it through the elements of the cycle that are in play and assure yourself that you now understand the one thing in RPG that most find most difficult to master – the RPG cycle. Congratulations.

Debugging for Learning and Decoding

RPG has a built in facility to help you figure out what is going on during the cycle or actually anytime you want. DEBUG has some disadvantages that skeptics may say make the tool worth less but I would argue that its simplicity and its ability to teach RPG make it a very powerful tool and one that deserves mention early in a book on learning about RPG.

The major disadvantage of the DEBUG is that you must alter your code to use it. Therefore, you must recompile your code. Then, when you have figured out the problem, you have to change the program to recompile it. Though this is true it is not as bad as all that.

The **first action** that you must take is to place a 1 in column 15 of the RPG Header Specification. This tells the compiler to honor the DEBUG calculations that are imbedded in the code. The **second thing** you must do is find a printer file or database file with a record length of at least 80 to accept the output of the debug. If your program has no such file then for the Debug to provide its output, you need to add one.

The disk option helps in debugging reports in which you do not want the output format changed and it also helps in the event that you are trying to trap an elusive problem and you never know when it will strike.

Notice that I had to change the QPRINT file specification by giving it a record length of 80 instead of 77 since DEBUG needs at least 80 to do its job. The **third thing** that you must do is to add DEBUG statements in the code where you would like RPG to provide program status information.

The modified PAREG code for the DEBUG problem is shown in Figure 12-5.

Figure 12-5 PAREG Program modified to support DEBUB Operation

```
0001.00      F* RPG HEADER SPECIFICATION FORMS
0002.00      H        1
0003.00      F*
0004.00      F* RPG FILE DESCRIPTION SPECIFICATION FORMS
0005.00      F*
0006.00      FPAYMAST IPEAE                    DISK
0007.00      FEMPTIM  ISEAE                    DISK
0008.00      FQPRINT  O   F        80     OF    PRINTER
0019.00      C* RPG CALCULATION SPECIFICATION FORMS
0020.00      C*
0021.00      C    01        'MR01'    DEBUGQPRINT     EMPNO
0022.00      C    02 MR     EMPRAT    MULT EMPHRS     EMPPAY  72
0023.00      C    02 MR     EMPPAY    ADD  CTYPAY     CTYPAY  92
0024.00      CL1            CTYPAY    ADD  STAPAY     STAPAY  92
0025.00      CL2            STAPAY    ADD  TOTPAY     TOTPAY  92
0026.00      CL2            'L1L2'    DEBUGQPRINT     TOTPAY
```

Statements 2 and 8 above are changed from the original PAREG program and statements 21 and 26 are added. In statement 21, you can see that I have asked RPG to give me a snapshot called MR01 whenever indicator 01 is on and with the snapshot, provide the value of the field called EMPNO in the snapshot output. Thus, only at 01 time will the debug be operation since as you can see, the DEBUG can be conditioned to execute only when you want it to execute. We get no output from this DEBUG statement when an 02 record is read.

I added statement 26 to the program to show the status of the indicators during the total calculations cycle. This information can be very revealing when you control breaks are not working correctly.

Figure 12-6 shows the way the report now looks with the DEBUGS on in the program. Notice that the first page headings worked fine as they did before since no DEBUG operations have occurred at all at this time (1P) in the program. Now, take a look down further in the report for more headings. For illustrative purposes, I have labeled this area as *** Second Page. This is not printed by the program.

Right after the 1P headings, during detail calculations after the first 01 record has been read by the input cycle, the first debug statement fires. You may recall that this is conditioned by indicator 01. Notice also that there are no detail lines printed before the DEBUG calculation. That is because the printout fired from detail calculations before RPG has even hit its second detail output cycle. During the first detail output cycle, of course, headings were printed but there were nor records read and thus, no non heading output was produced.

The field value for EMPNO in the first DEBUG is 1 or an edited "001" as the field data is available during the processing of the 01 record in calculations. Now look across the line to something called INDICATORS ON. There is a world of information there. You can see that five indicators, **MR IR L1 L2 01**, are on. So, w e can see that though the 02 record has never been read for this employee, RPG has turned on MR to designate that this 01 record matches the 02 record that will be read. The IBM RPG/400 Reference manual offers me no clue as to what indicator IR is and I have found no reference on the Internet so I guess it is something that RPG thinks it needs to be OK. Perhaps it means internal routine??

Why are L1 and L2 on while we are processing the first record that has been read? Can you figure that out? We are in the detail calculations phase right now. Why are L1 and L2 on when we have yet to have one in-between time. It has to do with the first cycle test. RPG does turn these indicators on and they stay on until right before RPG tests again to see if there is a break in the next record to be read. So, the L1 and L2 indicators stay on through detail calculations and detail output. What good is this and what can be done with it if it is good?

Well, it is good because it signifies to RPG that it is processing the first record of a new group. Whereas total level time is in-between, and we have yet to actually read the record that caused the break, detail L1 / L2 is when the record is actually being processed. It helps to know that this is the first record of a group because sometimes report designers like to group indicate.

Group indication is a formatting trick that provides just the first line of detail print with the control field value, say state for L2 and city for L1. The next line would not print the state since it is the same state. The same notion goes for City as you can see in the sample report shown in Figure 12-6A.

Figure 12-6 PAREG Report with RPG/400 DEBUG

```
          THE DOWALLOBY COMPANY GROSS PAY REGISTER BY STATE          3/11/06
   ST        CITY         EMP#      EMPLOYEE NAME        RATE     HOURS     CHECK
DEBUG = 2100        MR01       INDICATORS ON = MR IR L1 L2 01
FIELD VALUE =    1
   PA      Wilkes-Barre   001      Bizz Nizwonger       7.80     35.00    273.00
DEBUG = 2100        MR01       INDICATORS ON = MR IR 01
FIELD VALUE =    2
   PA      Wilkes-Barre   002      Warbler Jacoby       7.90     40.00    316.00
                                   TOTAL CITY  PAY FOR Wilkes-Barre     589.00
DEBUG = 2100        MR01       INDICATORS ON = MR IR L1 01
FIELD VALUE =    3
   PA      Scranton       003      Bing Crossley        8.55     65.00    555.75
DEBUG = 2600        L1L2       INDICATORS ON = MR IR L1 L2 01
FIELD VALUE =      114475

                                   TOTAL CITY  PAY FOR Scranton        555.75
                                   TOTAL STATE PAY FOR PA            1,144.75
DEBUG = 2100        MR01       INDICATORS ON = MR IR L1 L2 01
FIELD VALUE =    4
   AK      Fairbanks      004      Uptake N. Hibiter    7.80     25.00    195.00
DEBUG = 2100        MR01       INDICATORS ON = MR IR 01
FIELD VALUE =    5
   AK      Fairbanks      005      Fenworth Gront       9.30     33.00    306.90
                             006 NO MATCHING MASTER              40.00
DEBUG = 2100        MR01       INDICATORS ON = MR IR 01
FIELD VALUE =    7
   AK      Fairbanks      007      Bi Nomial            8.80     39.00    343.20
                                   TOTAL CITY  PAY FOR Fairbanks       845.10
DEBUG = 2100        MR01       INDICATORS ON = MR IR L1 01
FIELD VALUE =    8
   AK      Juneau         008      Milly Dewith         6.50     40.00    260.00
DEBUG = 2100        MR01       INDICATORS ON = MR IR 01
FIELD VALUE =    9
   AK      Juneau         009      Sarah Bayou         10.45     40.00    418.00
DEBUG = 2600        L1L2       INDICATORS ON = OF 1F 2F MR IR L1 L2 01
FIELD VALUE =      266785
                                   TOTAL CITY  PAY FOR Juneau          678.00
                                   TOTAL STATE PAY FOR AK            1,523.10
*** Second Page


          THE DOWALLOBY COMPANY GROSS PAY REGISTER BY STATE          3/11/06
   ST        CITY         EMP#      EMPLOYEE NAME        RATE     HOURS     CHECK
DEBUG = 2100        MR01       INDICATORS ON = OF MR IR L1 L2 01
FIELD VALUE =   10
   NJ      Newark         010      Dirt McPug           6.45     35.00    225.75
DEBUG = 2600        L1L2       INDICATORS ON = MR L1 L2 L3 L4 L5 L6 L7 L8 L9 LR
FIELD VALUE =      289360
                                   TOTAL CITY  PAY FOR Newark          225.75
                                   TOTAL STATE PAY FOR NJ              225.75
                      FINAL TOTAL PAY              2,893.60
```

Figure 12-6B Group Indication of PAREG Report

```
         THE DOWALLOBY COMPANY GROSS PAY REGISTER BY STATE        3/11/06
ST     CITY          EMP#     EMPLOYEE NAME        RATE     HOURS     CHECK

PA     Wilkes-Barre  001      Bizz Nizwonger       7.80     35.00    273.00
                      002      Warbler Jacoby       7.90     40.00    316.00

                               TOTAL CITY  PAY FOR Wilkes-Barre      589.00

       Scranton      003      Bing Crossley        8.55     65.00    555.75

                               TOTAL CITY  PAY FOR Scranton          555.75

                               TOTAL STATE PAY FOR PA             1,144.75
```

To make this work, you would use field indicators. On State, for example, on the detail record report line, you would place L2, as a field indicator and for city, you would place L1. Then the report would print just as in Figure 9-6. What makes it work is that L1 and L2 and the other L indicators stay on through detail output then they go off. When they are off, the state and city does not print. They print only on the first record of a new group – or detail L1 / detail L2 time.

Figure 12-7 Snippet of Debug Listing

```
  PA      Scranton        003      Bing Crossley      8.55      65.00     555.75
DEBUG = 2600      L1L2      INDICATORS ON = MR IR L1 L2 01
FIELD VALUE =      114475
                                   TOTAL CITY  PAY FOR Scranton           555.75
                                   TOTAL STATE PAY FOR PA             1,144.75
DEBUG = 2100      MR01      INDICATORS ON = MR IR L1 L2 01
FIELD VALUE =      4
  AK      Fairbanks       004      Uptake N. Hibiter  7.80      25.00     195.00
```

Figure 12-7 is a smaller snippet of the big debug listing shown first in Figure 12-6A. It shows the data that caused the first L2 control break in the program between states PA and AK. The last employee for Pennsylvania is shown on the top and the first employee for Alaska is shown on the bottom. Notice that the DEBUG marked L1L2 on the second line. It fired from an L2 calculation in the program at statement 26 as shown below:

0026.00   CL2   'L1L2'   DEBUGQPRINT

So, we know that in order for this DEBUG to fire, L2 must be on. The L1L2 in Factor 1 merely creates a marker in the reports so you can see where your DEBUGS are firing.

Clearly from Figure 12-7 we can see control field changes in both the city and the state fields and the DEBUG in line 2 shows us, that among a bunch of other particulars, L1 and L2 are on as you would expect. Notice also that at total calculation time, when this Debug fired, indicator 01 is also on. Yet, the last record processed for employee # 003 was an 02 (time card) record. So, why is 01 on?

It is the record identifying indicator of the next record to be processed. The fields for the 02 record still contain employee 003's data, however, RPG has turned off indicator 02 already at this point in the total calculations cycle and it has turned on the identifying indicator 01 of the next record to be read. This tells the programmer a bunch of interesting things.

First, it tells the programmer that record identifying indicators cannot be used at in-between time for prior groups. So, an 02 on line 26 would not fly. The other thing it says is that if need be, a programmer can know ahead of time, which record type was about to be read in. Sometimes this knowledge could help a programmer take a different logic path than otherwise.

It also shows us that record identifying indicators get turned off during "in- between time" and they get turned on during in-between time. When the 01 record data is actually read, the 01 record DI will continue to be on until in-between time when the next record is looked at.

For a detail lesson in RPG, take another go at running the data through this program and you will have a pretty good idea of how the RPG cycle works and when it turns on stuff and when it turns stuff off. After awhile, it will all seem logical because of course, it is. See the PAREG with an even more detailed RPG cycle in Figure 12-8.

Figure 12-8 PAREG and the RPG Cycle

Points in RPG Cycle	PAREG Activity- RPG Cycle
0. Start	PAREG program is loaded and started.
1. Heading & Detail Output -- What is there to output?	0028.00 OQPRINT H 206 1P 0029.00 O OR 206 OF 0034.00 OQPRINT H 3 1P 0035.00 O OR 3 OF
2.1 Turn off record id & Level Indicators. None on the first cycle	Time card or pay master records (01, 02). Level indicators between control fields -- L1, L2
2.2 Read a record from file just processed. At start, read a record from each file in sequence specified	Read primary and secondary at start to see which gets processed first.
2.3 Check for end of file	If all files are at end, set on the last record indicator and indicators L0 through L9
2.4 Are matching fields specified	Select highest priority record from appropriate file based on match field primary, secondary and match field value.
2.5 Turn on record ID indicator. You pick the #, the cycle turns it on7.	First cycle through the primary (01) record (Master) is selected, Subsequently the primaries and secondaries alternate based on matched field values.
3.0 Have any control fields changed, if so, turn on Level indicators – also test for first cycle... If first cycle, skip total calcs & total output by going to Step 6.0 If not first cycle, go to step 3.1	First cycle always creates a false control break because the control fields compare against a blank or zero value. When a city changes at this point, L1 turns on and when a state changes, L2 and L1 are turned on.

3.1 Perform total calcs (caused by control field change). You pick the control fields, RPG does the tests. When the fields change, the level indicator is turned on.	City and state total calculations are taken during this time in the cycle 23.CL1 CTYPAY ADD STAPAY STAPAY 92 24.CL2 STAPAY ADD TOTPAY TOTPAY
4.0 Perform total output(caused by control field change) You pick the field, RPG does the tests. Output conditioned with a T and a level indicator is performed.	City and state total output (subtotals) are performed at this time during the cycle 55.T 22 L1 56. 51 'TOTAL CITY PAY FOR' 57. EMPCTY 72 58. CTYPAY1B77 59.T 02 L2 60. 51 'TOTAL STATE PAYFOR' 61 EMPSTA 54 62 STAPAY1B77 63.T 2 LR 64. TOTPAY1 77 65. 50 'FINAL TOTAL PAY'
5.0 Check to see if LR is on. If LR is on, go to end of cycle and end job.	LR will not turn on in this program until the last secondary record (time card is read from the secondary file.
5.1 If LR not on, check to see if overflow has occurred and overflow indicator (s) are on.	RPG offers another time in the cycle not described in the 7 point cycle in which overflow printing occurs. It is close to detail cycle calculations and output but the data from the last record read has not yet become available.
5.2 If a print line has overflowed, perform overflow output cycle. Print those lines conditioned by an overflow indicator such as OF.	PAREG has overflow defined and in the debugged program, it occurs. 0028.00 OQPRINT H 206 1P 0029.00 O OR 206 OF 0034.00 OQPRINT H 3 1P 0035.00 O OR 3 OF
6.0 Move data from input area to fields	Fields are now available from the master or time card record – whichever was read last.
6.1 Is selected record a matching record? If so, turn on MR. Is there a match of the PAYR record from the master with the TIMR record from the time card file?	PAREG uses matched fields (M1) to identify matching records. 0012.00 IPAYR 01 0013.00 I EMPNO M1 0014.00 I EMPCTYL1 0015.00 I EMPSTAL2 0016.00 ITIMR 02 0017.00 I EMPNO M1
6.2 If there is a match, turn on the MR indicator. If	RPG processes just one record at a time. If the master is in process and there is a match with a to-be-read

there is no match, turn off the MR indicator.	secondary, then the record ID (01) for the master is also on. If the time card is in process, 02 is on.
7.0 Perform Detail Calculations	21.C 02 MR EMPRAT MULT EMPHRS EMPPAY 72 22.C 02 MR EMPPAY ADD CTYPAY CTYPAY
Repeat Cycle	PAREG goes another cycle

When you have the two machinations of the RPG fixed logic cycle digested and you want even greater detail on the cycle, it's time to get out the IBM reference manual. For your convenience we have provided a link to the RPG cycle in the IBM Boulder online books library:

http://publib.boulder.ibm.com/IBM i/v5r2/ic2924/books/c092508347.htm#FIGDETLOBJ.

Chapter Summary

In this chapter, we decode the trusty PAREG program that we have been working with throughout the book. In this way, we are now sure that we can decode it (read it with understanding) in anticipation of a potential maintenance change. In addition to a once through on the PAREG logic, you were introduced to the DEBUG operation.

The DEBIG operation has taken a hit since the mid 1990's in terms of acceptance because of the many other "better" ways to debug your programs. For learning the RPG cycle, however, as demonstrated in this chapter, there is no better tool.

The **first action** that you must take to debug a program is to place a 1 in column 15 of the RPG Header Specification. This tells the compiler to honor the DEBUG calculations that are imbedded in the code. The **second thing** you must do is find a printer file or database file with a record length of at least 80 to accept the output of the debug. The **third thing** that you must do is to add DEBUG statements in the code where you would like RPG to provide program status information.

Key Chapter Terms

Compile listing	First cycle	Maintenance
Control breaks	First page	Move data
Debug	First record	New group
DEBUG statement	Input cycle	NMR
Decoding	Intermediate output	RPG fixed logic cycle
Detailed RPG cycle	Last record indicator	UDATE
Error message	Link	VALUE
Final total		

Review Questions

1. Why is it a good idea to decoding the PAREG program again as a unit?

2. What is the DEBUG operation?

3. Does DEBUG provide source level debugging?

4. How does DEBUG help you learn the RPG cycle?

5. Code a DEBUG statement to display all of the indicators on at a given point in the RPG cycle? Include all code.

Chapter 13 Introduction to RPGIV

You've Already Seen RPGIV?

So far in this book as we decomposed and decoded the PAREG program using the RPG/400 specification templates, we also presented the formatting of the RPG/400 specifications used in PAREG for RPGIV. To an extent then, this chapter on RPGIV is somewhat redundant – at least as far as we have gotten in our study of the RPG language.

The Fact is, however, RPGIV is not just RPG/400 with a better coding sheet design. It's lots more than that and in this chapter we begin a series of chapters in which we differentiate the two languages better than was necessary in earlier chapters.

A Better RPG

In 1988, with the introduction of its highly successful AS/400 series of machines, IBM introduced a somewhat new name for an old language. The language was RPG III and the new moniker was RPG/400. There was little if any difference between RPG III on System/38 and the new version of RPG for the AS/400 known as RPG/400.

To be correct, RPG/400 is actually a compiler package that contains RPG II for System/36 compatibility, RPG III for System/38 compatibility and the RPG III for the AS/400 which also took on the name RPG/400.

As of OS/400 Version 3 release 1, IBM changed the name of this compiler package to "AS/400 ILE RPG/400." With this the company introduced the RPG IV language which is a version of RPG that targets the Integrated Language Environment (ILE).

ILE is the latest "native" runtime environment for programs on the IBM i. Way back in OS/400 Version 2 Release 3, IBM introduced this new program model that in many ways essentially changed the way the operating system works with languages. This new programming model now provides support for a mixed set of high-level languages. But, in V2R3, C/400 was the only ILE language and it became the basis for the other ILE languages soon to follow.

Prior to ILE, RPG for example had its own runtime environment. To be fair, CL had its own; COBOL had its own; and C also had its own. Thus, there were often issues trying to get two different languages to work well together in the same job. With ILE, all programming languages now run in ILE. Thus, the same "environment" is now used for COBOL, C, C++, RPG and CL.

To take advantage of the functionality built into the ILE, however, IBM had a lot of work to do. New compilers needed to be created. With its new RPG IV compiler introduced first in 1994, IBM decided to make full use of the ILE. This had the double advantage of providing a new version of RPG with an ILE targeted compiler.

Though ILE wasn't really ready for RPG IV in 1994 with V3R1 of CISC architecture OS/400, RPGIV made its debut and its initial syntax addressed many of the ills that programmers had begged IBM for years to correct – especially the multiple faces of RPG/400 input.

In 1994 in its CISC processors (that's all IBM had back then), Big Blue delivered a new language with a new syntax. Yet, this new language with its new syntax had a nice familiar flavor so that the RPG/400 programming community was able to almost immediately understand it as a new language. The new ILE notions were somewhat more problematic for the RPG community.

The new RPGIV defined a new look for all of RPG's specifications. The specs were revitalized and made much better. Since IBM had not really made any substantial changes to RPG for ten or more years at the time, there was lots of long overdue facility made available with this "new language."

Besides the changes to all the forms, IBM also added a new data specification – the 'D' spec. The 'D' spec helped make the formerly stodgy language much easier to learn and much more similar to other languages. The 'D' spec in many ways brought to RPG the capabilities that had been in COBOL's Data Division from the outset.

Programmers from other systems and other languages on the AS/400 were then able to learn RPG coding without having to learn the RPG cycle and many of the other RPG nuances that you have just learned in the prior 11 chapters. And, though this was mostly good, a disadvantage was that new RPG programmers often were not introduced to the old RPG. This created two RPG camps that today still have some disagreements. There are those that know, understand, and love the RPG cycle, and use it as a 4GL, and there are those who think that the RPG cycle is worth about as much as one of those primitive electromechanical monsters from which the cycle originated would be worth in today's world.

Popular thought has RPGIV first being developed for the RISC models but this is not true. IBM created RPGIV in 1994 and released it with V3R1 for its CISC processors. It originally ran under a programming model that got its name only after ILE was introduced. If the Integrated Language Environment was the new name for how IBM would bring all of the code produced by all of its compilers together, then, what was it that had existed prior to this new model? It was the same dilemma as RISC vs. CISC. CISC got its name when RISC came out.

With OS/400 V3R1, They christened the old "no name" model as "the original program model," or simply OPM. Thus OPM is just a name that has been given to the original runtime environment of RPG and CL under OS/400.

Since about 1995 with the availability of the RISC boxes, ILE has become the native mode and now the OPM a.k.a. the original native environment is emulated. Reading between the lines you can see that once ILE was the way, everything else became part of ILE. It was that good of an idea. ILE isn't really an environment at all; today it is in fact, the native OS/400.

So, where does that leave OPM? It still exists but it is a somewhat Rube Goldberg emulated environment running under ILE. Because of this emulation factor, and the machinations that IBM had to perform to perfect it, the new wave of RPG IV purists who understand the underpinnings of this issue in detail, do not think so well of RPG/400 in the ILE world.

Yet, despite their thoughts and the concerns of skeptics over the years, RPG/400 performs very well within its new ILE home. In many ways, RPG/400's fine performance is a big reason why there has been no compelling need for the full adoption of RPG IV in the one-language RPG shop. Twelve years after its introduction, full adoption of RPGIV is under 50%

Yet, as you will note RPGIV is a far superior language than is RPG/400. Just the specification changes alone with the addition of the 'D' spec were major improvements and enough to make the language a worthy replacement for RPG/400 code. You'll see for yourself shortly.

What is RPGIV?

As noted many times in this book so far, RPGIV is an evolutionary derivative of the IBM RPG from the late 1950s. Along the way, this RPG language was updated with powerful procedural op-codes and structured programming constructs and it has made the change from a problem oriented language to procedure oriented. With RPGIV in 1994, the language was modified and   extended for many purposes including a desire to make it more maintainable.

Who Needs It?

Why was a "New" RPG needed? For years before RPGIV, COBOL programmers, who had been introduced to RPG in System/38 and AS/400 shops, had given RPG high marks as a non-verbose language in which to write. COBOL of course goes down in history as one of the most verbose. The trick with verbosity, however, is that if you make the words in your program – record definitions and field names meaningful, they tell a better story about your program.

Early programming instructors made their points about flexibility in variable naming often by suggesting that you can call a field anything – buzz, crap, or any other four letter words. The compiler is not offended and thus, this is OK for the compiler – as long as you know what that field name actually means.

Teaching programming and teaching good programming style and conventions are two different things however. Just one year later, even the programmer who wrote the program using "CRAP" as a field name in all programs has no idea what the field named "CRAP" actually means.

In the same vein, one and two letter field names have no meaning. Six character RPG/400 field names give an opportunity for some meaning but not really much, yet that is all there is to work with in RPG/400 – just six characters. Thus, programmers in joking moments may call RPG a WRITE-ONLY language because it is very difficult to maintain programs where the field names and data records are not very intuitive.

Having said that, there are a number of RPG stalwarts out there who would suggest that they can get by without any issues from using six character meaningful names. Nonetheless, IBM got the message, a loud and clear one indeed, that it would be a good thing to give RPG fields and operations a bit more room.

The WRITE-ONLY tag is humorous but COBOL converts to RPG would argue that RPG programmers write more programs than COBOL programmers because "normal human beings" cannot read RPG code well enough to maintain it. Besides the short field names, here are a few other beefs:

- ✓ 6 character field names productive to write, not to read
- ✓ Input specs for data structures, constants records does not make sense
- ✓ Extension specs for arrays, tables – extensions of what?
- ✓ Calc specs for stand-alone fields – hard to find - where is working storage?
- ✓ K - continuation keywords – cryptic to understand; difficult to code correctly
- ✓ Indicators at will - Input, Calcs, wherever?
- ✓ Where do you define data – problem – wherever you want?

So, for these and a lot of reasons IBM felt that a new RPG was needed and they did a pretty nice job in the first iteration to address the anomalies and issues noted above. RPGIV was not the first attempt to make RPG code more like mainstream COBOL and other languages. For example, the structured operations in RPGIII made code reading much easier and it helped to alleviate the spaghetti rebellion.

Programmers new to RPG found code without indicators smattered everywhere much easier to read and maintain, but before RPGIV the anomalies remained, limits remained, and as features were added, the multi-purpose filled in blanks columns became more complex to read and write.

Therefore, high function RPG programs continued to be very difficult to read. For example, try to do even a simple math formula with RPG/400. It is often spread across many RPG calculation statements because the language has no mechanism for dealing with formulae. A more descriptive, more verbose, yet more productive RPG was required -- without forcing re-writes for existing programs.

When IBM announced RPGIV in 1994, in my ½ day overview seminar that I presented to my consulting clients (I left IBM in 1992 after 23 years), I would cap this discussion off by saying – "Done!" It's called RPG IV or ILE RPG. Anybody who looks at the further evolution of RPGIV over the past thirteen years knows that IBM did not rest on its laurels. Many more enhancements have been introduced to the language since 1994.

Many Beneficial Changes to RPGIV

So let's look at the comprehensive yet crisp list to see what's new in IV from III.!

7 Specification Sheets vs. 8

- ✓ E, L dropped
- ✓ + D(efinition) spec added

Functions Moved to More Logical Specification Sheet

- ✓ Non-IO data definitions to 'D' spec
- ✓ RAF moved to File Descriptions, etc.

Specifications Changed to Accommodate Extended Functions

- ✓ Field Name length increased to 10 characters
- ✓ Record length increased to 5 digits 99,999
- ✓ Decimal positions increased to 30
- ✓ Large function/keyword area for better code readability
- ✓ Field indentation for readability
- ✓ Op-Code & Extender in ( ), 10 spaces

Additional Functions Added To Language

- ✓ Date, Time, Timestamp operations
- ✓ Free form assignments / expressions
- ✓ Renamed op-codes
- ✓ Built in Functions (BIFs) -- %size, %trim
- ✓ Stand-Alone Fields
- ✓ Underscore now valid in field_name
- ✓ Upper/Lowercase names, upper internal
- ✓ Part of ILE Environment -- Static calls

Many RPG Limits Removed / Increased

- ✓ 50 file limit
- ✓ 200 Array limit
- ✓ program size limit
- ✓ File, Record, Field, Table Array Name size
- ✓ etc.

To get a great snapshot at the limits that were lifted with RPGIV, examine the chart in Figure 13-X1

Figure 13-X1 RPGIV Expanded Limits

RPG/400 Limit	ILE RPG Limit	Description
6	10	Field Name
6	10	Array/Table Name
8	10	File Name
8	10	Format Name
A-Z, 0-9, $, #, @	A-Z, 0-9, $, #, @, _	Valid Characters in Symbolic Name – but 1st character still may not be 0-9 or _
Upper Case	Upper &Lower Case	U/L case in symbolic names
256	32,767	Length of character field & array element
256	1024	Length of named constants
9	30	# of decimal positions
50	No published limit	# of files
200	No published limit	# of arrays
Varies	No published limit	Program Size
9,999	99,999	Program described file record length
9,999	32,767	# of elements in table or array
9,999	9,999,999	Length of single occurrence data structure
9,999	32,767	# of occurrences in mult occur DS
80	100	Length of compile time data arr/tab

RPGIV ILE Environment

Along with RPGIV came the use of ILE in RPGIV. Among other things, ILE allows for static binding of programs to accommodate modular programming and better performance in modular programming.

IBM i on Power Systems CALLS have always been dynamically bound using the original program model (OPM) and even the old extended programming environment (EPM). EPM was built for the C language and the notion of block structured languages existing within the AS/400 framework. Neither OPM nor EPM was efficient performance wise but the rest of the AS/400 facilities made up for that for most of my clients.

The new ILE RPG a.k.a. RPGIV uses activation groups and assures that static binds can be done and thus performance benefits occur. ILE removes this OPM / EPM issue. All IBM i on Power Systems programming languages benefit from ILE and all can talk to each other naturally because of it. Please see Chapters 25, 26, & 27 for a more detailed discussion of ILE, sub-procedures, and free-format RPG.

Pointer Example

ILE RPG has also introduced pointers which were introduced in the first version of RPGIV to be able to use static calls. Check out this D spec from the early RPGIV implementation:

D procpointr... S *... PROCPTR INZ(%paddr('proc_name'))

Using this mechanism, here is how you could effect static calls in RPGIV. This is then contrasted with the dynamic call method.

Static Calls

```
      CALLB     procpointr
      CALLB     'PREBOUNDPG'
```

Dynamic Calls

```
      CALL  'PGMNAME'
      CALL  Fieldname
```

In this case, Procpointr is a defined procedure pointer in ILE environment. Its internal data type is defined with an * in position 40. %PADDR is the get procedure address and is a built in function (BIF). BIFS were also new with RPGIV.

So, what is this CALLB operation in RPGIV? CALLB works similarly to an RPG/400 CALL but it is designed for a bound procedure vs. dynamic program call. The called procedure name can be a literal or a procedure pointer... not a variable as in dynamic calls. The compiler must know about the program in order to link it in at compile time so the name cannot be buried in a potentially changing variable name. The first RPGIV release permitted just one procedure in a module. That restriction was removed in the very next release with prototyped procedures.

Keyword Orientation

One of the most liked facilities introduced with RPGIV is keywords in the Header, Definition, and File Description specifications. The keyword area uses a syntax very much like DDS and thus for native database coders, the change is quite natural. Here is an example of two file description statements with keywords:

```
FFILEA UF... DISK    PREFIX(P1_) COMMIT
FFILEB UF... DISK    USROPN
```

In this example, all fields that come in from FILEA will have a prefix of "P1_" to differentiate the names from fields in other files or other items defined in this program. Commitment control will be used with the file. FILEB will not be opened automatically but will be opened by the user in the program with an OPEN operation.

> Note: No where you go in life, there is always somebody presenting you with a chicken or egg scenario. As much as I do not want to do that in this book, I have in this chapter. In order to fully introduce RPGIV in this chapter without making you jump around in the book here and there and everywhere, I am forced to show the RPG code for some things that we will not be covering for a few more chapters. When you encounter these, feel free to book mark the areas and come back after you have been introduced. The biggest issue here is examples showing arrays and tables and data structures which we do not cover until later chapters.

One of the tools that IBM built to help in the transition from RPG/400 to RPGIV is a program source conversion command. This tool converts RPG/400 to RPGIV in the most natural way. In other words, the flavor of the original program is preserved and the programmer can recognize the RPGIV version of the code quite readily without having to do substantial decoding.

The format of the CVTRPGSRC command is shown in Figure 13-1:

If you have never used the CVTRPGSRC command, it will definitely burp the first time because there is no log file (QRNCVTLG). The message you get will tell you exactly how to create the log file. The key things about this command and how the new RPGIV code is stored are as follows:

1. You specify the QRPGSRC file for the RPG/400 code.
2. You specify the library for the RPG/400 code – RPGBOOK.
3. You specify the source member –PAREG.
4. You specify the QRPGLESRC file for the RPGIV code
5. You specify the library in which QRPGLESRC is located.
    The record length is 112 characters to accommodate the
    expanded source record (100 characters in RPGIV).
6. You specify "yes" for source template to get formats intersperses
    inside of your program to more easily see the new RPG
    specification formatting.

Figure 13-1 IBM's CVTRPGSRC Command

```
                    Convert RPG Source (CVTRPGSRC)

Type choices, press Enter.
                                                From file  . . . . . . . . . . . >
QRPGSRC
  Library  . . . . . . . . . . . >    RPGBOOK
From member  . . . . . . . . . > PAREG
To file  . . . . . . . . . . .      QRPGLESRC
  Library  . . . . . . . . . . >    RPGBOOK
To member  . . . . . . . . . .      *FROMMBR


                      Additional Parameters

Expand copy member . . . . . .      *NO              Print conversion report  . . . .
*YES             Include second level text  . . .    *NO
Insert specification template .     *yes
Log file . . . . . . . . . . .      QRNCVTLG
  Library  . . . . . . . . . .        *LIBL
Log file member  . . . . . . .      *FIRST
                                        Bottom
```

The converted code for PAREG is shown in Figure 13-2. Before we examine the coding changes, let's take a look at some of the nuances that are shown in Figure 13-2. The first item of interest is the formatting lines themselves. Because I specified "yes" for a source template, lines, 2. 7, 14, 15, and 26 were automatically generated and included in the converted source as comments. These statements take us through calculations and then there are no more format records.

You cans see that each of added source records for formatting was also numbered by the converter. Yet, for some reason, this command did not place the format lines for output into the file. For our learning purpose, I had requested formats to make it easier to read the source. When I examined the code in the source file, I added the two SEU FMT lines for output and I left the FMT in the source to differentiate these lines from those auto-generated.

The other two nuances regarding the format lines are (1) in some cases, the format was inserted before the first spec form of a given type and in others it was after the first. and (2) for INPUT, the record format and the field format were added together, one line after the other, and were not separated by record and field form type.

To make the code easier for you to read, I highlighted the format statements as you can see in Figure 13-2. To make it easier for you to compare the programs, The RPG/400 version is shown in Figure 10-2.

The first difference you would notice is that the RPGIV program has 72 statements whereas the RPG/400 program has just 65. However, five of the RPGIV statements are used for formatting and none are used for formatting in the RPG/400 version. Therefore there are two extra lines in the RPGIV code. Where are they?

If you add up all the spec types, there is a one for once conversion in this program except for one specification type – calculations. With the structured operations that were placed in RPG III years ago, many RPG programmers had begun to use IF statements and DO statements to control conditioning. So, when IBM redesigned the calculation specification, rather than three "ANDed" areas on one calculation spec, RPGIV was designed with space fro just one conditioning indicator. The RPG/400 PAREG program uses both indicators 02 and MR to condition the detail calculations. Since RPGIV offers just one spot, to get MR and 02 as conditioning indicators, the converter needed two calc specs that use the AN linkage to extend the condition. See lines 25 to 29 in Figure 13-2. So now, everything else in this program is one to one.

Figure 13-2 RPGIV Version of PAREG

```
        67891123456789212345678931234567894123456789512345678961234567897 12
001.00 H* RPG HEADER SPECIFICATION FORMS
002.00 H*eywords++++++++++++++++++++++++++++++++++++++++++++++++++++++++++++
003.00 H
005.00 F* RPG FILE DESCRIPTION SPECIFICATION FORMS
006.00 F*
007.00 F*ilename++IPEASFRlen+LKlen+AIDevice+.Keywords++++++++++++++++++++++
008.00 FPAYMAST    IPE AE              DISK
009.00 FEMPTIM     ISE AE              DISK
010.00 FQPRINT     O   F   77          PRINTER OFLIND(*INOF)
011.00 I*
012.00 I* RPG INPUT SPECIFICATION FORMS
013.00 I*
014.00 I*ilename++SqNORiPos1+NCCPos2+NCCPos3+NCC...........................
015.00 I*...........Ext_field+Fmt+SPFrom+To+++DcField++++++++L1M1FrP1MnZr
016.00 IPAYR        01
017.00 I            EMPNO                     EMPNO          M1
018.00 I                                      EMPCTY       L1
019.00 I            EMPSTA                     EMPSTA       L2
020.00 ITIMR        02
021.00 I            EMPNO                     EMPNO          M1
022.00 C*
023.00 C* RPG CALCULATION SPECIFICATION FORMS
024.00 C*
025.00 C    02
026.00 C*0N01Factor1+++++++Opcode(E)+Factor2+++++++Result+++++++Len++D+HiLo
027.00 CAN MREMPRAT      MULT    EMPHRS       EMPPAY        7 2
028.00 C    02
029.00 CAN MREMPPAY      ADD     CTYPAY       CTYPAY        9 2
030.00 CL1    CTYPAY     ADD     STAPAY       STAPAY        9 2
031.00 CL2    STAPAY     ADD     TOTPAY       TOTPAY        9 2
032.00 O*
033.00 O* RPG OUTPUT SPECIFICATION FORMS
034.00 O*
FMT O  O*ilename++DF..N01N02N03Excnam++++B++A++Sb+Sa+...................
035.00 OQPRINT    H   1P                2 06
036.00 O          OR  OF                2 06
FMT P  O.............N01N02N03Field++++++++YB.End++PConstant/editword/DTfor
037.00 O                                    32 'THE DOWALLOBY COMPAN
```

Chapter 13 Introduction to RPGIV   171

```
038.00 O                                           55 'GROSS PAY REGISTER B
039.00 O                                           60 'STATE'
040.00 O                              UDATE     Y  77
041.00 OQPRINT    H     1P                         3
042.00 O          OR    OF                         3
043.00 O                                            4 'ST'
044.00 O                                           13 'CITY'
045.00 O                                           27 'EMP#'
046.00 O                                           45 'EMPLOYEE NAME'
047.00 O                                           57 'RATE'
048.00 O                                           67 'HOURS'
049.00 O                                           77 'CHECK'
050.00 O          D     02NMR              1
051.00 O                                           46 'NO MATCHING MASTER'
052.00 O                              EMPNO        27
053.00 O                              EMPHRS     1 67
054.00 O          D     02 MR              1
055.00 O                              EMPSTA        4
056.00 O                              EMPCTY       29
057.00 O                              EMPNO        27
058.00 O                              EMPNAM       52
059.00 O                              EMPRAT     1 57
060.00 O                              EMPHRS     1 67
061.00 O                              EMPPAY     1 77
062.00 O          T     L1                 2  2
063.00 O                                           51 'TOTAL CITY  PAY FOR'
064.00 O                              EMPCTY       72
065.00 O                              CTYPAY    1B 77
066.00 O          T     L2                 0  2
067.00 O                                           51 'TOTAL STATE PAY FOR'
068.00 O                              EMPSTA       54
069.00 O                              STAPAY    1B 77
070.00 O          T     LR                 2
071.00 O                              TOTPAY     1 77
072.00 O                                           50 'FINAL TOTAL PAY'
```

Figure 13-3 RPG/400 Version of PAREG

```
*************** Beginning of data *********************
       67891123456789212345678931234567894123456789512345678961234567 8
0001.00 H* RPG HEADER (CONTROL) SPECIFICATION FORMS
0002.00 H
0003.00 F*
0004.00 F* RPG FILE DESCRIPTION SPECIFICATION FORMS
0005.00 F*
0006.00 FEMPMAST IPEAE                   DISK
0007.00 FTIMCRD  ISEAE                   DISK
0008.00 FQPRINT  O   F      77      OF   PRINTER
0009.00 I*
0010.00 I* RPG INPUT SPECIFICATION FORMS
0011.00 I*
0012.00 IPAYR         01
0013.00 I             EMPNO                        EMPNO   M1
0014.00 I                                          EMPCTYL1
0015.00 I             EMPSTA                        EMPSTAL2
0016.00 ITIMR         02
0017.00 I             EMPNO                        EMPNO   M1
0018.00 C*
0019.00 C* RPG CALCULATION SPECIFICATION FORMS
0020.00 C*
0021.00 C   02 MR   EMPRAT   MULT EMPHRS    EMPPAY 72
0022.00 C   02 MR   EMPPAY   ADD  CTYPAY    CTYPAY 92
```

```
0023.00 CL1           CTYPAY      ADD  STAPAY      STAPAY   92
0024.00 CL2           STAPAY      ADD  TOTPAY      TOTPAY   92
0025.00 O*
0026.00 O* RPG OUTPUT SPECIFICATION FORMS
0027.00 O*
0028.00 OQPRINT   H   206       1P
0029.00 O         OR  206       OF
0030.00 O                                         32 'THE DOWALLOBY COMPANY'
0031.00 O                                         55 'GROSS PAY REGISTER BY '
0032.00 O                                         60 'STATE'
0033.00 O                             UDATE Y     77
0034.00 OQPRINT   H   3         1P
0035.00 O         OR  3         OF
0036.00 O                                          4 'ST'
0037.00 O                                         13 'CITY'
0038.00 O                                         27 'EMP#'
0039.00 O                                         45 'EMPLOYEE NAME'
0040.00 O                                         57 'RATE'
0041.00 O                                         67 'HOURS'
0042.00 O                                         77 'CHECK'
0043.00 O         D   1         02NMR
0044.00 O                                         46 'NO MATCHING MASTER'
0045.00 O                             EMPNO       27
0046.00 O                             EMPHRS1     67
0047.00 O         D   1         02 MR
0048.00 O                             EMPSTA       4
0049.00 O                             EMPCTY      29
0050.00 O                             EMPNO       27
0051.00 O                             EMPNAM      52
0052.00 O                             EMPRAT1     57
0053.00 O                             EMPHRS1     67
0054.00 O                             EMPPAY1     77
0055.00 O         T   22        L1
0056.00 O                                         51 'TOTAL CITY  PAY FOR'
0057.00 O                             EMPCTY      72
0058.00 O                             CTYPAY1B    77
0059.00 O         T   02        L2
0060.00 O                                         51 'TOTAL STATE PAY FOR'
0061.00 O                             EMPSTA      54
0062.00 O                             STAPAY1B    77
0063.00 O         T   2         LR
0064.00 O                             TOTPAY1     77
0065.00 O                                         50 'FINAL TOTAL PAY'
        ***************** End of data ******************************
```

Decoding the PAREG RPGIV Program

Before we give a general column definition for the newer RPGIV specs, let's see if the resulting program looks like RPG or something else. Since you are quite familiar with the RPG/400 version, take a good look at the RPGIV version before you read any more and see if you can decode it as we did the RPG/400 version in Chapter 12.

The RPGIV Header Specification

Let's start with the PAREG RPG/400 Header specification in Figure 13-4 and note its changes in RPGIV as shown in Figure 13-5. Then, let's move on to the rest of the specs from there.

Just as there is no H information at all provided for the RPG/400 version, there is none provided for RPG IV as you can see. The H entry has no entries at all – no keywords. However, the format line at statement 2 provides a clue that something is different.

Figure 13-4 Header RPGIV Spec – No Debug
```
          6789112345678921234567893123456789412345678951234567896123456789612345678
0001.00 H* RPG HEADER (CONTROL) SPECIFICATION FORMS
0002.00 H
```


Figure 13-5 Header RPGIV Spec – No Debug
```
          6789112345678921234567893123456789412345678951234567896123456789712345
001.00 H* RPG HEADER SPECIFICATION FORMS
002.00 H*eywords++++++++++++++++++++++++++++++++++++++++++++++++++++++++++++++++++++
003.00 H
```

H*eywords in line 2 of Figure 13-4 is a comment using a HEADER spec. This comment was inserted by CVTRPGSRC when it converted the RPG/400 source to RPGIV. If we replaced the asterisk with a 'k' it would read "Keywords."

That is the difference in a nutshell. The H spec now is keyword only. There are no columnar designations at all for the RPGIV Header.

In Figure 13-6, to demonstrate the DEBUG facility, we added a '1' in column 15 to the RPG/400 H spec to tell it to turn on debug for the program. Since there is no longer a spot for a 1 in column 15 of the RPGIV H specs, how do you handle the notion of debug as in RPG/400?

There is a keyword. And the keyword is DEBUG as shown in Figure 13-7. In fact, if you explored the H spec for RPG/400, you would find that those values that were once in H spec columns now are all represented by RPGIV keywords. It makes it easier to remember and hard to get in the wrong column.

Figure 13-6 Header RPGIV Spec Debug
```
          6789112345678921234567893123456789412345678951234567896123456789612345678
0001.00 H* RPG HEADER (CONTROL) SPECIFICATION FORMS
0002.00 H         1
```

Figure 13-7 Header RPGIV Spec with DEBUG Keyword
```
          6789112345678921234567893123456789412345678951234567896123456789712345
001.00 H* RPG HEADER SPECIFICATION FORMS
002.00 H*eywords++++++++++++++++++++++++++++++++++++++++++++++++++++++++++++++++++++
003.00 H DEBUG
```


RPGIV File Description Specification

Let's move on down to the File Description section. The RPGIV code is shown in Figure 13-8 and the RPG/400 code is shown in Figure 13-9.

Figure 13-8 RPG IV File Description Spec
```
          67891123456789212345678931234567894123456789512345674
07.00 F*ilename++IPEASFRlen+LKlen+AIDevice+.Keywords++++++
08.00 FPAYMAST    IPE AE              DISK
09.00 FEMPTIM     ISE AE              DISK
10.00 FQPRINT     O   F   77          PRINTER OFLIND(*INOF)
```
Figure 13-9 RPG/400 File Description Spec

```
        67891123456789212345678931234567894123456789512345 67
FMT...  Filename IPEAF........L..I........Device+......KExit
06.00 FEMPMAST IPEAE                      DISK
07.00 FTIMCRD  ISEAE                      DISK
08.00 FQPRINT  O   F     77        OF     PRINTER
```

Doing a quick compare, you can readily see that the RPGIV code is a little bit tighter and not as spread out. Moving from left to right, the first difference is that there are 10 spaces for the File name compared to 8. Since AS/400 objects have a natural max name length of 10 characters, this makes RPG capable of handling a file with a name length of 10.

Continuing the trek from left to right, you can see that there is a space between the glob of code for the primary and secondary files – IPEAE and ISEAE respectively. The new layout adds a column between the end of file designator and the ascending sequence columns. It is blank in the PAREG program.

Its meaning is File addition. In other words, the RPG/400 column 66 entry has been moved to column 20 of the new RPGIV File description specification.

Moving again from left to right, you will notice that the OF indicator from RPG/400 is removed completely and that the device name is moved further to the left, now starting in column 36 instead of column 40. The OF indicator is put back via a keyword starting in column 44.

OFLIND(*INOF)

The OFLIND keyword is one of many RPGIV File Description keywords. In this case, the keyword says to use the *INOF a.k.a. the reserved word OF as the overflow indicator. Its purpose is exactly the same as the OF entry in RPG/400. Ant that does it for the F spec RPGIV entries needed for the converted PAREG program.

RPGIV Input Spec Changes

One of my personal observations regarding the CVTRPGSRC command is that IBM did not invest a lot of resources in assuring that all was clean. Just as an example, the record format name PAYR in statement 12 of the RPG/400 input specs when converted shows a format line in statement 14 with *ilename and this is not correct even if you replace the asterisk with the 'F.'

It presents the internally described record format instead of the external format. For a facility that has been out for over ten years, this problem should already be fixed. In Figure 13-10, to make up for the wrong formatted provided by the converter, I placed correctly shaped format records on top of record line 16 and field line 21.

Figure 13-10 Converted RPGIV Input Specs
```
        6789112345678921234567893123456789412345678951234567896123456
14.00 I*ilename++SqNORiPos1+NCCPos2+NCCPos3+NCC..................
15.00 I*............Ext_field+Fmt+SPFrom+To+++DcField++++++++L1M1
FMTIX IRcdname+++....Ri.............
16.00 IPAYR            01
17.00 I                                        EMPNO          M1
18.00 I               EMPCTY                    EMPCTY         L1
19.00 I               EMPSTA                    EMPSTA         L2
20.00 ITIMR            02
FMTJX I.............Ext-field+.................Field++++++++L1M1
21.00 I               EMPNO                     EMPNO          M1
```

Figure 13-11 RPG/400 Input Specs
```
        6789112345678921234567893123456789412345678951234567896123 45
FM IX IRcdname+....In..........
FM JX.I..............Ext-field+......................Field+L1M1
12.00 IPAYR          01
13.00 I              EMPNO                            EMPNO    M1
14.00 I                                               EMPCTYL1
15.00 I              EMPSTA                           EMPSTAL2
16.00 ITIMR          02
17.00 I              EMPNO                            EMPNO    M1
```

Record ID in RPGIV

Let's walk down the specifications for Input first looking at RPG/400 right above and then RPGIV. Lines 12 and 16 in Figure 10-8 represent the record format. This converts to lines 16 and 20 in Figure 10-7. If you were glancing without concentrating at the RPG/400 and RPGIV record format statements, you might conclude that they were exactly the same. That's how close they are.

The both RPGs are extremely easy to read because of this. The two differences to the record format are that the format name area is expanded to 10 positions and that instead of positions 19 and 20, the Record ID Indicator in RPGIV is found in positions 22 and 23.

Input Field Spec in RPGIV

Four fields are defined in the RPG/400 program at statements 13, 14, 15, and 17. These are converted to statements 17, 18, 19, and 21 respectively. Besides all of the "from and to" positions changing, the major change to RPGIV is that the field name area is now 14 positions long.

The length of the field name itself has been increased to 10 positions but the area in RPG in which to specify the field has grown by an additional 4 positions so that indented. The field is specified from positions 49 to 62 of the record. And thus the programmer now has the latitude of indentation of input to make it more readable.

In case you want to rename a field, the external name is still in positions 21 – 30. The area in which group levels and match fields are coded has moved from positions 59 – 62 to 63 – 66 respectively. And, that's about it for significant change to INPUT.

RPGIV Calculation Spec Changes

The CALC Specification has gone through its own set of changes to better satisfy the readability requirement of RPGIV. Among the changes are the following:

- ✓ Factors 1 & 2 & Result Field are now 14 characters
- ✓ Maximum field length can be defined in calcs in 5 digits (99,999)
- ✓ Number of decimal places in definition increased from 1 to 2.(99)
- ✓ The space for the operation is now 10 characters
- ✓ Many operations have been stretched to make more sense -- READPE,CHECKR, RETURN, UNLOCK
- ✓ Op extender in parentheses not in 'H' 44
- ✓ From 3 to 1 conditioning indicator
- ✓ EVAL op-code can use an extended factor 2 as below:

```
C...   IF        (Hours <= 40)
C...   EVAL(H)   WeeklyPay = Rate * Hours
```

CALC Example 1

```
RPG/400
*.. 1 ...+... 2 ...+... 3 ...+... 4 ...+... 5 ...+... 6
CL0N01N02N03Factor1+++OpcdeFactor2+++ResultLenDHHiLoEqC
C           MYSAL     ADD  HISSAL     OURSAL 102
C                     MOVEL'BRIAN'    FNAME
C                     MOVE 'KELLY'    LNAME
C                     MOVELFNAME      FULNAM
C                     MOVE LNAME      FULNAM
-------
RPG IV
C
C... Mysalary   add   Hissalary   OURSalary         10 2
C...
CL0N01Factor1+++++++Opcode(E)+Extended-
Factor2++++++++++++++++++++++++++++++++++++++++++++++
C          ...      EVAL   Myname = 'BRIAN' + 'KELLY'
```

CALC Example 2

```
RPG/400
*.. 1 ...+... 2 ...+... 3 ...+... 4 ...+... 5 ...+...
CL0N01N02N03Factor1+++OpcdeFactor2+++ResultLenDHHiLoEq
C           KEY       REDPEARFMT                    01
C           *IN01     IFEQ *OFF
C           DZCOST    DIV  12        UNCOST 199
C                     ENDIF                                  ---
RPG IV
C... KEY     Readpe   ARFMT                     01
C... *IN01   IFEQ     *OFF
C... DZCOST  DIV(H)   12             UNCOST      2515
C           ENDIF
```

CALC Example 3

```
RPG/400
*.. 1 ...+... 2 ...+... 3 ...+... 4 ...+...
CL0N01N02N03Factor1+++OpcdeFactor2+++Result
C           x         DOWLT100
C           AR1,Y     ANDNE*BLANKS
C                     MOVE AR1,Y     AR2,Y
C                     ADD  1         X
C                     ADD  1         Y
C
----
RPG IV
CL0N01Factor1+++++++Opcode(E)+Extended Factor 2++++++
C                     DOW      X< 100 and AR1(Y) <> ' '
CL0N01Factor1+++++++Opcode(E)+Factor2++++++Result+++
C                     MOVE     AR1,Y       AR2,Y
C                     ADD      1           X
C                     ADD      1           Y
C                     ENDDO
```

As you can see in the DOW, there are a number of logical operators similar to those used in C language that are available in the formula permitted after the eval statement. Her are some of the C-like Arithmetic & Logical operators:

> = < ( ) NOT OR AND + - * / ** >= <= <>

The following table shows a number of renamed operation codes:

Renamed / Modified RPG OPCodes

RPG/400	RPG IV
BITOF	BITOFF
CHEKR	CHECKR
COMIT	COMMIT
DEFN	DEFINE
DELET	DELETE
EXCPT	EXCEPT
LOKUP	LOOKUP
OCUR	OCCUR
REDPE	READPE
RETRN	RETURN
SELEC	SELECT
SETOF	SETOFF
UNLCK	UNLOCK
UPDAT	UPDATE
WHXX	WHENXX

RPG IV Free-form Op-codes

RPGIV has had a number of free form op codes long before the recently released free format RPG. Though free form, the freeness of from only comes in on the Extended Factor 2 of the calculation specifications. SO, the free form comes after the op-code. The operations that can use this style are as follows:

- ✓ DOU & DOW
- ✓ EVAL   Answer = expression
- ✓ IF
- ✓ WHEN
- ✓ Arithmetic & Logical operators below:

```
> = <     (    )    NOT  OR    AND
+ -  *    /    **        >=         <=    <>
```

The operation extenders used in RPGIV operations of all kinds are as follows:

- ✓ (H) = Half adjust
- ✓ (N) = Record read but not locked
- ✓ (P)   =   Pad result field with blanks
- ✓ (D) = Date Field Test
- ✓ (T)   =   Time Field Test
- ✓ (Z) = Timestamp Field Test

CALC Example 4 – Semi Free Form in Action

```
RPG/400
C... ORDERCODE       IFEQ        "PROCESS"
C... QUANTITY        MULT(H)     PRICE...      EXTENSION
C...                 ELSE
C... PRICE           MULT(H)     .95...        DISC_PRICE... 5 2
C... QUANTIT         MULT        DISC_PRICE EXTENSION...  7 2
C...                 ENDIF
-------
RPGIV
C...         IF          (ORDERCODE = 'PROCESS')
C...         EVAL(H)     EXTENSION = QUANTITY * PRICE
C...         ELSE
C...         EVAL(H)     AMOUNT = (PRICE * .95) *Quantity
C...         ENDIF


RPG/400
C... Hours1          MULT        RATE          TOTALPAY
C*
C... RATE            ADD         DIFFRATE2  NEWRATE
C... Hours2          mult        newrate    shift2wage
C                    ADD         shift2wage TOTALPAY
C... RATE            ADD         DIFFRATE3  NEWRATE        7 2
C... HOURS3          MULT        NEWRATE    SHIFT3WAGE
C...                 ADD         SHIFT3WAGE TOTALPAY

RPGIV
C...         EVAL(H)     TotALPAY = hours1 *rate
C...            + (rate + diffrate2) *hours2
C...            + (rate + diffrate3) * hours3
C...         EVAL        MESSAGE1 = 'This method is much +        C...
easier than the +
C...                     constants in ROG/400 and -
C...                     much better than Move +
C...                     and MOVEL'
```

Figure 13-12 Converted RPGIV Calc Specs

```
        678911234567892123456789312345678941234567895123456789612345 67890
FMT C CL0N01Factor1+++++++Opcode&ExtFactor2+++++++Result++++++++Len++D+
23.00 C* RPG CALCULATION SPECIFICATION FORMS
24.00 C*
```

```
25.00 C    02
26.00 C*0N01Factor1++++++Opcode(E)+Factor2++++++Result++++++++Len++D+
27.00 CAN MREMPRAT          MULT      EMPHRS        EMPPAY          7 2
28.00 C    02
29.00 CAN MREMPPAY          ADD       CTYPAY        CTYPAY          9 2
30.00 CL1   CTYPAY          ADD       STAPAY        STAPAY          9 2
31.00 CL2   STAPAY          ADD       TOTPAY        TOTPAY          9 2
```

Figure 13-13 RPG/400 Calc Specs
```
          6789112345678921234567893123456789412345678951234567896123
          CL0N01N02N03Factor1+++OpcdeFactor2+++ResultLenDHHiLoEqComments+
0018.00 C*
0019.00 C* RPG CALCULATION SPECIFICATION FORMS
0020.00 C*
0021.00 C    02 MR   EMPRAT    MULT EMPHRS    EMPPAY  72
0022.00 C    02 MR   EMPPAY    ADD  CTYPAY    CTYPAY  92
0023.00 CL1         CTYPAY    ADD  STAPAY    STAPAY  92
0024.00 CL2         STAPAY    ADD  TOTPAY    TOTPAY  92
```

If it were not for the formatting lines and the two AN lines, the RPGIV calc specs in Figure 10-9 would very similar to the RPG/400 version in Figure 10-10. The biggest change so far in this program is that the number of "ANDed" conditioning indicators has been reduced from three to one per each RPG calculation statement.

Thus, for those heavily indicator driven calculations, as many as three RPGIV statements may be needed for each RPG/400 operation conditioned by three "AN" indicators. In this case, we need one extra statement for each detail calculation as shown in lines 25 and 28 of Figure 13-12.

Besides the AN indicator changes, the space for just about everything has become larger in the new RPG Calculations Specification. Factor 1 and Factor 2 and the Result Field now begin in columns 12 and 36 and 50 respectively and each entry has been widened to 14 positions. This enables indented calculations with ten character field names as well as larger literals / constants.

The operation code area is also larger providing from positions 26 to 35 supporting operation codes with extenders up to ten characters. The operation extender was formerly specified in column 53 and was traditionally labeled as the half-adjust column. For numeric operations, an H in column 53 told the compiler to round up. In RPG IV, operations such as an ADD with half adjust as you will see when we cover operations in Chapter 15 is specified as such:

ADD (H)

The parentheses are required. There are now many operations with RPGIV that can use the extender portion. Still, compared with the five position operations from RPG/400 that once were happy to exist in columns 28 to 32, there is plenty of room for the operation, the extenders as well as a lengthening of the base operation to make it more readable in English. Though I would like to tell you that IBM redid the multiply (MULT) in RPGIV but it did not. So, for me to give you an example, let me say that the operation for updating a record on disk in RPG/400 is UPDAT. That's about all you can get in a 5 character space. However, in RPGIV, IBM added the E at the end to make the new UPDAT command in RPGIV read much better as:

UPDATE

RPGIV Field Length and Decimals

The new field length columns (64-68) and the number of decimals in (69-70) have grown by one each from the RPG/400 calc spec and in V5R1 the largest numeric field has grown from 15 to 31 characters and the largest alphabetic field has gone from 256 to 65535. To support this, the length is now five columns and the length of the # of decimal positions in RPGIV is now 2, now permitting more than 9 decimal positions in a field.

Built-In-Functions (BIFs)

BIFS are covered in greater detail in Chapter 15 but it would be inappropriate in an RPGIV introductory chapter to leave without a discussion of one of the most powerful facilities in RPGIV, the built-in function. Moreover, in Chapter 26, you will be introduced to subprocedures and functions and afterwards, you will be able to create your own BIFS.

A function in any language must return a value to the expression. The BUILT-IN Functions merely mean that the functions are provided by the compiler. You do not have to write them. IBM i on Power Systems BIFS all begin with a percent (%) sign and are then followed by arguments. When there are multiple arguments permitted, they are separated by colons (:).

BIFs are supported by D-spec keywords and are used in calculations. The arguments to a BIF must be compile time values and they must have been defined previously in source. The BIF operations are used in the RPGIV Extended Factor 2 area as well as within the Free-Format RPGIV.

Many of today's string BIFs are very common and were introduced with the early RPGIV compiler. For example here are three BIFs that are fairly representative of what you can expect to be able to do:

%SUBST(string:start{:length})
Extracts a portion of a string

%TRIM(string)
Returns the string stripped of leading & trailing blanks

%TRIML(string)
Returns the string stripped of leading blanks

%TRIMR(string)   Returns the string stripped of trailing blanks

```
RPG/400
D STRING1…   S…    20    INZ('     Can it be done')
-------
RPGIV
C…EVAL        String1 = %TRIML(String1) + ' --- YES!'
C* String1 = 'Can it be done --- YES!'
```

Other BIFs

You can work up some fairly complex code with BIFS, especially those having to do with pointers.Check out this BIF

%ADDR(variable)

This function places the address of an item into a variable. The item can be a field, an element of an array, or an expression.

e.g.

```
IF %ADDR(FLD1) = %ADDR(FLD2)
    %ELEM(array_name) or
    %ELEM(Mul-Oc_DS)
```

This function places into a variable, the number of elements of an array or the number of occurrences of a multiple occurrence DS

%SIZE(name{*all})

This function places into a variable, the size of a field, literal, array, data structure, or named constant. If the name is an array or a multiple occurrence data structure, the variable contains the size of one element or occurrence. If *ALL is specified, the size received id the size of all the elements or occurrences.

Pointer Example 1 -- Pointer Variables

```
*.. 1 ...+... 2 ...+... 3 ...+... 4 ...+... 5 ...+... 6 ...+... 7
DName+++++++++++ETDSFrom+++To/L+++IDc.Keywords.................
D Pointer1        S                 *     INZ(%ADDR(Firstfld))
D Firstfld        S             100       INZ('123')
D SECNDFLD        S             100       BASED(Pointer2)
D aNSWER          S             100
D*
CLON01Factor1+++++++Opcode(E)+Factor2+++++++Result+++++++Len++
C                     EVAL      Pointer2 = %ADDR(firstfld)
C                     IF        Firstfld = secndfld
C        'EQUAL'      DSPLY
C                     ELSE
C        'Not Equal'  DSPLY
C                     ENDIF


---
D*
D* Sixmoarray is based on monvalues -allow access to month names
D* as elements of an arrray
*.. 1 ...+... 2 ...+... 3 ...+... 4 ...+... 5 ...+... 6 ...+... 7
DName+++++++++++ETDSFrom+++To/L+++IDc.Keywords.................
D Monvalues       DS
D    JAN                               INZ('January')
D    FEB                               INZ('February'
D    MAR                               INZ('March')
D    APR                               INZ('April')
D    MAY                               INZ('May')
D    JUN                               INZ('June'
D*
D Pointer         S                 *   INZ(%ADDR(Monvalues))
D*
D Sixmoarray      DS                    BASED(Pointer)
D    Monthname                   8      DIM(6)
```

In this example, Pointer1 is loaded with the address of firstfld. Secndfld is 100 characters long. Its address is to be supplied by the pointer field named pointer2

The code loads pointer2 with the address of firstfld. Since secndfld is based on the address in pointer2, firstfld and secfld now have the same address. Therefore, they have the same content.

RPGIV Output Spec Changes

Nothing that was in RPG/400 is in RPGIV. Well, not exactly but most!
Output is no exception. Since some fundamental things occurred to the language, all of the specifications had to be modified to react well to the changes. Following the most notable changes presented below, several examples of output in the RPGIV era are presented.

- ✓ 10 char field & file formats
- ✓ 10 char except label
- ✓ 14 char output field name space
- ✓ 3 pos space before / after
- ✓ 3 pos skip before / after

- ✓ Compile Tables / Arrays (name specified, sequence does not matter)

Output Example 1 -- RPGIV

```
RPG/400
*.. 1 ...+... 2 ...+... 3 ...+... 4 ...+... 5 ...+
Oname++++DFBASbSaN01N02N03Excnam.................
OAPMAST  EADD            ADMAST

O...............N01N02N03FldNAMYBEnd+PConstant/Ed
O                        CUSNO      6
O                        CHDATE     14
C                        AMTOWE     19P
---
RPG IV
Ofilename++DF..N01N02N03Excnam++++B--A++Sb+Sa+ ...
OAPMASTER  EADD          ADDMAST
O..............N01N02N03FldNAM+++++++YB.End++PConsta
O                        CUSNO              6
O                        CHDATE             14D*MDY/
O                        AMTOWE             19P
```

Output Example 2 -- RPGIV Printer Output

```
RPG/400
*.. 1 ...+... 2 ...+... 3 ...+... 4 ...+... 5 ...+
Oname++++DFBASbSaN01N02N03Excnam.................
OREPORT   E 3            PRNTIT
OREPORT   E 21           PRNTIT
O...............N01N02N03FldNAMYBEnd+PConstant/Ed
O                        CUSCOD      2
O                        CUSNO Z    10
C                        CHDATE     20
O                        AMTOWE3    32
----------
RPG IV
Ofilename++DF..N01N02N03Excnam++++B--A++Sb+Sa+ ...
OREPORT      E           PRINTIT     5 2
O.............N01N02N03FldNAM+++++++YB.End++PCon
O                        CUSNO       Z     2
O                        CUSCOD           10
O                        CHDATE           20
O                        AMTOWE      3    32
```

Some of the output specific changes include output spacing up to 255. Output is no longer limited to 3 spaces using multiple lines for spacing purposes.

Output Example 3 Literal End Positions

```
RPG/400
O...                 25 'It is a very nice feature'
O...                 50 ' Of the other RPG languag'
O...                 75 'e. But in this language I'
O...                100 ' unfortunately must calcu'
O...                125 'late end positions'
O...        AMTOWE3   32

RPG IV
O...                125 'It is a very nice feature'
O...                    ' of the other RPG languag'
O* Comment can come in between continuation
O* lines
O...                    'e. But in this language I'
O...                    ' unfortunately must calcu'
O...                    'late end positions'
```

So much for non-PAREG examples… to make it very convenient to compare the differences and mostly the similarities between RPGIV and RPG/400 output in Figure 13-14 and Figure 13-15, both programs are squeezed onto the same one page.

But, to contrast individual features of RPGIV with RPG/400, as we did for all other spec sheets, we will narrow in and blow-up lines for a more concentrated examination. For example, to get a better idea of the new output record format, take a look at Figures 13-14 and 13-15.

RPGIV Output Record Format and Control

Just as with every other RPGIV spec sheet, the size reserved for name lengths has increased for the output spec. From left to right on the output record format, the filename has grown to 10 positions starting at 7.

The detail or total (D or H) indication has been relocated to column 17 instead of 15 because of the longer file name.

The printer device control area has been completely moved from its original position of importance when RPG was a report writing language. The RPG IV designers, who have a mission to minimize the report writing facility of RPG and concentrate on its strong database and workstation facilities, seem to have hidden the printer control portion of output, but they have added a PRTCTL keyword to File Descriptions to help out.

Without printer control as was the next area of consequence in RPG/400, RPGIV goes right on to conditioning indicators. So, the new RPGIV output record form now finds its nine position conditioning indicator area starting in column 21. Yes, with a few more changes to the spec, IBM was able to line up the indicators just as they are in RPG/400. The next item is the Exception name.

The Exception name facility is described in Chapter 23. Just as in RPG/400, it begins in position 30 right after the three sets of indicators.

Continuing the examination of what's next for output, we eventually bump into the area in which the RPGIV designers chose to put the printer controls. Since printers of today have way more capabilities than RPG could ever have imagined in the 1950's, the designers extended the power of spacing and skipping to limits few had imagined or requested. So, with RPGIV, you now get to specify expanded print controls way down in the O spec in positions 40 through 51.

Figure 13-14 RPGIV New PAREG Output Record Format
```
        67891123456789212345678931234567894123456789512
FMT O   OFilename++DF..N01N02N03Excnam++++B++A++Sb+Sa+.
035.00  OQPRINT    H      1P                       2 06
036.00  O          OR     OF                       2 06
```

Figure 13-15 RPG/400 PAREG Output Record Format
```
        67891123456789212345678931234567894123456789512
FMT O   OName++++DFBASbSaN01N02N03Excnam..............
028.00  OQPRINT  H  206    1P
029.00  O        OR  206    OF
```

The definitions of spacing and skipping have not changed with RPGIV, but there are apparently no physical printer reasons for a programmer to use either skipping or spacing. Both are greatly enhanced and based on your printer with spooling, it may not even matter from a performance perspective.

Spacing still refers to advancing one line at a time, and skipping refers to jumping from one print line to another lines. But RPG has gotten lots smarter inside as to how it executes these operations.

Because choosing spacing and skipping before and after can get messy and there are since there are lots more spacing options than ever before, let's examine some facts in this area that can help bring some real order out of it all. If spacing and skipping are specified for the same line, it would help to know what happens first.

Figure 13-16 Converted RPGIV Output Specs

```
          678911234567892123456789312345678941234567895123456789612345 67
FMT O  O*ilename++DF..N01N02N03Excnam++++B++A++Sb+Sa+....................
035.00 OQPRINT      H    1P                        2 06
036.00 O            OR   OF                        2 06
FMT P  O.............N01N02N03Field+++++++++YB.End++PConstant/editword/DTfor
...
041.00 OQPRINT      H    1P                        3
042.00 O            OR   OF                        3
043.00 O                                               4 'ST'
...
049.00 O                                              77 'CHECK'
050.00 O            D    02NMR              1
051.00 O                                              46 'NO MATCHING MAS
052.00 O                      EMPNO                    27
053.00 O                      EMPHRS          1        67
054.00 O            D    02 MR              1
058.00 O                      EMPNAM                   52
059.00 O                      EMPRAT          1        57
060.00 O                      EMPHRS          1        67
061.00 O                      EMPPAY          1        77
062.00 O            T    L1                 2  2
063.00 O                                              51 'TOTAL CITY   PAY
064.00 O                      EMPCTY                   72
065.00 O                      CTYPAY         1B        77
066.00 O            T    L2                 0  2
067.00 O                                              51 'TOTAL STATE PAY
068.00 O                      EMPSTA                   54
069.00 O                      STAPAY         1B        77
070.00 O            T    LR                 2
071.00 O                      TOTPAY          1        77
072.00 O                                              50 'FINAL TOTAL PAY
```

Figure 13-17 RPG/400 Output Specs

```
028.00 OQPRINT   H  206   1P
...
033.00 O                           UDATE Y    77
034.00 OQPRINT   H  3     1P
035.00 O         OR  3    OF
036.00 O                                  4 'ST'
037.00 O                                 13 'CITY'
038.00 O                                 27 'EMP#'
039.00 O                                 45 'EMPLOYEE NAME'
040.00 O                                 57 'RATE'
041.00 O                                 67 'HOURS'
042.00 O                                 77 'CHECK'
043.00 O         D 1    02NMR
044.00 O                                 46 'NO MATCHING MASTER'
045.00 O                     EMPNO       27
046.00 O                     EMPHRS1     67
047.00 O         D 1    02 MR
048.00 O                     EMPSTA       4
049.00 O                     EMPCTY      29
050.00 O                     EMPNO       27
051.00 O                     EMPNAM      52
052.00 O                     EMPRAT1     57
053.00 O                     EMPHRS1     67
054.00 O                     EMPPAY1     77
055.00 O         T 22   L1
056.00 O                                 51 'TOTAL CITY   PAY FOR'
```

```
057.00 O                                EMPCTY     72
058.00 O                                CTYPAY1B   77
059.00 O           T 02      L2
060.00 O                                           51 'TOTAL STATE PAY FOR'
061.00 O                                EMPSTA     54
062.00 O                                STAPAY1B   77
063.00 O           T 2       LR
064.00 O                                TOTPAY1    77
065.00 O                                           50 'FINAL TOTAL PAY'
```

The spacing and skipping operations are processed in the following sequence:

```
Skip before
Space before
Print a line
Skip after
Space after.
```

If the PRTCTL (new RPGIV printer control option) keyword is not specified on the file description specifications, an entry must be made in one of the following positions when the device is PRINTER:

```
40-42 (space before)
43-45 (space after)
46-48 (skip before)
49-51 (skip after)
```

If a space/skip entry is left blank, the function on the record line with the blank entry (such as space before or space after) does not occur.

If entries are made in positions 40-42 (space before) or in positions 46-51 (skip before and skip after) and no entry is made in positions 43 - 45 (space after), no space occurs after printing.

When PRTCTL is specified, it is used only on records with blanks specified in positions 40 through 51. If a skip before or a skip after a line on a new page is specified, but the printer is already on that line, the skip does not occur.

Considering that there were just two positions for skipping and one for spacing in RPG/400, it will be interesting to see if print programs for printers of the future can ever take advantage of the vastly expanded printer capabilities in RPGIV.

RPG IV Field and Control Specification

As a sample of a field and control specification from the converted PAREG program, let's pick some print lines that have both variable detail time data (fields) and constant detail time data (literals.). Looking first at the RPG/400 code, statements 43 – 46 show exactly the type of print line that demonstrates the major change with RPGIV. This code snippet in RPG/400 form is shown in Figure 13-19 below. The corresponding RPGIV code is shown in Figure 13-18.

Figure 13-18 Converted RPGIV Output Field Specs

```
          67891123456789212345678931234567894123456789512345678961234567 0
FMT P  O..............N01N02N03Field++++++++++YB.End++PConstant/editword/DTfo
050.00 O          D    02NMR            1
051.00 O                                         46 'NO MATCHING MASTER'
052.00 O                       EMPNO             27
053.00 O                       EMPHRS       1    67
```

Comparing statement 44 in RPG/400 to Statement 51 in RPGIV, if there were no template, the trained RPG programmer would not be able to tell them apart. With RPGIV, one noticeable change is that the end position length is now 5 positions ending in column 51 v. 4 positions in RPG/400 ending in column 43. Additionally, the constant area begins in position 53 v. 45 in RPG/400.

Figure 13-19 RPG/400 Output Field Specs

```
          67891123456789212345678931234567894123456789512345678961 2345
FMT P  O..............N01N02N03Field+YBEnd+PConstant/editword
043.00 O          D 1    02NMR
044.00 O                                         46 'NO MATCHING MASTER'
045.00 O                       EMPNO             27
046.00 O                       EMPHRS1           67
```

Looking at the field names in RPG/400 and RPGIV respectively, the six position space for EMPNO from statement 45 begins in position 32 whereas the 14 positions of space permit up to 10-character field names that begins anywhere from column 30 to 33 and end anywhere from column 39 to 43.

IBM provides all this space for field names so that the programmer can indent subfields, thereby making the program more readable. The end position for the length of the field is column 51.

With 5 positions available, the largest record position that can be defined in this space for a field is 65535. Of course, we wouldn't be expecting that field to be printed on a real print line any time soon.

The changes in the other lines of the PAREG program follow the same principals that we have outlined for all of the code that has been transitioned to RPGIV.

Wrap-Up RPGIV with Similar Forms

You now have seen how to code RPG Fixed logic cycle programs in both RPG/400 and RPGIV. From what you have learned in this chapter, you should already be able to conclude that with the expanded capabilities and minimal additional learning required for moving to RPGIV, there is no real technical reason, even for what some might call "legacy code" to stay in the RPG/400 environment for new program development..

The RPGIV Definition 'D' Specification

The RPGIV Definition specifications are the most natural innovation to hit the RPG language from its conception. Just a walk down the many faces of RPG/400 input and you can readily see that IBM was running out of places for programmers to code the most innovative new notions to the language.

The 'D' spec was long overdue when it hit the streets in 1994. Though there are no 'D' specifications required in the PAREG RPGIV version, this is the natural place to cover this most revealing RPGIV topic.

Many of us want to call it the Data Definition specification but that is not correct. IBM does not limit itself to data, though lots of data can be coded and coded logically using the "new" 'D' spec. For example, the D spec can be used to define:

✓ Data Structures and their subfields

✓ Arrays (no E Spec)
✓ Stand-alone fields
✓ Indented items to show structure
✓ Named constants
✓ Prototypes
✓ Procedure interface
✓ Prototyped parameters

After about 9 examples of the 'D' Spec in action, none of which use a 'D' continuation spec, we introduce the continuation spec in case you need it. After this, the full 'D" spec itself is examined column by column.

D Spec Example 1 Indentation

```
D Personal... DS...                    INZ

D Name...                         30
D    FirstName...           15

D* DIM operation means that this is
D* an array of 10 elements
D StrayArray...     S          5   0 DIM(10)
D StrayField...     S          5   2
```

D Spec Example 2 – DS From / To

Here is a contrasting example of an RPG/400 data structure with an RPGIV data structure using from and to positions:

```
*.. 1 ...+... 2 ...+... 3 ...+... 4 ...+... 5
IName++....EUDSExterName+...OccrLnth......
ISTRUC       DS
I...........Ext-field+....PFromTo++DField+L1M1
ISTRUC       DS
I                            1  10 PART1
I                            6  10 PART1B
I                           11  20 PART2
--

DName+++++++++++ETDSFrom+++To/L+++IDc.Keywords......
DSTRUC            DS
D Part1                    1      10
D    Part1B                6      10
D Part2                   11      20
```

As you can see, indentation makes code easier to read. The DS in 24, 25 makes D spec a data structure definition.

D Spec Example 3 DS Using Length

DS Using Length vs. From / To
```
RPG/400
*.. 1 ...+... 2 ...+... 3 ...+... 4 ...+... 5 ...+
IName++....EUDSExterName+...OccrLnth....
ISTRUC        DS...
I...........Ext-field+....PFromTo++DField+L1M1..
ISTRUC        DS
I                              1  10 PART1
I                              6  10 PART1B
I                             11  20 PART2


RPGIV-----
DName++++++++++ETDSFrom+++To/L+++IDc.Keywords...
DSTRUC              DS
D Part1                            10
D   Part1B                          5      OVERLAY(PART1:6)
D Part2                            10
```

As you can see in the example, the code is easier to change with length vs. having to calculate the from and to positions. The subfield name & start position are parms in the OVERLAY keyword. Now, let's look at a multiple occurrence data structure.

D Spec Example 4 Multiple Occurrence DS

```
RPG/400
*.. 1 ...+... 2 ...+... 3 ...+... 4 ...+... 5 ...+
IName++....EUDSExterName+...OccrLnth....
ISTRUC        DS...                    10
I...........Ext-field+....PFromTo++DField+L1M1
ISTRUC        DS
I                              1  10 PART1
I                              6  10 PART1B
I                             11  20 PART2

RPG IV
DName++++++++++ETDSFrom+++To/L+++IDc.Keywords....
DSTRUC              DS                   occurs(10)
D Part1                 1    10
D   Part1B                    6      overlay(part1:6)
D Part2                      10
```

In RPGIV as you can see, the occurs keyword on the 'D' spec is used to specify the # of occurrences. The I spec is not needed in RPGIV.

D Spec Example 5 Named Constant

```
RPG/400
*.. 1 ...+... 2 ...+... 3 ...+... 4 ...+... 5 ...+...
I...............NamedConstant++++++++C.........Fldnme.
I
I               'RESIDENCES'           C         RES
I               'UNOCCUPIED'           C         UNOC
I               '_____-C              ULINE
I               '_____'
I               'ABCDEFGHIJKLMNOPQRST-C          UC
I               'UVWXYZ'
I               'abcdefghijklmnopqrst-C          LC
I               'uvwxyz'
I               'ABCDEFGHIJKLMNOPQRST-C          VALID
I               'UVWXYZ'


RPGIV
DName++++++......c.Keywords.....
D res         C     'RESIDENCES'
D uNOC        C     'UNOCCUPIED'
D ULINE       C     '_____'
D UC          C     'ABCDEFGHIJKLMNOPQRSTUVWXYZ'
D lc          C     'abcdefghijklmnopqrstuvwxyz'
D Valid       C     'ABCDEFGHIJKLMNOPQRSTUVWXYZ'
```

D Spec Example 6 Stand-Alone Fields

```
RPG/400 (has no such mechanism)
*.. 1 ...+... 2 ...+... 3 ...+... 4 ...+... 5 ...+
IName++....EUDSExterName+............OccrLnth....
I          DS
I..........Ext-field+.............PFromTo++DField+L1M1
I
I                                 1  10 ALFA10
I                                11  15 PACK92


RPGIV
DName+++++++++++ETDSFrom+++To/L+++IDc.Keywords....
D ALFA10          S           10
D PACK92          S            9P
```

Standalone fields can be coded with with length or From / To but they cannot be coded within a DS. The 'S' in 24 designates the field as standalone field but it can also be an array or table.

When using IBM's source conversion, the program will move named constants outside of the DS definition area.

The next logical question for those who are already familiar with Tables and Arrays is "How do we do Tables & Arrays?"

D Spec Example 7 Tables & Arrays

```
E....FromfileTofile++Name++N/rN/tbLenPDSArrnamLenPDSComments+++++
* Compile-time arrays in alternating format. Both arrays have
* eight elements (three elements per record). In both arrays, the
* length of each element is 12, with 4 decimal positions
E                       ARC      3    8 12 4 ARD     12 4
Dame++++++++++ETDsFrom+++To/L+++IDc.Functions++++++++++++++++
DARC            S              12  4 DIM(8) CTDATA PERRCD(3)
D ARD           S              12  4 DIM(8) ALT(ARC)
* Pre-run item array  ARE, which is to be read from file ARRFILE
* has 250 character elements (12 elements per record). Each elem
* is five positions long. The elements are arranged in ascending
* sequence.
E   ARRFILE          ARE    12 250  5  A
Dame++++++++++ETDsFrom+++To/L+++IDc.Functions++++++++++++++++
DARRFILE         S               5    DIM(250) ASCEND PERRCD(12)
D                                     FROMFILE(ARRFILE)
*
* Run-time array.  ARI has 10 numeric elements, each 10 positions
* with zero decimal positions.
E                       ARI      55 10 0
Dame++++++++++ETDsFrom+++To/L+++IDc.Functions++++++++++++++++
D ARI           S              10  0 DIM(55) INZ(*HIVAL)
* Pre-run time table specified as combined file. TABH is written
* back to the same file from which it is read.  TABH has 250
* character entries (12 entries per record). Each entry is 5
* positions long. The entries are arranged in ascending order.
E   DISKOUT DISKOUT TABH   12 250  5  A
Dame++++++++++ETDsFrom+++To/L+++IDc.Functions++++++++++++++++
D TABH          S               5    DIM(250) CTDATA PERRCD(12)
D                                     ASCEND
*-------------------------------------------------------------
```

D Spec Example 8 Compile Time Tables

RPG/400
```
 ...+... 2 ...+... 3 ...+... 4 ...+... 5 ...+... 6 ...+
FromfileTofile++Name++N/rN/tbLenPDSArrnamLenPDSComments
E                     TABSML  1  26  1 ATABCAP  1
E
```

RPG IV
```
Dname++++++++++ETDsFrom+++To/L+++IDc.Functions++++++++++++++++
D   TABSMLETTR       S            1    DIM(26) CTDATA PERRCD(1)
D   TABCAPLTR        S            1    DIM(26) ALT(TABSMLETTR)
```

D Spec Example 9 Ext. Described DS

```
RPG/400
*.. 1 ...+... 2 ...+... 3 ...+... 4 ...+... 5 ...+..
IDSName....EUDSExterName+.............OccrLnth......
ISTRUC    E DSSTRCFILE
I...........Ext-field+.............PFromTo++DField+
I           PART1                        STPT1
I           PART1B                       STPT1B
I           PART2                        STPT2
CL0N01N02N03Factor1+++OpcdeFactor2+++ResultLenDHHiLoEq
C           *INZSR    BEGSR
C                     MOVE *ALL'5'   STPT1B
C                     ENDSR
------------
RPG IV
DName++++++++++ETDS............Keywords........
DSTRUC          E DS... EXTNAME(STRCFILE) PREFIX(ST)
D STPart1B            INZ(555)
D NSPart3         E...  EXTFLD(PART3)
```

In this example, there is an externally defined format named STRUCTUR. The Program data structure name is STRUC. Two fields in the externally defined structure are used with in D specs. STPart1B is referenced using the ST prefix per the PREFIX(ST) keyword and it is initialized to "5"s. NSPart3 is a program field which overrides the external field name referenced in the EXTFLD(PART3) keyword

D Spec Example 9 Data Area DS

```
RPG/400
*.. 1 ...+... 2 ...+... 3 ...+... 4 ...+... 5 ...+
IDSName....NODSExterName+...OccrLnth....
INXTCHK     DS
I...........Ext-field+....PFromTo++DField+L1M1
I                        1   60CHKNO1
I                        7  120CHKNO2
I            CL0N01N02N03Factor1+++OpcdeFactor2+++Result.....
C           *NAMVAR   DEFN APVALS     NXTCHKRPGIV
DName++++++++++ETDSFrom+++To/L+++IDc.Keywords
D NXTCHK       UDS                  DTAARA(APVALS)
D   CHKNO1                6S 0
D   CHKNO2                6S 0
```

*In this example, the U in col. 23 designates the DS as a data area. For Named system object data areas, specify the name in between parentheses e.g. DTAARA(APVALS. Use (*LDA) for local data area. Use (*PDA) for PIP - Program Initialization Parameters data area. As in RPG/400, you can also define Data Area Data Structure in C specs with the *DTAARA DEFINE as*

```
C...   *DTAARA   DEFINE   APVALS   NXTCHK (DS UDS)
```

For more information on arrays, data structures and constants see Chapter 9. For more information on the more advanced RPGIV notions such as Prototypes, Procedure Interfaces, and Prototyped parameters, see Chapter 26..

D Spec Keyword Continuation Line

Because RPGIV is so keyword oriented, it makes sense before we cover the columns of the 'D' spec to show the 'D' continuation spec. As you begin to code RPGIV, you will be looking for more space fro more 'D' keywords and the continuation spec provides a nice and easy vehicle for you to accomplish this.

If additional space is required for keywords, the keywords field can be continued on subsequent lines as follows:

Position 6   Continuation line must contain a 'D'
Positions 7 to 43   Continuation line must be blank
Positions 44 – 80   Continue the prior D spec keywords here
Positions 81 – 100   Comments

Figure 13-20   D Continuation Line Specification
```
*.. 1 .....4 ...+... 5 ...+... 6 ...+... 7 ...+... 8 ...+... 9 ...+... 10
D.............Keywords+++++++++++++++++++++++++++++++++Comments++++++++++++
```

'D' Spec Continued Name Line

There are a number of surprises in RPGIV even if you already think you have an idea of what it is all about. One of the surprises is the 'D' Spec Continued Name Line. Here's where this comes into play. A name that is up to 15 characters long can be specified in the Name entry of the definition specification without requiring continuation.

Any name (even one with 15 characters or fewer) can be continued on multiple lines by coding an ellipsis (...) at the end of the partial name. A name definition consists of the parts identified in Table 13-21. The format for the spec line is shown in Figure 13-22

Table 13-21 Three Parts to Name Definition

Parts 1 to 3	Description
(1) Zero or more continued name lines	Continued name lines are identified as having an ellipsis as the last non-blank character in the entry. The name must begin within positions 7 to 21 and may end anywhere up to position 77 (with an ellipsis ending in position 80). There cannot be blanks between the start of the name and the ellipsis character. If any of these conditions is not true, the line is parsed as a main definition line.
(2) One main definition line,	Contains name, definition attributes, and keywords. If a continued name line is coded, the Name entry of the main definition line may be left blank.
(3) Zero or more kwd cont lines	Self explanatory

Figure 13-22 D Continuation Line Specification
```
*.. 1 ...+... 2 ..... 7 ...+... 8 ...+... 9 ...+... 10
DContinuedName++++...++++++++++++++Comment s++++++++++++
```

D – Columns 7-21 Name

Use columns 7-21 of the D spec to supply the name for whatever you are defining. Besides the name, you may leave this position blank if the purpose is to define filler fields in data-structure subfield definitions, or an unnamed data structure in data-structure definitions.

The name can begin in any position in the space provided. Thus, indenting can be used to indicate the shape of data in data structures. For continued name lines, a name is specified in positions 7 through 80 of the continued name lines and positions 7 through 21 of the main definition line. As with the traditional definition of names, case of the characters is not significant. For an externally described subfield, a name specified here replaces the external-subfield name specified on the EXTFLD keyword.

For a prototype parameter definition, the name entry is optional. If a name is specified, the name is ignored. (A prototype parameter is a definition specification with blanks in positions 24-25 that follows a PR specification or another prototype parameter definition. See Chapter 26.

D – Column 22 External Definition

This column is used to identify a data structure or data-structure subfield as externally described. If a data structure or subfield is not being defined on this specification, then this field must be left blank.

The allowable entries for data structure are as follows

E   Identifies a data structure as externally described: subfield definitions are defined externally. If the EXTNAME keyword is not specified, positions 7-21 must contain the name of the externally described file containing the data structure definition.

Blank Program described: subfield definitions for this data structure follow this specification. The allowable entries for data structure subfields are as follows

E   Identifies a data-structure subfield as externally described. The specification of an externally described subfield is necessary only when keywords such as EXTFLD and INZ are used.

D – Column 23 Type of Data Structure

When you are defining a data structure, code the type of data structure in column 23. This entry is used to identify the type of data structure being defined. If you are not defining a data structure then this space must be left blank.

The allowable entries are as follows:

Blank The data structure being defined is not a program status or data-area data structure; or a data structure is not being defined on this specification

S   Program status data structure. Only one data structure may be designated as the program status data structure.

U   Data-area data structure. RPG IV retrieves the data area at initialization and rewrites it at end of program. If the DTAARA keyword is specified, the parameter to the DTAARA keyword is used as the name of the external data area. If the DTAARA keyword is not specified, the name in positions 7-21 is used as the name of the external data area. If a name is not specified either by the DTAARA keyword, or by positions 7-21, *LDA (the local data area) is used as the name of the external data area.

D - Columns 24-25 Definition Type

Specify the type of definition that this D statement line represents. The allowable entries are as follows:

Blank The specification defines either a data structure subfield or a parameter within a prototype or procedure interface definition.

C   The specification defines a constant. Position 25 must be blank.

DS   The specification defines a data structure.

PR   The specification defines a prototype and the return value, if any.

PI   The specification defines a procedure interface, and the return value if any.

S   The specification defines a standalone field, array or table.
Position 25 must be blank.

Definitions of data structures, prototypes, and procedure interfaces end with the first definition specification with non-blanks in positions 24-25, or with the first specification that is not a definition specification.

D Columns 26-32 (From Position)

Positions 26-32 may contain an entry only if the location of a subfield within a data structure is being defined. The allowable entries are as follows:

Blank   A blank FROM position indicates that the value in the TO/LENGTH field specifies the length of the subfield, or that a subfield is not being defined on this specification line.

nnnnnnn   Absolute starting position of the subfield within a data structure. The value specified must be from 1 to 65535 for a named data structure (and from 1 to 9999999 for an unnamed data structure), and right-justified in these positions.

Reserved Words: Reserved words may also be specified. Reserved words for the program status data structure or for a file information data structure are allowed (left-justified) in the FROM-TO/LENGTH fields (positions 26-39). These special reserved words define the location of the subfields in the data structures.

Reserved words for the program status data structure are *STATUS, *PROC, *PARM, and *ROUTINE. Reserved words for the file information data structure (INFDS) are *FILE, *RECORD, *OPCODE, *STATUS, and *ROUTINE. This information is given for completeness only. These keywords are not covered in any detail in this book.

Columns 33-39 (To Position / Length)

The allowable entries and their explanations follow:

Blank   If columns 33-39 are blank: a named constant is being defined on this specification line, or the standalone field, parameter, or subfield is being defined LIKE another field, or the standalone field, parameter, or subfield is of a type where a length is implied, or the subfield's attributes are defined elsewhere, or a data structure is being defined. The length of the data structure is the maximum value of the subfield To-Positions.

Nnnnnnn   Columns 33-39 may contain a (right-justified) numeric value, from 1 to 65535 for a named data structure (and from 1 to 9999999 for an unnamed data structure) If the From field (position 26-32) contains a numeric value, then a numeric value in this field specifies the absolute end position of the subfield within a data structure. If the From field is blank, a numeric value in this field specifies : the length of the entire data structure, or the length of the

standalone field, or the length of the parameter,
or the length of the subfield. Within the data
structure, this subfield is positioned such that its
starting   position is greater than the maximum
to-position of all previously defined
subfields in the data structure.
Padding is inserted if the subfield is defined with
Type basing pointer or procedure pointer to ensure that
The subfield is aligned properly.

+|-nnnnn   This entry is valid for standalone fields or subfields
defined using the LIKE keyword. The length of the
standalone field or subfield being defined on this
specification line is determined by adding or subtracting
the value entered in these positions to the length of the
field specified as the parameter to the LIKE keyword.

Reserved Words : Reserved words may also be specified in these columns. If columns 26-32 are used to enter special reserved words, this field becomes an extension of the previous one, creating one large field (positions 26-39). This allows for reserved words, with names longer than 7 characters in length, to extend into this field. See Columns 26-32 (From Position), 'Reserved Words' above.

D - Column 40 (Internal Data Type)

This entry allows you to specify how a standalone field, parameter, or data-structure subfield is stored internally. This entry pertains strictly to the internal representation of the data item being defined, regardless of how the data item is stored externally on disk if it is stored on disk or tape or other media. To define variable-length character, graphic, and UCS-2 formats, you must specify the keyword VARYING to have it take effect; otherwise, the format will be fixed length. The allowable entries and explanations are as follows:

Blank When the LIKE keyword is not specified: If the decimal
positions entry is blank, then the item is defined as character. If the decimal positions entry is not blank, then the item is defined as packed numeric if it is a standalone field or parameter; or as zoned numeric if it is a subfield.

Note: The entry must be blank when the LIKE keyword is specified.

A	Character (Fixed or Variable-length format)
B	Numeric (Binary format)
C	UCS-2 (Fixed or Variable-length format)
D	Date
F	Numeric (Float format)
G	Graphic (Fixed or Variable-length format)
I	Numeric (Integer format)
N	Character (Indicator format)	
O	Object
P	Numeric (Packed decimal format)
S	Numeric (Zoned format)

T	Time
U	Numeric (Unsigned format)
Z	Timestamp
*	Basing pointer or procedure pointer.

Note: The RPG/400 datatypes are similar to those above.

D -- Columns 41-42 (Decimal Positions)

Use Columns 41-42 to indicate the number of decimal positions in a numeric subfield or standalone field. If the field is non-float numeric, there must always be an entry in these positions. If there are no decimal positions enter a zero (0) in position 42. For example, an integer or unsigned field (type I or U in position 40) requires a zero for this entry.

The allowable entries and explanations are as follows:

Blank The value is not numeric (unless it is a float field) or has been defined with the   LIKE keyword.
0-30   Decimal positions: the number of positions to the right of the decimal in a numeric field. This entry can only be supplied in combination with the TO/Length field. If the TO/Length field is blank, the value of this entry is defined somewhere else in the program (for example, through an externally described data base file).

D -- Column 43 Reserved for Future Use

D -- Columns 44-80 (Keywords)

Columns 44 to 80 are provided for definition specification keywords. Keywords are used to describe and define data and its attributes. This area is used to specify any keywords necessary to fully define the field. If you don't have enough room for all the keywords you need, use the continuation form which was described at the beginning of this section.

D -- Columns 81-100 Optional Comments

D Specification Keywords.

From column 7 to 42 the D specification provides a standard means of defining data and other items to the RPGIV compiler. However, there are lots more options that the D specification handles besides what can be specified within the 7 – 42 column boundaries. As with the other RPGIV specifications, these other items are enabled through the use of keywords in positions 44 – 80 of the D spec. Table 13-23 provides a look at these powerful keywords as well as an explanation as to what they are all about.

Table 13-23 D Specification Keywords & Parameters

ALIGN	The ALIGN keyword is used to align float, integer, and unsigned subfields. When ALIGN is specified, 2-byte subfields are aligned on a 2-byte boundary, 4-byte subfields are aligned on a 4-byte boundary and 8-byte subfields are aligned on an 8-byte boundary. Alignment may be desired to improve performance when accessing float, integer, or unsigned subfields.
ALT	**(array_name)** The ALT keyword is used to indicate that the compile-time or pre-runtime array or table is in alternating format.

ALTSEQ	(*NONE) When the ALTSEQ(*NONE) keyword is specified, the alternate collating sequence will not be used for comparisons involving this field, even when the ALTSEQ keyword is specified on the control specification.
ASCEND	The ASCEND keyword is used to describe the sequence of the data in arrays, tables, or prototyped parameters
BASED	(basing_pointer_name) When the BASED keyword is specified for a data structure or standalone field, a basing pointer is created using the name specified as the keyword parameter. This basing pointer holds the address (storage location) of the based data structure or standalone field being defined. In other words, the name specified in positions 7-21 is used to refer to the data stored at the location contained in the basing pointer.
CCSID	(number | *DFT) This keyword sets the CCSID for graphic and UCS-2 definitions. The number must be an integer between 0 and 65535. It must be a valid graphic or UCS-2 CCSID value.
CLASS	(*JAVA:class-name) This keyword indicates the class for an object definition. Class-name must be a constant character value
CONST	{(constant)} The CONST keyword is used to specify the value of a named constant or to indicate that a parameter passed by reference is read-only.
CTDATA	The CTDATA keyword indicates that the array or table is loaded using compile-time data. The data is specified at the end of the program following the ** or **CTDATA(array/table name) specification.
DATFMT	(format{separator}) The DATFMT keyword specifies the internal date format, and optionally the separator character for a Date; standalone field; data-structure subfield; prototyped parameter; or return value on a prototype or procedure-interface definition
DESCEND	The DESCEND keyword is used to describe the sequence of the data in arrays, tables, or prototyped parameters
DIM	(numeric_constant) The DIM (Dimension) keyword defines the number of elements in an array; a table; a prototyped parameter; or a return value on a prototype or procedure-interface definition. The numeric constant must have zero (0) decimal positions. It can be a literal, a named constant or a built-in function.
DTAARA	{(data_area_name)} The DTAARA keyword is used to associate a standalone field, data structure, data-structure subfield or data-area data structure with an external data area. You can create three kinds of data areas: (1) *CHAR Character, (2) *DEC Numeric, and (3) *LGL Logical. You can also create a DDM data area (type *DDM) that points to a data area on a remote system.
EXPORT	{(external_name)} The EXPORT keyword allows a globally defined data structure or standalone field defined within a module to be used by another module in the program. The storage for the data item is allocated in the module containing the EXPORT definition. The external_name parameter, if specified, must be a character literal or constant. The EXPORT keyword on the definition specification is used to export data items and cannot be used to export procedure names. To export a procedure name, use the EXPORT keyword on the procedure specification.
EXTFLD	(field_name) The EXTFLD keyword is used to rename a subfield in an externally described data structure. Enter the external name of the subfield as the parameter to the EXTFLD keyword, and specify the name to be used in the program in the Name field (positions 7-21).
EXTFMT	(code) The EXTFMT keyword is used to specify the external data type for compile-time and prerun-time numeric arrays and tables. The external data type is the format of the data in the records in the file. This entry has no effect on the format used for internal processing (internal data type) of the array or table in the program. The values specified for EXTFMT will apply

	to the files identified in both the TOFILE and FROMFILE keywords, even if the specified names are different. The possible values for the parameter are: **B** The data for the array or table is in binary format. **C** The data for the array or table is in UCS-2 format. **I** The data for the array or table is in integer format. **L** The data for a numeric array or table element has a preceding (left) plus or minus sign. **R** The data for a numeric array or table element has a following (right) plus or minus sign. **P** The data for the array or table is in packed decimal format. **S** The data for the array / table is in zoned decimal format. **U** The data for the array or table is in unsigned format. **F** The data for the array or table is in float numeric format.
EXTNAME	**(file_name{:format_name})** Use the EXTNAME keyword to specify the name of the file which contains the field descriptions used as the subfield description for the data structure being defined. The file_name parameter is required. Optionally a format name may be specified to direct the compiler to a specific format within a file. If format_name parameter is not specified the first record format is used. If the data structure definition contains an E in position 22, and the EXTNAME keyword is not specified, the name specified in positions 7-21 is used
EXTPGM	**(name)** Use the EXTPGM keyword to indicate the external name of the program whose prototype is being defined.
EXTPROC	**({*CL|*CWIDEN|*CNOWIDEN|{*JAVA:class-name:}}name)** There are a number of formats as noted that can be used with this keyword. The EXTPROC keyword indicates the external name of the procedure whose prototype is being defined.
FROMFILE	**(file_name)** Use the FROMFILE keyword to specify the input data file for the prerun-time array or table.. The FROMFILE keyword must be specified for every prerun-time array or table defined/used in the program.
IMPORT	**{(external_name)}** Use the IMPORT keyword to specify that storage for the data item being defined is allocated in another module, but may be accessed in this module.
INZ	**{(initial value)}** The INZ keyword initializes the standalone field, data structure, |data-structure subfield, or object to the default value for its data type or, |optionally, to the constant specified in parentheses.
LIKE	**(name)** Use the LIKE keyword to define an item like an existing |one. When you specify the LIKE keyword, the item you are defining takes on the length and the data format of the item specified as the parameter. You may define standalone fields, prototypes, parameters, and data-structure subfields using this keyword.
LIKEDS	**(data_structure_name)** Use the LIKEDS keyword to define a data structure, prototyped return value, or prototyped parameter like another data structure. The subfields of the new item will be identical to the subfields of the other data structure.
NOOPT	The NOOPT keyword indicates that no optimization is to be performed on the standalone field, parameter or data structure for which this keyword is specified. Specifying NOOPT ensures that the content of the data item is the latest assigned value. This may be necessary for those fields whose values are used in exception handling.

OCCURS	(numeric_constant) Use the OCCURS keyword to specify (in the num constant parm) the number of occurrences of a multiple-occurrence data structure.
OPDESC	The OPDESC keyword specifies that operational descriptors are to be passed with the parameters that are defined within a prototype.
OPTIONS	(*NOPASS *OMIT *VARSIZE *STRING *RIGHTADJ) The OPTIONS keyword is used to specify one or more parameter passing options: (1) Whether a parameter must be passed (2) Whether the special value *OMIT can be passed for the parameter passed by reference. (3) Whether a parameter that is passed by reference can be shorter in length than is specified in the prototype. (4) Whether the called program or procedure is expecting a pointer to a null-terminated string, allowing you to specify a character expression as the passed parameter. The single parameter passed can have different values.
OPTIONS	(*NOPASS) Use this option so that the called program or procedure will simply function as if the parameter list did not include that parameter.
OPTIONS	(*OMIT) Use this to allow the value *OMIT for that parameter. *OMIT is only allowed for CONST parameters and parameters which are passed by reference
OPTIONS	(*VARSIZE) Use this for parameters passed by reference that have a character, graphic, or UCS-2 data type, or that represent an array of any type.
OPTIONS	(*STRING) Use this for a basing pointer parameter passed by value or by constant-reference. You may either pass a pointer or a character expression.
OPTIONS	(*RIGHTADJ) Use this for a CONST or VALUE parameter in a function prototype. In this case, the character, graphic, or UCS-2 parameter value is right adjusted.
OVERLAY	(name{:pos | *NEXT) Use the OVERLAY keyword to overlay the storage of one subfield with that of another subfield, or with that of the data structure itself. This keyword is allowed only for data structure subfields. The Name-entry subfield overlays the storage specified by the name parameter at the position specified by the pos parameter. If pos is not specified, it defaults to 1.
PACKEVEN	Use the PACKEVEN keyword to indicate that the packed field or array has an even number of digits. The keyword is only valid for packed program-described data-structure subfields defined using FROM/TO positions.
PERRCD	(numeric_constant) Use the PERRCD keyword to specify the number of elements provided per record for a compile-time or a prerun-time array or table.
PREFIX	(prefix{:nbr_of_char_replaced}) Use the PREFIX keyword to change the field names of all of the fields from a particular external data structure so there is no conflict with fields already coming in to the program. Specify a character string or character literal, which is to be prefixed to the subfield names of the externally described data structure being defined. In addition, you can optionally specify a numeric value to indicate the number of characters, if any, at the beginning of the existing name to be replaced.
PROCPTR	The PROCPTR keyword defines an item as a procedure pointer. The internal Data-Type field (position 40) must contain a *.
QUALIFIED	Use the **QUALIFIED** keyword to specify that the subfields of a data structure will be accessed by specifying the data structure name followed by a period and the subfield name.
STATIC	Use the STATIC keyword to specify that a local variable is stored in static storage and thereby hold its value across calls to the procedure in which it is defined or to specify that a Java method is defined as a static method.

`TIMFMT`	`(format{separator})` Use the TIMFMT keyword to specify an internal time format, and optionally the time separator, for type Time: standalone field; data-structure subfield; prototyped parameter; or return value on a prototype or procedure-interface definition.
TOFILE	`(file_name)` Use the TOFILE keyword to specify a target file to which a prerun-time or compile-time array or table is to be written.
VALUE	Use the VALUE keyword to indicate that the parameter is passed by value rather than by reference. Parameters can be passed by value when the procedure they are associated with are called using a procedure call.
VARYING	Use the VARYING keyword to indicate that a character, graphic, or UCS-2 field, defined on the definition specifications, should have a variable-length format. If this keyword is not specified for character, graphic, or UCS-2 fields, they are defined as fixed length.

Built-In Functions / Pointers

A host of built-in functions and other facilities have been introduced with RPGIV. Chapter 15 explores these in substantially more detail . However, in 1994 when all of this came out, there was another facility that was made available for the first time in an RPG language – pointers.

Address pointers are the mainstay of low-level languages such as C and they have slowly been walking forward into higher level languages. With the first RPGIV edition, pointers stared the RPG programmer right in the face. Of course, nobody really had to use them.

There were not a whole lot of them at first and their use was packaged inside of BIFS. The following are a sample of three BIFS using pointers:

```
%ADDR     gets address of variable

%ELEM     gets # of elements in array

%SIZE     gets length of variable

Etc.
```

Date & Time Operations

Before RPGIV RPG programmers has to rough it whenever trying to calculate dates or times or get durations by subtracting dates. The Date and time operations support introduced with RPGIV has been well heralded and they have simplified the date and time mission substantially.

Three new data types are now supported. These are as follows:

- ✓ T = Time
- ✓ D = Date
- ✓ Z = Timestamp

As an example of the power of these operations, using one of the new operations called "add duration," let's calculate a future date by adding a duration to a date. In this case we advance a due date by xx years and yy months:

```
C        ADDDUR      xx:*Years      DueDate
C        ADDDUR      yy:*Months     DueDate
------
```

In this next example, let's set the loan date as being earlier than the due date.

C DueDAte SUBDUR xx:*Y LOANDate

Date, time and timestamp values have been stored by programmers for years as numeric variables. Sometimes the field designers were astute enough to also include separate fields for year, month, and day values, and perhaps a century field for date. For time, of course, it is sometimes nice to have hours, minutes and seconds segregated for certain operations.

Though desirable, sometimes our designer just did not do the job and we have to work with six- or eight-digit numeric fields holding some form of a date. Of course, there are other variants making the matter even more complex, such as seven-digit fields with six digits with a century character.

Of course, nothing says that the date designer had to use numeric data types. Lots of files out there us character field versions of date. Some have separators; some no separators; some leading zeroes; some with suppressed zeros. With all of the different US and international ways of formatting a date, working with dates of any format has been an exercise in pot luck.

So, how do you handle dates? The answer always has been, "It depends." Even after date data types were permitted in the database, they were not usable in RPG/400. So, when looking at a date field, you have to ask yourself, "Is it a real date, or a numeric or character field pretending to be a date?"

The notion of a real date, time, or timestamp value comes about because the AS/400 system long ago decided to support these data types. But, RPG did not. Now, RPGIV supports just about any data type that is available by storing real dates etc. as real dates etc. The compiler worries about formatting the date at a later time.

In an RPGIV program then, a real date is a program or a file variable that is actually defined as a date variable. It is easy to do this with a standalone field definition with an internal data type of d as shown below:

d TheDate   s   d

With no value provided for this field, it will default to 0001-01-01, or the first day of the first month of the first year. Just as when you define a date variable to the database, there is no need to define a length declaration or say whether the date is numeric or character. That's because the system knows what a real date, a real time, or a real timestamp actually is. There are three different variable types – one for each.

A date, time, or timestamp value, regardless of format, is stored by the IBM i on Power Systemsn a raw binary manner that only the operating system can access and manipulate. In an RPG IV program, that data is accessed through variables, using a specified format.

Thus, date, time, and timestamp fields exist in RPGIV independent of their format. The format is applied after the fact based on defaults or explicit use of date type symbols. Many of the available date and time formats are given in the two charts below. Note in the charts that all of these options include separator characters.
Include chart

DATFMT OPTIONS

Name	Description	Format	Sep	Len	Example
*MDY	Month/Day/Year	mm/dd/yy	/-.,&	8	1/15/06
*DMY	Day/Month/Year	Dd/mm/yy	/-.,&	8	15/01/06
*YMD	Year/Month/Day	Yy/mm/dd	/-.,&	8	06/01/15
*JUL	Julian	Yy/ddd	/-.,&	6	06/015
*ISO	International Standards org.	yyyy-mm-dd	-	10	2006-01-15
*USA	IBM USA Standard	mm/dd/yyyy	/	10	01/15/2006
*EUR	IBM European Standard	dd.mm.yyyy	.	10	15.01.2006
*jis	Japanese Industrial Lang	yyyy-mm-dd	-	10	2006-01-15

TIMFMT Options

Name	Description	Format	Sep	Len	Example
*HMS	Hours:Minutes:Seconds	hh:mm:ss	:.,&	8	14:00:00
*ISO	Internat. Stds. Org.	yyyy.mm.dd	.	8	14.00.00
*USA	IBM USA Std.	hh:mm A.M.	:	8	02:00
*EUR	IBM European Standard	hh.mm.ss	.	8	14.00.00
*JIS	Jaoanese Ind. Standard	hh:mm:ss	:	8	14:00

Let's work on our date example again. You can create the date field with a default value as follows:

```
D TheDate…   s…   d…  inz(d'2006-08-01')
```

Hopefully you immediately see the three items of note in this example. First, you must precede the literal value in the initialization parameter with a 'd' for date data type and second, you must wrap the literal in single quotes. This is also true for time (t) and timestamp (z) values and for comparing such values in conditional statements as shown below:

```
If TheDate = d'2007-08-01' ;
 // insert your code
endif ;
```

Third, the format used to initialize the date is *ISO: the default DATFMT (date format) for date literals is also *ISO. From the tables above, you can see a number of the other options.

RPG is a little finicky if you use date formats but you use the wrong date format. For example, what if instead of year first, you specify the date with the month first as in the following:

d TheDate... s...   d... inz(d'05/01/2004')

The RPGIV compiler will not like this because you have not used the default *ISO format. The format you used, as you can see in the charts is *USA> So, RPG burps and gives you an RNF0305 error, which means that "the date literal is not valid," You can fix this by adding an H-spec in your program for DATFMT or add the DATFMT keyword to an existing H specification:

H   DATFMT(*USA)

Now all the date fields in your program require literals to be in the *USA format. Whatever format you use, you must be consistent throughout your program.

There are lots more permutations of these examples that you will probably run into in your date activities. To cover them all would take way too much space in this book. But, this is enough to get you going. Now, let's look at a few more date / time / timestamp operations before showing a few more examples.

Date and Time Op-Codes

ADDDUR   Adds the duration in factor 2 to factor1 or result field creating a new date, time, or timestamp.

SUBDUR   Subtracts duration - Factor2 from Factor1

EXTRCT   Extracts requested component of a date, time, or timestamp

TEST   Tests if a field contains a valid date, time, or timestamp

Date Example 1 – Four Operations

```
C...MyBdate     adddur     21:*Y          Drinkdate
C*
C...NewYears    subdur     7:*d           Christmas
C*
C...            Extrct     MyBdate:*y     Year_born
C*
C...*ISO        TEST(D)                   ISODATE...     40
```

As you can see, duration codes may be used in Factor 2 of the ADDDUR, EXTRCT, or SUBDUR operations, and in the result field for SUBDUR. Let's take a look at what these codes mean:

Date/Time Duration Codes

- ✓ *YEARS or *Y
- ✓ *MONTHS or *M
- ✓ *DAYS or *D
- ✓ *HOURS or *H
- ✓ *MINUTES or *MN
- ✓ *SECONDS or *S
- ✓ *MSECONDS or *MS

Duration codes may be used in Factor 2 of the ADDDUR, EXTRCT, or SUBDUR operations, and in the result field for SUBDUR

Date Example 2 OP-CODES In Use

```
C...Todaydate      adddur 10:*D            DUEDate
C*
C...PURDATE        ADDDUR WARTYYRS:*Y      EndWarrnty
C*
C...Todaydate      ADDDUR 3:*MOnths        OVR90Date
C*
C...TODAYDATE      SUBDUR DUEDATE          NUMMONTHS:*M
C...
C...todayDate      SUBDUR DATOFBIRTH       AGE:*Y
C*
C...PAYMNTDATE     SUBDUR TODAYDATE        DAYSOVRDUE:*D
C*
C...               Extrct YOURBDate:*y     YOURYEAR
C...               EXTRCT GRAD_date        Year
C...               EXTrct DueDate          Month
C*
C...      TEST                  NEWDATE...      61
C...*YMD       TEST(D)               DATEFLD...      40
```

RPGIV is fairly flexible in providing tools to deal with dates of many origins. For example, an extender of D, T, or Z is used to test a non-D, T, or Z field type to determine whether it contains a valid date of the type in Factor 1. But, where do you specify these?

Where to specify D, T, Z Formats?

H Spec

- ✓ Specifies default for internal fields/literals
- ✓ Defaults to *ISO

F Spec

- ✓ Defaults for date/time in pgm described files
- ✓ If not specified, Use H Spec as default

I & O Specs
- ✓ Overrides F spec for pgm described fields

D Specs

- ✓ Overrides H spec
- ✓ INZ or CONST must use H spec format

C Specs

- ✓ Used in Factor 1 for certain op-codes
- ✓ TEST, MOVE, etc.

Before we finish this chapter, let's look at a few more Date operation examples:

Date Example 3 More Operations

```
*.. 1 ...+... 2 ...+... 3 ...+... 4 ...+... 5 ...+... 6 ...+... 7
HDATEDIT(*DMY) DATFMT(*YMD) TIMFMT(*HMS)
DName+++++++++++ETDSFrom+++To/L+++IDc.Keywords.................
DDate             S              D    DATFMT(*MDY)INZ(D'99 03 31')
DtIME             s              T    TIMFMT(*HMS)INZ(D'15 02 00')
D numdatfld       S              6  0INZ(870623)
D alphdatfld      S              6   INZ('870623')
D DateMarry       S              D    DATFMT(*USA)
D DATElost        S              D    DATFMT(*ISO)
D TimeLost        S              T    TIMFMT(*USA)
D hold                           6  0
CL0N01Factor1+++++++Opcode(E)+Factor2+++++++Result+++++
C                     move       date          datelost
C* datelost is now = to '1999-03-31'
C                     move       time          timelost
C* timelost is now = to '03:02 PM'
C    *YMD             MOVE       numdatfld     datemarry
C* datemarry is now = to '06/23/1987'
C                     move       alphdatfld    hold
C    *YMD             move(d)    hold          date
C* date is now = to '06/23/1987'  (move could not
C* be done directly,
C* Would have needed an 8 char date field with
C* separators
C    *HMS             MOVE       '05 30 00'    Timelost
C* Timelost now = '05:30 AM'
```

Chapter Summary

RPGIV is not just RPG/400 with a better coding sheet design. It's lots more than that and in this chapter we examined some of the features that make it one of the best languages of today. It works hand in glove with ILE, the latest "native" runtime environment for programs on the IBM i on Power Systems. Way back in OS/400 Version 2 Release 3, IBM introduced this new program model that in many ways essentially changed the way the operating system works with languages

To take advantage of the functionality built into the ILE, however, IBM had a lot of work to do. In 1994, the RPGIV compiler facilities were built to address the need for a full ILE implementation in RPG. The result was the new RPG IV compiler introduced first in 1994 / 1995.

The new RPGIV defined a new look for all of RPG's specifications. The specs were revitalized and made much better. Needed changes to all forms and the elimination of the E and L specs, IBM also introduced a new form known as the definition specification -- the 'D' spec.

The 'D' spec helped make the language much easier to learn and much more similar to other languages. Programmers from other systems and other languages on the AS/400 are now able to learn RPG coding without having to learn the RPG cycle and many of the other RPG nuances that you have just learned in the prior 11 chapters.

IBM also introduced a new tool, the CVTRPGSRC command which converts RPG/400 to RPGIV in the most natural way. In other words, the flavor of the original program is preserved and the programmer can recognize the RPGIV version of the code quite readily without having to do substantial decoding.

The Header spec has been changed to include a free format notion that is all keyword driven. The L and E specs were eliminated. Input and output were changed to deal with longer field names. Calculations were also stretched as well as providing for the EVAL statement which is an almost extended version of a free-form RPG. BIFS were added in a subsequent release and more and more BIFS are added each new release of the language.

The most dramatic change to RPGIV is the D specification. It is the most natural innovation to hit the RPG language from its conception which provides the following:

- ✓ Standalone fields
- ✓ Named constants
- ✓ Data structures and their subfields
- ✓ Prototypes
- ✓ Procedure interface
- ✓ Prototyped parameters

At the time of its introduction another of the most heralded facilities in RPGIV were Date operations in which dates and time durations, times and dates could be calculated almost as easily as regular numeric values.

Key Chapter Terms

%ADDR	DDS	OPDESC
%ELEM	DEBUG	OPEN
%PADDR	DEC	Operation code
%SIZE	Decimal Pos	Operation extender
%TRIM	Decoding	OPM
%TRIML	DEFINE	OPTIONS
%TRIMR	DEFN	OVERLAY
*DMY	DESCEND	PACKEVEN
*FILE	DIM	Pad
*HIVAL	DIV	PARM
*HMS	DO	PERRCD
*INZSR	DOU	PGMNAME
*ISO	DOW	PIP
*JUL	DSPLY	Pointers
*LDA	DTAARA	PREFIX
*MDY	Duration	Procedural op-codes
*NAMVAR	Duration codes	Procedure interface
*OFF	Dynamic program call	PROCPTR
*OPCODE	ELSE	Prototyped parameters
*PDA	ENDSR	Prototyped procedures
*RECORD	EPM	PRTCTL
*ROUTINE	EVAL	Purists, RPG
*STATUS	EXCEPT	QRPGLESRC
*USA	EXCPT	QRPGSRC
*Years	Expanded source	QUALIFIED
*YMD	EXPORT	READPE
'D' spec	Ext. Described DS	REDPE
Activation groups	Extended functions	REL
ADDDUR	Extended pgm env.	Renamed op-codes
ALIGN	EXTFLD	Result Field
ALT	EXTFMT	RETRN
ALTSEQ	EXTNAME	RETURN
ASCEND	EXTPGM	SELEC
BASED	EXTPROC	SELECT

BEGSR	EXTRCT	SETOF
BIF	Factor 2	SETOFF
BITOF, 23	Factor 1	Spaghetti code
BITOFF, 23	From position	Stand-alone fields
Block struc languages	FROMFILE	STATIC
Bound procedure, 10	Half adjust	SUBDUR
CALL	IMPORT	Subprocedures
CALLB	Indented calcs	SUBST
CCSID	ILE	TEST
CHECK	Internal data type	TIMFMT
CHECKR	INZ	TOFILE
CHEKR	LIKE	UDATE
CISC	LIKEDS	UNLCK
CLASS	LOKUP	UNLOCK
COMIT	LOOKUP	UPDAT
COMMIT	Module	UPDATE
Compiler package	MOVEL	USROPN
Conditioning indicators	Multiple Occ. DS	VALUE
CONST	Named constant	VARYING
Control specification	NEXT	Verbosity
CTDATA	NOOPT	WHENXX
CVTRPGSRC	OCCUR	WHXX
Data Structure	OCCURS	WRITE
Date & Time Ops	OF indicator	WRITE-only language
Date type symbols	OFLIND	

Review Questions

1. Is RPGIV merely another RPG/400 with a better coding sheet design? Why?

2. Though we refer to RPG/400 as the version of native RPGIII that runs on the IBM i on Power Systemsi, how does IBM see the term RPG/400?

3. What is the difference between ILE RPG and RPGIV?

4. Which specifications were dropped for RPGIV?

5. Which specifications were added for RPGIV?

6. Does RPG still have a cycle and support for internally described data elements? Explain?

7. What came before ILE?

8. Has RPGIV been well accepted in its lifetime?

9. What is the means that an RPG programmer would use to convert their RPG/400 programs into RPGIV?

10. If the IBM command is used to convert to RPGIV, does the resultant code use any of the more advanced RPG facilities such as the EVAL statement, BIFs, or Free-Form RPG?

11. Describe the parameters of the IBM source conversion tool and how to set it up for a conversion?

12. The format lines inserted by the tool are not precise. Explain?

13. How is debug implemented in RPG/400 and RPGIV?

14. Many columnar values in File Descriptions (FD) are converted to columnar values in RPGIV FDs. Which former columnar value used in PAREG requires a keyword? Why?

15. Where is the File Add column in RPGIV?

16. Other than column shifts and enlargements, and the elimination of the multiple faces, there are no substantive changes to normal program described or externally described Input specs in RPGIV? Comment?

17. What is the most significant change on the Calculation Specification for RPGIV?

18. What are the two most significant changes to operation codes? (Hint – one column eliminated)

19. Has there been a change to the maximum field size in RPGIV as shown in the calc spec.

20. What are the significant changes to RPGIV output?

21. What is the most natural innovation to hit the RPG language from its conception?

22. List six things that can be defined in RPGIV using the new D specification?

23. What is the purpose of the D specification continuation line?

24. What are the three parts to a name definition in RPGIV?

25. Why is the name area in the D specification 15 spaces in length?

26. What column of the D specification is used to designate a data structure or subfield as externally described? What entry is used?

27. What types of data structures can be specified on the D specification and what entries are possible?

28. What is the definition type entry (columns 24-25) of the D spec used for in RPGIV?

29. What is the purpose of the reserved words area in the D specification?

30. What are the possible internal data types in RPGIV and what does this mean?

31. What are columns 44 – 80 of the D specification used for?

32. Pick five D spec keywords and explain their purpose?

Chapter 14   RPG (/400) Operations

How RPG Gets Things Done!

In RPG/400 and RPGIV, if you are not fixed on the fixed cycle, you will quickly see that almost all of the action occurs in the calculations (calc) specifications. Moreover, the heart of the CALC spec as you learned earlier in this book is the operation area in which you place the specific op-code to tell RPG which operation to conduct on your behalf.

In Chapter 9 we examined the CALC spec and how it is formatted for fill-in the blank operations. In this chapter, we take a real close look at those operations in their RPG/400 format. Better than 90% of these operations are also usable with RPGIV. We'll get to RPGIV calculations are covered in Chapter 15..

There are many different operations available and they are implemented via the codes that a programmer can specify in the op-code column (28 in RPG/400 and 26 in RPGIV) of the CALC form. RPG operations can be classified in a number of ways. The various op-code charts and tables shown in this chapter starting with Figure 14-1 provide a complete picture of all of the operations available in RPG and RPGIV.

The first chart, shown in Figure 14-1 is a summary of all operations by type and it shows the classification and a number of specific the op code examples that are available in each classification.

This chapter breaks PAREG tutorial-like stride temporarily to present the complete set of RPG/400 operations that you can deploy in calculation specifications. It covers major language elements in RPG/400 to familiarize the student with the full capabilities of the RPG/400 language.

It would be impossible to teach all of this with examples and text in an introductory book. By showing all of the RPG/400 operations in this chapter, which by default is over 90% of the RPGIV operations developed by IBM in this chapter, it might seem like next chapter (RPGIV Operations) might be unnecessary but it is not. This chapter is simply the operations warmup. We resume the case study work in RPG & RPGIV in Chapter 23 with PAREG2 and Chapter 24 with PAREG3..

As you will see, in most cases, the operations for RPG/400 are the same in RPGIV, other than the expanded columns in RPGIV and of course the truly free form operations released between 1994 and today.

So, to repeat somewhat, the intent of this chapter is to demonstrate the programming capabilities of the language by examining the operations that are found in both modern forms of the RPG language – RPG/400 and RPGIV. By doing this, you can see and learn operations in one form (RPG/400 in this chapter) and unless otherwise noted, the same operation is available in just about the same form in RPGIV. In other words, when the reader learns an operation in RPG/400, the corresponding RPGIV operation is understandable by default.

You are about to see that in this chapter, I have taken every RPG operation and have condensed its explanation into something that is germane and understandable without losing its meaning in simplicity. In fact, the RPG charts in this chapter are so comprehensive that they can be used as a reference for how to code operations without having to understand all of the intricacies and options that are provided in IBM's four RPG manuals.

When you become an RPG programmer instead of an RPG learner, because of these operation charts and other unique function charts, this book will continue to provide value to you to quickly recap your learning. However, when you are moving deeper into the language, you will be pleased that IBM's entire library for the AS/400 is included on-line in reference form.

To get to the IBM RPG manuals go to www.IBM i.ibm.com and look for the RPG/400 and RPGIV reference and/or user manuals. They're free for the downloading.

With this book and IBM's manuals, you have all the tools you need to become and to serve as an effective RPG programmer.   For those enjoying the tutorial nature of this book, please note that the PAREG tutorial example set breaks for some intensive training on RPG topics but continues in Chapter 23. In the next set of chapters we are stopping to take a by-example look at a number of major RPG operations.

After several chapters showing detailed examples of arrays, data structures, structured programming, strings, interactive programming, subfile progrmmaing and database programming, you will be well prepared to move on to tutorial mode again in Chapters 23 & 24.

You will find that the PAREG program that we have been working with so far in this book goes through many metamorphoses to be able to provide all of its function without the use of the RPG fixed logic cycle – no level time and no MR match fields. But, there is lots to learn first!

RPG Operations

To introduce you to the plethora of operations in RPG, let's first take a look at Table 14-1. This table provides a quick summary of the types of operations that you will find in RPG along with a number of representative operations as shown by their op-codes. The detail for these types of operations is provided in the subsequent tables.

Basic Operations - Including Arithmetic

It can be readily argued that COBOL is the most English-like language ever devised. With its lengthy field names, data attributes are able to be naturally explained well within the confines of the variable name itself. As you examine the list of operations in 14-1, you can see that the five character operation names available in RPG/400, though reasonably easy to understand are no match for COBOL.

RPG operations are logical and they are somewhat English-like. Once read and understood, they are difficult to forget.

These op-codes are very unlike the computer science languages operations available in languages such as C. Moreover, it can be argued that despite their conciseness, the RPG operations resemble COBOL, the Common **Business** Oriented Language more than any other language.

Table 14-1 Types of Operations & Op-Codes

Types Of Operations	Representative Op- Codes
Basic Operations	ADD– add two numbers BEGSR– begin a subroutine MULT-- multiply two numbers
Compare & Branch Operations / Subroutines	GOTO -- Go to EXSR – Execute a subroutine CABXX -- Compare and branch if EQ,GT…. .
Data Manipulation Operations	CLEAR– houseclean a structure BITON– Turn bits on RESET– Reset a structure
Database & Device File Operations	READ—read a record REDPE– read a prior equal record SETLL-- set file index position EXFMT– write then read a screen
Data Structure, Table, Array, String Operations	LOKUP—find item in table/array MOVEA– move data to-from array

Program Control Operations	DUMP—take a dump ACQ-- acquire a device in program
Structured Operations	DOWXX—do while EQ, GT etc. SELEC-- Select ITER—Repeat Do loop
RPGIV Free Form Syntax Calculation spec	Eval—evaluate expression EvalR-evaluate expression, rt adjust
RPGIV Free Form Operations	/FREE compiler directive signifies free form RPGIV is coming /END-FREE self explanatory

Clearly RPG is much more concise and thus much more precise than COBOL, PL/1 and any other business language. In fact, compared to mostly all languages, RPG is the most concise, rendering many less statements per equivalent program than all of the other languages du jour. There is no room for verbosity in RPG operations. The language is built to solve business problems. In earlier chapters we demonstrated the utility of RPG for basic input and output and report writing facilities. Now, let us move from the overview in Table 14-1 to a look at a number of the most elemental operations available in the RPG language.

For your review, the columns of the CALC spec are as follows:

Column 6	C for calc spec
Columns 7- 17	Level and detail conditioning indicators
Column 18- 27	Factor 1
Column 28- 32	Operation Code
Column 33- 42	Factor 2
Column 43- 48	Result Field
Column 49- 53	Field Length- 3, Decimals-1, Op Extender-1
Column 54- 58	HI LO EQ Resulting Indicators

As you can see in Table 14-2, RPG Basic Operations, the operation is shown on the left, followed by the provided function on the right.   The first area within the provided function is a one phrase shortened synopsis of the operation. This is then followed by a detailed description of the function and purpose of the operation and how it needs to be coded in RPG/400 to achieve the desired result. To prepare you better for the operations journey you are about to take, we begin this tour with a concise definition of the calculation specifications for RPG/400. The operation codes that we explain in the many tables that follow place the operation in column 28 of the calc spec.

Table 14-2 RPG Basic Operations

Operation	Provided Function
ADD	Add two factors to produce a result. The ADD operation adds Factor 1 to Factor 2 and places the sum in the Result field. If Factor 1 is not specified, the contents of Factor 2 are added to the Result field and the sum is placed in the Result field. Factor 1 and Factor 2 and the Result field must be defined as numeric.
CHAIN	Random Retrieval from a File. The CHAIN is a very powerful operation in RPG and is used in most programs for record retrieval by relative record # or by key. The operation retrieves a record from a full procedural file (F in position RPG/400 position 16) of the file description specifications), and places the data from the record into the input fields. The search argument is provided in Factor 1. It must contain the key or the relative record number used to retrieve the record. Factor 2 specifies the file or record format name (externally described files) that is to be read. For a

WORKSTN subfile, the CHAIN operation retrieves a subfile record. Files specified as input, read all records without locks and position 53 in RPG/400 must be blank. **To lock all records**, the file must be specified as update and RPG/400 position 53 is blank. Specify an "N" in RPG/400 53 so that no lock should be placed on a record when it is read. **The HI positions** 54 and 55 must contain an indicator that is set on if no record in the file matches the search argument. The LO positions can contain an indicator that is on if the CHAIN operation is not completed successfully Error). The EQ positions must be blank. A successful chain repositions the file cursor such that if it is followed by a READ operation the next sequential record following the retrieved record is read. If an update (on the calculation or output specifications) is done on the retrieved record after a successful CHAIN operation and before other access to that file, the last record retrieved is updated.

DEBUG   Shows internal variables and indicators. Output is to A print device or a disk file at specific points in calcs.

DELET   Delete a specific record in a database. If no search argument is   placed in Factor1, this operation deletes the last locked record retrieved from the file or record format specified in Factor 2. If a search argument is specified and the record is found, it is deleted. A status indicator area is provided in the HI (not found) and LO (error) indicator areas to show the results of the DELET. When indicators are specified and none are turned on, the delete is successful.

DIV   Divide two numbers, produce a result and a **remainder.** The DIV operation divides Factor 1 by Factor 2. Without Factor 1 specified, it divides the result field by Factor 2. The quotient (result) is placed in the result field. If Factor 1 is 0, the result of the divide operation is 0. Any remainder resulting from the divide operation is lost unless the move remainder (MVR) (See this table) operation is specified as the next operation. If move remainder is the next operation, the result of the divide operation cannot be half-adjusted

DSPLY   Display function - show values immediately. The DSPLY operation allows the program to communicate with the display work station that requested the program. The operation can display a message from Factor 1 and send a value in the result field into which can be keyed a response. Specify a literal of a field in factor 1 to be used as the message to be displayed. The result field is optional. If specified, the user response is placed in it and the program can take immediate action based on this communication with the user. The result field can contain a field name, a table name, or an array element the contents of which are displayed and into which the response is placed. If no data is entered, the result field is unchanged. The DSPLY can also be used as a handy and quick interactive debugger because it does not mess   up printouts or displays to get its job done.

EXCPT   Calculation Time Exception Output. This program described file operation initiates immediate output to internally described disk or printer files. Output triggered for this operation is coded with a special "E" designation for exception output record headers in place of the RPG cycle's typical H or D records. The lines of output can be conditioned or unconditioned using record indicators. The EXCPT also has a special name facility that can be specified in Factor 2. When the EXCPT is executed with an except name, only the records with that particular name in the output record area are written to a printer or a disk file.

EXFMT   Write/then Read Interactive Screen Format. This powerful operation is a combination put screen, wait, and get screen operation. The format name specified in Factor 2 is defined in a display file that is typically created using the Screen Design Aid. A display file can have multiple record formats (screen panels) defined. A screen panel with input fields can be sent using the EXFMT operation, specifying the panel name, to a display. The program then waits for the user to enter data and signify they are finished. The user provides input and presses Enter or a function key. Control is then returned to the statement in the RPG program following the EXFMT.

MOVE Move data field right to left. This operation moves each corresponding character from the Factor 2 field to the Result field starting with the rightmost char and stopping w/ the leftmost char in Factor 2.

MOVEL   Move data field left to right. This operation moves each corresponding character from the Factor 2 field to the Result field starting with the leftmost position to the leftmost position and stopping with the last character in Factor 2.

MOVEA   Move Array – Array to Field and Vice Versa. This operation moves each corresponding character from the array or field specified in   Factor 2 field to the field or array specified in   the result field -- starting with the leftmost position of the field or array to the leftmost position and stopping with the last character in Factor 2.

MULT   Multiply one field or value by another and store the **result.** Factor 1 is multiplied by Factor 2 and the product is placed in the result field. The Result field must be large enough to hold it. If Factor 1 is not specified, Factor 2 is multiplied by the Result field and the product is placed in the Result field. The fields in Factor 1, Factor 2, and the Result field must be defined as numeric. You can specify half adjust (position 53 in RPG/400).

MVR   Move the remainder after a divide operation into a **field.** This operation moves the remainder from the previous DIV operation to a separate field named in the result field. Factor 1 and Factor 2 must be blank. The MVR operation must immediately follow and be processed after the DIV operation. The MVR operation Be careful with conditional operations surrounding an MVR operation. If the MVR operation is processed before the DIV operation, undesirable results occur.

READ   Read a record from a file or format. The READ operation reads the current record, from a procedural file (identified by an F in position 16 of the RPG/400 file description specifications). Factor 2 must contain the name of a file. A record format name in Factor 2 is allowed only with an externally described file (E in pos. 19 of the RPG/400 F spec. A READ-by- format-name operation will receive a different format than the one you specified in factor 2. If so, the READ operation ends in error. This operation is most often associated with database files but it also works with other files including WORKSTN files in which the record format name on the READ. In database operations, specify an indicator in the EQ indicator position to have the READ operation check for end of file (no more records left to read). The indicator turns on when the file is at end.

SQRT   Take the square root of a number and store it in a **field**. The SQRT operation derives the square root of the field named in Factor 2 and it places it in the Result field. If the value of the factor 2 field is zero, the Result field value is also zero. If the value of the Factor 2 field is negative, the RPG/400 exception/error handling routine receives control.

SUB   Subtract one field from another and store the result. Factor 2 is subtracted from Factor 1 and the difference is placed in the result field. If Factor 1 is not specified, the contents of Factor 2 are subtracted from the contents of the Result field and the results are stored in the Result field. Indicators specified in the HI, LO, EQ resulting indicator area are turned on depending on a +, -, or 0 value in the result field.

TIME   Get time of day and store in a field. The TIME operation accesses the system time of day and, if specified, the system date at any time during program processing. The system time is based on the 24-hour system clock. The result field must specify the name of a 6-, 12- or 14-digit numeric field (no decimal positions) into which the time of day or the time of day and the system date are written. To access the time of day only, specify the result field as a 6-digit numeric field. To access both the time of day and the system date, specify the result field as a 12- (2-digit year portion) or 14-digit (4-digit year portion) numeric field. The time of day is always placed in the first six positions of the result field in the following format: hhmmss (hh=hours, mm=minutes, and ss=seconds)

UPDAT   Modify Existing Record The UPDAT operation rewrites (updates) the last record retrieved for processing from an update disk file or subfile. Data changes that occurred through normal processing will be made to the updated record. No other file operation should be performed between the input operation that retrieved the record and the UPDAT operation. Specify the file or record format name in factor 2 for the database file to be updated. For externally defined files, the record format name must be used with this operation. UPDAT follows a read type operation. Data in the record's fields are updated in program memory then they are written over the former contents of the record in the database.

WRITE   Create new DB Records (Add Records) or write a format to a display screen.   The WRITE operation writes a new record to a file. In essence, it creates new

	records. Factor 2 must contain the name of a file or a record format name for an externally described file. A file name in factor 2 is required with a program described file. In this case, a data structure must be defined in for the result field. For program described files, the record is written directly from the data structure to the file. The result field must be blank if factor 2 contains a record format name. The Write operation can also be used to send a panel (screen) to a display station.
XFOOT	Sums the elements of an array. Powerful operator that adds each of the elements of an array to create a total and it stores the total in a result field.
Z-ADD	**Zero and Add.** Zeroes out a result field first and then adds the content of the Factor 2 field or constant to the zeroed total. Similar to a numeric MOVE operation. Indicators specified in the resulting HI, LO, EQ area are turned on according to their +, - 0, result.
Z-SUB	**Zero and Subtract** Zeroes out a result field first and Then subtracts the content of a Factor 2 field or a constant from the zeroed result creating in most cases a negative value. Has the same arithmetic result as subtracting a number from zero to create its negative. Indicators specified in the resulting HI, LO, EQ area are turned on according to their +, - 0, result.

Compare & Branch / Subroutine Operations

The basic operations in Table 14-2 consist of mostly database and arithmetic operators. Though you definitely need a computer with nice healthy disk drives for database, the arithmetic operations in Table 14-2 are done just as handily with a calculator.

Besides database capability, the major factor which differentiates computers from calculators is logic. The logic of a computer machine provides the ability to compare values, and based on those values take different courses of actions. The term used for taking those "different courses of action" is called branching.

Through comparisons of values and branches which alter the sequential pattern of instructions, computer systems achieve a somewhat human-like, logical capability that enables them to far surpass the capabilities of the most advanced calculator.

As a language known for providing an easy means to quantify business rules for programmed decision making, RPG is well equipped for the tasks necessary to provide programs the compare and branch instructions necessary to run the business on the AS/400 or IBM i. Table 14-4 below summarizes all of the compare and branch operations that an RPG programmer their disposal.

As you examine the table, it will help you in deciphering the meaning of the operations that provide the decision making capabilities for RPG. This notion also applies to the operations listed under Structured Operations as shown in Table 14-8.

A number of compare and branch and structured decision operations are listed with XX as the last two characters of the operations. XX is a convenient means of specifying the type of test that you can call upon using the operation. For example, the IFXX is much more meaningful if it is coded as IFEQ (If Equal) or IFGT (IF Greater Than). The meaning of these operation suffixes are shown in Table 14-3.

Table 14-3 XX Operation Meanings

```
XX          Meaning
GT          Factor 1 is greater than factor 2.
LT          Factor 1 is less than factor 2.
EQ          Factor 1 is equal to factor 2.
NE          Factor 1 is not equal to factor 2.
GE          Factor 1 is greater than or equal to factor 2.
LE    F     actor 1 is less than or equal to factor 2.
Blanks      Unconditional processing  -- (CAS ).
```

Table 14-4 Compare & Branch Operations

Operation	Provided Function
ANDxx	And if another condition is true, then... This operation links two operations together. If you specify this optional operation, it must immediately follow a ANDxx, DOUxx, DOQxx, IFxx, ORxx, or WHxx. With ANDxx, you can specify a complex condition for the DOUxx, DOWxx, IFxx, and WHxx operations. The ANDxx operation has higher precedence than the ORxx operation. The comparison of factor 1 and factor 2 follows the same rules as those given for the compare operations. See COMP in this table.
BEGSR	Beginning of Subroutine. Defines the beginning point of a subroutine. Subroutine ends with an ENDSR opcode. Factor 1 contains the name of the subroutine.
COMP	Compare Two values and set on status indicators Based on the relationship of the first value (field or literal) in Factor 1 to the second value (Factor 2). Status indicators can be specified for HI, LO, EQ. The COMP operation compares Factor 1 with Factor 2. As a result of the comparison, indicators are set on in RPG/ 400 and RPG IV as follows: HI – if Factor 1 is greater than Factor 2; LO – if Factor 1 is less than Factor 2; EQ – if Factor 1 equals Factor 2. When specified, the resulting indicators are set on or off each time through the operation to reflect the results of the latest compare.
CABxx	Compares two values and branches if the tested **condition is satisfied.** The condition, xx = EQ or GT etc is specified as part of the op-code. The branch-to label is taken if the condition is satisfied. This combination operation first compares Factor 1 with factor 2. If the condition specified by xx in the op-code is true, the program branches to the TAG operation associated with the label specified in the result field. Otherwise, the program continues with the next operation in the sequence.
CASxx	Conditionally Invoke Subroutine on Compare. Very similar to the CABXX operations. Instead of a straight go to like branch, a specified subroutine is invoked if the conditions are met. This operation allows you to conditionally select a subroutine for processing. The selection is based on the relationship between Factor 1 and Factor 2, as specified by the "xx" portion of the op-code.. If the relationship denoted by xx exists (true) between Factor 1 and Factor 2, the subroutine specified in the result field is processed.

DO	Starts a straight Do loop – Loop ends with ENDDO The DO operation begins a group of operations and indicates the number of times the group will be processed. You specify an index field, a starting value, and a limit value. You also specify an ENDDO statement to mark the end of the DO group. Specify the numeric starting value in Factor1 with no decimal positions. If you do not specify Factor 1, the starting value is 1. Specify the limit value in Factor 2. If you do not specify a limit, the default is 1. Specify the current index value in the Result field. (The loop does not have to begin with "1.") Any value in the index field is replaced by Factor 1 when the DO operation begins. Factor 2 of the associated ENDDO operation specifies the value to be added to the index field, otherwise, 1 is the default.
DOUxx	Starts a Do until loop xx = the relationship. Loop Ends with ENDDO Do until xx is true. DO until and DO while are similar operations. The Do until (DOUxx) operation begins a group of operations you want to process more than once (but always at least once). The group of instructions in the loop are sandwiched between the statement defining the beginning of the loop (DOUxx) and the statement defining the end of the loop (ENDDO). Factor 1 and Factor 2 are required. On the DOUxx statement, you indicate a relationship xx. However, you can specify a more complex condition by pacing ANDxx or ORxx statements immediately following the DOUxx. The instructions within the DO loop are processed once, and then the group is repeated until the ENDDO test. At the end of the loop, when the ENDDO is processed, if the relationship xx exists between Factor 1 and Factor 2 or the specified condition exists, the DO group is finished and control passes to the next calculation operation after the ENDDO statement.
DOWxx	Starts a Do while loop xx = the relationship. Loop ends with ENDDO Do while xx continues to be true. DO while and DO until are similar operations. The Do while (DOWxx) operation begins a group of operations you want to process while the relationship xx exists between Factor 1 and Factor 2. The group of instructions in the loop are sandwiched between the statement defining the beginning of the loop (DOWxx) and the statement defining the end of the loop (ENDDO). Factor 1 and Factor 2 are required. On the DOWxx statement, you indicate a relationship xx. However, you can specify a more complex condition by pacing ANDxx or ORxx statements immediately following the DOUxx. If the relationship xx between factor 1 and factor 2 or the condition specified by a combined operation does not exist, the DO group is finished and control passes to the next calculation operation after the ENDDO statement. If the relationship xx between factor 1 and factor 2 or the condition specified by a combined operation exists, the operations in the DO group are repeated.
DO****	This is a further Doxx explanation, not an operation.

	DOUxx tests at the end of the loop and **always** gets executed at least once. DOWxx tests for the condition first, before executing the loop and thus it is possible that no instructions in the DOW loop get executed.
ELSE	The ELSE operation is an optional part of the IFxx operation. If the IFxx comparison is met, the instructions before ELSE are processed; otherwise, the instructions after ELSE are processed.
ENDSR	**End of Subroutine.** Use this as the ending statement in A subroutine that would begin with a BEGSR operation. There are no other operands (Factor 1, Factor 2, Result)
END	Generic End of If or Do Operations. This Generic operation will end a DO block or an If block of instructions. There are no other operands (Factor 1, Factor 2, Result)
ENDDO	Ends DO, DOUXX or DOWXX Operations. There Are no other operands (Factor 1, Factor 2, Result)
ENDIF	**Ends If Operations.** There are no other operands (Factor 1, Factor 2, Result)
EXSR	**Invoke Subroutine.** This operation branches to an in-line subroutine, causes the subroutine code to be executed, and when the subroutine ends, it passes control to the statement following the EXSR operation. The EXSR (execute subroutine) operation causes the RPG subroutine provided in Factor 2 to be performed. The subroutine name must be a unique symbolic name and must appear as Factor 1 of a BEGSR operation in another section of the same program. Whenever the EXSR appears in calculations, the subroutine that is named is immediately executed. Following the processing of all the subroutine, control is passed to the statement following the EXSR operation except when a GOTO within the subroutine sends the program to a label outside the subroutine or when the an error subroutine is being processed.
GOTO	Unconditional branch statement. This operation causes the next operational instruction to be the statement following a named (labeled) TAG Statement. The GOTO Label is provided in Factor 2.
IFxx	If a condition xx is true, execute statements that follow the IFxx statement and continue to the group-ending END or ENDIF statement. Other than the requisite RPG columnar formatting, the RPG standard IFxx operation is similar in function to the "IF" statement varieties in other languages. As such it allows a group of calculations to be processed if a certain relationship, specified by xx, exists between Factor 1 and Factor 2. The "ENDIF" statement is the last statement in an "IF Group." The If tests can be made more complex by adding the "ANDxx" and "ORxx." operations. The If statement itself can have conditioning indicators but it does not use resulting indicators. Factor 1 and Factor 2 are compared just like the RPG COMP operation. If the relationship specified by the IFxx and any associated ANDxx or ORxx operations exists, the statements are executed, if it does not exist, control passes to the calculgion operation immediately following the associated ENDIF operation. If an "ELSE" is also specified as described above under ELSE, when the

	group is finished, control passes to the first calculation operation that can be processed following the ELSE op.
ITER	Iterate the instructions in a Do group from the beginning. Run through Do group another time, bypassing the instructions between the ITER and the ENDDO. There are no operands (Factor 1, Factor2, or Result)
ORxx	OR -- if another Condition is True, then... the "or" operation works with a preceding operation that has established a condition, (HI, LO, EQ). This operation ties the prior operation with this operation so that if either are true, the statement is true .
OTHER	The "Otherwise Select" or (OTHER) operation Begins the sequence of operations to be processed if no WHxx condition is satisfied in a SELEC group. The Sequence ends with the ENDSL or END operation. See SELEC and WHxx operations. There are no operands (Factor 1, Factor2, or Result)
LEAVE	**Leave a Do Group.** A very similar statement to ITER, but very different. Whereas an ITER causes the loop to repeat, the Leave statement says that the Do loop is over... move on to an instruction after the DO. There are no operands (Factor 1, Factor2, or Result)
SELEC	The SELEC operation begins a selection grouping. The "select group" conditionally processes one of several alternative sequences of operations. It works with the WHxx group operation, and optionally with the OTHER group operation. A SELEC group ends with an ENDSL or END statement. The SELEC packaging consists of the SELEC statement, zero or more groups, an optional OTHER group, and the requisite ENDSL or generic END statement. It works like this: When the SELEC operation is processed, control passes to the statement following the first WHxx condition that is satisfied. All statements within the WHxx group are then executed until the next WHxx operation. Control then passes to the ENDSL statement. If no WHxx condition is satisfied and an OTHER action is specified, control passes to the statement following the OTHER operation. If no WHxx condition is satisfied and no OTHER operation is specified, control transfers to the statement following the ENDSL operation of the select group. There are no operands (Factor 1, Factor2, or Result)
TAG	Destination label for a GOTO operation. "Where a 'GOTO' goes.
TESTB	**Test Bit**– Individual Bit Testing. Each individual bit in a byte can be tested for on /off (0, 1) status. RPG has a number of bit operations that can be used to test and manipulate the individual bits in characters. The TESTB operation compares the bits identified in factor 2 with the corresponding bits in the field named as the result field. Only one character is tested in this operation so the result field must be a one-position character field. Resulting indicators in HI, LO, EQ, reflect the status of the result field bits. Factor 2 is always a source of bits for the result field. The bits to be tested are identified by the numbers 0 through 7. (0 is the leftmost bit.) The bit numbers must be enclosed in apostrophes, and the entry

must begin in the first position of Factor 2.

TESTN   **Test Numeric:** The TESTN operation tests a character result field for the presence of zoned decimal digits and blanks. The result field must be a character field. To be considered numeric, each character in the field, except the low-order character, must contain a hexadecimal F zone and a digit (0 through 9). The low-order character is numeric if it contains a hexadecimal C, hexadecimal D, or hexadecimal F zone, and a digit (0 through 9). An indicator is turned on in the HI indicator area if either the result field contains numeric characters, or it contains a 1-character field that consists of a letter from A to R. An indicator is turned on in the LO area if the result field contains both numeric characters and at least one leading blank. For example, the values b123 or bb123 set this indicator on. An indicator is turned on in the EQ area when the result field contains all blanks

TESTZ   **Test Zone:** The TESTZ operation tests the zone of the leftmost character in the result field. Resulting indicators are set on according to the results of the test. The characters &, A through I, and any character with the same zone as the character A set on the indicator in the HI position. characters - (minus), J through R, and any character with the same zone as the character J set on the indicator in the LO position. . Characters with any other zone set on the indicator in the EQ position

WHxx   "When True Then Select" (WHxx) These are the operations of a select group which determine where control passes after the "SELEC (Begin a Select Group)" operation is processed. The WHxx conditional operation is true if factor 1 and factor 2 have the relationship specified by xx If the condition is true, the operations following the WHxx are processed until the next WHxx, OTHER, ENDSL, or END statement is encountered.

Call Operations (Inter-program)

One of the simplest ways to create applications is to build small programs / routines and link them together to form a cohesive complete application system. In Table 14-4, we introduced the notion of an inline subroutine which is a set of "stand-alone" instructions which get invoked independently throughout a program.

Though the notion of building small modules does work somewhat with subroutines, being able to get outside your program and link to routines that are not buried within one big program provides an even more powerful and flexible way to build applications.

Without getting into a computer science discussion about call by name/value or call by reference, let's just say that the natural way to call a program in RPG/400 and the simplest way in RPGIV has always been to use the dynamic call.

The beauty of this is that there is little thinking and as a new RPG programmer before you can even see the value of various calling mechanisms, you are using the AS/400's innate ability to dynamically call programs from one language to the same or another.

For argument purposes, let's just say that you need to write an application that needs some major calculations to produce your answers. Let's also say that there is an existing RPG/400 program written by your predecessor that provides all of these calculations. You merely have to pass it a few parameters and receive a few back and that's all there is.

Let's also say that each set of answers that are provided need to be stored in the database and be indexed for later access. Let's also say that your predecessor has written a routine in CL that accepts parameters from a program and calls other programs and does all the work necessary to create a new database for each new program run. There is no reason for you to have to rewrite these programs. RPG/400 has a very nice and very easy to use dynamic program call facility that is at your disposal.

The operations to call, pass parameters, return, and deal with program resources are shown in Table 14-5. The list is not long and for RPG/400, that's all there is. With RPGIV, the language has been expanded to use what are called bound programs / procedures and / or prototyped procedures with various flavors of CALL operations. We'll pick that up in Chapters 15 and 26. For now, Table 14-5 shows you all you need to make inter program communication work for you in RPG/400.

Table 14-5 CALL Operations

Operation	Provided Function
CALL	**Calls a program** written in the same or a different language from the same system. The program name to call can be provided in a quoted literal name or in a variable. A parameter list can be provided via multiple PARM statements following the CALL operation or a PLIST operation provided in the result field
FREE	**Deactivate a Program.** The RPG/400 – only FREE operation removes a program from the list of activated programs that have been "called," frees static storage, and ensures that program initialization (first cycle processing) occurs the next time the program is called. This operation does not close files or unlock data areas. It is not supported in RPGIV.
PARM	**Identify Parameters for Program.** The "Identify Parameters" operation defines the parameters that compose a parameter list (PLIST). PARM operations can appear anywhere in calculations as long as they immediately follow a PLIST or a CALL operation to which they refer. PARM statements must be in the order expected by the called program. One PARM statement, or as many as 255 PARM statements in RPG/400, can follow a PLIST or CALL.
PLIST	**Identify a Parameter List for Program**. The "Identify Parameter List" (PLIST) operation defines a unique symbolic name for a list of parameters (PARMs) to be specified in a CALL operation. The PLIST operation must be immediately followed by at least one PARM operation. The name of the list is supplied in Factor 1. For programs that are passed parameters by a calling program a special factor 1 entry containing "*ENTRY" must be provided to catch the parameters passed by a calling program. The list is ended when an operation other than PARM is encountered.
RETRN	Return to Caller (Calling Program). The RETRN operation causes a return to the calling program. If a halt indicator (H1 to H9) is on, the program ends abnormally. In this case, all open files are closed and an error is sent to the caller. If no halt indicators are on, the last record LR indicator is checked. If it is on, the called program

ends normally and closes files and data areas. If no halt
condition exists and LR is not on, the program returns to
the calling routine. Data is preserved for the next time
the program is called. Files and data areas are not written.

Data Manipulation Operations

Business computer systems need lots of ways to manipulate and shape data for testing and for storage
purposes. As a business-first language RPG has operations ranging from the bit level to the byte level to the
field level that provide they types of data manipulation facilities that you would expect in a high-quality
business programming language. Table 14-6 gives us a good look at these operations.

Table 14-6 Data Manipulation Operations

Operation	Provided Function
BITOF	Set Bits Off – Individual Bit Manipulation. Each individual bit in a byte can be set off to a binary "0" value. Similar to BITON.l
BITON	Set Bits On -- Individual Bit Manipulation. Each individual bit in a byte can be set on to a binary "1" value. The BITON operation causes bits identified in factor 2 to be set on (set to 1) in the result field. Bits not identified in factor 2 remain unchanged. Therefore, when using BITON to format a character, you should use both BITON and BITOF
CLEAR	**Clear a structure.** The CLEAR operation sets elements In a structure (record format, data structure, array, or table) or a variable (field, subfield, or indicator), to zero, blank or '0', depending on field type (numeric, char, or indicator). It is a convenient way to clear structures on a global basis, as well as element by element, during run time. Factor 1 must be blank unless factor 2 contains a DISK record format name; in which case, it can contain *NOKEY to indicate that all fields except key fields are to be cleared.
MOVE	Move data from one field to another right to left. See Table 14-2 Basic Operations
MOVEA	Move data from an array to a field or vice verse, left **to right.** See Table 14-2 Basic Operations
MOVEL	Move data from one field to another, left to right. See Table 14-2 basic Operations
MHHZO	Move High to High Zone Nibble Operation. The Move High to High Zone (MHHZO) operation moves a half-byte or "nibble" of data. It moves the zone portion of a character from the leftmost zone in the character field in Factor 2 to the leftmost zone in the Result field.
MHLZO	Move High to Low Zone Nibble Operation. The Move High to Low Zone (MHHZO) operation moves a half-byte or "nibble" of data. It moves the zone portion of a character from the leftmost zone in the character field in Factor 2 to the rightmost zone in the result field.
MLHZO	Move Low to High Zone- Nibble Operation. The Move Low to High Zone (MHHZO) operation moves a half-byte or "nibble" of data. It moves the zone portion of a character from the rightmost zone in the character

	field in Factor 2 to the leftmost zone in the result field.
MLLZO	Move Low to Low Zone-- Nibble Operation. The Move Low to Low Zone (MLLZO) operation moves a half-byte or "nibble" of data. It moves the zone portion of a character from the rightmost zone in the character field in Factor 2 to the rightmost zone in the result field.
RESET	**Reset a structure**. The RESET operation is similar to the CLEAR operation. It sets elements in a structure (record format, data structure, array, or table) or a variable (field, subfield, or indicator), to its initial value, It is a convenient way to reset structures on a global basis, as well as element by element, during run time. This initial value can be established using data structure initialization, or you can use the initialization subroutine to assign an initial value to the structure or variable. The RESET operation causes a snapshot of the variable or structure to be taken and this becomes the RESET value. Factor 1 must be blank unless factor 2 contains a DISK record format name; in which case, it can contain *NOKEY to indicate that all fields except key fields are to be reset.
SETON	**Turn Indicator ON.** This operation immediately sets the indicators specified in the HI LO EQ area to the "on" or "1" condition.
SETOF	**Turn Indicator OFF**. This operation immediately sets the indicators specified in the HI LO EQ area to the "off" or "0" condition

Database & Device File Operations

Just as a business computer system needs its compare and branch operations to provide business logic, a business programming language needs natural integrated database operations to maximize the productivity of programmers and minimize the need for high-priced database administrators.

The RPG/400 and the RPGIV language compilers have been built from the ground up with full knowledge of the system's integrated database. As such programmers are not burdened with coding input or output or update specifications in RPG programs. The compiler fetches the descriptions right from the database at compile time. This makes RPG business programmers the most productive programmers in the world.

Add to this notion a series of powerful database record at a time operations unprecedented on any other computer system or any other language. For example the CHAIN operation provides random read or random read by key.

The UPDAT operation is always ready to update the record just read by a CHAIN, or any type of READ operation. The WRITE operation adds records to a database file and of course the DELET operation can delete the record just read or it can be used to directly access a record via a search argument for deletion.

How many different ways do you want to read data? In addition to the CHAIN operation, for example the SETXX (EQ or GT) positions the database to a specific record from which a subsequent READ operation can be performed. So speaking of read operations, you can READ the next record consecutively, READP (READ prior) the prior record one back and one back after that etc.

You can also READE (READ equal) the next record whose key is equal to a search argument and you can specify. You can also REDPE (READ prior equal) if you want to read backwards by key.

RPG programmers bred on other systems don't like RPG because it is simple. Most do not like it all but if they do, the truth is they like it because it is rich in function and easy to use as witnessed by the host of database operations shown in Table 14-7.

But, then again, that's just database. A number of these operations also work with other types of devices such as tape drives. Despite all of the accolades I can get from showing these types of operations against database and media, there is no set of operations more powerful than those dealing with the IBM-unique notion of a WORKSTN file. You just cannot beat it.

In its traditional Program Development Manager toolset, for example, and in its WebSphere Development Studio Client IDE (intelligent development environment) IBM offers a facility that enables workstation screens to be designed in a WYSIWYG style. Groups of these screens or panels as they are sometimes called are combined and compiled for use in a specific program.

The result of the compilation is an AS/400 object called a display file. It is a *File type object but it is associated with a device that has the characteristics of an IBM 5250 terminal.

Just as RPG removes the requirement for programmers to code database input and output specifications, it provides the same facilities for WORKSTN device files. Each record format in a Workstation device file is in essence a display panel with both output and input fields available on the display.

When you write a program that is to use screen panels, you first send out prompts and then you read in the input that was entered. On many systems this is a very difficult task and requires highly skilled programming. IBM has made the notion of interactive much more easy than traditional methods by including compiler operation codes within the COBOL and RPG compilers.

So, if an RPG programmer wants to send out a screen panel, they would first specify the device file name as a WORKSTN file in the File Description specifications. Then, as you would expect the first operation to the screen would be a WRITE op-code. You would then want the program to wait a bit for input before continuing and as it turns out, if you immediately follow-up with a READ operation, the program will wait for input before continuing. As simple as this is, it is actually simpler. The RPG compiler designers recognized that the typical sequence of operations is a WRITE followed by a READ, so they devised a new operation specific to the WORKSTN file that does both a WRITE and a READ. The operation is called EXFMT for Execute Format.

This operation as well as all of the wonderful RPG database and device file operations is included in Table 14-7 for your review and learning pleasure.

Table 14-7 Database & File Operations

Operation	**Provided Function**
ACQ	Acquire a device for program use
CHAIN	Random retrieval from a file. The chain is a read operation by either relative record number or via a search argument against a key value in an indexed file database.. See Table 14-2 Basic Operations.
CLOSE	**Close files.** This operation closes the file specified in Factor 2
COMIT	Commit records to DB and post to journal. For applications using commitment control with database journaling, this operation commits the last set of writes and updates to the database.
DELET	Delete DB File Record. See Table 14-2 Basic Operations
DSPLY	Displays variable values during program execution. Unlike Debug, this command sends its results immediately to the job's message queue from where it can be viewed. See table 14-2 Basic Operations
EXCPT	Calculation Time Output – outside RPG cycle. This commend immediately outputs disk records or print lines

	from within calculations rather than through the fixed logic cycle. See Table 14-2 Basic Operations
EXFMT	Write/then read a screen format for interactive Programming. This is the major op code for sending a Screen panel to a display and then waiting for input from The user to the program. When the user inputs data it is returned to the program in this one operation. It is a combination of a Write screen operation followed by a wait followed by a read screen. See table 14-2 Basic Operations.
FEOD	Force End of Data on File. The FEOD operation Signals the logical end of data for a primary, secondary, or full procedural database file. By placing a file at end of data it effectively means that the next READ operation for the file will return an "end of file" condition; no record will be read, an error indicator will be returned, and no data will be received by the program. A CHAIN or SETLL operation against a file will undo the FEOD and reposition the file cursor on some record someplace before end of data.
FORCE	Force Certain DB File to Read Next RPG Cycle. This operation permits the program to change the Normal sequencing of a primary or secondary file by picking the file to be read (input) and processed on the next RPG cycle.
NEXT	Causes Specific Device to Be Read Next. Similar in nature to FORCE, this operation selects the specific device in a multi-device file that will be selected next cycle for input.
OPEN	Open file NOW for processing. To simplify the language, RPG files are by default opened automatically when the program is invoked. However, there may be times that it would best serve a program to open the files only if and when they are needed. Files that are opened by the explicit RPG OPEN operation, named in factor 2, must be designated as user controlled by specifying "UC" (user control) in positions 71 and 72)of the RPG/400 file description specifications. The OPEN operation requires that Factor 2 contain the name of the file to be opened.
POST	Post – Loads File Info Data Structure. This infrequently used operation posts information in an INFDS (file information data structure). The information is either on the status of a specific program device or I/O feedback associated with a file. In Factor 1, you can specify a program device name to get information about that specific program device. If a program has no POST operation code, or if it has only POST operation codes with factor 1 specified, the INFDS is updated with each input/output operation or block of operations. If you leave factor 1 blank, you get I/O feedback information. Specify a file name in Factor 2. The information for this file is posted in the INFDS associated with this file.
READ	Read a Record from a file at the point of the file cursor. Also used to read a display format form a WORKSTN file. See Table 14-2 Basic Operations for more detail.

READC Read Next Changed Record – Subfile. The READC operation can be used only with an externally described WORKSTN file to obtain the next changed record in a subfile. When a subfile is displayed to a user, the RPG program "disconnects." The user may then roll through the file changing any of many records. The Read changed (READC) operation looks for only the records that were changed after the disconnect and before the reconnect. to the RPG program. Factor 2 is required and must be the name of a record format defined as a subfile by the SFILE keyword on the File Description specifications.

READE **Read Equal by key.** The READE operation retrieves the next sequential record from a full procedural file. (F in position 16 of the RPG/400 file description specs) if the key of the record matches the search argument. If the key of the record does not match the search argument, the indicator that must be specified in RPG/400 positions 58 and 59 (EQ) is set on, and the record is not returned to the program.

READP Read Prior Record (Consecutive) The READP operation reads the prior record from a full procedural file (F in position 16 of the F spec). This operation goes against the data and does not use an index. Place the name of a file or record format to be read in Factor 2. A record format name in factor 2 is allowed only with an externally described file. If a record format name is specified in factor 2, the record retrieved is the first prior record of the specified type (in the event of a multi format logical file). Intervening records are bypassed.

REDPE Read Prior Equal (Key) The REDPE operation retrieves the next prior sequential record from a full procedural file if the key of the record matches the search argument. In essence it reads backwards by key and only picks those records equal to the search argument specified in Factor 1. If the key of the record does not match the search argument, the indicator in RPG/400 positions 58-59 (EQ) is set on and the record is not returned to the program. Factor 1, is optional and it identifies the record to be retrieved. If factor 1 is left blank and the full key of the next prior record is equal to that of the current record, the next prior record in the file is retrieved. The full key is defined by the record format or file specified for Factor 2.

REL **Release the program device** (WORKSTN) acquired Via the ACQ operation.

ROLBK Roll Back uncommitted DB records. When program operations write or update records to a database while under commitment control, the before and after images are also written to a journal. If after performing these operations a program wants to undo the transactions and updates, the ROLBK operation does just that. It takes the database back to where it was before the transaction began (transaction boundary).

SETGT Set Greater Than Key or Relative Record # The SETGT operation positions a database file at the next record with a key or relative record number (RRN) that is greater than the key or relative record number specified in factor 1. The file must be a full procedural file (F in position 16 of FD). The operation requires that

	Factor 1 be specified as the key or RRN search argument. Factor 2 is also required and can contain either a file name or a record format (externally described file only).
SETLL	Set Lower Limit – key or relative record #. The SETLL operation positions a file at the next record that has a key or relative record number RRN that is greater than or equal to the search argument (key or RRN) as specified in factor 1. The file must be full procedural (F in position 16 of FD) Factor 1 is required. Factor 2 is also required and can contain either a file name or a record format (externally described file only).
UNLCK	Unlock a Data Area or release a locked record. Use the UNLCK operation to unlock data areas and release database record locks in a program. Specify the name of the data area or the name of an update disk file or the word, *NAMVAR. The data area must already be specified in the result field of an *NAMVAR DEFN statement. When *NAMVAR is specified in factor 2, all data areas in the program that are locked are unlocked. Using the UNLCK operation releases the most recently locked record for an update disk file.
UPDAT	Modify an existing database record. Follows a read Type operation. Data in the record's fields are updated In program memory and then the new contents of the record are written over the former contents of the record in the database. See Figure 14-2 Basic Operations.
WRITE	Create (Add) new records to file. Unlike a file update which writes an existing record back to the database, the WRITE operation creates or adds a brand new record to the database. See Figure 14-2 Basic Operations

Data Structure, Data Area, Table, Array, String Operations

In Table 14-6, we took a good look at the basic operations that are available in RPG to manipulate data once it arrives in memory. As you may from this section, recall the data manipulation operations that we studied are based on field, character, or bit data elements.

Though the list in Table 14-6 is comprehensive for basic structures, it does not include all of the manipulation operations. We saved some special operations on some special structures for Table 14-8 below.

The operations in this table are provided to work with data structures. A data structure is a superset of the other types of data that we studied in Table 14-6. Other than the disk and device operations described in Table 14-7, a "field" is the largest data element that we have covered to this point.

A data structure, as a superset of a field, can contain multiple fields or data elements. As the title of this section suggests, the four different types of data structures that we are about to discuss are as follows:

1. Data Structure
2. Table
3. Array
4. String

The various operations that can be used against these structures are described in detail in Chapters 16, 17 & 18. You may have noticed that we did not list the "Data Area" as one of the structures under study.

That is because it is not a data structure. However, as you will learn in Chapter 17, a Data Area is an AS/400 object, similar in nature to a one field, one record, database file. For the data that is contained in a Data Area to make sense when it arrives in a program, IBM has provided the ability for a Data Area to use a Data Structure for its data definition.

All of us have learned that we should not use the word we are defining as the definition of the word itself. Yet, here we are, about to explore the operations provided in Table 14-8 for all sorts of data structures and yet, against the rules, one of them is actually named Data Structure.

Data Structure (as a data structure)

A Data Structure is a particular structure of data that combines a number of different fields of varying length and type into a meaningful structure that can be referenced and manipulated by one name, rather than having to reference each item in the structure individually. In essence, a Data Structure is the memory equivalent of a record format in a database file, though it does not have to be associated with a database file.

So, the Data Structure is a memory artifact into which data can be applied and manipulated. Data Structures can be one record or multiple records in nature. When there are multiple records in a data structure, it is known as a Multiple Occurrence Data Structure.

Table

A Table is a data structure (grouping of data) of similar sized and shaped elements in tabular form. Tables can either be one column or two columns wide. A single column table, for example might consist of the fifty states as in the United States, properly spelled. A programmer could check this table to assure that a valid state abbreviation was used in an application.

A two-column table is officially called an Alternating Table. Carrying the states example into two columns, by adding a second column or alternating table, the name of the state could be provided in the alternate table.

Then, in addition to verifying the validity of the state code in the look up, the operation could also return the name of the state in the same operation. Thus, PA would beget Pennsylvania and NJ would beget New Jersey, etc. As you will learn in Chapter 16, tables in RPG always begin with the three letters "TAB."

An Array is a data structure that consists of all similarly sized and typed data elements. Each element in an array for example is a field in its own right but once defined it is accessible only through array operations. A common application example for arrays over the years is to store monthly sales figures.

By definition, all of the monthly totals would be stored in fields of the same size and type – often in the neighborhood of nine numeric digits, two of which would represent decimal positions. Programmers learned quickly that they could define an array of 108 characters to hold the twelve sales values for the year.

Arrays also permit indexing. Thus, January can be accessed in an array called SAL, for example as SAL,1. That is read SAL sub 1. In RPGIV, the index is in parentheses as in SAL(1). The index can also be a variable so that all elements of the array can be processed individually in a loop by adding 1 to the index value. Arrays can also be processed using the lookup that is often used with tables. Once the lookup operation completes, the specific array element can be processed, just as with a table.

Strings

A String in all computer languages is a group of alphameric characters. In the AS/400 RPG world, strings are held in fields. Thus, the String operations to which you are about to be introduced in Table 14-8 operate within the AS/400 type called "field," which, for the String operations, works just fine.

Though RPG's basic string operations provide many of the same facilities as provided by other languages, please do not read that to mean the structure of the string in RPG (a field) is the same as the structure of the string in languages which treat a string as something special to the language. For example, an RPG string is not compatible with a Java String object. Thus when RPG and other languages exchange strings, it is not a straight-forward process.

Table 14-8 Data Area, Table, Array, String Operations

Operation	**Provided Function**
CAT	Concatenate two character strings. The concatenate (CAT) operation combines the character string specified in Factor 2 to the end of the character string specified in Factor 1 and places it in the result field. If no Factor 1 is specified, factor 2 is concatenated to the end of the result field string.
CHECK	Check for Certain Chars in a String (L to R) The CHECK operation verifies that each character in the base string (Factor 2) is among the characters indicated in the comparator string (Factor 1). All of the string operations are complex instructions with many specifications. See Chapter 18. Checking begins at the leftmost character of factor 2 and continues character by character, from left to right. Each character of the base string is compared with the characters of factor 1. If a match for a character in factor 2 exists in factor 1, the next base string character is verified. If a match is not found, an integer value is placed in the result field to indicate the position of the first incorrect character. The whole base string does not have to be checked, however. You can specify a start position in factor 2, separating it from the base string by a colon. This start position is optional and defaults to 1. If it is > 1, the value in the result field is still relative to the leftmost position in the base string, regardless of the start position. If no incorrect characters are found, the result field is set to zero.
CHEKR	Check Reverse for Chars in a String (R to L). This command works very similarly to the CHECK command. However, checking is done from right to left. Although checking is done from the right, the position placed in the result field will be relative to the left. See Chapter 18.
CLEAR	Sets values in structure to zero or blank. See details in Table 14-6 Data Manipulation Operations
IN	Retrieve a Data Area Object into Program. The IN operation retrieves a data area and optionally allows you to specify whether the data area is to be locked from update by another program. For a data area to be retrieved by the IN operation, it must be specified in the result field of an *NAMVAR DEFN statement. See "DEFN" for information on *NAMVAR DEFN. in Table 14-9, Pgm Control, Declarative & Informational Operations. Factor 1 can contain the reserved word *LOCK or can be blank. The lock is held until (1) an UNLCK operation or (2) an OUT operation with no Factor 1 or (3) when the RPG program ends. Factor 2 must be either the name of the result field used when you retrieved the data area or the reserved word *NAMVAR. When *NAMVAR is specified, all data areas defined in the program are retrieved.
LOKUP	Look up argument in a memory table or array. The LOKUP operation causes a search to be made for a

particular element in an array or table. Factor 1 is the search argument (data for which you want to find a match in the array or table named). For a table LOKUP, the result field can contain the name of a second table from which an element (corresponding position with that of the first table) can be retrieved. The name of the second table can be used to reference the element retrieved. The result field must be blank if Factor 2 contains an array name. Resulting indicators can be assigned to EQ and HI or to EQ and LO. The program searches for an entry that satisfies either condition with equal given precedence; that is, if no equal entry is found, the nearest lower or nearest higher entry is selected.

MOVEA
Move Array to Field and Vice Versa. See Table 14-6 Data Manipulation Operations for details

OCUR
Specifies occurrence of the DS to be used. When there is more than one record in a data structure it is called a multiple **occur**rences data structure. Similar to an array index, the records in the DS can be retrieved by their relative position in the structure. For a DS, this is called an occurrence. For example, record 3 would be occurrence3. The OCUR operation code specifies which Occurrence (record) of the data structure that is to be used next within the program. After an OCCUR op is specified, the occurrence of the data structure that was established by the OCUR operation is used.   Factor 1 is optional. If specified, it sets the occurrence of the DS. If blank, the value of the current occurrence of the data structure in factor 2 is placed in the result field during the OCUR operation. The result field is optional. The value of the current occurrence of the data structure specified in factor 2 is placed in the result field.

OUT
Write out a data area object from a program. The OUT operation updates the data area specified in Factor 2. The rules for this operation include the following: (1) The data area must also be specified in the result field of a *NAMVAR Statement. (See "DEFN" for information on *NAMVAR DEFN. in Table 14-9, Program Control, Declarative & Informational Operations.) and (2) The data area must have been locked previously by a *LOCK IN statement or it must have been specified as a data area data structure by a U in position 18 of the RPG/400 input specifications. The RPG language implicitly retrieves and locks data area data structures at program initialization. When factor 1 contains *LOCK, the data area remains locked after it is updated. When factor 1 is blank, the data area is unlocked after it is updated. Factor 2 must be either the name of the result field used when you retrieved the data area or the reserved word *NAMVAR. When *NAMVAR is specified, all data areas defined in the program are updated.

RESET
Resets structure values. See Table 14-6 Data Manipulation Operations for details

SCAN
Scan Character String for a Certain String. The SCAN operation scans a character string (base string) contained in Factor 2 for a substring (compare string) contained in Factor 1. The scan begins at a specified location contained in Factor 2 and continues for the length of the compare string which is specified in Factor

1. Factor 1 must contain either the compare string or the compare string, followed by a colon, followed by the length. If no length is specified, it is that of the compare string. Factor 2 must contain either the base string or the base string, followed by a colon, followed by the start location of the SCAN. If no start location is specified, a value of 1 is used. The result field contains the numeric value of the leftmost position of the compare string in the base string, if found. The result field is set to 0 if the string is not found. If the result field is specified and the start position is greater than 1, the result field contains the position of the compare string relative to the beginning of the source string, not relative to the start position. If no result field is specified, a resulting indicator in RPG/400 positions 58 and 59 (EQ) must be specified. See Chapter 18 for more detail & examples.

SUBST   Substring – Results in a Portion of a String   The SUBST operation returns a substring from factor 2, starting at the location specified in factor 2 for the length specified in Factor 1, and places this substring in the result field. If factor 1 is not specified, the length of the string from the start position is used. Factor 1 can contain the length value of the string to be extracted from the string specified in factor 2. Factor 2 must contain either the base character string, or the base character string followed by a colon, followed by the start location. If the start position is not specified, SUBST starts in position 1 of the base string. The result field must be character If the substring is longer than the field specified in the result field, the substring will be truncated from the right. See Chapter 18 for detail.

SORTA   Sort an array in ascending or descending sequence. Factor 2 contains the name of an array to be sorted. The array is sorted into sequence (ascending or descending), depending on the sequence specified for the array in position 45 of the RPG/400 extension specifications. If no sequence is specified, the array is sorted into ascending sequence.

XLATE   Translate String (eg Upper Case to Lower Case). Characters in the source string (Factor 2) are translated according to the from and to strings (both in Factor 1) and put into the result field. Source characters with a match in the from string are translated to corresponding characters in the to string. XLATE starts translating the source at the location specified in Factor 2 and continues character by character, from left to right. If a character of the source string exists in the from string, the corresponding character in the to string is placed in the result field. Any characters in the source field before the starting position are placed unchanged in the result field. Factor 1 must contain the from string, followed by a colon, followed by the to string. Factor 2 must contain either the source string or the source string followed by a colon and the start location. If no start location is specified, a value of 1 is used. The result field must be specified – typically as a character field. See Chapter 18 for more detail and string examples.

XFOOT   Sum the elements of an array to a result field. See

UNLCK
Table 14-6 Data Manipulation Operations for details
Unlock a data area or release a record.
See Table 14-7 - Database & File Operations for details

Program Control, Declarative, Informational & Other Operations

Table 14-9 provides a description for a number of operations that can make coding easier and / or provide additional information without a lot of work during the programming cycle. Starting with the Field Definition operation, which permits like fields and special constructs to be defined to the KFLD and KLIST operations to make using composite keys easier, to the PARM and PLIST operations which help line up data for program passage, to the DEBUG, SHTDN (shutdown) and TIME operations, this table offers a lot of variety and utility and the operations contained herein will come handy as you become an accomplished RPG programmer.

Table 14-9 Program Control, Declarative, Informational & Other Operations

Operation	Provided Function
DEBUG	Show Internal Variables and Indicators. See Table 14-2 RPG Basic Operations
DEFN	**Field Definition.** Depending on the Factor 1 entry, the declarative DEFN operation can do either of the following: (1) ***LIKE** -- Define a field based on the attributes (length and decimal positions) of another field. (2) ***NAMVAR** Define a field as a data area. You can use DEFN operation anywhere within calculations The ***LIKE DEFN** operation defines a new field based up-on the attributes (length, decimal positions) of another field. Factor 2 must contain the name of the field being referenced, and the result field must contain the name of the field being defined. The ***NAMVAR DEFN** oper-ation associates an RPG program defined field, a data structure, a data-structure subfield, or a data-area data structure with an AS/400 data area (outside your RPG program). In factor 2, specify the external name of a data area. Use *LDA for the name of the local data area or use *PDA for the Program Initialization Parameters (PIP) data area. If you leave Factor 2 blank, the result field entry is both the RPG name and the external name of the data area. In the result field, specify the name of one of the following that you have defined in your program.
DUMP	Program dump to help debug programs. The UMP operation provides a dump (all fields, all files, indicators, data structures, arrays, and tables defined) of the program.
KFLD	Define parts of a key search argument – by **field name.** The KFLD operation is a declarative operation that indicates that a field is part of a search argument identified by a KLIST name. The result field must contain the name of a field that is to be part of the search argument. The result field cannot contain an array name or a table name. Each KFLD field must agree in length, data type (character or numeric), and decimal position with the corresponding field in the composite key of the record or file.
KLIST	Define a composite key of KFLDs. The KLIST operation is a declarative operation that gives a name to a

list of KFLDs used as a search argument to retrieve records from files that have a composite key. Factor 1 must contain a unique name.

PARM   Identify parameters for a program. See Table 14-5 CALL Operations

PLIST   Identify a parameter list for program. See Table 14-5 CALL Operations.

TAG   Tag – Destination for a GOTO.   Label "Where a 'GOTO' goes.

SHTDN   Test for system shut down request.   The SHTDN operation provides a means for the programmer to test whether the system operator has requested a system shutdown. If the system operator has requested shutdown, the resulting indicator specified in RPG/400 positions 54 and 55 (HI) is set on.

TIME   Get time of day and store in a field. See Table 14-2 Basic Operations

Structured Operations

Some time after RPGIII was introduced; IBM substantially enhanced the RPG language with the addition of a number of structured operations. These are fully covered in Chapter 19. As you will see as you examine the structured operations in Table 14-10 you may notice the brief function descriptions. That is because each of these operations has been explained fully in a previous table arlier in this chapter. For your convenience in being able to recognize this powerful RPG structured operators, we repeat them below together and provide specific reference to the table in which they are more fully explained.

Table 14-10 Program Control, Declarative, & Informational Operations

Operation	**Provided Function**
ANDxx	And If another condition is true, then.. See Table 14-4 Compare & Branch Operations
CASxx	Conditionally Invoke Subroutine on compare. See Table 14-4 Compare & Branch Operations
DO	**Straight DO Loop.** See Table 14-4 Compare & Branch Operations
DOUxx	**Do until xx is true.** See Table 14-4 Compare & Branch Operations
DOWxx	**Do while xx is true.** See Table 14-4 Compare & Branch Operations
ELSE Else. See Table 14-4 Compare & Branch Operations	
ENDSL	**End of Select Group.** See Table 14-4 Compare & Branch Operations
ENDSR	**End of Subroutine.** See Table 14-4 Compare & Branch Operations.
ENDyy	End a Group yy = IF or DO etc. See Table 14-4 Compare & Branch Operations
IFxx	If a condition is xx, perform a set of operations. See Table 14-4 Compare & Branch Operations
ITER	Iterate– run through do group another time. See Table 14-4 Compare & Branch Operations
LEAVE	Leave a do group after ENDxx. See Table 14-4 Compare & Branch Operations
ORxx	Or If another condition is true, then... See Table 14-4 Compare & Branch Operations

OTHER	Otherwise select operation in select group. See Table 14-4 Compare & Branch Operations
SELEC	**Begin a select group**. See Table 14-4 Compare & Branch Operations
WHxx	When true then select. See Table 14-4 Compare & Branch Operations

All RPG Operations / Parameters

Now that we have examined all of the RPG/400 operations in this chapter, we have just one more task to accomplish. In the next short section, we provide a comprehensive table of all the RPG/400 operations.

This table shows the Factor 1, Factor 2, and Result Field components and the potential status of resulting indicators after the operation. It can serve as a very handy reference in future programming assignments.

To help in our examination of all these op-codes, there are a number of abbreviations and symbols that we must briefly define in Table 14-11. You may find these anywhere in Table 14-12 but primarily, you will see them in the resulting indicators area. This shows which operations turn on indicators for what purpose.

Table 14-12 can serve as a very handy summary guide to RPG operations. It shows how most of the RPG/400 operations that we described in terms of capabilities earlier in this chapter are used in actual calculation specifications. Additionally, the resulting indicators are explained according to the following key:

To make it much easier to look up operations in Table 14-12, the operations are presented in alphabetic sequence by op-code. If you need more information than the format and options of the operations in this table, check out the first column. It is a direct link to the first Table in which the operation is explained in more detail. For example, B is basic operations, C is Compare, D is database/device, M is manipulation, P is program call, S is data structure, and O is other operations.

Table 14-11 Op Code Symbols / Indicators

+	If the result is positive, the indicator placed in these columns is set on.
-	If the result is negative, the indicator placed in these columns is set on.
0	If the result is zero, the indicator placed in these columns is set on.
BL	Blank(s)
BN	Blank(s) then numeric
BOF	Beginning of file
EOF	End of database file has been reached via READ type operations
ER	Error – indicator specified in these columns is set on indicating that an error occurred in the operation
EQ	Equal condition also If factor 1 is equal to factor 2, set on indicator specified in these columns
FD	Found
HI	If factor 1 is greater than factor 2, set on indicator specified in these columns
IN	Indicator
LO	If factor 1 is less than factor 2, set on indicator specified in these columns
LR	Last record indicator
NA	Not applicable
NR	No record found – indicator is set on signifying no record found

NU	Numeric
Of	Indicator to be set off
On	Indicator to be set on
Z	If the result is zero, the indicator placed in these columns is set on.
ZB	Zero or blank

Table 14-12 All RPG Operations / Parameters Alphabetical

T	Code	Factor1	Factor2	Result	I1	I2	I3
D	Acq	Device name	Workstn file		NA	ER	NA
B	ADD	Addend	Addend	Sum	+	-	0
C	ANDxx	Comparand	Comparand				
C	BEGSR	Subr. Name					
M	BITOF		Bit #s in byte	Char field			
M	BITON		Bit #s in byte	Char field			
C	CABxx	Comparand	Comparand	Go to instr. label	HI	LO	EQ
P	CALL	&OS	'Program name' or variable name	Plist name optional	NA	ER	LR
M	CAT	Source str 1	Source string 2: #blanks	Target string			
C	CASxx	Comparand	Comparand	Subroutine label	HI	LO	EQ
B	CHAIN	Search arg.	File/record name		NR	ER	NA
M	CHECK	Comparator str	Base string: start pos	Left-pos	NA	ER	FD
S	CHEKR	Comparator str	Base string: start pos	Right-pos	NA	ER	FD
M	CLEAR	*nokey	Structure, variable, record				
D	CLOSE		File name		NA	ER	NA
D	COMIT	Boundary			NA	ER	NA
C	COMP	Comparand	Comparand		HI	LO	EQ
B	DEBUG	Identifier	Output file name	Debug Info			
M	DEFN	*like	Reference field	Defined field			
M	DEFN	*namvar or *extrn	External / internal data area	Internal program area			
B	DELET	Search arg.	File / record name		NR	ER	NA

B	DIV	Dividend	Divisor	Quotient	+	-	0
C	DO	Start value	Limit value	Index val			
C	DOUxx	Comparand	Comparand				
C	DOWxx	Comparand	Comparand				
O	DUMP	Identifier					
D	DSPLY	Msgid or literal	Outq or variable to view	Response	N A	ER	N A
C	ELSE						
C	END			Increment val			
C	ENDCS						
C	ENDDO			Increment value			
C	ENDIF						
C	ENDSL						
C	ENDSR	Label	Return point				
D	EXCPT		EXCPT name				
B	EXFMT		Screen name		N A	ER	N A
C	EXSR		Subroutine name				
D	FEOD		File name		N A	ER	N A
D	FORCE		File name				
P	FREE		Program name		N A	ER	N A
C	GOTO		Program Label				
C	IFxx	Comparand	Comparand				
S	IN	*Lock	Data Area name		N A	ER	N A
C	ITER						
O	KFLD			Key field name			
O	KLIST	Klist name					
C	LEAVE						
S	LOKUP	(Array) Search arg.	Array name		HI	L O	E Q
S	LOKUP	(Table) Search arg.	Table Name	Alternate Table name	HI	L O	E Q
M	MHHZO		Source field	Target fld			
M	MHLZO		Source field	Target fld			

M	MLHZO		Source field	Target fld			
M	MLLZO		Source field	Target fld			
B	MOVE		Source field	Target fld	+	-	ZB
B	MOVEL		Source field	Target fld	+	-	ZB
B	MOVEA		Source array or field	Target array/field	+	-	ZB
B	MULT	Multiplicand	Multiplier	Product			
B	MVR			Remainder	+	-	Z
D	NEXT	Program device	File name		NA	ER	NA
S	OCUR	Occurrence value	Data structure name	Occurrence value	NA	ER	NA
D	OPEN		File name		NA	ER	NA
C	ORxx	Comparand	Comparand				
C	OTHER						
S	OUT	*lock	Data Area name		NA	ER	NA
P	PARM	Target field	Source Field	Parameter			
P	PLIST	Plist name					
D	POST	Program device	File Name	INFDS name	NA	ER	NA
B	READ		File/record name	Data structure	NA	ER	EOF
B	READC		Record Name / SFL		NA	ER	EOF
D	READE	Search arg.	File/record name	Data structure	NA	ER	EOF
D	READP		File/record name	Data structure	NA	ER	BOF
D	REDPE	Search arg.	File/record name	Data structure	NA	ER	BOF
D	REL	Program device	File Name		NA	ER	NA
M	RESET	*NKEY	Structure or variable				
P	RETRN						
D	ROLBK				NA	ER	NA

S	SCAN	Comparator string : lgth	Base string : start	Left-most position	NA	ER	FD
C	SELEC						
D	SETLL	Search arg.	File/record name		NR	ER	EQ
D	SETGT	Search arg.	File/record name		NR	ER	NA
M	SETON				OF	OF	OF
M	SETOF				ON	ON	ON
O	SHTDN				ON	NA	NA
S	SORTA		Array name				
B	SQRT		Field name/ value	Square root			
B	SUB	Minuend	Subtrahend	Difference	+	-	Z
S	SUBST	Length to extract	Base string: start	Target string	NA	ER	NA
C	TAG						
C	TESTB	Label	Bit #s	Char field	OF	ON	EQ
C	TESTN			Char field	NU	BN	BL
C	TESTZ			Char field			
B	TIME			Num field			
D	UNLCK		Data Area or file name		NA	ER	NA
B	UPDAT		File / record format name	Data structure	NA	ER	NA
C	WHxx	Comparand	Comparand				
B	WRITE		File / record format name	Data structure	NA	ER	NA
S	XFOOT		Array name	Sum	+	-	Z
S	XLATE	From : To	String : Start	Target string	NA	ER	NA
B	Z-ADD		Addend	Sum	+	-	Z
B	Z-SUB		Subtrahend	Difference	+	-	Z

Chapter Summary

There are many different operations available and they are implemented via the codes that a programmer can specify in the op-code column (28 in RPG/400 and 26 in RPGIV) of the CALC form.

RPG operations can be classified in a number of ways. In most cases, the operations for RPG/400 are the same in RPGIV, other than the expanded columns in RPGIV.   The RPG operations are classified as follows:

- ✓ Basic Operations
- ✓ Compare & Branch Operations / Subroutines
- ✓ Data Manipulation Operations
- ✓ Database & Device File Operations
- ✓ Data Structure, Table, Array, String Operations
- ✓ Program Control Operations
- ✓ Structured Operations
- ✓ RPGIV Free Form Operations

This chapter in many ways is a reference document for RPG operations. It covers every operation in every classification and the operation is repeated when it works in multiple classification areas. Starting with RPG basic operations, working through the list above, each operation is shown in tabular form with eh operation code on the left followed by the provided function on the right.

The first area within the provided function is a one phrase shortened synopsis of the operation. This is then followed by a detailed description of the function and purpose of the operation and how it needs to be coded in RPG/400 to achieve the desired result.

Key Chapter Terms

*ENTRY	DOWxx	READP
*LDA	DSPLY	REDPE
*LIKE	DUMP	REL
*LOCK	ELSE	RESET
*NAMVAR	ENDSR	RETRN
*PDA	EXCPT	ROLBK
5250	EXFMT	RPGIV Free Form Ops
ACQ	EXSR	RPGIV Free Syntax
Basic Operations	FEOD	SCAN
BEGSR	FORCE	SELEC
BITOF	FREE	SETGT
BITON	GOTO	SETLL
CABxx	IFxx	SETOF
CALC	ITER	SETON
CALL	KFLD	SETXX
CASxx	KLIST	SHTDN
CAT	LEAVE	SORTA
CHAIN	LOKUP	SQRT
CHECK	MHHZO	String ops
CHEKR	MHLZO	Structured Ops
CLEAR	MLHZO	SUB
CLOSE	MLLZO	SUBST
COMIT	MOVE	TAG
COMP	MOVEA	TESTB
Compare & Branch Ops	MOVEL	TESTN
Data Manipulation Ops	MULT	TESTZ
Data Structure	MVR	TIME
Database Operations	NEXT	UNLCK
Device Operations	OCCUR	UPDAT
DEBUG	OPEN	WHxx
DEFN	ORxx,	WORKSTN
DELET	OTHER	WRITE
DIV	OUT	WYSIWYG
DO	PARM	XFOOT
DOU	PIP	XLATE
DOUxx	READC	Z-ADD

DOW   READE

Review Questions

1. Are any of the calculations operation codes that are available in RPG/400 also available in RPGIV?

2. In what columns do you specify the op-code in RPG/400? RPGIV?

3. What are the two major IBM publications about RPGIV that all RPG students should download?

4. What are the types of operations that can be performed in RPG calculations?

5. How many characters is the op-code in RPG/400 and RPGIV?

6. Where is the op code extender located in RPG, RPGIV?

7. What programming language is the most English-like?

8. Which language is known for its concise operations?

9. Explain the purpose and meaning of the following basic operations – CHAIN, DELET, EXFMT, UPDAT, Z-ADD.

10. What is meant by compare and branch?

11. Which RPG op-code is used to perform a compare and a branch in one operations?

12. What is a subroutine?

13. What operations can cause a subroutine to be executed?

14. A number of operations begin with three letters and then there is a double 'XX' which means relationship. Describe two such operations and the meaning of the XX in those operations?

15. What function does AND and OR perform as RPG operations?

16. What two operations are necessary to define a subroutine?

17. Are there any restrictions on the placement of a subroutine?

18. Is GOTO a preferred operation in structured programming?

19. What are the differences among the ENDDO, ENDIF, and END operations?

20. What is the difference between DOUXX and DOWXX?

21. What defines an IF group?

22. Describe the TESTN, TESTB, and TESTZ operations?

23. What purpose does a TAG operation provide?

24. What is a Select Group?

25. What is the difference between an ITER and a LEAVE operation?

26. Which operation begins a sequence of operations to be processed if no condition is met in a select group?

27. What is the purpose of inter-program operations?

28. What is a call operation?

29. What is a dynamic call?

30. What is a parm?

31. What operation defines a parameter list?

32. What operation is used to send control back to the calling program?

33. How do BITON and BITOF help form special characters (byte configurations)?

34. Why would you use a CLEAR operation instead of a RESET??

35. Why are there seven MOVE operations?

36. What operation permits you to set on an indicator?

37. Why is there more than one READ operation?

38. Does a READC operate on a memory file? How?

39. Why would you use a DSPLY operation?

40. If RPG can open and close files automatically, why are there OPEN and CLOSE operations in RPG/400?

41. What operation would you use to set the file cursor equal to a record key so that your READ operations would read from that point in the file?

42. Under what circumstances would an UNLCK operation be appropriate?

43. What are the four different structures upon which RPG structure-type operations can perform functions?

44. What operations can be used with strings? Describe the purpose of each operation?

45. When Data Areas are not automatically read and written by RPG, they can be manipulated in calculations with which operations?

46. Which operation provides a function to find a search argument in a table or array?

47. Which operation permits data movement between fields and whole arrays?

48. To set the "record number" in a data structure, you would use which operation?

49. What are the two powerful operations against arrays that enable the array (1) to be put in sequence or to have the elements cross-footed?

50. What operation enables you to define a name as a data area?

51. How would you build a list of keys that could be used with the chain operation to access a record with a composite key?

52. Why do you suppose IBM add the structured operation codes to RPG/400?

Chapter 15   RPGIV Operations and Built-In Functions

What Is the Same in RPGIV?

After studying all the RPG/400 operations in Chapter 14, the best place to start now for RPGIV is to examine what is the same. Let's look at what you already know and how much of your new knowledge is portable to RPGIV. Let's start with what is gone.

Of the 101 RPG/400 op codes that we studied in Chapter 7, only one, the FREE op-code has been eliminated. Surely IBM has its reasons but you can think of it as IBM's attempt to bring the number of operations to an even hundred. IF Big Blue had not added another 22 instructions (Table 15-2) and a bunch of built-in functions (Table 15-9) to RPGIV, then maybe that supposition would stand.

To make it easy for you to know how much you already know about RPGIV, we have included the 100 operations and the name of its equivalent in RPGIV. It should be a pretty quick exercise because only fifteen operations have changed and the change in all cases was or readability. So, without more ado, take a look at Table 15-1 below so you can learn about how much you already know.

Table 15-1 RPG/400 and RPGIV OP-Code Differences

RPG/400 OP-Code	RPGIV OP-Code	RPG/400 OP-Code	RPGIV OP-Code
ACQ	ACQ	BITOF	BITOFF *
ADD	ADD	BITON	BITON
ANDxx	ANDxx	CABxx	CABxx
BEGSR	BEGSR	CALL	CALL
RPG/400 OP-Code	RPGIV OP-Code	RPG/400 OP-Code	RPGIV OP-Code
CAT	CAT	KLIST	KLIST
CASxx	CASxx	LEAVE	LEAVE
CHAIN	CHAIN	LOKUP	LOKUP
CHECK	CHECK	LOKUP	LOOKUP *
CHEKR	CHECKR *	MHHZO	MHHZO
CLEAR	CLEAR	MHLZO	MHLZO
CLOSE	CLOSE	MLHZO	MLHZO
COMIT	COMMIT *	MLLZO	MLLZO
COMP	COMP	MOVE	MOVE
DEBUG	DEBUG	MOVEL	MOVEL
DEFN	DEFINE *	MOVEA	MOVEA
DELET	DELETE *	MULT	MULT
DIV	DIV	MVR	MVR
DO	DO	NEXT	NEXT
DOUxx	DOUxx	OCCUR	OCCUR
DOWxx	DOWxx	OPEN	OPEN
DUMP	DUMP	ORxx	ORxx
DSPLY	DSPLY	OTHER	OTHER
ELSE	ELSE	OUT	OUT
END	END	PARM	PARM
ENDCS	ENDCS	PLIST	PLIST
ENDDO	ENDDO	POST	POST
ENDIF	ENDIF	READ	READ

ENDSL	ENDSL	READC	READC
ENDSR	ENDSR	READE	READE
EXCPT	EXCEPT *	READP	READP
EXFMT	EXFMT	REDPE	READPE *
EXSR	EXSR	REL	REL
FEOD	FEOD	RESET	RESET
FORCE	FORCE	RETRN	RETURN *
FREE	NA	ROLBK	ROLBK
GOTO	GOTO	SCAN	SCAN
IFxx	IFxx	SELEC	SELECT *
IN	IN	SETLL	SETLL
ITER	ITER	SETGT	SETGT
KFLD	KFLD	SETON	SETON
RPG/400 OP-Code	RPGIV OP-Code	RPG/400 OP-Code	RPGIV OP-Code
SETOF	SETOFF *	TIME	TIME
SHTDN	SHTDN	UNLCK	UNLOCK *
SORTA	SORTA	UPDAT	UPDATE *
SQRT	SQRT	WHxx	WHENxx *
SUB	SUB	WRITE	WRITE
SUBST	SUBST	XFOOT	XFOOT
TAG	TAG	XLATE	XLATE
TESTB	TESTB	Z-ADD	Z-ADD
TESTN	TESTN	Z-SUB	Z-SUB
TESTZ	TESTZ		

RPGIV-Only Operations

In 1994, the major changes in no particular order that everybody was talking about for the "new" RPGIV included the following:

1. Columns expanded to support longer field names.
2. Keywords for column functions
3. EVAL statement with extended Factor 2
4. Elimination of the E specification
5 D specification for defining fields, arrays, and structures
6. New date operations including date arithmetic.

Some might suggest that the major change immediately in 1994 was the introduction of the EVAL operation that provided RPG with the ability to enable equations and expressions following this operation code. Eventually RPGIV became a fully functional ILE language and IBM gave many more facilities to the language. Not all of these were provided with new operation codes but a number were.

Procedures and prototyped procedures were quick to arrive giving the language some of the flavor of the traditional block structured languages. As the supply of RPG-trained programmers dwindled, this language change helped C programmers from other platforms more readily understand RPG and its benefits. Pointers and pointer operations were also added to the language extending it into areas that had been reserved for low-level functions written in other languages.

To make the language even more likeable to those who had become accustomed to the FOR Loops in BASIC, the FOR Loop was also made available. In the last few years additional expression logic was added to the EVAL statement along with a fully free form of RPGIV. In essence, IBM enhanced the EVAL statement and then eventually removed its requirement for free- form operations

Error monitoring facilities were also added as operations to make the language more similar in its ability to trap various errors during execution. Additionally, IBM began work on providing full XML facilities into the language with the first installment being included in the operations shown in Table 15-2.

Table 15-2 RPGIV-Only Operations

Operation   Provided Function

ADDDUR   **Add a Duration to a Date** (Days, Months, Years) The ADDDUR is an original RPGIV operation that works with dates. It adds the duration specified in Factor 2 to a date or time or timestamp field or constant specified in the Result field and places the resulting Date, Time or Timestamp in the result field. Factor 1 is optional if The programmer prefers the longer way of coding the operation. If factor 1 is not specified the duration is added to the field specified in the result field. Factor 2 is required and contains two sub-factors. The first is a numeric duration and the second must be a valid duration code indicating the type of duration (year *Y, month *M, etc.). The duration code must be consistent with the result field data type. For example, You can add a year, month or day duration but not a minute duration to a date field. For list of duration codes and their short forms see Table 15-3.

ALLOC   Allocates main storage and sets a pointer. RPGIV has extended the RPG language with pointer operations. The ALLOC operation allocates storage in the default heap of the numeric length specified in Factor 2. The Result field is a pointer set to point to the new heap storage. This storage, though allocated is uninitialized and thus needs additional work to be usable. The result field must be a basing pointer scalar variable (a standalone field, data structure subfield, table name, or array element).

CALLB   Call Bound Procedure written in any ILE Language. RPGIV is an ILE language. As such it uses the ILE programming model which permits incomplete modules to be bound (linked) together to create executable programs or *PGM objects. RPGIV also supports procedures. Procedures are most often referred to as the natural building blocks for ILE applications. You can think of a procedure then as a hybrid between subroutines and external called programs. The CALLB operation is used to call bound procedures written in any of the ILE languages. The notion of an operation extender as implemented in the RPG/400 half-adjust column has been expanded with RPGIV. Extenders are now suffixes to normal op-codes. The operation extender "D" may be used to include operational descriptors for the procedure call. Operational descriptors provide the programmer with run-time resolution of the exact attributes of character or graphic strings passed (that is, length and type of string). Factor 2 is required and must be a literal or constant containing the name of the procedure to be called, or a procedure pointer containing the address of the procedure to be called. See RPGIV procedure operations in Chapter 26 for more details.

CALLP   Call Prototyped Procedure or Program. CALLP uses

a "free-form" syntax. You use the name operand to specify the name of the prototype of the called program or procedure, as well as any parameters to be passed. (similar to calling a BIF) The compiler uses the prototype name to obtain an external name, if required, for the call. If the keyword EXTPGM is specified on the prototype, the call will be a dynamic external call; otherwise it will be a bound procedure call. A prototype for the program or procedure being called must be included in the definition specifications preceding the CALLP. See RPGIV procedure operations in Chapter 26 for details

DEALLOC   Deallocates storage back to the default heap.   The operation frees one previous allocation of heap storage. The pointer name that you provide in Factor 2 is a pointer that must be the value previously set by a heap-storage allocation operation (either an ALLOC operation in RPG, or some other heap-storage allocation mechanism). It is not sufficient to simply point to heap storage; the pointer must be set to the beginning of the specific allocation that is to be deallocated. The storage pointed to by the pointer is freed for subsequent allocation by this program or any other in the activation group. If operation code extender N is specified, the pointer is set to *NULL after a successful deallocation.

DOU   **Do Until (Free Form)** RPGIV also brings with it free format operations (covered in Chapter 27.) The DOU operation code is a free format RPG operation that precedes a group of operations which you want to execute at least once and possibly more than once. Its function is similar to that of the DOUxx operation code. As with the DOUxx, the associated ENDDO statement marks the end of the group. It differs in that the logical condition is expressed by what is called an "indicator valued expression." An example of such an operation follows: dou *in01 or (Field2 > Field3). As with normal DO operations, those instructions within the loop are performed until the indicator valued expression is true. There are also two op code extenders, "M" & "R" available which may be needed to affect the precision of the operation.

DOW   **Do While (Free Form)** DOW is a free format operation code that precedes a loop of instructions, which you want to process when a given condition exists. It is very similar in function to that of the DOWxx operation code but it differs in form. An associated ENDDO statement marks the end of the Do group. Rather than a mix of op-code and factors, the logical condition of the DOW is expressed by an "indicator valued expression." The loop is performed while the indicator valued expression is true. "M" and "R" op-code extenders are available to affect the precision of the expression if necessary.

ENDFOR   **Ends a FOR Group.** An ENDFOR operation indicates the end of the FOR group. There are no operands.

ENDMON   **Ends a Monitor Group.** An ENDMON operation Indicates the end of the MONITOR group. There are no operands.

ELSEIF   **Else and IF Combination Operation**. The ELSEIF operation is a clever combination of an ELSE operation with an IF operation. Its major advantage over the split operation is that it avoids the need for an additional level of nesting. It uses the extended Factor 2 facility of RPGIV to provide the space for what is called the "indicator valued expression." The IF part of the operation code allows a series of operation codes to be processed if a condition is met. Its function is similar to that of the IFxx operation code. Rather than comparing Factors, the IF expression is evaluated. The operations controlled by the ELSEIF operation are performed when the expression in the indicator-expression operand is true (and of course the expression for the previous IF or ELSEIF statement was false).

EVAL **Evaluate Expression.** The EVAL operation code permits semi-free form expressions to be used in the Extended Factor 2 area of the RPG calculations statement. It evaluates an assignment statement of the form result=expression. The expression is evaluated and the result placed in result (left side of equal sign). The expression may yield any of the RPG data types. On a free-form calculation specification, the EVAL operation code name itself may be omitted if no op-code extenders are needed.

EVALR   Evaluate Expression – Right Adjust Result. The EVALR is similar to EVAL. However, the result will be right justified and padded with blanks on the left, or truncated on the left as required. Unlike the EVAL operation, the result of EVALR can only be of type character, graphic, or UCS-2.

EXTRCT   Extracts part of date / time/ timestamp into a field. The EXTRCT operation code is a very powerful RPGIV operator which returns to the Result field, the requested sub field from the date, time, or timestamp specified in Factor 2. This can be (1) the year, month or day part of a date or timestamp field, (2) the hours, minutes or seconds part of a time or timestamp field, (3) the microseconds part of the timestamp field to the field specified in the Result field. The duration code (Table 15-3) must be consistent with the data type of Factor 2. For a character result field, the data is put left adjusted into the result field.

FOR   FOR loop with index and increment. FOR is another loop type made famous in the BASIC language that is similar in function to a DO loop. The FOR operation begins the loop which consists of a group of operations and it controls the number of times the group will be processed. The operation uses only the Extended Factor 2 form and is thus specified in much the same way as an Extended Factor 2 expression. To indicate the number of times the group of operations is to be processed, you specify an index name, a starting value, an increment value, and a limit value. The optional starting, increment, and limit values can also be used in an RPG free-form expression. The ENDFOR or an associated END statement marks the end of the FOR group.

IF   **If statement (Free form).** The IF operation uses the Extended Factor 2 form of RPGIV calculations. The operation code starts a group that allows a series of operation codes to be processed if a condition is true. Its function is similar to that of the IFxx operation code The difference is that the logical condition is expressed by an "indicator valued expression." The operations controlled by the IF operation are performed when the expression is true.

LEAVESR **Exits Subroutine from Any Point.** The LEAVESR operation exits a subroutine from any point within the subroutine. Control passes to the ENDSR operation for the subroutine. LEAVESR is allowed only from within a subroutine. There are no operands.

MONITOR Begin Monitor Group -- Monitors for Errors **with ON-ERROR.** To enable more control of exception handling in RPG IV, the MONITOR operation code (Or group) is added. It consist of the following: (1) A MONITOR block, (2) One or more ON-ERROR blocks, and (3) an ENDMON operation (Or END opcode). If an error occurs when the monitor block is processed, control is passed to the appropriate ON-ERROR group. There are no operands.

ON-ERROR **Specifies Types of Errors to Monitor.** This operation works with Extended Factor 2 to provide a list of error IDs. You specify which error conditions the on-error block handles in the list of exception IDs. You can specify any combination of the following, separated by colons: (1) nnnnn -- A status code, (2) *PROGRAM – Handles all program-error status codes, from 00100 to 00999, (3) *FILE -- Handles all file-error status codes, from 01000 to 09999, (4) *ALL – This default handler, takes care of both program-error and file-error codes, from 00100 to 09999. When all the statements in an on-error block have been processed, control passes to the statement following the ENDMON statement.

REALLOC Reallocate main storage with a new length. This operation alters the prior memory allocation by changing the length of the heap storage pointed to by the Result-field pointer to the new length as specified in Factor 2. The result field of REALLOC contains the basing pointer variable, which must contain the value previously set by a heap-storage allocation operation (either an ALLOC or REALLOC operation in RPG -- or some other valid heap-storage function.) As with the DEALLOC, it is not sufficient to simply point to heap storage; the pointer must be set to the beginning of an allocation. The new storage amount is allocated and the value of the old storage is copied to the new storage. Following this, the old storage is deallocated. If the new length is shorter, the value is truncated on the right. If the new length is longer, the new storage to the right of the copied data is uninitialized. The Result field pointer is set to point to the new storage.

SUBDUR Subtract a Duration to a Date (Days, Months, **Years).** The SUBDUR operation can be used to subtract a duration specified in factor 2 from a field or constant specified in factor 1 and place the resulting Date, Time or Timestamp in the field specified in the Result field. If factor 1 is not specified then the duration is subtracted from the field specified in the result field.

Factor 2 is required and contains two subfactors. The first is a numeric field. The second subfactor must be a valid duration code indicating the type of duration (YR, Mo Day, etc. See Table 15-3 for valid duration codes. The Result field must be a date, time or timestamp data type field, array or array element. The SUBDUR operation can also be used to calculate a duration between: two dates, a date and a timestamp, two times, a time and a timestamp, and two timestamps. The result is a number of whole units, with any remainder discarded. For example, 62 minutes is equal to 1 hour and 57 minutes is equal to 0 hours. The result field consists of two subfactors. The first is the name of a numeric element in which the result of the operation will be placed. The second subfactor contains a duration code with the type of duration.

XML-INTO   **Bring in an XML document.**   The XML-INTO operation has two forms as follows:
(1) XML-INTO{ (EH) } variable %XML(xmlDoc { : options });
(2) XML-INTO{ (EH) } %HANDLER(handler : commArea) %XML(xmlDoc { : options });
The newest IBM RPGIV op codes include XML-INTO which reads the data from an XML document in one of two ways: (1) directly into a variable or (2) gradually into an array parameter that it passes to the procedure specified by %HANDLER. Various options may be specified to control the operation. The first operand specifies the target of the parsed data. It can contain a variable name or the % HANDLER built-in function. The second operand contains the %XML built-in function specifying the source of the XML document and any options to control how the document is parsed. It can contain XML data or it can contain the location of the XML data. From the looks of this XML operation and the next, XML and its RPG debut are not really ready for prime time. Look at how simple the other RPG codes have been constructed to understand that IBM has lots of work to do in this area..

XML-SAX   **Parse XML using SAX.**   The newest IBM RPGIV op codes include XML-SAX which initiates a SAX parse for the XML document specified by the %XML built-in function. The syntax of this basically free-form expression is as follows: **XML-SAX{ (e) }** %HANDLER(eventHandler : commArea) %XML(xmldocument { : saxOptions });
The XML-SAX operation begins by calling an XML parser which begins to parse the document. When the parser discovers an event such as finding the start of an element, finding an attribute name, finding the end of an element etc., the parser calls the eventHandler with parameters describing the event. The commArea operand is a variable that is passed as a parameter to the eventHandler providing a way for the XML-SAX operation code to communicate with the handling procedure. When the eventHandler returns, the parser continues to parse until it finds the next event and calls the eventHandler again.

Table 15-3 Duration Codes for Date Operations

Unit	Built-In Function	Duration Code
Year	%YEARS	*YEARS or *Y
Month	%MONTHS	*MONTHS or *M
Day	%DAYS	*DAYS or *D
Hour	%HOURS	*HOURS or *H
Minute	%MINUTES	*MINUTES or *MN
Second	%SECONDS	*SECONDS or *S
Microsecond	%MSECONDS	*MSECONDS or *MS

Taking a look at the old and new RPGIV op-codes makes it easy to conclude that RPGIV is both the same and lots more than RPG/400. The additions to RPGIV have stretched the capabilities of the language to the point that it can provide the best business function as well as very powerful operations that may be rightfully categorized in the computer science area.

Table 15-4 takes these new operations described in detail in Table 15-2 and places them in their most simplistic form –> op-codes with a mission and a format. Each of the operations described in Table 15-2 are outlined in terms of their parameters and their format in Table 15-4. After checking out table 15-2 and its adjunct, Table 15-3, Table 15-4 is the right medicine for the RPG programmer wanting to see how the operations look when in action.

Table 15-4 All New RPG IV Operations / Parameters Alphabetical

Code	Factor1	Factor2	Result	I1	I2	I3
ADDDUR	Date/Time	Duration: Duration code	Date/Time	NA	ER	NA
ALLOC(E)		Length	Pointer	NA	ER	NA
CALLB (D,E)		Procedure name or procedure pointer	PLIST name	NA	ER	LR
CALLP		name{ (parm1 {:parm2...}) }	Extended Factor 2	NA	NA	NA
DEALLOC (E/N)			Pointer-name	NA	ER	NA
DOU (M/R)		indicator-expression	Extended Factor 2			
DOU (M/R)		indicator-expression	Extended Factor 2			
ENDFOR						
ENDMON						
ELSEIF (M/R)		indicator-expression	Extended Factor 2			
EVAL (H M/R)		Assignment Statement	Extended Factor 2			
EVALR (M/R)		Assignment Statement	Extended Factor 2			
EXTRCT (E)		Date/Time: Duration Code	Target	NA	ER	NA
FOR		index-name = start-value BY increment TO | DOWNTO limit	Extended Factor 2			

IF (M/R)		indicator-expression	Extended Factor 2			
LEAVESR						
MONITOR						
ON-ERROR		List of exception IDs	Extended Factor 2			
REALLOC		Length	Pointer	NA	E R	N A
SUBDUR (E) (Duration)	Date/time/ Timestamp	Date/Time/ Timestamp	Duration: Duration code	NA	E R	N A
SUBDUR (E) (New Date)	Date/time/ Timestamp	Duration: Duration code	Date/ Time/ Time – stamp	NA	E R	N A
XML-INTO		receiver %XML(xmlDoc {: options })	Extended Factor 2			
XML-INTO		%HANDLER(handlerProc : commArea) %XML(xmlDoc {: options })	Extended Factor 2			
XML-SAX		%HANDLER(handlerProc : commArea) %XML(xmlDoc {: options })	Extended Factor 2			

RPGIV Built-In Functions (BIFs)

Besides additional resources provided via new op-codes, RPGIV also provides a wealth of new and/or easier to use capabilities by its "Buuilt-In Functions or BIFs. The BIFS are similar to operation codes in that they perform operations on data that you specify. Built-in functions can be used in expressions in Free-Form RPG IV or with the EVAL statement described in more detail with an example below. Additionally, constant-valued built-in functions can be used in named constants. These named constants can be used in any specification. All built-in functions have the percent symbol (%) as their first character. The general syntax of RPGIV built-in functions is:

```
function-name{(argument{:argument...})}
```

Arguments for the function may be variables, constants, expressions, a prototyped procedure, or other built-in functions. An expression argument can also include a built-in function.

The list of all BIFs and the functions they provide is included in Table 15-8. Even before getting there, you can examine the individual built-in function descriptions used in the examples in Figures 15-6 and 15-7 for a look at the types of arguments that are allowed in BIF operations. It helps to remember that unlike operation codes, built-in functions return a value rather than placing a value in a calc spec Result Field.

The examples in Figure 15-6 and 15-7 illustrate this difference. Let's set up the examples now so they have more meaning as you look at the first very powerful one line BIF in Figure 15-6. It springs from the EVAL operation and it will give you your first look see at the RPGIV Extended Factor 2 operation for the first time. Explanations of the three built-in functions used in the Figure 15-6 example are shown in Table 15-5.

The short example below in Figure 15-6 returns a value to the field named RES that has been defined elsewhere in the RPGIV program. RES will contain the trimmed string that consists of a field named "A" containing "Toronto" and the substring of "Ontario, Canada" starting with the C in Canada for a length provided by the %Size function of a field named "B" (30 characters) containing 'Ontario Canada ' minus the constant digit 20.

At the end, RES will contain 'Toronto, Canada' with just one blank between the comma and the "C" in Canada. The first line of the example in Figure 15-5 shows the right-side of the C-spec with the extended Factor 2 form of RPGIV.

The Figure 15-6 example is from IBM's RPGIV Reference Manual. It illustrates a compound expression with multiple BIFs.

Table 15-5 Three BIFS for the Example

%TRIM	Purpose: Trims blanks at edges; Format: %TRIM**(string)** Returns string less any leading and trailing blanks.
%SUBST	Purpose: Get SubString; Format: %SUBST(string:start{:length}) The %SUBST returns a portion of an argument string – a.k.a a substring. It may also be used as the result of an assignment with the EVAL operation code. The start parameter represents the starting position of the substring. The length parameter represents the length of the substring.
%SIZE	**Purpose: Get Size in Bytes**. Returns size of variable or literal Formats: %SIZE(variable) %SIZE(literal) %SIZE(array{:*ALL}) %SIZE(table{:*ALL}) %SIZE(multiple occurrence data structure{:*ALL}) %SIZE returns the number of bytes occupied by the constant or field. If the argument is an array name, table name, or multiple occurrence data structure name, the value returned is the size of one element or occurrence. If *ALL is specified as the second parameter for %SIZE, the value returned is the storage taken up by all elements or occurrences. Returns size of variable or literal

Figure 15-6 RPGIV Extended Factor 2, EVAL, & BIF

```
C...+Opcode(E)+Extended-factor2++++++++++++++++++++++++ * *
C ...+ EVAL    RES = %TRIM(A + %SUBST(B:11:%SIZE(B) - 20))
```

To evaluate this statement it helps to know the following:

A   is equal to the string, ` Toronto,"
B   is equal to the string, ` Ontario, Canada '
RES becomes the string,   'Toronto, Canada'

The above example shows a complex expression with multiple nested built-in functions.

%TRIM takes as its argument a string.

In this example, the argument is the concatenation of string A and the string returned by the %SUBST built-in function. The %SUBST BIF returns a substring of string B starting at position 11 and continuing for the length returned by %SIZE minus 20. %SIZE will return the length of string B.

If A is the string ' Toronto,' and B is the string ' Ontario, Canada ' then the argument for %TRIM will * be ' Toronto, Canada ' and RES will have the value 'Toronto, Canada'.

Now, let's make this all a bit easier by providing a full RPGIV program complete with data definitions in Figure 15-7. The BIFs used don't make real sense unless you know how big the fields really are. To make the code readable in this narrow context, as you can see, we took some liberties by chopping off some space within the D & C specification (Op-code and Factor 1) and we squeezed the LR into the picture though it deserves its own column way out to the right.

Figure 15-7 Full RPGIV Program to demonstrate BIFS

```
DName++++++ETDsFrom+++To/L+++IDc.Keywords+++++++++
DA              S             12      INZ('   Toronto,')
DB              S             30      INZ(' Ontario, Canada ')
DRES1           S             20
DRES2           S              4S 0
DRES3           S             21
DLEFT           S              4
CL0N01Factor1++OpcodeExtExtended-factor2+++++++++
C               EVAL    RES1=%TRIM(A+%SUBST(B:11:%SIZE(B)-20)
C               EVAL    RES2=%SIZE(B)
C               EVAL    RES3=%SUBST(B:11:%SIZE(B)- 20)
C      'RES1='  DSPLY                       RES1
C      'RES2='  DSPLY                       RES2
C      'RES3='  DSPLY                       RES3
C               MOVEL   'LEFT'              LEFT
C      'LEFT='  DSPLY                       LEFT
C               SETON                                      LR
```

So, what does this code in Figure 15-7 do? The major BIF itself has already been explained. However, when you are learning RPG or any language, it is good to learn the language incrementally for example by walking through the smallest parts of big expressions. That's what we did.

Notice we took the one big EVAL and made two more out of it. RES2 returns the length value that is actually used in the %SUBST BIF. RES2 brings back the substring value "Canada," so you can see how the trimmed version RES1 actually gets built. Notice that the length of field "B" is 30. This code does not work as well if it is anything else.

Once the program calculates the three results (RES1, RES2, and RES3) to communicate the results to us, we use the very handy DSPLY operation. I use DSPLY all the time for debugging when I don't believe my problem is serious enough for the fine DEBUG tools that are available. The three DSPLY operations project the constant in Factor 1 to the job log and next to it DSPLY places the value of the field in the Result field.

You can even put an indicator in the Result field if that is what you are interested in examining. Finally, you see a four position alpha field called LEFT getting filled with a MOVEL operation with the word "LEFT." I put this in so that on the DSPLY view, you would know the leftmost position of the data being shown so that you would believe there were no blanks to the left of the trimmed RES1 field. Finally, so the RPG program knows that it is OK to end, the code sets on LR using the SETON operation. The job log results are shown in Figure 15-8.

Figure 15-8 Job Log "Printout" of DSPLY Operations

```
 *N
 DSPLY   RES1=      Toronto, Canada
 *N
 DSPLY   RES2=         30
 *N
 DSPLY   RES3=      Canada
 *N
 DSPLY   LEFT=      LEFT
```

Now that we have taken a big byte out of the mystery of BIFS, let's get adventurous and show them all with a brief description in Table 15-9. Then, let's follow that with a more lengthy description of each BIF in Table 15-10.

After these two charts, you will have a pretty good idea of what BIFS have been made available in RPGIV and how they can be valuable in your coding. You can also expect a number of additional BIFS of various flavors in the next release of RPGIV.

Since all of these BIFS operate without any help from Factor1, Factor2, the Result field or the resulting indicators, there is no need for a formatted operation table as we did in Chapter 7 for all operations and as we did in Table 15-4 for the new RPGIV operations.

Table 15-9	BIFs and Functions Provided
BIF Name	Provided Function
%ABS	Numeric absolute value of expression
%ADDR	Variable name address of variable
%ALLOC	# of bytes storage to allocate pointer storage
%BITAND	Char, numeric bit wise ANDing bits of all args
%BITNOT	Char, numeric bit-wise reverse of bits of the args
%BITOR	Char, numeric bit-wise ORing bits of all args
%BITXOR	Char, numeric bit-wise exclusive ORing two args
%CHAR	Graphic, UCS-2, numeric, date, etc. in char fmt.
%CHECK	Check for Certain Chars in a String (L to R)
%CHECKR	Check Reverse for Chars in a String (R to L)
%DATE	Date -- system date if none is specified
%DAYS	# days as a duration
%DEC	Changes expression to packed decimal
%DECH	Changes expression to packed decimal – rounded up
%DECPOS	Numeric expression -- # of decimal digits
%DIFF	Difference between two dates, times
%DIV	Divide two #s function
%EDITC	Edit value using an edit code.
%EDITFLT	Convert to Float External Representation.
%EDITW	Edit value using an Edit word:
%ELEM	# of elements or occurrences
%EOF	Test for End of File
%EQUAL	Return exact match condition.
%ERROR	Most recent operation was an error
%FIELDS	List of fields to be updated not applicable
%FLOAT	Convert value to floating format.
%FOUND	Successful found record
%GRAPH	Expression in graphic format
%HOURS	# of hours as a duration
%INT	Change to integer format
%INTH	Change to integer format – rounded up
%KDS	Data structure with keys
%LEN	Get or set length.
%LOOKUPxx	argument: array with index
%MINUTES	# of minutes as a duration
%MONTHS	# of months as a duration
%MSECONDS	# of microseconds as a duration
%NULLIND	Null-capable field name value in indicator
%OCCUR	Current occurrence of multiple-occurrence DS
%OPEN	Opens a closed file
%PADDR	Get procedure address
%PARMS	# of parameters passed to procedure
%REALLOC	Numeric pointer: to allocated storage
%REM	Division - the remainder from div of 2 args

%REPLACE	Replacement string
%SCAN	Returns searched for value or zero
%SECONDS	# of seconds as a duration
%SHTDN	Returns value indicating shutdown (1 or 0)
%SIZE	Returns size of variable or literal
%SQRT	Square root of a numeric value
%STATUS	0 if no I/O error for file
%STR	String characters addressed by pointer argument
%SUBARR	Return a subset of an array
%SUBDT	Returns a portion of date or time value
%SUBST	Returns a substring
%THIS	The class instance for the native method
%TIME	Brings back system time if none is specified
%TIMESTAMP	Brings back current timestamp if none specified
%TLOOKUPxx	Checks for match and returns '*ON' or '*OFF'
%TRIM string	Trims string with left, right blanks or specified
%TRIML string	Trims string with left blanks or specified
%TRIMR string	Trims string with right blanks or specified
%UCS2	Brings back value in UCS-2 format
%UNS	Brings back value in unsigned format
%UNSH	Brings back rounded-up value - unsigned format
%XFOOT	Array expression sum of the elements
%XLATE	Translate String (eg Upper Case to Lower Case).
%YEARS	# of years as a duration

Table 15-10 BIFs and Functions Details

BIF Name	**Provided Function**
%ABS	Numeric absolute value of expression. Format: %ABS(numeric expression) Example: **F8 = %abs (F8);** %ABS returns the absolute value of the numeric expression specified as the parameter. %ABS may be used either in expressions or as parameters to keywords.
%ADDR	Variable name address of variable. Format: %ADDR(variable); %ADDR(variable(index)); %ADDR(variable(expression)) Example: IF %ADDR (CHAR10) = %ADDR (SUBF); %ADDR returns a value of type basing pointer. The value is the address of the specified variable. It may only be compared with and assigned to items of type basing pointer.
%ALLOC	# of bytes storage to allocate pointer storage. Format: %ALLOC(num) Example: **Pointer = %ALLOC(200);** %ALLOC returns a pointer to newly allocated heap storage of the length specified. The newly allocated storage is uninitialized. The length specified must be between 1 and 16776704.
%BITAND	Char, numeric bit wise ANDing bits of all arguments. **Format::** %BITAND (Bitwise AND Operation) %BITAND(expr:expr{:expr...}) Example below from IBM manual courtesy of IBM: %BITAND returns the bit-wise ANDing of the bits of all the arguments. That is, the result bit is ON when all of the corresponding bits in the arguments are ON, and OFF otherwise. The arguments to this BIF can be either character or numeric. For numeric arguments, if they are not integer or unsigned, they are first converted to integer. %BITAND can have two or more arguments. All arguments must be the same type, either character or numeric. The result type is the same as

the types of the arguments. For numeric arguments, the result is unsigned if all arguments are unsigned, and integer otherwise. The length is the length of the largest operand. If the arguments have different lengths, they are padded on the left with bit zeros for numeric arguments. Shorter character arguments are padded on the right with bit ones. %BITAND can be coded in any expression. It can also be coded as the argument to a File or Definition Specification keyword if all arguments are known at compile-time. If all arguments of this built-in function are hex literals, the compiler produces a constant-folded result that is a hex literal.

Examples for &BITAND and &BITOR

```
D const          c                 x'0007'
D ch1            s           4a    inz(%BITNOT(const))
 * ch1 is initialized to x'FFF84040'

D num1           s           5i 0 inz(%BITXOR(const:x'000F'))
 * num is initialized to x'0008', or 8

D char2a         s           2a
D char2b         s           2a
D uA             s           5u 0
D uB             s           3u 0
D uC             s           5u 0
D uD             s           5u 0

C                eval    char2a = x'FE51'
C                eval    char2b = %BITAND(char10a : x'0F0F')
 * operand1   = b'1111 1110 0101 0001'
 * operand2   = b'0000 1111 0000 1111'
 * bitwise AND:    0000 1110 0000 0001
 * char2b = x'0E01'
C                eval    uA = x'0123'
C                eval    uB = x'AB'
C                eval    uc = x'8816'
C                eval    uD = %BITOR(uA : uB : uC)
 * operand1   = b'0000 0001 0010 0011'
 * operand2   = b'0000 0000 1010 1011'(fill w x'00')
 * operand3   = b'1000 1000 0001 0110'
 * bitwise OR:     1000 1001 1011 1111
 * uD = x'89BF'
```

%BITNOT   Char, numeric bit-wise reverse of bits of the arguments.   Format:
%BITNOT(expr)

Example:
```
D const     c                 x'0007'
D ch1       s           4a    inz(%BITNOT(const))
            * ch1 is initialized to x'FFF84040'
```

%BITNOT returns the bit-wise inverse of the bits of the argument. That is, the result bit is ON when the corresponding bit in the argument is OFF, and OFF otherwise.
The argument to this built-in function can be either character or numeric. For numeric arguments, if they are not integer or unsigned, they are first converted to integer. If the value does not fit in an 15-byte integer, a numeric overflow exception is issued. %BITNOT takes just one argument. The result type is the same as the types of the arguments. For numeric arguments, the result is unsigned if all arguments are unsigned, and integer otherwise. The length is the length of the largest operand. If the arguments have different lengths, they are padded on the left with bit zeros for numeric arguments.

%BITOR   Char, numeric bit-wise ORing bits of all arguments.
              Format: %BITOR(expr:expr{:expr...})
              Example: See under %BITAND

%BITOR returns the bit-wise ORing of the bits of all the arguments. That is, the result bit is ON when any of the corresponding bits in the arguments are ON, and OFF otherwise. The arguments to this built-in function can be either character or numeric. For numeric arguments, if they are not integer or unsigned, they are first converted to integer. If the value does not fit in an 15-byte integer, a numeric overflow exception is issued. %BITOR can have two or more arguments. All arguments must be the same type, either character or numeric. However, when coded as keyword parameters, these two BIFs can have only two arguments. The result type is the same as the types of the arguments. For numeric arguments, the result is unsigned if all arguments are unsigned, and integer otherwise. The length is the length of the largest operand. If the arguments have different lengths, they are padded on the left with bit zeros for numeric arguments. Shorter character arguments are padded on the right with bit zeros. %BITOR can be coded in any expression. It can also be coded as the argument to a File or Definition Specification keyword if all arguments are known at compile-time. If all arguments of this built-in function are hex literals, the compiler produces a constant-folded result that is a hex literal.

%BITXOR Char, numeric bit-wise exclusive ORing two arguments.
Format: Format: %BITXOR(expr:expr)
Examples: **&BITXOR X'12' X'22'**   *results in* X'30'
            &BITXOR X'1211' X'22'   *results in* X'3011'
%BITXOR returns the bit-wise exclusive ORing of the bits of the two arguments. That is, the result bit is ON when just one of the corresponding bits in the arguments are ON, and OFF otherwise. The argument to this BIF can be either character or numeric. For numeric arguments, if they are not integer or unsigned, they are first converted to integer. If the value does not fit in an 15-byte integer, a numeric overflow exception is issued. %BITXOR takes just two arguments. The result type is the same as the types of the arguments. For numeric arguments, the result is unsigned if all arguments are unsigned, and integer otherwise. The length is the length of the largest operand. If the arguments have different lengths, they are padded on the left with bit zeros for numeric arguments. Shorter character arguments are padded on the right with bit zeros. %BITXOR can be coded in any expression. It can also be coded as the argument to a File or Definition Specification keyword if all arguments are known at compile-time. If all arguments of this built-in function are hex literals, the compiler produces a constant-folded result that is a hex literal.

%CHAR Graphic, UCS-2, numeric, date, etc. in char fmt. Format:
%CHAR(expression{:format})
Example:
Res = 'Time now ' + %SUBST (%CHAR(time):1:5) + '.';
%CHAR converts the value of the expression from graphic, UCS-2, numeric, date, time or timestamp data to type character. The converted value remains unchanged, but is returned in a format that is compatible with character data. If the parameter is a constant, the conversion at compile time.

%CHECK Check for Certain Chars in a String (L to R). Format:
%CHECK (comparator : base {: start})
Example: pos = %check (delimiters : string);
%CHECK returns the first position of the string base that

contains a character that does not appear in string comparator.
If all of the characters in base also appear in comparator, the
function returns 0. The check begins at the starting position
and continues to the right until a character that is not
contained in the comparator string is found. The starting
position defaults to 1. The third parameter is optional.

%CHECKR   Check Reverse for Chars in a String (R to L). Format:
%CHECKR(comparator : base {: start})
Example: %len(string1) = %checkr(padChars:string1);
%CHECKR returns the last position of the string base that
contains a character that does not appear in string comparator.
If all of the characters in base also appear in comparator, the
function returns 0. The check begins at the starting position
and continues to the left until a character that is not contained
in the comparator string is found. The starting position
defaults to the end of the string The first parameter must be of
type character, graphic, or UCS-2, fixed or | varying length.
The third parameter is optional.

%DATE   Date --returns system date if no parms specified. Format:
%DATE{(expression{:date-format})}
Example: date = %date(string:*MDY0);
%DATE converts the value of the expression from character,
numeric, or timestamp data to type date. The converted value
remains unchanged, but is returned as a date. The first
parameter is the value to be converted. If you do not specify a
value, %DATE returns the current system date. The second
parameter is the date format for character or numeric input.
Regardless of the input format, the output is returned in *ISO
format. If the first parameter is a timestamp, *DATE, or
UDATE, do not specify the second parameter. The system
knows the format of the input in these cases.

%DAYS   # days as a duration. Format:
%DAYS(number)
Example: newdate = date + %DAYS(5);
%DAYS converts a number into a duration that can be added
to a date or timestamp value. %DAYS can only be the right-
hand value in an addition or subtraction operation. The left-
hand value must be a date or timestamp. The result is a date or
timestamp value with the appropriate number of days added
or subtracted. For a date, the resulting value is in *ISO
format.

%DEC   Convert to packed decimal format. Format:
%DEC(numeric expression{:precision:decimal places})
Example: Result = %dec (s9 : 5: 0);
%DEC converts the value of the numeric expression to
decimal (packed) format with precision digits and decimal
places decimal positions. The precision and decimal places
must be numeric literals, named constants that represent
numeric literals, or built-in functions with a numeric value
known at compile-time. Parameters precision and decimal
places may be omitted if the type of numeric expression is not
float. If these parameters are omitted, the precision and
decimal places are taken from the attributes of numeric
expression.

%DECH   Convert to packed decimal format Half adjust. Format::
%DECH(numeric expression :precision:decimal places)
Example: Result = %dech (f8: 5: 2);
%DECH is the same as %DEC except that if numeric
expression is a decimal or float value, half adjust is applied to

the value of numeric expression when converting to the desired precision. Unlike, %DEC, all three parameters are required.

%DECPOS   Numeric expression -- # of decimal digits. Format:
%DECPOS(numeric expression)
Example: Result = %decpos (p7);
%DECPOS returns the number of decimal positions of the numeric variable or expression. The value returned is a constant, and so may participate in constant folding. The numeric expression must not be a float variable or expression.

%DIFF   Difference between 2 dates, times, timestamps. Format:
1. %DIFF(op1:op2:*MSECONDS|*SECONDS|
    *MINUTES| *HOURS|*DAYS|*MONTHS|*YEARS)
2. %DIFF(op1:op2:*MS|*S|*MN|*H|*D|*M|*Y)
Example: Num_days = %DIFF (loandate: duedate: *DAYS);
%DIFF produces the difference (duration) between two date or time values. The first and second parameters must have the same, or compatible types. Many combinations are possible.

%DIV   Divide two #s function Return integer quotient: Format:
%DIV (n:m)
Example: Result = %DIV (A:B);
%DIV returns the integer portion of the quotient that results from dividing operands n by m. The two operands must be numeric values with zero decimal positions.

%EDITC   Edit value using an edit code. Format:
   %EDITC(numeric : editcode {: Value))
Value choices = *ASTFILL | *CURSYM | currency-symbol
Example: EVAL Result = 'Annual salary is ' +
        %trim(%editc(salary * 12:'A': *CURSYM))
The &EDITC function returns a character result representing the numeric value edited according to the edit code. In general, the rules for the numeric value and edit code are identical to those for editing numeric values in output specifications. The third parameter is optional, and if specified, must be one of the values shown above. The result of %EDITC is always the same length, and may contain leading and trailing blanks.

%EDITFLT   Convert to Float External Representation. Format:
%EDITFLT(numeric expression)
Example: Reslt = 'Float value is' + %editflt (f8 - 4E4) + '.';
%EDITFLT converts the value of the numeric expression to the character external display representation of float. The result is either 14 or 23 characters. If the argument is a 4-byte float field, the result is 14 characters. Otherwise, it is 23 characters

%EDITW   Edit value using an Edit word: Format:
 %EDITW(numeric : editword)
Example: D editwd   C   '$, , **Dollars& &Cents'
Result = 'Annual salary ' + %editw(salary * 12 : editwd);
This function returns a character result representing the numeric value edited according to the edit word as in the above example. The rules for the numeric value and edit word are identical to those for editing numeric values in output specifications. The edit word must be a character constant.

%ELEM   # of elements or occurrences: Format:
%ELEM(table_name) %ELEM(array_name)
%ELEM(multiple_occurrence_data_structure_name)
Example: Resultary = %elem (arr1d);
               Resulttbl = %elem (table);

ResultDS = %elem (mds);

%ELEM returns the number of elements in the specified array, table, or multiple-occurrence data structure. The value returned is in unsigned integer format (type U). It may be specified anywhere a numeric constant is allowed in the definition specification or in an expression in the extended Factor 2 field. The parameter must be the name of an array, table, or multiple occurrence data structure.

%EOF   Test for End of File. Format:
%EOF (Return End or Beginning of File Condition)
%EOF{(file_name)}
Example: IF %EOF(FILE1) AND %EOF(FILE2);
%EOF returns '1' if the most recent read operation or write to a subfile ended in an end of file or beginning of file condition; otherwise, it returns '0'. The operations that set %EOF are: READ, READC, READE (Read Equal Key), READP, READPE, WRITE (subfile only). The following operations, if successful, set %EOF(filename) off. If the operation is not successful, %EOF(filename) is not changed. %EOF with no parameter is not changed by these operations: CHAIN, OPEN, SETGT, SETLL. When a full-procedural file is specified, this function returns '1' if the previous operation in the list above, for the specified file, resulted in an end of file or beginning of file condition. For primary and secondary files, %EOF is available only if the file name is specified. It is set to '1' if the most recent input operation during *GETIN processing resulted in an end of file or beginning of file condition. Otherwise, it returns '0'. This function is allowed for input, update, and record-address files; and for display files allowing WRITE to subfile records.

%EQUAL   Return exact match condition. Format:
%EQUAL{(file_name)}
Examples: Setll Cust CustRec;
                if %equal;
            C   WHEN   %EQUAL
%EQUAL returns '1' if the most recent relevant operation found an exact match; otherwise, it returns '0'. The operations that set %EQUAL are: SETLL (Set Lower Limit), LOOKUP (Look Up a Table or Array Element) If %EQUAL is used without the optional file_name parameter, then it returns the value set for the most recent relevant operation. For the SETLL operation, this function returns '1' if a record is present whose key or relative record number is equal to the search argument. For the LOOKUP operation with the EQ indicator specified, this function returns '1' if an element is found that exactly matches the search argument.

%ERROR   Most recent operation was an error. Format:
%ERROR (Return Error Condition)
Example: if %error; exsr ErrorSub; endif;
Format: %ERROR returns '1' if the most recent operation with extender 'E' specified resulted in an error condition. This is the same as the error indicator being set on for the operation. Before an operation with extender 'E' specified begins, %ERROR is set to return '0' and remains unchanged following the operation if no error occurs. All operations that allow an error indicator can also set the %ERROR built-in function. The CALLP operation can also set %ERROR.

%FIELDS   List of fields to be updated not applicable
%FLOAT   Convert value to floating format. Format:

%FLOAT(numeric expression)
Example; Result = %float (p1) / p2;
%FLOAT converts the value of the numeric expression to
float format. This built-in function may only be used in
expressions.

%FOUND   Successful found record. Format:
%FOUND{(file_name)}
Example: If %found (Master) and not %found (Gold);
%FOUND returns '1' if the most recent relevant file operation
found a record, a string operation found a match, or a search
operation found an element. Otherwise, this function returns
'0'. The operations that set %FOUND are: CHAIN,
DELETE, SETGT, SETLL, CHECK, CHECKR, LOOKUP,
SCAN (Scan String – however, the %SCAN BIF does not
change the value of %FOUND.) If %FOUND is used
without the optional file_name parameter, then it returns the
value set for the most recent relevant operation. When a
file_name is specified, then it applies to the most recent
relevant operation on that file.

%GRAPH   Expression in graphic Format:
%GRAPH(char-expr | graph-expr | UCS-2-expr { : ccsid })   Example:

```
D*Name+++++ETDsFrom+++To/L+++IDc.Keywords+++++++++++++++++++++++++
D  char      S             5A   inz('abcde')
 * %GRAPH built-in function is used to initialize a graphic field
D  Result    S            10G   inz (%graph ('oAABBCCDDEEi'))
D  ufield    S             2C   inz (%ucs2 ('oFFGGi'))
                /FREE
```

Result = %graph (char) + %graph (ufield);
%GRAPH converts the value of the expression from
character, graphic, or UCS-2 and returns a graphic value. The
result is varying length if the parameter is varying length. The
second parameter, ccsid, is optional and indicates the CCSID
of the resulting expression. The CCSID defaults to the graphic
CCSID related to the CCSID of the job. If CCSID
(*GRAPH : *IGNORE) is specified on the control
specification or assumed for the module, the %GRAPH built-
in is not allowed. If the parameter is a constant, the conversion
will be done at compile time. In this case, the CCSID is the
graphic CCSID related to the CCSID of the source file. If the
conversion results in substitution characters, a warning
message is issued at compile time. At run time, status 00050 is
set and no error message is issued.

%HOURS   # of hours as a duration. Format:
%HOURS(number)
Example   // Determine the time in 3 hours
              Newtime = time + %HOURS(3);
%HOURS converts a number into a duration that can be
added to a time or timestamp value. %HOURS can only be
the right-hand value in an addition or subtraction operation.
The left-hand value must be a time or timestamp. The result is
a time or timestamp value with the appropriate number of
hours added or subtracted. For a time, the resulting value is in
*ISO |format.

%INT Change to integer format. Format:
%INT(numeric expression)
Example Result = %int (p7) + 0.011;
%INT converts the value of the numeric expression to integer.
Any decimal digits are truncated. This built-in function may
only be used in expressions. %INT can be used to truncate the

decimal positions from a float or decimal value allowing it to be used as an array index.

%INTH   Change to integer format – rounded up. Format:
             %INTH(numeric expression)
             Example Result1 = %int (p7)
             %INTH is the same as %INT except that if the numeric expression is a decimal or float value, half adjust is applied to the value of the numeric expression when converting to integer type.

%KDS   Data structure with keys. Format:
             %KDS(data-structure-name{:num-keys})
             Example: Chain %kds(CustRecKeys) custRec;
             %KDS is allowed as the search argument for any keyed Input/Output operation (CHAIN, DELETE, READE, READPE, SETGT, SETLL) coded in a free-form group. The search argument is specified by the subfields of the data structure name coded as the first argument of the built-in function. The key data structure may be (but is not limited to), an externally described data structure with keyword EXTNAME(...:*KEY) or LIKEREC(...:*KEY).. The first argument must be the name of a data structure. This includes any subfield defined with keyword LIKEDS or LIKEREC. The second argument specifies how many of the subfields to use as the search argument. The individual key values in the compound key are taken from the top level subfields of the data structure. Subfields defined with LIKEDS are considered character data.

%LEN   Get or set length. Format:
             %LEN(expression)
             Example: Length = %len(num1);
             %LEN can be used to get the length of a variable expression or to set the current length of a variable-length field. The parameter must not be a figurative constant.

%LOOKUPxx   Look up an array element: Generic Format:
             %LOOKUP xx with xx = type of match
             %LOOKUP(arg : array {: startindex {: numelems}})
                     – exact match
             %LOOKUPLT(arg : array {: startindex {: numelems}})
                     – closest but less than
             %LOOKUPGE(arg : array {: startindex {: numelems}})
                     -- equal or closest but less than
             %LOOKUPGT(arg : array {: startindex {: numelems}})
                     -- closest but greater than
             %LOOKUPLE(arg : array {: startindex {: numelems}})
                     – equal or closest but greater than
             Example: Result = %LOOKUP('Paris':arr);
             If no value matches the specified condition, zero is returned. The search starts at index startindex and continues for *numelems* elements. By default, the entire array is searched. The first two parameters can have any type but must have the same type. They do not need to have the same length or number of decimal | positions. The third and fourth parameters must be non-float numeric values with zero decimal positions.

%MINUTES   # of minutes as a duration Format:
             %MINUTES(number)
             Example: // Determine the time in 3 minutes
                            Newtime = time + %MINUTES(3);
             %MINUTES converts a number into a duration that can be

added to a time or timestamp value. %MINUTES can only be the right-hand value in an addition or subtraction | operation. The left-hand value must be a time or timestamp. The result is a time or timestamp value with the appropriate number of minutes | added or subtracted. For a time field, the resulting value is in *ISO | format.

%MONTHS   # of months as a duration. Format: %MONTHS(number)
Example: Resultdate = duedate - %MONTHS(6);
%MONTHS converts a number into a duration that can be added to a date or timestamp value. %MONTHS can only be the right-hand value in an addition or subtraction | operation. The left-hand value must be a date or timestamp. The result is a date or timestamp value with the appropriate number of months added or subtracted. For a date, the resulting value is in *ISO format.

%MSECONDS   **Convert to # of microseconds as a duration. Format: %MSECONDS(number)**
Example: // Determine the time in 360 microseconds
Newtime = time + %MSECONDS(360);
%MSECONDS (convert to microsoeconds) converts a number into a duration that can be added to a time or timestamp value. %MSECONDS can only be the right-hand value in an addition or subtraction operation. The left-hand value must be a time or timestamp. The result is a time or timestamp value with the appropriate number of microseconds added or subtracted. For a time, the resulting value is in *ISO format.

%NULLIND   Null-capable field name value in indicator. Format: %NULLIND(fieldname)
Example: if %nullind (DBField1);
The %NULLIND BIF can be used to query or set the null indicator for null-capable fields. %NULLIND can only be used in expressions in extended factor 2 or free-form RPG. When used on the right-hand side of an expression, this function returns the setting of the null indicator for the null-capable field. The setting can be *ON or *OFF. When used on the left-hand side of an expression, this function can be used to set the null indicator for null-capable fields to *ON or *OFF. The content of a null-capable field remains unchanged.

%OCCUR   Returns current record of multi-occurrence DS. Format: %OCCUR(dsn-name)
Example:
                    /FREE
Form 1:   Result = %OCCUR(mds);
Form 2:   %OCCUR(mds) = 7;
%OCCUR gets or sets the current position of a multiple-occurrence data structure. When this function is evaluated for its value, it returns the current occurrence number of the specified data structure as an unsigned numeric value. When this function is specified on the left-hand side of an EVAL statement, or a free form equation, the specified number becomes the current occurrence number.

%OPEN   Opens a closed file. Format: %OPEN(file_name)
Example:
        If not %open (PRINTFILE);
        Open PRINTFILE;
%OPEN returns '1' if the specified file is open. A file is

considered "open" if it has been opened by the RPG program during initialization or by an OPEN operation, and has not subsequently been closed. If the file is conditioned by an external indicator and the external indicator was off at program initialization, the file is considered closed, and %OPEN returns '0'.

%PADDR   Get procedure address. Format:
%PADDR(string|prototype)
Example: **EVAL   PROC1 = %PADDR ('NextProg')**
%PADDR returns a value of type procedure pointer. The value is the address of the entry point identified by the argument. %PADDR may be compared with and assigned to only items of type procedure pointer. The parameter to %PADDR must be a character constant or a prototype name. When a character constant is used, this identifies the entry point by name. The prototype must be a prototype for a bound call. The EXTPGM keyword cannot be used. The entry point identified by the prototype is the procedure identified in the EXTPROC keyword for the prototype. If the EXTPROC keyword is not specified, the entry point is the same as the prototype name (in upper case).

%PADDR   Used with a Prototype. Same format
Example C   Eval   procptr = %paddr(TheProc)
The argument of %PADDR can be a prototype name, with restrictions: (1) It must not be a prototype for a Java method. (2) It must not have the EXTPGM keyword. (3) If its EXTPROC keyword has a procedure pointer for an argument, %PADDR |cannot be used in definition specifications. |

%PARMS   # of parameters passed to procedure. Format:
%PARMS – returns the # of parms
Example: **IF   %PARMS < 1**
%PARMS returns the number of parameters that were passed to the procedure in which %PARMS is used. For the main procedure, %PARMS is the same as *PARMS. The value returned by %PARMS is not available if the program or procedure that calls %PARMS does not pass a minimal operational descriptor. The ILE RPG compiler always passes one, but other languages do not. So if the caller is written in another ILE language, it will need to pass an operational descriptor on the call. If the operational descriptor is not passed, the value returned by %PARMS cannot be trusted.

%REALLOC   Numeric pointer: to allocated storage. Format:
%REALLOC(ptr:num)
Example: RESpointer = %REALLOC(pointer:500);
%REALLOC changes the heap storage pointed to by the first parameter to be the length specified in the second parameter. The newly allocated storage is uninitialized. The first parm must be a basing pointer value. The second parm must be a non-float numeric value with zero decimal places. The length specified must be between 1 and 16776704. The function returns a pointer to the allocated storage. This may be the same as ptr or different.

%REM   Division - remainder from div of 2 arguments: Format:
%REM(n:m)
Example: Result = %REM(A:B);
%REM returns the remainder that results from dividing operands n by m. The two operands must be numeric values with zero decimal positions

%REPLACE   Replacement string. Format

%REPLACE(replacement string: source string{:start position {:source length to replace}})

Example: Result = %replace ('Scranton': result);

%REPLACE returns the character string produced by inserting a replacement string into the source string, starting at the start position and replacing the specified number of characters. The first and second parm must be of type character, graphic, or UCS-2 and can be in either fixed- or variable-length format. The second parm must be the same type as the first. If the third parm is not specified, the starting position is at the beginning of the source string. The value may range from one to the current length of the source string plus one. The fourth parm represents the number of characters in the source string to be replaced. If zero is specified, then the replacement string is inserted before the specified starting position. If the parm is not specified, the number of characters replaced is the same as the length of the replacement string.

%SCAN   **Forat:** %SCAN (search

Argument : source string {: start})

Example: Position = %scan ('D' : source : 2);

%SCAN returns the first position of the search argument in the source string, or 0 if it was not found. If the start position is specified, the search begins at the starting position. The result is always the position in the source string even if the starting position is specified. The starting position defaults to 1. The type of the return value is unsigned integer. This BIF can be used anywhere that an unsigned integer expression is valid. Unlike the SCAN operation code, %SCAN cannot return an array containing all occurrences of the search string and its results cannot be tested using the %FOUND built-in function.

%SECONDS   # of seconds as a duration. Format:

%SECONDS(number)

Example: // Determine the time in 36 seconds

         Newtime = time + %SECONDS(36);

%SECONDS converts a number into a duration that can be added to a time or timestamp value. %SECONDS can only be the right-hand value in an addition or subtraction operation. The left-hand value must be a time or timestamp. The result is a time or timestamp value with the appropriate number of seconds added or subtracted. For a time, the resulting value is in *ISO format.

%SHTDN   Returns value indicating shutdown (1 or 0) Format:

%SHTDN

Example:

         IF %SHTDN;

         QuitProgram();

         ENDIF;

%SHTDN returns '1' if the system operator has requested shutdown; otherwise, it returns '0'.

%SIZE Returns size of variable or literal.   Formats:

%SIZE(variable)

%SIZE(literal)

%SIZE(array{:*ALL})

%SIZE(table{:*ALL})

%SIZE(multiple occurrence data structure{:*ALL})

Example: Result = %SIZE(field1);

%SIZE returns the number of bytes occupied by the

constant or field. If the argument is an array name, table name, or multiple occurrence data structure name, the value returned is the size of one element or occurrence. If *ALL is specified as the second parameter for %SIZE, the value returned is the storage taken up by all elements or occurrences. Returns size of variable or literal

%SQRT   Square root of a numeric value. Format:
           %SQRT (numeric expression)
           Example: Result = %SQRT (239874);
           %SQRT returns the square root of the specified numeric expression.

%STATUS   0 if no I/O error for file. Format
           %STATUS{(file_name)}
           Example: When %status = 01331;
                         Exsr SUBOVER999
           %STATUS returns the most recent value set for the program or file status. %STATUS is set whenever the program status or any file status changes, usually when an error occurs. If %STATUS is used without the optional file name parameter, then it returns the program or file status most recently changed. If a file is specified, the value contained in the INFDS *STATUS field for the specified file is returned. The INFDS does not have to be specified for the file. %STATUS starts with a return value of 00000 and is reset to 00000 before any operation with an 'E' extender specified begins. %STATUS is best checked immediately after an operation with the 'E' extender or an error indicator specified, or at the beginning of an INFSR or the *PSSR subroutine.

%STR String characters addressed by pointer argument. Format:
           %STR (Get or Store Null-Terminated String)
           1. Get: %STR(basing pointer{: max-length})(right-hand-side)
           2. Store: %STR(basing pointer : max-length)(left-hand-side)
           Example 1 Get: ResultGet = '<' + %str(String1 : 2) + '>';
           Example 2 Store   %str(StoreStr(25))= 'abcdef';
           %STR is used to create or use null-terminated character strings, which are very commonly used in C and C++ applications. The first parameter must be a basing-pointer variable. The second parameter, if specified, must be a numeric value with zero decimal positions. If not specified, it defaults to 65535. The first parameter must point to storage that is at least as long as the length given by the second parameter When used on the right-hand side of an expression, this function returns the data pointed to by the first parameter up to but not including the first null character (x'00') found within the length specified. When used on the left-hand side of an expression, %STR(ptr:length) assigns the value of the right-hand side of the expression to the storage pointed at by the pointer, adding a null-terminating byte at the end. The maximum length that can be specified is 65535. This means that at most 65534 bytes of the right-hand side can be used, since 1 byte must be reserved for the null-terminator at the end. The length indicates the amount of storage that the pointer points to. This length should be greater than the maximum length the right-hand side will have. The pointer must be set to point to storage at least as long as the length parameter. If the length of the right-hand side of the expression is longer than the specified length, the right-hand side value is truncated. Make sure that the length parameter is not greater than the actual length of data addressed by the pointer and that the length of

the right-hand side is not greater than or equal to the actual length of data addressed by the pointer. You must keep track of the length that you have allocated.

%SUBARR   Return a subset of an array. Format:
%SUBARR(array:start-index{:number-of-elements})
Example: ResultArr = %subarr(a:4:n);
%SUBARR returns a section of the specified array starting at start-index. The number of elements returned is specified by the optional number-of-elements parameter. If not specified, the number-of-elements defaults to the remainder of the array. The first parameter of %SUBARR must be an array. That is, a standalone field, data structure, or subfield defined as an array. The first parameter must not be a table name or procedure call. The start-index parameter must be a numeric value with zero decimal positions. A float numeric value is not allowed. The value must be greater than or equal to 1 and less than or equal to the number #of elements of the array. The optional number-of-elements parameter must be a numeric value with zero decimal positions. A float numeric value is not allowed. The value must be greater than or equal to 1 and less than or equal to the number of elements remaining in the array after applying the start-index value. Generally, %SUBARR is valid in any expression where an unindexed array is allowed.

%SUBDT   Returns a portion of date or time value.
Format 1 %SUBDT(value:*MSECONDS|*SECONDS |*MINUTES|*HOURS|*DAYS|*MONTHS|*YEARS)
Format 2 %SUBDT(value:*MS|*S|*MN|*H|*D|*M|*Y)
Example: Numval = %subdt(date:*YEARS);
%SUBDT extracts a portion of the information in a date, time, or timestamp value. It returns an unsigned numeric value. The first parameter is the date, time, or timestamp value. The second parameter is the portion that you want to extract. The following values are valid: For a date: *DAYS, *MONTHS, and *YEARS. For a time: *SECONDS, *MINUTES, and *HOURS. For a timestamp: *MSECONDS, *SECONDS, *MINUTES, *HOURS, *DAYS, *MONTHS, and *YEARS. For this function, *DAYS always refers to the day of the month not the day of the year (even if you are using a Julian date format).

%SUBST   Returns a substring. Two Formats
%SUBST Form1 : Used for its value
Format: %SUBST (string: start position, length)
Example: C   IF   %SUBST (CITY:C+1) = 'Scranton'

%SUBST Form 2 : Used as the Result of an Assignment
Format: %SUBST (string: start position, length)
Example: C   EVAL   %SUBST (A:3:4) = '****'

%SUBST used for its value (Form 1) returns a substring from the contents of the specified string. The substring begins at the specified starting position in the string and continues for the length specified. If length is not specified then the substring continues to the end of the string.
%SUBST used as the result of an assignment (Form 2) refers to certain positions of the argument string. The result begins at the specified starting position in the variable and continues for the length specified. If the length is not specified then the string is referenced to its end. If the length refers to

characters beyond the end of the string, then a run-time error is issued. When %SUBST is used as the result of an assignment, the first parameter must refer to a storage location such as a field or structure. Any valid expressions are permitted for the second and third parameters of %SUBST when it appears as the result of an assignment with an EVAL operation.

%THIS   The class instance for the native method. Format
             %THIS -- returns object value reference to class
             Example: C   Eval   Id_Num = getId(%THIS)
             %THIS returns an Object value that contains a reference to the class instance on whose behalf the native method is being called. %THIS is valid only in non-static native methods. This BIF gives non-static native methods access to the class instance. A non-static native method works on a specific instance of its class. This object is actually passed as a parameter to the native method by Java, but it does not appear in the prototype or procedure interface for the native method In a Java method, the object instance is referred to by the Java reserved word this. In an RPG native method, the object instance is referred to by the %THIS BIF.

%TIME   Brings back system time if none is specified. Format:
             %TIME{(expression{:time-format})}
             Example: Time = %time(string:*USA);
             %TIME converts the value of the expression from character, numeric, or timestamp data to type time. The converted value remains unchanged, but is returned as a time. The first parameter is the value to be converted. If you do not specify a value, %TIME returns the current system time. The second parameter is the time format for numeric or character input. Regardless of the input format, the output is returned in *ISO format.

%TIMESTAMP   Brings back current timestamp if none specified. Format:
             %TIMESTAMP{(expression{:*ISO|*ISO0})}
             Example: Times = %timestamp(string);
             %TIMESTAMP converts the value of the expression from character, numeric, or |date data to type timestamp. The converted value is returned as a timestamp. The first parameter is the value to be converted. If you do not specify a value, %TIMESTAMP returns the current system timestamp. The second parameter is the timestamp format for character input. Regardless of the input format, the output is returned in *ISO format.

%TLOOKUPxx   Checks for match and returns '*ON' or '*OFF.'
             The "xx" is the specific type of match
             Formats:
             %TLOOKUP(arg : search-table {: alt-table})
                   – Exact match
             %TLOOKUPLT(arg : search-table {: alt-table})
                   – Closest but less than
             %TLOOKUPGE(arg : search-table {: alt-table})
                   – Exact match or closest but less than
             %TLOOKUPGT(arg : search-table {: alt-table})
                   – Closest but greater than
             %TLOOKUPLE(arg : search-table {: alt-table})
                   – Exact or closest but greater than
             Example: IF %TLOOKUP('Goose Bay':tab1:tab2);
             If a value meets the specified condition, the current table element for the search table is set to the element that satisfies

the condition, the current table element for the alternate table is set to the same element, and the function returns the value *ON. If no value matches the specified condition, *OFF is returned. Unlike the %LOOKUP operation code, %TLOOKUP applies only to tables. To look up a value in an array, use the %LOOKUP BIF.

%TRIM string   **Trims string with left, right blanks or specified. Format:**
%TRIM(string)
Example:
Name = %trim (FirstName) + '' + %trim (LastName);
Returns string less any leading and trailing blanks.

%TRIML string   Trims string with left blanks or specified. Format
%TRIML(string)
Example: Location = %triml('   Wilkes-Barre, PA'));
%TRIML returns the given string less any leading blanks
When specified as a parameter for a definition specification keyword, the string parameter must be a constant.

%TRIMR string   Trims string with right blanks or specified Format:
%TRIMR(string)
Example: Location = %trim (' Wilkes-Barre, PA   ');
%TRIMR returns the given string less any trailing blanks.
When specified as a parameter for a definition specification keyword, the string parameter must be a constant.

%UCS2   Brings back value in UCS-2 format. Format:
%UCS2 --converts to UCS2 type of value
Example: C eval ufield = %UCS2(char) + %UCS2(graph)
%UCS2 converts the value of the expression from character, graphic, or UCS-2 and returns a UCS-2 value. The second parameter, ccsid, is optional and indicates the CCSID of the resulting expression. The CCSID defaults to 13488. If the parameter is a constant, the conversion will be done at compile time.

%UNS   Brings back value in unsigned format. Format:
%UNS(numeric expression)
Example Result = %uns (NumValue);
%UNS converts the value of the numeric expression to unsigned format. Any decimal digits are truncated. %UNS can be used to truncate the decimal positions from a float or decimal value allowing it to be used as an array index.

%UNSH   Brings back rounded value - unsigned format. Format:
%UNSH(numeric expression)
Example   Result = %unsh (FloatValue);
%UNSH is like %UNS except that if the numeric expression is a decimal or a float value, half adjust is applied to the value of the numeric expression when converting to unsigned type.

%XFOOT   Array expression sum of the elements. Format:
%XFOOT (array-expression)
Example: Result = %xfoot(MothSales)
%XFOOT results in the sum of all elements of the specified numeric array expression. The precision of the result is the minimum that can hold the result of adding together all array elements, up to a maximum of 30 digits. The number of decimal places in the result is always the same as the decimal places of the array expression. This built-in function is similar to the XFOOT operation, except that float arrays are summed like all other types, beginning from index 1 on up.

%XLATE   Translate String (eg Lower Case to Upper Case). Format:
%XLATE (from:to:string{:startpos})

Example: String = %XLATE (locase:upcase:'our dept');
                      // string now contains 'OUR DEPT'
%XLATE translates string according to the values of from, to, and startpos. The first parameter contains a list of characters that should be replaced, and the second parameter contains their replacements. For example, if the string contains the third character in from, every occurrence of that character is replaced with the third character in to. The third parameter is the string to be translated. The fourth parameter is the starting position for translation. By default, translation starts at position 1. The first three parameters can be of type character, graphic, or UCS-2. All three must have the same type. The value returned has the same type and length as string. The fourth parameter is a non-float numeric with zero decimal positions.

%YEARS
# of years as a duration Format: Format: %YEARS(number)
Example: **FutureDat = Today + %YEARS(4);** *add 4yr to date.*
%YEARS converts a number into a duration that can be added to a date or timestamp value. %YEARS can only be the right-hand value in an addition or subtraction operation. The left-hand value must be a date or timestamp. The result is a date or timestamp value with the appropriate number of years added or subtracted. For a date, the resulting value is in *ISO format. If the left-hand value is February 29 and the resulting year is not a leap year, February 28 is used instead. Adding or subtracting a number of years to a February 29 date may not be reversible. For example, |20015-02-29 + %YEARS(1) – %YEARS(1) is 20015-02-28.

Table 15-11 BIF Arguments and Values

Name	Arguments	Value Returned
%ABS	numeric expression	absolute value of expression
%ADDR	variable name	address of variable
%ALLOC	number of bytes to allocate	pointer to allocated storage
%BITAND	character, numeric	bit wise ANDing of the bits of all the arguments
%BITNOT	character, numeric	bit-wise reverse of the bits of the argument
%BITOR	character, numeric	bit-wise ORing of the bits of all the arguments
%BITXOR	character, numeric	bit-wise exclusive ORing of the bits of the two arguments
%CHAR	graphic, UCS-2, numeric, date, time, or timestamp expression {: date, time, or timestamp format}	value in character format
%CHECKError! Bookmark not defined.	comparator string:string to be checked{:start position}	first position of a character that is not in the comparator string, or zero if not found
%CHECKR	comparator string:string to be checked{:start position}	last position of a character that is not in the comparator string, or zero if not found
%DATE	{value {: date format}}	the date that corresponds to the specified *value*, or the current system date if none is specified
%DAYS	number of days	number of days as a duration
%DEC	numeric expression {:digits:decpos} character expression: digits:decpos	value in packed numeric format

	date, time or timestamp expression {:format}	
%DECH	numeric or character expression: digits:decpos	half-adjusted value in packed numeric format
%DECPOS	numeric expression	number of decimal digits
%DIFF	Date or time expression: date or time expression: unit	difference between the two dates, times, or timestamps in the specified unit
%DIV	dividend: divisor	the quotient from the division of the two arguments
%EDITC	Non-float numeric expression:edit code {:*CURSYM | *ASTFILL | currency symbol}	string representing edited value
%EDITFLT	numeric expression	character external display representation of float
%EDITW	Non-float numeric expression:edit word	string representing edited value
%ELEM	Array, table, or multiple occurrence data structure name	number of elements or occurrences
%EOF	{file name}	'1' if the most recent cycle input, read operation, or write to a subfile (for a particular file, if specified) ended in an end-of-file or beginning-of-file condition; and, when a file is specified, if a more recent OPEN, CHAIN, SETGT or SETLL to the file was not successful
		'0' otherwise
%EQUAL	{file name}	'1' if the most recent SETLL (for a particular file, if specified) or LOOKUP operation found an exact match
		'0' otherwise
%ERROR		'1' if the most recent operation code with extender 'E' specified resulted in an error
		'0' otherwise
%FIELDS	list of fields to be updated	not applicable
%FLOAT	numeric or character expression	value in float format
%FOUND	{file name}	'1' if the most recent relevant operation (for a particular file, if specified) found a record (CHAIN, DELETE, SETGT, SETLL), an element (LOOKUP), or a match (CHECK, CHECKR, SCAN)
		'0' otherwise
%GRAPH	character, graphic, or UCS-2 expression	value in graphic format
%HANDLER	handling procedure : communication area	not applicable
%HOURS	number of hours	number of hours as a duration
%INT	numeric or character expression	value in integer format
%INTH	numeric or character expression	half-adjusted value in integer format
%KDS	data structure containing keys {: number of keys}	not applicable
%LEN	any expression	length in digits or characters

%LOOKUPxx	argument: array{:start index {:number of elements}}	array index of the matching element
%MINUTES	number of minutes	number of minutes as a duration
%MONTHS	number of months	number of months as a duration
%MSECONDS	number of microseconds	number of microseconds as a duration
%NULLIND	Null-capable field name	value in indicator format representing the null indicator setting for the null-capable field
%OCCUR	multiple-occurrence data structure name	current occurrence of the multiple-occurrence data structure
%OPENError! Bookmark not defined.	file name	'1' if the specified file is open
		'0' if the specified file is closed
%PADDR	procedure or prototype name	address of procedure or prototype
%PARMS	none	number of parameters passed to procedure
%REALLOC	pointer: numeric expression	pointer to allocated storage
%REM	dividend: divisor	the remainder from the division of the two arguments
%REPLACE	replacement string: source string {:start position {:source length to replace}}	string produced by inserting replacement string into source string, starting at start position and replacing the specified number of characters
%SCAN	search argument:string to be searched{:start position}	first position of search argument in string or zero if not found
%SECONDS	number of seconds	number of seconds as a duration
%SHTDN		'1' if the system operator has requested shutdown
		'0' otherwise
%SIZE	variable, array, or literal {:* ALL}	size of variable or literal
%SQRT	numeric value	square root of the numeric value
%STATUS	{file name}	0 if no program or file error occurred since the most recent operation code with extender 'E' specified
		most recent value set for any program or file status, if an error occurred
		if a file is specified, the value returned is the most recent status for that file
%STR	pointer{:maximum length}	characters addressed by pointer argument up to but not including the first x'00'
%SUBARR	array name:start index{:number of elements}	array subset
%SUBDT	Date or time expression: unit	an unsigned numeric value that contains the specified portion of the date or time value
%SUBST	string:start{:length}	substring
%THIS		the class instance for the native method
%TIME	{value {: time format}}	the time that corresponds to the specified *value*, or the current system time if none is specified
%TIMESTAMP	{(value {: timestamp format})}	the timestamp that corresponds to the specified *value*, or the current system timestamp if none is specified
%TLOOKUPxx	argument: search table {: alternate table}	'*ON' if there is a match
		'*OFF' otherwise

%TRIM	string {: characters to trim}	string with left and right blanks or specified characters trimmed
%TRIML	string {: characters to trim}	string with left blanks or specified characters trimmed
%TRIMR	string {: characters to trim}	string with right blanks or specified characters trimmed
%UCS2	character, graphic, or UCS-2 expression	value in UCS-2 format
%UNS	numeric or character expression	value in unsigned format
%UNSH	numeric or character expression	half-adjusted value in unsigned format
%XFOOT	array expression	sum of the elements
%XLATE	from-characters: to-characters: string {: start position}	the string with from-characters replaced by to-characters
%XML	Xml document { : options }	not applicable
%YEARS	number of years	number of years as a duration

Chapter Summary

All RPG/400 instructions except for the FREE operation are included in RPGIV. In addition to the 100 from RPG/400, RPGIV has another 22 instructions that are not found in RPG/400.

Besides additional resources provided via new op-codes, RPGIV also provides a wealth of new and/or easier to use capabilities by its "Built-In Functions or BIFs. The BIFS are similar to operation codes in that they perform operations on data that you specify. Built-in functions can be used in expressions in Free-Form RPG IV or with the EVAL statement described in more detail with an example below.

Additionally, constant-valued built-in functions can be used in named constants.

Key Chapter Terms

%ABS	%UNS	ITER
%ADDR	%UNSH	KFLD
%BITAND	%XFOOT	KLIST
%BITNOT	%XLATE	LEAVE
%BITOR	%YEARS	LEAVESR
%BITXOR	*DATE	LOOKUP
%CHAR	*FILE	MHHZO
%CHECK	*GETIN	MHLZO
%CHECKR	*OFF	MLHZO
%DATE	*ON	MLLZO
%DAYS	*PARMS	MONITOR
%DEC	*PROGRAM	MOVEA
%DECH	*PSSR	MOVEL
%DECPOS	*STATUS	MVR
%DIFF	ACQ	NEXT
%DIV	ADDDUR	OCCUR
%EDITC	ALLOC	ON-ERROR
%EDITFLT	ANDxx	OPEN
%EDITW	BEGSR	ORxx
%ELEM	BITOFF	OTHER
%EOF	BITON	OUT
%EQUAL	CABxx	PARM
%ERROR	CALL	PLIST
%FIELDS	CALLB	POST
%FLOAT	CALLP	READ
%FOUND	CASxx	READC
%GRAPH	CAT	READE
%HOURS	CHAIN	READP
%INT	CHECK	REALLOC
%INTH	CHECKR	READPE2
%KDS	CLEAR	REL
%LEN	CLOSE	RESET
%LOOKUPxx	COMMIT	RETURN
%MINUTES	COMP	ROLBK
%MONTHS	DEALLOC	SCAN

%MSECONDS	DEBUG	SELECT
%NULLIND	DEFINE	SETGT
%OCCUR	DELETE	SETLL
%OPEN	DIV	SETOF
%PADDR	DO	SETON
%PARMS	DOU	SHTDN
%REALLOC	DOUxx	SORTA
%REM	DOW	SQRT
%REPLACE	DOWxx	SUB
%SCAN	DSPLY	SUBDUR
%SECONDS	DUMP	SUBST
%SHTDN	ELSE	TAG
%SIZE	ELSEIF	TESTB
%SQRT	ENDFOR	TESTN
%STATUS	ENDMON	TESTZ
%STR	ENDSR	TIME
%SUBARR	EVAL	UDATE
%SUBDT	EVALR	UNLOCK
%SUBST	EXCEPT	UPDATE
%THIS	EXFMT	WHxx
%TIME	EXSR	WRITE
%TIMESTAMP	Extended Factor 2	XFOOT
%TLOOKUPxx	EXTRCT	XLATE
%TRIM	FEOD	XML-INT
%TRIML	FORCE	XML-SAX
%TRIMR	GOTO	Z-ADD
%UCS2	IFxx	

Review Questions

1. Discuss the function and purpose of the new RPGIV operation codes whose first letter is within the range A through D.

2. Discuss the function and purpose of the new RPGIV operation codes whose first letter is within the range E through L.

3. Discuss the function and purpose of the new RPGIV operation codes whose first letter is within the range M through X.

4. Which operation provided RPG IV with the ability to enable equations and expressions following this operation code.

5. What facilities of RPGIV provide some of the flavor of the traditional block structured languages?

6. What type of operations added to RPGIV extending it into areas that had been reserved for low-level functions written in other languages.

7. What is the difference between a CALLB and a CALLP?

8. How many date operations are there in RPGIV and what functions do they provide for the language?

9. What is a FOR Group?

10. Which operation does for a subroutine what the LEAVE operation does for a Do Loop?

11. What functions do the XML operations provide?

12. RPGIV also provides a wealth of new and/or easier to use capabilities in a more free form context by use of a mechanism similar to operation codes but more conducive to free form use. These are called?

13. What is the general format of a BIF?

14. What types of general components can make up a BIF?

15. Which BIFS have counterparts or similarities with RPGIV operation codes?

Chapter 16 RPG Arrays and Programming Structures

Advanced RPG/400 Elements

When RPG II hit the streets in the 1970's, two of the features that were touted heavily were tables and arrays. Over time in addition to tables and arrays, various structures were added to the language such as data structures and data areas.

In the early 1990's I included this material in what I billed as an advanced RPG class that I had designed. Half of the attendees believed that RPG structures were an advanced topic and the other half thought that they were a natural and necessary part of the language.

I can say with certainty that in the 1970's tables and arrays were thought of as advanced features by the many who had gained their language experience with the RPG cycle. Among other things, this had to do with the unfriendly look of the Extension spec and this made tables and arrays look more difficult than they needed to be.

The RPG structures that we will examine in this chapter and the next are the following:

✓ Tables
✓ Arrays
✓ Named Constants
✓ Figurative Constants
✓ Data Structures
✓ Data Areas
✓ Data Area Data Structures
✓ Initialization
✓ RESET operation
✓ CLEAR operation
✓ Performance Implications

IBM Definitions

IBM defines an array as a systematic program-internal arrangement of data fields (called array elements) with the same field length, data type (char or numeric), and number of decimal positions (if numeric).

You can search an array sequentially for an identifiable array element or you can refer to an array element by its position within the array via a technique called subscripting. One of the big advantages of arrays is it helps you code more efficiently. For example, when you use arrays, some operations permit you to refer to all of array elements merely by using the array name, rather than having to refer to each element of the array.

If we were performing a database design and we wanted to create a file that would hold the history of a particular value for a year or several years, an array would be an ideal mechanism in RPG to reference all that data merely by specifying the array name. So if you defined an array with 24 monthly sales figures, we would call it a 24 element array with each of the 24 elements being referenced by a subscript from 1 to 24. The first element for example might be January's sales to a particular customer and the second might be February's sales on out to December of two years ago.

Note: Ironically in database design arrays are known as repeating groups and are not recommended. Yet, they have so much power when used in RPG that RPG coders over the years have figured out how to define databases properly and still gain the benefits of array processing.

What is an RPG Table?   A table is also a systematic program-internal arrangement of data fields (table elements) with the same field length, data type (char or numeric), and number of decimal positions -if numeric. Just as with an array, you may search a table sequentially using the table lookup operation (LOKUP in RPG/400, LOOKUP in RPGIV) to find a uniquely identifiable table element and any associated data.

Unlike arrays, however, you cannot refer to table elements by their position within the table As you will see, however, from the LOKUP operation, you can access table elements individually since after a LOKUP operation, the table name itself when used in RPG calculations or output refers to the last table element found in a prior LOKUP operation.

There are two more major differences between tables and arrays. Unlike an array name, (1) the table name does not refer to the entire set of table elements and (2) the table name must begin with the letters "TAB." With a six character field name in RPG/400, that sure does not give a lot of creativity to the programmer for creating meaningful table names.

Three Types of Arrays in RPG

There are three types of arrays that you can use in an RPG program. Each of the types of arrays is defined using the RPG Extension specification. The types of array are as follows:

1. Compile Time Array

Just as the name implies, compile time arrays are loaded from the program when the program is compiled. The array contents become a permanent part of the compiled object program. The data for the first array defined in the extension specifications must be provided two statements after the last executable RPG statement in the program. In between the last RPG statement and the first record of the compile time array is a record with two asterisks (positions 1 & 2). If there is more than one compile time array coded in the Extension specifications, the array records at the back of the program must be in the sequence of the extension specifications, with each array's records separated from the one before by double asterisks.

2. Execution Time Array

The execution time array is also referred to as a run time array. Programmers use this form of array when data is coming in from disk files as arrays or when it makes sense to load and process an array for programming efficiency. In essence, the array gets loaded by your program while it is running. Consider the example noted above with 24 monthly sales figure buckets per customer. Each time a customer record would be read in with this data, the array would be reloaded with that customer's data.

3. Pre-Execution Time Array

Pre-execution time arrays are very similar to compile time arrays but for two differences: (1) The data is provided by a disk file prior to execution and (2) The data can be modified and written out to the same or a different disk file when the program ends. So, before the RPG cycle ever begins, the data from the pre-execution array is loaded from a disk file.

Because tables are typically used for reference and look up purposes rather than for data storage, tables can be loaded only at compile & pre-execution (right before the program starts) time.

What does an array look like in memory and how would a programmer reference an array or an array element when coding a program?. Suppose we have an array that for simplicity sake we want to name simply as "A." Suppose there are 24 elements in the array. Suppose that each array element is five positions long and each has two decimal places. The A array in figure 16-1 shows you how these elements would be laid out in memory. Likewise, you can reference the whole array by using A in your program, and you can reference each element individually by using the array name, a comma, and a variable or a constant.

Figure 16-1 A Look at the "A" Array

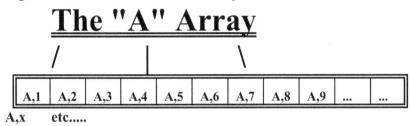

Thus arrays can be referenced in two ways:

1.   Array Name
2.   Array Element

Array elements can be referenced using the following notation::

✓ The array name
✓ Followed by a comma (,)
✓ Followed by an index which indicates the specific *ith* element in the array which is referenced

If an array were named ARR, elements could be referenced as in the following examples:

✓ ARR,1 (constant index)
✓ ARR,IX (variable index)

Array Syntax Rules

Just as RPG fields, arrays have a set of syntax rules which include the following:

✓ Unique symbolic name
✓ Length is 6 characters
✓ Length includes comma & index
✓ When used in Factor 1 or Factor 2, length can be 10)
✓ Index is a numeric field with no decimal positions, or it is a numeric constant
✓ The Index value must be within the range of the # of values specified for the array – i.e. if there are 9 elements, the index value can never be 10.
✓ A 0 index value or a # too high = exception error

For a look at some valid and invalid array references, see Figure 16-2

Figure 16-2 Valid & Invalid Array References

Valid / Invalid	Examples	Explanation
Valid	AR,1 X,YY2	1st element of array AR An element of X The value of YY2 determines which element
Invalid	AR,+1	Invalid signed index

	AR,0	Index must be between 1 and # of elements
Valid Sometim es	BAL,xx1	More than 6 characters OK for Factor 1 & Factor 2 Not OK for Result Field

Let's review the **File Extension** specification form in Figure 16-3 now starting with what I would like to call the essential array columns in bold.

When you work with arrays it helps to remember that all arrays require at least the first three bolded and underlined entries in Figure 16-3. Those with just these 3 entries or if the data is numeric, with four entries, or if the data has special attributes such as packed or binary, with five entries in the E spec, are **RUN TIME** (execution) arrays.

Figure 16-3 Essential Extension Spec Array Columns (bold)

Columns	Extension Spec Field
11-18	Name of File Holding Pre-run time data
19-26	Name of optional output file
27-42	Array name
33-35	# Entries per record
36-39	# Entries in this Array
40-42	Length of each entry (element)
43-43	Data Format for 1st table/ array Specify a P if data is packed decimal format, Specify a "B" if binary format. **Specify an "L" if sign is on left** **Specify an "R" if sign is on right** Otherwise leave blank
44-44	# of decimals in each entry (element)
45	Table / Array Sequence (This is where you specify the A or D so the LOKUP operation knows the table or array is in sequence.
46-51	Alternating Table/Array Name
52-44	Alternating Table/Array Entry length
55-55	Alternating Table/Array Data Format See 43-43.
56-56	Alternating Table/Array # of decimals
57-57	Alternating Table/Array Sequence

As an example, the following **File Extension** specification shows the ARC array defined with just the first three bold entries noted. The first example shows RPG/400 and the second shows the conversion to RPGIV as it looks on the new "D" spec..

RPG/400
```
E....E....FromfileTofile++Name++N/rN/tbLenPDS
     E                    ARC        12  3
```

```
RPGIV
D ARC       S       3  DIM(12)
```

Let's take yet another crack at defining an execution time array. This time, let's call the array IN and let's provide two different sets of input field specs for a file from which the array can be loaded at execution time, whenever a record from the file is read.

Option 1 in Figure 16-4 shows how the entire array can be read with just the array name. Option 2 shows how to load the array with the individual elements defined in input. Both work. Option 1 is less coding.

Figure 16-4 Two Options for Loading an Array at Input Time

```
Options 1 & 2
E....E....FromfileTofile++Name++N/rN/tbLenPDSArrnamLenPDS
     E                      IN        6 12

Options 1 & 2
I....IFilenameSqNORiPos1NCCPos2NCCPos3NCC.................
     IARRFILE AA   01

Option 1
J....I.................................PFromTo++DFldnme
     I                              1  72 IN
     I*
Option 2
J....I.................................PFromTo++DFldnme
     I*
     I                              1  12 IN,1
     I                             12  24 IN,2
     I                             25  36 IN,3
     I                             37  48 IN,4
     I                             49  60 IN,5
     I                             61  72 IN,6
```

Compile Time Arrays

Now that we have examined the execution array type, which is the most common, let's look at how to code the compile time array. Let's define a compile time array called ARC with 12 elements. Each element is 3 characters alphabetic. For a compile time array, one more entry is necessary than with execution. Take notice to the "12" directly under the N/r piece of the E format below. This is the *# of entries per record* entry and it exists in columns 33 to 35 of the E spec.

```
RPG/400
E....E....FromfileTofile++Name++N/rN/tbLenPDSArrnam
     E                      ARC    12 12  3

RPGIV
D ARC            S              3    DIM(12)
                                     CTDATA
                                     PERRCD(12)
```

Since a compile time array needs to be loaded into program memory when the program is compiled, there must be a way to tell the compiler how many records are to be read after the program so that the compiler doesn't go nuts looking for more when there isn't more. Thus, the "12" above stands for number of entries in each record that will be used to lad the array at compile time.

It has nothing to do with the actual shape of the array in memory. The other entries do that. Instead, its value is in telling the compiler the shape of the records that it will be reading at compile time and providing a means for the compiler to calculate how many records there will be.

In the example above, the ARC array has 12 entries per record and 12 entries for the entire array. Therefore, it will take just one compile time record (12/12) to load the array. Each element is 3 characters. This tells the compiler how to chop up the input record and it tells the compiler how to carve up memory in 12 three byte elements.

A representative compile time record for the ARC array, including the ** separator, with 12 entries per record would look like the entry below:

**
48K16343J64044H12648A47349K34650B125

If the above were represented as 1 entry per record, there would be twelve records as follows:

**
48K
163
43J
640
44H
126
48A
473
49K
346
50B
125

When the compile time data is loaded in memory within the object program, it will look similar to the format shown in Figure 16-5

Figure 16-5 The shape of an Array in Memory

48K	163	43J	640	44H	126	48A	...	...

Compile Time Array Record Rules:

Everything has rules and thus if you want to use compile time arrays effectively, you must play by the compile time rules as follows:

- ✓ Each record must have same # of entries
- ✓ Each entry must fit on one line (no continuation)
- ✓ Input can be for separate or alternating format
- ✓ All elements must have same length, format & decimal positions
- ✓ A record with **b (b = blank) must precede 1st data record
- ✓ Character elements can be no larger than 80 bytes
- ✓ Arrays can be ascending, descending sequence or unordered (A. D, or blank in pos 45 & 57 of E spec)
- ✓ If L or R is specified in 43 & 55 of E spec, the length must include the sign (+ or -)

Pre-run Time Array

Besides the essential entries, there are additional Entries for the E Spec needed to load and update pre-run time arrays. The new entries are shown in Figure 16-3 as underlined. They are as follows:

11 - 18	Name of File holding array data
19 - 26	Name of optional output file

When you choose to load a file before the program runs, rather than at compile time, it gives you much more flexibility since you can update that file right until the time or times that you run the program that loads. Moreover, your program may be written so that it is smart enough to write out better array records after processing data than the program read in. In other words, the table can be updated and written back or to a new file for a subsequent program to read.

To get this coded right, you must specify the name of the file that holds the array data in columns 11-18 of the E spec. Code the file name that you wish to write out when the program is complete in columns 19-26..

The names you choose for both files must also be coded on the File Description specifications for the program with a few special entries. In addition to a matching file name, specify a T in column 16 of File Description to tell the compiler that the file being defined is a table / array file and it will be loaded into memory prior to run time. Specify a "T" for the file description of the data base file containing the array data.

The example below shows the ARP array being defined to load from the disk file named ARFILE. As you can see, there are 12 entries per record, 250 entries for the table, and each entry is five positions alphabetic.

RPG/400

```
E....E....FromfileTofile++Name++N/rN/tbLenPDSArrnam
     E     ARRFILE          ARP    12 250   5   A
RPGIV
D ARP...      S             5     DIM(250) FROMFILE(ARRFILE)
D...                              PERRCD(12) ASCEND
*Sample 1
E....FromfileTofile++Name++N/rN/tbLenPDSArrnamLenPDSComments
* Compile-time arrays in alternating format. Both have
* eight elements (3 elements per record). In both arrays, the
* length each element is 12, with 4 dec. positions. There are
* three (3) table entries for each record after the ** at the
* bottom of the program. The entire array consists of only 8
* elements
*
*Sample 2
E....FromfileTofile++Name++N/rN/tbLenPDSArrnamLenPDSComments
E                    ARC    3   8 12 4 ARD     12 4
*
* Pre-run item array ARE, to be read from file ARRFILE
* 250 char elements (12 elements per record). Each element
* five positions. The elements are arranged in ascending
* sequence.

Samples Continued below
*Sample 3
E....FromfileTofile++Name++N/rN/tbLenPDSArrnamLenPDSComments
E    ARRFILE          ARE    12 250   5   A
*
* Run-time array. ARI has 10 num. elements, each w/ 10 pos
* & zero dec. positions. Execution arrays are buit within
* the pgm and therefore do not need entries per record.
*
*Sample 4
E....FromfileTofile++Name++N/rN/tbLenPDSArrnamLenPDSComments
E                    ARI         10 10 0
*Sample 5
* Pre-run time array specified as combined file. ARH written
* back to the same file from which it is read.  ARH has 250
* character elements (12 elements per record). Each is 5
* positions long. The elements are in ascending order.
E....FromfileTofile++Name++N/rN/tbLenPDSArrnamLenPDSComments
E    DISKOUT DISKOUT ARH    12 250   5   A
*-------------------------------------------------------------
```

When defining arrays, more than one array type can be defined for inclusion prior to execution. Compile and Pre run-time arrays as well as run-time arrays can all be mixed on the E specification. In fact arrays and tables can be mixed as long as the compile records are in the sequence of the E specifications.

Alternating Arrays or Tables

Two arrays or tables can be specified on one E spec line, by entering a second array or table name, length, and decimal positions in columns 46-57 of the same extension specification. See Figure 16-3. Despite all the flexibility with mixing tables and arrays on E specifications, tables and arrays cannot be defined on the same E specification in alternating format or any format.

The rules for specifying tables or arrays in alternating format are as follows:

- ✓ Records for storing the array data in alternating format have the first element of the first array,
- ✓ Followed by the first element of the second array,
- ✓ Followed by the second element of the first array etc.
- ✓ Continually alternating until the end.
- ✓ Corresponding elements must appear on the same input record
- ✓ # Entries per record (33-35) applies to both arrays

The E specification coding for alternating PART# and COST arrays is shown immediately below followed by the compile or pre-run data that would be loaded to fill the arrays.

```
RPG/400
E....FromfileTofile++Name++N/rN/tbLenPDSArrnamLenPDS
E                      PART   1   5   5 0 COST     4 2
RPGIV
D PART... S               5   0 DIM(5) CTDATA PERRCD(1)
D COST... S               4   2 DIM(5) ALT(PART)
```

The raw data with PART (5 positions) alternating with COST
(4 positions) is shown immediately below following the ** separators:

```
**
000102000
035107900
055604225
032102300
060207500
```

Figure 16-6 shows the data after it is loaded into memory as a visual for how programmers should consider both alternating arrays and alternating tables.

Figure 16-6 Alternating Arrays PART & Cost in Memory

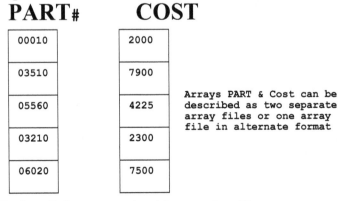

PART#   COST

PART#	COST
00010	2000
03510	7900
05560	4225
03210	2300
06020	7500

Arrays PART & Cost can be
described as two separate
array files or one array
file in alternate format

Related Arrays w/o Alternating Format

Though the alternating format is very convenient in working with tables and arrays, the processing of related arrays and tables does not have to be done in alternating format. In fact, if the arrays are defined individually, each related array can be viewed as another data element to a whole. Thus, instead of just two fields PART & COST being in alternating format to create the relationship, three, four, five or "n" arrays and tables can be related using the singular format below.

The trick, of course is that the elements of each array are related. If a third array, such as NAME were added to the relationship, for example, when PART,X were referenced with X being equal to 1, the related elements of COST,X and NAME,X would provide the data associated with PART in the same fashion as if they were loaded in alternating format.

For this exercise, let's load the records of PART & COST in straight forward. The E specifications look like those below and the arrays would look like the records in Figure 16-7 when described as two separate array files.

```
E....E....FromfileTofile++Name++N/rN/tbLenPDSAr
       E                        PART     5   5  5 0
       E                        COST     5   5  4 2
```

Figure 16-7 PART & COST in Straight Array Format
This record contains PART entries in positions 1 - 25

PART Entry 1.....	PART Entry 6.....	PART Entry 11....	PART Entry 16....	PART Entry 21....

This record contains COST entries in positions 1 – 20

COST Entry 1....	COST Entry 5....	COST Entry 9....	COST Entry 13....	COST Entry 17....

Tables

Let's look at the PART and COST arrays a little differently now. Let's define these as tables TABPAR and TABCST rather than arrays. In the examples below, the only difference is that the data is being stored in tables rather than arrays. Basically that means that the table name must begin with TAB and that the elements cannot be indexed.

The E specification coding for alternating PART# (TABPAR) and COST (TABCST) arrays is shown immediately below followed by the compile or pre-run data that would be loaded to fill the tables.

```
RPG/400
E....FromfileTofile++Name++N/rN/tbLenPDSArrnamLenPDS
E              TABPAR 1  5  5 0 TABCST 4 2
RPGIV
D TABPAR...S          5 0 DIM(5) CTDATA PERRCD(1)
D TABCST...S          4 2 DIM(5) ALT(TABPAR)
```

The raw data with TABPAR (5 positions) alternating with TABCST
(4 positions) is shown immediately below following the ** separators:

```
**
000102000
035107900
055604225
032102300
060207500
```

If this data looks just like the array data, it's because it is. Arrays and tables are often used interchangeably for similar purposes. Figure 16-8 shows the table data after it is loaded into memory as a visual for how programmers should consider both alternating arrays and alternating tables.

Figure 16-8 Alternating Tables TABPAR & TABCST in Memory

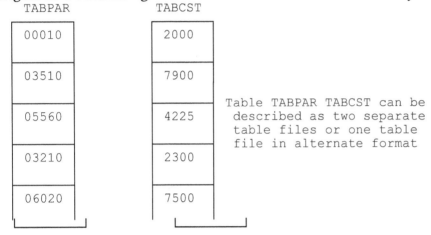

Table TABPAR TABCST can be
described as two separate
table files or one table
file in alternate format

Related Tables w/o Alternating Format

Though the alternating format is very convenient in working with tables and arrays, the processing of related arrays and tables does not have to be done in alternating format. In fact, if the arrays are defined individually, each related array can be viewed as another data element to a whole. Thus, instead of just two fields PART & COST being in alternating format to create the relationship, three, four, five or "n" arrays and tables can be related using the singular format below.

The trick, of course s that the elements of each array are related. If a third array, such as NAME were added to the relationship, for example, when PART,X were referenced with X being equal to 1, the related elements of COST,X and NAME,X would provide the data associated with PART in the same fashion as if they were loaded in alternating format.

For this exercise, let's load the records of PART & COST in straight forward. The E specifications look like those below and the arrays would look like the records in Figure 16-9 when described as two separate array files.

```
E....E....FromfileTofile++Name++N/rN/tbLenPDSAr
     E                    TABPAR    5    5  5 0
     E                    TABCST    5    5  4 2
```

Figure 16-9 PART & COST in Straight Array Format
This record contains TABPAR entries in positions 1 - 25

TABPAR Entry 1.....	TABPAR Entry 6.....	TABPAR Entry 11....	TABPAR Entry 16....	TABPAR Entry 21....

This record contains TABCST entries in positions 1 – 20

TABCST Entry 1....	TABCST Entry 5....	TABCST Entry 9....	TABCST Entry 13....	TABCST Entry 17....

Searching Arrays & Tables

The RPG LOKUP operation is used to search arrays & tables. The format of the LOKUP is shown in Figure 16-10

Figure 16-10 RPG/400 LOKUP, RPGIV LOOKUP Operation

Code	Factor 1	Factor2	Result	Ind.
LOKUP (array) (table)	srch arg srch arg	arrnam tabnam	tabnam	HILOEQ HILOEQ

Checking out Figure 16-10, the Code is LOKUP and it can be used against a table or an array. In Factor 1, you put an argument – the data for which you want to find a match in the array or table. In Factor 2, you put the name of the table name or array name that you are searching.

The specification of the result field depends on whether you are searching a table or an array. If you are searching a table, you put the name of the table in the result field. At the end of the search if you get a hit, the indicator specified in EQ will be turned on and the matched value will be stored in table name as specified in the result field.

When a search is done on the left side of an alternating table, the corresponding alternate value of the matched value is placed in the field referenced by the alternate array name. So that if TABPAR is searched for example, the corresponding cost will be in TABCST after the operation is successful.

Because the data will be lost when the next LOKUP occurs, most often the next operation a programmer performs after a successful table lookup is to move the table name (TABCST for example) to another field for later use.

If you are searching an array, you do not specify a result field. If you specify an array name and no index, the HILOEQ indicators that you specify will reflect the search. If the EQ indicator is on, for example, you got a hit.

If you would like to work with the element of an alternate array after a hit, then in Factor 2, you specify the array name, a comma, and an index value. At the end of the search, the index value is set so that can be used to access the element from the alternating array.

When LOKUP is processed on an array and an index is used, the LOKUP begins with the element specified by the index. The index value is set to the position number of the element located. An error occurs if the index is equal to zero or is higher than the number of elements in the array when the search begins.

The index is set equal to one if the search is unsuccessful. If the index is a named constant, the index value will not change. The message there is that for the most part, do not use a named constant since its value by definition cannot change.

The search argument can be any of the following types:

- ✓ Character or numeric literal,
- ✓ Field name
- ✓ Array element,
- ✓ Table name,
- ✓ Named constant,
- ✓ Figurative constant

LOKUP Example

The following example shows the components that we have discussed and can help solidify the information already presented. Let's say that our objective is to use a keyed part number, look up the part and find the corresponding cost and the corresponding description for the part number.

To do this we store the cost in an array, and the description in a table. The example uses LOKUP to find each. After the array look-up, use the index (COST,X) as the cost and after the table lookup, use the TABDSC referenced field.

Figure 16-11 Array and Table Example

```
E....FromfileTofile++Name++N/rN/tbLenPDSArrnamLenPDS
E                       PART    5   5   5 0A
E                       COST    5   5   4 2
E                       TABPAR  5   5   5 0 TABDSC 30

CL0N01N02N03Factor1+++OpcdeFactor2+++ResultLenDHHiLoEq
C               PARTNO  LOKUPTABPAR    TABDSC         20
C                       MOVE TABDSC    DESCR 30
C   20          TABPAR  LOKUPPART,X                      21
C   21                  Z-ADDCOST,X    PCOST 42
C   N20
CORN21                  GOTO NOTFND
C*
```

Decoding the example in Figure 16-11, we have two related arrays in straight format and a table in alternating format defined on the E specifications. PARTNO is a variable that contains the search argument.

Using PARTNO, the TABPAR table is searched and the TABDSC alternating table name is used in the result field to catch the name of the department when a match is found. The matching department is then moved to a field, DESC for safe keeping. Then, TABPAR is used for the lookup on the PART array.

Indicator 20 is on because we got a hit on the description lookup. PARTNO could just as easily have been used. If there is a hit, indicator 20 comes on and since the letter X is being used as the array index on the lookup, after the match, the field X is primed with the value of the index for the matching element.

Since the COST array is loaded with related (corresponding) elements, COST,X contains the cost for the matched part. To save this cost for later processing, it is moved to another field, PCOST.

The Meaning of the LOKUP Resulting Indicators

As you saw in the example in 16-11, the HI LOEQ resulting indicators can be used to provide additional information about a LOKUP operation. The meaning of these indicators is explained below:

HI   Find the entry nearest to, yet higher in sequence than the search
         argument

LO   Find the entry nearest to, yet lower in sequence than the search
         argument

EQ   Find the entry equal to the search argument

If only the EQ indicator is specified, the by default the LOKUP searches the entire table/array for a match, even if data is in sequence. For better performance, (to limit the search), you can specify both an A for ascending sequence on the E spec, and a HI indicator on the LOKUP. This will end the search when the HI indicator is turned on.

Let's try another LOKUP example in Figure 16-12.

Figure 16-12 LOKUP Example 2
```
E....FromfileTofile++Name++N/rN/tbLenPDSArrnamLenPDSCom
E                     PART    5   5   5 0A
E                     COST    5   5   4 2
E                     TABPAR  5   5   5 0 TABDSC 30


CL0N01N02N03Factor1+++OpcdeFactor2+++ResultLenDHHiLoEq+
C            PARTNO     LOKUPTABPAR     TABDSC        20
C     20     PARTNO     LOKUPPART,X                   21
C...
```

If a table name is used as Factor 1 as in Figure 16-12, then the specific table entry used is the element of the table last selected in the last table LOKUP operation, or the default is the 1st element if no LOKUP has been performed. For a table LOKUP, the result field (TABDSC) can contain the name of a second table (alternating format) from which a corresponding element can be retrieved. Take the two examples shown in Figure 16-13.

Figure 16-13 Sample Alternating Table Data

Left Table (TABPAR)	Right Table (TABDSC)
03000	Bi-focal Glasses
06300	Tinted Contact Lenses

If PARTNO is 06300, then after the LOKUP operation, the TABDSC name is Tinted Contact Lenses. It's actually that straight forward. Now, let's try another LOKUP example against an array in Figure 16-14.

Figure 16-14 Array LOKUP Example
```
E....FromfileTofile++Name++N/rN/tbLenPDSArrnamLenPDS
E                     PART    5   5   5 0 A
E                     COST    5   5   4 2


CL0N01N02N03Factor1+++OpcdeFactor2+++ResultLenDHHiLo
C            PARTNO     LOKUPPART,X
C     21                MOVE COST,X    WSCOST   40
```

LOKUP (LOOKUP in RPGIV) Review

In review, for an array LOKUP, the LOKUP begins with the current index value (if x= 3, the 3rd element of PART). A Match is indicated by the EQ indicator. After a match, index points to matched element (if match is with second element, then X is 2). This can be used with a structurally similar or an alternating array.

Some tips for searching arrays with an index include the following:

- ✓ Leave enough room for the index when choosing the name
- ✓ Start the search at a particular element by specifying array name, a comma, & the index in factor2
- ✓ The index can be a numeric constant, or a numeric field
- ✓ When matched, the numeric field will contain the position of the matched element

Now, let's use Figure 16-15 and try searching an array w/o an index. This type of LOKUP uses the status of the EQ resulting indicator (on or off) to determine whether a particular element is present in the array. It is often used for validity checking to determine if an entered item is present in a list of valid items.

Figure 16-15 Searching Pre-Run Time Array for a Match

```
F*
FFilenameIPEAF..........I........Device+......KExit++E
FARRFILE IT  F       5           EDISK
E*
E....FromfileTofile++Name++N/rN/tbLenPDSArrnamLenPD+
E    ARRFILE          DPTNOS  1  50  5 0A
C*
CL0N01N02N03Factor1+++OpcdeFactor2+++ResultLenDHHiLoEQ
C            DPTNUM    LOKUPDPTNOS                    20
C  N20                 EXSR BADNUM
C            ...       ETC            ...
C            BADNUM    BEGSR
* ------ ------------- ------ ----------------------
```

An RPGIV lookup is shown below:

C... DPTNUM   LOOKUP   DPTNOS   20

In decoding Figure 16-15, you can see in the File descriptions that the ARRFILE is a table file (T in 16) and that it is program described (F in 19) and that the record length is 5 (5 in record length). Notice the E immediately to the left of the DISK device on the File Description specification.

This tells the compiler that this file is further defined on the Extension specification. Besides the name ARRFILE being the same in Extension and File Descriptions, this, as well as the T in column 16, is one of the links that are necessary.

At the beginning of the program the ARRFILE containing the pre run-time array as defined in Figure 16-15 is read from disk. It is used to load the DPTNOS pre-run time array. Each record in the ARRFILE as you can see in the E spec has just one entry (# entries per record = 1) and there are fifty records in the file.

The first action finds the DPTNUM search argument looking up the department # in DPTNOS. If it does no t find it, then there is a problem and indicator 20 comes on to tell the program there was no hit. From here, the BADNUM subroutine e gets run to do what is necessary.

For the next example, let's search an array with an index one more time as shown in Figure 16-16.

Figure 16-16 – Searching an Array with an Index

```
FARRFILE    T  F          5                EDISK
E      ARRFILE            DPTNOS  1  50   5 0ADPTDSC 20
C*
C                         Z-ADD1            X
C              DPTNUM     LOKUPDPTNOS,X                    20
C   N20                   EXSR BADNUM
C                         MOVE DPTDSC,X    DPTNAM
C              ...        ETC              ...
C              BADNUM     BEGSR
```

In Figure 16-16, again there is the ARRFILE pre run-time array just as in Figure 16-15. This time we extend the code so that if there is a hit on department number, we capture the department name by using the index value on the alternate array named DPTDSC.

Changing Entries in Arrays

Now, let's do a little more with our examples. This time, let's change some entries in the pre-run array and write it back at the end of the program. Here is the additional code to get that job done in with a real easy sample.

```
C              25         LOKUPARFL,X                      10
C   10                    MOVE 30          ARFL,X
C   10                    MOVE 500         ARLI,X
```

In the above example, after finding the entry with 25 in the ARFL array, the program replaces the value with 30 and then also replaces the value of a corresponding array ARLI with 500.

The TOFILE entry in the E specification determines which files get updated at end of job. The ARFL and the ARLI arrays are changed for the duration of the program and will be changed for good if there is a TOFILE entry on the E specification.

There are always rules for performing functions on arrays and changing their values is no different.

Pre-run time array entries can be changed before, or during program execution. The simplest approach is to use something like DFU or a simple update program to change the values in the array in the disk file that holds it prior to the program even running. For compilation arrays, the array at the back of the program – after the *** can be modified and the program can then be recompiled. before running

Yet, in a programmer's world, that is not enough. The genius of programmers, dictates that this be not the only way. IBM has accommodated this by permitting RPG to modify pre-run time arrays and tables during execution. The entries can be changed as we did above via various operations such as MOVE, MOVEL etc.
    Of course, if the TOFILE entry is not used, the changes are temporary. If the TOFILE entry is used, then, right before the program gracefully ends, it writes out the file from memory replacing the contents of the array or table file on disk.

Adding Entries to Arrays

Just like the update facility described above, you can also add entries to arrays. For compile time arrays, You can add entries after the ** and before the highest element #. You can add records to the pre run-time array in the disk file, or you can use operations within the program to reference unoccupied areas of the array and fill tem up during execution using MOVE, MOVEL type operations

Unused index entries are used to store the adds. These are found by using 000 as search argument. Just as with the update function, if TOFILE is not used, the changes are temporary. Here is some sample code:

```
* Adding
*
C   01        000         LOKUPARRA,X              35
C   35 01                 MOVE NEWA     ARRA,X
C   35 01                 MOVE NEWB     ARRB,X
```

If you get a hit on the 000 LOKUP, 35 comes on. Then, you have found a clean spot to put your new entry.

The information that we just rpresented regarding the updating and adding of entries to arrays also pertains to tables, with the following differences:

✓ Tables must have a unique symbolic name that begins with the letters -- TAB

✓ Tables can be loaded only at compilation and prerun-time.

✓ The LOKUP operation is the only way to search tables. There is no index option

✓ Prior to 1st LOKUP, the 1st element is used

Figure 16-17 Table LOKUP Example
```
E....FromfileTofile++Name++N/rN/tbLenPDSArrnamLenPDS
E                   TABPAR  5    5   5 0 TABDSC 30
E                   TABEMP  5    5   4 0 TABPAY  4 0


CL0N01N02N03Factor1+++OpcdeFactor2+++ResultLenDHHiLoEq+
C             PARTNO    LOKUPTABPAR    TABDSC      19 20
C N20                   GOTO ERROR
C                       MOVE TABDSC    DESC   30
C             EMPNUM    LOKUPTABEMP    TABPAY         09
C N09                   GOTO ERROR
C    09       HRSWKD    MULT TABPAY    AMT    62H
C             DPTNUM    LOKUPDPTNOS,X             20
```

Decoding this example we see four tables as two pairs of alternating compile time tables defined in the E specs. The five (5) entries per record (N/r) is the giveaway for a compile time table. Decoding with little knowledge we would conclude that there is parts table (TABPAR) with an alternating parts description table (TABDSC) and there is an employee table (TABEMP with an alternating pay table (TABPAY).

The program action starts with the PARTNO field as the search argument against the TABPAR table. If indicator 20 is on, there is a match. Since there is no A specified for ascending in the E spec and there is a 20 in the EQ area, the whole table will be searched. In other words, the search will not stop when a higher than search argument entry is found because without an A, the compiler does not know whether the table is loaded in PARTNO sequence.

If 20 is not on, the GOTO operation takes a branch to a routine (TAG operation) called ERROR that is not included in the sample code. Otherwise, the next statement gets executed and TABDSC holds the name of the description that matches the part. This value is then stored in a field called DESC for later operations.

The next LOKUP involves the EMPNUM field as the search argument looking for an employee # match in TABEMP. If there is not a match, the code takes a branch to the ERROR routine. If 09 is on the PAY (rate) field in TABPAY is multiplied by hours worked (HRSWRK) to create a field called AMT. Finally, to make the TABLE code look legitimate, a DPTNUM search argument goes against the DPTNOS array looking for a match.

Example – Table LOKUP with one Table

Let's use one simple table defined in the following E specification and the operations in the C specifications to present the summary for a LOKUP with one table.

```
E....Tofile++Name++N/rN/tbLenPDSArrnamLenPDS
E             TABEMP  5    5  4 0

C...N03Factor1+++OpcdeFactor2+++ResultLenDHHiLoEq
C      EMPNUM     LOKUPTABEMP                      09
```

The LOKUP needs:

✓ Factor1, Factor2, and at least one resulting indicator
✓ Conditioning indicators may be used
✓ Whenever a hit is encountered on the table lookup the following items numbered A through D occur:

A.   The system places the found element in a reserved area.

B.   The element can then be referenced by using the table name. (name points to element)

C.   If no LOKUPs performed, the reserved area points to the 1st   table entry

D.   If no-hit, the table name refers to the 1st element

Let's wrap up LOKUP with tables and arrays with a rehash of the rules for two tables in alternating format. The code below can be used as a reference:

```
E....FromfileTofile++Name++N/rN/tbLenPDSTabnamLenPDSCom
E                       TABEMP  5    5  4 0 TABRAT  4 2

CL0N01N02N03Factor1+++OpcdeFactor2+++ResultLenDHHiLoEq
C              EMPNUM   LOKUPTABEMP    TABRAT            09
C*
C      09               Z-ADDTABRAT    RRATE
C              1.5       MULT RATE      OTRATE  42
```

In this case, TABEMP is searched to find the rate in TABRAT. Then, in this routine the rate is used to calculate an overtime rate.

The specifics about an alternating table LOKUP are as follows:

✓ Only one table is actually searched
✓ Factor1, Factor2, result field, and at least one resulting indicator are required
✓ Conditioning indicators may be used.

With table LOKUP with two tables, whenever a hit is encountered on the table lookup the following occurs:

A. The system places the corresponding elements of both
     tables in a reserved area

B. The elements can then be referenced by using the
     respective table name

C. If no LOKUPs have been performed, the reserved area points to
     the 1st entry in both tables

D. If there is not a hit, the table names refer to the 1st element of
     Each respectively

Speeding up Array Searches

An array can be loaded in a particular sequence or no particular sequence. Most often arrays are loaded in a particular sequence. However, it is not necessary to tell the compiler that the array is in sequence. The results will be the same.

So, sometimes programmers take the time to put an array in sequence as in Figure 16-18, but never tell the compiler it is in sequence. Since the compiler does not know that the data is in sequence, it will search the whole array, element by element looking for an equal condition. Only when it reaches the last element can it know that it has not gotten a hit.

On the other hand, if a programmer tells the compiler the array is in ascending or descending sequence, the compiler can use a much better search technique to find an element and it knows immediately as soon as a higher value is encountered than the search argument that there is no hit.

Thus, no-hits are processed substantially faster. When the compiler knows the data is in sequence, then, it is not necessary to search the entire array. The search continues only until an equal or greater than condition.

Figure 16-18 Using Sequenced Arrays for Faster Processing

```
E                         AI            60  1  A
E*                                             A = ASCENDING
E*  RPG LOKUP ON ORDERED ARRAY UNTIL MATCH OR NOT FOUND
E*  ( > THAN)
E*
C* Indicator 10 comes on if greater
C* Indicator 20 come on if equal
C* Key benefit - Search stops when greater than
C* Unordered array searches all items always to assure an
C* EQUAL condition can be found
C*
C           ARG           LOKUPTAB                 10   20
C           *IN20         IFEQ *ON
C*                        ETC
C*
C*
C*   END ORDERED ARRAY LOKUP CODE
C*
C* ------------------------------------------------------------
```

Faster Processing for Unordered Arrays

The indexing for arrays has traditionally been done in IBM compilers using multiply to get to the correct element. Thus, array processing has traditionally been a dog in RPG. Traditionally multiply has been an inefficient operation using successive additions in software rather then hardware. Performance improvement techniques for arrays then almost always have to do with limiting the array element accesses if possible.

This next set of code in Figure 16-19 speeds up processing again by eliminating processing. The technique is to fill an execution array from the end instead of from the beginning when adding elements. To do this, you use the beginning entry on the RPG LOKUP. In this way, only the elements at the back of the array are searched.

Figure 16-19 Processing Unordered arrays for performance

```
F*
E           AI    2000 1
E*  BLNK=UNORDERED
E*  RPG LOKUP ON FULL UNORDERED ARRAY RESULTS IN
E*  2000 COMP OPERATIONS IF NOT FOUND
C*
C       ARG   LOKUPTAB          20
C*                 = ONLY TEST
C*
C** STARTS AT ELEMENT 1 & SEARCHES THE ENTIRE ARRAY
C*
C       *IN20   IFEQ *ON
C*          ETC
C*
C*
C** END UNORDERED ARRAY LOKUP CODE...
C**     ELEMENT 1 TO END
C*------------------------------------------------
C*
C** SEARCH FROM LAST ARRAY ELEMENT ADDED ..
C** PRIME X With a VALUE
C*
C           Z-ADD2000   X
C*               X = # ELEMENTS
C*               X = ELEMENT #
C*   ...   ETC      ...
C** LOAD ARRAY FROM LAST POSITION TO FIRST
C           MOVELDATA   A1,X       C*              LAST POS.
C           SUB 1   X         C*            NEXT TO LAST
C*   ...   ETC      ...
C*
C* At the end of above routine X = last element
C* loaded – front of array is blank. Use X as start
C** RPG LOKUP FROM LAST ELEMENT LOADED
C** TO END (X TO END OF ARRAY)
C*
C       ARG   LOKUPA1,X          20
C*              X=1ST USED  20 = Hit
C*
C** END UNORDERED ARRAY LOKUP CODE. ELEMENT X TO END
C*
C* ------------------------------------------------
```

Consider Keyed Files Vs. Arrays

Arrays have been such a bugaboo to performance that an alternative that can be faster is to use a keyed file (indexed) instead of an array where appropriate. If the elements are unordered and there are at least 250 to 300 elements in the array, moving the file to the database may help performance. Performance is even faster if the keyed file is in memory in its own storage pool. We show you how to do this in Figure below.

The command is **SETOBJACC** and after you type it in on a command line, press F4 to get a prompt which brings up a screen similar to that shown in Figure 16-20.

Figure 16-20 Set Object Access Command

```
*...+... 1 ...+... 2 ...+... 3 ...+... 4 ...+... 5 ...+... 6
****************************************************************
*            Set Object Access (SETOBJACC)               * 01
*                                                         * 02
* Type choices, press Enter.                              * 03
*                                                         * 04
* Object . . . . . . . .     MYFILE      Name             * 05
*   Library  . . . . . .     RPGBOOK     Name, *LIBL, *USRLIBL* 06
* Object type  . . . .       *FILE       *FILE, *PGM      * 07
* Storage pool:                                           * 08
*   Shared pool or subsystem QINTER      Name, *JOB, *BASE...* 09
*   Pool identifier  . . . . 3           1-10             * 10
*                                                         * 11
*                                                         * 20
*                                             BOttom * 21
* F3=Exit   F4=Prompt   F5=Refresh    e                   * 22
* F12=Cancel   F13=How to us   F24=More keys              * 23
*                                                         * 24
****************************************************************
 *...+... 1 ...+... 2 ...+... 3 ...+... 4 ...+... 5 ...+... 6 ..78
```

The Set Object Access (SETOBJACC) command temporarily changes the speed of access to an object by bringing the object into a main storage pool. In the example above in Figure 16-40, MYFILE from library RPGBOOK is going to be brought into main storage

The object is a *FILE type and it will occupy the storage in subsystem QINTER subsystem pool ID # 3. As long as pool ID 3 exists in QINTER and it has been allocated enough memory, the file object will be brought into memory and the very fast routines to access the file will be used and the data will be grabbed from memory rather than from disk.

Named Constants

What is a named constant? A constant is something that never changes in a program. It has traditionally manifested itself in something called a literal which was defined in RPG output or in calculations just for that particular operation.

Sometime there was so much constant data and the constants were so large, arrays were used to bring them into programs. The notion of being able to define and name a constant in RPG has provided more flexibility than any of the techniques of the past.

The Format of the named constant specification is covered in detail in Chapter 8. It is a derivative of the input specification.

Figure 16-21 provides a quick review of the format of the Input spec to support naming a constant:

Figure 16-21 Named Constant Use of Input Specification

Columns	Name	Specify
6	Form Type	I
7-20	Leave blank	Blank
21-42	Constant Value	Value
43	Data Type (C for constant)	C, Blank
44-52	Leave blank	Blank
53-58	Constant Name	Name
59-74	Leave Blank	Blank

Named Constant Examples

A picture is worth a thousand words. Check out Figure 16-22 for some informative "pictures" of RPG named constants in action.

Figure 16-22 Named Constants in Action

```
C*        NAMED CONSTANTS: e.g.
C*
C*
I..............Namedconstant+++++++++C.........Fldnme.....
I             'RESIDENCES'            C          RES
I             '  ,    ,$0.  -'        C          @EDMSK
I             'UNOCCUPIED'            C          UNOC
I             'Press Enter to con-    C          CONTNU
I             'tinue operation'
I             'Kelly Consulting'      C          CNAME1
I             'Professional Trainin-C            CNAME2
I             'g Company of America-
I             '- ProTrain'
I             '                    -C            ULINE
I             '          '
OQPRINT  E 00                BOLD
O                            FRSPRT   45
O                            AMOUNT   60 @EDMSK
O                            AMTDUE   75 '  ,    ,$0.  -'
O                            AMTO30   90 @EDMSK
OQPRINT  E 00                UNDER
O                 50         ULINE    40
O                 51         ULINE    75
```

The RPGIV entries for several constants are shown below:

```
D RES...     C                    CONST('RESIDENCES')
D @EDMSK...  C                    CONST('  ,    ,$0.  -')
D UNOC...    C                    CONST('UNOCCUPIED')
```

When these constants print or are displayed on terminals, they will appear as follows:

```
RES         RESIDENCES
@EDMSK      $25.10-
UNOC        UNOCCUPIED
CONTNU      Press Enter to continue operation
CNAME1      Kelly Consulting
CNAME2      Professional Training Company of America - ProTrain
ULINE       _____
```

Now let's look at the rules that govern the use of named constants in RPG/400. Similar rules / notions apply in RPGIV.

- ✓ 'C' in pos. 43 of INPUT, TEXT in 21 - 42
- ✓ Appearance anywhere among the I specs
- ✓ Up to 256 bytes for a character constant
- ✓ 20 char/line continued over multiple lines
- ✓ SAVES many MOVE, MOVEL commands, or arrays
- ✓ Can be used for edit masks / edit words
- ✓ Can be used to initialize DS subfields
- ✓ SEU Prompt type is "N"

Figurative Constants

Now that we have explored named constants, let's continue our look at constants by examining Figurative Constants and their use within RPG. The list of possible Figurative constants in RPG is shown in Table 16-23.

Figure 16-23 Figurative Constants

Figurative Constant	Meaning
*LOVAL	Factor1 to set pointer to BOF
*HIVAL	Factor1 to set pointer at EOF
*ZERO	Zero Fill
*BLANKS	Blank Fill
*ON	All Ones (1)
*OFF	All Zeros (0)
*INxx	Indicator as a field
*IN	All indicators as an large array

The figurative constants *BLANK, *BLANKS, *ZERO, *ZEROS, *HIVAL, *LOVAL, *ALL'x..", *ALLX'x1..' and *ON, *OFF are implied literals that can be specified without a length, because the implied length and decimal positions of a figurative constant are the same as those of the associated field. (For exceptions, see the following section, "Rules for Figurative Constants" on page 385.)

Figurative constants can be specified in positions 18 through 27 (factor 1) and in positions 33 through 42 (factor 2) of the calculation specifications.

The following shows the reserved words and implied values for figurative constants:

Table 16-24, Figurative Constants and Meanings

Figurative Constant	Meaning, Implied Values and Further explanation
***BLANK /
*BLANKS**	All blanks – valid only for character fields
*ZERO /
*ZEROS	All zeros – valid for character and numeric fields
*HIVAL	Hexadecimal "FF" Provides the highest collating character for the system. For numeric fields *HIVAL provides all nines with a positive sign
*LOVAL	Hexadecimal "00" Provides the lowest collating character for the system. For numeric fields *LOVAL provides all nines with a negative sign
*ALL'x..'	Character/numeric fields: Character string x . . is cyclically repeated to a length equal to the associated field. If the field is a numeric field, all characters within the string must be numeric (0 through 9). No sign or decimal point can be specified when *ALL'x..' is used as a numeric constant.
*ALLX'x1..'	Character fields: The hexadecimal literal X'x1..' is cyclically repeated to a length equal to the associated field.

*ON / *OFF	*ON is all ones. *OFF is all zeros. Both are only valid for character fields. Often used to test the value of an indicator
*IN, *INxx	Indicator array as a field; specific indicator # as a field

The figurative constants *BLANK/ *BLANKS, *ZERO/ *ZEROS, *HIVAL, *LOVAL, *ALL'x..', *ALLX'x1..' and *ON/ *OFF are implied literals that can be specified without a length, because the implied length and decimal positions of a figurative constant are the same as those of the associated field.

Rules for Figurative Constants

The use of powerful RPG objects always come with a set of rules. The rules for Figurative constants are as follows:

1. Figurative constants are considered elementary items. Except for MOVEA, figurative constants act like a field if used in conjunction with an array. For example with ARR defined in E specs as an array:

```
MOVE        *ALL'XYZ'              ARR
```

If ARR has 4-byte character elements, then each element will contain 'XYZX'.

2. MOVEA is a special case for figurative constants. The constant is generated with a length equal to the portion of the array specified. Examples follow:

```
MOVEA       *BLANK            ARR,X
```

In this move array operation, beginning with element X, the remainder of ARR will contain blanks.

```
MOVEA       *ALL'XYZ'              ARR,X
```

In this example, ARR has 4-byte character elements. The element boundaries are completely ignored, as is always the case with character MOVEA operations. Beginning with element X, therefore, after this operation, the remainder of the array would contain 'XYZXYZXYZ...'

Note that the results of MOVEA are different from those of the MOVE example.

3. Figurative constants are valid in compare operations such as COMP, CAB, DOU, DOW, and IF; when the associated field in the compare operations is the field with which the figurative constant is to be compared.

Figurative constants are not allowed in factor 1 of a DEBUG or DSPLY operation or in factor 2 of MHLZO, MLHZO, MHHZO, MLLZO, BITON, BITOF, TESTB, or SQRT operations. The figurative constants, *BLANK/ *BLANKS, are actually replaced by zeros when moved to a numeric field in a MOVE operation.

Figurative Constant Example 1

Let's take a look at one of the most common uses of Figurative constants,

*OFF, and *ON. These constants make it very handy to "spray "1's" or "0's" into Result Fields. *ON and *OFF can be used handily MOVE and comparison statements. They are valid for char fields only and their use is very similar to that of *ZERO's and *BLANKS. It makes a lot of sense to use *ON and *OFF to set the value of an indicator at 1 or 0 and because we become accustomed to referring to indicators as being on or off, not as to whether they contain ones or zeros. The example in Figure 16-25, stretches the notion of *ON and *OFF somewhat.

Figure 16-25 Figurative Constants - *ON / *OFF Example 1

```
CL0N01N02N03Factor1+++OpcdeFactor2+++ResultLenD
C*------------------------------------------
C*  Conventional Way
C                     MOVE *ALL'0'   FIELD1 100
C*
C                     MOVE *ZEROS    FIELD1 100
C*------------------------------------------
C*  New Way
C*
C                     MOVE *OFF      FIELD1 100
C*
C                     MOVE *ON       FIELD1 100
```

Figurative Constant Example 2

This example uses a CAS group (conditionally invoke subroutine)
in calculations to test for indicator conditions and then execute a particular subroutine based on the value, which is a very handy way to test conditions and then immediately execute the function to handle the condition.

The CASxx operation allows you to conditionally select a subroutine for processing. The selection is based on the relationship between factor 1 and factor 2, as specified by xx. The examples in Figure 16-26 use an "EQ" (equal) test.

If the relationship denoted by xx exists between factor 1 and factor 2, the subroutine specified in the result field is processed. All CAS operations are looked upon as a group and the group must end with an END or ENDCS statement as it does in the example.

It helps to know that only one of the CASxx or CAS entries will be executed. Once the subroutine is completed, the next executable statement is the ENDCS. The CAS is an unconditional execution. Since just one CAS or CASxx gets executed in a group, the CAS as a catchall is always placed last. Otherwise, none of the other tests would eb made since after the CAS the program would execute the ENDCS and get out of the group.

Let's look at this example in Figure 16-24 now as a nice way of using the *INxx Figurative constant in a comparison. You can see that there is a DO loop controlling the screen "cycle" in this program. Each time that the loop goes around, the operator has the opportunity to press Function keys. Since F3 is the default end of job indicator, it makes sense that it would turn on indicator 03 and that the Do loop would thus be conditioned to continue until the user pressed end-of-job (F3).

Using indicator 03 as a field permits the DO loop to test the value for a "1" or an on condition. The new way in the bottom half of the example shows that the Figurative constants fit nicely in this scenario.

Figure 16-26 *INxx Use in CASxx Operations

```
C*----------------------------------------------
C*
C*   Conventional Way
C            *IN03       DOUEQ'1'
C                        EXFMTSCREEN1
C*
C                        MOVEA*ALL'0'    *IN,80
C*
C            *IN01       CASEQ'1'        HELP
C            *IN03       CASEQ'1'        EOJ
C            *IN06       CASEQ'1'        SIX
C            *IN10       CASEQ'1'        RTEN
C                        CAS             ENTER
C                        ENDCS
C*
C                        ENDDO
C*----------------------------------------------
C*
C* New Way
C            *IN03       DOUEQ'1'
C                        EXFMTSCREEN1
C*
C                        MOVEA*OFF       *IN,80
C*
C            *IN01       CASEQ*ON        HELP
C            *IN03       CASEQ*ON        EOJ
C            *IN06       CASEQ*ON        SIX
C            *IN10       CASEQ*ON        RTEN
C                        CAS             ENTER
C                        ENDCS
C                        ENDDO
C            HELP        BEGSR
                          . .
C                        ENDSR
```

When the indicators are used as data fields or an array, it helps to think of the reserved word *IN as a 99-element array, with each element one byte in length. This can be used anywhere array elements can be specified except as a subfield of a data structure, a result field of a PARM operation or in a SORTA operation.

The MOVEA operation prior to the CASEQ operations in the top and bottom moves all zeros in both cases to the indicator array *IN starting at indicator 80 and continuing for 19 more indicators until indicators 80 to 99 are off. This is a very handy way of setting off a group of indicators with just one operation.

Since a DO Until tests the DO condition at the end of the loop, when indicator 03 comes on, indicating the last record F3 key has been hit, the second case (after the *IN01 case) that begins with *IN03 is executed and the EOJ subroutine completes.

If command key 01, 06, or 10 is hit, and if the Display format maps them to indicators 01, 06, and 10 respectively, then the HELP, SIX, or RTEN subroutines would be executed based on the value of the indicators as fields. In the top half, the operation looks for a "1" while in the second half, the operation looks for the *ON figurative constant which is another way of testing for the value of "1."

Let's take a look at a simpler example:

```
C*  SET OFF INDICATORS 50 THROUGH 99
C        MOVEA   *ZERO    *IN,50
```

The above example sets off indicators 50 to 99. Now, let's look at another example of the single name field for an indicator. In the example in Figure 16-27, we are working with indicator 10 as *IN10.

Figure 16-27 Indicator as Data

```
C...        *IN10  DOWEQ     *ZERO
C...               READ      VENDMST               10
C...        *IN10  IFEQ      *ZERO
C...               MOVE      'XXX'      FLD1
C...               UPDAT     RECORD1
C...               ENDIF
C...               ENDDO
```

Here are a few other examples to show you how Figurative Constants can be used:

```
C* Initialize Fields
C     MOVE        *ZERO      NEW   50
C     MOVE   *BLANKS         NEW1  10
C* Fill with repeating pattern:
C     MOVE        *ALL'ABC'  NEW1
C     MOVE        *ON        *IN20
C     MOVE        *OFF       *IN35
C* Five Zeros
C     MOVE        *OFF       FIELD  5
C *LOVAL  SETLL       DIR2
C *HIVAL  SETLL       DIR2
```

Before we move on to Data Structures, let's take a look in a general way at the other reserved words and special values that can be used in RPG/400.

Other RPG/400 Reserved Words

In addition to Figurative Constants, a number of RPG/400 reserved words have special functions within a program. These include UDATE, *DATE, UMONTH, *MONTH, UYEAR, *YEAR, UDAY, and *DAY. These allow the RPG programmer to access the system date, or a portion of it, to be used in the program.

The reserved words, PAGE, and PAGE1-PAGE7 can be used for numbering the pages of a report, for record sequence numbering, or to sequentially number output fields.

In this teaching / learning guide to RPG, we have chosen not to devote substantial space to notions that do not enhance the initial learning experience. Yet, to be fairly complete, we have included the other reserved words that are not seen or used as frequently.

For example, RPG has a notion called the File Information Data Structure (INFDS) which can be queried after I/O operations to get status information on the success / failure of the operation. To make it easier for programmers to access elements of the INFDS, the following reserved words define symbolic locations within the structure: *FILE, *OPCODE, *PARMS, *PROGRAM, *RECORD, *ROUTINE, *STATUS.

As another convenience for programmers doing heavy duty work, .RPG/400 also has reserved words that provide symbolic labels for the ENDSR operations for the file and program exception/error subroutines or for the INFDS. These reserved words make it easier to refer to the point in the cycle or the routine in which an event occurs:

✓	*CANCL	Cancel the program
✓	*DETC	Detail calculations
✓	*DETL	Detail lines
✓	*GETIN	Get input record
✓	*INIT	Program initialization
✓	*OFL	Overflow lines
✓	*TERM	Program ending
✓	*TOTC	Total calculations
✓	*TOTL	Total lines

There are also a number of RPG/400 special words that are used with specific operation codes. There are some examples of the use of these words throughout his text. The words are shown in Table 16-28.

Table 16-28 RPG Special Words with RPG Operations

*ENTRY	Entry List Initial parameter list in PLIST Operation
*INZSR	Program initialization subroutine -- A specific subroutine that is to be run at program initialization time can be defined by specifying *INZSR in factor 1 of the subroutine's BEGSR operation. When used in Factor 2, this specifies that the program initialization subroutine is to be processed.
*LDA	Local Data Area used in the RPG program. For example, you can specify *LDA in factor 2 of a *NAMVAR DEFN statement to define the LDA data structure for use in the program..
*LIKE	Define one field like another field. For example, the *LIKE DEFN The "DEFN (Field Definition)" operation with *LIKE in Factor 1 defines a field based upon the attributes (length and decimal positions) of another field.
*LOCK	Lock a data area. Used with the IN and OUT data area operations to lock the specified data area. to associate a field, a data structure, a data-structure subfield, or a data-area data structure (within your RPG/400 program) with an AS/400 data area (outside your RPG/400 program). See DEFN operation in Chapters 9 and 13.
*PDA	Program Data Area. Used with the *NAMVAR option of the DEFN operation with *PDA in Factor 2 to define the name in the result field as the PDA data area.
*PSSR	Program Status Subroutine Used with EXSR operation. *PSSR used in Factor 2 specifies that the program exception/error subroutine is to be processed.

Chapter Summary

The earliest features of RPG for dealing with structures of data are tables and arrays. In many ways tables and arrays are similar. Both are defined on the RPG/400 "E" specification or the RPGIV "D" specification.

A table however, must begin with TAB and in RPG that just leaves three positions to differentiate one table from another. Arrays can use subscripts to address specific elements whereas table access cannot be subscripted.

There are three types of arrays and two types of tables. The compile time array and the compile time tables uses records keyed and stored after a double asterisk (**) record in the source program as the input for the array or table.

Pre-execution or pre-run arrays and tables are typed into database files and are loaded into the program at run time right before the program begins to execute. These can be changed and written back.

A third type of array can also be used at execution time to bring in data that is stored in an array format in normal databases. These are called execution time arrays or run-time arrays.

Two arrays or tables can be specified on one E spec line, by entering a second array or table name, length, and decimal positions in columns 46-57 of the same extension specification. This type of array or table is called an alternating table or array.

When an element is found in the first table, the corresponding element in the alternate array is then usable. The RPG LOKUP or RPGIV LOOKUP operation is used to search arrays & tables.

Named constants are items that never change in a program. The notion of being able to define and name a constant in RPG has provided more flexibility than any of the past techniques to bring constant data into a program.

Figurative Constants are also used within RPG and RPGIV The figurative constants *BLANK *BLANKS, *ZERO, *ZEROS, *HIVAL, *LOVAL, *ALL'x..', *ALLX'x1..' and *ON, *OFF are implied literals that can be specified without a length, because the implied length and decimal positions of a figurative constant are the same as those of the associated field.

In addition to Figurative Constants, a number of RPG/400 reserved words have special functions within a program. These include UDATE, *DATE, UMONTH, *MONTH, UYEAR, *YEAR, UDAY, and *DAY.

These allow the RPG programmer to access the system date, or a portion of it, to be used in the program. The reserved words, PAGE, and PAGE1-PAGE7 can be used for numbering the pages of a report, for record sequence numbering, or to sequentially number output fields.

RPG also has a notion called the File Information Data Structure (INFDS) which can be queried after I/O operations to get status information on the success / failure of the operation.

Key Chapter Terms

*ALL'x.'	*ON	Compile time array
*BLANK	*OPCODE	CTDATA
*BLANKS	*PARMS	Data Areas
*CANCL	*PDA	Data Structure
*DATE	*PROGRAM	DEFN,
*DAY3	*PSSR	DIM -arrays
*DETC	*RECORD	DSPLY
*DETL	*ROUTINE	Execution time array
*ENTRY	*STATUS	Figurative constants
*FILE	*TERM	Keyed Files
*GETIN	*TOTC	LOKUP
*HIVAL	*TOTL	LOOKUP
*IN	*YEAR	Named constants
*INIT	*ZERO	Performance
*INxx	*ZEROS	PERRCD
*INZSR	"D" spec	Pre-execution arrays
*LDA	"E" spec	Pre-run time tables
*LIKE	Adding entries	RESET
*LOCK	Alternating format	SETOBJACC
*LOVAL	Array elements	SORTA
*MONTH3	Array searches	Subscripts
*NAMVAR	Array syntax	Tables
*OFF	Changing entries	TOFILE
*OFL	CLEAR	

Review Questions

1. Which two structures have been in the RPG language with the introduction of RPGII.

2. What is an RPG array?

3. How are arrays searched?

4. Can arrays be used in data files – Give an example?

5. What is an RPG table?

6. What are the differences between arrays and tables? What are the similarities?

7. What are the three types of arrays? When would you use each?

8. What are the two types of tables? When would you use each?

9. What are the syntax rules for arrays? tables?

10. Is the syntax of this array element invalid, valid, or valid sometimes?
JOE,XA3

11. Which form is used in RPG/400 and which form is used in RPGIV to define an array or table?

12. Write the RPGIV equivalent of this array?
```
E....E....FromfileTofile++Name++N/rN/tbLenPDSArrnamLenPDS
    E                      ARC           12   3
```

13. What is an alternating array or table?

14. Write the RPGIV equivalent of the following alternating array? What would need to be done for this to be an alternating table?
```
E....FromfileTofile++Name++N/rN/tbLenPDSArrnamLenPDS
E              PART   1 5 5 0 COST   4 2
```

15. What operation in RPG/400 and what operation in RPGIV is used to find an entry in a table or array.

16. ARC,9 in RPG/400 would equate to what in RPGIV?

17. How do you define a Table File in RPG/400 and in RPGIV?

18. What is a named constant?

19. What is a figurative constant?

20. What is a reserved word?

Chapter 17   RPG Data Structures

What is a Data Structure?

Technically speaking an array and a table and a field and a constant are all data structures since they are structures in which data resides. Thus, having a special notion of a data structure that is called a data structure may at first not make sense.

If I had been consulted on the naming of the notion of data structure that we are about to study, I might have suggested that IBM call it a defined memory record, for that is in fact what we are about to talk about.

In other words an RPG or RPGIV data structure is a stand-alone record designed for use in memory. It has no association with a database file or a data area unless one is explicitly given. It is merely a defined memory record. So, what is a defined memory record, a.k.a. data structure?

A data structure is an area in storage which allows for items of different sizes and shapes to be grouped. It is a means of referencing some or many fields, called subfields, within the storage area of the data structure. To visualize the shape of a typical data structure, the best means is to think of a record format in a database.

In other words, for an example we studied in this book already think of the field definitions all grouped together for the EMPMAST from Chapter 15. Better yet, the HLDMAST data structure is exactly the type of data structure that we are about to discuss in detail for the rest of this chapter.

What are some purposes for RPG data structures? A date structure:

- ✓ Allows for the division of a field into subfields without requiring calculation operations such as MOVE and MOVEL. For example, a data structure to store a date would break down nicely into year month and day.

- ✓ Can change based on operations performed on a subfield which change its contents and therefore the DS itself

- ✓ Redefine the same internal area more than once using different data formats

- ✓ Permits a structure of data to be defined with sub fields in the same way a record is defined, without any required association with a database.

- ✓ Is analogous to a record

- ✓ Can have multiple occurrences or a set of data. In other words, a data structure can be defined with multiple records without an associated file.

- ✓ Can group non-contiguous data into contiguous internal locations

----

Special Types of Data Structures

Besides the typical record-like data structure that is used frequently in RPG programs, there are a number of special data structures that are described in Figure 17-1.

Figure 17-1 Types of Data Structures

DS Type	Description
Data Area Data Structure (DADS)	Points to a data area object on the system. When the data area is red into the program, its shape (length and subfields) is governed by the data structure. A data area data structure is identified by a "U" in column 18 of the DS variant of the Input statement
File Information Data Structure (INFDS)	Provides feedback on file operations. It comes into play when it is referred by the keyword INFDS on a File Description specification continuation line.
Program-Status Data Structure (PSDS)	This special data structure providinf progam status information is defined to RPG by specifying an "S" in column 18 of the DS variant of the Input statement.

These special data structures look just like the normal data structures other than the presence of the U or S in column 18 of the DS form or the reference on File Continuation for the INFDS. Before we examine the very powerful notion of the multiple occurrence data structures, let's see what a simple data structure actually looks like. As a review, it helps to remember that a data structure can be used for the following purposes:

✓ Divide a field into sub-fields without using the MOVE or MOVEL operation

✓ Operate on a subfield and change the contents of a sub-field

✓ Redefine the same internal area more than once using different data formats

✓ In RPG/400, data structures are defined on the input specifications
✓ the same way records are defined.

A multiple occurrence data structure is a data structure whose definition is repeated in a program to form a series of data structures with identical formats. You can think of it as a 2-dimensional data structure. It is defined with one set format, but has multiple entries to it.

Data can be grouped into different 'levels' called occurrences and access can be made by level. The OCUR operation code sets the current level of the data structure.

Some other important facts about data structures include the following:

✓ Data Structures can be elements of an array?
✓ Data structures can include Arrays as elements
✓ Data structures can have more than one occurrence (dimension)

How Are Data Structures (DS) Defined?

With a quick review of data structures, you may recall the following

- ✓ Defined via Input Specifications Record Specification line
- ✓ DS in 19 & 20
- ✓ Field Specifications contain DS subfields
- ✓ DS spec must follow all input specifications
- ✓ All entries for a particular DS must appear together

Moving Data into Data Structures

Mostly everything in RPG gets moved naturally merely by using the same name for from and to. For example, you do not have to use a MOVE operation in your program if an output field is the same name as input. RPG does the move under the covers. The same applies to a data structure.

The compiler generates necessary code to "move" fields into their associated data structure as long as the names are the same. It also provides data conversions as necessary such as from a packed field on disk to a zoned decimal field in the DS. The data conversions occur when a record is being read from a database or at detail or total calculation time or at detail or total output time

Since a multiple occurrence data structure is a superset of a data structure, the next few examples use multiple occurrence data structures to show you how to code simple data structures.

There is just one trick. After you code the multiple occurrence data structure to make it a single occurrence, just remove the # of occurrences entry.

The RPG/400 /RPGIV operation that sets the DS occurrence is OCUR. Some might suggest that if your initial DS was an array, then a multiple occurrence data structure is a means for you to have a "poor man's" way of RPG two dimensional arrays.

Data Structure Example 1

The example in Figure 17-2 has one record for each of 50 states with each state having 12 monthly totals.

Figure 17-2 Loading a Multiple Occurrence Data Structure

```
E                 MTOT      12  5 0

ISTOT       DS                50
I                             1   20RECNO
I                             3    4 ST
I                             6  120TOTAL
I                            13   72 MTOT
...
C        1         DO    50    X
C                  READ  STFILE                    21
C        X         OCUR  STOT
C                  Z-ADDX      RECNO
C                  MOVE  STATE ST
C                  Z-ADDMONTH# Z         20
C                  Z-ADDSTAMT  MTOT,Z
C                  XFOOTMTOT   TOTAL
...
...
C                  ENDDO
```

A Do loop reads 50 records from the STFILE to pull in some state information. The OCUR operation code sets the current level of the data structure to the DO loop index value. In the example, the data structure STOT is defined as having three subfields: record # (RECNO), total dollars for year (TOTAL), and an array of 12 monthly totals (MTOT). The STOT DS has 50 occurrences – one for each state.

At the OCUR operation, the value of the DO index field, X determines which occurrence of STOT will be updated in memory. It goes from 1 to 50 as the DO loop index increments. Each time, the OCUR causes the RECNO field to contain the index value as a record #. The ST subfield contains the state abbreviation, and the MTOT array is loaded directly from the STFILE as an execution time array.

The STAMT value is also read in from the STATES file. This is the current month's totals which have not yet been moved to the correct month in the MTOT array. The numeric month # from 1 to 12 is also read in from the STFILE.

To make the variable index for MTOT a small name, the value of the field MONTH# is moved with a Z-ADD to the field Z. The current amount that is stored in STAMT is then moved via Z-ADD to the current month # bucket in the MTOT array for that state record. The occurrence value (X) determines which memory record actually is updated.

When the MTOT array is updated with STAMAT reflecting the current amount for the Zth element as the new month total, a cross-foot (XFOOT) operation is executed to get a yearly total for months 1 to 12. This is then stored in the TOTAL subfield of the STOT data structure.

At the end of the Do loop, the 50 occurrences of the STOT multiple occurrence data structure have been loaded with new data and they have been cross-footed.

Data Structure Example 2

In the example shown in Figure 17-3A, a multiple occurrence data structure is defined with 100 occurrences. It therefore contains 100 "records" in memory. Each record known as an "occurrence" has the same format: Name, ADDR1 etc as shown in the example.

Accessing Multiple Occurrence Data Structures

The RPG code is the same for one occurrence as for many. There is no subscripting of the fields as in arrays. Instead that which would be the subscript value for an array is called the occurrence value in a multiple occurrence data structure. The occurrence value reflects the record # being processed in the memory file? The occurrence is set each time a different "record" in the multiple occurrence data structure is to be used. When looking at the code, however, other than the OCUR, it is not obvious that a multiple occurrence DS is being used since the Field names look like normal field names as opposed to the special names (subscripts) as in arrays.

Figure 17-3A Reading Records from a Multiple Occurrence Data Structure

```
IDATAS1      DS                      100
I                                      1   30 NAME
I                                     31   60 ADDR1
I                                     61   90 ADDR2
I                                     91  110 CITY
I                                    111  112 STATE
I                                    113 1170ZIP
I                                  P 118 1252AMDUE
C            1          DO    100   RRN     30
C            RRN        OCUR  DATAS1
C*           . . .      ETC          . . .
C                       ENDDO1
```

```
C       RRN     OCUR DATAS1
```

Using RRN in the statement above, the DO loop in Figure 16-27 "reads" each occurrence of the data structure in a similar fashion to a database READ. RRN chooses an occurrence from 1 to 100 of the data structure as it is looping and in so doing the associated sub-fields for that occurrence are then usable as denoted by the ETC in the code above..

Data Structure Example 3

In Chapter 23, this book continues the PAREG example. You will see how the program is expanded to be able to perform matching and control level processing without the benefit of a primary or secondary file or the RPG cycle. To perform the control field checks, for example, as you will see in the PAREG2 program set, a data structure called HLDMST is used to hold the prior record so that the control fields of the current record can be compared with the prior record to see if an L1 or L2 break has occurred.. The single occurrence HLDMST data structure is shown in RPG/400 form in Figure 17-3B.

Figure 17-3B HLDMST Data Structure from PAREG2
```
049  IHLDMST        DS
050  I                                           1    30HLDNO
051  I                                           1    70 HREC
052  I                                           4    33 HLDNAM
053  I                                           4    23 HLDNM
054  I                                          34    382HLDRAT
055  I                                          39    58 HLDCTY
056  I                                          59    60 HLDSTA
057  I                                          61    650HLDZIP
058  I                                          66    66 HLDSCD
059  I                                          67    70 HLDDPT
```

Data Structure Example 4

Looking further ahead to Chapter 24, the PAREG2 program is enhanced with a history file that captures all of the variables regarding a particular payroll for each employee. Since the mythical Dowalloby Company has less than 100 employees, we have built a 100 record data structure as shown in Figure 17-3C to hold the payroll information temporarily while it is being calculated.

The occurrence number in this case is the employee number. At the end of processing, the PAREG3 program reads this data structure by record number (occurrence) and writes the 512 byte history records to a database for permanent archive storage. Notice in Figure 17-3B that we do not show all of the fields. The data structure is shown in RPGIV format using the D specification rather than the E specification for RPG/400. The OCCURS keyword is used to set the occurrences to 100.

Figure 17-3C MLHMST Data Structure from PAREG2

```
082 D*
083 D* MLHMST Holds updated records used for this payroll
084 D* This multiple occurrence DS has 100 record slots to
085 D* store data prior to writing to the history file.
086 D*
087 D MLHMST          DS                      OCCURS(100)
088 D   MLHRC1                 1     256
089 D   MLHRC2               257     512
090 D   MLHE#                  1       3  0
091 D   MLHRC3                 1      70
092 D   MLHNAM                 4      33
093 D   MLHRAT                34      38  2
094 D   MLHCTY                39      58
...
099 D   MLHHRS                71      74  2
100 D   MLHSAL                75      80  0
101 D   MLHPAY                81      87  2
102 D   FILLH1                88      90
103 D   MLHDAT                91      96  0
104 D   FILLH2                97     113
...
123 D   MLHRNO               503     505  0
124 D   MLHYR                506     507  0
125 D   MLHPWK               508     509  0
126 D   MLHNO                510     512  0
```

Working with IBM i on Power Systems Data Areas

Unlike a PC or Unix box, the **IBM i on Power Systems** is an object based system. When an RPG program brings in external devices into the system, those devices always represent IBM i on Power Systems objects. For example, the EMPMAST file that we have been using from the early chapters of this book is a database file object.

The print file from PAREG known as QPRINT is a printer file object. Now, we are about to work with another system object type. It is known as a data area and it is similar to a database object in several respects. For example, it can contain data and that data is shaped like a database record. However, a data area contains just one "record." Thus, a data area is like a one record file.

Data areas are often used to communicate variable information across tasks (programs) within a job and between jobs.

Very often designers will place important numbers such as the next order # to be used or the next check # to be used or the next employee number to be used in a data area to help completely automate functions that once required trigger input or database records to achieve that end.

Data areas are created by a user on IBM i on Power Systems with the CRTDTAARA CL command. A data area can be of variable Size, in character (*CHAR), decimal (*DEC) or logical (*LGL) format. Once created, it remains permanently on the system until it is deleted.

An additional point on data area use in programs is that multiple named data areas are allowed per job. Theoretically at least there is no limit of the # of data area objects that can be used in an RPG program.

*LDA Local Data Area

There is a special data area that exists for every job (signon to signoff or batch submission) that ever is initiated on the IBM i on Power Systems. This object is a data area that is associated with the job and it is called the local data area. System/36 environment programs often make extensive use of the local data area.

A different local data area exists for every job that is alive on the IBM i on Power Systems. When data is written from a program to the *LDA in one job, it does not affect the *LDA in any other job. The IBM i on Power Systems handles all of that internally. The *LDA is like any other data area plus it has some of its own special attributes as follows:

- ✓ Automatically created by System at job startup
- ✓ Deleted by system at job-end
- ✓ Constant Size - 1024
- ✓ Character data type (*CHAR) only

Several pages ago in this chapter we discussed the notion of a data structure and described that several special forms of data structures can be used in RPG. One of them is called a data area data structure.

You may recall that it is identified by a U in column 18 of the DS spec. When you tell the RPG compiler (with a U in column 18) that a data structure relates to a data area, the compiled RPG program automatically retrieves the external data area object of the same name at program initialization time.

If you have updated the data area via the structure in the program during the program run, the compiled RPG program does even more for you. It automatically updates the external data area of the same name at program close before the program ends.

There are some tricks, some of which seem unnatural to cause this all to happen. For example, the *NAMVAR DEFN statement can be used to change the name of the data structure or it can be used to point the structure to the *LDA.

Otherwise, the name that is used in the RPG program must match the name of data area object. So, the data structure is the means by which the data area is chopped into subfields.

When defined, the data structure itself behaves as a 6 char max character field. If the name is not provided for the data structure, that is the signal to the compiler to use the *LDA instead of a named data area.

A quick look at the general format of a data area data structure, brought in automatically by RPG is shown in Figure 17-4.

Figure 17-4 RPG Compiler Controlled Data Area

```
Name Of DS
   |            Data Area Data Structure
   |                 |
IORDNBR          UDS
I                                       1    50ORDNO
```

An RPGIV DS is defined immediately below:

```
D ORDNBR         UDS
D   ORDNO               1       5   0
```

Looking at the general structure for a named data area with the appropriate programmer controlled definition statement; the sample shape would be as shown in Figure 17-5

Figure 17-5 Programmer Controlled Data Area

External Name of DA
|
Internal Name

```
C           *NAMVAR   DEFN   ORDERNUMB   ORDNBR
C           *LOCK     IN     ORDNBR
C                     Z-ADD  ORDNO       NXTNBR   50
C                     ADD    1           ORDNO
C                     OUT    ORDNBR
C                     UNLCK  ORDNBR
```

Even though the term *NAMVAR means absolutely nothing to anybody I know, the *NAMVAR DEFN data area data structure in Figure 17-5 above is recommended rather than defining the data area data structure as in Figure 17-4 with a "U" in position 18.   It is simply a matter of flexibility and control. Both methods work. The "U" in 18 reads and immediately locks the data area from the point of program initialization until termination, while the *NAMVAR option gives the programmer substantially more control. It locks the data area only for the time needed for its update.

Now, let's move to the Local Data Area and see how that can be used effectively in an RPG/400 program. Keep in mind that the typical use of the *LDA is for Program A to perform some work and then to pass some information to Program B via the *LDA rather than having to use a separate database file or multiple parameters in a CALL statement.

Figure 17-6 *LDA Example

External Name of LDA
|
Internal Name

```
C     *NAMVAR DEFN *LDA      LDTA
C           IN   LDTA
C           ADD  1      ORDNO  50
C           MOVE ORDNO     LDTA
...
C           OUT  LDTA
```

The ignominious *NAMVAR again is required in the programmer controlled version of the data area data structure saga to use the *LDA. *NAMVAR links the *LDA to the internal name LDTA which refers to a 5 byte data structure defined elsewhere in the program, the IN command brings the contents of the local data area *LDA into the program.

The LDTA data structure has a field called ORDER mapped to positions 1 - 5 of the *LDA as a 5 0 zoned decimal field. When the value for ORDNO is read in and gets moved to LDTA, it maps perfectly to the ORDER field within the LDTA data structure. The +1 increment updates the LDTA data structure as well as the ORDNO subfield.

The OUT operation then updates the *LDA with the new "next" order number ORDNO. Overall, this technique as shown only will work when order #s are unique to a job or terminal because the *LDA disappears when the job ends. For it to really work another step in the job stream would have to grab a global order # and present it to the *LDA for subsequent processes in that job to access. The RPGIV version operates the same.

Additional Data Area Data Structure Info

As shown in the examples, data areas may be effectively used in RPG and brought into the program formatted as a data structure. Considering that data areas consist of one big blob of unformatted data and data structures are a wonderful RPG means of formatting data, the marriage works well.

Data areas are nice places to keep things that change and are used by several different programs. As noted previously, a good example would be next order number. As several users process order entry programs and start to enter orders, it is always nice to keep track of the next order number that is to be used. You could always put this into a file, but that takes a lot of overhead to open, update and then close a file. By putting the order number into a named data area data structure and have several people accessing it, there is not as much overhead.

In the example in 17-5, the data area ORDERNUMB is being used as a data structure (ORDNBR) in the program. It contains the subfield ORDNO in positions 1 - 5.

The lock condition in Figure 17-6 using the *LDA doesn't really matter since the *LDA is a temporary job structure and non-sharable. The example in Figure 17-5 does matter because ORDERNUMB is a IBM i on Power Systems object. So, the system 'locks' the data area once to read the next order number and then 'unlocks' the data area immediately after the field ORDNO has been incremented by 1 and written back (OUT) to the data area.

This prevents a lot of lockout problems between users. If the data area were locked for the entire time the user was entering an order, then no other user could get to the next order number. The code in Figure 17-5 is a nice way of sharing a Data Area Data Structures

More on *NAMVAR DEFN

Let's now use the below figure to summarize how you define a data area within a data structure within an RPG/400 or RPGIV program:

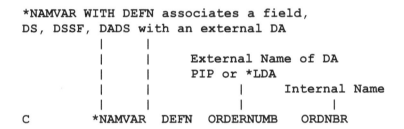

```
*NAMVAR WITH DEFN associates a field,
DS, DSSF, DADS with an external DA
            |       |
            |       |        External Name of DA
            |       |        PIP or *LDA
            |       |             |        Internal Name
            |       |             |            |
   C        *NAMVAR  DEFN   ORDERNUMB     ORDNBR
```

The *NAMVAR DEFN defines a data area data structures for RPG program control. As you can see, Factor 2 can contain the *LDA. (local Data Area) or PIP (Program Initialization Parameters), or an External data area name. If Factor 2 is blank, then internal name placed in the Result Field is also the external data area name.

The Result Field is really how the DA is defined and the name by which it is referenced in an RPG/400 PGM. The name can reference a field, a data structure, a data structure subfield, or a data area data structure (DADS). When DADS is specified, RPG Implicitly reads the DS at the beginning and writes at the end of the program. As noted in the examples above, the IN and OUT operations can also be used to bring in and write back the data areas.

Now that we have been introduced to just about all there is regarding data area data structures, let's look at a chunk of code that uses some of what we just learned. Take a look at Figure 17-7 before you read the code explanation below to see if you can decode it to help solidify your learning.

Figure 17-7 RPGIV Data Area Data Structure Summary Example

```
6 Characters max, optional, can contain name of DS. If DS is externally described, and
positions 21-30 are blank, this must contain the name of the data area. In RPGIV, the D
spec would be used but the calcs would be very similar.
      |
      |               Externally described DS
      |               |    External File Name for Desc.
      |               |    |
      |               |    |  Rename / Initialize field
      |               |    |  |
01 IORDNO       E  DSORDNODEF
02 I*                   |
03 I                  ORDEXT                    ORD
04 I                DS  |
05 I I              'KELLY CONSULTING'  1  20 CONAME
...
06 I*
07 C              *LIKE     DEFN  COST           PRICE
08 C              *NAMVAR   DEFN                 ORDNO
09 C              *NAMVAR   DEFN                 ORDTTL
10 C              *NAMVAR   DEFN                 ORCOST
11 C*
12 C              *LOCK     IN    ORDNO
13 C                        Z-ADD ORD            NXTNBR 50
14 C                        ADD   1              ORD
15 C              *LOCK     OUT   ORDNO
16 C                        UNLCK ORDNO
```

The code starts with the ORDNO data structure defined in line 1. A physical file named ORDNODEF contains the description (sub field names) of the data structure that is internally named ORDNO.

The data structure subfield names will appear in the compile listing. Line 2 shows that one of the fields in the external description (ORDEXT) is to be renamed as ORD for use in the program.

In line 4, there is an unnamed data structure defined. In line 5, one of the subfields called CONAME for company name, is primed with the constant information 'Kelly Consulting.' This occurs because in column 8 of line 5, there is an I for initialization.

This data structure subfield code says to take the initialization value that is provided data in columns 21 to 42 and move it into the subfield named in columns 53 to 58.

In Line 7, the *LIKE DEFN defines the Result Field PRICE with the same attributes (length decimals and type) as COST. In Line 8, the data area action begins with the *NAMVAR DEFN. This code says that the data area named ORDNO is defined by the data structure ORDNO and when ORDNO is retrieved it will fill up the ORDNO data structure.

ORDTTL and ORCOST are also defined as data areas but there are no other references in the block of code to tell us what types of data they represent. In Line 12, the ORDNO data area is brought into the ORDNO data structure and the data area is locked.

The next order number field called ORD is then moved to the NXTNBR field. Since this # is now used, the ORD field is incremented by one to reflect the next order number to be given and in line 15, the updated data structure information is written to the data area and the ORDNO data area on the system remains locked.

f Factor 1 were blank and the OUT operation finished writing out the data area, it would naturally unlock the data area. However, the *LOCK keeps it locked until a subsequent OUT without a *LOCK in Factor 1 or an UNLCK operation as shown in Statement 16.

Summary of Data Area Operations

As a point of note, when you specify the U in column 18 of a data structure typing the data area to the data structure and causing automatic input and output of the data area, the *NAMVAR DEFN is not required in calculations to complete the linkage

The operations we have studied in this section that permit data areas to be manipulated in RPG programs are as follows:

- ✓ IN: Explicitly retrieves data area

- ✓ OUT: Explicitly writes/rewrites data area

- ✓ UNLCK: Explicitly unlocks data area previously locked by
                     your program.

We also learned that the local data area can be used by specifying no name in columns 7-12 of the DS Input statement. To Name the LDA structure for use with the program, the good ole *NAMVAR DEFN is used with *LDA in Factor 2 and the program name for the LDA in the Result Field.

There is another caveat before we move on to a few more examples shown in Figure 17-8: A data area data structure (DADS) cannot be used in the result field of a PARM operation.

More Data Area Data Structure Examples:

Figure 17-8 has five additional examples of the effective use of data ara data structures in RPG programs. Both Program 1 & Program 2 use the same external data area object named TOTALS on the IBM i on Power Systems.

When the programs begin, they implicitly access the data area TOTALS because of the U in column 18 of the DS specifications (Lines 4 & 17). This loads the program data structure named TOTALS.   At end of job, program 1 writes the updated totals back to the data area object

When Program 1 finishes, Program 2 is called as the next job in the job stream. Program 2 uses the fields in the data area that were updated by Program 1 to perform additional calculations. Program 2 does NOT update these fields. Nonetheless, at EOJ, the same data area is written back. Program 2 also contains a data area data structure (U in column 18) called DIVTOT for Division Totals. During calculations, the division totals are created in lines 27 to 28 and at EOJ, the DIVTOT data area is also updated.

In both of these programs, the data area TOTALS is locked from all other processes on the system until the programs end at which time the system automatically unlocks all of its locked data areas. In Program 2 the same goes for DIVTOT.

Figure 17-8 Five Good Data Area Examples
```
01   *
02   * PROGRAM 1 EXAMPLE --- Named Data Area Update
03   *
04 ITOTALS     UDS
05 I                                        1    82TOTAMT
06 I                                        9   182TOTGRS
07 I                                       19   282TOTNET
08 C*          ---      ETC        ---
09 C*          ---      ETC        ---
10 C                    ADD   AMT        TOTAMT
11 C                    ADD   GROSS      TOTGRS
12 C                    ADD   NETAMT     TOTNET
13   *
14   *-------------------------------------------------------
15   * PROGRAM 2 EXAMPLE --- Named Data Area Use
16   *
```

```
17 ITOTALS      UDS
18 I                                              1    82TOTAMT
19 I                                              9   182TOTGRS
20 I                                             19   282TOTNET
21 IDIVTOT      UDS
...
22 I                                              1    82DIVAMT
23 I                                              9   182DIVGRS
24 I                                             19   282DIVNET
25 C*           ---        ETC           ---
26 C*           ---        ETC           ---
27 C                       ADD   TOTAMT   DIVAMT
28 C                       ADD   TOTGRS   DIVGRS
29 C                       ADD   TOTNET   DIVNET
30  *
31  *------------------------------------------------
32  *
33  * PROGRAM 3 EXAMPLE --- External Data Area
34  *
35 IDIVTOT      EUDSDIVTOTEX
36 I                DIVISIONNM                        NAME
37 I                                   1   29 NAMAMT
38 I*
39 ITOTALS      EUDSTOTALSEX
40 I                AMT                               TOTAMT
41 I                GRS                   9   182TOTGRS
42 I                NET                  19   282TOTNET
43 I*
Program 3 Continued

44 C*           ---        ETC           ---
46 C*           ---        ETC           ---
47 C                       ADD   TOTAMT   DIVAMT
48 C                       ADD   TOTGRS   DIVGRS
49 C                       ADD   TOTNET   DIVNET

56  *------------------------------------------------
57  *
58  * PROGRAM 4 EXAMPLE --- Local Data Area
59  *
60 ITOTALS      UDS
61 I                                              1    82TOTAMT
62 I                                              9   182TOTGRS
63 I                                             19   282TOTNET
64 C            *NAMVAR    DEFN *LDA     TOTALS
66 C*           ---        ETC           ---
67 C*           ---        ETC           ---
68 C                       ADD   AMT      TOTAMT
69 C                       ADD   GROSS    TOTGRS
70 C                       ADD   NETAMT   TOTNET
71 C*           ---        ETC           ---
72 C                       CLEARTOTALS
73  *
74  *------------------------------------------------
75  *
76  * PROGRAM 5 EXAMPLE --- Data Area Explicit Association
77  *
78 ITOTALS      DS
79 I                                              1    82TOTAMT
80 I                                              9   182TOTGRS
81 I                                             19   282TOTNET
82 C            *NAMVAR    DEFN          TOTALS
83 C*
84 C* Either *LOCK OR BLANK FOR DON'T LOCK
85 C*
86 C   10                 IN    TOTALS
87 C   10      *LOCK      IN    TOTALS
88 C*
89 C* Unlock immediately upon retrieval
```

```
90 C*
91 C    10                  UNLCKTOTALS
92 C*               ---     ETC                    ---
93 C*               ---     ETC                    ---
94 C                        ADD   AMT       TOTAMT
95 C                        ADD   GROSS     TOTGRS
96 C                        ADD   NETAMT    TOTNET
97 C*               ---     ETC                    ---
98 C    LR                  OUT   TOTALS
99 C*   ------------------------------------------------
```

Program 3 uses the same two data structures as Program 2, TOTALS and DIVTOT. In function it is identical with Program 2. In program 3, however, we learn that there are many more fields in DIVTOT and they are defined in a database physical file named DIVTOTEX for division totals external file. The data definitions for TOTALS are also described in an external physical file named TOTALSEX for totals external..

Again the function of PROGRAM 3 is basically the same as Program 2 other than the use of the externally defined data structure. This means that the record definition of the data structures is described in the two database files DIVTOTSEX and TOTALSEX.

At compilation time, the RPG compiler goes to the database file headers and grabs the field definitions and brings them into the program as the subfields for the two data structures. After compilation, those external data definitions mean nothing. When the program begins executing, the contents of the data area objects TOTDIV and TOTALS are pulled into data area data structures TOTDIV and TOTALS.

In Program 3 the DIVISIONNM (division name) field definition from the external file DIVTOTEX is too big for RPG/400. So, it is renamed at statement 36 to name. Additionally, it is redefined in statement 37 as a new 29 character field (1 to 29) called NAMAMT. Three fields from the TOTALSEX definition are renamed also in statements 40 to 42.

When the program ends, just like Program 2, the DIVTOT data area is updated and not TOTALS. TOTALS is written back but Program 3 does not change it in any way.

Program 4 uses the local data area with a data area data structure (U in 18). At PGM startup the LDA is dumped into the data area data structure named in the result field at statement 64. It is a typical *NAMVAR statement as follows:

*NAMVAR   DEFN   *LDA   TOTALS

TOTALS is defined in line 60. At program end, the LDA is written
back automatically.

Program 5 uses a regular named data area with a data structure access in the program (not a data area data structure – U in col 18). Therefore, RPG will not bring in the data area automatically at startup, nor will RPG write the data area at PGM end. The UNLCK and *LOCK are shown as ways to unlock the data area to make it available to other jobs.

Data Structure Initialization

There are two methods of data structure initialization: global & individual subfield. Initialization of data structures is very helpful to programming in that it can eliminate many causes of data decimal errors from bad (unprimed) data in fields being written to databases.

Data structures and subfields can also be RESET to these initial values. Named Constants & Literals can be used to set the initial values. As a rule, subfields are initialized according to the order in which they are defined in the data structure.

Let's look at both methods of data structure initialization:

Method 1 -- Global Initialization

- ✓ Specify an I in column 18 of DS Statement
- ✓ Num fields initialized to zeros
- ✓ Alpha fields initialized to blanks
- ✓ Subfields initialized in order of definition
- ✓ Programmer is responsible for proper ordering
- ✓ Occurs during first part of RPG *INIT routine

Figure 17-9 Global Data Structure Initialization

```
IDATES        IDS
I                                    |    1    20MM
I                                  /|    3    40DD
I                                 /  |    5    60YY
I                                /   |    1    60DATEN
I                               /    |    1    6 DATEA
I*                      CAUTION
I*    All subfields will be blank
I*    because last overlapping field
I*    prevails (DATEA)
I                                        15   21 OTHER
I                                  /|  P  25  270PAKNUM
I                                 /  |  B  29  300BINNUM
 *                               /
 *    Both of these fields will be set to zero
 *
```

Method 2 - Subfield Initialization

- ✓ Specify an I in column 8 of subfield spec & values in cols 21-42
- ✓ Can be used in concert with Method 1
- ✓ Values can be named constant or literal
- ✓ Fields initialized in order of definition
- ✓ Multiple occurrence data structures can be initialized using both methods. All occurrences have the same value after initialization
- ✓ Arrays in data structures will have all elements initialized to the defined value
- ✓ SEU "SV" Format is used for code entry

Figure 17-10 Subfield Initialization
Example 1 Subfield initialization for externally described

```
I*
IMASTER       EIDSPMASTER
I I           'Kelly Consulting'              CONAME
I I           'A'                             ACREC
I I           'PA'                            STATE
I I           'Wilkes-Barre'                  CITY

Example 2 Data Structure Initialization
 *----------------------------------------------------------
```

```
*    Multiple occurrence data structure and arrays
*
E              DED        3  3 0
I              'Western'            C         @DIV
ITHREE    IDS                    3
I*
I I        00000                      1   4 EMPNO
I                                     5  29 LAST
I I        'X'                        30  30 MINIT
I                                     31  51 FIRS
I                                     52  570BIRTH
I I        75                         58  660DED
I*
I I        @DIV                       67  74 DIV
I*
I*    Data in each DS occurrence is represented below
I*       after initialization
I*
*|00000|  ...    |X|    ... |000000|075|075|075|Western
*|00000|  ...    |X|    ... |000000|075|075|075|Western
*|00000|  ...    |X|    ... |000000|075|075|075|Western
```

Initialization Subroutine

RPG comes with its own initialization subroutine capability called *INZSR. The initialization subroutine is performed at the end of the *INIT routine. Its purpose is to eliminate the need for one time setup type of routine in the mainline of the program. It happens before 1P time output and only on "cold" call to a program, not after a return from a called program.

It can also be executed directly with EXSR, & CASXX operations and it can execute other subroutines from itself. It works by taking a snapshot of variables to be used with the RESET operation which will be described in a few more pages. The code used in Figure 17-11 is non functional, but is included for you to get a perspective for how the *INZR facility might be used.

Figure 17-11 Sample Initialization Subroutine
```
C*
C         *INZSR    BEGSR
C                   OPEN FILEA
C         USER      CHAINFILEA                    60
C         *IN60     IFEQ *OFF
C                   MOVE PARTA     PARTB
C                   Z-ADDNUM1      NUMRES
C                   CLOSEFILEA
C                   ELSE
C                   EXSR *PSSR
C                   ENDIF
C*
C         *NAMVAR   DEFN *LDA      LDA
C                   MOVE OKMSG     MSG35
C                   MOVE OTHMSG    NXTMSG
C*
C                   ENDSR
C*
```

The rules for writing a valid the initialization subroutine routine are as follows:

- ✓ *INZSR must be specified in Factor 1 of the BEGSR
- ✓ The subroutine is automatically called at the end of the internal RPG program initialization step.
- ✓ All OP-codes are permitted in the subroutine except for RESET
- ✓ The *INZSR routine can also be called via EXSR or CASXX

The RESET and CLEAR Operations

RESET and CLEAR are very handy operations that can save a lot of time in clearing and resetting subfields in structures. The valid structures for the RESET and CLEAR operations to operate include the following:

- ✓ Record Format
- ✓ Data Structure
- ✓ Array
- ✓ Table
- ✓ Variable (Field)

The RESET Op-Code

The function of the RESET operation is to set all elements of a data structure or array etc. equal to their values as of the end of INIT or *INZSR.

The rules for understanding how to use RESET and what it will do for you are provided below:

- ✓ All structures/variables for which there is a RESET operation are saved at *INIT (adds to store req't)
- ✓ It sets elements in a structure or a variable to its initial value
- ✓ Structures include - record format, data structure, array, table
- ✓ Variables include - field, subfield, indicator
- ✓ RESET sets Factor2 to the value it was at the end of the *INZSR function of the *INIT routine. *INZSR Overrides any DS initialization
- ✓ Factor 2 can be any structure or variable
- ✓ If Factor 2 is a multiple occurrence DS, only the current occurrence is reset

When resetting a record format, only those fields that are output in that record format are affected (input only fields are unaffected)

When resetting a DB format, Factor 1 can be *NOKEY which directs all fields in the format that are outputted except the KEY field to be RESET

The CLEAR Op-Code

The rules for CLEAR are very similar to RESET. The result is just substantially different. The CLEAR operation sets elements in the structure or variable specified in factor 2 to blank or zero depending on the data characteristics of the structure or variable

The format of both operations is simple and is demonstrated in the six example sets shown in Figure 17-12. Each of the examples and code snippets are explained within the Figure itself via comment statements.

Figure 17-12 RESET and CLEAR Examples
Reset / Clear Example 1 - Data Structure is reset
```
C*
C                     RESETDS1
C*
C*    *    USE *NOKEY in Factor1 if factor 2 is a
C*         DISK record format name
C*
```

Reset / Clear Example 2 - Data Structure is cleared

```
C*
C*    CLEAR Op-code
C*
C*    *   Sets all elements to zero or blank based on type
C*
C*
C                      CLEARDS1
C*
```

Reset / Clear Example 3 - Clear the old way

```
C*   Consider all of the work it used to take to reset
C*   data items
C*   CLEAR is a substantial reduction in coding
C*
C                 MOVE SPACES    A1
C                 MOVE SPACES    NAME
C                 MOVE SPACES    FIRST
C                 Z-ADD0         RATE
C                 Z-ADD0         AMOUNT
C                 MOVE ZEROS     NEWAMT
C                 MOVE *BLANK     ADDR1
C                 MOVE *BLANKS    ADDR2
C                 MOVE *ZEROS     YEAR
C                 MOVE *ZERO      DIGIT
*----------------------------------------------------------
```

Reset / Clear Example 4 - Clear & Reset operations

```
  *  . 1....+... 2 ...+... 3 ...+... 4 ...+... 5 ...+... 6
  *
FFilenameIPEAF........L..I........Device+......KExit++Entr
FARMASTERO    E                  DISK
  *
  * The file ARMASTER contains one record format
  * RECFMT containing the character fields NAME and ADDR1,
  * and The numeric fields Num1 & Num2
  *
IDsname....NODsExt-file++.............OccrLen+............
IDS1      IDS
I.I............Init-value+++++++++++PFromTo++DField+.....
I I          'Tuesday'               1   8 DAY3
I I          'Thursday'              9  18 DAY5
I I              .                  17  22 DATE
CL0N01N02N03Factor1+++OpcdeFactor2+++ResultLenDHHiLoEqComm
  *
  * The below operation clears (blanks) DAY3, DAY5,
  * and DATE
C                      CLEARDS1
  * The below operation resets DAY3, DAY5, and DATE to
  * their values as they were immediately after
  * the *INZSR routine 'TUESDAY', 'Thursday', UDATE
  * respectively .... Note that although DAY3 was
  * initialized to both small and caps, the *INZSR
  * takes precedence over the INIT of the data structure
  *
  *
C                      RESETDS1
  * The below operation sets NAME, ADDR1 to blanks and
  * NUM1 and NUM2 to zero.
C                      CLEARRECFMT
  * The below operation resets NAME, ADDR1, NUM1 and
```

```
 * NUM2 to THEIR INITIAL VALUES  of JONES and '14 P ST.'
 * respecively. These were set in the *INZSR
C                     RESETRECFMT
 *
C          *INZSR     BEGSR
C                     MOVELUDATE     DATE
C                     MOVE 'TUESDAY' DAY3
C                     MOVEL'JONES    'NAME
C                     MOVEL'14 P ST.'ADDR1
C                     Z-ADD1         NUM1
C                     Z-ADD2         NUM2
C                     ENDSR
 *
 *------------------------------------------------------------
```

Reset / Clear Example 5--   Reset multiple occurrences

```
 *
 * FIRST is a data structure of which several fields are
 * initialized with values from constants or literals.
 * There are 66 occurrences of this multiple occurrence
 * data structure (length 155).
 *
 * The DO loop sets the occurrence of each of the 66
 * "records" in FIRST and it RESETS them to the values
 * they were after initialization
 *
I..............Namedconstant++++++++C.........Fldnme.....
I              'Wilkes-Barre'        C          @CITY
IFIRST       DS                       66 155
I I          'Kelly Consulting'       1  30 CONAME
I                                    31  60 ADDR21
I                                    61  90 ADDR31
I                                    91 120 ADDR41
I I          @CITY                  121 143 CITY
I                                   144 145 STATE1
I                                   146 150 ZIP1
I I          11111                  151 1550SEQ#
C                     DO   66        INDEX
C          INDEX      OCUR FIRST
C                     RESETFIRST
C                     ENDDO
 *
 *
 *------------------------------------------------------------
```

Reset / Clear Example 6 – Clear Screen Format

```
 *
 * In the display format DDS for format SCREEN1 below
A* FIELD2 & FIELD3 are defined as output fields and can be
A* affected by the CLEAR Operation. Indicator 15 can
A* also be changed by the CLEAR, even though it conditions
A* an INPUT only field... This can happen because all
A* field indicators are treated as output fields
A*
A.........T.Name+++++RLen++TDpB......Functions++++++++++

A          R SCREEN1
A  15       FIELD1         20A  I  2 40
A           FIELD2         20A  O  3 40
A           FIELD3         20A  B  4 40
```

```
      FFilenameIPEAF........L..I........Device+......KExit++EntrFSCREENS CF   E
WORKSTN
I.............Namedconstant++++++++C.........Fldnme.....
I              'Constant Input'      C          INPUT
C*
C* At program startup, the screen format is cleared
C* Then it is written to the screen for viewing and input
C*
CL0N01N02N03Factor1+++OpcdeFactor2+++ResultLenDHHiLoEqComm
C                    CLEARSCREEN1
C                    WRITESCREEN1
C*  This Program loops until EOJ (F3) is depressed
C           *IN03    DOWEQ*OFF
C                    READ SCREEN1                          LR
C*
C* IF PF9 is pressed, move input fields to output fields
C*
C           *IN09    IFEQ '1'
C                    MOVELFIELD3    FIELD2
C                    MOVELFIELD1    FIELD3
C                    CLEAR*IN09
C*                   CLEAR*IN
C* (CLEAR *IN would set off all indicators)
C*
C                    ENDIF
C                    MOVELINPUT     FIELD1
C*
 *                   ETC
C                    WRITESCREEN1
C                    ENDDO
C* -------------------------------------------------------
```

Data Structure Performance Trick

One of the most frequently used data structure techniques is referred to as data reformatting. Prior to data structures, RPGII programmers were forced to use a clever multiplication routine which always works to reformat a date from MMDDYY format to YYMMDD.

Speeding up Date Reformatting

The routine works by truncating the left four digits with a size exception. This worked fine except for one thing. Multiplication operations as well as size exceptions are very expensive in the amount of processing resources used

Figure 17-13 Multiplication and DS Date Reformatting
```
C*
C* Method1 - Multiplication - just one statement
C*
C          DATIN      MULT 10000.01  DATOUT  60
C*
C*
C*
C* Method 2 Data structures -- more statements but
C* a substantially better way
C*
IDI         DS
I                                        1   6 DATIN
I                                        1   4 MMDDIN
I                                        5   6 YYIN
IDO         DS
```

```
I                                          1   6 DATOUT
I                                          1   2 YYOUT
I                                          3   6 MMDDOT
C*
C              MOVE MMDDIN    MMDDOT
C              MOVE YYIN      YYOUT
C*
C*    IBM's Benchmarks indicate the following timings:
C*
C*    Method 1:    approx  400 microseconds (B60)
C*    Method 2:    approx.   9 microseconds (B60)
C*
C* -------------------------------------------------
```

Chapter Summary

An RPG or RPGIV data structure is a stand-alone record designed for use in memory. It has no association with a database file or a data area unless one is explicitly given. It is an area in storage which allows for items of different sizes and shapes to be grouped. It is a means of referencing some or many fields, called subfields, within this storage area.

Data structures have many purposes in programming and save the programmer many calculations and move operations when formatting data records in memory.

There are also three special purpose data structures as follows:

- ✓ Data Area Data Structure (DADS)
- ✓ File Information Data Structure (INFDS)
- ✓ Program-Status Data Structure (PSDS)

A multiple occurrence data structure is a data structure whose definition is repeated in a program to form a series of data structures with identical formats. It is basically a 2-dimensional data structure. Data areas are often used to communicate variable information across tasks (programs) within a job and between jobs. When read into a program, they are stored in data structures. There is a special data area that exists for every job (signon to signoff or batch job) that ever is initiated on the IBM i on Power Systems. It is called the local data area.

There are two methods of data structure initialization: global & individual subfield. Initialization of data structures is very helpful to programming in that it can eliminate many causes of data decimal errors from bad (unprimed) data in fields being written to databases. There is also an RPG provided initialization subroutines called *INZSR. The RESET and CLEAR operations are very handy tools for the data structure tool chest. RESET takes you back to where the DS was in the beginning and the CLEAR clears out the data structure.

Key Chapter Terms

*BLANK	CLEAR	OCCUR
*BLANKS	CRTDTAARA	OCCUR
*IN,	Data area data struc	One record file
*INIT	Data areas	OUT
*INZSR	Data conversions	Performance
*LDA	Data structure	PIP
*LIKE	Date reformatting	RESET
*LOCK	DEFN	Special data structures
*NAMVAR	DEFINE	Stand-alone record
*OFF	IN	Sub-fields
*PSSR	INFDS	Subscripts

*ZERO	Initialization	Two dimensional arrays
BEGSR	Local data area	UNLCK
CALL	Named Constants	

Review Questions

1. What is a data structure?

2. What are four purposes for an RPG data structures?

3. What are the special types of data structures and what role do they play?

4. How do data structures save calculations?

5. What specification is used to define an RPG/400 and an RPGIV data structure?

6. What is a multiple occurrence data structure?

7. How is data "moved" into a data structure?

8. What is a data area?

9. What is a data area data structure?

10. How do you code a data area data structure in RPG/400, RPGIV?

11. What is *NAMVAR used for?

12. Why would you use a data area in a program?

13. Why would you use IN, OUT, or UNLCK rather than have the RPG program handle the data area work automatically?

14. What are the two methods of data structure initialization?

15. What is an initialization subroutine?

16. Describe the RESET and the CLEAR operations and relate them to initialization.

17. What are some tricks for making programs perform better using data structures as an alternative to calculations?

Chapter 18   String Coding In RPG

Strings Are an RPG Later Arrival

String processing is one of the more recent additions to the RPGIII part of the RPG/400 language. Since the last upgrade to the language was some time before 1994, however, it does not mean that strings are anything close to new. The String operations in RPG are very powerful, yet, they are somewhat cryptic (hard to learn and hard to remember) in their format.

Let's start this chapter by discussing the notion of a string generically, then look at the notion of a string in RPG and then look at some of the powerful operations that permit major manipulation of strings in the RPG language and finally we'll take the basic concepts and form some complex string code to perform some valuable functions.

String Characteristics:

So just what is a string? The simple answer is that a string is series of characters and as such it can also be called a character string. A character string is typically composed of a set of alphabetic and numeric characters (A- Z, a-z, 0-9,   and special characters @#$ etc.).

A string also can consist of certain characters that are not present on a typical keyboard, such as hexadecimal literals

Strings are typically of variable length. RPG Strings, however, are fixed length fields with variable length contents padded with blanks. The RPG String operations have many rules for truncation and padding.

When using RPG string operations, one simple rule it helps to remember is that they are left justified by default – but there are also some right hand / reverse operations.

Basic String Handling Functions

The basic string handling functions that are typically found in all programming languages are as follows:

1. Define/ Create a string and give it a value.
      (Declare or define a variable and give it
      an initial value)
2. Extract a substring from another string
3. Concatenate two strings to form a new string
4. Compare Two Strings
5. Search within string for substring
6. Determine the length of a string
7. Assign the value of a string to another string

Figure 18-1 Basic String Handling Functions

String Function	RPG Implementation
1. Define/ Create a string and give it a value.	1. RPG uses field or subfield definition; subfield initialization, MOVE, MOVEL, Z-ADD
2. Extract a substring from another string	2. RPG uses manual array loops, SUBST op-code. Same in RPGIV
3. Concatenate two strings to form a new string	3. RPG uses manual array loops, MOVE, MOVEL, MOVEA, CAT op-code. Same in RPGIV plus EVAL.
4. Compare Two Strings	4. RPG uses IFxx, WHxx, COMP, CASxx,ANDxx, ORxx, CABxx . Same in RPGIV plus EVAL and BIFs.
5. Search within a string for a substring	5. RPG uses manual array loops, SCAN op-code. Same in RPGIV
6. Determine the length of a string	6. RPG uses manual array loops, CHEKR op-code. CHECKR is the replace operation in RPGIV.
7. Assign the value of a string to another string	7. RPG uses MOVE, MOVEL, MOVEA. EVAL is often used in RPGIV

Complex String Handling Functions

By combining basic operations, and using special functions, string processing capabilities can be expanded to provide a number of valuable, yet, more complex facilities. These include the following:

1. Center a string of text in a field
2. Left Justify a string of text in a field
3. Delete a substring of text in a field
4. Replace a substring of text with another string
5. Insert a string of text into another string
6. Return a substring that is composed of only the valid characters in a given pattern
7. Verify that a string consists of only valid characters
8. Translate a string (such as upper case to lower case)

For this 'complex" string handling as noted above, there is not a one to one correspondence of these advanced string functions to RPG constructs. Instead, these are implemented via routines which employ the basic building block operations for string manipulation.

Following a description of primitive string handling in RPG, we demonstrate a series of coding examples that perform the above functions in RPG/400 and RPGIV.

RPG String Implementation

Of all the wonderful business functions that can be performed in RPG, nobody has ever accused the language of being text based. RPG is not a text based language and no amount of basic string functions is about to change that. There are some exotic languages found in research institutions, such as SNOBOL4 that are very specific to text. Today's powerful word Processing programs in fact are based on SNOBOL research

Word Processing is the proper metaphor for text based operations. Word processing software must deal with the notion of text, text strings and ad hoc text manipulation.

Text Processing

Thinking through word processing and the types of actions that the software must support, it is clear that to manipulate strings, facilities must exist in the software to handle the following:

- ✓ String identification: functions must exist to find the beginning and ending positions of substrings (smaller pieces of text) within strings

- ✓ Copy, Move, Delete, Insert, Search, and Replace (parsing purposes)

Outside of SNOBOL, most modern languages do a poor job of dealing with strings of text. Yet, with relational databases taking on more facilities regarding variable length text, it is clear that strings are here to stay. Text and string type data are a reality of information systems.

Prior to the primitive string operations being made available in RPG/400, the programmer was faced with defining string type data using arrays that were typically composed of 1 character elements.

For example, for RPG to store a 30 character name for string manipulation purposes, the programmer would build a 30-byte array. When a 30-byte character field such as name were read from a database for example, the 30-bytes would be moved using the MOVEA (move array) RPG operation to an array for manipulation.

In RPG of course, fields and arrays are structurally different. Thus using the regular operations, MOVE and MOVEL would be invalid. So, the MOVEA operation was created to solve this so that data can be moved from an array to a field or from a field to an array.

Individual character positions in the array can then be examined and manipulated by using variable or constant subscripting.

Text Processing Examples

For example, assume the text below originated in a field called NAME:. The contents of NAME would have to be moved via MOVEA to an Array (NAM) The "F" in LaFong, could then be accessed directly.

As you can see, it is the third element of the array NAM which in RPG/400 is referenced as NAM,3 and in RPGIV is referenced as NAM(3).

```
LaFong, Carl
```

This or any element (individual piece or position) of a one byte element length array could be moved into a one byte field. To move the "F" in LaFong to a field called LETTR3, the following RPG code would be used:

```
C... MOVEANAME...    NAM       (NAM is array)
C... MOVE NAM,3    LETTR3    1
```

So, you can see that this technique, though cryptic does permit substrings to be manipulated, though not naturally. Let's look at another example. A common string processing requirement in business databases is to change the format of a *Name* type field.

Almost every business at one time has had data that had to be moved from a last name first format that permitted name alphabetizing to a first name first format that permitted envelope addressing and label preparation. Prior to string operations in RPG/400, this task also was accomplished using arrays. In this case, of course, you would need to use variable array subscripting since names come in all sizes and shapes:

1. **LaFong, Carl**
2. **Stonebreaker, Mike**
3. **Monumentous, Shirley**
4. **Etc.**

Looking at this simple set of data, it is clear that counting across, the comma in LaFong is at position 7 and the blank separating the names is in position 8. Using array processing, this could be referenced nicely with constant subscripts as NAM,7 and NAM,8 respectively.

What about the next name? Is the comma and space in positions 7 & 8? It doesn't look that way. In fact, assuming that any name can be any length, the notion of a constant subscript cannot work in all cases.

Being right every now and then is not a reason for companies to invest in computer technology. So, a better technique needs to be deployed that is consistently correct. Check out the following data breakdown more closely to see what I mean.

```
          11111111112
 12345678901234567890
'Stonebreaker, Mike'
```

The comma is at 13 and the blank is at 14. We can count on the lengths being different and the separators being in different places for each set of text. Again, this task is not readily made for constant subscripting.

But, with some nicely honed array coding, it can be accomplished. "Pre-string" RPG needs to use variable subscripting to work with strings. For example, take the following simple RPG operations:

```
ADD    1              X
MOVE   NAM,X          ONEBYT
```

To work with arrays for string manipulation, one or several programming loops are required. The COMP and GOTO operations might be used along with indicators. In more modern RPG, structured operations such as DO loops, and IFxx SELEC etc. can be used to control the manipulation loops.

Variable Subscripting for String Manipulation:

In order for the array notion to work in manipulating strings there are a number of things that need to be considered. A partial list of considerations is shown immediately below, followed by several assumptions.

✓   The variable subscript (index) name would have to be no more than 1 or 2 positions, since there are only six spaces available in the Result Field for field name.

✓ "NAM," with the comma takes up 4 of 6 positions. The name X for index is often used as an array index. Some very creative programmers may choose to use a "creative" name such as "Y." for the output array.

✓ When the comma is encountered, the last name would have been captured and could then be moved.

✓ Following the space after the comma, the program would need to look for the next space or position 30 of the array to signify the end of the first name. Once the first name was discovered, it could be moved.

✓ The lengths of the fields would need to be kept for determining the reformatted output positions.

✓ In a "final" output array, the first name would be placed at the beginning. Then a space, followed by the last name. The output array would then get moved to the Name field and the data would be converted.

For a simple notion, this can be a complex routine. The code considerations as noted above would need a few assumptions on the data contents in order to work properly.

✓ Last name is left justified. Thus, the programmer does not have to test for blanks initially to find where the first letter of the last name would be.

✓ There is no middle name or initial and no second middle name or initial.

String Program Logic

The logic for such a program to perform the string manipulation to change the Name format would include the following:

1. Two arrays are set up by the programmer-- one for analyzing the input, and the other for preparing the output. Two additional arrays are defined to hold the first name, FST, and the last name, LST, as they are being parsed.

2. The program first tests the first position of the input array for a comma by using a variable subscript referring to the position in the array. The supposition is that the comma ends the last name.

3. The Input array is primed by a MOVEA of the NAME Field to the NAM array. MOVEA provides an RPG means of taking a field structure and moving it, character by character to an array structure.

4. The program cycles via several DO loops through the input ARRAY (NAM) looking first for the comma which separates the last name from first name.

5. As each letter of the last name is examined, the letter contained within that array position is moved to the corresponding position in the last name array and the last name subscript used for the processing, (X) as in LST,X is as it is in the NAM input array.

6. Each time through the loop the subscript X is incremented to capture the next letter and to move it to the right place in the last name array.

7. When the comma is found in position X, position X minus 1 contains the last character of the last name. The index variable, "X" points to the comma in the input array.

8. Considering that there is always a blank (according to the rules) between the comma and the first letter of the first name, the value of X needs to be incremented by 2, not 1 to point to the first character of the first name in the NAM array.

9. To keep the notion simpler than it might otherwise be, the code passes to a second DO loop at position "X" of the input array. In other words, when the DO loop begins, the X subscript refers to the first character of the first name. The second DO loop also uses the index "X" starting at the value pointing to the first character of the first name. Its objective is to capture the first name in the FST array. Since the next position of the NAM array needs to be placed in the first position of the FST array, a new array index (Y) needs to come in to play, primed to begin at position 1.

10. Incrementing both the NAM array with X and the FST array with Y respectively, by the time the second loop considerations are met, the first name has been tucked nicely into the FST array.

11. The Loop ends when the program finds a blank or it reaches the end of the first name field (length = 20). As noted in item 10, at this point, the first name and last name are isolated in the LST and FST arrays, respectively.

12. With the first name in FST and the last name in LST, the very next step is to move these guys into the proper positions of the output array (OUT) The MOVEA operation is perfect with the FST array in Factor 2 and the output array OUT in the result field. When the MOVEA completes, the First name occupies the first positions in the OUT array.

13. At this time, the Y index is set for the position of the last letter in the first name. Since the last name should be separated by a space, the Y index gets 2 added two it, one for the space and one to position it to the first position in the OUT array to which the last name (LST array) should begin loading.

14. The load is accomplished with a MOVEA again with the destination OUT array being subscripted with the Y index to get the last name loaded in the right spot from left to right.

15. The next and final step is to use the handy MOVEA operation again and move the OUT array into the NAME field. By default the MOVEA moves the leftmost position of the from-array to the leftmost position of the to-field. The name reversal is now complete.

No attempt has been made to add the code necessary for this operation to be repeated. As in every routine, housekeeping for fields left unchanged at the end of the routine would need to be cleared in order for the code to work the same way the second and subsequent times in the same program invocation

In order to appreciate the work necessary in the manipulation of strings of data, it would serve the student well to analyze and decode the example code in Figure 18-2 before moving on to other String topics.

Simpler Example

Let's now look at a much more simple example. In this case, let's take the values and create a last name first; first name last scenario. Assume the last name field (LAST) has already been segregated and it contains the last name. Also, assume that the first name / middle initial field (FRSTMD) contains the first name followed by the middle initial. Knowing the shape of the data simplifies this code a great deal. Here are the tasks to accomplish this new mission.

1. The OUT array is again used as in the prior example to form the output. The array is first cleared by moving blanks to all of the elements.

2. It will then used to capture the desired end result: last name (LAST), comma, blank, first name / middle initial (FRSTMD). The remainder of OUT, from the end of FRSTMD to the end of the OUT array are blank.

3. Since Last Name is of variable size, the routine must determine in which position of the OUT array to place the comma and the blank position following the comma.

4. The routine must also determine the position in the array to begin to load the first name / middle initial (FRSTMD) field.

5. The code begins by priming the OUT array with the last name field (LAST) which is assumed to have just been read in from a data base.

6. Since the length of last name is no larger than the field size (20) of LAST, a DO LOOP is used to increment through the LAST array 20 times and exiting when a space is found or then the loop index (IN) hits 21. If either condition is true, this signifies the end of the last name field (LAST).

Figure 18-2 Name Reversal String Code with Arrays

```
E                       NAM          30   1
E                       OUT          30   1
E                       LST          20   1
E                       FST          20   1
C* BEGIN LAST NAME / FIRST NAME REVERSAL
C*
C           NAMRV       BEGSR
C                       Z-ADD0         Y        20
C                       MOVEANAME      NAM
C                       MOVEA'CHIK, JO'NAM
C*
C*   FIND LAST NAME
C*
C                       DO   31        X        20
C           NAM,X       IFNE ','
C           X           ANDNE21
C                       ELSE
C                       LEAVE
C                       ENDIF
C                       ENDDO
C*
C*   SKIP ANOTHER TO GET TO START OF FIRST NAME -
C*   FIND FIRST NAME
C*
C                       Z-ADD0         Y
C                       ADD  2         X              C* ABOVE CODE ENABLES THE BYPASS
OF THE BLANK
C           X           DO   31        X
C* NAME REVERSAL CODE CONTINUED:
C*
C           NAM,X       IFNE ' '
C           Y           ANDNE21
C                       ADD  1         Y
C                       MOVE NAM,X     FST,Y
C                       ELSE
C                       LEAVE
C                       ENDIF
C                       ENDDO
C*
C* AT END OF LOOP, THE Y INDEX IS PRESERVED.
C* IT WILL BE USED AFTER THE BELOW MOVEA
C* OF THE FIRST NAME.  BY ADDING 2 TO Y,
C* A BLANK SPACE IS LEFT IN THE OUTPUT
C* ARRAY. THEN THE LST ARRAY IS MOVED VIA
C* MOVEA TO THE OUT ARRAY
C*
C                       MOVEAFST       OUT
C                       ADD  2         Y              C* LEAVE A SPACE
C                       MOVEALST       OUT,Y
C                       MOVEAOUT       NAME     30
C                       ENDSR
C*   END LAST NAME FIRST NAME REVERSAL
```

7. The value of IN at the time the blank is discovered is one greater than the length of the last name. If this code were implemented, please note that it would need to be spiffed up a bit to deal with last names such as VAN HORN etc. which contain an embedded blank.

8. Upon finding a blank, the routine moves a comma into the position after the last name in the OUT array

9. It then adds 2 to the subscript IN, to make room for the comma and the blank between last name and first name.

10. At this point, the FRSTMD field can be moved to OUT at the right beginning position using a MOVEA to the INth position of the OUT array.

11. When the OUT array is fully formed, a MOVEA is used to dump its contents back into the name field.

After the moves, there will always be a comma and a blank between the last name and the first name / middle initial as structured in the OUT array and subsequently into the NAME field.

The code to perform this is shown in Figure 18-3.

Figure 18-3 Simplified Name Reversal Code, Last Name First

```
C* BEGIN NAME BLANK SEARCH ROUTINE
C* TO DETERMINE LENGTH OF LAST NAME
C*
C* PRIME LAST NAM TO THE NAM ARRAY
C                    MOVEA*BLANKS     OUT
C                    MOVEALAST        OUT
C* CHECK 1ST 20 POSITIONS OF NAM ARRAY
C* TO ISOLATE LAST NAME
C          1         DO   21          IN          20
C          NAM,IN    IFEQ ' '
C          IN        OREQ 21
C* WHEN ISOLATED, PLACE COMMA AND A BLANK IN NAM
C                    MOVE ','         OUT,IN
C                    ADD  2           IN
C* USE SUBSCRIPTD IN AS START POSITION FOR FRSTMD
C                    MOVEAFRSTMD      OUT,IN
C                    MOVEANAM         NAME
C          'NAME'    DSPLY            NAME
C* LEAVE DO LOOP WHEN REVERSAL IS COMPLETE
C                    LEAVE
C                    ENDIF
C                    ENDDO
```

Convert Upper/Lower (U/L) Case of State Field

Before we begin RPG string operations using the STRING op-codes, let's look at another common example of string operations being performed via tables/arrays. It is depicted in the code highlighted in Figure 18-4.

In this example, the objective is to change the entire STATE name from Upper/lowercase to Uppercase only.

The application requiring this conversion was a directory listing by state which performed a series of functions at the time a State name changed in the report (control break). One of the requirements was to print the state name in capital letters even though in the database, it is stored in capitals and small letters.

To accomplish this, an array named ST is defined with 25 1-character elements, which is large enough to hold the largest state field for this database. An alternating table is defined with each side being 26 characters in length with 26 1 character table elements. Lower case is on the one side and upper case is on the other.

The routine to translate the state field from lower to upper case is quite simple.

1. A "ST" array is set up, cleared to blanks and then primed with the STNAME (state name) field.

2. A DO loop is then used to roll through the ST array checking each character for lower case. When a lower case character is found in the state name, the alternating table value provides an uppercase A.

3. The TABCAP value is moved in over the top of the formerly lowercase position (a in this case).

4. If the position already contains a capital letter or another character such as a #, the original character remains in that position of the ST array.

5. After the array is changed to caps, the ST array is then moved via MOVEA back to the STNAME field. At this point it is all upper case. The code for this translation using arrays and tables is shown in Figure 18-4.

Figure 18-4 Translating Lower to Upper Case

```
E*
E* Compile TIME Table - Data at end of program
E*
E                         TABSML  1  26  1  ATABCAP  1
E               ST              25  1
C*
C* STATE UPPER / LOWER (U/L) CASE TRANSLATION
C* WITH TABLE / ARRAY
C*
C           ULSTAT     BEGSR
C*
C* CHANGE STATE LOWERCASE TO UPPERCASE
C*
C* PRIME ST ARRAY WITH THE NAME OF THE STATE
C* TO TRANSLATE
C                       MOVEA*BLANKS   ST
C                       MOVEASTNAME    ST
C           1           DO   25        IN      20
C* LOOK UP EACH LETTER IN THE STATE NAME...
C* WHEN A LETTER IS FOUND IN THE SMALL TABLE,
C* THE CORRESPONDING CAPITAL IS REFERENCED
C* BY THE NAME TABCAP
C           ST,IN      LOKUPTABSML    TABCAP          83
C* MOVE CAPITAL LETTER TO WHERE SMALL LETTER
C* ONCE WAS IF HIT (83)
C   83                  MOVE TABCAP    ST,IN
C                       ENDDO
C* USE MOVEA TO MOVE THE STATE ARRAY BACK TO THE
C* STATE NAME FIELD
C                       MOVEAST        STNAME 25
C           'STNAME'    DSPLY          STNAME
C                       SETOF                          60
C                       ENDSR
**
aA
bB
cC    (etc to zZ)
```

In the three examples above, because the size of the data elements varied, arrays were the best approach to capture the data and accomplish the string operation. MOVE, MOVEL, and MOVEA were the tools used to accomplish the realignments. If, the shape of the data were fixed in size, the MOVE and MOVEL could have been used without the arrays and tables to accomplish basic string reformatting.

These operations can be used in combination to provide a level of concatenation that often is "good enough." Although the control of blanks between fields is irritatingly difficult to achieve using these two operations, MOVE, and MOVEL have been used together frequently over the years for text (string) manipulation purposes.

A few often cited examples would include the creation of a composite key as well as the building of a date field from the three pieces of date -- MM, DD, YY. With the introduction of data structures in RPG III, the use of MOVE and MOVEL for these purposes has been even more minimized.

With the data structure function, as explained below, data could be laid out in memory to achieve the desired result without having to code a long series of MOVEs and MOVELs.

RPG Fields

The notion of a field in RPG is somewhat different than in many of the block structured languages such as Pascal and C Language. (integer, floating point, character, string). It can be argued, however, that a field is merely a string of characters which may consist of further substrings.

RPG provides implicit MOVE functions for fields defined on INPUT and on OUTPUT merely by use of the same field name in both places. In other languages, such as COBOL, data must be moved from INPUT to OUTPUT explicitly.

So, although string operations in RPG have been primitive, the implicit functions, data structures, MOVE & MOVEL operations, and arrays have given programmers the opportunities over the years to perform this primitive text manipulation with a "minimum of pain". In other words, what could be done could be done reasonably, though arguably, not naturally.

And now we come to a more natural way of accomplishing the text manipulation mission. Over the years, RPG/400 has been extended to support string functions which extend the capabilities of the RPG language into the text processing domain. These new functions allow a programmer to more naturally and more productively manipulate strings of data than with the prior RPG methods discussed above.

String Coding In RPG/400

String operations can only be performed on char fields. RPG operations to support String functions are shown in Table 18-5.

Figure 18-5 String Operations in RPG

RPG String Operation	Explanation
CHECK (E)	Search for a non-match in string looking from left to right with verification if non match
CHEKR (E)	Search for a non-match in string looking from right to left with verification if non match
CAT (P)	Concatenate two strings
SCAN (E)	Scan a String for a match
SUBST (P)	Substring – separate parts of a string
XLATE (E,P)	Translate one string to another

The (P) operation code extender in RPG/400 is placed in column 52. The P extender means that the result should be padded with blanks. In RPGIV, two operation extenders (E and P) are permitted on string operations a shown for the specific operations in Figure 18-5. In RPGIV, the extenders do not use column 52. They are written next to the operation code within parentheses. To handle certain exceptions, such as a program status code 100, either the operation code extender 'E' or an error indicator ER can be specified in RPGIV, but not both.

The CAT Operation (CAT RPGIV)

The CAT RPG operation concatenates the character string specified in Factor 2 to the end of the character string specified in factor 1 and places it in the result field. If no factor1 is specified, factor 2 is concatenated to the end of the result field string. The # of blanks between the fields is specified as a second part of Factor 2.

Figure 18-6 Two Forms of RPG/400, RPGIV CAT Operation

Code	Factor1	Factor2	Result	Indicators
CAT (P)	Source String 1	Source String 2: # of blanks	Target String	No indicators
CAT (P)		SS1	Target/ SS1	

In CAT example 1 below, the code begins by filling up the BOTH field with asterisks. For demonstration purposes a first name with two blanks to the right is placed in NAMEC and a last name is moved to LASTC with one blank to the right. The CAT operation concatenates LASTC to NAMEC with 1 blank in between [LASTC:1] as defined in the second half of Factor 2.

```
C*
C*    CAT   EXAMPLE 1
C*
C...              MOVE *ALL'*'   BOTH   15
C...              MOVE 'HERR  '  NAMEC   6
C...              MOVE 'HECTOR ' LASTC   7
C... NAMEC        CAT  LASTC:1   BOTH
C...              DSPLY          BOTH
```

The DSPLY produces the result at the end of the code. The value in BOTH is as follows:

DSPLY = HERR HECTOR *

Why are there three asterisks? The answer to this question gives insights into how CAT actually works. First HERR within NAMEC is placed into BOTH at the beginning of the concatenate operation. The padding value of one tells the CAT operation to trim the two blanks to just one in between. Five positions of BOTH are now occupied in this example. The next thing that the CAT does is take the seven position value in LASTC and place it, left justified right after the blank in the fifth position. Five plus seven are twelve so twelve asterisks are removed from the BOTH field which had been set up originally with 15 asterisks. And, thus you have the result as presented above.

In CAT example 2 below, just as in the above operation, the MOVE operation fills the field BOTH with asterisks. The code them moves "/400" into a field called HOLD. The CAT operation then concatenates 'AS' to HOLD to form the term AS/400 with no blanks in between left justified in the BOTH field, which is fifteen characters long. The DSPLY results look as follows:

```
DSPLY = AS/400*********
```

You can that see the eight asterisks of fill in positions 7 to 15 in field BOTH remain in the Result Field since there is no request for padding in this operation. The code is as follows:

```
C*
C* CAT   EXERCISE 2
C*
C...              MOVE *ALL'*'    BOTH
C...              MOVE '/400'     HOLD      4
C... 'AS'         CAT   HOLD      BOTH     15
C... 'AS400*'     DSPLY           BOTH
```

In this example, the CAT operation concatenates the literal 'AS' to HOLD to form the term "AS/400" in the field named BOTH. The Move of all the asterisks into the both field primes it from 1 to 15 with asterisks. The CAT operation fills in the first 12 positions of the BOTH field l

The difference between Example 2 and Example 3 is the CAT operation itself. The results of the code are as follows:

```
DSPLY = AS/400b̶b̶b̶b̶b̶b̶b̶b̶b̶
```

Padding on cat replaces the *s with blanks. The b̶'s above represent the 9 blanks that are padded to the right by the P op code extender placed in column 52 of the CAT operation as shown below:

```
C*
C*    CAT   EXERCISE 3
C*
C... CAT3       BEGSR
C...              MOVE *ALL'*'    BOTH     15
C...              MOVE '/400'     HOLD      4
C... 'AS'         CAT   HOLD      BOTH          P
C... 'AS400'      DSPLY           BOTH
C...              ENDSR
```

The following code snippet sets the NAMET field up with "AS/ and two blanks after the slash in the first operation. The value '400' is then moved left justified with two blanks to the right of LASTT. A typical CAT operation on these two fields would yield two blanks in between – the two blanks at the end of the field in Factor 1 (NAMET). The technique that is used to remove the two in-between blanks from the end of the first field in the CAT operation is to set the padding value in the second half of Factor 2 to zero for no spaces.

In the below example, the padding factor is contained in the field named BL#, a variable instead of a constant. So, in the third statement this variable is primed to zero and then the CAT operation uses that value to determine the # of blanks.

```
C...              MOVE  'AS/  '    NAMET      5
C...              MOVE  '400  '    LASTT      5
C...              Z-ADD0           BL#       10
C... NAMET        CAT   LAST:BL#   BOTHT     10 P
```

BL# set to zero causes blanks in Factor 1 that are between AS/ and 400 to be removed. The result is as follows:

```
    1234567891
             0
    >AS/400    <
```

Only the trailing blanks in factor 1 are affected by the # of blanks portion of the CAT operation. If there were three leading blanks in Factor 2, for example, they would be included in the output stream regardless of the BL# value.

The CHECK Operation (CHECK RPGIV)

CHECK is a very handy string operation that verifies that each character in the base string (Factor 2) is among the characters indicated in the comparator string (Factor 1)

Code	Factor1	Factor2	Result	Indicators
CHECK (E)	Compara- tor string	Base String: start	Left Position	_ ER NF

CHECK Example 1

Since Factor 1 is a blank, the CHECK operation below returns the position of the first non-blank character. If STRING contains the value 'b̶b̶b̶b̶dog', then NUM will contain the value 5 and indictor 20 will be on indicating a not found condition.

```
C...' '           CHECKSTRING       NUM       20
```

CHECK Example 2

In the CHECK example below, after the code is executed, N=7 and the "found" indicator 99 is on. Since the start position is 2, the first non-numeric character found is the period '.'. In this example, a constant is primed with all of the digits from 0 to 9. The SALRY field is checked from left to right starting in position 2 (SALRY:2) for any of the digits in Factor 1. The "$" sign is bypassed and the CHECK hits the 4, 0, 0, 0, and the last 0, all of which are in the comparator string in Factor 1, before the CHECK hits the period. Counting from left to right, the period is the seventh character in the string and the # 7 is returned to the variable N. Additionally since there was a non-numeric value found, the found indicator 99 is turned on.

```
I...   '0123456789...     C            NUMBRS
-------
C                MOVE '$40000.'  SALRY 7...  NF
C NUMBRS         CHECKSALRY:2    N                99
```

CHECK Example 3

This set of CHECK code checks that FIELD contains only the letters A to J. The LETTRS constant is primed at the top of the code with these letters. A search argument is moved to the field, FIELD. When the CHECK is executed, the array ARRAY contains the positions of the characters in the search argument that are not found in the LETTRS constant. ARRAY contains 136000 after the operation . The three zeroes also indicate that there were three hits.

```
I...   'ABCDEFGHIJ'...     C            LETTRS
------
C...             MOVE '1A=BC*'  FIELD 8   NF
C... LETTRS      CHECKFIELD     ARRAY           99
```

In the below 3example, the FIELD contains only letters within the range A thru J, ARRAY = (000000). Therefore, indicator 99 (String not found) turns off since all of the letters in Factor 2 were found in Factor 1.

```
I...   'ABCDEFGHIJ'...     C            LETTRS
-----
C                MOVE 'CDCDCD'  FIELD 6 NF
C LETTRS         CHECKFIELD     ARRAY           99
```

CHEKR CHECKR(RPGIV)

Just like the CHECK operation, CHEKR or CHECKR in RPGIV also verifies that each character in the base string (factor 2) is among the characters indicated in the comparator string (factor1). The CHEKR differs from CHECK in that the checking is done from the right... although the position placed in the result field is relative to the left

Code	Factor1	Factor2	Result	Indicators
CHEKR (E)	Compara- tor string	Base String: start	Right Position	__ ER NF

CHEKR Example 1

Let's start right in with the examples. Since Factor 1 is a blank in the example below, the results indicate the position of the first non-blank character coming from right to left. Another way of saying this is that by identifying the first non-blank from the right by its position in the string, the CHEKR operation allows you to readily determine the length of a string. If STRING contains 'dogbbbb', for example in the sample code below, lthen NUM will contain the value 3

```
C... ''      CHEKRSTRING   NUM    20
```

N=1 after this code is executed against the string field containing '$40000.', and the found indicator 99 is on. Since the start position is 6, the first non-numeric character found is the '$'.

```
I... '0123456789...      C           NUMBRS
-----
C...            MOVE '$40000.' SALRY 7   NF
C...NUMBRS      CHEKRSALRY:6   N          99
```

Checking from the right, this next set of code checks that FIELD contains only the letters A to J. Therefore, after the CHEKR function, ARRAY = 876310. Indicator 99 turns on

```
I...          'ABCDEFGHIJ...  C           LETTRS
-----
C             MOVE '1A=BC***'FIELD 8   NF
C...LETTRS    CHEKRFIELD      ARRAY      99
```

SCAN Operation (RPG/400 & RPGIV)

The SCAN operator is also very handy and very powerful. It scans a character string (base string) contained in Factor 2 for a substring (compare string) contained in Factor 1. The scan begins at the specified location contained in factor 2 and continues for the length of the compare string which is specified in factor 1

Code	Factor1	Factor2	Result	Indicators
SCAN (E)	Compara- tor string: length	Base String: start	Left-most Position	__ ER FD

Working through the SCAN operation in the next example, we discover that the SCAN encounters the substring 'ABC' starting in position 3 as defined in Factor 2. Thus, a "3" is placed in the result field signifying that the left most position is 3. Indicator 99 is set on because the string is found. Because no starting position is used default 1 is used

```
C...  'ABC'...    SCAN  'XCABCD'   RESULT          99
```

The SCAN operation scans the string in Factor 2 for an occurrence of the string in Factor 1 starting at position 3. The operation places the values 5 and 6 in the first and second elements of the array. Indicator 99 is set on

```
C...              MOVE  'ARRAYY'   FIELD1     6
C...              MOVE  'Y'        FIELD2     1
C...FIELD2        SCAN  FIELD1:3   ARRAY
```

How is the SCAN different from the CHECK operation? The best answer to this question begs that the interrogator recall that the comparison in the CHECK operation is by character and the comparison in the SCAN operation is by string.

In other words, it would not be OK in a scan if the ZYZ were located because there was an A in position 2, a B in position 7, and a C in position 93 of a string. This would yield results in a CHECK operation and a CHEKR. The SCAN, on the other hand wants there to be one or multiple occurrences of XYZ in the string being examined. The ARRAY option in the Result field of the SCAN provides for the notation of all of the occurrences found of a comparator string against a base string in a SCAN.

The SCAN begins at the leftmost character of Factor 2 (as specified by the start location) and it continues character by character, from left to right, comparing each characters in factor 2 to those in factor 1 – for the length specified. If the result field is not an array, the SCAN operation will locate only the first occurrence of the compare string.

To continue scanning beyond the first occurrence, you may use the result field from the previous SCAN operation to calculate the starting position of the next SCAN. Again, if the result field is a numeric array, as many occurrences as there are elements in the array are noted. If no occurrences are found, the Result Field is set to zero. If the Result Field is an array, all its elements are set to zero.

Taking the generic explanation forward against the next example, the SCAN operation scans the string in Factor 2 called FIELD1, starting in the position specified after the colon. Since this is X and X is a variable, we see that X is primed in the Z-ADD with a "2."

This X value directs the SCAN to proceed from the second position of the contents of FIELD1, looking for an occurrence of the string specified in Factor 1, for a length of 4 (also specified in Factor 1). Because 'TOOL' is not found in FIELD1, WHERE is set to 0 and indicator 99 is set off.

```
C...              Z-ADD2         X      10
C...              MOVE 'TESTING' FIELD1 7
C...              MOVE 'TOOL'    FIELD2 5      FD
C...FIELD2:4      SCAN FIELD1:X  WHERE 20      99
```

SUBST Substring Operation -- RPG/400 & RPGIV

The substring (SUBST) RPG operation returns a substring from Factor 2 starting at the location specified in factor 2 for the length specified in factor 1, and it places this substring in the result field. Factor 2 must contain either the base string, or the base string followed by ':', followed by the start location. If Factor 1 is not specified, the length of the string from the start position is used.

Code	Factor1	Factor2	Result	Indicators
SUBST (P)	Length to extract	Base String: start	Target string	__ ER __

In the following example, the SUBST operation extracts the substring from Factor 2 starting at position 3 for a length of 2. The value 'CD' is placed in the RESULT field. Indicator 99 is not set on because no error occurred.

```
C...          Z-ADD3          T          20
C...          MOVEL'ABCDEF'   STRING 10...      ER
C... 2        SUBSTSTRING:T   RESULT 20         99
```

In the below substring operation, the length (5 specified in Factor 1) is greater than the length of the string minus the start position plus 1.
Since the length of 'ABCDEF' is 6 and T is 4, the following depicts the calculation. $(6 - 4 + 1 = 3)$ As a result, indicator 90 is set on and the result field is not changed.

```
C...          MOVE  'ABCDEF'  STRING  6
C...          Z-ADD4          T          10...   ER
C... 5        SUBSTSTRING:T   RESULT            99
```

XLATE Translate Operation—RPG/400 & RPGIV

The translate (XLATE) operation is very handy when simple code translations need to take place, such as upper to lower case. Characters in the source string (Factor 2) are translated according to the From and To strings (both in Factor1) and the result is put into a receiver field (Result field). Source characters with a match in the From string are translated to corresponding characters in the To string.

XLATE starts at the location specified in factor 2 and continues character by character left to right. If a character of the source string exists in the From string, the corresponding character in the To string is placed in the result field.

Any characters in the source field preceding the starting position are placed unchanged in the result field.

Code	Factor1	Factor2	Result	Indicators
XLATE (P, E)	From: To	Source string: start	Target string	__ ER __

To analyze the following code, first note that an 8 position field called NUMBER is loaded in the first line with '999 9999.' There is a space after the third nine. Then, note that the *translate from* and *translate to* areas of Factor 1 contain a literal blank and a literal dash. This, of course means that when a blank is found in the source string (NUMBER), the XLATE operation is to translate that blank to a dash in the Result Field. Therefore, the following code translates the blank in NUMBER to '-'.

The contents of the Result Field then are **999-9999**.

```
C...              MOVE  '999 9999'NUMBER     8
C... ' ':'-'      XLATENUMBER     RESULT     8
```

In the next example, all values in the string are translated to lower case. Therefore RESULT = **'rpg dep'**

```
I... 'ABCDEFGHIJKLMNOPQRST-C...        UC
I... 'UVWXYZ'
I... 'abcdefghijklmnopqrst-C          LC
I... 'uvwxyz'
------
C...              MOVE  'RpG Dep' STRING     7
C... UC:LC        XLATESTRING     RESULT     8
```

In the below example, all values in the string are translated to upper case. Therefore RESULT = **'RPG DEP'**

```
C...              MOVE  'RpG Dep' STRING     7
C... LC:UC        XLATESTRING     RESULT     8
```

The above example is the last basic string operation example. In this section we examined the structure of all of the basic string operations that are used in RPG/400 and RPGIV. We are now poised to use this knowledge in building some more useful and in fact, more complex examples using multiple basic operators to accomplish each.

Complex String Examples

The following set of constants will be used in various places in this section for building the complex string example code:

```
I... 'ABCDEFGHIJKLMNOPQRST-C             UC
I              'UVWXYZ'
I   'abcdefghijklmnopqrst-C              LC            I
'uvwxyz'
I... 'ABCDEFGHIJKLMNOPQRST-C             VALID
I              'UVWXYZ'
I...X'B8'              C         HALF
```

The calculation specification below creates an underline field 30 characters long for use in the complex string code

```
C...              MOVEL*ALL'_'     ULINE     30
```

Complex String Example 1: Hex Literals & Named Constants

The next example uses the HALF (1/2 ½) named constant that is defined above. The QUARTR hexadecimal literal (1/4 ¼) is created on the fly

```
C...              MOVEL'QUARTER'  FIELD      9 P
C...              MOVE X'B7'      FIELD
C... 'OUTPUT'     DSPLY           FIELD
C...              MOVEL'HALF'     FIELD        P
C...              MOVE HALF       FIELD
C... 'OUTPUT'     DSPLY           FIELD
```

?

———

RESULTS OF 2 DSPLY OPS:

```
DSPLY OUTPUT    QUARTER ¼
DSPLY OUTPUT    HALF    ½
```

Please note that in the above examples, Factor 2 is shorter than the result field and P (for padding) is specified in the operation extender field. Therefore, on a MOVE operation, padding occurs to the left and on a MOVEL operation padding occurs on the right. That is why it is perfectly OK to use the field FIELD in all of the above examples without concern for "crap" being left by another operation.

Complex String Example 2: Extract & Identify a String

The string for this example is as follows:

```
Beginning Full Name
FULNAM = 'MISSƀKATIEƀKELLYƀƀƀƀ'
```

```
C*
C...       SUBSTFULNAM:12    LASTNM  20 P
```

The end result is in field **LASTNM.   Last Name is 'KELLYƀƀƀƀ...'**
The following code identifies the last name as KELLY

```
C*    Now to identify the string as KELLY
C*
C...      'KELLY'    IFEQ LASTNM
C...                    .
C...                    .
C...                    .
C              ENDIF
```

Complex String Example 3: Find the Length of a String

Now, let's use our string techniques in the next example to find the length of a string. The string is:

The string for this example is as follows:

```
Beginning Full Name
FULNAM = 'MISSbKATIEbKELLYbbbb'
```

```
C*
C...   ' '      CHEKRFULNAM      LENGTH  20 P          C*
```

The end result is in field **LENGTH**

```
LENGTH is 16
```

Complex String Example 4: Convert Last, First to First Last

Now, let's use our string techniques in the next example to convert a last name first string to a first name last string. This is the string operation equivalent of the work we did at the beginning of the chapter with arrays.

The string for this example is as follows:

```
Beginning Full Name (40 characters)
FULL = 'KELLY,KATIEbbbbbbbbbbbbbb...b'
```

```
C*
C...   'KEY NAME' DSPLY          FULL    40
C...   ','        SCAN FULL      COMMA   20
C...   COMMA      SUB  1         LENL    20
C...   LENL       SUBSTFULL:1    LNAME   20
C...   COMMA      ADD  1         FBEG    20
C...   ' '        CHEKRFULL      FEND    20
C...   FEND       SUB  COMMA     LENF    20
C...   LENF       SUBSTFULL:FBEG FNAME   20
C...   FNAME      CAT  LNAME:1   FULL    40  P
C...   'NEW NAME' DSPLY          FULL
```

The information gained by the SCAN and the CHEKR is as follows:

```
12345678901234567
KELLY,KATIE    ...
```

... becomes ...

```
12345678901234567
KATIE KELLY    ...
```

Beginning Position of first name (FBEG) = 7
Ending position of first name (FEND)= 11
Length of last name (LENL) = 5
Length of first name LENF = 5
Comma position = 6
Last name = LNAME (KELLY)
First name = FNAME (KATIE)

Complex String Example 5:
Convert LastFirst to FirstLast, Mixed Case

Now, let's up the string ante a bit with the next example to convert an upper case string to lower case. This is the string operation equivalent of the work we did at the beginning of the chapter with the compile time array..

The string for this example is as follows:

```
Beginning Full Name (40 characters)
FULL = 'bbbKELLYbbbKATIEbbbb'
```

```
I...      'ABCDEFGHIJKLMNOPQRST-C             UC
I...      'UVWXYZ'
I...      'abcdefghijklmnopqrst-C             LC
I...      'uvwxyz'
C*
C...      ' '           CHECKFULL         BEG1      20
C...      ' '           SCAN  FULL:BEG1 END1        20
C...      ' '           CHECKFULL:END1 BEG2         20
C...      ' '           SCAN  FULL:BEG2 END2        20
C...      END1          SUB   BEG1       LENL       20
C...      END2          SUB   BEG2       LENF       20
C...      LENL          SUBSTFULL:BEG1 LNAME        20
C...      LENF          SUBSTFULL:BEG2 FNAME        20
C*
C...      UC:LC         XLATEFNAME:2     FNAME
C...      UC:LC         XLATELNAME:2     LNAME
C...      FNAME         CAT   LNAME:1    FULL       40
```

The information gained by the SCAN and the CHEKR is as follows:

```
12345678901234567890
bbbKELLYbbbKATIEbbbb
```

… becomes …

```
12345678901234567890
KatiebKellybbbbbbbbb
```

Beginning position of last name (BEG1) = 4
Ending position of last name +1 (END1)= 9
Beginning position of first name (BEG2) = 12
Ending position of first name (END2)= 11
Length of last name (LENL) = 5
Length of first name (LENF) = 5
Last name = LNAME (Kelly)
First name = FNAME (Katie)

The output of the program is as follows:

```
DSPLY   BEG1       4
DSPLY   END1       9
DSPLY   BEG2      12
DSPLY   END2      17
DSPLY   LENL       5
DSPLY   LENF       5
DSPLY   LNAME      Kelly
DSPLY   FNAME      Katie
DSPLY   FUL2       Katie Kelly
```

Complex String Example 6: Center a Line of Text

Now, let's move the ante up even more with this next example to center a string. Yes, it would be nice if there were a command that you could type in that said "center" and that's all you had to do. But, since there is not, this little technique will show you how in just six executable statements.

The string for this example is as follows:

```
Beginning Title (26 characters)
TITLE = 'SouthbW-BbSkyhawksbbbbbbbb'
```

```
I        'South W-B Skyhawks    -C       TITLE
I        '             '
C*
C... CENTER       BEGSR
C... ' '          CHEKRTITLE       LEN        20
C... 'LEN'        DSPLY            LEN
C... 26           SUB  LEN         DIFFR      20
C... 'DIFFR'      DSPLY            DIFFR
C... DIFFR        DIV  2           PAD        20
C... 'PAD'        DSPLY            PAD
C...              CAT  TITLE:PAD   HEADNG 26
C... 'HEADNG1'    DSPLY            HEADNG
C...              MOVEL'F'         HEADNG
```

```
C...              MOVE 'L'        HEADNG
C... 'HEADNG2'    DSPLY           HEADNG
C...              ENDSR
```

When all is said and done, the beginning string has been centered as follows:

```
123456789012345678901123456
```
`SouthbW-BbSkyhawksbbbbbbbb`

… becomes …

```
123456789012345678901123456
```
`bbbbSouthbW-BbSkyhawksbbbb`

Without some guidance, looking at the code here in this example would bring you to the conclusion that the TITLE field which is already left justified and starting in position 1, would be concatenated with the blanks on the right.

Moreover, the untrained eye would see those blanks not being centered at all.

However, that is not how CAT works. The reason this works so nicely is because of the nature of a CAT operation with blank padding and a blank result field. If Factor 1 is not specified (as in the CAT in this sample code) the Result Field string is used.

The padding blanks are added following the last nonblank character. Then Factor 2 is appended to this result.

In other words, if the number of blanks is specified after the colon in Factor 2 as it is, with no Factor 1 specified in the operation, the trailing blanks of the Result Field are ignored. The HEADNG field in the example starts off as all blanks so all are trailing blanks and thus, all are ignored.

Only as many blanks as specified after the colon are included in the result between the last nonblank character in the result field (there are none) and the first character of Factor 2.

Any leading blanks in Factor 2 are always included but again, there are none in TITLE for this example. So, the magic occurs because HEADNG is all blank and all of the blanks are viewed as trailing blanks.

So, the PAD (4 characters) gets inserted into the result followed by Factor 2 (TITLE) and that's how the result appears centered. This is a trick worth remembering.

The DSPLY operations in the program reveal what is going on. Take notice to HEADNG1 and HEADNG2 below. Since it is difficult to discern a blank in a field from a printed blank, the code above places an F in the first position and an L in the last position of the field named HEADNG.

```
DSPLY LEN    18
DSPLY DIFFR  8
DSPLY HPAD   4
DSPLY HEADNG1   bbbbSOUTH W-B SKYHAWKSbbbb
DSPLY HEADNG2   FbbbSOUTH W-B SKYHAWKSbbbL
```

Complex String Example 7: Justify a Line of Text

Now, let's start with the string that we just centered and see what it takes to left justify it. The string for this example is as follows:

Beginning Title (26 characters)
TITLE = '~~bbbb~~SouthbW-BbSkyhawks~~bbbb~~'

```
I     '    South W-B Skyh   -C       LJUST
I     'awks      '
---
C...   ' '        CHECKTITL2      POS      20
C...   'POS'      DSPLY           POS
C...   POS        IFGT 1
C...              SUBSTTITL2:POS LJUST   26 P
C...   'LJUST1'   DSPLY           LJUST
C...              MOVEL'F'        LJUST
C...   'LJUST2'   DSPLY           LJUST
C...              ENDIF
```

To demonstrate that the code is left justified at completion, the results of the DSPLY operations are included below:

```
DSPLY   POS       5
DSPLY   LJUST1      South  W-B  Skyhawks
DSPLY   LJUST2      Fouth  W-B  Skyhawks
```

Complex String Example 8: Substring Insertion

Now, let's start with the string that we just centered and see what it takes to left justify it. The string for this example is as follows:

Beginning Title (40 characters)
CORS = 'This is a course in RPG. ...'
REQD = 'required'

```
I...   'This is a course in -C       CORS
I...   'RPG.'
I...   'required'           C        REQD
-------
C* Insert text in a sentence
C...              MOVELCORS       THIS   40
C...   'THIS'     DSPLY           THIS
C...   9          SUBSTTHIS:1     PART1  20
C...   'PART1'    DSPLY           PART1
C...              SUBSTTHIS:11    PART2  20
C...   'PART2'    DSPLY           PART2
C...   PART1      CAT  REQD:1     RESULT 40 P
C...   '1RESULT'  DSPLY           RESULT
C...   RESULT     CAT  PART2:1    RESULT
C...   '2RESULT'  DSPLY           RESULT
```

To demonstrate that the code has inserted the word required where appropriate, the results of the DSPLY operations are included below:

```
DSPLY THIS              This is a course in RPG.
DSPLY PART1             This is a
DSPLY PART2             course in RPG.
DSPLY 1RESULT           This is a required
DSPLY 2RESULT           This is a required course in RPG.
```

Complex String Example 9: Substring Text Replace

Now, let's start with the string that we just centered and see what it takes to left justify it. The string for this example is as follows:

```
Beginning Title (26 characters)
CORS2 = 'THIS IS A NASTY COURSE IN RPG'...
REQD = 'required'
I... 'This is a nasty cour-C          CORS2
I... 'se in RPG.'
I...  'required'                C           REQD
-------

C* Replace text in a sentence
C*
C...              MOVELCORS2        THIS    40
C... 'THIS'       DSPLY             THIS
C... 9            SUBSTTHIS:1       PART1   20
C... 'PART1'      DSPLY             PART1
C...              SUBSTTHIS:17      PART2   20
C... 'PART2'      DSPLY             PART2
C... PART1        CAT   REQD:1      RESULT  40 P
C... '1RESULT'    DSPLY             RESULT
C... RESULT       CAT   PART2:1     RESULT
C... '2RESULT'    DSPLY             RESULT
C                 ENDSR
```

To demonstrate that the code has been replaced where appropriate, the results of the DSPLY operations are included below:

```
DSPLY THIS              This is a nasty course in RPG.
DSPLY PART1             This is a
DSPLY PART2             course in RPG.
DSPLY 1RESULT           This is a required
DSPLY 2RESULT           This is a required course in RPG.
```

Complex String Example 10: Substring Text Deletion

Now, let's start with the string that we just centered and see what it takes to left justify it. The string for this example is as follows:

Beginning Title (26 characters)
DELET = 'Can this U/Lcase teXT BE DELETED'

```
I... 'Can this U/Lcase teX-C              DELET
I... 'T BE DELETED'
-------
C* Delete text in a sentence
C*
C...            MOVELDELET      THIS    40
C... 'THIS'     DSPLY           THIS
C... 9          SUBSTDELET:1    PART1   20
C... 'PART1'    DSPLY           PART1
C...            SUBSTDELET:18   PART2   20
C... 'PART2'    DSPLY           PART2
C... PART1      CAT   PART2:1   RESULT  40 P
C... 'RESULT'   DSPLY           RESULT
```

To demonstrate that the code has been deleted where appropriate, the results of the DSPLY operations are included below:

DSPLY THIS   Can this U/Lcase teXT BE DELETED
DSPLY PART1   Can this
DSPLY PART2   teXT BE DELETED
DSPLY RESULT   Can this teXT BE DELETED

Complex String Example 11: Scan and Replace Text

Now, let's start with the string that we just centered and see what it takes to left justify it. The string for this example is as follows:

Beginning Title (26 characters)
INPUT1 = 'THE 1992 Schedule'
SRCH = '1992'
CHGS = 'NEW 1993'

```
 1  I...'THE 1992 SCHEDULE'  C...    INPUT1
 2  I...'1992'           C...    SRCH
 3  I...'NEW 1993'          C...    CHGS
-------
11  C...  SCANRP        BEGSR
13  C...  ' '           CHEKRSRCH        LEN      20
14  C...                MOVELINPUT1      THIS     40
15  C...  'INPUT1'      DSPLY            THIS
16  C...                MOVELSRCH        SRCHF    40
17  C...  'SRCH'        DSPLY            SRCHF
18  C...  'LNSRCH'      DSPLY            LEN            FD
21  C...  SRCH:LEN      SCAN INPUT1      BG1      20 ...01
23  C...  'IN01'        DSPLY               *IN01
25  C...  'BG1'         DSPLY            BG1
27  C...  *IN01         IFEQ *ON
29  C...  BG1           SUB  1           LEN1     20
30  C...  'LEN1'        DSPLY            LEN1
31  C...  LEN1          SUBSTINPUT1      PARTA    30
33  C...  'PARTA'       DSPLY            PARTA
35  C...  BG1           ADD  LEN         BG2      20
36  C...  'BG2'         DSPLY            BG2
38  C...                SUBSTINPUT1:BG2PARTB      30
39  C...  'PARTB'       DSPLY            PARTB
43  C...  ' '           CHEKRPARTA:LEN1BLK#
44  C...  'BLK#1'       DSPLY            BLK#     20
47  C...  LEN1          SUB  BLK#        BLK#     20
48  C...  'BLK#2'       DSPLY            BLK#     20
51  C...  PARTA         CAT   CHGS:BLK#  OUTPUT 30 P
52  C...  'OUTPUT1'     DSPLY            OUTPUT
53  C...  OUTPUT        CAT   PARTB:0    OUTPU2 40
54  C...  'OUTPUT2'     DSPLY            OUTPU2
55  C...                ENDIF
```

To demonstrate that the code has been found and replaced with the proper # of blank separators where appropriate, the results of the DSPLY operations are included below:

```
DSPLY    INPUT1       THE 1992 SCHEDULE
DSPLY    SRCH         1992
DSPLY    LNSRCH       4
DSPLY    IN01         1
DSPLY    BG1          5
DSPLY    LEN1         4
DSPLY    PARTA        THE
DSPLY    BG2          9
DSPLY    PARTB        SCHEDULE
DSPLY    BLK#1        3
DSPLY    BLK#2        1
DSPLY    OUTPUT1      THE NEW 1993
DSPLY    OUTPUT2      THE NEW 1993 SCHEDULE
```

The essence of the code in this example is to scan for a value (1992 in this case) and replace that value with another value (NEW 1993). Unlike the other examples so far in this chapter, this one tries to make the routine somewhat generic so that it can be used with other search criteria for other search strings.

The code starts with a few constant definitions shown below:

```
1   I...'THE 1992 SCHEDULE'    C...      INPUT1
2   I...'1992'                 C...      SRCH
3   I...'NEW 1993'             C...      CHGS
```

INPUT1 is the string that will be searched for content. SRCH is the value that will be used to search the string and CHGS will be the new string to replace 1992 in the INPUT 1 string.

```
13  C...   ' '       CHEKRSRCH    LEN      20
14  C...             MOVELINPUT1  THIS     40
15  C...   'INPUT1'  DSPLY        THIS
16  C...             MOVELSRCH    SRCHF    40
17  C...   'SRCH'    DSPLY        SRCHF
18  C...   'LNSRCH'  DSPLY        LEN
```

As you can see in the above snippet, the code begins with a CHEKR operation to find out that the length of the SRCH string data is 4 characters for this search. The INPUT1 constant is then moved into a field only so it can be displayed. Then it is displayed and the SRCH constant is moved into a field so it also can be displayed. When these values are displayed the length field LEN of 4 from the CHEKR in line 13 is also displayed

```
21  C... SRCH:LEN   SCAN INPUT1    BG1      20      01
23  C... 'IN01'     DSPLY          *IN01
25  C... 'BG1'      DSPLY          BG1
27  C... *IN01      IFEQ *ON
```

Since all STRING operations do not have the same meaning for Factor 1 and Factor 2, until you understand the nuances among the six string operations, like most programmers, you may have to look up the format of the command and sometimes the explanation of the command. In this book, these are in Chapters 14 (RPG/400) and 15 (RPGIV).

The first operation above in line 21 is a scan which takes the search argument (the thing you are searching for) and its length of 4 (calculated in statement 13), and it compares those four characters to each set of four characters in the INPUT1 string starting from the first position in the string to the end.. Any set of four characters in the input stream causes a found condition. When the string, which contains the value 1992 is found, the beginning of *string found field,* BG1 is loaded with the value of 4 representing the position of the found item (1992) for which the search occurred. The value of indicator 1 (ON) and the value of the BG1 field (5) is displayed and then the code tests for the status of the indicator 01. If 01 is on which it is, the following code gets executed.

```
29 C... BG1          SUB   1          LEN1     20
30 C... 'LEN1'       DSPLY            LEN1
31 C... LEN1         SUBSTINPUT1      PARTA    30
33 C... 'PARTA'      DSPLY            PARTA
35 C... BG1          ADD   LEN        BG2      20
36 C... 'BG2'        DSPLY            BG2
38 C...              SUBSTINPUT1:BG2PARTB      30
39 C... 'PARTB'      DSPLY            PARTB
```

The value (5) of the beginning position of the found search argument (1992) is used in line 29 to calculate another value which is minus 1 and represents the length (4) of the part of the string up to the first character of 1992 but not including the 1 in 1992. This value is then displayed.

Using the length that needs to be grabbed from the input string (4), the SUBST operation takes the four characters in the beginning of the string and it places them in a field called PARTA.

The contents of PARTA at this time for the constant value being compared is "THE ." That's the letters T – H – E followed by a blank.

This is then displayed for verification that all is going well. The next operation adds the LEN value of 4 to BG1 which is 5 to come up with the value 9 as stored in BG2. This value is then displayed. BG2 represents the beginning position of the second string of data after '1992' in the string has been bypassed.

Using the beginning of the second string, BG2 after the colon in Factor 2 of the substring operation in line 38, the remainder of the values in INPUT1 is moved to the field named PARTB. The next operation in line 39 displays the value of PARTB showing that it is primed for the concatenation coming up.

```
43 C... ' '          CHEKRPARTA:LEN1BLK#
44 C... 'BLK#1'      DSPLY            BLK#     20
47 C... LEN1         SUB   BLK#       BLK#     20
48 C... 'BLK#2'      DSPLY            BLK#     20
```

This next section of code directly above begins with a CHEKR (check Reverse) operation that looks for the first non blank character moving from right to left of the starting position given after the colon in Factor 2. PART A at this point holds the value **'THE '** clearly showing a blank in position 4.

Moving from position 4 to the left from the right looking for the first non-blank, the code would quickly find the "E" in THE in position 3 and it would store that in the field called BLK#.

LEN1 holds the value 4 representing the total length of the first string. When the operation in line 47 is completed, BLK# contains the result of a subtraction of 3 (current value of BLK#) from a value of 4 (length of the PARTA string.

The difference is the number of trailing blanks that would also need to be reinserted into the modified string. Since the only thing originally in INPUT1 that was between the three letters THE and 1992 was a space (blank) it is clear that the result of executing this code captures that fact.

The result of the # of blanks found (4 – 1) is then displayed using BLK# as the vehicle.

```
51 C... PARTA       CAT   CHGS:BLK# OUTPUT 30 P
52 C... 'OUTPUT1' DSPLY           OUTPUT
53 C... OUTPUT      CAT   PARTB:0   OUTPUT
54 C... 'OUTPUT2' DSPLY           OUTPUT
55 C...              ENDIF
```

In the home stretch, the next real code occurs at statement 51 above as the change value (CHGS) -- **'NEW 1993'** is concatenated (CAT) with the "THE ' from PART1, rendering The "NEW 1993" in OUTPUT, displayed in OUTPUT1 at line 52. Moving towards completion of the string the combination of PARTA with CHGS in OUTPUT needs to be again concatenated with PART. This is done in statement 53 followed by the printing of the completed replacement string in statement 54.

Complex String Example 12: Translate Numbers

Now, let's start with the string below and see what it takes to translate all the digits to asterisks. The string for this example is as follows:

Beginning FROM (31 characters)

```
FROM = 'The balance due is 255 dollars'
TO = 'The balance due is *** dollars'
```

```
I... '1234567890'          C    FROM
I... '**********'          C    TO
---
C* ONE for ONE Positional TRANSLATE
C... FROM:TO     XLATEINPUT        OUTPUT  30
C... 'OUTPUT'  DSPLY            OUTPUT
```

To demonstrate that the code has been translated where appropriate, the results of the DSPLY operation are included below:

DSPLY OUTPUT   The balance due is *** dollars

Complex String Example 13: Remove Leading Zeros

Now, let's start with the string below and see what it takes to translate all the leading zeros top blanks.. The string for this example is as follows:

Beginning INPUT (9 digits)

```
INPUT =   000079031
OUTPUT = 79031
```

```
C* first non zero or non blank position
C...  '0 '          CHECKINPUT       N
C* Are there lead zeroes / blanks yes(5)
C...  N             IFNE *ZERO
C* Change '0' in INPUT to ' ' in OUTPUT
C...  '0':' '       XLATEINPUT       OUTPUT
C...  'OUTPUT1'     DSPLY            OUTPUT
C* Change non-leading '0' back to zeros
C* Translation begins at N - 1st non zero
C...  ' ':'0'       XLATEOUTPUT:N    OUTPUT    20
C...  'OUTPUT2'     DSPLY            OUTPUT
C...                ENDIF
```

The code above is self explanatory with the comments. Examine each statement and you will first see the beginning of the non-zero text found as the first digit is found. If any digits are found, the two basic translations occur.

The first translation changes all zeroes to blanks including the zero in the middle of the digits (shown below).

The second translation starts at the N (N=5) position of the OUTPUT and changes all blank digits in the middle, back to zeros. To demonstrate that the code has been translated where appropriate, the results of the DSPLY operations are included below:

```
DSPLY   OUTPUT1     79 31
DSPLY   OUTPUT2     79031
```

Complex String Example 14: Find a # in an Address

Now, let's start with the string below and see what it takes to find a number in the given address. The string for this example is as follows:

```
Beginning TEXT1 (31 characters)
```
```
TEXT1 = My Address is 1432 Prill Avenue
NUMADD = 1432
```
```
I...  'My Address is 1432 P-C        TEXT1
I...  'rill Avenue'
I...  'ABCDEFGHIJKLMNOPQRST-C        ALPBET
I...  'UVWXYZabcdefghijklmn-
I...  'opqrstuvwxyz '
I...  '1234567890         C          DIGITS
-------
C...                MOVELTEXT1       TEXT     40
C...     'TEXT'     DSPLY            TEXT
C* To extract the # part of the address,
C* we must know the start of the # text &
C* the length of the numeric text...
C* Find the start of the Numeric text
C* Store in the field named BEGIN below FD
C...  ALPBET        CHECKTEXT        BEGIN    20
C...  'BEGIN'       DSPLY            BEGIN
C* CHECK finds first non alpha char pos.
C* Where does the Numeric Text End?
C...  DIGITS        CHECKTEXT:BEGINEND
C...  'END'         DSPLY            END
```

```
C* CHECK finds first blank after #
C* How long is the Numeric Text?
C...  END           SUB  BEGIN       LENGTH
C...  'LENGTH'      DSPLY            LENGTH
C* Extract the # portion of the address
C...  LENGTH        SUBSTTEXT:BEGINNUMADD   100
C...  'NUMADD'      DSPLY              NUMADD
```

The code above is self explanatory when read with the comments.

Examine each statement and you will first see the original text being moved to a field so it could be displayed. The TEXT is then compared against the whole alphabet of upper and lower case characters to find the first non- alphabetic character.

The CHECK operation brings back the beginning position of the numeric part of the address which is then displayed.

From the beginning position of the numeric portion of the address, (BEGIN) the CHECK operation looks for the first non digit by comparing each character of TEXT, starting at BEGIN, looking for a non-digit. The non-digit means that the position of the blank after 1432 in the address has been located and it is stored in a field called END.

The position in END is then subtracted by the position in BEGIN to find the length of the numeric portion of the address which is to be extracted. The length is then displayed. Now, the code knows beginning, end and length of the numeric portion of the address. The next step is to grab it and place it in a field.

The SUBSTRING operation uses the length of the number in Factor 1 against the TEXT field starting at the beginning of the numeric portion (TEXT:BEGIN) and it places the extracted numeric text into the NUMADD field which is then displayed. To demonstrate that the code has been translated where appropriate, the results of the DSPLY operations are included below:

```
DSPLY   TEXT      My Address is 1432 Prill Avenue
DSPLY   BEGIN     15
DSPLY   END       19
DSPLY   LENGTH    4
DSPLY   NUMADD    1432
```

Complex String Example 15: Replace All Blanks in a Text Line

Now, let's start with the string below and see what it takes to find a number in the given address. The string for this example is as follows:

Beginning TEXT1 (31 characters)

```
TEXT1 = MarysbbbbbAddressbbisb1432bbbPrillbbbbAvenue
FINAL = Marys Address is 1432 Prill Avenue
```

```
I...  'Marys     Address   i-C        TEXT1
I...  's 1432    Prill     Av-
I...  'enue'
-------
C* FIND THE LENGTH OF THE INPUT TEXT
C...            MOVELTEXT1     TEXT    45
C...  'TEXT1'   DSPLY          TEXT
C...  ' '       CHEKRTEXT      TXTLEN   20
```

```
C... 'TXTLEN'   DSPLY            TXTLEN
C* SCAN for the first blank - end of part1
C... ' '        SCAN TEXT:1    END      20        01
C...            'END1'  DSPLY            END
C* PERFORM DO 'til end of string or no blanks
C... END        DOWLTTXTLEN
C... *IN01      ANDEQ*ON
C* FIND START OF NEXT WORD IN TEXT STRING
C* STARTING FROM THE END OF PART1-NXT changes
C... ' '        CHECKTEXT:END  NXT
C... 'NXT1'     DSPLY            NXT
C* Determine # of blanks in between words
C... NXT        SUB  END       BLNKS    20
C... 'BLNKS'    DSPLY            BLNKS
C... BLNKS      IFGT 1
C* Get First Part of text
C... END        SUBSTTEXT        PART01 45 P
C... 'PART01'   DSPLY            PART01
C* Get 2nd part of text
C...            SUBSTTEXT:NXT    PART02 45 P
C... 'PART02'   DSPLY            PART02
C* Concat Part01 & Part02 w 1 blank separator
C* PART01 and PART02 change each loop
C... PART01     CAT  PART02:1   TEXT
C... 'TEXT2'    DSPLY            TEXT
C* Determine new text length after blanks are
C* removed
C... ' '        CHEKRTEXT        TXTLEN   20
C... 'TXTLN2'   DSPLY            TXTLEN
C...            ENDIF
C* NXT ADJUSTED BECAUSE TEXT HAS SHIFTED LEFT
C... END        ADD  1         NXT      20
C... 'NXT2'     DSPLY            NXT
C* Find end of the next word in text string
C... ' '        SCAN TEXT:NXT  END               01
C... 'END2'     DSPLY            END
C...            ENDDO
C... 'FINAL'    DSPLY            TEXT
```

The code above is a literal cavalcade of string operations with CAT, CHECK, CHEKR, SCAN, and SUBST all being used for their specific qualities in this operation to remove multiple blanks from text.

This routine is generic and thus, most of it can be copied into any program with field name modifications and be run against various data strings. Since we did not want to complicate the routine to include dealing with an apostrophe in text we did take poetic license on Marys as opposed to using the correct, Mary's.

The basic logic of the program is to continually isolate two parts of the big 45-byte text field, which contains the starting 44-character string of data. We call these parts, PART01 and PART02.

After the first loop, PART1 contains "Marys" and then "Marys address" with just one blank and then "Marys address is" and so on until the end position is calculated to be past the final character of text at which time the program ends and the FINAL text is perfect with just one blank in between each word.

To demonstrate that the code has been translated where appropriate, the results of the DSPLY operations are included below.

To follow the logic of this program completely, walking through the program along with the DSPLY operation results below should be quite revealing to the new RPG programmer.

```
DSPLY  TEXT1     Marys   Address  is 1432  Prill   Avenue
DSPLY  TXTLEN    44
DSPLY  TXTLEN    44
DSPLY  END1      6
DSPLY  NXT1      11
DSPLY  BLNKS     5
DSPLY  PART01    Marys
DSPLY  PART02    Address  is 1432  Prill   Avenue
DSPLY  TEXT2     Marys Address  is 1432  Prill   Avenue
DSPLY  TXTLN2    40
DSPLY  NXT2      7
DSPLY  END2      14
DSPLY  NXT1      16
DSPLY  BLNKS     2
DSPLY  PART01    Marys Address
DSPLY  PART02    is 1432  Prill   Avenue
DSPLY  TEXT2     Marys Address  is 1432  Prill   Avenue
DSPLY  TXTLN2    39
DSPLY  NXT2      15
DSPLY  END2      17
DSPLY  NXT1      18
DSPLY  BLNKS     1
DSPLY  NXT2      18
DSPLY  END2      22
DSPLY  NXT1      25
DSPLY  BLNKS     3
DSPLY  PART01    Marys Address is 1432
DSPLY  PART02    Prill   Avenue
DSPLY  TEXT2     Marys Address is 1432 Prill   Avenue
DSPLY  TXTLN2    37
DSPLY  NXT2      23
DSPLY  END2      28
DSPLY  NXT1      32
DSPLY  BLNKS     4
DSPLY  PART01    Marys Address is 1432 Prill
DSPLY  PART02    Avenue
DSPLY  TEXT2     Marys Address is 1432 Prill Avenue
DSPLY  TXTLN2    34
DSPLY  NXT2      29
DSPLY  END2      35
DSPLY  FINAL     Marys Address is 1432 Prill Avenue
```

Complex String Example 16: Check a Name for Valid Characters

Now, let's start with the string below and see what it takes to check a name for valid characters. The string for this example is as follows:

Beginning INPUT (4 characters)

```
Name  =  'TEXT'
Name  =  '*EXT'
Name  =  'T*XT'
```

```
I... 'ABCDEFGHIJKLMNOPQRST-C        TEST1
I... 'UVWXYZ'
I... 'ABCDEFGHIJKLMNOPQRST-C        TEST2
I... 'UVWXYZ$#&1234567890'
-----
C*  VALID CHARS
C*
C... VALCHR      BEGSR
C...            MOVEL'TEXT'     TXT01    4
C... 'TEXT'     DSPLY           TXT01
C* FIND LENGTH OF TXT01 (INPUT STRING)
C... ' '        CHEKRTXT01      TXTLEN
C... 'TXTLEN'   DSPLY           TXTLEN
C* CHECK 1ST POS OF NAME FOR VALID #1 CHAR
C... 1          SUBSTTXT01      POS1     1
C... 'POS1'     DSPLY           POS1
C... TEST1      CHECKPOS1...                  99
C* 99 = INVALID
C... 'IN99'     DSPLY           *IN99
C*
C... *IN99      IFEQ *OFF
C* If off,then 1ST Character is valid
C... TEST2      CHECKTXT01:2    POS2ND  20... 98
C... 'IN98'     DSPLY           *IN98
C... 'POS2ND'   DSPLY           POS2ND
C*
C* IS THE REST OF THE NAME VALID?
C* OR IS THE INVALID POSITION > THAN THE
C* LENGTH OF THE TEXT (TRAILING BLANKS)
C... *IN98      IFEQ *OFF
C... POS2ND     ORGT TXTLEN...    OR TEST OVER
C...            MOVEL'GOOD'     RESLT
C... 'RESULT1'  DSPLY           RESLT
C...            ELSE
C...            MOVEL'BAD'      RESLT    4 P
C... 'RESULT2'  DSPLY           RESLT
C...            ENDIF
C* FIRST CHARACTER IS INVALID
C...            ELSE
C...            MOVEL'BAD'      RESLT
C...            ELSE
C...            MOVEL'BAD'      RESLT
C... 'RESULT3'  DSPLY           RESLT
C...            ENDIF
C...            ENDSR
```

The code above is understandable with the comments included. It uses three string operations in trying to assure that all characters are valid in a set of text.

The first character of text must be a capital letter and so, the criteria (TEST1) used for the first character is different from that used for the second and subsequent characters (TEST2).

As a reminder, the CHECK operation does its job by verifying that each character in the base string as defined in Factor 2 (TXT01) is among the characters indicated in the comparator string as specified in Factor 1 using either TEST1 for the first character of text or TEST2 for the second and subsequent characters as shown in Factor 1.

Verification begins at the leftmost character of Factor 2 and continues character by character, from left to right. In this code, that is why there are just two CHECK operations. One is for the first character and the other is for the second and subsequent characters.

The "*" character was selected as the substitute to force an invalid hit. As you can see the first iteration with "TEXT" as TXT01 has no invalid characters. Since the "*" character is not in either comparator string (TEST1 or TEST2) it is invalid any place in the test.

The results of the code are shown below with three variations to show an invalid first, second, and subsequent character in the test.

The way this was accomplished was by changing one line of code and running the program again. The line of code changed and the variations are as follows:

```
C...        MOVEL'TEXT'  TXT01  4
C...        MOVEL'*EXT'  TXT01  4
C...        MOVEL'T*XT'  TXT01  4
C...        MOVEL'TE*T'  TXT01  4
```

Test 1 TEXT Results:

DSPLY	TEXT	TEXT
DSPLY	TXTLEN	4
DSPLY	POS1	T
DSPLY	IN99	0
DSPLY	IN98	0
DSPLY	POS2ND	0
DSPLY	RESULT1	GOOD

Test 2 *EXT Results:

DSPLY	TEXT	*EXT
DSPLY	TXTLEN	4
DSPLY	POS1	*
DSPLY	IN99	1
DSPLY	RESULT3	BAD

Test 3 TE*T Results:

DSPLY	TEXT	T*XT
DSPLY	TXTLEN	4
DSPLY	POS1	T
DSPLY	IN99	0
DSPLY	IN98	1
DSPLY	POS2ND	2
DSPLY	RESULT2	BAD

Test 4 TE*T Results:

DSPLY	TEXT	TE*T
DSPLY	TXTLEN	4
DSPLY	POS1	T
DSPLY	IN99	0

```
DSPLY    IN98     1
DSPLY    POS2ND   3
DSPLY    RESULT2  BAD
```

Arrays vs. String Ops Example 17: Combine First & Last Name

Now, let's start with the string below and see what it takes to translate all the leading zeros top blanks.. The string for this example is as follows:

Beginning INPUT (4 characters)

FIRST = CARL

LAST = LAFONG

```
E*  Array code first
E                     A1        30  1
I...   'CARL          '    C         FIRST
I...   'LAFONG        '    C         LAST
IDS1          DS
I...                          1   30 A1
I...                          1   30 NAME
C*
C...          MOVE *BLANKS   NAME
C*  Load first name into NAME array
C...          MOVEAFIRST     A1
C...          Z-ADD1         X
C... A1,X     DOUEQ' '       X
C* FIND END OF FIRST NAME ' ' stored as X
C...          ENDDO
C* Add 1 to X for first letter last name
C...          ADD  1         X
C* Load LAST name after blank separator
C...          MOVEALAST      A1,X
C*            ...       ETC            ...
C*  CODE FINDS BLANK AFTER FIRST NAME
C*  LOOP INCREMENTS X AFTER LOCATING THE
C*  SPACE ALLOWING A BLANK TO SEPARATE THE
C*  FIRST NAME FROM THE LAST
C*

I*  String code second
I*  THE BELOW CODE SHOWS HOW CRAFTY AND
I*  CODE EFFICIENT ONE CAN BE WITH THE RPG
I*  OP-CODES FOR STRING MANIPULATION
I*
I...   'CARL          '    C         FIRST
I...   'LAFONG        '    C         LAST
C... FIRST     CAT  LAST:1    NAME    30
C*
C*  This operation simply concatenates
C*  the LAST name to the FIRST
C*  WITH 1 BLANK SEPARATING THEM
C* ------------------------------------------
```

The comments in the code above makes the code self explanatory. Both the array version and the string version perform the same function.

We began this chapter with a thorough look at the use of arrays to perform string operations and so it is fitting that we end this way. As you can see, the simple CONCAT RPG string operation can save a tremendous amount of coding when used instead of array processing.

Arrays vs. String Operations Example 18:
Separate / Reverse First & Last Name

Now, let's start with the string below and see what it takes to translate all the leading zeros top blanks.. The string for this example is as follows:

Beginning CNAM (20 characters)

CNAM =   'CARL LAFONG   '

```
E...                      A1          15 1
E...                      A2          15 1
I...    'CARL LAFONG         'C        CNAM
C...    ARRSTR    BEGSR
C...              MOVE *BLANKS  NAM1
C...              MOVE *BLANKS  NAM2
C* LOAD FULL NAME INTO A1
C...              MOVEACNAM     A1
C...              MOVELCNAM     DNAME  30
C...    'CNAME'   DSPLY         DNAME
C...              Z-ADD1        X
C* PRIME INDX TO 1
C...    A1,X      DOUEQ' '
C* FIND BLANK AFTER ENDING L IN CARL
C...              MOVE A1,X     A2,X

C...              ADD  1        X
C...              ENDDO
C...              MOVEAA2       NAM1   15
C...    'FIRST'   DSPLY         NAM1
C*  ABOVE CODE FINDS BLANK AFTER FIRST NAME
C*  AT THIS POINT ARRAY A2 CONTAINS THE
C*  FIRST NAME SO IT IS MOVED TO NAM1
C*  (FIRST NAME IS FOUND AND STORED in NAM1
C* -------------------------------------
C*
C* FIND BEGINNING of LAST NAME (Non BLANK)
C...    A1,X      DOUNE' '
C...    'X '      DSPLY         X
C...    'A1,X'    DSPLY         A1,X
C...              ADD  1        X
C...              ENDDO
C*  THE ABOVE LOOP INCREMENTS X AFTER
C*  LOCATING THE SPACE SEPARATING
C*  THE FIRST NAME FROM THE LAST.
C*
C...              MOVEAA1,X     NAM2   15
C*  Above MOVEs LASTNAME FROM ARRAY TO NAM2
C*  THE SECOND DO LOOP ABOVE CONTINUES
C*  SEARCHESING THE A1 ARRAY LOOKING FOR
C*  THE FIRST CHARACTER OF THE LAST NAME,
C*  SINCE THERE MAY BE MORE THAN ONE BLANK
C*  SEPARATING THE NAMES
C*  UPON LOCATING THE 1ST CHARACTER OF THE
C*  LAST NAME, THE X INDEX IS USED ON THE
```

```
C*    MOVEA,X TO DIRECT THE MOVE OPERATION
C*    TO BEGIN WITH THE XTH CHARACTER, WHICH
C*    IS THE 1ST CHAR OF THE LAST NAME, AND
C*    THEN TO LEFT JUSTIFY IT IN THE FIELD
C*    CALLED NAM2
C...     'LAST'      DSPLY           NAM2
C*           ...           ETC                   ...
C*    LAST AT X     *
C*
----------------------

C*    String Version
C*
C*    BELOW CODE SHOWS HOW CRAFTY AND CODE
C*    EFFICIENT ONE CAN BE WITH THE NEW OP-
C*    CODES FOR STRING MANIPULATION
C*
C*
C*    1.  SCAN THE NAME FIELD LOOKING FOR
C*    THE POSITION OF THE FIRST BLANK.
C...               MOVELCNAM       CNM1   20
C...     'NAME'    DSPLY           CNM1
C...     ' '       SCAN CNAM       BLK1   30
C...     'BLK1'    DSPLY           BLK1
C*    2.   USE THE POSITION HELD IN BLK1 TO
C*      SPECIFY THE LENGTH OF THE 1ST NAME TO
C*    THE SUBSTRING OP-CODE.   THE END RESULT
C*    OF THE SUBST IS TO CAPTURE FIRST NAME
C...     BLK1      SUBSTCNAM       NAM01  16 P
C...     'FIRST'   DSPLY           NAM01
C*    3.   CHECK THE NAME FIELD STARTING WITH
C*    THE FIRST BLANK AFTER FIRST NAME TO
C*      DETERMINE WHERE THE LAST NAME BEGINS
C*    THIS ALLOWS FOR MULTIPLE BLANKS
C*      BETWEEN 1ST & LAST NAMES
C...     ' '       CHECKCNAM:BLK1 BLNM    20
C*    4.   SUBTRACT THE BEGIN POSITION OF THE
C*    LAST NAME (BLNM) FROM
C*    THE LENGTH OF THE NAME FIELD (20) TO
C*    DETERMINE THE LENGTH OF THE REMAINING
C*    STRING TO BE "MOVED" TO NAM02 LAST
C...     20        SUB  BLNM       LENNM  20
C...     'LEN'     DSPLY           LENNM
C*
C*    5.   SUBSTRING THE NAME FIELD TO
C*    COLLECT LAST NAME BY SPECIFYING THE
C*    CALCULATED LENGTH OF LONGEST POSSIBLE
C*    LAST NAME IN FACTOR1. USE THE BEGIN
C*    POSITION OF THELAST NAME (BLNM FIELD)
C*    AS THE STARTING POINT FOR THE
C*    SUBSTRING TO BEGIN "MOVING" DATA FROM
C*    THE NAME FIELD
C*    (NAME:BLNM  IN FACTOR2 OF SUBST).
C*    THE REST OF NAME LEFT JUSTIFIED IS
C*    CONSEQUENTLY STORED IN NAM02
C*
C...     LENNM     SUBSTCNAM:BLNM NAM02   16 P
C...     'LAST'    DSPLY           NAM02
C*
C* -----------------------------------------
```

The comments in the code above makes the code self explanatory. Both the array version and the string version perform the same function.

We began this chapter with a thorough look at the use of arrays to perform string operations and so it is fitting that we end the chapter once again by showing how powerful the string operators are compared to all of the work necessary with arrays. As you can see, the use of the string operations saves a tremendous amount of coding when used instead of array processing.

To demonstrate that both sets of code (arrays and strings) has accomplished the name capture mission, the results of both sets of the DSPLY operations are included below, separated by a blank line:

Array Processing
DSPLY CNAME CARL LAFONG
DSPLY FIRST   CARL
DSPLY X   5
DSPLY A1,X
DSPLY LAST   LAFONG

String Processing
DSPLY NAME   CARL LAFONG
DSPLY BLK1   5
DSPLY FIRST   CARL
DSPLY LEN   14
DSPLY LAST   LAFONG

RPGIV for String Manipulation

The examples in this chapter are all portable to RPGIV using the CVTRPGSRC command as previously described. You can also perform string manipulation using RPGIV BIFS with EVAL type op-codes or with /Free form text. Many of the experts who lead the RPGIV revolution would tell you not to use anything other than function available in BIFS and free form when the facility is also implemented using these more "modern" techniques.

I do not necessarily share this recommendation in all cases. That is a topic for you to pursue as you become an expert in RPG. If you like BIFS, there once was an inexpensive product on the Web that implements the center text and some other string manipulation facilities with black-box RPGIV BIFS. It was Called COOLBIFs at www.jcasi.com/coolbifs.htm. I can no longer find it but things like this do exist. Here are some places to go for more information and sample BIFS"

http://www.itjungle.com/fhg/fhg022509-story01.html
http://www.mcpressonline.com/programming/rpg/use-string-manipulation-built-in-functions-to-process-external-files.html
https://publib.boulder.ibm.com/iseries/v5r2/ic2924/books/x091315219.htm
https://publib.boulder.ibm.com/iseries/v5r2/ic2924/books/c092508429.htm
http://www.mcpressonline.com/programming/rpg/use-rpg-string-manipulation-built-in-functions-to-remove-spaces.html

Since this book teaches you to use all flavors of RPG so that you can both develop and maintain both the RPG/400 style and the RPGIV style of programming, we have included the string manipulation facilities available in both languages in this chapter.

BIFS and /Free form RPG are RPGIV only topics.

Chapter Summary

String processing is one of the more recent additions to the RPGIII part of the RPG/400 language. The same facilities are available in RPGIV operations as well as BIFS.

A string is series of characters and as such it can also be called a character string. Strings are typically of variable length. RPG Strings, however, are fixed length fields with variable length contents padded with blanks.

The basic string handling functions that are found in RPG include the following:

- ✓ Define/ Create a string and give it a value.
- ✓ Extract a substring from another string
- ✓ Concatenate two strings to form a new string
- ✓ Compare two Strings
- ✓ Search within string for substring
- ✓ Determine the length of a string
- ✓ Assign the value of a string to another string

As we progressed through this chapter from handling strings processing with arrays to basic string operations, we described with examples how basic string operations could be combined to form complex string operations that could perform the following functions:

- ✓ Center a string of text within a field
- ✓ Left Justify a string of text within a field
- ✓ Delete a substring of text within a field
- ✓ Replace a substring of text with another string
- ✓ Insert a string of text into another string
- ✓ Return a substring that is composed of only the valid characters in a given pattern
- ✓ Verify that a string consists of only valid characters
- ✓ Translate a string (such as upper case to lower case)

Many examples were used throughout this chapter to demonstrated how these functions could be accomplished using arrays, as well as simple and complex string handling techniques using the six RPG/400, RPGIV string op-codes as shown below:

- ✓ CAT   Concatenate 2 Strings
- ✓ SCAN   Scan a String for a match
- ✓ SUBST   Substring.. Separate parts of a string
- ✓ CHECK   Search for a non-match, left to right
- ✓ CHEKR   Search for a non-match, right to left
- ✓ XLATE   Translate one string into another

Key Chapter Terms

Adv String functions	COOLBIFs	Return a substring
Alternating table	Copy	SCAN
ANDxx	CVTRPGSRC	Search
Array	Database	SELEC
BIFS	Date field	SNOBOL
CASE	Delete	Special characters
CAT	Extract	String
Center a Line	GET	String handling
Center a string	GOTO	Subscript
Character string	Housekeeping	SUBST
CHECK operation	Insert a string	Substring
CHECKR operation	Loop	Text based
CHEKR operation	Move	Text manipulation
COMP	MOVEA	Translate a string

Complex string	MOVEL	Valid characters
Concatenate	Operation extenders	Variable length
Constant subscripts	Prim string handlng	Variable subscript
Control break	Replace a substring	XLATE

Review Questions

1. What is a string?

2. What are the attributes of a string in RPG?

3 - 9. Match the RPG implementation with the string function?

String Function	RPG Implementation
3. Define/ Create a string and give it a value.	A. RPG uses IFxx, WHxx, COMP, CASxx, ANDxx, ORxx, CABxx . Same in RPGIV plus EVAL and BIFs.
4. Extract a substring from another string	B. RPG uses field or subfield definition; subfield initialization, MOVE, MOVEL, Z-ADD
5. Concatenate two strings to form a new string	C. RPG uses MOVE, MOVEL, MOVEA. EVAL is often used in RPGIV.
6. Compare Two Strings	D5. RPG uses manual array loops, SCAN op-code. Same in RPGIV
7. Search within a string for a substring	E. RPG uses manual array loops, SUBST op-code. Same in RPGIV
8. Determine the length of a string	F. RPG uses manual array loops, CHEKR op-code. CHECKR is the replace operation in RPGIV
9. Assign the value of a string to another string	G. RPG uses manual array loops, MOVE, MOVEL, MOVEA, CAT op-code. Same in RPGIV plus EVAL.

10- 17. Describe the array or string examples to handle each of the following types of operations:
10. Center a string of text in a field
11. Left Justify a string of text in a field
12. Delete a substring of text in a field
13. Replace a substring of text with another string
14. Insert a string of text into another string
15. Return a substring that is composed of only the valid characters in a given pattern
16. Verify that a string consists of only valid characters
17. Translate a string (such as upper case to lower case)

Chapter 19   RPG/400 & RPGIV Structured Programming

What is Structured Programming?

A program, of course, is simply a set of computer instructions to get a job done. Programming then is the writing of those tasks, entering them into the machine, compiling and testing them and getting them to work.

So far in this book, we have been doing a lot of unstructured programming (antonym of structured programming) or at least programming that has not been markedly or intentionally structured. It's like driving a car. You first learn how to manipulate the vehicle and then you learn how to drive according to the rules. It's time for some rules.

What exactly does structured mean?

Dictionary.com presents three generic definitions which apply. They are as follows:

1. Something made up of a number of parts that are held or put together in a particular way: hierarchical social structure.
2. The way in which parts are arranged or put together to form a whole; makeup: triangular in structure.
3. The interrelation or arrangement of parts in a complex entity: political structure; plot structure.

With structure then, there is implied order. The General Services Administration, Federal Standard 1037C suggests that structured programming is defined as follows:

Structured programming: A technique for organizing and coding computer programs in which a hierarchy of modules is used, each having a single entry and a single exit point, and in which control is passed downward through the structure without unconditional branches to higher levels of the structure. Three types of control flow are used: sequential, test, and iteration.

This is a very good definition though a bit involved for the neophyte RPG programmer. Wikipedia has a very simple definition:

Structured programming can be seen as a subset or subdiscipline of procedural programming, one of the major programming paradigms. It is most famous for removing or reducing reliance on the GOTO statement (also known as "go to.")

The notion of no "GOTO" statements is at the heart of the Wikipedia definition and in many ways it captures the essence of structured programming. GOTOs inevitably produce spaghetti code, which is another term for unstructured code. Such code goes anywhere in the program and comes from anywhere and it is very difficult to follow and thus it is difficult to maintain. Moreover, because of its lack of structure it is prone to error.

Some of the topics that we will cover in this chapter along with their relative sequence are shown below.

   ✓ Why Structured Programming
   ✓ Implementing Structured Programming
   ✓ RPG Structured Programming
   ✓ Miscellaneous Operations
   ✓ RPG Structured Enhancements

Why Structured Programming?

In examining the straight definition of structured programming we have already hit on a number of the advantages of structured programming. Most experts aggress that the following three benefits are always included when a shift to structured programming occurs:

- ✓ Effective Program Development
- ✓ Easier Program Maintenance
- ✓ Improved Program Efficiency

Effective Program Development

Effective program development is achieved by the following:

- ✓ Structured Logic
- ✓ Functional Pieces
- ✓ Easier Debugging
- ✓ Better Communication
- ✓ Programmer Productivity

Easier Program Maintenance

Easier program maintenance is achieved by a number of factors including readability and flexibility.

Readability

When developing structured code, the programmer can read the code already written more easily than unstructured code and thus can apply new code more efficiently. The major readability benefit comes in the maintenance of code.

Working with code that has an expected structure helps the programmer who has not written the code or the programmer who wrote the code years ago to better understand what the code is trying to do.

Flexibility

Because the code is more easily readable and understandable, programmers have more flexibility when adding new code or when dissecting chunks of logic to create a more efficiently running or operating program.

Improved Program Efficiency

Improved program efficiency is delivered in many ways. Structured programming typically reduces the size of the program thereby conserving system resources. Since the programmer is smaller, it is less to carry around and it reduces the virtual paging overhead.

Additionally, because it is structured instead of all over the place, the chance for a branch to be satisfied without a page refresh is higher thereby increasing the efficiency of virtualization. Overall, such efficiency saves processing time which causes jobs to finish faster or for more work to be absorbed in the same time period.

Back when the System/38 was announced RPG programmers quickly learned that the idea of a multifunction structured program, though productive to write, because of memory constraints was not productive to run. Then, as memory became less expensive and more available, rather than split logic into multiple programs, IBM recommended building these large programs again.

Today, with ILE, it is most often better to build service programs with which other programs can gain efficient function without bundling it all together in the same program. ILE is examined in Chapter 25.

So, if you have seen with the IBM i on Power Systems for some time, you would have seen these various paradigms. The big approach was preferred, then not preferred, and now again preferred but with module separation in ILE.

When you address performance issues or efficiency on programming some of the things you like to do are included in the following list:

- ✓ Reduce the # of open files
- ✓ Decrease the size of job
- ✓ Save Processing Time

To achieve this, the program must be properly structured. In some cases it may be appropriate to have similar function be coded in several programs but the extra program maintenance load caused by extra modules does prompt programmers to try to use the idea of a service program, not many modules in many programs to achieve this end.

When coding for a multifunction, structured program, some of the steps to take to make the code even more efficient are included in the list below:

1. Files: Open by sequence of usage

2. Code: Write top down code with the primary functions on top. Use structured operations and structure your inline routines so that the most used are closest to the top of the program. This may reduce unnecessary program paging in virtual systems.

3. Subroutines: Sequence in the program by usage which gives more opportunity for code block to be resident

Control Logic Structures

The three control logic structures and their uses are described in the following short list:

- ✓ Sequence -- simple sequence of functions
- ✓ Selection -- selection of function path
- ✓ Iteration – structured loop control

Implementing Structured Programming

Today all programming languages have structured operations. In fact, RPG was one of the last languages to be equipped with structured operations more than twenty years ago. Table 19-1 shows the standard structured figures and the RPG operations that implement the figures. Let's look at these one at a time

Table 19-1 Structured Programming Figures & RPG Operations

Structured Programming Figures	RPG Structured Operations
Sequence	ADD, MULT, EXSR
If Then Else	IFXX, ELSE, ENDIF
CASE	CASEQ, CAS, ENDCAS
Iteration -- Do While	DOWXX, ENDDO
Iteration -- Do Until	DOUXX, ENDDO
Iteration – Do	DO
Leave Do Loop	LEAVE
Next iteration	ITER

Sequence

Sequence merely suggests that operations are performed in sequence from top to bottom in the program. There is nothing special about this. Thus it would be implemented by the stacking of these operations:

ADD
SUB
MULT

If Then Else

"If Then Else" is implemented primarily with the IFxx statement in which xx is greater than (GT), less than(LT), equal(EQ), not equal (NE), greater than or equal (GE) or less than or equal (LE). The ELSE verb is also implemented as well as an ELSEIF in RPGIV.

When an IFxx statement is invoked, there are always at least three statements involved in the group. The code between the IFxx and ELSE or the ELSE and the END execute as a group.

An else is an optional element, thus there will always be (1) an IF at the beginning, (2) at least one line of functional RPG code that is not a structured operation, and (3) and ENDIF operation.

There are various forms of the END operation. The RPG developers have helped the user community over the years by permitting different END statements though all END statements basically perform the same group ending function.

The fact is that an END by any other name is still an end. The END possibilities are listed below

✓ END   End all structured groups
✓ ENDCS   End CASE groups
✓ ENDDO   End Do groups
✓ ENDIF   End If groups
✓ ENDSL   End Select groups

If statements can be structured in many different combinations. For example, IF statements can be "nested" within other IF statements. Additionally, complex conditions can be specified using ANDxx or ORxx and ELSE as you can see in the snippet below:

```
C...    BALOWE  IFGT       400
C...    X       ANDLE      10
C...            MOVE       NAME        ARR,X
C...            ADD        1           X
C...            ELSE
C...            MOVE       NAME        SAVE1
C...            ENDIF
```

The IFxx operation allows the processing of a group of calculations one or more times based on the results of comparing factor 1 and factor 2. In therefore, the above code reads as follows: If balance owed is greater than 400 and X is less than or equal to 10, move name into ARR,X and add 1 to X, but if the condition specified by the IF / AND is not true, move NAME into SAVE1 and end the IF group.

So, as you have now seen, if the expanded condition (AND / OR) is true then the calculations between the IF and the ELSE are executed. If the condition is not true, then the calculations between the ELSE and the END or ENDIF are executed. It helps to remember that there is an associated END for every IF.

The above code also showed us that IF statements may be combined and this next block of code will show that they can be nested into very complex conditions. The use of AND or OR operations allows for even more complex conditions. Let's look at a few other IF code snippets as examples:

```
C* IF Shell Code Example 1
C...        FACT1   IFXX       FACT2
C...                . . .
C...                . . .
C...                . . .
C...                ELSE
C                   . . .
C*                  END   (only one end)
C                   ENDIF


C* IF Shell Code Example 2
C       FACT1   IFEQ       FACT2
C               . . .
C               EXSR       SUBREQ
C* Above processed if equal
C               . . .
C               ELSE
C               . . .
C               EXSR       SUBRNE
C* Above EXSR processed if not equal
C               . . .
C* Above block processed if not equal
C               ENDIF



C* IF Shell Code Example 3
C     FACT1   IFEQ    FACT2       IF#1
C     FACT3   IFGT    FACT4       IF#2
C             EXSR    SUBR01      IF#2 Part1
```

```
C            ELSE                     IF#2 Part2
C    FACT5   IFEQ    100              IF#3
C            EXSR    SUBR02           IF#3 Part1
C            ELSE                     IF#3 Part2
C            EXSR    SUBR03           IF#3 Part2
C            ENDIF                    End of IF#3
C            ENDIF                    End of IF#2
C            ELSE                     IF#1 Part2
C    FACT6   IFEQ    50               IF#4
C            EXSR    SUBR04           IF#4 Part1
C            ELSE                     IF#4 Part2
C            EXSR    SUBR02           IF#4 Part2
C            ENDIF                    End of IF#4
C            ENDIF                    End of IF#1
```

Here is another complex snippet with ORs and ANDs mixed in:

```
C...       FLD1    IFEQ    FLD2
C...       FLD3    ANDGT   FLDD
C...       FLDE    OREQ    100
C...               EXSR    SUBR01
C...               ELSE
C...               EXSR    SUBR02
C...               ENDIF
```

This code reads as follows: If FLD1 is equal to FLD2 and FLD3 is greater than FLDD execute subroutine SUBR01. Regardless of whether the above is true or not, test Field E to see if it is equal to 100 and if it is, execute SUBR01. If none of the above are true then execute subroutine SUBR02. and end the IF group.

Select Groups - SELEC - WHXX- OTHER

The SELEC operation begins a selection grouping. The "select group" conditionally processes one of several alternative sequences of operations. It works with the WHxx (When true then select) group operation, and optionally with the OTHER (otherwise select) group operation.

Like all structured operations, a SELEC group ends with an ENDSL or END statement. The SELEC packaging consists of the SELEC statement, zero or more groups, an optional OTHER group, and the requisite ENDSL or generic END statement.

It works like this: When the SELEC operation is processed, control passes to the statement following the first WHxx condition that is satisfied. WHxx is also structured in group form but each WHxx ends its influence when it reaches the next WHxx statement.

In other words, all statements within the WHxx group are then executed until the next WHxx operation. Control then passes to the ENDSL statement. If no WHxx condition is satisfied and an OTHER action is specified, control passes to the statement following the OTHER operation.

If no WHxx condition is satisfied and no OTHER operation is specified, control transfers to the statement following the ENDSL operation of the select group. There are no operands (Factor 1, Factor2, or Result) in this operation.

The **"When True Then Select"** (WHxx) operations make up the logic in a select group. They determine to where in the program control passes after the "SELEC (Begin a Select Group)" operation is processed.

The WHxx conditional operation is true if factor 1 and factor 2 have the relationship specified by xx. If the condition is true, the operations following the WHxx are processed until the next WHxx, OTHER, ENDSL, or END statement is encountered.

The **"Otherwise Select"** or (OTHER) operation begins the sequence of operations to be processed if no WHxx condition is satisfied in a SELEC group. The sequence ends with the ENDSL or END operation.

See SELEC and WHxx operations above. Just like the WHxx operations, there are no operands (Factor 1, Factor2, or Result). The following snippet shows how the SELEC group functions:

```
C...                 SELEC
C...      FACT1      WHXX      FACT2
C...                 . . .
C...      FACT1      WHXX      FACT3
C...                 . . .
C...                 OTHER
C...                 . . .
C...                 ENDSL
```

The above snippet reads as follows: Select the group of code that is true when Fact 1 (SAY XX is equal) is equal to FACT2. If first WHxx not satisfied keep going. If none are satisfied, run the set of code that follows the OTHE ((otherwise select) and end the Select group.

Here is another SELEC snippet:

```
C...                 SELEC
C...      PAYYTD     WHGE      75000
C...                 ADD       20          BONUS   20
C...      PAYYTD     WHGE      50000
C...                 ADD       15          BONUS
C...      PAYYTD     WHGE      25000
C...                 ADD       10          BONUS
C...                 OTHER
C...                 ADD 5                 BONUS
C...                 ENDSL
```

This reads as follows: Select the group of code starting with ADD 20 when PAYYTD is greater than or equal to 75000. If this group is not true select the next group (ADD 15) when PAYYTD is greater or equal than 50,000.

If this group condition is not true then select the group of code starting with ADD 10 whenever the PAYYTD is greater or equal to 25000. If none of the above tests are true, then (otherwise) run the OTJER group of code and add 5 to the BONUS and end the select group.

That about does it for SELEC. Now, let's move to the CASE operator

Conditionally Invoke Subroutine on Compare (CASE)

One of the implementations of structured programming in RPG/400 is the use of CASE. Case structure allows a subroutine to be conditionally
selected for processing based on the relationship between Factor 1 and Factor 2.

CASxx stands for **Conditionally Invoke Subroutine on Compare.** It is very similar to the CABXX operations. Instead of a straight GOTO like branch, a specified subroutine is invoked if the conditions are met.

This operation allows you to conditionally select a subroutine for processing. The CAS with no relationship is the same as an unconditional execute subroutine.

The selection is based on the relationship between Factor 1 and Factor 2, as specified by the "xx" portion of the op-code.. If the relationship denoted by xx exists (true) between Factor 1 and Factor 2, the subroutine specified in the result field is processed. The Result field is subroutine name

The following CASE snippets drive home the facility presented with this powerful structured operation.

```
C* CASE Example 1
C...    BALOWE CASGE     400        SUBR1
C...    BALOWE CASLT     300        SUBR2
C...           CAS                  SUBR3
C...           ENDCS
----------------
C...    SUBR1  BEGSR
C...           etc.
```

Unlike the SELEC operation, there is no group header. Instead, the first CASxx operation begins the group. The CASxx operations work together as a group. However if one is true and the subroutine is executed, none of the others are tested or executed.

In this example, if balance owed is greater or equal to 400, the programs runs SUBR1 and then passes to the instruction after ENCCS. If it is not true, the next case is tested. If it is true, SUBR2 is executed and control is passed to the instruction after the ENDCS. If none are true, the third CAS statement executes unconditionally and fires off SUBR3 after which control is passed to the statement following ENDCS.

The result field is the subroutine name that will be processed if the relationship is true. Thus CASE performs similar function of comparing values, setting conditions and then exiting to a subroutine. CASE example 2 below is as readable as example 1. The ellipses in the op-code area indicate that there are quite a number of cases prior to the unconditional CAS operation. Example 3 is the generic equivalent of the prior two examples and it shows the CASE operations in their most simple form.

```
C* CASE Example 2
C...    TRANID CASEQ 'A'       SUBRA
C...    TRANID CASEQ 'B'       SUBRB
C...           . . .
C...           . . .
C...           CAS             SUBNOK
C...           ENDCS .
```

```
C* CASE Generic Example 3
C...    FACT1   CASXX      FACT2      SUBR1
C...            . . .
C...            CAS                   SUBRX
C...            ENDCS
```

In the next example, a number of cases, A through Z are tested. If true a subroutine that starts with SUBR concatenated with the letter of the case is executed and the code passes to the statement following the ENDCS. If none are selected (CODE is not upper case alphabetic) the CAS operation is taken and SUBRSM is taken prior to exiting the CASE group.

This example also shows a snippet of the three subroutines tested above to better demonstrate how this actually happens in the program. The subroutines are in a completely separate section of the program as depicted by the dash lines separating them from the CASE code.

```
C* CASE Big Example 4
C...            . . .
C...    CODE    CASEQ      'Y'        SUBRY
C...    CODE    CASEQ      'Z'        SUBRZ
C...            CAS                   SUBRSM
C...            ENDCS
C...            . . .

C...            . . .
C...            . . .
-----------------
C...    SUBRY   BEGSR
C...            . . .
C...            ENDSR
-----------------
C...    SUBRZ   BEGSR
C...            . . .
C...            ENDSR
-----------------
C...    SUBRSM  BEGSR
C...            . . .
C...            ENDSR
```

The following subroutines get executed in a particular case:

```
SUBRY     Performed when code = "Y"
SUBRZ     Performed when code = "Z"
SUBRSM    default case - performed
          when neither of the above are true.
```

Iteration Do While / Do Until / Do

Do loops are very handy operations. The basic DO loop had its origins in the FORTRAN language, one of the first if not the first high level programming languages. The Do While and Do Until variants of the Do operation came later to help programmers more easily write structured code.

Another structured programming implementation in RPG/400 and RPGIV is the use of DO type logic. This is done with the DO, DOWxx, and DOUxx operation codes.

Do While DOWxx

The DOWxx, operation tests the xx relationship between Factor 1 and Factor 2 and executes the code in between the DOWxx and the END or ENDDO one or more times while the condition is satisfied. The xx of course is replaced by GT, LT, EQ, NE, GE or LE in the actual operation.

The primary purpose is to execute a block of code repetitively while a particular condition is true. The comparison is made prior to execution of the code between DOWxx and an associated END or ENDDO statement marking the end of the group. The notion of when the comparison is made is important in trying to figure out how many iterations a DO While may travel.

Complex conditions can be specified using ANDxx or ORxx. The loop ends when comparison on DOWxx is false or when conditioning indicators on DOWxx or on ENDDO are not satisfied. You can ANDxx or ORxx more complex conditions in order to attain the desired function.

The group or block of code is executed while the condition is true and as noted, that condition is determined PRIOR to execution of the group of code. The Do While loop ends when the condition is no longer true.

In the example below, the calculations between the DOWLE and the ENDDO will be performed WHILE X is less than or equal to 10. When X has a value greater than 10, the condition is not met and the calculations are not performed.

```
C...                Z-ADD     1         X
C...       X        DOWLE     10
C...       ARR,X    COMP      0                   10
C... 10             ADD       ARR,X     TOT
C...                ADD       1         X
C...                ENDDO
```

Do Until DOUxx

Do until and Do while are basically the same operation other than the point of view. Just about everything said about Do while can be said about Do until other than when the test is made. Unlike the DOWxx, the Do until comparison is made after execution of the group of code between DOUxx and ENDDO. DOUxx, uses the same xx values, GT, LT, EQ, NE, GE or LE based on the relationship of Factor 1 and Factor 2.

Like DOWxx, DOUxx is used execute a block of code repetitively Complex conditions can be specified using ANDxx or ORxx. The loop ends when comparison on DOUxx is true or when conditioning indicators on DOUxx or END (ENDDO) are satisfied

DOUxx begins a group of operations you want to process more than once (but always at least once). DOWxx may not process any in the group since the test is done prior. An associated END (DO) marks the end of the group.

In the below example, (Example 2) the first example shows the two Dos, While and Until on top of each other in a loop within a loop scenario, The second example (Example 3) is structured so the code between DOUGT and ENDDO will be executed at least once and continue executing until X is greater than 10.

```
C* DO While / Until Generic Example 2
C...      FACT1   DOUXX      FACT2
C...      FACT1   DOWXX      FACT2
C...              . . .
C...              . . .
C...              ENDDO
C...              ENDDO
```

   XX = GT, LT, EQ, NE, GE, LE

```
C* DO Until Example 3
C...              Z-ADD    1        X
C...      X       DOUGT    10               EQ
C...      ARR,X   COMP     0                10
C...N10           ADD      ARR,X   TOTAL
C...              ADD      1        X
C...              END
```

Do Groups DO

Do groups are used to repeat a block of code a fixed number of times. There is no comparison other than against an indexing value that keeps track of how many times the loop has been executed. The DO loop has a number of rules that are easy to learn and that are just as easy to forget so the more times you see these rules the better:

- ✓ Factor 1 is starting value, default is 1
- ✓ Factor 2 is limiting value, default is 1
- ✓ Field name in result field contains current index value
- ✓ Loop ends when limit exceeded or conditioning indicators on DO or END not satisfied

In summary, the DO operation allows the processing of a group of calculations one or more times starting with the value in Factor 1   incrementing each time through the loop by a value on the associated END operation or 1 if none specified on END, until the limit, specified in Factor 2 is reached.

The DO loop capabilities in RPG and RPGIV are very similar to those in all other languages. However, the format is substantially different. The DO operation itself begins the group of operations you want to process a fixed number of times. If you do not specify an index field, RPG/400 generates one for internal use.

In the first example below (Example 4), DO operations will perform 10 times, starting with a value of 1, incrementing each time by 1, until the loop has been done 10 times. In the second example (Example 5), the DO operation will be done only once. The default values are all taken in which the starting value is 1, the increment is 1, and the number of times is 1.

```
C*.....DO Example 4
C...      1       DO      10      X
C...      ARR,X COMP     0                    10=
C... N10...      ADD     ARR,X TOTAL
C...            ENDDO     1


C*.....DO Example 5 below
C...15...        DO
C...            MOVE    NAME    NAME1
C...            MOVE    CITY    CITY1
C...            ADD     1       NUM1
C...    FACT1   COMP    FACT2                 15=
C...            END     1
```

Above loop executes 1 time.
What if factor 2 of the DO were 100? (100 times)

```
C* Do While Example 6 with
C* Indicators as fields
C...   *IN65  DOWEQ     '1'
C...           . . .
C...          EXFMT     SCREEN1
C...           . . .
C...          ENDDO
```
Above DO loop performed while indicator 65 is on

```
C* Do While Example 7
C* Do While with Indicators as
C* fields, figurative constants
C...   *IN65  DOWEQ     *ON'
C...           . . .
C...          EXFMT     SCREEN1
C...           . . .
C...          ENDDO
```
Same as above using figurative constant.

```
C* Do Until Example 8 with
C* Indicators as fields
C              *IN65  DOUEQ     '0'
C                      . . .
C                     EXFMT     SCREEN2
C                      . . .
C                     ENDDO
```
Above DO loop is performed until indicator 65 is off.

```
C* Do Until Example 9
C* Do Until with Indicators as
C* fields,  figurative constants
C...     *IN65   DOUEQ     *OFF
C...             . . .
C...             EXFMT     SCREEN2
C...             . . .
C...             ENDDO
```

Same as above using figurative constant

Do Loop Leave Option (LEAVE)

The LEAVE operation in a DO loop of any kind causes an immediate "ejection" from the loop and the control is passed to the instruction following the ENDDO in the loop in which the LEAVE was executed. There are times within a DO loop that a condition occurs that would make it best for no more instructions in the loop should be executed.

The LEAVE operation is perfect for this situation. The sample code below shows the LEAVE conditioned by an IFxx group.

```
C* Leave causes the control to Leave
C...     *IN65   DOXXX     *OFF
C...             . . .
C...     *IN23   IFEQ      *ON
C...             LEAVE
C...             ENDIF
C...             . . .
C...             ENDDO
```

LEAVE takes leave of the do loop and goes to the statement following the ENDDO

Do Loop Iterate Option (ITER)

The ITER operation in a DO loop of any kind causes an immediate end of that particular iteration of the loop and control is passed to the ENDDO operation within that loop. In other words, it bypasses the rest of the code to get to the end of the loop.

Then based on whether loop conditions are satisfied, it moves out of the loop or back for another iteration. The sample code below shows the use of ITERi

```
C...     *IN65   DOXXX     '1'
C...             . . .
C...             ITER
C...             . . .
C...             ENDIF
C...             . . .
C...             ENDDO
```

"Structured" Misc. Operations – CABXX

At the same time that the structured operations first appeared in RPG, the Compare and Branch on condition xx was also introduced. The operation looks like CABxx in which xx is GT, LT, EQ, NE, GE or LE. The operation is very efficient in that it replaces a COMP operation and a conditioned GOTO.

In just one operation this op-code performs the comparison and branches to a TAG specified in the Result Field if the comparison is true. The sample line of code below demonstrates a comparison to see if BALOWE is greater than 400 and if it is, the program makes the next instruction be the executable line after the tag, named TAG1.

```
BALOWE CABGT      400           TAG1
```

ThE CABxx operations provide another set of op-codes that allows for easier implementation of comparing and then branching to calculations based upon the results of the compare. Technically, it is not a structured operation but it came out with the RPG structured operations and has typically been presented with them. It certainly is an efficient operation.

The CABxx operation compares Factor 1 and Factor 2. If the comparison condition is true, the program branches to the TAG operation associated with the label specified in the result field. Otherwise the program continues with the next process-able operation in the sequence.

Chapter Summary

Three benefits derived from structured programming are as follows:

- ✓ Effective Program Development
- ✓ Easier Program Maintenance
- ✓ Improved Program Efficiency

The tools of structured programming that help achieve those benefits include functional pieces and structured logic. Writing modular code in functional pieces provides for easier debugging, better communication, and overall programmer productivity – both diring creation and during maintenance.

Easier program maintenance is achieved by a number of factors including the following

1. **Code Readability**. The programmer can read the code already written more easily than unstructured code and thus can apply new code more efficiently.
2. **Flexibility**. The programmer has more flexibility when adding new code because the structures are well defined and more readily understood..
3. **Efficiency**. Structured code is more tuned for virtual systems that use paging – such as the IBM i on Power Systems.

Though not as rich of a programming implementation as RPG/IV, RPG/400 also allows for good, structured programming techniques to be implemented using the following operations:
- ✓ Sequence -- ADD, MULT, EXSR
- ✓ If Then Else -- IFXX, ELSE, ENDIF
- ✓ CASE -- CASEQ, CAS, ENDCAS
- ✓ Iteration – Do While, DOWXX, ENDDO
- ✓ Iteration -- Do Until, DOUXX, ENDDO
- ✓ Iteration – Do, DO
- ✓ Leave Do Loop – LEAVE
- ✓ Next iteration -- ITER

Key Chapter Terms

Better communication
CABXX operation
CAS operation
CASE operation
Code, readable
COMP operation
Compiling, 1
Conditionally Invoke
Control Logic Structures
Do Groups
Do Until DOUxx
Do While DOWxx
Easier Debugging
ENDCS operation
ENDDO operation
ENDIF operation
ENDSL operation
EXFMT operation
Federal Std 1037C
FORTRAN
Functional pieces
GOTO operation

If Then Else
IFxx
ILE
Index
ITER
Iteration
LEAVE
Loop
Loop control
Memory constraints
Modular code
Modular programming
Modules
MULT operation
Multi-function program
Open files
ORxx operation
Otherwise select
Program development
Program efficiency
Program maintenance

Program Maintenance
Programmer Productivity
Programming languages
Programs
Readability
SELEC
Selection, 6
Sequence
Service program, 5
Structured code, 3, 18
Structured figures, 6, 28
Structured logic, 3
Structured programming
Structured prmg technique
SUB
Subroutines
System resources
System/38
Testing
WHXX
Wikipedia

Review Questions

1. What is structured programming?

2. Name three benefits of structured programming?

3. How can effective program development be achieved?

4. How can easier program maintenance be achieved

5. With ILE is it best to write large, multi-function programs or is it better to write modular code? Why?

6. What are some factors that make modular programming more efficient?.

7. What are control logic structures. Name three and provide examples.

8. What are the standard structured figures and what operations does RPG use to implement these?

9. In a Select group in RPG, what operation I used for catchall?

10. What options do you have to end a DO loop?

11. For CASE to work, must subroutines be coded in the same program?

12. Is CABXX really a structured operation?

Chapter 20 Interactive RPG Programming

The WORKSTN Device

The numerous examples of RPG code that have been presented in this book have predominately been batch / report oriented. As we decoded the PAREG versions, starting at the top, it was not long before we examined the many capabilities of the File Description specifications.

To explain how interactive programming is accomplished in RPG and RPGIV, it is time to explore a magical device known as WORKSTN, for it through this mechanism that the language gets to talk and literally interact with both real and emulated workstation display devices.

Prior to 1977 (and that is a long time ago), for an RPG or COBOL program to talk to a terminal workstation device, it was not very easy. A separate software product such as the mainframe's Customer Information Control System (CICS) or the System/3's Communication Control Program (CCP) was an absolute necessity.

Strange operations such as PUT and GET and PUT OVERRIDE, and INVITE INPUT were needed with hex values in output along with heavy parsing routines in input as a means of communicating with CCP or CICS. These "software programs," CCP and CICS then spoke to the operating system on the program's behalf. It was painstakingly difficult and not even close to "fun."

Today, mainframes still use CICS and Unix boxes use a similar programs (in terms of transaction function) such as Tuxedo to get their interactive work done.

In the spring 1977, 30 years ago, I was in Philadelphia with a few other IBM Systems Engineers from our branch office in Scranton for the announcement of a new machine called the System/34.

This little machine (for the time) was about the size of two desks stacked on each other. It came with a maximum of 27Meg of hard disk and 64 K of main memory. As small as that seems now, it was not a lot of resource even for 1977. The system also came with a hardware facility and a software facility that would change interactive computing for the good and possibly forever – since it is still done that way.

The hardware was a semi-intelligent twin-axial terminal controller and a CRT device called the IBM 5250, which worked with the "twinax" controller. The speed from the inboard controller to the terminal was 1,000,000 bits per second, as speed which was unusually fast for the times.

Compared with how terminals had spoken to systems prior to this, it was the difference between a slow modem connection to the Internet and DSL. The terminal protocol itself was far superior to the 3270 protocol of the day in that it supported blinking, underline, column separators, and reverse image characteristics as compared with the simple high intensity and low intensity options provided by 3270s of that day.

Impressive as the System/34 was for a 1977 unit, none of these hardware milestones were close to the groundbreaking improvement that IBM had made to its operating system support for display workstations.

In many ways, RPG and COBOL are structured similarly. In COBOL, for example, the devices to be used in the program are defined in a division called the Environment Division. The attributes of the Environment Division are just about all available in the RPG File Description. So, to communicate with devices in RPG, the programmer would make standard entries for disk devices, tape devices, printers, -- even card readers and card punches.

However, despite the popularity of display workstations from the early 1970's, the compiler writers and the operating system developers had chosen to treat display workstations as special entities requiring special device treatment. It was not a device choice in the early RPG or COBOL languages. Instead, to communicate with CCP, the File Description needed to use the "SPECIAL" device, which was in turn handled by a special routine that was adjunct to the operating system.

The System Support Program (SSP) of the System/34 ended all of that and the RPG compiler for the System/34 introduced the simplest notion of dealing with terminals that had ever been conceived. The IBM developers in Rochester Minnesota decided to make the display workstation a natural device to the operating system.

The compiler writers in Rochester (later Toronto) likewise decided to make the display workstation a natural device to the RPG compiler. Prior to this innovative development, display workstations were treated as unnatural because neither the OS nor the compiler had a natural means of communicating with them. The WORKSTN OS support and the WORKSTN RPG device changed all that.

In my humble opinion (IMHO), the WORKSTN device with System/34 was so revolutionary, and its support in RPG was so revolutionary that the language should have been upgraded in name from RPGII to RPGIII. RPGIII would come but it would not be until the Device File was invented by IBM for use with the System/38. Yet, the device name for the WORKSTN device file in System/38 remained as WORKSTN, the name it got in 1977 with the introduction of the IBM System/34.

When the System/38 was announced in 1978, it carried the new workstation paradigm to its natural conclusion. Though workstations were substantially easier to use with System/34 and later System/36 than CCP or CICS or Tuxedo, the coding was still somewhat obscure and the treatment of multiple displays in one program was problematic. For example, there were Single Requester Terminal programs (SRTs) and there were Multiple Requester Terminal programs (MRTs) and there were procedures that needed to understand the SRT or MRT notions in order to support multiple users running the same program.

The introduction of multithread programming and the Display File interface for the WORKSTN device with System/38's RPGIII significantly raised the bar on interactive programming simplicity. In testimony for the productivity achieved with the WORKSTN device and display files, programmers who have worked with both language approaches have offered that up to five times the amount of work can be accomplished with the System/38 method vs. the System/34 and its follow-on, the System/36. Of course, today's IBM i on Power Systemsuses an even better version of the System/38 approach.

Web Programming

Those who teach how to program for the Web caution their students that the old logic paradigms for display programming, in which user interface code and program logic are intermingled, no longer apply. The Web page implementation via HTML or PHP or Java server pages (or whatever the chosen UI) is to be kept separate from the business logic. This is known as the separation of the user interface (UI) from business logic (BL) and it is a very effective technique for writing programs that deal with Web front ends.

Not only is such separation a good idea for Web programming but it is also a good idea for interactive programming with interactive display workstations. Moreover, it's not a new idea at all. The Systen i uses the UI/BL technique first introduced with the display file of the System/38 in 1978 to keep the design and execution of the display panels separate from the design and execution of the business logic with which the panels interact.

Data Description Language

With the delivery of the System/38, IBM also introduced a new data language named after its specification form. It is called Data Description Specifications or quite simply, DDS and it is still used with IBM i on

Power Systems. DDS can be used for externally defined communication files, database files, printer files, and workstation display files. It is the native all-purpose data language for the IBM i on Power Systems.

DDS is far too large a topic for this book. In fact, to help student's gain a command of the DDS language for display files and native database files, I have written three books. All are advertised on the last pages of this book. Their names are <u>The AS/400 and IBM i Pocket Developer's Guide;</u> <u>The AS/400 and IBM i Pocket Database Guide;</u> <u>The AS/400 and IBM i Pocket Query Guide;</u> <u>The AS/400 and IBM i Pocket SQL Guide; The IBM I RPG & RPGIV Tutorial & Lab Exercises; and Getting Started With WebSphere Development Studio Client</u>. All books but the last have been refreshed for IBM I technology.

So, if DDS is too large a topic for this book and it is needed to create display files, and display files are needed for interactive programming, how can a neophyte RPG programmer create a display file without knowing DDS?

There are two answers to this question. On the still bleeding edge but clotting fast is the very powerful Rational Developer for i and its internal screen creation facility known simply as the Designer. The second but the most used method is the integrated Program Development Manager (PDM). It is the launching pad for its Screen Design Aid facility. All of these products as well as the RPG and COBOL, C, and C++ compilers were once shipped by IBM in its programmer kit, product number 5722-WDS. Today, they are orderable as The Rational Developer for i product. Application development other than the original tools has been in flux in IBM for many years and still is. Few IBM i clients know what to order or how. Therefore, since it is likely changing as we speak, it is always best to consult your IBM Sales Representative from your own source to ask the particulars about ordering AD software.

What is IBM SDA i?

In much the same fashion as the Designer, without the use of a mouse, SDA allows a programmer or analyst to interactively design, create, and maintain display screen panels and menus for applications.

When designing screen panels for programs, SDA allows the user to:

1. Define fields and constants for the screen
2. Select a data base file and fields from that file
3. Change attributes (blinking, highlighted, colors, etc.) for fields and constants
4. Move, copy, or remove a field from the screen
5. Display or change the conditions that control when a field will be displayed
6. Define cursor-sensitive help areas for the screen.

Menus

In addition to providing a tool to build workstation display file panels, highlighting the inherent separation of the user interface from the business logic, SDA also provides a facility to test the panels prior to even writing the RPG program to help assure that the panels look and behave properly prior to deployment in an RPG or COBOL program. The third capability provided on the SDA main menu is the ability to create and maintain menus with little programming skill required. Menus are a tremendous aid in building applications. This powerful SDA menu build capability takes all of the heavy work from this important task.

IBM i on Power Systemsmenus are very similar to a menu in a restaurant. They tell you what you can have. In essence, they present a list of options. The workstation operator can then make a selection from the available options, and the system does the work of getting that application alive and ready for the user. Online help information can also be built for menus, making it even that much easier to navigate through the options. Online RPG programs are most often launched from menus rather than by name. Since this book deals only with RPG programming factors, the creation of SDA menus is not on the topic list.

Display Panels

Display panels (a.k.a. screens or panels) define the screens a user works with when using interactive application programs. The display files which are produced by SDA have a natural affinity for inclusion in RPG, COBOL, and other high level language programs. Moreover, with the introduction of the WebSphere Development Studio Client, the DDS source produced by SDA for display files can be readily WebFaced into java server pages. This provides the same function for the Web as the display file does for interactive green screen applications. Just as with SDA menus, you can also build online help information for your SDA-created displays.

You do not need extensive knowledge of DDS coding, its forms, keywords or syntax to use SDA. In fact, with a few simple commands, you will be able to move fields and/or constants or groups of fields and/or groups of constants around on the screen to suit your end user's needs – even before even creating the screen panel or program.

SDA Features

In a nutshell, SDA provides tremendous facility for programmers. Some of its major features are as follows:

1. Generate data description specifications (DDS)
2. Create menus with message files
3. Present displays in functional groups at file, record and field level
4. Test displays with data and status of condition indicators
5. See the display being designed and changes as work is being done.

Not only does SDA remove the burden of creating DDS from the back of the programmer, but it also provides a very nice testing facility. Using the test display option, a developer can test different data inputs, provide specific status conditions for indicators, and observe the look, feel, and overall behavior of the display file object, even before linking the display with a program. This not only provides the developer with a way of quickly assuring his or her work, but it also serves as a powerful prototyping facility, permitting users to approve, disapprove, or modify panel design before programs are even written.

Getting Started

You begin using SDA by invoking the STRSDA command from an AS/400 or IBM i on Power Systems command line. If you press F4 with the command, you will be presented with a fill-in screen. The last option is your first major decision. Do you want to create your display panels or menus in AS/400 mode (*STD), System/38 mode (*S38), or System/36 mode (*S36)? For different reasons, you may choose any of these options. As you would probably expect, AS/400 mode is the default, and there is no IBM i mode. For IBM i on Power Systems, you can use any of the provided options...   but there is no specific IBM i on Power Systems choice.

The first SDA panel you see is shown in Figure 20-6.

Figure 20-6 SDA Prompt Panel

```
                         Start SDA (STRSDA)

Type choices, press Enter.

SDA option . . . . . .    *SELECT         *SELECT, 1, 2, 3
Source file  . . . . .    *PRV            Name, *PRV
  Library  . . . . . .      *PRV          Name, *PRV, *LIBL,
Source member  . . . .    *PRV            Name, *PRV, *SELECT
Object library . . . .    *PRV            Name, *PRV, *CURLIB
Job description  . . .    *PRV            Name, *PRV, *USRPRF
  Library  . . . . . .      *PRV          Name, *PRV, *LIBL,
Test file  . . . . . .    *PRV            Name, *PRV
  Library  . . . . . .      *PRV          Name, *PRV, *LIBL,
Mode . . . . . . . . .    *STD            *STD, *S38, *S36

                                                    Bottom

F3=Exit    F4=Prompt    F5=Refresh    F12=Cancel
F13=How to use this display  F24=More keys
```

If you make no choices on this panel, it will be as if you just typed in STRSDA and did not hit the F4 prompter. You can see in Figure 20-6 that almost all of the options are defaulted to *PRV. This specifies that SDA is to use the name of the source file and library used in your last SDA session for the AS/400 system. There is actually a little item on the AS/400 which the system keeps for each user. It is called your interactive profile, and the system uses it to remember what parameters you may have used the last time you were in an interactive session with a product. This comes in very handy. For our purposes at this time, let's assume you changed no option on the display panel selected.

Screen Design Aid Menus

When you hit ENTER on this panel or after typing STRSDA, you will see the main SDA Menu. When you examine Figure 20-7, you will notice that it looks a lot like the standard PDM panel but, believe me it is much different.

Figure 20-7 Main Screen Design Panel

```
                    AS/400 Screen Design Aid (SDA)

Select one of the following:

    1. Design screens
    2. Design menus
    3. Test display files

Selection or command
===>2


F1=Help    F3=Exit    F4=Prompt    F9=Retrieve
F12=Cancel   ©) COPYRIGHT IBM CORP. 1981, 2000.
```

Creating a Display File

In Figure 20-7, you are presented with the main SDA Menu. It is good to remember when using SDA that just as many other of the WebSphere Development Studio utilities, SDA comes with significant help facilities. In fact, cursor-sensitive help is always available. This means that whatever field or option you have the cursor on, when you press the help key, detail help text will be displayed. To proceed with the next SDA menu, pick the option of creating a menu. I would recommend at this point that you press the help key just to display the definitions of all the function keys. This will help immensely as you begin designing screen panels. For now, select option 1 and press ENTER. You will be taken to a panel similar to that in Figure 20-8

Figure 20-8 Design Screens Initial Panel

```
                    Design Screens
Type choices, press Enter.

    Source file . . . . . . . . QDDSSRC___   Name, F4 for list
      Library . . . . . . . . . RPGBOOK___   Name, *LIBL, *CURLIB
    Member  . . . . . . . . . . NEW_____   Name, F4 for list


  F3=Exit    F4=Prompt    F12 = Cancel
```

Screen Panel Exercise Objectives

In Figure 20-8, specify the new member name, source file, and library where the generated DDS resides (or will reside when generated). As you attempt to create the member named *NEW* in the QDDSSRC file in the HELLO library, let's suppose it is already there. On your systems, this will not happen to you. But, for this exercise, let's just suppose that somebody before you has created this display file object. Let's also say that later you learn that it is an unnecessary, bogus object and you are authorized to delete it. Then, you will be able to create your own version of *NEW* from scratch.

That's exactly what this coming display file exercise is all about. You are about to find (in this book exercise) that the file *NEW* already exists. Then, you will bring up the *NEW* member and take a look at it with SDA's full screen panel editor. From here, you will try to delete it and you will discover that there is no easy way to get all the pieces. Along the way, you will be shown the tools you need to delete all of the entrails of the SDA application, and you will begin again from scratch.

Before we get into the thick of the exercise, let's review a few items that will help put display file DDS in perspective. After all, SDA creates DDS on its way to building the display file object from the DDS that it generates. Sometimes DDS operations can be designed to relate to certain portions of a display file. Some operations pertain to all the panels in a the display file; some pertain to one file, while others may pertain to just one field.

The following brief section is designed to put this in perspective as well as present the nature and consistency of a display file object and its relationship to a calling program.. Then we resume the case study.

Levels: Files, Records, Fields

It is important to understand the relationship between Files, Record Formats, and Fields within DDS. These important relationships have even more bearing in display formats than in database.

Each record in any display file specifies all the characteristics of one display panel. Thus, operations occurring on one panel are known as **Record Level** operations. A record is composed of fields, which exist within a panel and are designated as input, output or both (input and output). Operations on individual fields are known as **Field Level** operations. Operations that occur in all records within a file are referred to as **File Level** operations. The sum total of all of the screens (record formats, panels etc.), with all of the associated fields and attributes, is referred to as the *display file object*.

The name of the file is important. The RPG programs reference the display file by name. Therefore the link from program to display file is through the display file name as specified in the program. In RPG for example the display file name would appear in the File Description Specifications as a WORKSTN device file.

That's it for the diversion. Now, let's get back to this mini case study. When you have your panel from Figure 20-8 completed, press ENTER to get to the *Work with Display Records* panel as shown in Figure 20-9.

Figure 20-9 Work with Display Records SDA Panel

```
Work with Display Records
```

```
File  . . . . . . :  QDDSSRC            Member  . . . . . . :  NEW
  Library . . . . :  HELLO              Source type . . . . :  DSPF

Type options, press Enter.
  1=Add          2=Edit comments       3=Copy            4=Remove
  7=Rename       8=Select keywords    12=Design image

Opt  Order   Record       Type   Related Subfile Date     DDS Error
 __   ____
 __    __10   VENDFMT      RECORD                 10/04/90



F3=Exit                   F12=Cancel     F14=File-level keywords
F15=File-level comments   F17=Subset     F24=More keys
```

Working with an Existing Source Member

The NEW member already exists. Therefore, SDA goes inside the member and picks up the information about the one record format within the DDS that has been previously built. As you can see in Figure 20-9, the record format name is VENDFMT.

To add a new format (display panel), from this panel, you would specify the option (OPT) to add (1) and specify the name of the record format. If you want to update the existing format, type the appropriate option number (12) next to the record format name.

As you can see by looking at the options, including option 12, you can use this panel to change information about an existing format, add or change comments, select record level keywords (option 8), or file level keywords (F14), etc. You can also change the image itself.

Look at an Existing Screen Image

Press ENTER with option 12 specified and you will see a panel similar to that shown in Figure 20-10.

Figure 20-10 Screen Image Existing Format

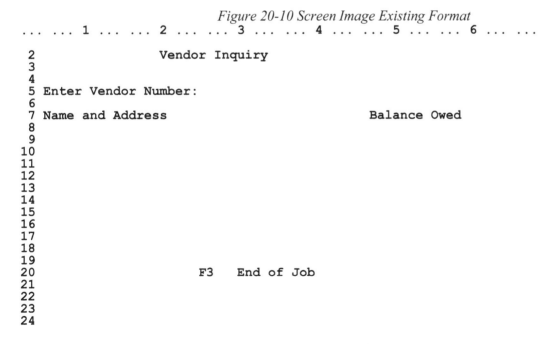

In order to get your work panel to look like the panel in Figure 20-10, you must press PF14. This brings up the "rule." The *ruler* will give you a numeric columnar grid on the left and top so you have an idea on which row and which column you are placing your design.

Building SDA Image from Scratch

Start your session by typing the start SDA command (STRSDA). The SDA main menu would appear as in Figure 20-7. Type "1" for Design screens. The Design Screens option panel is presented as shown in Figure 20-8 and filled in as in Figure 20-10. After completing the panel in 20-10 and pressing ENTER, you will see a panel as in Figure 20-11 with one big difference. There would be no record format in the file. In fact when you arrive, it says very clearly at the bottom, (**No records in file**) as shown in Figure 20-11.

Figure 20-11 Creating The First Display Panel for the Display File
```
                    Work with Display Records

File  .   .   .   .   .   .  :   QDDSSRC         Member  .   .   .   .   .   .  :   NEW
   Library  .   .   .   .  :     HELLO           Source type  .   .   .  :   DSPF
Type options, press Enter.
   1=Add                  2=Edit comments          3=Copy            4=Delete
   7=Rename               8=Select keywords       12=Design image
Opt  Order  Record     Type    Related Subfile   Date          DDS Error
 1          VENDFMT
    (No records in file)                                        Bottom


F3=Exit                    F12=Cancel        F14=File-level keywords
F15=File-level comments    F17=Subset        F24=More keys
```

So, the mission is to create one record format for this display file. In the end, the panel you create will look like that in Figure 20-10. To begin this process, place a "1" in the options column as shown in Figure 20-11, and place the name of the new format (VENDFMT) in the Record column. Press the ENTER key to get the process under way. You will then be asked what *type* of record to add to the display file. This question is shown in Figure 20-12.

Figure 20-12 Add a New Record Selection
```
                      Add New Record

File  .   .   .   .   .   .  :   QDDSSRC         Member  .   .   .   .   .   .  :   NEW
   Library  .   .   .   .  :     HELLO           Source type  .   .   .  :   DSPF

Type choices, press Enter.

   New record  .   .   .   .   .   .   .   .   .   .   .   .   .  VENDFMT       Name

   Type  .   .   .   .   .   .   .   .   .   .   .   .   .   .   .  RECORD        RECORD,  USRDFN
                                                                   SFL,     SFLMSG
                                                                   WINDOW,  WDWSFL
                                                                   PULDWN,  PDNSFL
                                                                   MNUBAR


F3=Exit      F5=Refresh      F12=Cancel
```

Specify Record Format Type

You can see in Figure 20-12 that we answered the question by filling in the word RECORD for the type. There are nine choices for the record type, from which you can choose. A normal display file is known as a record. That's what you want to create for this case study. That's what you pick. When you pick RECORD and hit ENTER, SDA makes that panel image part of the display file SDA source.

SDA is most helpful in being able to build most, if not all of the powerful display facilities supported by DDS. The panel types in Figure 20-12 include record type keywords for subfiles, windows, pull-down menus, and menu bars. As noted, the correct choice for a regular display panel, such as that which we are selecting is *RECORD*. After making this selection, press the ENTER key.

The No-Nonsense Design Image Panel

You will immediately be taken to a completely black design screen. It will look somewhat like Figure 20-10 but there will be nothing filled in. There will be no hints at all as to what you should do next. The closest thing to help you at this point is a little message at the bottom of the black void which says:

Work screen for record VENDFMT: Press Help for function keys.

If you follow the message and hit either the Help key or the F1 (Help) key, you will get a ton of help. Among other things, this Help text will "help" you know what to do next. As soon as you get into the design panel, on your own, take the Help trip and study how much text is available. Then, when you need to get a question answered, you know where to find the Help text. Roll through all the Help if you can spare the time. Everything you are about to do in this exercise is covered in the Help text after a "few" rolls.

Typing Your Screen Constants

When you are finished with the HELP text review, press F14 so that you can see the reference lines on the top and left as shown in Figure 20-10. After you see the lines, type the constant information as shown in Figure 20-10.

When you have this typing done, you have one more task to do before this phase is completed. On your design panel, after it looks exactly as Figure 20-10, place a single quote around (*in front of and after*) each set of constant text. Do not place quotes around each individual word. When you finish, you should have ten single quotes in total, in five pairs, surrounding the five different clumps of text on the panel. When your display looks like this, press the ENTER key.

You will notice that the quotes disappear. The purpose for the quotes is to define blocks of text to be treated in the same fashion. If, for example, you wanted to highlight just the title text, *Vendor Inquiry*, you could do so by placing the highlight (h) code immediately to the left of the text such as:

hVendor Inquiry

When you press the ENTER key from the design panel, immediately, you would see this text highlighted, such as the following:

Vendor Inquiry

Instantaneous Feedback upon ENTER

You may also notice that after you press ENTER, any SDA commands on the design screen, such as the quotes to block text together or the "h" command to highlight a block of text, are all gone. ENTER causes a design panel interaction with SDA. SDA does its work during these interactions. The panel returns to a WYSIWYG form so that you know what the effect of your change has been immediately. For example, your highlighted field will immediately appear highlighted

At this point, the panel is almost complete. You keyed the constants at the desired locations and it is starting to look like a real display. However, the panel is really incomplete. It does not yet include any variable fields - either input or output. You are about to add fields from the database to this panel.

Intermediate Exit and Creation

To know which command keys to hit for ending the database design session (F3 or F12) and to know the various attribute commands, such as "h" for highlight, you already toured the Help text by hitting the Help key or F1. During the tour, the Help text told you about using F14 for the ruler and it also told you that the F10 key is to be used to bring in field descriptions from the data base file – for both prompt and field reference purposes.

As a final review point before moving on, we also discussed the notion of multi word constants, and we suggested enclosing them in quotes. Overall, blocking constant text in this fashion, results in fewer DDS statements, and it makes working with / examining the SDA-created DDS substantially easier.

Before we add to the display file DDS that SDA is about to create, let's exit SDA from the display panel, without adding any variables. Do this by pressing F12 twice. Then hit ENTER after reviewing the "defaults" specified on the SDA exit panel. When you get to a command line, the file *NEW* has been created, though it is incomplete. SDA has created DDS specs for you in a source member. Take a look at the DDS in Figure 20-13, as it exists now before you proceed to complete the panel.

Figure 20-13 NEW Source with Only Constant DDS

```
Columns . . . :    1  71              Edit           HELLO/QDDSSRC
SEU==>                                                         NEW
A*. 1 ...+... 2 ...+... 3 ...+... 4 ...+... 5 ...+... 6 ...+... 7
********** Beginning of data *********************************
A*%%TS  SD  20020512  171200  BKELLY      REL-V5R1M0  5722-WDS
A*%%EC
A                                  DSPSIZ(24 80 *DS3)
A           R VENDFMT
A*%%TS  SD  20020512  171012  BKELLY      REL-V5R1M0  5722-WDS
A                            2 24'Vendor Inquiry'
A                            5  9'Enter Vendor Number:'
A                            7  9'Name and Address'
A                            7 51'Balance Owed'
A                           20 29'F3   End of Job'
************ End of data ***************************************

F3=Exit   F4=Prompt F5=Refresh  F9=Retrieve F10=Cursor F11=Toggle
F16=Repeat find      F17=Repeat change       F24=More keys
                  ©) COPYRIGHT IBM CORP. 1981, 2000.
```

Checking Intermediate DDS with SEU

The quick way to check your DDS is as follows:

Use PDM to *Work with members*; select QDDSSRC in the HELLO library. Press ENTER to get the list of SDA members. Display member *NEW* (PDM option 5), which is the newly created DDS from SDA. The source should look similar to that in Figure 20-13. Notice the big chunks of text. If you had not used the quotes around the constant text blocks as suggested, there would be many more, but smaller DDS statements. SDA would make each word a statement by default.

Looking at the DDS in Figure 20-13, you can see ten lines of DDS. You can also see that of the ten lines, there is one line for each quoted block of constant text and there is a record format ("R" in column 17) statement line in which the screen panel is named. The file level keyword DSPSIZ is created and there are no other keywords. Moreover, as predicted, there are no variable fields defined in DDS.

The numbers you see prior to the text represent the screen panel location information for the row and column starting positions. This is where you placed the text on the screen. These positions are determined based on where you keyed the text on the design panel.

This is one of the major timesaving benefits of SDA. Can you imagine manually coding these DDS statements in such detail, as well as having to specify the exact "from" and "to" positions?

Adding Variable Fields from the Database

Let's exit SEU and PDM and bring back our SDA design panel as it was in Figure 20-10. We get there by the following:

1. F3 from PDM
2. STRSDA
3. Design Screens - option 1
4. Specify QDDSSRC in HELLO, member NEW
5. Place a 12 next to New in the record list.

Begin by adding input and output information to this panel. First press F10 to get at the database. Pick the VENDORP database file that exists in the RPGBOOK library. You will see a panel similar to that in Figure 20-14.

Figure 20-14 Select Database Files For Screen Reference

```
                       Select Database Files

  Type options and names, press Enter.
    1=Display database field list
    2=Select all fields for input (I)
    3=Select all fields for output (O)
    4=Select all fields for both (B) input and output

  Option    Database File   Library      Record
    1          VENDORP        HELLO       VNDMSTR



  F3=Exit    F4=Prompt    F12=Cancel
```

To get a look at all of the fields in the VENDORP file, which you might choose to use as input or output references, select option 1, and specify the location for the VENDORP database file as shown in Figure 20-14. In this panel, select the data base file, library and the specific record format, to serve as a reference for the fields being defined on the screen image panel.

Of course, this all depends on the VENDORP database file already having been created.

Figure 20-15 Select Database Fields for use on Design Display

```
                        Select Data Base Fields

  Record . . . :    VNDMSTR
Type information, press Enter.
 Number of fields to roll . . . . . . . . . . . . . . .   __8
  Name of field to search for . . . . . . . . . . .  _____


Type options, press Enter.
 1=Display extended field description
 2=Select for input (I),3=Select for output(O),4=Select/both(B)

 Option  Field        Length   Type     Column Heading
    4     VNDNBR        5,0      P       VENDOR NUMBER
    3     NAME           25      A       NAME
    3     ADDR1          25      A       ADDRESS LINE 1
    3     CITY           15      A       CITY
    3     STATE           2      A       STATE
    3     ZIPCD         5,0      P       ZIP CODE
    _     VNDCLS        2,0      P       VENDOR CLASS
    _     VNDSTS          1      A       ACTIVE CODE
                                                         More...
 ...
    3     BALOWE        9,2      P       BALANCE OWED

 F3=Exit    F12=Cancel
```

Selecting Database Fields for Use

After picking F10 from the image panel, it is time to pick the fields that should appear in the particular image panel that you are building with SDA. As you pick the fields, you also must tell SDA to select the field for use on the panel for input, output or both purposes. Both is short for both input and output. Fore each database field that you want to be used in the panel, Enter a "2" to select it for input, a "3" for output, and a "4" for both (input and output). Notice that in the panel shown in Figure 20-15, we have already selected the VNDNBR field as both (option 4), and we have selected six other fields as output only (3).

To get to see field six, BALOWE on this panel, you must hit Page Down or Roll Down. Then, select the field as an output field (3). In Figure 20-15, field BALOWE is superimposed at the bottom of the panel, so you could see it in better context.

The idea with this application as you may have already surmised is that this one panel is to be used to enter a vendor number. The program will then look up the vendor information, and redisplay the vendor number as an output field. Additionally, after looking up the vendor information, the program writes the data to the same display panel with the same "write" operation.

Because the vendor information is sent to the screen as output, it cannot be read in. Since it cannot be read, it cannot be changed. In fact, SDA produces DDS which will send the data out, but will lock the keyboard if the user tries to change one of the output fields.

When you are done with this panel hit F3 or ENTER to return to the design panel. When you get back to the design panel, you should be pleased to see that the selected fields are displayed on the bottom row of the work screen where you design your display. Press page down (Roll on some terminals) to display more data base fields if all of them are not visible.

Exiting the Data Base Option

Press ENTER on the display shown in Figure 20-15 to return to the *Select data base files* display if you want to reference another file for input, or if you are on your way to exiting. In this example, press F3 or ENTER again from the database files display, to return to the design panel. You will see a screen similar to that shown in Figure 20-16.

Figure 20-16 Vendor Inquiry Panel With Fields in On-Deck Circle

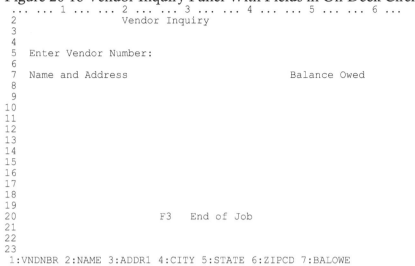

```
... ... 1 ... ... 2 ... ... 3 ... ... 4 ... ... 5 ... ... 6 ...
 2                    Vendor Inquiry
 3
 4
 5   Enter Vendor Number:
 6
 7   Name and Address                      Balance Owed
 8
 9
10
11
12
13
14
15
16
17
18
19
20                       F3    End of Job
21
22
23
 1:VNDNBR 2:NAME 3:ADDR1 4:CITY 5:STATE 6:ZIPCD 7:BALOWE
```

Look at the bottom of Figure 20-16 for the new stuff. When you are looking for a field and it is not in the list, remember that the bottom line holds only so many. The fields are inserted and appear in a multiple-field mode at the bottom of the work screen as shown in Figure 20-16. This is what we referred to as the "On-Deck Circle." A "+" at the end of the field name list indicates there are more field names. Just position the cursor in that area of the screen and press page down to display more field names.

SDA Image Commands

Notice in Figure 20-16 that the text fields are in tact, and the design panel is in somewhat of a wait state. It is waiting for you to do something with these fields. They don't just pop up into the screen panel. You have to place them. To do this, SDA has given you some handy commands. The first command is the " &." With this command, you tell SDA to "place a database field right here!"

Following the "&" command, you then tell SDA which database field number to place. We already pre-typed the SDA database commands "&" in the panel in Figure 20-17. These reference, by number, the on-deck fields that SDA lists at the bottom of the panel after you select them in the panel shown in Figure 20-15. You may also notice that we did one more thing with Figure 20-17.

In real life, you would not split your design by (1) implementing the constant fields, (2) saving the panel, (3) creating the file, and (4) coming back in update mode to add the variables with database fields, as we did for this training example. Thus, Figure 20-17 shows how the panel as it should look when you build it with all the necessary information specified at once. In other words, the quote commands surround the text as they should have at the time we built the constants-only panel.

Figure 20-17 Database Fields Selected for Action
```
... ... 1 ... ... 2 ... ... 3 ... ... 4 ... ... 5 ... ... 6 ... ...
    2                'Vendor Inquiry'
    3
    4
    5'Enter Vendor Number:' &1
    6
    7'Name and Address'                      'Balance Owed'
    8
    9 &2                                     &7
   10 &3
   11 &4               &5 &6
   ..
   20                        'F3   End of Job'
   21
   22
   23
    1 VNDNBR 2 NAME 3 ADDR1 4 CITY 5 STATE 6 ZIPCD 7 BALOWE
```

Column Headings from the Database

As you can see in Figure 20-17, in addition to the blocked text shown with quotes, we have placed the "&" command plus the field number at the location desired for each field. If you want to be more productive than this, or perhaps you are feeling a little lazy during your design trip, SDA gives you a few more tools to eliminate even more keying and more guesswork.

You can ask SDA to get you the column headings from the database and you can then use them as your prompts. If you have good column headings, the idea is that there should be lots less keying and lots less opportunity for misinterpretation of field meanings. Moreover, you can tell SDA to place the prompt text to the left or to the right of the inserted database input or output field, so you have initial design flexibility. Additionally, you can tell SDA to place the column heading right on top of the field being defined.

You add the column heading and provide its placement with one-letter commands. You place the letter "L" for left, or the letter "R" for right or the letter "C" for center, along with the "&" command and the field number. This is how you tell SDA to grab the column heading, along with the field definition, and place them on your design panel – based on the specific command you used.

When you press ENTER on the display, you see how nice or how ugly the text prompts appear in the work display. If they are not so nice, without re-keying or excess typing, you can simply change them and move them accordingly.

After hitting ENTER on Figure 20-17, your display panel should look similar to that in Figure 20-18.

Figure 20-18 The Resulting Display Panel
```
... ... 1 ... ... 2 ... ... 3 ... ... 4 ... ... 5 ... ... 6 ... ...
    2              Vendor Inquiry
    3               .
    4
    5 Enter Vendor Number:*99999-
    6
    7 Name and Address                    Balance Owed
    8
    9 OOOOOOOOOOOOOOOOOOOOOOOOOO          *666666666
   10 OOOOOOOOOOOOOOOOOOOOOOOOOO
   11 OOOOOOOOOOOOOOOO  OO*66666
   12
   13
   14
   15
   16
   17
   18
   19
   20              F3   End of Job
   21
   22
   23
   24
```

The field *Vendor Number*, which is represented by all 99999s, is an output/input (both) field, and it is defined as numeric. The fields defined at lines 9 to 11 are a combination of alphabetic output (O) and numeric output (6). If you were not using SDA database referencing to supply the field attributes and lengths, you would have had to count field spaces and assure that your coding lined up properly. This would be another thing you would have to do that would not be much fun! SDA helps keep it light-hearted. The database referencing ability is just another way that SDA saves this type of drudgery, and in so doing, it saves time. Who wants to be counting O's as you are hitting the O key, hoping not to have one too many or one too few?

Adding Fields & Changing Field Attributes

Oh! It's not that you can't make a mistake with SDA. You can make as many as you please, and you can fix them just as fast – long before you'd know you'd made them if you were dealing just with DDS. You can add fields and/or change the attributes of fields after they are on your work display — years after you've first created your display file. As you can see in Figure 20-18, we are doing exactly that for the vendor number field and the balance owed field by placing asterisks "*" next to fields to be edited for highlighting or perhaps to display their attributes. The "*" is just another tool that enables you to open the fields up for many different combinations of changes, without once having to refer to your DDS manual.

Field Manipulation Commands

There are also one-character commands which immediately highlight a field. You have already seen the highlight command. A few more examples include the "r" for reverse image, and the "u" for an underline.

Delete Field Command

Some one-character commands do more than just highlight. They are much more powerful. The "d" command, for example, is for *dangerous*. OK, it is not. But it is dangerous! You can place a "d" next to any field you want to delete from the panel. It's that easy. Press ENTER and it's gone.

Two Forms of Move Commands

Two other powerhouse commands are the two forms of "move." To move fields you have two choices. And, they are both good! To move them a little, use the symbols " >>>>" and "<<<<." There is a one-to-one relationship between symbols used and characters moved. These field move commands move fields, and blocks of fields, to the left (<) or to the right (>) as many positions as symbols you type. If you type four ">>>>" signs, for example, and you place them next to the rightmost character of text to be moved, when you press ENTER, the text will be four positions over to the right. Likewise if you wanted to move to the left, you would type the "<" symbols to the left of the text to be moved.

Another tremendous tool is the "block move" operation. To move fields a lot, use this command. This move command is a simple dash "-" preceding the field or text block to be moved. Just like SEU, it needs a corresponding to-position indicator to get its job done. SDA has chosen the equal sign "=" for this. An example of the way this works is as follows: If you place a dash on text at, say line 23, and you put an equal sign in some column on say, line 5, after you hit the ENTER key, the block of text from line 23 is now on line 5, starting at your designated column position. It is no longer on line 23. The move operations make it so easy to redesign the work panel on the fly that it actually isn't any fun getting it right the first time.

Adding a New Field to Your Display

There will also be times that you must add a field to the panel which is not in a database. For example, if your program is calculating a result which goes nowhere else but the screen panel, your panel must know about that field somehow. SDA handles it. You can easily add your own fields to the work screen. Just key a "+" to specify a user-defined field. For numeric, "3" is input, "6" is output and "9" is both. For alphabetic, "I" is input, "O" is output, and "B" is both. For example: +6 (8,2) creates a field named FLD001 (default field name) with a length of eight, and with two decimals for output only.

Changing Display Attributes

It's been so long, we would like to remind you that, in our example panel in Figure 20-18, we have placed asterisks "*" next to the vendor number field (VNDNBR), the balance owed field (BALOWE), and the zip code (ZIPCD) field . When you hit ENTER, with these asterisks positioned where they are, you will first see a panel similar to that in Figure 20-19.

Figure 20-19 Select Field Keywords

```
                    Select Field Keywords

Field . . . . . :  VNDNBR    Usage . . :  B
Length . . . . :   5,0       Row . . . :  5    Column . . . :  31

Type choices, press Enter.
                                   Y=Yes  For Field Type
    Display attributes . . . . . . .  Y    All except Hidden
    Colors . . . . . . . . . . . .  __    All except Hidden
    Keying options . . . . . . . .  __    Hidden, Input or Both
    Validity check . . . . . . . .  __    Input or Both, not float
    Input keywords . . . . . . . .  __    Input or Both
    General keywords . . . . . . .  __    All types
    Editing keywords . . . . . . .  Y    Numeric Output or Both
    Database reference . . . . . .  __    Hidden, Input, Output, Both
    Error messages . . . . . . . .  __    Input, Output, Both
    Message ID (MSGID) . . . . . .  __    Output or Both

    TEXT keyword . . . . . . . . . .  VENDOR NUMBER
F3=Exit   F4=Display Selected Keywords   F12=Cancel
```

You will see a panel similar to Figure 20-19 once for each of the fields selected with the "*" command. From this panel, for VNDNBR, change the *Display attributes* and *Editing keywords* by placing "Y" responses in this panel. For BALOWE and ZIPCD, change just the *Editing keywords* by typing a "Y." To proceed from this panel for the field VNDNBR, type "Y" in the appropriate columns as shown in Figure 20-21. You will first be taken to a panel similar to the *Select Display Attributes* panel as in Figure 20-20.

By placing the "*" next to the vendor number field (VNDNBR), you first get the panel in Figure 20-19. From there, you determine which type of attribute you want to change. By selecting a "Y" for Display Attributes, you get to work with the panel in Figure 20-20. By selecting a "Y" for editing keywords, you get to work with a panel similar to that in Figure 20-21.

Figure 20-20 Select Display Attributes

```
                Select Display Attributes

Field . . . . . :  VNDNBR       Usage . . :  B
Length . . . . :   5,0          Row . . . :  5    Column . . . : 26

Type choices, press Enter.
                                        Keyword   Y=Yes   Indicators/+
    Field conditioning . . . . . . . . . .
    Display attributes:                     DSPATR
       High intensity . . . . . . . . . . .  HI
       Reverse image . . . . . . . . . . .   RI      Y      44  __  __
       Column separators . . . . . . . . .   CS      __     __  __  __
       Blink . . . . . . . . . . . . . . .   BL      __     __  __  __
       Nondisplay . . . . . . . . . . . . .  ND      __     __  __  __
       Underline . . . . . . . . . . . . .   UL      __     __  __  __
       Position cursor . . . . . . . . . .   PC      __     __  __  __
       Set modified data tag . . . . . . .   MDT     __     __  __  __
       Protect field . . . . . . . . . . .   PR      __     __  __  __
       Operator ID magnetic card . . . . .   OID     __     __  __  __
       Select by light pen . . . . . . . .   SP      __     __  __  __

   F3=Exit    F12 = Cancel
```

Making the Attribute Change

Our display objective for the VNDNBR field is to make it a reverse-image, if a certain condition occurs in the program. To display the field in reverse-image (like a negative) under certain conditions, specify the attributes as shown in the panel in Figure 20-20. When you come back to the design work panel, the field VNDNBR will show in reverse-image.

Conditional Attributes Using Indicators

However, it will not be shown in reverse-image when put out by the program unless indicator 44 is on in the controlling program at the time of the output operation. You set the condition (indicator 44 in this case) for the field to be shown in reverse-image within the hig20-level language program. If the indicator is on, the VNDNBR field will be lit up in reverse-image when the program sends out this screen panel. Field conditioning and un-conditioning can be achieved by entering a "Y" by the desired display attribute (DSPATR) when you select an indicator to condition the attribute.

Adding Editing Keywords

When you have changed the attributes in Figure 20-20 to your satisfaction, press the ENTER key until the display changes to *Select Editing Keywords* for VNDNBR. This panel is shown in Figure 20-21. Notice that we used the "3" edit-code for the field since, for this field type, we found it desirable to edit it so that zero value vendor numbers will show, and there will be no commas, and no decimals in the vendor number field.

Figure 20-21 Selecting Editing Keywords or Codes.

```
                        Select Editing Keywords
Field . . . . . :    VNDNBR  Usage . . :  B
Length  . . . . :    5,0     Row . . . :  5  Column . . . :   31


Type choices, press Enter.
                                        Keyword              More
    Edit code  . . . . . . . . . . . .  EDTCDE     3 A-D,J-Q,W etc.
      Replace leading zeros with . . . .             *, $

    Edit word  . . . . . . . . . . . .  EDTWRD

    Edit mask  . . . . . . . . . . . .  EDTMSK

F3=Exit    F12=Cancel
```

After you finish with the VNDNBR field for both attributes and editing, keep pressing the ENTER key until the field name changes to BALOWE. It should be right away. By having placed the "*" next to the balance owed field, you also get a panel similar to that in Figure 20-19. However, the field name is primed with BALOWE instead of VNDNBR, since that is the field you now want to adjust. Since it is a nice big numeric field, it would be nice for it to show up edited on the final display.

You do not need a Y for *Display Attributes*, as in VNDNBR, since the attributes are fine. However, to make the field look right, you need to do some editing of the output. If you look down, near the bottom of the panel in Figure 20-19, you will notice Editing Keywords. Place your "Y" in this field. Make sure there is not a "Y" in any of the other attributes, and press ENTER. You will see a panel similar to that in Figure 20-21. Instead of *VNDNBR*, however, the field name will be *BALOWE*.

If you hit Help on the Edit-codes field, it will tell you which code produces which level of editing. This is very handy. I like to show dollar fields with commas and have zero balances appear on the report rather than be hidden. Also, I like to have a minus sign show to the right of the number if the value is negative. If you hit the Help or F1 key now, you will see that the edit-code to do all of that is a "J." To select "J," type it into the edit-code instead of the "3" as in Figure 20-21 and press Enter.

You should see the panel as in Figure 20-19 again, except this time, the field name should be *ZIPCD*. Follow the same process for editing this field as you did for *VNDNBR*, but leave the attributes alone. Change the edit-code to "3". When you have made all of your editing and attribute changes for the asterisked "*" fields, you should return to the SDA work panel. Your display should no longer show the "-" sign to the right of *VNDNBR* and *ZIPCD* and the *BALOWE* field should appear nicely edited. See Figure 20-22 for the final display panel.

Figure 20-22 Final Version of Display Panel

```
... ... 1 ... ... 2 ... ... 3 ... ... 4 ... ... 5 ... ... 6 ... ... 7 ... ..
  2              Vendor Inquiry
  3
  4
  5 Enter Vendor Number: 99999
  6
  7 Name and Address                Balance Owed
  8
  9 OOOOOOOOOOOOOOOOOOOOOOOOO        $6,666,666.66-
 10 OOOOOOOOOOOOOOOOOOOOOOOOO
 11 OOOOOOOOOOOOOOO  OO 66666
 12
 13
 14
 15
 16
 17
 18
 19
 20              F3   End of Job
 21
 22
 23
 24
```

The example in Figure 20-24 shows the final form of the screen as it was just designed. Remember, even now, you can move any of the fields around, delete fields, or add more fields and more constants.

Assigning End-of-Job Indicator

Before you close this out, there is one more job to do. You need to enable a command key (CF03) and assign an indicator (switch) value to the command key so that the program can get a signal from the display panel when the operator decides that it is time to end it. Since there is only one display panel, and since other panels, if added, may very well want to end the program in the same fashion, the recommendation is to add the CF03 function key at the file level so it applies to all display panels (formats).

From Figure 20-22, press F24 to return to the *Work with Display Records* panel similar to that in Figure 20-9. From this screen, if you were assigning the indicator to just this one panel design, you would type an "8" next to the format name. You would then press ENTER, and select *Indicator keywords* by placing a "Y," next to the prompt. You would then see a panel similar to Figure 20-23. On this panel, you would type *CF03* for keyword. You would pick response indicator 03. And, you would type *"end-of-job"* for text. This would create the indicator reference at the record format (display panel) level.

Figure 20-23 Defining Command Keys and Indicators

```
              Define Indicator Keywords

Member . . . :   NEW

Type keywords and parameters, press Enter.
  Conditioned keywords:    CFnn CAnn CLEAR PAGEDOWN/ROLLUP
                           PAGEUP/ROLLDOWN
                           HOME HELP HLPRTN
  Unconditioned keywords: INDTXT VLDCMDKEY

Keyword    Indicators/+ Resp Text
CF03       ___ ___ ___  03  end-of-job


    ...
                                        Bottom
F3=Exit    F12=Cancel
```

Indicator at File Level

However, you would want this command key to work for all display panels, even those not yet built. To do this, from the panel shown in Figure 20-9, you would press F14 for "File-level keywords." You would then select "Indicator keywords" as above for the record level. After all that, you would get a panel, which looks the same as the panel used for record function keys, as shown in Figure 20-23.

Press ENTER to return to the Work with Display Records panel. After defining the command keys, we have no more design work to do. From here then, it is time to compile and test your display file. Press F3 to exit. You will get the SDA exit panel. Take the options to exit and create the objects. The source will be saved and your updated file will be created. At this point of success, you now have a display file to test.

Display File in an RPG Program

After testing the SDA panel using the SDA testing facility (option 3 from the SDA Main menu - Figure 20-7), the next step is to merge the file with your RPG program. This is the merging of the user interface with the business logic. For your edification, Figure 20-24 shows a sample RPG program named NEW, which sends out a display of vendor information from the database using this panel we created. The logic of the program is as follows:.

RPG Display File Program Logic

The program starts with a Do-While-Equal (DOWEQ) statement. This tells the compiler to keep running the same set of statements, from 0005 to 0011 until something happens. That "something" occurs if indicator 03 (a switch that gets tested) has turned to the ON state from the OFF state.

Figure 20-24 RPG program (NEW) for Display File (NEW)

```
Columns . . . :   1  71          Browse     HELLO/QRPGSRC
SEU==>                                       NEW
FMT FX.....FFilenameIPEAF........L..I........Device+...
      ************** Beginning of data ******************
0001.00     FNEW     CF  E                   WORKSTN
0002.00     F* LOGICAL FILE VENDMST BUILT OVER VENDORP W/ KEY
0003.00     FVENDMST IF  E        K          DISK
0004.00     I               'VENDOR NOT FOUND    'C...  ERRMSG
0005.00     C         *IN03     DOWEQ*OFF
0006.00     C                   EXFMTVENDFMT
0007.00     C         VNDNBR    CHAINVENDMST                90
0008.00     C         *IN90     IFEQ *ON
0009.00     C                   MOVELERRMSG    NAME
0010.00     C                   ENDIF
0011.00     C                   ENDDO
0012.00     C                   MOVE *ON      *INLR
      **************** End of data ************************
```

F3=Exit F5=Refresh F9=Retrieve F10=Cursor F11=Toggle F12=Cancel
F16=Repeat find   F24=More keys
©) COPYRIGHT IBM CORP. 1981, 2000.

You may recall that in our SDA display panel, we assigned Command Key 03 to the indicator 03. Thus, when indicator 03 (*IN03) is turned on by the user of the display file while on a workstation pressing the F3 key, it is a signal to the program that the program user wants to end the program. F3 is changed to indicator 01 by the user interface. The DOWEQ then moves to statement 0012 and sets on LR (last record), which as we know is how RPG programs end.

Within the repeating Do-Loop, at statement 0006, the program sends out the VENDFMT panel from our SDA-built display file. The EXFMT operation in RPG sends a panel and then waits in the program for a user to enter data and hit ENTER. When the user types the vendor number and hits ENTER, the typed information becomes available in the program, inside the field *VNDNBR*.

In the next statement, 0007, the program uses the VNDNBR data to CHAIN to (access) the vendor file. If the vendor number entered is on file, the database information for that vendor is available to the program immediately after the CHAIN operation. If the record is not found, the operation turns on switch # 90 (indicator 90) to let the program know that a record was not found.

At statement 0008, the program tests the status of indicator 90 to see if it is on - meaning that a record was not found. At statement 0009, if the record was not found, the program loads an error message into the *Vendor Name* field of the display panel. Statement 10 ends this not-found error routine that began at statement 0009.

The next statement at 0011 is the ENDO. This works with the DOWEQ in statement 0005 to define the part of the program which repeats until the user hits Command Key 3. The ENDDO passes control back to statement 0005 and if the user has not hit Command Key 3, control is passed to the "loop" at statement 6.

At statement 0006, the second and subsequent times through the DOWEQ loop, the output part of the operation sends out the data from the database, or the error message in NAME, while the input part of the operation brings in the next VENDOR number as well as an indication that the ENTER key or Command key 03 has been pressed. The program continues in the loop until the user takes the appropriate ending action - by pressing Command key 03.

Simple RPG Inquiry with Display File

In this inquiry example, the input is vendor number and the output is name and address information, as defined on the panel, which you built in this Chapter. After you have compiled your RPG program, you can call the program (CALL NEW), enter a vendor number, and press ENTER. The name, address and balanced-owed information are then displayed. When this happens, your efforts have been successful.

Other Display Operations

The **EXFMT** (execute format) operation is very powerful and is the most used of the RPG interactive display operations. Without IBM implementing EXFMT, the programmer would be forced to use the WRITE operation followed by the READ operation to perform the same function. When a WRITE followed by a READ occurs to a displays station and the panel contains input fields or command keys, the RPG program halts so that the user can interact with the workstation. When the user hits a command key or other function key or the ENTER key, the READ operation brings in the input or both data from the workstation. If line 6 of the interactive program in Figure 20-29 were replaced by the WRITE / READ operations, the code would look as follows:

```
0006.00 C...     WRITEVENDFMT
0006.01 C...     READ VENDFMT
```

A WRITE operation is also used when the programmer wants to output information to a display and accept no input. The READ operation cannot be used without a prior WRITE operation since the WRITE places the format on the workstation that the READ accepts. However, there are mechanisms, using facilities referred to on the IBM i on Power Systems as shared access paths that permit program A to use a WRITE operation to place a panel on the workstation, set on LR and end, and then have program B come alive and READ the panel sent by program A. This notion is called request under format (sharing formats) and was used frequently when memory was expensive and processor speeds were very limited. While the user was typing in the data on the panel sent by program A, the system would be loading program B, thereby giving the illusion of better performance.

Chapter Summary

In this chapter on Interactive programming, we examined the creation of a display panel using SDA in a brief tutorial fashion. You can now use the results of your efforts in this chapter to move on to bigger and more sophisticated programming examples, using subfiles and other different advanced interactive techniques such as green screen windows.

They key device in RPG which makes workstation files and interactive programming possible is WORKSTN. It is through this mechanism that RPG gets to talk and literally interact with both real and emulated workstation display devices. This device was introduced with the System/34 in 1977, and perfected with the display file as introduced in 1978 with the System/38. AS/400 and IBM i on Power Systems use the same device facility.

The WORKSTN file gets created using the Data Description language for its externally defined workstation files. DDL is also used in IBM i on Power Systems for communication files, database files and printer files. It is the native all-purpose data language for the IBM i on Power Systems.

The Rational for IBM i has a facility called the Designer that in the same spirit of SDA can creates the DDS that creates the display files. SDA is a green screen tool, originally introduced with the System/34 that permits a programmer or analyst to interactively design, create, and maintain display screen panels and menus for applications.

The display panel is the operative part of a WORKSTN file built by DDS. They have a natural affinity for inclusion in RPG, COBOL, and other high level language programs. The strong point of SDA as well as the WDSC designer is that you do not need extensive knowledge of DDS coding, its forms, keywords or syntax to use them.

Though programmers do not have to understand DDS per se to work with SDA or the Designer, it is better if they do. The DDS structure for example enables WORKSTN keywords to be applied to files, fields and formats. When applied to files, the function key for example is applicable to all panels in the display file. When applied at the format level, it has meaning at the screen panel level. And when a keyword is applied at the field level, it has governance only for that particular field.

One of the main productivity features of SDA and the GUI Designer is that they both provide for database definition inclusion during the design phase. This assures the proper database definitions being used for workstation fields.

In addition to being able to design new panels, the tools also provide a means of adding panels or adding or changing fields or field attributes one existing panels. To use the display file in the RPG program, code the name of the display file in File descriptions. Make it combined and fully procedural and place the WORKSTN device in the device column. Then, in calculations use the appropriate interactive operation, EXFMT, WRITE, or READ to send and receive the specific panels that you request.

Key Chapter Terms

3270 protocol	ERRMSG keyword	RPG device
3270	EXFMT operation	RPG interactive program
5250 protocol	Field Level	RPGIII
5250	File Description	RSE
Calling program	File SAVE	Screen Design Aid
CCP1	GET	SDA
CF03	Green screen	SEU
CHAIN operation	GUI Designer	SFLMSG
CICS	Help facilities,	Source Edit Utility
CODE Designer	HTML	Source editor
CODE/400,	In-between time	Source file
Command key	Indicator keywords	Source member
Command line	Indicator reference	SRT, 3
Compile	Inquiry	SSP, 3
Copy	Interactive programming	STRSDA
Database	Internet	Subfile
DDL	Java server pages	System/34
DDS language	Loop	System/36
DDS operations	Modem	System/38
Delete	Move	Systems Engineers

Design Panel	MRT	Test display
Devices	Native method	Testing
Display devices	Outline View	Text editing
Display file object	PAYINPUT	The Designer
Display programming	PDM	Toronto IBM
Display workstations	PR	Twinax,
DSL	Procedures	Unix boxes,
DSPATR keyword	Prototyping	WDSC
Eclipse	PUT, 1	Web Programming,
Edit-codes	QDDSSRC	Windows
Editing	QRPGSRC	Workstation operator
EDTCDE keyword	Record Level	WORKSTN
End of job	Remote Systems Explorer	WRITE
ENDDO operation	Replace	WRITE / READ
ENDIF operation	Rochester Minnesota	WYSIWYG
Environment Division		

Review Questions

1. Which device in RPG/400 enables interactive programming?

2. Which device in RPGIV enables interactive programming?

3. Name two other methods that use interactive programming prior to 1977?

4. Which machine first introduced interactive programming to RPG?

5. What type of object was built for System/38 to create the screen format member in System/34?

6. What specifications are used on IBM i on Power Systems to create a display file?

7. What two productivity tools can be used on IBM i on Power Systemsi to create the display file DDS?

8. What is AS/400 SDA?

9. What is another name for display panel?

10. Is a display panel an object why? Why not?

11. What are the five main features of SDA?

12. What is the command used to begin an SDA session?

13. If you did not use SDA or designer to create screen files, how would you create them?

14. What are the three levels in a display file? Which levels relate to command keys?

15. Is there such a thing as an SDA source member? Explain?

16. How do you get database field names and attributes to be sued for fields defined on a display panel using SDA?

17. Can you place just field prompts on a design panel without taking the database field? How?

18. Provide an example of an SDA "Image" command?

19. How do you change the attributes of a field on an SDA design panel?

20. How do you delete a field on an SDA design panel?

21. How do you add a field on an SDA design panel?

22. With SDA, how do you move a field to another line on the screen?

23. With SDA, how do you move a field over to the left two spaces?

24. What is an SDA editing keyword?

25. With SDA, how do you add Editing keywords?

26. Describe the process of adding and end of job description, function key and indicator.

27. Does it matter if you type in your RPG interactive program source and compile it before you create and compile your display file? Why? Why not?

28. Which operation sends out a display format and waits until the operator finishes keying before processing the results and moving on to the next sequential statement in the program?

Chapter 21   RPG Subfile Programming

Subfile Lists

Now that we have worked through a simple interactive program, it's time to up the ante with subfile programming. From the onset of workstation display programming, systems analysts have been designing list panels for one purpose or another.

Often the data of the list that can be shown on one screen panel is merely a small portion of the total list. RPG Programmers of course then had the job of implementing the lists across as many panels as it took to display them.

Once the user has a list in front of them, they would want to page back and forward through the list, type new entries in the list, or select, update or delete entries in the list Though it is very simple as a user or an analyst to say that is what the program has to do, without subfiles, it was not all that easy to get the job done.

Old –Time Display List Management

Display files and screen specifications from way back had techniques for programmers to be able to send lists of output to display panels but no real good ways of accepting input. For example the SLNO RPG parameter interfaces with a display file so that the programmer can loop through a disk file and send one record at a time to the screen and the screen will automatically position the one line to the next line of the panel until it fills up or reaches the defined end.

Using this technique, the programmer also had to store each of the values put out in an array, multiple occurrence data structure or a work database file structured for the mission.

When IBM introduced subfiles with RPGIII, it was a major breakthrough. All of the facilities that programmers needed to operate lists were included and the coding required was minimal. So what then is a subfile? In simple terms it is a memory file associated with a display file that provides temporary storage for items written to the display file.

Suppose for example, a user is able to type a short description of an item in inventory in an order entry program for an alphabetic search but the short description can be so generic that there may be as many as 1000 returned records from the inventory file that meet the search criteria.

In conventional programming if the programmer were able to fit ten on one panel, the loop would continue through 100 iterations in order to get all of the items displayed once. The user would then need a means of interacting with the program to request one or several of the records that were displayed. This can require substantial coding.

The Subfile Method

With subfiles (a.k.a. memory files) the programmer defines just one record that will appear multiple times in the list. The entire list or parts of the list are shown on the screen panel when displayed.

When the subfile is defined, DDS permits the programmer to say how many records (capacity) the subfile should hold and how many should be displayed at one time. So, when the programmer is reading from the inventory file in this case, they can be writing records to the display file subfile record format.

Rather than displaying the records as they are written, the subfile holds them and numbers them from 1 to the end of the subfile. Until the programmer tells the program in the RPG code to display the subfile, all of this work goes on behind the scenes. Then, when the subfile is full or all records meeting the condition have been found and written, the program than can display the first page of the subfile.

The RPG subfile logic then provides the bulk of the facility. Without any additional coding, once the subfield control record is displayed with the subfile, the user can roll through the records, backwards and forwards, making changes as they go. Only when the user tells the program by pressing the Enter key or a Function key that all of th entering, selecting, maintaining or deleting has been done does the program again gain control.

The program can then read through this in a similar fashion to it being a disk file but with a special operation called Read Changed or READC. With the READC operation, all of the records that the user changed (as many as the entire subfile or just one) are returned for the programmer to then perform the action(s) requested.

Learn Subfiles By Example

This chapter uses an example to make almost all of the points on subfile programming in RPG. The data for the example is shown in Figure 21-1.

Figure 21-1 Data For Subfile Example

```
                    VENDOR MASTER INQUIRY      09:43:05   6/09/93

     ENTER VENDOR NO:      25          F3       END OF JOB
     VENDOR NO.      VENDOR   NAME         STATE    BALANCE OWED
        00025        A MACHINE CORP.         IL        7,500.00
        00026        B MACHINERY             IL        1,495.55
        00028        C ENGRAVING CO          IL          100.00
        00030        D CONTROLS INC.         IL          900.25
        00032        I POWER EQUIPMENT       IL          250.00
        00034        ROBIN   COMPANY         IL          153.00
        00036        F STEEL CO.             IL          290.00
        00038        J B COMPANY             IL             .00
        00040        CHICAGO INC             IL          150.00
        00042        PASS BOX INC            IL          299.50
```

Actually, the panel shown in Figure 21-1 is a screen showing the successful execution of a subfile search from a program called VENDSRCH.

The DDS for this subfile is shown in Figure 21-2.

Figure 21-2 VENDSUBF Subfile DDS for Program VENDSRCH

```
A* VENDSUBF Display File DDS
A                                         DSPSIZ(24 80 *DS3)
A                                         PRINT
A                                         REF(VENDORP)
A>>>          R VENSUB                    SFL
A*
A               VNDNBR    R         O  7 12TEXT('VENDOR NUMBER')
A               NAME      R         O  7 23TEXT('NAME')
A               STATE     R         O  7 50TEXT('STATE')
A               BALOWE    R         O  7 54TEXT('BALANCE OWED    ')
A                                         EDTCDE(J)
A>>>          R VENDCTL                   SFLCTL(VENSUB)
A*
A                                         CF03(99 'end of job')
A  88                                     SFLINZ
A  81                                     SFLDSP
A  81                                     SFLDSPCTL
A N81                                     SFLCLR
A                                         SFLSIZ(0500)
A                                         SFLPAG(0010)
A  98                                     SFLMSG('INVALID VENDOR      A
1 29'VENDOR'
A                                      1 36'MASTER'
A                                      1 43'INQUIRY'
A                                      1 54TIME
A                                      1 63DATE
A                                         EDTCDE(Y)
A                                      3 10'ENTER'
A                                      3 16'VENDOR'
A                                      3 23'NO:'
A               VENDNO        5   0B  3 28DSPATR(HI)
A                                         EDTCDE(4)
A                                      3 41'F3 '
A                                      3 45' '
A                                      3 48'END'
A                                      3 52'OF'
A                                      3 55'JOB'
A                                      5 10'VENDOR'
A                                      5 17'NO.'
A                                      5 23'VENDOR'
A                                      5 31'NAME'
A                                      5 48'STATE'
A                                      5 56'BALANCE'
A                                      5 64'OWED'
```

As we have discussed previously in this course, DDS is used for a number of good purposes in IBM i on Power Systemsdevelopment. For example, you use it to define database files and printer files. Now, of course we are using it to describe display files. Whether we use Rational's Designer or we use SDA, the output is DDS as shown in this example.

So, since this DDS is simple and we don't have to type it in to understand it, let's take a shot at looking at this thing in its entirety.

First of all, there are only five fields in the whole thing. Looking at the Figure, you can see these names:

VNDNBR
NAME
STATE
BALOWE
VENDNO

The first four of these are underneath a line of code that looks like this.

A>>>... R VENSUB...   SFL

Pretend the >>> are not there since they are only tools I am using to highlight the two record formats ("screens") defined in this display file DDS. The R says this is a record format. Notice that there are only two. **VENSUB** is the name of the subfile. The keyword on the right is **SFL** declaring that this is the subfile for the display file.

VNDNBR, NAME, STATE, and BALOWE are the fields defined for this subfile. In many ways this display file record (memory file) will be treated as a disk file in RPG processing.

Moving down in the ode, we get to see another Record Format called VENDCTL. It is shown below:

A>>>... R VENDCTL...   SFLCTL(VENSUB)

The R designates this as a record format so it is a screen panel. The keyword SFLCTL is very important. It links this control format to the actual subfile definition. It is called the subfile control record and thus the keyword SFLCTL.

VENSUB is the parameter for the keyword showing that the VENSUB format is the specific subfile that will be controlled (displayed, cleared etc.) using this special control mechanism.

Most of the text typed right side of the DDS specifications are literals and are positioned with the row and column number to display at a certain junction of column and row. For example, at row 3, column 29, the literal 'VENDOR' will begin its display when the control panel is written.

The other text in this area is for keywords. For example, immediately after the BALOWE field in the subfile is an EDTCDE keyword telling the display to format the balance owed field using the J edit code (comma, zero suppression, minus sign to the right if negative) when it is displayed.

The VENDNO field in the VENDCTL format is defined as being five positions in length with zero decimals and its sue is **BOTH** meaning it will be out put and it will be input back into the program.

The four fields in the VENSUB are not defined in this program because of the REF keyword above the VENSUB format. Notice it says VENDORP. This means that any fields that do not have their lengths and types specified in this DDS are defined in VENDORP and the DDS compiler should go to VENDORP at compile time to get those definitions. The R designation to the right of the field tells DDS which fields definitions to fetch.

To complete the description of the DDS in Figure 21-2, let's look at the special operations that are enabled for the subfile control record.

```
1. A   88...                    SFLINZ
2. A   81...                    SFLDSP
3. A   81...                    SFLDSPCTL
4. A  N81...                    SFLCLR
5. A...                         SFLSIZ(0500)
6. A...                         SFLPAG(0010)
```

Looking at these one at a time in the order of their importance to the program we begin with number 5. All subfile keywords begin with SFL so there are only three characters to get something meaningful. SFLSIZ is where you specify how many records in memory to reserve for this subfile.

SFLPAG in line 6 tells DDS to display 10 records at a time starting at line 7. We know it is line 7 because that is where the subfile fields as defined tin Figure 21-2 are to be written.

When subfiles are to have data entered, since RPG does not clear ot memory first, the SFLINZ operation at line 1 will do that trick. In this case, the program will turn on indicator 88 when the subfile is to be initialized. The Subfile control record VENDCTL is to be written based on line 3 whenever indicator 81 is on.

Additionally, as specified in line 2, the tem lines of the subfile are also to be displayed if indicator 81 is turned on. Finally, if there is an output operation to the subfile control record and 81 is not on, and then the subfile is to be cleared. It would be good to condition this record with N88 also so that a clear does not occur when an initialize is being effected. That wraps up our discussion of the display file for a simple subfile

VENDSRCH RPG Subfile Program

Every great display file needs a program to drive it. In this case, the RPG program name is VENDSRCH and it is shown in Figure 21-3. Starting at the top of the program at line 01, in File Descriptions, you find the VENDSUBF display file defined as combined and fully procedural. This means it can be used both for input and output operations. It is externally described using the device WORKSTN.

Statement 02 is the kicker that is needed for all subfile definitions in RPG programs. The "K" in the continuation line at column 53 means that line 02 is a continuation of Line 01. Columns 47 to 52 contain RRN which we have chosen as the name for the relative record number ("RECNO") field to be used to access records in the subfile. Positions 54-59 contain the SFILE keyword and the name of the subfile itself from the display file (VENSUB) is specified in columns 60-67 to ling the subfile with the file description at the program level. All of the continuation entries as specified are important for subfiles.

The next file specified is the VENDMST, a database file for vendors. This is an input, fully procedural file meaning random ands sequential input operations can be used against the file. It will be processed by key and the RPG device for database of course is DISK.

Figure 21-3 RPG Subfile Program-VENDSRCH

```
01.FVENDSUBFCF   E                 WORKSTN
02.F                                   RRN   KSFILE VENSUB
03.FVENDMST IF  E          K     DISK
04.C                       MOVE *ON        *IN88
05.C                       WRITEVENDCTL
06.C                       MOVE *OFF       *IN88
07.C            *IN99      DOWEQ*OFF
08.C                       MOVE *ON        *IN81
09.C                       EXFMTVENDCTL
10.C                       MOVE *OFF       *IN81
11.C                       WRITEVENDCTL
12.C                       MOVE *OFF       *IN60
13.C                       Z-ADD0          RRN      50
14.C            VENDNO     SETLLVENDMST
15.C            *IN60      DOWEQ*OFF                    EQ
16.C                       READ VENDMST                 60
17.C   .        *IN60      CABEQ*ON        FULL
18.C                       ADD  1          RRN          EQ
19.C                       WRITEVENSUB                  82
20.C            *IN82      CABEQ*ON        FULL
21.C                       ENDDO
22.C            FULL       TAG
23.C                       ENDDO
24.C                       MOVE *ON        *INLR
```

Because both files in the VENDSRCH program have an E in column 19 of File Description, the input and output specifications for the files will automatically be included in the program at compilation time. There is no need to code input for the display or database and output for the display. This work is accomplished already in the display file and the database file.

Now that we have handled the mechanics of how the display file with subfile and the RPG program are linked, let's look at the logic (C-specs). The program first sets on *IN88 at line 04 to prepare the SFLINZ keyword in the display file to initialize the subfile.

The program then WRITES the VENDCTL format to cause the initialization to occur. So that the file will never be initialized again, at line 06, *IN06 is turned off for the duration of the program.

Starting at line 7 through line 23, the "DO while loop" controls the action of the program from here on in. These steps will be repeated until the DO While is satisfied. The first step in the loop is to turn on indicator 81 which prepares the subfile and the subfile control display prompts (literals) to appear on the workstation. The EXFMT at line 09 sends the control format to the workstation which causes both the prompts and the empty subfile to appear (the first time)

In subsequent passes, the subfile will be full as will the first page. The other important thing that the EXFMT causes is for the user to be able to type in the next or first vendor number to use as the starter for filling up the subfile So, after the EXFMT, the program now has a vendor number search argument in the field called VENDNO. Following this, indicator 81 is turned off and a write operation goes against the subfile control record with *IN81 off and this causes the subfile to be cleared.

At statement 12 *IN60 is turned off for housekeeping reasons for the second time through the next do loop to assure it is off at the beginning of the loop starting in line 15. At statement 14, the SETLL using the VENDNO field positions the first read to the database file at the record containing the VENDNO field.

The DO loop starting at line 15 continues until the end of file is hit or the subfile is full. At line 16 the VNDMST file is read and indicator 60 comes on if it is at end of file. This will end this do loop. S Line 17 sends the program to the FULL Tag at line 22 if indicator 60 meaning end of file has been reached on the READ.

Now, the subfile action is about to begin. At line 18, the code adds 1 to the RRN value so that the record just read can be written to the subfile. The subfile is then written to adding the record. Indicator 82 is sued to test if the subfile (500 records) has been filled during this series of do loops. At statement 20, Indicator 82 is tested to see if the subfile is full and if so control is passed to the FULL Tag on a CABEQ branch operation.

Statement 21 ends the inner DO loop and if neither the end of the VENDMST file has been reached nor the subfile is full, the loop goes on again and again writing out subfile record 1, 2, 3 etf. Until either of the conditions are true.

When the conditions are true, the inner loop is complete and the control passes to the line 23, the ENDDO for the outer Do loop. If CF03 has not been pressed, this loop continues with statement 8 to set on 81 so that the subfile that we just filled can now be written out. The user can then page back and forth through the subfile records in the ten line window from lines 7 to 16 of the display.

The user can then enter another vendor number and the process tarts all over again until F3 is depressed. Then the code falls to line 24 which sets on LR and ends the program.

SDA Design Panel

If we had used SDA to design the panel, it would look very similar to the screen design shown in Figure 21-4

Figure 21-4 VENDSUBF Created With SDA

```
****************************************************************
*...+... 1 ...+... 2 ...+... 3 ...+... 4 ...+... 5 ...+...6..
01 *                 VENDOR MASTER INQUIRY    TT:TT:TT DD/DD/DD
02 *
03 * ENTER VENDOR NO:    99999-            F3      END OF JOB
04 *
05 *   VENDOR NO. VENDOR NAME               STATE   BALANCE OWED
06 *
07 *     66666    OOOOOOOOOOOOOOOOOOOOOOOOOOO  OO    66,666,666-
08 *     66666    OOOOOOOOOOOOOOOOOOOOOOOOOOO  OO    66,666,666-
09 *     66666    OOOOOOOOOOOOOOOOOOOOOOOOOOO  OO    66,666,666-
10 *     66666    OOOOOOOOOOOOOOOOOOOOOOOOOOO  OO    66,666,666-
11 *     66666    OOOOOOOOOOOOOOOOOOOOOOOOOOO  OO    66,666,666-
12 *     66666    OOOOOOOOOOOOOOOOOOOOOOOOOOO  OO    66,666,666-
13 *     66666    OOOOOOOOOOOOOOOOOOOOOOOOOOO  OO    66,666,666-
14 *     66666    OOOOOOOOOOOOOOOOOOOOOOOOOOO  OO    66,666,666-
15 *     66666    OOOOOOOOOOOOOOOOOOOOOOOOOOO  OO    66,666,666-
16 *     66666    OOOOOOOOOOOOOOOOOOOOOOOOOOO  OO    66,666,666-
17 *
...
23 *
24 *     Function Key 3 - E-O-J
 *...+... 1 ...+... 2 ...+... 3 ...+... 4 ...+...5...+.....6...+

****************************************************************
```

So, now that we have examined a subfile program set from DDS to RPG to SDA, let's take a walk back and explain the general notion of subfile processing. The diagram in Figure 21-5 almost perfectly represents the activities that take place in the most complex subfile program.

Figure 21-5 Using a Subfile

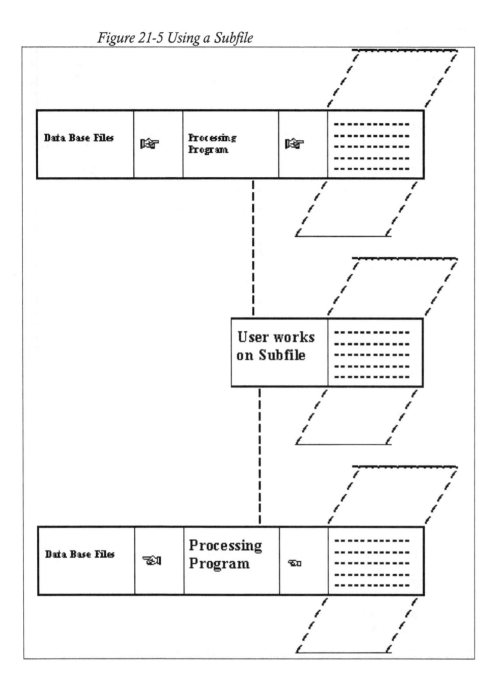

Figure 21-5 shows three boxes from top to bottom. Two are fairly wide and the middle box is lots smaller. Little pointer hands show the flow of data within the top box and the bottom box. Let's first examine the top box. Keep in mind that this diagram does not depict the entire processing program, only the interaction of the subfile with the program.

On the left side of the top box, you see the database file as input to the processing program and its output is added to the subfile. The box on the very right represents the page size of the subfile and the extensions above and below represent the fact that the subfile page (SFLPAG) is merely a window into the larger subfile, which of course is a file that gets loaded in memory.

Once the file is loaded, the PC or terminal user can get control. For the user to get control the programmer sends out the subfile control format with the SFLDSPCTL and SFLDSP keywords operative. This shows the control headers as well as the page size of the subfile to the user.

The middle box shows what can happen next in the program. The middle box depicts that the subfile is now displayed on the user workstation. The user can page forward and backward through the subfile; can change delete, and add items to the subfile, and finally can release the subfile back to the program with a mere depression of the ENTER key.

The part that you see in the middle on the right side of the middle box is the subfile page with full access via paging to the rest of the subfile. Once control is passed back to the program, we find ourselves at the bottom box or the third phase of subfile processing.

This bottom box looks very much like the top box except for one thing. The fingers on the little hands are pointing away from the subfile. At this point, the subfile has been loaded with initial data from the database and the user has manipulated the data in the subfile to suit their needs. If the program ended now, the subfile changes would not be applied to any permanent files and thus, the purpose of this last step.

Using operations such as the READC (read changed data from a subfile) the data changes are extracted and the databases are updated to reflect the manipulation of the user in the middle section of Figure 21-5. In a nutshell, the three steps we just examined are what subfile processing is all about

Subfile Records

Two record types in DDS do all the work for subfiles, the subfile record, shown below named data in this example and the subfile control record, named CTL in this example below:

R DATA   SFL

R CTL   SFLCTL(DATA)

In this example, DATA record is the subfile (SFL) record description. Using this record format, the programmer defines the subfile data and in so doing, the first record of the subfile page as it appears on the screen. Together the subfile and control record formats define the heading, body, file size, page size, and control information. Now, let's review some of the subfile keywords.

SFL Main Keywords

Figure 21-6 Review of Main Subfile Keywords

```
    A              R VENSUB          SFL
                     |  |
    A              R VENDCTL          SFLCTL(VENSUB)
    A                                 SFLSIZ(0500)
    A                                 SFLPAG(0010)
    A   88                            SFLINZ
    A   81                            SFLDSP
    A   81                            SFLDSPCTL
    A  N81                            SFLCLR
    A   40                            SFLEND
    A   98                            SFLMSG('INVALID VEND...')
```

We covered most of these earlier in the chapter but we did not look at the SFLEND back then. This keyword is to be turned on when the programmer would like to place a "more" on the screen indicating that there are more records to see. Additionally, the SFLMSG appears on the bottom of the screen in line "25" so to speak even though the panel has but 24 lines. The user can position the cursor at the bottom to see this message.

So now that we have seen just about it all, let's review what we have learned. First of all, a subfile is a memory File. You write records to memory subfile via the SFL record in much the same way you write records to a direct file. The records do not display. When you want to show the work to the user, you write screen panels using the subfile control record. You also perform control functions by writing to the control record. As we have seen in our VENDSRCH example, the indicators that are on and off when the CTL record is written determine what is actually done.

Let's look at some very specific sample code:

```
SETON                                    8292
EXFMT           CONTROL
SETOF                                    8292
```

In this sample, the code first sets on 82 and 92 to perform one or several functions against the subfile as determined by the subfile keywords. Then the EXFMT sends out the panel and waits for a response. EXFMT is typically used when the subfile is to be displayed. Following the receipt o the response, the code shuts off those specific indicators since the function is complete. In the sample code, CONTROL is name of SFL Control format. Control is passed back from EXFMT when the operator presses the enter key. The workstation's Roll Keys (Page up / Page down) are operative without coming back to the program.

The WRITE operation is used for control functions and functions not requiring a response from the user. Some sample code follows:

```
SETON                                    60
WRITE           CONTROL
SETOF                                    60
```

In the sample code above, either a initialize or a clear or some other function may be occurring which does not involve the user. However, write can be used to send out literals or constants or other output-only fields which light up the screen. In these instances, the program does not wait for the operator to hit ENTER when the display is actually sent

The write operation is also used to put data into the subfile. The write occurs with the relative record number field defined in File Continuation specs. As the RRN is incremented, each record is written the subfile with the WRITE operation. The relative record or RRN field in our examples determines where in which record, the contents of the WRITE operation is placed. Four RPG entries for the subfile sample code follow:

```
       Device      Symbolic    K       Key           ENTRY
                   Device              Word
       40 - 48     47 - 52     53      54 - 59       60-65
F..    WORKSTN
F..                RRN         K       SFILE         DATA
```

The RRN field is the relative record # used to write /read records to/from the memory subfile. DATA is the name of the subfile record format in the display file. Let's look at the code to actually write to the subfile:

```
ADD            1       RRN     2 0
WRITE          DATA                    50
```

In this sample, DATA is the name of the subfile record format and 50 is specified in EQ to signal when the subfile has been filled.

Three Major Purposes for Subfiles

When a subfile is the proper solution for an application, it serves one fo three major purposes as follows:

1. Inquiry for multiple records

2. Inquiry w/ update for multiple records

3. Data entry for multiple records

Inquiry for Multiple Records

Let's first look at subfiles for inquiry purposes. If you look back at Figure 21-5, stop the diagram at the second box from the top. The top two boxes diagram the inquiry function. Data is written to the subfield and the user gets to review it when the panel is displayed. It's that simple. The VENDSRCH program was a good example of an inquiry program in which multiple records are returned in response to the query.   What must the programmer do? The four steps required for inquiry that answer that question are as follows:

1. Activating
2. Loading
3. Displaying
4. Processing

What is Activation?

The simple answer to the activation question is: a write to the subfile causing a single active record. Without the write, the subfile is not ready to go. Once activated, subfiles are loaded, displayed and processed. The processing occurs if there are more records to be delivered since an inquiry by definition does not update records.

Let's look at a simple structured programming process in Figure 21-7 to demonstrate:

Figure 21-7 Structured Process

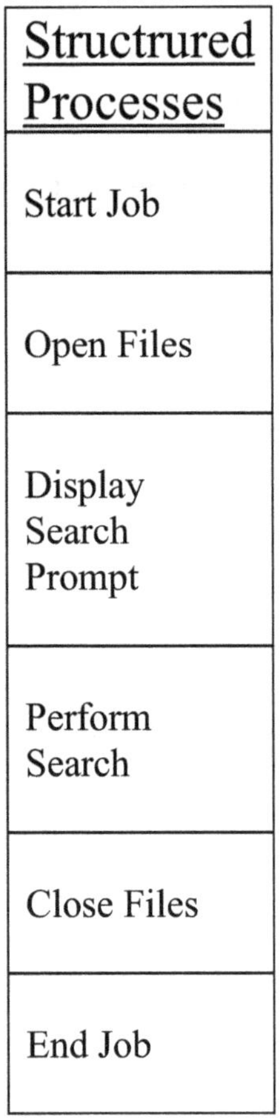

Structrured Processes
Start Job
Open Files
Display Search Prompt
Perform Search
Close Files
End Job

Figure 21-8 The Subfile Search -- Detail Chart

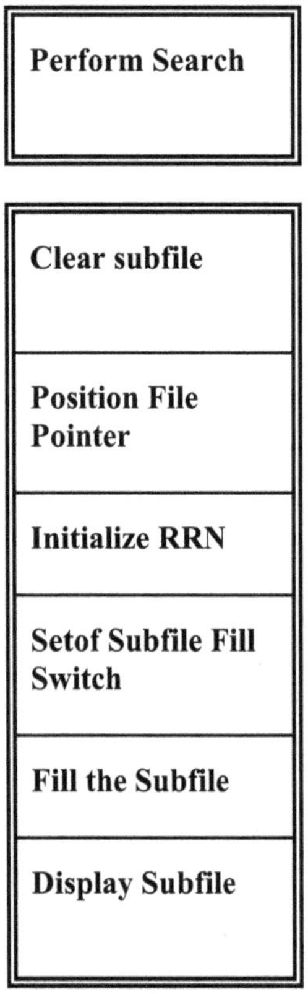

Perform Search

Clear subfile
Position File Pointer
Initialize RRN
Setof Subfile Fill Switch
Fill the Subfile
Display Subfile

The subfile fill portion of the inquiry subfile process is exploded in Figure 21-8. In this process, as you can see, there are two major tests performed in the code

1. During the read of the Database Master, there is a required test for EOF. If there is no more input, the filling is done.

2. During the writing of the subfile, with an allocation of 500 records, it is possible that the subfile might be filled before all of the records meeting the search criteria are found. Therefore, there is the test for a full condition which again ends the fill since there is no more room to put more records.

If you were paying close attention, back at Figure 21-4, you would have noticed that I slipped an extra line of display at line 24. In order to accomplish this, I needed to define a third format on the display. The DDS to accomplish this is shown in Figure 21-9 and the program to accomplish this is shown in Figure 21-10..

As you can see below, the new format name is CFKEY and it is unconditioned.

```
A...    R CFKEY
A...                           24  2'Function Key 3 -
```

Since a subfile works only on the last panel sent to a display, CFKEY, though it is the third format is sent out before the subfile so it is not the active format on the display. The *Overlay* keyword is new to this scenario and is used so that the subfile can be displayed along with the headers without wiping out the information already on line 24 from the WRITE operation in the new VENDSRCH for format CFKEY.

User / Program Control of Subfile Display

If you do nothing special, on its own, a display of a subfile starts with the first record of the subfile. This does not have to be the way the subfile page behaves. If you would like to begin displaying a record other than the first, you may use the SFLRCDNBR keyword. On this keyword in parentheses, you would specify the specific subfile record that you wish to be the first record on the subfile page that you see. This can be done via program or via a screen field from the subfile control record

Figure 21-9 DDS for Expanded VENDSUBF

```
A* SUBFILE DDS -- VENDSRCH
A                                          REF(VENDORP)
A            R VENSUB                      SFL
A              VNDNBR    R         O  7 12TEXT('VENDOR NUMBER')
A              NAME      R         O  7 23TEXT('NAME')
A              STATE     R         O  7 50TEXT('STATE')
A              BALOWE    R         O  7 54TEXT('BALANCE OWED   ')
A                                          EDTCDE(Y)
A
A            R VENDCTL                     SFLCTL(VENSUB)
A*
A                                          CF03(99 'end of job')
A   95                                     SFLDSP
A   85                                     SFLDSPCTL
A   75                                     SFLCLR
A   40                                     SFLEND
A                                          SFLSIZ(025)
A                                          SFLPAG(0010)
A                                          OVERLAY so CFKEY doesn't
A                                             disappear
A                                        3 29'VENDOR'
A                                        3 36'MASTER'
A                                        3 43'INQUIRY'
A                                        3 54TIME
A                                        3 63DATE
A                                        5 10'ENTER'
A                                        5 16'VENDOR'
A                                        5 23'NO:'
A              VENDNO        5  0B    5 28DSPATR(HI)
A                                          EDTCDE(4)
A                                        5 41'F3 '
A                                        5 45' '
A                                        5 48'END'
A                                        5 52'OF'
A                                        5 55'JOB'
A                                        7 10'VENDOR'
A                                        7 17'NO.'
A                                        7 23'VENDOR'
A                                        7 31'NAME'
A                                        7 48'STATE'
A                                        7 56'BALANCE'
A                                        7 64'OWED'
A            R CFKEY
A                                       24  2'Function Key 3 - EOJ'
```

Figure 21-10 Expanded VENDSRCH RPG Subfile Program

```
FVENDSUBFCF  E                        WORKSTN
F                                             RRN    KSFILE VENSUB
FVENDMSTRIF  E           K            DISK


Write the CFKEY screen + prompt for vendor # -begins search
C                       WRITECFKEY
C                       MOVE '1'        *IN85
C                       EXFMTVENDCTL
C                       MOVE '0'        *IN85
C* Repeat until indicator 99 (ON)  representing EOJ
C           *IN99       DOWEQ'0'
Clear the Subfile by writing the control record with *IN75
C                       MOVE *ON        *IN75
C                       WRITEVENDCTL
C                       SETOF                         75
C                       Z-ADD0     RRN    50
C           VENDNO      SETLLVENDMSTR
C* Fill the subfile with records from the Vendor Master
C           *IN40       DOWEQ'0'
C                       READ VENDMST                 40
C           *IN40       CABEQ'1'    FULL
C                       ADD  1      RRN
C                       WRITEVENSUB                  82
C           *IN82       CABEQ'1'    FULL
C                       ITER
C           FULL        TAG
C                       LEAVE
C                       ENDDO
```

Additional Subfile Controls (Appearance)

The following subfile keywords govern the appearance of the display:

SFLDROP (CFXX)

This provides a toggle switch for text that overflows. The default is to truncate.

SFLFOLD (CFXX)

This also provides a toggle switch for text that overflows. With this toggle switch, the default is to fold the records. The user can toggle between the default and the other form.

SFLLIN (#)

This keyword permits the programmer to specify the #spaces between columns. It is used if there is more than one column for a subfile. This keyword permits you to specify the column spacing.

Inquiry w/ Update for Multiple Records

Let's now look at Subfiles for inquiry with update capabilities for multiple records. If you take a look back at Figure 21-5, this whole diagram plays in this type of subfile activity. All three diagrams describe this type of action. The database fills up the subfile. The user manipulates the subfile data and the program must then update the database from the changed records in the subfile. The steps the programmer must do are basically the same as with inquiry but there is a lot more processing:

- ✓ Activating
- ✓ Loading
- ✓ Displaying
- ✓ Processing

The key item here is that the records in the subfile must be accessed by another routine after the "inquiry" facility fills the subfile. So, how are records accessed in a subfile? The answer is as simple as basic disk file processing, though the file is in memory and it is associated with a display, not a disk device. Once the records are there and you want to fetch then, you have two choices:

```
1.  Chain Operation -- CHAIN (BY RRN)
2.  Read Changed Operation -- READC
```

A snippet of code to access a subfile is shown below:

```
C...   RRN...      CHAIN...  DATA...            50
```

In this scenario, RRN is the relative record # pointer of the subfile records defined in the RPG File Description Continuation specification. Indicator 50 turns on if the RRN is too high and the record requested is not found ... not there! DATA is the subfile format name as defined in the subfile and in File Description Continuation.

Now, let's use the Read changed operation, READC to access the subfile data:

```
C...            READCDATA               50
C... *IN50      DOWEQ*OFF
        ...
        ...
C               READCDATA               50
C               . . .
C               ENDDO
```

The beauty of the READC operation is that the subfile keeps track of the records that the user changed, added, or deleted during the page up / page down session. It presents one record at a time to the program until no more records have been changed. It skips over unchanged records in the subfile.

Command Key Specification

When you are working with command keys in display formats, it helps to know which type of format for the key definition itself you should use because they behave totally differently. Just like ENTER, both CA and CF keys provide an interruption to keying on the workstation and they request that the program read from the workstation.

There's where the similarities mostly end. On the workstation itself, there are no CA keys and CF keys. The programmer decides in the construction of the display file which function keys will be used as CF and which will be used as CA.

When the user presses a CF key, all of the changed data on the display goes along with the command ke is shipped back – just the indication as to which key was depressed. This then is translated to an indicator based again on the display file keyword CA or CF and sent to the program.

So, how is the update processed for the Subfile after it is changed and after the records are fetched? The steps are as follows:

1. Read the subfile for changed records
2. Read and lock the VENDMST record
3. Re-Read the subfile record for verification of data – assure match
4. Update VENDMST record
5. Read the subfile again for the next changed record until end of subfile

The SDA panel is shown in Figure 21-11; the DDS in Figure 21-12, and the RPG program in 21-13.

Figure 21-11 Subfile SDA .. Inquiry with Update

```
****************************************************************
*...+... 1 ...+... 2 ...+... 3 ...+... 4 ...+... 5 ...+...6..
01 *                    VENDOR MASTER INQUIRY     TT:TT:TT DD/DD/DD
02 *
03 * ENTER VENDOR NO:      99999-              F3        END OF JOB
04 *
05 *    VENDOR NO. VENDOR NAME                 STATE    BALANCE OWED
06 *
07 *      66666    BBBBBBBBBBBBBBBBBBBBBBBBB     OO      66,666,666-
08 *      66666    BBBBBBBBBBBBBBBBBBBBBBBBB     OO      66,666,666-
09 *      66666    BBBBBBBBBBBBBBBBBBBBBBBBB     OO      66,666,666-
10 *      66666    BBBBBBBBBBBBBBBBBBBBBBBBB     OO      66,666,666-
11 *      66666    BBBBBBBBBBBBBBBBBBBBBBBBB     OO      66,666,666-
12 *      66666    BBBBBBBBBBBBBBBBBBBBBBBBB     OO      66,666,666-
13 *      66666    BBBBBBBBBBBBBBBBBBBBBBBBB     OO      66,666,666-
14 *      66666    BBBBBBBBBBBBBBBBBBBBBBBBB     OO      66,666,666-
15 *      66666    BBBBBBBBBBBBBBBBBBBBBBBBB     OO      66,666,666-
16 *      66666    BBBBBBBBBBBBBBBBBBBBBBBBB     OO      66,666,666-
17 *
18 *
19 *
20 *
21 *
22 *
23 *
24 * Function Key 3 - EOJ          Function Key 11 - Update
 *...+... 1 ...+... 2 ...+... 3 ...+... 4 ...+...5...+.....6...+

****************************************************************
```

The new code for update comes in the documented program in Figure 21-12. The code is documented so that you can decode it to find out exactly how it accomplishes our defined mission of inquiry with multiple update via subfile. Now it's time for us to turn our attention to the workstation equivalent of heads down multiple direct record entry.

Figure 21-12 Subfile DDS .. Inquiry with Update

```
A* SUBFILE Inquiry w/ Update
A                                        REF(VENDORP)
A              R VENSUB                  SFL
A*
A                VNDNBR    R       12 10
A                NAME      R     B 12 18DSPATR(PC)
A                STATE     R       12 46
A                BALOWE    R       12 54
A
A              R VENDCTL                 SFLCTL(VENSUB)
A*
A                                        CF03(99 'end of job')
A                                        CF11(11 'Update')
A  95                                    SFLDSP
A  85                                    SFLDSPCTL
A  75                                    SFLCLR
A  40                                    SFLEND
A                                        SFLSIZ(025)
A                                        SFLPAG(0010)
A                                        OVERLAY
A                                      3 29'VENDOR'
A                                      3 36'MASTER'
A                                      3 43'INQUIRY'
A                                      3 54TIME
A                                      3 63DATE
A                                        EDTCDE(Y)
A                                      5 10'ENTER'
A                                      5 16'VENDOR'
A                                      5 23'NO:'
A                VENDNO     5  0B    5 28DSPATR(HI)
A                                        EDTCDE(4)
A                                      5 41'F3 '
A                                      5 45' '
A                                      5 48'END'
A                                      5 52'OF'
A                                      5 55'JOB'
A                                      7 10'VENDOR'
A                                      7 17'NO.'
A                                      7 23'VENDOR'
A                                      7 31'NAME'
A                                      7 48'STATE'
A                                      7 56'BALANCE'
A                                      7 64'OWED'
A              R CFKEY
A  N95                                24  2'Function Key 3 - EOJ'
A  95                                 24 40'Function Key 11 - Update'
```

Figure 21-13 RPG Subfile Program Inquiry with Update

```
FVENDSUBFCF   E                       WORKSTN
F                                     RRN    KSFILE VENSUB
FVENDMST UF  E          K         DISK
C*
C* Write the CFKEY screen and prompt for vendor # to begin search
C*
C                       WRITECFKEY
C                       MOVE '1'        *IN85
C                       EXFMTVENDCTL
C                       MOVE '0'        *IN85
Do until EOJ
C           *IN99       DOWEQ'0'
C*
C*     Clear the subfile
C*
C                       MOVE *ON        *IN75
C                       WRITEVENDCTL
C                       SETOF                        75
C                       Z-ADD0          RRN     50
C* Position the VENDMSTR file to right before the first record
C*
C           VENDNO      SETLLVENDMSTR
C*
C* READ records from the VENDMST format until EOF and /or
C* Fill subfile full condition is reported (*IN40 = on)
C           *IN40       DOWEQ'0'
C                       READ VENDMST                 40
C           *IN40       CABEQ'1'        FULL
C                       ADD  1          RRN
C                       WRITEVENSUB                  82
C*
C           *IN82       CABEQ'1'        FULL
C                       ITER
C           FULL        TAG
C                       LEAVE
C                       ENDDO
C*  Write CFKEY format and overlay the next Subfile
C*
C                       SETON                        8595
C                       WRITECFKEY
C                       EXFMTVENDCTL
C                       SETOF                        8595
C*
C* Update after reading changed records
C*
C           *IN11       IFEQ '1"
C                       READC                        40
C*
C           *IN40       DOWEQ'0'
C           VENDNO      CHAINVENDMAST                41
C           RRN         CHAINVENSUB                  41
C                       UPDATVENDMST
C                       READCVENSUB                  40
C*
C                       SETON                        85
C                       WRITECFKEY
C                       EXFMTVENDCTL
C                       SETOF                        855
C*
C                       ENDIF
C                       ENDDO
C*
C                       MOVE '1'        *INLR
```

Data Entry Subfiles

Let's now look at subfiles for date entry for multiple records. If you take a look at Figure 21-13A, you will see a depiction of what happens in a data entry scenario using subfiles. Instead of multiple WRITE operations in RPG adding records to this subfile, this record holder gets its records directly from the screen panel as the user keys each page. There can be some user manipulation of the keyed data but, by and large, what is keyed is going to get processed. That's the nature of the application.

So, as you see in Figure 21-13 for data entry, the first step here is to interact with the user. Once the user fills the subfile as in the top figure, the user directs that entry of a page or a series of pages is complete and as you can see in the bottom the databases are populated with the data from the subfile The steps the programmer must perform do are far different from inquiry though there is a resemblance to the second half of the inquiry with multiple update.

Figure 21-13A Data Entry Process via Subfile

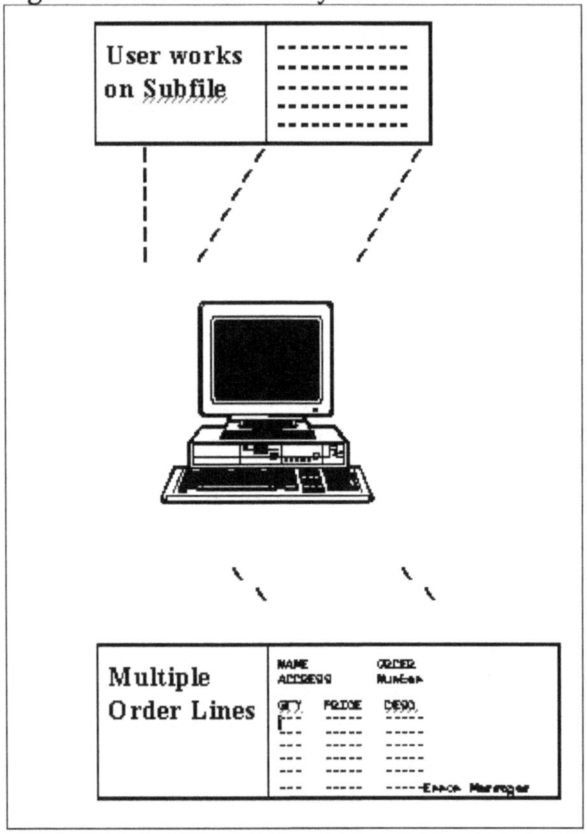

Besides the notion of straight key to disk entry, this example gives the idea of order entry which is more intelligent of a process than data entry. Order entry can serve as an effective example for this type of subfield action since it typifies those applications requiring more than one line of entry (order line item) per order. In this scenario, the line item information is entered through the subfile and after entry it has to go through an additional step prior to updating the databases. It must be validated. The first thing for us is to set the stage by examining three subfile interaction keywords that help in pulling this off.

```
SFLNXTCHG
DSPATR
SFLMSG / SFLMSGID
```

SFLNXTCHG Keyword

You use this record-level keyword; subfile next changed SFLNXTCHG on the subfile record format to force the work station user to correct errors that the program detects. In the first part of the data entry scenario in Figure 21-13, the program has already captured the records in the subfile. It next must read the records and perform validation checks on the data after it gains control from the workstation user.

The problem with this approach may be obvious. How does the editing function tell the user which records are bad? The READC cannot be used in its normal form because all records in the file have changed – that is the nature of entry. So, there must be a way that the program can mark a record in error so that it appears to have been changed and can be processed by the READC. That's what SFLNXTCHG does. It makes bad records that were keyed at the workstation and flagged by the program validation to reappear to the workstation user. It's pretty neat especially since there are not many good ways to edit blobs of data at once rather than one at a time. This trick gives the program the ability to make the user see these records so they can be fixed prior to sending them on to further processing. When this keyword is applied, the next get-next-changed operation (READC) must read the "bad" record.

DSPATR Keyword

The display attributes keyword permits various highlighting to be shown on erroneous data, when the subfile is displayed. This is a nice way of pointing out that data needs correction.

SFLMSG / SFLMSGID Keyword

This special keyword permits errors to be flagged and highlighted within the subfile. When the subfile is displayed the error record is highlighted and a straight message or a message with an ID from a message file cane be displayed at the bottom of the panel to inform the user what is wrong with the highlighted item. Figure 21-14 shows the bottom half of a generic order entry panel in subfile form for the "blank customer."

Figure 21-14 Order Entry Panel

```
NAME          _____
ADDRESS       _____
              _____
              _____
Order Number      _____

ITEM          QTY               PRICE

101           355               93
745           35                225

____          ____              ____
____          ____              ____
____          ____              ____
```

The programmer must be concerned with more steps with Data Entry than with the other subfield methods.

1. Activation
2. Data Entry
3. Re-Display of Errors
4. Error Correction
5. Processing

Process of Activation

For an entry file, let's look at how the activation piece actually works by looking at the various processes shown in Figure 21-15:

Figure 21-15 Process of Activation

Process Of Activation		
Write to Subfile Record	Write to Subfile Control Record SFLINZ	Write to Subfile Control Record SFLINZ / SFLRNA
	-------------------	-------------------
	-------------------	-------------------
	-------------------	-------------------
	-------------------	-------------------
	-------------------	-------------------
	-------------------	-------------------
	-------------------	--
A single Active Record	All Subfile records are active	All Subfile records are inactive

In order to have the subfile page display to a user, the subfile itself must already be activated. The normal means of getting records from a database and having the first record activate the subfile does not work for entry. However, the initialize function does. It not only writes one record, it writes to every record in the subfile thereby permitting initialized (pristine) records to appear on the entry screen for keying of real data.

However, though you want the subfile to be active, you do not want the records to be active when they are displayed for keying. Thus, you use the SFLNRA with the SFLINZ keyword on the subfile control record format so that your program can initialize a subfile with no active records. When the subfile is displayed and the user types records in, then the records will become active.

Performing Data Entry with Subfiles

Subfiles provide a very productive means of keying data into programs. The way this is accomplished includes the following:

✓ Data is entered at screen
✓ Fields defined as input
✓ All records have same shape
✓ DDS Validity checking allowed
✓ SFL Records read by READC (all are read 1st)
✓ SFL Records are changed by UPDAT

Check out the following code snippet:

```
C           READC...                    60
C  *IN60    IFEQ'0'
C           . . .
C           . . .
C           UPDATVENSUB
C                     END
```

Suppose that you have already keyed in your records into the subfile. The READC will read all of the records that you keyed. You then go through an editing routine and you write back the errors to the subfile so that they can be shown on the next panel and be corrected. In essence this process writes error conditions back to records

To have the user correct the errors that exist in the subfile, a good technique is to make use of the DSPATR keyword to highlight the errors so they are known when the subfile is displayed. Moreover, as noted above the SFLNXTCHG keyword forces the user to fix the error because it keeps coming up, the READC gets it each time and redisplays the error until it passes the edit.

It forces user to fix the error before continuing. It causes the changed attribute to be on in the subfile record in error. The next READC gets the record, ENTER cannot bypass it so chances are the user will fix it to move on.

As noted previously another good technique is to use the SFLMSG keyword to specifies a message to be displayed on the message line. The programmer is in charge of highlighting with DSPATR or ERRMSG if this technique is used. The SFLMSGID keyword can also be sued to provide the same function. It is basically the same as SFLMSG with a message file. The SFLPGMQ keyword is used for a message subfile. Multiple messages can be written / retrieved to/from a message subfile so it can work hand in glove with multiple errors in the subfile.

Should you use SFLMSGID or SFLMSG? After some sample code look for the considerations:

```
A* SFLMSGID - Predefined Messages
A                      REF(VENDORP)
A          R SFLCTL    SFLCTL(VENSUB)
A  20                  SFLMSGID(USR0020 MYLIB/MFILE)
```

In this example, the message ID is USR0020 and it is a user defined message, stored in the MFILE message file in the MYLIB library. Second level message text is available if it is defined by the programmer when building the message.

```
A* SFLMSG - Impromptu Messages
A                           REF(VENDORP)
A           R SFLCTL        SFLCTL(VENSUB)
A 30                        SFLMSG('Correct & Retry' 30)
A*
```

In this example, there is no message ID given since it is impromptu. The message comes out and makes its demands in a less formal way than a message in a file.

Now, let us examine the code for the data entry work follow-on to the VNDSRCH examples including the SDA layout-- Figure 21-16, DDS—Figure 21-17, and the RPG program --Figure 21-18. Following this are two additional diagrams that show the input side of the transaction – Figure 21-19 and the Output side of the transaction – 21-20.

As you decode the source for these objects remember the data entry steps discussed earlier in this chapter. Data Entry programs must go through activation, data entry, re-display of errors, and error correction processing. Look for these areas in the DDS and the RPG code in tandem.

Watch what indicators get turned on at what point and the effect they have on the display. Look for SFLCHGNXT, SFLINZ and SFLRNA as the new SFL keywords for the entry type programs. Also, remember the objective is to have the data correct.

.

Figure 21-16 Entry Subfile Design Layout SDA -- Input fields for SFL

```
******************************************************************
*...+... 1 ...+... 2 ...+... 3 ...+... 4 ...+... 5 ...+...6..
01 *                  VENDOR MASTER ENTRY      TT:TT:TT DD/DD/DD
02 *
03 *                            F3       END OF JOB
04 *
05 *   VENDOR NO. VENDOR NAME              STATE   BALANCE OWED
06 *
07 *     33333    IIIIIIIIIIIIIIIIIIIIIIIII  II    33333333
08 *     33333    IIIIIIIIIIIIIIIIIIIIIIIII  II    33333333
09 *     33333    IIIIIIIIIIIIIIIIIIIIIIIII  II    33333333
10 *     33333    IIIIIIIIIIIIIIIIIIIIIIIII  II    33333333
11 *     33333    IIIIIIIIIIIIIIIIIIIIIIIII  II    33333333
12 *     33333    IIIIIIIIIIIIIIIIIIIIIIIII  II    33333333
13 *     33333    IIIIIIIIIIIIIIIIIIIIIIIII  II    33333333
14 *     33333    IIIIIIIIIIIIIIIIIIIIIIIII  II    33333333
15 *     33333    IIIIIIIIIIIIIIIIIIIIIIIII  II    33333333
16 *     33333    IIIIIIIIIIIIIIIIIIIIIIIII  II    33333333
17 *
18 *
19 *
20 *
21 *
22 *
23 *
24 * Function Key 3 - EOJ
  *...+... 1 ...+... 2 ...+... 3 ...+... 4 ...+...5...+.....6...+

******************************************************************
```

Figure 21-17 Entry Subfile DDS -- Input fields for SFL

```
A* DDS for ENTRY Subfile
A                                      REF(VENDORP)
A             R VENSUB                 SFL
A*
A  15                                  SFLNXTCHG
A             VENDNO    R       I  9 12TEXT('VENDOR NUMBER')
A                                      CMP(GT 0)
A                                      DSPATR(PC)
A  11                                  DSPATR(PR)
A  10                                  DSPATR(RI)
A             NAME      R       I  9 23TEXT('NAME')
A                                      COMP(NE ' ')
A  11                                  DSPATR(PR)
A             STATE     R       I  9 50TEXT('STATE')
A                                      COMP(NE ' ')
A  11                                  DSPATR(PR)
A             BALOWE    R       I  9 54TEXT('BALANCE OWED   ')
A                                      EDTCDE(J)
A                                      COMP(GT 0)
A  11                                  DSPATR(PR)
A* -----------------------------------------------------------
A             R VENDCTL                SFLCTL(VENSUB)
A*
A                                      CF03(99 'end of job')
A*
A  85                                  SFLDSP
A  85                                  SFLDSPCTL
A*
A  65                                  SFLINZ
A  65                                  SFLRNA
A                                      SFLSIZ(010)
A                                      SFLPAG(0010)
A  20                                  SFLMSG('INVAL VEN NO.' 20)
A*
A                                      OVERLAY
A             PAGEND           I  2  2CHECK(FE)
A*
A                                   3 29'VENDOR'
A                                   3 36'MASTER'
A                                   3 43'ENTRY'
A                                   3 54TIME
A                                   3 63DATE
A                                      EDTCDE(Y)
A                                   5 41'F3 '
A                                   5 45' '
A                                   5 48'END'
A                                   5 52'OF'
A                                   5 55'JOB'
A                                   7 10'VENDOR'
A                                   7 17'NO.'
A                                   7 23'VENDOR'
A                                   7 31'NAME'
A                                   7 48'STATE'
A                                   7 56'BALANCE'
A                                   7 64'OWED'
A*
A             R CFKEY
A  N95                             24  2'Function Key 3 - EOJ'
```

Figure 21-18 Entry Subfile RPG Program

```
F* Data Entry Program - Subfiles
F*
FVENDSUBFCF   E                         WORKSTN
F                                       RRN   KSFILE VENSUB
FVENDMST UF  E           K      DISK                         A
F*
F*   Initialize the subfile for entry
C                        MOVE *ON        *IN65
C                        WRITEVENDCTL
C                        MOVE '0'        *IN65
C*
C*    While END of JOB not selected, prompt for data entry
C*
C           *IN99        DOWEQ'0'
C                        MOVE '1'        *IN85
C                        EXFMTVENDCTL
C                        MOVE '0'        *IN85
C*
C*  Process the records as entered
C*
C           *IN99        IFEQ '0'
C                        READCVENSUB                        40 EOF
C           *IN40        DOWEQ'0'        DO
C           VENDNO       SETLLVENDMST                       10 EQ FD
C*
C           *IN10        IFEQ '0'
C                        WRITEVENDMST
C                        SETON                              11
C*  Protect fields with indicator 11
C                        ELSE
C                        SETON                            1520
C*                                            For SFLNXTCHG
C*                                            & SFLMSG
C                        ENDIF
C*
C*    Update Error Indicator Status in record
C*
C                        UPDATVENSUB
C                        SETOF                          101115
C*
C                        READCVENSUB
C                        ENDDO           ENDDO
C*  C*
C*    When there are no records in subfile in error.
C*         re-initialize subfile for add'l input
C*
C           *IN20        IFEQ *OFF
C                        SETON                              65
C                        WRITEVENDCTL
C                        SETOF                              65 INZ
C                        ENDIF
C                        ENDDO
C                        ENDDO
C                        SETON                              LR
```

Figure 21-19 Entry Subfile Input Side

Subfile Control Record

IN03	PAGEND

Subfile Data Records

VENDNO	NAME	STATE	BALOWE

**Indicator status is determined by what the operator does!

Figure 21-20 Entry Subfile Output Side

Subfile Control Record: **Indicator Status is managed by OS/400**

*IN20	*IN65	*IN85

Subfile Data Records: **Program must manage indicators as fields**

*IN10	*IN11	*IN15	VENDNO	NAME	STATE	BALOWE

How to Correct Errors in Subfile?

Anytime there can be multiple input records entered into a program before any corrections can occur, there is a problem for both the user and the programmer. The user is happy being able to enter ten or fifteen records on a display without having the delay of an interaction with the system. However, chances are high that a number of those interactions with multiple records will have some type of keying error. It's just human nature.

Since the mission of entry programs is to gain clean data for applications, the bad data cannot be tolerated. Coming to the program in subfile form makes it more difficult to handle errors interactively. The simplest approach for a programmer is to store the data in a temporary file, produce an error list and permit the user to go back into the temporary file to make the changes one at a time. The programmer can then make an immediate edit of the one record input and the user can correct any second or third-time errors for the same record without moving on. This approach can also work in the subfile environment by feeding error records one at a time to users for correction.

Two Subfiles for Error Correction

Two subfiles is another common approach for correcting errors in a subfile. It is the programmer's decision how frequently to notify the operator of errors. Some applications may be better served if the user were able to key all the data once and then go back and check for errors; others might be better to correct the errors each time a page or so is entered. In the first scenario, the subfile would be larger than the page size and in the latter scenario it subfile size and page size would be the same.

Using the two subfile approach, only the errors that are found would be placed in the second subfile for reediting. When all records were checked the second subfile would be displayed with just the error records. Of course the edit routines to check for good data would have to be run against the second subfile and any errors collected again for display either through a third subfile or by holding the records and rewriting them to the second subfile.

A variation of the approach that requires just two subfiles is as follows: The user enters data to SFL1. The program puts good records in a temporary database and puts errors in SFL2. User then makes changes to SFL2. Then the program switches to SFL2 for editing and it puts good records in same database and it puts bad records in SFL1. User then edits the SFL1 errors again and so on until all errors are eliminated. The techniques are endless but the goal is the same. – provide clean data for the system.

The code might look something like that shown in Figure 21-21.

Error Correction Using One Subfile

In this scenario, the user enters data to the subfile. The program flags records in the subfile as errors and redisplays the subfile pages with errors. The user then corrects the error records in the subfile interactively. When there are no more errors, the program writes all DB records that were entered from the subfile to the database file

Representative code for this example is shown in Figure 21-22. Again this is not fully tested code and is presented here to demonstrate a technique.

Figure 21-21 Two Subfiles - Error correction

```
FVENDSUBFCF  E                       WORKSTN
F                                          RRN    KSFILE VENSB1
F                                          RRN2   KSFILE VENSB2
FVENDMST UF  E           K        DISK                       A
F*
F* Initialize first subfile for entry
C                    MOVE *ON       *IN65
C                    WRITEVENCTL1
C                    MOVE '0'       *IN65
C*
C*      Display First Subfile
C*
C                    MOVE '1'       *IN85
C                    EXFMTVENDCTL
C                    MOVE '0'       *IN85
C*
C*      Process first subfile
C*      Write error records to second subfile
C*
C                    READCVENSB1                       40 EOF
C          *IN40     DOWEQ'0'       DO
C          VENDNO    SETLLVENDMST         |           10 FD
C          *IN10     IFEQ '0'
C                    WRITEVENDMST         |
C                    ELSE
```

```
C                           ADD  1          RRN2
C                           SETON                    |          1520
C*  SFLNXTCHG & SFLMSG SET above
C                           WRITEVENSB2
C                           SETOF                               15
C                           ENDIF
C                           READCVENSB1
C                           ENDDO           ENDDO
C*
C*  Clear First Subfile to prepare for records
C*
C                           SETON                               75
C                           WRITEVENCTL1
C                           SETOF                               75
C*
C*  If errors, show the second display file to user
C           *IN20     IFEQ '1'
C                           SETON                               86
C                           EXFMTVENCTL2
C                           SETOF                               86
C*
C*      Now process the second SFL,
C*      Write your error records to first subfile
C*
C                           ...
C                           ...
```

Figure 21-22 Correct Entry Errors: Process Same Subfile Twice

```
FVENDSUBFCF   E                     WORKSTN
F                                        RRN   KSFILE VENSUB
FVENDMST UF  E          K       DISK                    A
F*
C*  Initialize subfile for entry
C                           MOVE *ON        *IN65
C                           WRITEVENDCTL
C                           MOVE '0'        *IN65
C*
C*  When not EOJ, display subfile for data entry
C*
C           *IN99     DOWEQ'0'         C
C                           MOVE '1'        *IN85
C                           EXFMTVENDCTL
C                           MOVE '0'        *IN85
C*
C*  Edit the records entered on last enter key depression
C*
C                           READCVENSUB                  40 EQ -EOF
C           *IN40     DOWEQ'0'
C           VENDNO    SETLLVENDMST                 10 EQ FD
C           *IN10     IFEQ '1'
C                           SETON                        1520
C* SFLNXTCHG & SFLMSG set above
C                           UPDAT VENSUB
C                           SETOF                        1015
C                           ENDIF
C                           READCVENSUB                  40
C                           ENDDO
C*
C*
C* If errors,  re-display the subfile for correction
```

```
C                  *IN20      IFEQ '1'
C                             SETON                          85
C                             EXFMTVENDCTL
C                             SETOF                          85
C*
C* IF No errors, re-read the subfile and write it to the database
C*
C                             ELSE
C                             Z-ADD1          RRN
C                  *IN41      DOWEQ'0'
C                  RRN        CHAINVENSUB                    41   HI=NF
C                  *IN41      IFEQ '0'
C                             WRITEVENDMST
C                             ADD  1          RRN
C                             ELSE
C*
C*  If all records are processed initialize the subfile
C*  for add'l entry
C*
C                             MOVE *ON        *IN65
C                             WRITEVENDCTL
C                             MOVE '0'        *IN65
C*
C                             ENDIF
C                             ENDIF
C                             ENDDO
C                             ENDDO
C*
C                             MOVE *ON        *INLR
```

Data Entry Approach Correct Errors: Heads Down w/ Batch Edit

The term "Heads Down" data entry means that the user's mission is power keying and thus, they are not to stop for errors. Somebody else will correct the errors. The person keying is keying because they can get lots of data into the system fairly accurately in a short period of time.

The approach is as follows: A User enters data into a subfile. The subfile program writes the subfile data to the entry database with no editing. A batch program reads the data from the entry database and produces edit lists for correction. A user examines a list, calls a correction program to fix errors or make reversing entries

Figure 21-23 Partial DDS: Correct Errors: Heads down / Batch Edit

```
A*
A                                           REF(VENDORP)
A          R VENSUB                         SFL
A*           ...                            ...
-----------------------------------------------------------
A          R VENDCTL                        SFLCTL(VENSUB)
A                                           UNLOCK(*ERASE *MDTOFF)
A*
A                                           CF03(99 'end of job')
A*
A                                           SFLDSP SFLDSPCTL
A              SFLSIZ(010) SFLPAG(0010)
```

Figure 21-24 Partial RPG Correct Errors: Heads Down / Batch Edit

```
FVENDSUBFCF   E                         WORKSTN
F                                                RRN    KSFILE VENSUB
FVENTRAN UF   E           K             DISK                        A
F*
C*
C*    Send out initial Entry screen
C*                      ...
C                       EXFMTVENDCTL
C*
C*    When not EOJ, read records placed in subfile and write to DB
C*
C           *IN99       DOWEQ'0'          C
C                       READCVENSUB                       40 EQ  -EOF
C           *IN40       DOWEQ'0'
C                       WRITEVENDTFMT
C                       READCVENSUB                       40
C                       ENDDO
C                       EXFMTVENDCTL
C                       ENDDO
C*
C*    Some time later, correct the errors
```

Subfile Heads-Down Entry Considerations

There are a number of things that come into play when you need to enter more than one record at a time for heads down data entry. The list of considerations includes the following:

- ✓ Subfile size
- ✓ Operator Error Correction
- ✓ Programmer Error Correction

Subfiles are best when used for heads down data entry with a small subfile. The fact is that multiple record error correction done interactively is not fun for anybody – user or programmer.

Another Subfile Technique for Data Entry

This is the last subfile tip that we offer regarding correction of multiple error records. In this scenario, you enter data in a non-subfile screen. You can also define a subfile to the program. Write the data from the normal entry to the subfile to permit easy data review but no direct manipulation. In this way, the user can be informed of errors or can spot errors but not be able to change them immediately.

To change a record, the program could access it by a key field, like line number and the data can be sent back to the non-SFL display. The user can then make the changes, enter them and the program can write them back. This approach is one of many. It is less complex and would be less performance intensive than using subfiles for all actions.

Hopefully, while we were examining all of these various techniques, you spotted one you like better than others or perhaps you would prefer a variation of a technique that we described.

When you write your programs, you make the call. But, you may very well be maintaining programs using a variety of clever techniques for multiple data entry correction. You are now better prepared to handle those situations. That's about it for subfile, but we have one more clever technique coming up that is similar to using a subfile but it does not.

Poor Person's Subfile

There is another method of multiple line display / entry that we discussed earlier in this chapter. It does not use subfiles and for its utility it is very code efficient. I like to call this notion, using a starting line number (SLNO), a poor person's subfile. It's just another good technique to put in your bag of coding tricks.

Figure 21-25 Poor Person's Subfile

```
************************************************************
*...+... 1 ...+... 2 ...+... 3 ...+... 4 ...+... 5 ...+...6..
01 *                 VENDOR MASTER ENTRY     TT:TT:TT DD/DD/DD
02 *
03 *                               F3      END OF JOB
04 *
05 *   VENDOR NO. VENDOR NAME                STATE   BALANCE OWED
06 *
07 *     66666    OOOOOOOOOOOOOOOOOOOOOOOOOO   OO     66,666,666-
08 *     66666    OOOOOOOOOOOOOOOOOOOOOOOOOO   OO     66,666,666-
09 *     66666    OOOOOOOOOOOOOOOOOOOOOOOOOO   OO     66,666,666-
10 *     66666    OOOOOOOOOOOOOOOOOOOOOOOOOO   OO     66,666,666-
11 *     66666    OOOOOOOOOOOOOOOOOOOOOOOOOO   OO     66,666,666-
12 *     66666    OOOOOOOOOOOOOOOOOOOOOOOOOO   OO     66,666,666-
13 *     66666    OOOOOOOOOOOOOOOOOOOOOOOOOO   OO     66,666,666-
14 *     66666    OOOOOOOOOOOOOOOOOOOOOOOOOO   OO     66,666,666-
15 *     66666    OOOOOOOOOOOOOOOOOOOOOOOOOO   OO     66,666,666-
16 *     66666    OOOOOOOOOOOOOOOOOOOOOOOOOO   OO     66,666,666-
17 *
18 *
19 *
20 *
21 *
22 *     33333    IIIIIIIIIIIIIIIIIIIIIIIIII   II     33333333
23 *
24 * Function Key 3 - EOJ
 *...+... 1 ...+... 2 ...+... 3 ...+... 4 ...+...5...+.....6...+
```

Variable Line Numbering

The poor person's subfile requires a little trick called variable line numbering. Just as in a subfile, you define just one record on the screen, and then by changing the line # on which the record will display, you can paint the screen from top to bottom – from line 1 to line 24 by changing the line number where the record is displayed.

The DDS keyword to pull this off is the starting line number keyword or just SLNO. When you use the SKNO keyword, you have two choices. You can use a definite value such as SLNO(7) and each time the format is displayed it will appear beginning on line 7. Or, you can be much cuter.

You can use the variable option and thus, instead of a constant line number, by specifying SLNO(*VAR) in DDS, the RPG or COBOL program can supply the actual line number where the first line of the format will be displayed at execution time.

Just as when you used subfiles, the nosy RPG compiler wants to know all you can tell it about the fact that you have decided to use the starting line number facility of DDS in RPG. The RPG Entries for starting line number are shown in the code below:

Device	Symbol Device	K	Key Word	ENTRY
40 - 48	47 - 52	53	54 - 59	60-65
---------	---------	----	---------	-------
F.. WORKSTN				
F..		K	SLN	LINNBR

In the continuation spec, SLN is the keyword that you must use and in the ENTRY column, you place the variable in the program that you will use to specify the starting line number for the display. In our example the record is just one line but that does not have to be the case, There may be programs that require more information written in the middle of the screen at times and this technique permits a format of any number of lines (not past the end) to be specified anywhere on the screen.

To mimic a subfile, the format that you create will be a one-liner and if you want lines to appear between say, line 7 and 16 as in Figure 21-25, then as you get the data to display, you would increment the LINNBR field starting at 7, then 8, then 9 etc. With each increment the format would be written to the display causing many more interactions than would typically be needed with a subfile. To the user, it would all appear at once but would not really be sent until you have filled up the screen at line 16.

In line 22 of Figure 21-25, you may have noticed an input field. This format would be sent out last as an overlay. Though this technique is not perfected with the panel, you can theoretically use this area of the screen for new input, changes, or deletions.

For example, if a line number were presented on the record display, this could be a reference number from which the input area on the bottom could reference a displayed record for change or deletion. However you choose to use, it, the variable line number is a powerful tool for those applications that can use a more simple approach than subfiles.

In Chapter 20, we examined how to use SDA to create basic display files. The same SDA or even the WDSC designer tool can be used to create the DDS for subfiles. When using the SDA tool, keep in mind that the subfile and the subfield control record both need to be created and linked and SDA has the tools and the help text to get you there.

Chapter Summary

In this chapter, we took the simple notion of a display file and expanded it with numerous coding examples. We learned about how to look at a subfile as a memory file and we saw how subfiles can be used for three basic purposes:

1. Multiple record inquiry
2. Multiple record inquiry with update
3. Multiple record data entry with / without correction.

For the first two types of subfiles, the examples showed the SDA design panel, the DDS and the RPG code for the subfile program. RPGIV could use the same exact logic as RPG/400. For the third example, since data entry can have errors, we also explored a number of techniques that can be used to correct data in subfiles prior to updating permanent database files.

Finally, we showed a non subfile technique that many programmers use to keep the program coding and interactions less complex. The variable starting line number approach offers many of the advantages of the subfile without the complexity.

Subfiles help the programmer in those applications that present lists of records for viewing or maintenance. They can also be used for the entry of multiple records per display panel. Subfiles are memory files associated with the shape of a subfile record defined by DDS in a display file.

The records that are displayed and changed or newly keyed remain in memory until the program process them, typically with a read changed (READC) operation. With subfiles, the programmer defines just one record that will appear multiple times in a list thereby saving much coding.

The RPG subfile logic then provides the bulk of the facility. Without any additional coding, once the subfield control record is displayed with the subfile, the user can roll through the records, backwards and forwards, making changes as they go. Only when the user tells the program by pressing the Enter key or a Function key that all of the entering, selecting, maintaining or deleting has been done does the program again gain control.

To define a subfile in DDS, you need a memory file which is called a subfile record in DDS along with a second format known as a subfile control record. The subfile control record is used to determine when operations, such as initialize or clear are performed against the subfile and also whether the subfile contents are displayed on the screen.

A subfile needs a companion RPG program to drive it. The WORKSTN file that is used with a subfile is defined with a continuation record in File Descriptions to define the record number field for reading the subfile in the program.

Key Chapter Terms

Activating	Inquiry	SFLEND keyword
Activation	ITER	SFLFOLD keyword
Adding records	Iteration	SFLINZ keyword
Array	Key to disk	SFLLIN keyword
COBOL,	LEAVE operation	SFLMSG keyword
Command Key	LINNBR keyword	SFLNRA keyword
COMP,	Loading	SFLNXTCHG keyword
Continuation	Memory file	SFLPAG keyword
CTL record	Multiple occurrence DS	SFLRCDNBR keyword
Data Entry Subfile	Poor person's subfile	SFLSIZ keyword
DB records	PR	SLN keyword
Design panel	Read Changed	SLNO keyword
Disk file processing	READC operation	Subfile
Display attributes	Record at a time	Subfile data
Display files	Record description	Subfile keywords
Display of Errors	RPG device	Subfile page
Display programming	RPGIII	Subfile pages
DO loop	RRN field	Subfile Records
DO While loop	SDA design	UPDAT operation
Editing	Search	Variable Line Numbering
EDTCDE keyword	SETLL operation	VENDMS
ERRMSG keyword	SETON operation	VENDORP
Error Correction	SFLCHGNXT,	VENDSRCH
EXFMT operation	SFLCLR keyword	VENDSUBF
File Description	SFLDROP keyword	WDSC
Function key	SFLDSP keyword	WORKSTN
Heads down data entry	SFLDSPCTL keyword	WRITE
Housekeeping		

Review Questions

1. What is a subfile?

2. What are the typical uses for subfiles?

3. For a complete subfile program, what two components are necessary?

4. What is meant by a subfile page?

5. What is a list?

6. Which parameter interfaces with a display file so that the programmer can send one record at a time to the screen and fill up a list page without a subfile?

7. What operation reads through all of the records that are changed in the subfile and only those changed?

8. Which of the following three items are needed to create a display file containing a subfile: 1. WDSC Designer, 2. SDA; 3. DDS?

9. Define the following keywords and give a one line DDS example and brief explanation as to why the keyword would be needed:: SFL; SFLCTL; SFLCLR; SFLINZ; SFLSIZ; SFLPAG; SFLDSPCTL; SFLMSG; SFLNXTCHG; SFLRNA; SFLDROP; SFLFOLD; SFLLIN

10. Why would an EXFMT be used instead of WRITE in a subfile program?

11. What are the three main purposes for subfiles?

12. What are the four steps in subfile processing?

13. What is activation?

14. Once the records are there and you want to fetch then, what re the two RPG operation choices? Give an example of each?

15. What are the steps to process update for a subfile after it has been displayed.

16. Why might there be times that two subfiles are needed for error correction?

17. When would the heads down / batche dit approach for error correction be best?

18. What is a poor person's subfile?

Chapter 22 RPG Database & Inter-Program Operations & Examples

Input-Output Operations

RPG is rich with many native database operations. With the RPG compiler developers knowing from day one that they were working with a database machine, they were able to fashion a compiler that is database aware.

Whether the database object is formed by native DDS or through SQL CREATE commands, the RPG operations can deal with them all, and quite well, I might add.

We examined all of RPG's database operations in some level of detail in Chapters 14 & 15. The list of operations by category, shown in Table 22-1 is a reminder of the bounty of op-codes available for use by the RPG programmer.

Before we get into some serious examples of using these operations, let's take a look at each individually so that we are prepared to decode the snippets that use these DB op-codes.

Figure 22-1 RPG Database / Device Operation Codes

General	Workstation I/O	Disk I/O
OPEN	EXFMT	CHAIN
FEOD	READ	COMIT
CLOSE	WRITE	DELET
	CHAIN (subfiles)	READ/READE/READP
	READC (subfiles)	REDPE
	UPDAT (subfiles)	ROLBK
		SETLL/SETGT
		UPDAT
		WRITE

General Operations

The code next to the operation in this section represents the purpose of the HI LO EQ indicator areas in RPG/400 and RPGIV. Each operation has its own set of resulting indicators (HILOEQ) indicators that are turned on to signify things like not found (NF), found (FD) error (ER) End of file (EF), Beginning of File (BF), Not applicable (NA), etc. as shown above before the operation description

OPEN – NAERNA Enables you to open a file within the program under program control at any time and not under control of RPG logic which would typically occur at the start of the program.

FEOD – NAERNA Enables you to force the end of a file condition to occur. It is like a dummy close of the file and then a re-open of the file. This is really helpful when you are printing and want to do a forms eject without having to end the program or close the printer file.

CLOSE – NAERNA Allows you to close an open file within the program -- under program control and not under RPG control at the end of the program.

Workstation I/O Operations

EXFMT-- NAERNA Does a write and then a read to display file

READ – NAEREF Reads a display file format

WRITE -- NAERNA Writes a display file format

CHAIN -- NFERNA Reads a specific record in a subfile

READC -- NAEREF Reads only the changed records in a subfile

UPDAT -- NAERNA Updates a specific record that was read in a subfile

Disk I/O Operations

CHAIN -- NFERNA Reads a specific data base record by key or relative record #.

COMIT -- NAERNA Completes a Commitment Control boundary

DELET -- NAERNA Deletes a specific record in a data base file

READ -- NAEREF Read from a specific file or record format,

READE – NAEREF Read if equal as long as a certain field value remains equal to the condition

READP -- NAERBF Read the previous record format specified.

REDPE – NAERBF Reads / retrieves the next prior sequential record if the key of the record matches the search argument.

ROLBK -- NAERNA Do not complete a commitment control boundary and rollback all records in the commit group to the last complete commitment control boundary

SETLL -- NRERFD Set the file cursor (position the file) at the next record that has a key or relative record number that is greater than **or equal to** the search argument (key or relative record number) operand specified)

SETGT -- NFERNA Set the file cursor (position the file) at the next record with a key or relative record number that is greater than the search argument (key or relative record number) operand specified.

UPDAT – NAERNA Update a database record from the record format that was previously read

WRITE – NAERNA Add a data base record to a database file.

Each operation has its own set of resulting indicators (HILOEQ) indicators that are turned on to signify things like not found (NF), found (FD) error (ER) End of file (EF), Beginning of File (BF), Not applicable (NA), etc. as shone above before the operation description

Data Base File Processing

How do you access data in RPG? Data can be accessed by file name using externally described data or program described data. It can also be accessed by record format name for externally described data. The Chain operation is one of the most frequently used database operations of all time in RPG. Programmers love the CHAIN operation. The term chain is analogous to a lasso that goes out and grabs (chains) a record on the disk.

CHAIN Operation

Chain by file: CHAIN is used in this context to access a file by file name, given a key or search argument, and if the record is not found, an indicator (NF) is set on. Its job is to get the first record in the file, which matches the search argument. Yes, the fact that the word first is used here means that the database may have duplicate keys – as foreign a notion as that may be to relational database purists.

Chain by Record Format Name: This CHAIN operation gets the first record of the specified format, which matches the search argument. With the IBM i on Power Systems's DB2 database, logical files (native DB views) can be built over (linked together) multiple physical files (real files). The resulting file has multiple formats – one for each of the underlying physical files. Each format has its own name. Thus, the CHAIN by record format name returns only a matched record from the physical file referenced by the format name or it returns a not found condition.

Traditional CHAIN coding follows:

CHAIN by Key

```
                              key
FFILE1     IF  E          K       DISK
                                       NF
C... KEY       CHAIN   FILE1           51
```
The above code is a chain by file name. If not found, 51 cones on.

```
                                       NF
C... KEY       CHAIN   FORMATA         51
```
      This Chain is by record format name –
      (1st record hit in specified record format)

CHAIN by Relative Record Number

The key point in a chain by relative record number is that there is no key involved. As you can see in the code immediately below, the file description has no K specified. It does not matter whether the file is indexed or not, the lack of a K here means that any random access chains to the file will be by relative record number by definition – since no key is specified.

```
                          nokey
FFILE2      IF   E                      DISK
                                              NF
                                              ──
C...  RRN       CHAIN   FILE2               51
      Chain to file name with RR#
                                              NF
                                              ──
C...  RRN       CHAIN   FORMATB             51
        Chain to record format name with RR#
```

The not found situation was always something that programmers had to deal with and RPG provided a no hit area (HI) in which you can specify an indicator. If the indicator you specify is on after the operation, the record has not been found. – key or no key. A few releases ago in an attempt to make RPG not like your Father's RPG, IBM added a few more goodies so that a left hand indictor condition was not the most natural way to deal with not founds.

IBM's innovations were the %Error reserved word and the %Found . In the code above if we had specified indicator 50 for example to the immediate right of indicator 51, it would turn on if there were an error condition. So, the %Error provides that function and the %Found provides the test for found / not found. The code shells below show how this is implemented:

```
C... Key      CHAIN      File1
C            If          %Error
C*    Error handling follows
C...          ENDIF
C*
C...          If          %Found
C... Insert Found Routine Here
C...          Else
C... Insert not found routine here
C...          ENDIF
```

Of course any time you hear the word recent enhancement, you can bet one thing" "Not available in RPG/400." That's right, these enhancements to RPG are only to RPGIV.

IBM also gave the CHAIN a few other facelifts recently with the addition of a composite key, extended free form notation, Chain to expression values and read directly into data structures. These new offerings are a bit beyond the scope of this book but they are there for you to use when you become he expert you are destined to be.

READ (consecutive)

The READ operation can read directly from a database file consecutively by the data or consecutively by the key. The first code snippet is sequential by file name and the second is sequential by format name. Neither of the first two snippets use the key. The snippets are repeated to demonstrate how the key would be used.

```
                         No key
FFILE3      IF  E                       DISK


C...            READ    FILE3                   60
```
Read to file name -- internally or externally described &
not using the index.

```
                                                EF
C...            READ    FORMATB                 60
```
READ record format name -- externally described &
not using the index.

```
                         key
FFILE3      IF  E        K               DISK


C...            READ    FILE3                   60
```
Read to file name -- internally or externally described &
using the index.

```
                                                EF
C...            READ    FORMATB                 60
```
READ record format name -- externally described &
using the index.

Set Lower Limit SETLL (Indexed)

By definition the SETLL must work against an indexed file. The following snippet does a SETLL to a file
name.

```
                            key
FFILE4      IF  E           K            DISK
                                                FD
C...    KEY     SETLL   FILE4                   51
C...    *IN51   IFEQ    '1'                     FD
C...            READ    FORMATB                 52
C...            . . . .
C...            END
```
SETLL to file name (not recfmt) with KEY. READ to Format name

READ EQUAL (READE)

The READE operation retrieves the next sequential record from a full procedural file if the key of the record
matches the search argument. This is like a read with intelligence. If the key of the record does not match
the search argument, the indicator that must be specified in positions 58 and 59 is set on (NF / EF), and the
record is not returned to the program.

```
                         key
FFILE5      IF  E        K           DISK
C* Chain to file name w KEY vs SETXX
                                     NF
C...  KEY      CHAIN   FILE5         51
C...  IN51     DOWEQ   *OFF
C...           . . .                      NF
C...  KEY      READE   FILE5       N 52
```

N in col 53 requests a READE without a temporary update lock

```
C...           READE   FILE5
               ENDDO
```

If factor 1 is blank the default for the read equal is the full key of the current record

Set Greater Than SETGT (Indexed)

The following is a snippet portraying the SETGT operation:

```
                    key
FFILE5      IF  E   K           DISK
C...  KEY      SETGT   FILE5       51
C...  *IN51    IFEQ    '0'
C...           READ    FORMATB       52
C                      . . . .
C              END
```

SETGT against file name with KEY sets a pointer to the file

Read Prior Record (READP)

```
                    key
FFILE6  IF  E       K       DISK    NF
C...  KEY      SETGT   FILE6           51
C...  *IN51    IFEQ    *OFF
C...  KEY      READP   FORMATB
C...           END
```

Position file cursor with SETGT

ReadPrior Equal (REDPE)

```
                        key
FFILE7      IF  E    K      DISK
C...     KEY    CHAIN  FILE7        51
C... N51 KEY    READE  FILE7             51
C...     *IN51  IFEQ    '0'
C...      KEY   REDPE  FILE7             41
C...            . . .
```
Chain to file name with KEY

```
C...            REDPE  DIR2              41
C...     *IN41  IFEQ    '0'
C...            ENDIF
C...            ENDDO
C...            ENDIF
```

If factor 1 is left blank, default is current record key
If factor 1 is blank the default for the read prior equal is the full key
of the current record.

Composite Key

Quite often in the design of a database, such as a student registration system the transaction file will have a composite key. In the academic example, the student takes a class and thus there is an interaction of a student with a class. The key to capture this transaction as unique so that the student appears in the class list and the class appears in the student's schedule is to use a composite key of student and class.

In random processing, you would chain by file or format name with a composite key to access records. The. If the file key is composite (2 or more), then the search argument must be built in the program using the KLIST and KFLD operations as shown in the code snippet below

```
                        key
FFILE8      IF  E    K         DISK
C...  COMKEY  KLIST
C...          KFLD           FLDA
C...          KFLD           FLDB
C...  COMKEY  SETLL  DIR2              22
C...  COMKEY  CHAIN  FILE8        51
C...  *IN22   IFEQ   *ON
C...  COMKEY  READE  FORMATB           44
C...          ENDIF
```

Update & Delete (UPDAT & DELET)

To update a record, the record must be read first. In most programs this is accomplished via a random read or chain but it can also occur via a READ operation. A valid input operation must occur prior to the update. The update or Delete record can be to a format or a file. Use a format for internally described data and a file with a data structure for internally described data.

In the DELET operation, when Factor 1 is specified on DELET, a read does not have to occur prior to the DELET because the presence of Factor 1 causes the seek to the record. In this case, because it is like an implied CHAIN, indicators 54-55 must be specified for the "Not Found" test.

```
                           key
FDIR2     UF  E        K        DISK
FFILE9    IPEAF 512 10AI     1DISK
C... KEY       CHAIN  DIR2                   51
C... *IN51     IFEQ   *OFF
C...           UPDAT  FORMATB
C...           ENDIF
C... KEY       DELET  PERS11          73
```

Output Delete / Add / Update

When using program described data in RPG, there are some old ltime techniques from RPGII days that still can be used. One of these is the Delete Option and another is the Add option ands till another is the update option right from the output specs.

Since many externally described files have no output specs at all, the DEL, ADD, and update in output are not used much anymore but you still may find them out there in their respective roles for deleting records, adding records or updating records. The output record definitions for these three options are shown in column definition form below:

```
6           Form Type O
7-14        Filename (internal),
            Format name (external)
15          D,T, E
16-18       DEL----------DELETE THE RECORD

15          D,T, E
16-18       ADD ---------ADD THE RECORD

15          D,T, E
16-18       NO Entry -----UPDATE THE RECORD
```

Note: For the ADD operations above and below an "A" needs to be placed in RPG/400 File Description in column 66 and in RPGIV File Description in column 20.

Add Record with Externally Described File

In addition to adding records the old fashioned way as shown above, RPG and RPGIV support the notion of adding records in calculations specifications with the WRITE operation. Whereas UPDAT updates a record previously read, WRITE is an output-only operation and its job is to write anew record using the format name in Factor 2. In this example, the file to which the record is added is keyed (indexed) and the key is used in the program.

```
C*    Writing records by KEY
                     key                 ADD
FFILEA    UF  E   K        DISK      A
C...         WRITE   FORMATB
```

Writing Records by RRN

When writing records by relative record number, the continuation specification KRECNO is required for output files processed by relative record. There really is no such thing as a direct file organization on the IBM i on Power Systems. Therefore, to use a normal physical file as a direct file, the programmer must allocate the proper number of records on the creation of the file and then use the CL command called initialize physical file (INZPFM) to prime the file with default records (often blanks and zeros) so that it can be processed in a direct fashion. Direct files built using this convention cannot be "written" using the WRITE command or any other method because by definition the INZPFM creates a full file with no room for additional records. Even though no records can get added to the back of the file, the KRECNO keyword provides the relative record processing to mimic real output operations when using the WRITE op-code.

```
F* Write Records by RRN
                 nokey
FDIR2     UF  E        DISK    KRECNO RRN
C...         ADD     1       RRN    20
C...         WRITE   FORMATB
```

Printer File Processing

Since we are discussing output, it is appropriate to offer some instruction on the use of printer files in RPG and RPG/400 using the RPG/400 columns in the examples. When specifying output print positions for fields or constants, the end positions in output can be specific. They can also be relative to last field on the print line

```
                  END
                  POSITION
                  IN
                  OUTPUT
                  RECORD
                  (40-43)
                  (46-51) RPGIV
        NAMEX.......10
        NAMEY.......25
        NAMEZ+..... 3
```

When coding printer output, the notion of edit words quick edit codes provided in RPG can be very helpful in dressing up your output. For your convenience Figure 22-2 shows a number fo the edit codes that you may select for editing output fields.

Figure 22-2 Edit Codes for Dressing Up Printed Output

commas	Zero Balances to print-	No Sign	CR	-	F L O A T	x=no plus sign y=date z= zero suppress	5 - 9 user defined CRT- EDTDSC
YES	YES	1	A	J	N		
YES	NO	2	B	K	O		
NO	YES	3	C	L	P		
NO	NO	4	D	M	Q		

Group Name for Exception Output

For printed output as well as database output, the notion of using indicators and / or exception names for output is often used (especially for printer files). The EXCPT works only with program described files so you won't see this operation if the file is defined with an E in column 19 of the File Description spec.

The following code separated by a solid line shows the calculations that are necessary in the old method of using indicators and the new method of using an exception output name. In the first block of code, you will see an indicator being turned on, followed by the EXCPT operation followed by the same indicator being set off.

In the output area, there would be E records defined that had specific indicators assigned for the type of record that was being outputted. The SETON / SETOF combination was necessary so that just the records that were conditioned for the exception output were printed or other wise written.

Notice in the second block of code that there is no such indicator work and the typical three statements required is reduced to just one by using the efficient exception name notion rather then indicators:

```
C* Exception Output by indicator
C...              SETON                 10
C...              EXCPT
C...              SETOF                 10
O...    E...       10
O...                         25 ADDR1
```

```
C* Exception Output by EXCPT Name
C...           EXCPT      GROUP1
C...           . . .
C...           EXCPT      GROUP2
C...           . . .
C...           EXCPT      GROUP3
O...         E...                  GROUP1
O...                            25 NAME
O...         E...                  GROUP1
O...                            25 ADDR1
O...         E...                  GROUP1
O...                            25 ADDR2
```

EXCPT Externally Described File Output

This last example of Exception output comes from an externally described database file but the update operations are clearly written the same way for internally described processing. As you can see the output in this snippet is directed to the EXCPT name and not the File Name

```
C*   Update files with EXCPT
C...           EXCPT      ADD1
C...           . . .
C...           EXCPT      UPDAT1
OFMT EADD...                    ADD1
O...                         25 NAME
O     E...                      UPDAT1
O...                         25 ADDR1
```

File Control Options

RPG uses an implicit method to open and close files. That is another of the major rime saving coding techniques provided in the base language. However, some applications are built so that options selected by a user may eliminate the need for one file and create the need for another. Rather then have RPG use system resources to open and close files whether or not they are needed, the compiler developers added the OPEN and CLOSE operations so that files can be selectively opened.

Just about all systems have a mechanism called a job switch in which they can specify options that will be read by the program upon startup. The IBM i on Power Systems is no different in that respect. The switches are numbered from 1 to 8 and in RPG, they are treated as special indicators, U1 to U8 respectively.

The external switch can be used to condition whether a file is opened by RPG or not (without the OPEN command). When an external (Ux) indicator is placed in column 72 in RPG/400 or the EXTIND(*INUx) is used to condition the file, RPG opens the file only if the switch is set to on.

There is a third option called UC for user control (USROPN keyword) in RPGIV. From my point of view the second option is better termed user control but IBM did the naming. I would call the UC option PC for program control because the program actually decides whether to open the file or not.

With the external switch, prior to running the program, the user would have to pick a procedure to set the switch or set it manually. With the UC option, the program decides while it is executing whether t use the OPEN statement or not. Regardless of how a file is opened (any of the three ways) the CLOSE file operation closes the file. If the file is not closed and LR is on, RPG closes it for you.

As noted in the beginning of the chapter, the FEOD operation signals the logical end of data for a primary, secondary, or full procedural file. An example is included in the below code snippets.

RPGIV PARM or Column 72	Means
Blank	RPG controls open and close
U1 – U8	User controls open with external switch
UC / USROPN	Program controls open with OPEN

```
C...    FEOD DIR4
C...    OPEN DIR5
C...    CLOSE       DIR5
C...    SETON                      LR
C*
C* Can close and re-open file which
C* has been opened by RPG
```

FEOD vs CLOSE

What is the difference between the Force End of Data (FEOD) operation and the CLOSE operation. FEOD does not close the file. The output buffer is written to disk (single level storage); the file cursor positioned at end of data.

A real end-of-file condition occurs on the next read. The program is not disconnected from the file (or device). Thus, the file can be used again for subsequent file operations without an explicit OPEN operation being specified to the file

With a CLOSE, the output buffer is written to disk and the file is disconnected completely from the module / program. The file cannot be used again in the module / program unless you specify an explicit OPEN for that file. A CLOSE operation to an already closed file does not produce an error.

External Subroutines

External subroutines are a technique of permitting a programs to be divided into logical portions. In RPGIV with the ILE environment, this may involve the creation of modules and service programs to fully complement the application. RPG/400 provides similar facility but the IBM i on Power Systemss not as prepared for modularized programming using the original RPG programming model as with ILE and thus the technique is not as efficient.

External subroutines facilitate the use of multiple programmers to build a large application program. It permits commonly-used routines to be changed independently of the big application without having to recompile all using programs

In this scenario, a "calling program" can pass data to the "called program" and it can receive data from the called program when that program returns or ends. Fields within the called program can be "refreshed" every time if LR is used in the subprogram (called program) or they can be retained if the RT indicator or the RETRN operation is used in the subprogram. Let's look at some simple examples to demonstrate how this is achieved.

In the two examples below, the same program PGM1 is called. In the first example, the PARM statement parameters (fields that are passed from program to program) are specified immediately after the CALL statement. In the second snippet, a parameter list operation is used to specify the parameters that are to be passed.

At first blush it appears that the first option is more code efficient in that the PLIST operation is not required and both snippets perform the same function. PLISTS are used for two purposes.

1. They help organize the non executable code in a program. In this way, the PLIST can be closer to the I specs or the D specs in RPGIV – not in the middle of executable code as the PARM statements need to be.

2. A large program may have to call a program in various places within the program code and having parameters defined in one place permits the second and subsequent CALL with a PLIST to be made without the need to specify parameters a second, third or fourth time.

```
C* Call Program with PARMS
C...          . . .
C...          CALL      'PGM1'
C...          PARM                  FLD1
C...          PARM                  FLD2
C...          . . .
```

```
C* Call Program with PLIST
C...          . . .
C... PLIST1 PLIST
C...          PARM                  FLD1
C...          PARM                  FLD2
C...          . . .
C...          CALL      'PGM1'      PLIST1
```

More -- Inter-Program Communication

External subroutines can be programs of different languages as well as the same language. This allows programs to be divided into logical (function) portions. As noted above, this has a side benefit of permitting multiple programmers to work on a 'single program' by each doing different functions of the program. The single program would then actually be a   program that would call multiple external subroutines (or programs) that perform different functions.

Suppose, for example that there is a common routine (FICA calculation for example) that is changed. If the code is modular, any programs that call it would not have to change. IN RPGIV, the code may have to be "recompiled because of ILE rules." But, overall, with RPG/400 and RPGIV, maintenance of the programs is easier.

The program that calls another program can pass along data to the called program. Once the called program is finished it can pass back data to the calling program. The fields in the called program can be reset after the program has been called and used, or the data in the fields can remain intact waiting for the next call.

There always is some type of 'agreement' between the calling and called programs thus data is not inadvertently changed or destroyed. This means that using external subroutines or programs requires more control and there is a bit more detailed work for the programmers.

In order to pass data, the calling program must pass parameters to the called program and the called program must be written to accept them and it must be written to return data through parameters. As you saw in the snippet, these parameters are defined either individually after a CALL operation or are defined in a parameter list (PLIST)

To Subprogram or Not to Subprogram

A little checklist to examine in making the decision as to whether to subprogram or write big programs follows:

- ✓ Ease of maintenance
- ✓ Testing sub-functions
- ✓ Routine more appropriate in a non-RPG language?
- ✓ Separate infrequently used code?
- ✓ Performance?
- ✓ ILE & RPGIV

The subprogram that is called must be coded a bit differently than the calling program. In fact, other than the call and the PARMS, nothing out of the ordinary is required for calling programs. In ILE there are a number of additional techniques to link programs including procedures / prototyped procedures. These are examined in Chapters 25 & 25. RPG/400 is not at all complicated but the called program needs a notion called am *ENTRY parameter list in order to catch the parameters passed from the calling program. This technique also works in RPGIV as you would see if you converted the code.

In the two code snippets below, take notice that the names of the parms in the calling and called programs may be different. However, the attributes must match

```
C*   Calling Program
C...           MOVE  PGMC  PGMNAM        6
C...           CALL  PGMNAM
C...           PARM              PASS1


-------------------------------------

Called Program


C... *ENTRY   *PLIST
C...           PARM...      PASSB        6
C*   Use the field PASSB,
C*   Now, perform subprogram functions
C...           RETRN
```

Good and Bad Inter-program Techniques

The short list below includes the good techniques that you should consider using when writing programs that require other programs. If you choose not to use these techniques, then that is a bad programming technique.

- ✓ Use local copies of parameters
- ✓ Use parameter lists
- ✓ Call using literal program name

Steps for Inter-program Communications

From the "calling" program to the "called" program, the play by play is most often as follows:

1. PGMT calls PGMC

2. If Factor 2 of PGMT's PARM statements is/are used, the data is copied from factor 2 to the result field of the PARMs for PGMT prior to calling them to PGMC

3. PGMT calls PARMT fields to PGMC after calling PGMC

4. PGMC catches the field(s) in the RESULT field(s) of the associated PARM] statement(s) as specified on the *ENTRY PLIST

5. If a field is specified in Factor1 of the called program's PARMs, PGMC moves the data from its result field to the field in Factor1

6. If the called program (PGMC) changes the field received in the result field, the actual storage for this field exists in the calling program, not the called. Therefore, the field name in the result field of the calling program can be changed by the called program.

7. The new value is received in the result field of the calling (PGMT) program.

8. To avoid the altering of Calling program data, use Factor2 on the PARM to store the name of the local variable to pass to the called program, and specify a different name (global variable)in the result field.

9 Just before sending the parms to the called program, the calling program copies the local variable's data (factor2) into the result field of the PARM for inter-program communication / modification.

10 Prior to returning control to the calling program, the called program takes what has been specified in factor 2 of its *ENTRY PLIST PARMs and moves these to the result field for passing back to PGMC (the calling program).

11 Upon return, the calling program places the data received in the result field(s) of its PARMs into the fields specified in Factor 1 of its PARMs -- if Factor 1 is specified.

12 Factor 2 in both programs is unaffected by work being performed in the companion program.

Here is the code

```
C*   Calling Program (PGMT)
C...    PARMT       PLIST
C...                PARM        CUSTNO
C...                PARM ITM    ITEMNO
C...    *IN36       PARM *IN35  IND35
C...                CALL PGMC   PARMT

C* Called Program (PGMC)
C...    *ENTRY      PLIST
C...                PARM        CUSNBR
C...                PARM        ITEM
C...    *IN35       PARM *IN36    LOG35
C...                . . .
C...                SETON                    RT
```

Running a CL command in RPG

There may be times in your RPG programming career that you must communicate with the operating system to perform a function needed by your RPG program. The most appropriate way to do this is to use the IBM supplied program called QCMDEXC to execute the IBM command that you need to be performed. Of course you can create your own CL program with the command and work with it as if it were another program to which you were communicating using the parameter passing rules that we already discussed. However, QCAEXC is a nice and efficient way to accomplish the mission without having to write a program.

The way you get this done is as follows:

✓ Specify CL command in first PARM
✓ Specify the length of the command in second parm

A sample code snippet is as follows:

```
C...         IFXX
C...         . . .
C...         CALL 'QCMDEXC'
C...   PARM 'DSPMSG'      COMMD    6
C...         PARM 6       LENGTH  15 5
C*
C...         END
```

Data Retention with Program Calls

When you call a program from a program, the called program may keep the contents of the fields intact and alive when it returns control or it may reset the contents of each passed field each time it is called. To retain the fields and keep the called program alive in RPG/400, there are two RPG operations that cane be used – RETURN and the special RT indicator.

RETRN Operation and RT Indicator

The following code snippet shows both the RETRN and RT options for returning control to the calling program. Either approach causes the called program to return but does not destroy contents of fields. Please note that you would use just one of these techniques in the called program:

```
C...             RETRN
C...             SETON                           RT
```

Of course, there may be times that you would likely want to remove the called program upon your return. This is accomplished by turning on LR in the called program. If the called program ends normally with LR, then the contents of the fields are not maintained.

In RPG/400, there is also the notion of the FREE op-code to free resources that otherwise would exist in the called program even after LR. causes normal termination. The FREE operation in the calling program destroys subprogram field contents. If you get into heavy inter-program work, IBM suggests that you watch any non-shared open data paths to assure that your application maintains integrity. See the well documented example from IBM's RPG/400 Reference Manual in Figure 22-3.

Figure 22-3 Using the FREE Operation in RPG/400
```
*...1....+....2....+....3....+....4....+....5....+....6...
CL0N01N02N03Factor1+++OpcdeFactor2+++ResultLenDHHiLoEqCom+
C*
C*   When the CALL operation is processed, the data in the
C*   result fields of the parameter list can be accessed by
C*   PROGA.  The parameter list ends when the first
C*   calculation operation other than a PARM operation is
C*   encountered.
C                 CALL  'PROGA'
C                 PARM            FLDA    30
C                 PARM            FLDB    30
C                 PARM            FLDC    50
C*
C*   When the FREE operation is processed, PROGA is removed
C*   from the list of activated programs.  Removing it from
C*   the list ensures a fresh copy of all fields in PROGA
C*   the next time the program is called.  Indicator 55 is
C*   set on if the FREE operation is not completed
C*   successfully.
C*
C                 FREE  'PROGA'                    55
C*   55 = NO SUCCESS
```

FREE Operation in RPGIV

You won't find much written about the FREE operation in RPGIV because the operation does not exist. FREE was needed in RPG/400 to clean up entrails and to assure that a program when called got a fresh start with new internal structures from the calling program's perspective.

Many RPG experts suggest that FREE was never a good op-code even when it was supported.. The program being freed had its static storage cleared, but it didn't have its files closed. Files would stay open until the job ended, or until a major resource reclamation on the system (RCLRSC) was done.

Though FREE seemed to be a good idea and since IBM made it available to the calling program, programmers used it sometimes as if it were required for all types of CALLs. It created its own share of issues, such as performance collapse, that would manifest themselves in ways that were not very easy to discern and that might disappear as quickly as they appeared. There seems to be a consensus that IBM did the RPG community a favor by eliminating the operation.

In those cases that a programmer is moving from RPG/400 to the ILE environment with RPGIV, the simplest way to assure that data is fresh each time if that is the goal is to end the called program with an LR.

If the function of a FREE is desired, the called program can be modified so that it accepts a signal from the calling program (in a new parameter perhaps) to end the program rather then to gently return.

RPGIV has several very sophisticated ways to handle inter-prpgram communications. These are covered in Chapters 25 & 26.

To Exit From a Sub Program

As noted above, the way to exit from a subprogram is to set on LR or to return through one of the return methods. Using LR is a way of assuring everything is the same each time since variables are replenished each time. LR for example, frees static storage, closes files, and then returns control to the higher invocation

When the program is called a second time, RPG initializes the variables again, reopens the files, does its thing, and again closes and flushes everything and returns control to next higher invocation. Thus, variable values and file status is refreshed on each call.

When all is not done correctly and floating programs remain, IBM recommends that periodically you run the reclaim resource command. This command rids the system of unnecessary items such as unused open data paths that were knocked out by the FREE command as well as other resources that get disconnected from running jobs.

Chapter Summary

In this chapter, we learned that RPG is rich with many inherent database operations. This is unusual in modern compilers since on most systems the database is optional and thus when deployed, the compilers have no affinity for it. IBM's RPG compiler developers knew from day one that the system had relational database capabilities and they integrated the compiler function to fit those capabilities.

Database Operations in the general category include the OPEN, FEOD and the CLOSE operations which are used to meet the needs of programmers needing control of these important processes.

The Disk IO category of operations includes a wealth of operations to provide the programmer with flexibility in picking the right tool for the job. Random processing tool include CHAIN, SETLL and SETGT operations. Sequential and consecutive processing include the READ, READE, READP, and REDPE operations. These are used to process the whole file sequentially or to process records from a given point forward or backward.

The UPDAT and WRITE and DELET operations offer a simple and natural means to maintain databases, to add new records to database files or to delete records from them. The COMIT operation permits the enforcement of commitment control and the ROLBK enables records that will not be committed to be rolled back in one simple operation.

Besides the operations for updating, adding, and deleting, records can be maintained in the same way using the program cycle and detail or exception output. On the record line in RPG output, the programmer places ADD to add records (in concert with an A in column 66 in RPG/400 or an A in column 20 in RPGIV); DEL to delete records and   no entry to update the record just read.

Inter-program communications is well supported in RPG. In this environment, a "calling program" can pass data to a "called program" and it can receive data from the called program when that program returns or ends. In some cases using RETRN or the RT indicator the called program data stays intact for subsequent calls and in other situations, such as setting on LR it is like starting over with newly initialized structures.

The FREE operation in RPG/400 and better parameter passing techniques in RPGIV can be used to more effectively clean up lost resources. Finally if all else fails, the RCLRSC system command always does the trick but it is not a function that should be taken lightly.

To support modular programming both RPG and RPGIV support dynamic binding of programs at execution time using " external subroutines." Of course RPGIV also has support for static binding and procedure prototyping as described in Chapters 25 & 26.

Key Chapter Terms

%Error	File key	Prototyping
%Found	File name	QCMDEXC
Add Record	FREE operation	READ operation
Called program	Full procedural file	READC operation
Calling program	Global variable	READE operation
CHAIN operation	Inter-program	READP operation
CLOSE operation	INZPFM command	REDPE operation
COMIT operation	Job switch	RETRN operation
Composite Key	KFLD operation	RETURN operation
Data retention	KLIST operation	ROLBK operation
DELET operation	KRECNO parameter	Scope
Direct files	Local variable	Service program
Edit codes	Modular programming	SETGT operation
Edit words	Modules	SETLL operation
Editing, 16	OPEN	SETOF operation
Exception name	Open data path	SETON operation
Exception output	Parameter list	Static binding
EXCPT operation	PARM	Subprogram
EXFMT operation	Pass data	Subroutine
External subroutine	PLIST operation	System resources
Externally described data	Print positions	U1 to U8
Externally described file	Printer file	UPDAT operation
EXTIND keyword	Printer output	Updating records
FEOD	Procedures	USROPN keyword
File Control	Program calls	WRITE operation

Review Questions

1. Why can RPG compiler operations work directly upon a database without a database package such as Oracle, or Ingress?

2. Does RPG care whether a DB2 UDB database is created with RPG or SQL?

3. If RPG uses automatic OPEN and CLOSE, why are there operations to perform these functions?

4. Is READC ever used against a database? Why? Why not?

5. How do you access data in RPG?

6. What is one of the most frequently used database operations of all time in RPG?

7. Does a chain require a key argument in Factor 1?

8. Are composite keys supported by the database operations?

9. What is a composite key and how do you create a search argument for one?

10. What are the %FOUND and %ERROR functions?

11. In an RPG program what determines whether a READ operation is reading sequentially by key or consecutively by record #?

12. What is the purpose of SETLL and SETGT? What do the resulting indicators mean

13. Can SETLL work against a consecutive (non-indexed file?

14. Which operation retrieves the next sequential record from a full procedural file if the key of the record matches the search argument?

15. How do you specify an update or delete or add using program described output?

16. Which output operation works best with program described printer files?

17. How do you prevent files from being opened at program start time?

18. What are External subroutines?

19. What are the two ways to cause a return to the calling program without ending the program?

20. Is the RPG/400 FREE operation supported in RPGIV?

21. What are the reasons for writing subprograms?

22. What is a PARM?

23. What is a PLIST?

24. What is an *ENTRY PLIST?

25. Describe the steps for inter-program communications?

26. How can you run CL programs in RPG/400 and RPGIV?

27. With regard to inter-program communications, what is meant by data retention?

Chapter 23 Case Study Part I: RPG Operations in Action

The Once and Future PAREG2

There is no better way to learn programming than by programming. Almost every new programmer entering the programming world is first faced with maintenance programming. Yes, this is programming of course but the first task is decoding, not coding. To help you in this effort we have taken the very popular PAREG program with which you have become familiar in this book and have created version PAREG2 for your decoding pleasure.

PAREG2 as shown in Figure 23-1 is the reincarnation of PAREG without the use of the RPG cycle. In all fairness, the program is not really 248 statements because in order to demonstrate the new routines more clearly we used more commenting within the program. In fact, there are 61 additional comment lines. over and above those in the program described version of PAREG.

In Figure 5-2, we introduced the program described version of PAREG with 69 statements, 13 of which were comments. Thus, there were 56 operative statements in this PAREG. So, if we take the 61 additional plus the 13 original comments from PAREG2 (74 comment statements in total) from the 248 statements in this program, there are and we le 174 operative statements in PAREG2 gram.

Yes, we did add a little bit of new function. For example, we added two additional fields to the Employee Master, – a department # (EMPDPT) and a Salary code. We also added a new file. Rather than extend the Payroll master further, we borrowed a technique from the days of old when disk space was expensive. Since these programs exist today, we placed the new salary payroll option in its own file. Thus, to calculate pay with a salaried employee, we must access this file using a random read (CHAIN). Overall, it took eleven statements for processing the salary file and the department file in PAREG2 after they were added to the mix. That brings us to 163 operative statements to perform the same function as PAREG in Figure 5-2.

Figure 23-1 PAREG2 Program – Register with No Cycle, MR, Levels

```
       *PAREG2P internally described PAREG - no MR, No LX totals
001  H* RPG HEADER (CONTROL) SPECIFICATION FORMS
002  H
003  F*
004  F* RPG FILE DESCRIPTION SPECIFICATION FORMS
005  F*
006  FEMPMAST IF  F     70  3AI     1 DISK
007  FTIMCRD  IF  F      7  3AI     1 DISK
008  FSALFILE IF  F      9  3AI     1 DISK
009  FQPRINT  O   F     77     OF     PRINTER
010  FERROR   O   E                   PRINTER
011  I*
012  I* RPG INPUT SPECIFICATION FORMS
013  I*
014  I*
015  I*   EMPMAST is the employee master file
016  I*   One record per employee - pay rate and dept
017  I*   For salaried employees, Salary is in SALFILE
018  I*
019  IEMPMAST AA   01
020  I                                 1  70 EREC
021  I                                 1    30EMPNO
022  I                                 4  23 EMPNM
023  I                                 4  33 EMPNAM
```

```
024  I                                        34   382EMPRAT
025  I                                        39   58 EMPCTY
026  I                                        59   60 EMPSTA
027  I                                        61   650EMPZIP
028  I                                        66   66 EMPSCD-SALCOD
029  I                                        67   70 EMPDPT-DPTCOD
030  I*
031  I*  TIMCRD is updated in an independent process.
032  I*  Provides current time records for the PAYROLL process
033  I*  For salaried employees, no hours provided but TIMcard
034  I*  is needed for person to be paid.
035  I*
036  ITIMCRD  AB  02
037  I                                        1    30EMPNO
038  I                                        4    72EMPHRS
039  I*
040  I*  SALCRD is updated in an independent process.
041  I*  Mimics an extension to the PAYMAST file
042  I*  For salaried employees, Salary stored in this file
043  I*
044  ISALFILE AC  03
045  I                                        1    30SALENO
046  I                                        4    90SALYR
047  I*  HLDMST is the working file for level chacking
048  I*
049  IHLDMST      DS
050  I                                        1    30HLDNO
051  I                                        1    70 HREC
052  I                                        4    33 HLDNAM
053  I                                        4    23 HLDNM
054  I                                        34   382HLDRAT
055  I                                        39   58 HLDCTY
056  I                                        59   60 HLDSTA
057  I                                        61   650HLDZIP
058  I                                        66   66 HLDSCD
059  I                                        67   70 HLDDPT
060  I*
061  C*
062  C* RPG CALCULATION SPECIFICATION FORMS
063  C*
064  C*  Run default register with no prompt input
065  C                    EXSR RUNREG
066  C                    SETON                          LR
067  C*
068  C*  Body of Code- Controls running of Payroll Register
069  C          RUNREG    BEGSR
070  C*  Check to see if there is a missing master
071  C                    EXSR CHKMST
072  C*  Clear fields from CHKMST run to begin fresh register
073  C                    EXSR CLR
074  C                    CLOSEEMPMAST
075  C                    OPEN EMPMAST
076  C*  First read ahead to be able to check for Levels
077  C                    READ EMPMAST                   91
078  C                    EXCPTHEADER
079  C                    EXSR PROCES
080  C*  Run register until end of file
089  C          *IN91     DOUEQ*ON
090  C*  SECOND READ -- UNTIL EOF NEED FOR LEVEL CHECK
091  C                    READ EMPMAST                   91
092  C          91        LEAVE
093  C*  Replaces L1 coding as in PAREG
```

```
094  C*    LEVEL 1 TEST -- See if current city is different
095  C              EMPCTY    IFNE HLDCTY
096  C              EMPSTA    ORNE HLDSTA
097  C                        SETON                    L1
098  C                        EXSR LEVEL1
099  C                        ENDIF
100  C*   Level 2 test -- See if state changed
101  C              EMPSTA    IFNE HLDSTA
102  C                        SETON                    L2
103  C                        EXSR LEVEL2
104  C                        ENDIF
105  C                        SETOF                    L1L2
106  C                        EXSR PROCES
107  C                        ENDDO
108  C                        EXSR LEVEL1              L1Break
109  C                        EXSR LEVEL2              L2Break
110  C                        EXCPTLROUT              LRBreak
111  C                        ENDSR
112  C*
113  C*   Level 1 Subroutine - Control break on City
114  C*
115  C              LEVEL1    BEGSR
116  C              CTYPAY    ADD  STAPAY    STAPAY  92
117  C                        EXCPTL1OUT
118  C                        ENDSR
119  C*
120  C*   Level 2 Subroutine - Control break on State
121  C*
122  C              LEVEL2    BEGSR
123  C              STAPAY    ADD  TOTPAY    TOTPAY  92
124  C                        EXCPTL2OUT
125  C                        ENDSR
126  C*
127  C*   PAYCLC  Calculates Gross PAY from HRS or Salary
128  C*   Also calculates "net pay" and updates YTD files.
129  C*   Calculate pay for HELD record
130  C*   If Salaried, do not use RATE multiplier
131  C*
132  C              PAYCLC    BEGSR
133  C                        SETOF                    9298
134  C                        Z-ADD0         HLDSAL  60
135  C* REPLACES MR CYCLE WORK
136  C              HLDNO     CHAINTIMCRD             92    No TC
137  C     92                 EXCPTNOTIME                  ERROR
138  C    N92       HLDRAT    MULT EMPHRS    HLDPAY  72    CALCPAY
139  C    N92                 Z-ADDEMPHRS    HLDHRS  92
140  C    N92       HLDPAY    ADD  CTYPAY    CTYPAY  92    ADDCity
141  C    N92       HLDNO     CHAINSALFILE            98    Get Sal
142  C    N98N92               Z-ADDSALYR    HLDSAL  60
143  C    N98N92    SALYR     DIV  52        HLDPAY        CalcSal
144  C    N98N92    HLDPAY    ADD  CTYPAY    CTYPAY  92    City
145  C    N98N92               Z-ADD0        HLDHRS        No HRS
146  C                        ENDSR
147  C*
148  C* Write error msg for no master to separate Ext print file
149  C*
150  C              NOMAST    BEGSR
151  C                        WRITEHDR
152  C                        WRITEDTL
153  C                        ENDSR
154  C*
155  C*   Process line item
```

```
156  C*
157  C              PROCES     BEGSR
158  C                         EXSR MOVMS1
159  C                         EXSR PAYCLC
160  C                         EXSR PRNTLN
161  C                         ENDSR
162  C*
163  C* Print Detail Line on Register
164  C*
165  C              PRNTLN     BEGSR
166  C    OF                  EXCPTHEADER
167  C    OF                  SETOF                          OF
168  C                        EXCPTPRTLN1
169  C                        ENDSR
170  C*
171  C* Move Fields to Hold Area- Level Info/ Comparison
172  C*
173  C              MOVMS1     BEGSR
174  C                         Z-ADDEMPNO      HLDNO
175  C                         MOVELEMPNAM     HLDNAM
176  C                         Z-ADDEMPRAT     HLDRAT
177  C                         MOVELEMPCTY     HLDCTY
178  C                         MOVELEMPSTA     HLDSTA
179  C                         Z-ADDEMPZIP     HLDZIP
180  C                         MOVELEMPSCD     HLDSCD
181  C                         MOVELEMPDPT     HLDDPT
182  C                         ENDSR
183  C*
184  C* CLR Clear fields used in the missing master test
185  C*
186  C              CLR        BEGSR
187  C                         Z-ADD0          EMPNO
188  C                         MOVE *BLANKS    EMPNAM
189  C                         Z-ADD0          EMPRAT
190  C                         MOVE *BLANKS    EMPCTY
191  C                         MOVE *BLANKS    EMPSTA
192  C                         Z-ADD0          EMPZIP
193  C                         MOVE *BLANKS    EMPSCD
194  C                         MOVE *BLANKS    EMPDPT
195  C                         Z-ADD0          EMPHRS
196  C                         ENDSR
197  C*
198  C*   CHKMST Read time cards for missing masters & report
199  C*
200  C              CHKMST     BEGSR
201  C              *IN93      DOUEQ*ON
202  C                         READ TIMCRD                        93
203  C              EMPNO      CHAINEMPMAST                94
204  C    94                  EXSR NOMAST
205  C                         ENDDO
206  C                         ENDSR
207  O*
208  O* RPG OUTPUT SPECIFICATION FORMS
209  O*
210  OQPRINT  E  206           HEADER
211  O                                    32 'THE DOWALLOBY COMPA'
212  O                                    55 'GROSS PAY REGISTER '
213  O                                    60 'STATE'
214  O                         UDATE Y    77
215  O           E  3          HEADER
216  O                                     4 'ST'
217  O                                    13 'CITY'
```

```
218  O                                         27  'EMP#'
219  O                                         45  'EMPLOYEE NAME'
220  O                                         57  'RATE'
221  O                                         67  'HOURS'
222  O                                         77  'CHECK'
223  O        E 11                 NOTIME
224  O                             HLDSTA        4
235  O                             HLDCTY       29
236  O                             HLDNO        27
237  O                                         53  'No Time Card th pay'
238  O                                         71  ' period for below:'
239  O        E 01                 PRTLN1
230  O                             HLDSTA        4
231  O                             HLDCTY       29
232  O                             HLDNO        27
233  O                             HLDNM        52
234  O               N92           HLDPAY1B     77
235  O               N92           HLDHRS1B     67
236  O                             HLDRAT1      57
237  O               92                         76  '** No Time Card **'
238  O        E 22                 L1OUT
239  O                                         51  'TOTAL CITY   PAY FOR'
240  O                             HLDCTY       72
241  O                             CTYPAY1B     77
242  O        E 02                 L2OUT
243  O                                         51  'TOTAL STATE PAY FOR'
244  O                             HLDSTA       54
245  O                             STAPAY1B     77
246  O        E 2                  LROUT
247  O                             TOTPAY1      77
248  O                                         50  'FINAL TOTAL PAY'
```

The Cycle Is Efficient

So, what happened that it cost us almost three times the code in order to perform the same functions without the RPG cycle. The additional lines of code can be characterized as in Table 23-2.

Table 23-2 Reasons for Code Increases from PAREG to PAREG2

Reason For Code Increase	# Stmts
No RPG Cycle Input	5
No RPG Cycle Output	13
No Matching records logic – Includes missing master test	26
No Cycle Control Break testing / Processing	44
Miscellaneous DOs and Ifs	15

The RPG Cycle Does Lots of Work

As we decode the major areas of this program, it will become clear as to why it takes so much coding to replace the RPG cycle when the objective is to prepare a simple report. The net of it is, however, that the RPG cycle does lots of work for you that you never see. When there is no RPG cycle, you must do that work.

Looking at the PAREG2 program in File Description for example, you notice that there is no primary and there is no secondary file. Therefore, at input time, you must do your own reading. At output time, since there is no handy cycle to do the printing as you designate, you must take over the action using exception output (EXCPT op-code) during calculations to get the heading and detail and total lines printed.

Since there is no opportunity to place an A in column 18 of file description for ascending and / or a D for descending sequence, as you could easily do for a primary or secondary file, you must do sequence checking yourself to assure your input is in the proper order (by EMPNO in this program).

Since we did not really want to complicate this program further by introducing a sequence check routine, and since we rigged the input so that if the data were in EMPNO sequence, it would also be in City within State sequence, we took the easy way out on sequence checking. We used the AS/400 database facilities to define the new EMPMAST and the TIMCRD files, as well as the new SALFILE for salaries, as indexed files.

Primary File vs Fully Procedural

When you compare the file description of EMPMAST in Figure 5-3 with the primary file version in Figure 23-4, it is all but too obvious that there are major differences. By defining the key field information for EMPMAST in line 6 of Figure 23-3, we tell RPG that the key is 3 positions long, that there will be alphabetic keys, the file is indexed and the key starts in position 1. By defining the key information in the RPG program that tells RPG to process the file by key.

So, what does that have to do with assuring ascending sequence by EMPNO? Notice that the EMPMAST, TIMCRD, and SALFILE all have an "F" designation in column 16. In RPG parlance, that makes the file use in the program fully procedural. Fully procedural means that operations supporting random reads, writes, and updates as well as operations supporting sequential reads, writes and updates are fully supported against this file

Figure 23-3 PAREG2 No Cycle File Description – Internally Described

```
004   F* RPG FILE DESCRIPTION SPECIFICATION FORMS
005   F*
006   FEMPMAST IF   F      70  3AI     1 DISK
007   FTIMCRD   IF   F       7  3AI     1 DISK
008   FSALFILE IF   F       9  3AI     1 DISK
009   FQPRINT   O    F      77      OF    PRINTER
010   FERROR    O    E                    PRINTER
```

Figure 23-4 RPG Cycle Program PAREG – Internally Described Data

```
0004.00 F* RPG FILE DESCRIPTION SPECIFICATION FORMS
0005.00 F*
0006.00 FEMPMAST IPEAF      55            DISK
0007.00 FTIMCRD  ISEAF       7            DISK
0008.00 FQPRINT  O    F      77      OF   PRINTER
```

In line 77 of the PAREG2 program, you can see the following coded operation:

```
077   C...    READ EMPMAST...            91
```

This operation reads the EMPMAST file using the RPG READ consecutive operation. Since the file is defined to be processed by key in File Descriptions, when a READ is issued against EMPMAST, the index, which is always maintained in sequence, just as the index in the back of a book, is read first under the covers.

Then RPG uses the address of the record found in the index to bring the record into the program. For the next read, the next sequential index record is read and its data record is brought into the program. From RPG's perspective the data is being processed in city within state sequence and thus for PAREG2, it is always read in EMPNO sequence by key.

The database in this program assures that the data will be presented in EMPNO sequence. Without having made the EMPAST file an indexed file, however, there would have been lots more work involved.

Is the Data All Wrong Here?

If the program report is sequenced city within state, then how is it that by sorting on EMPNO or using EMPNO as the key causes the data to be sequenced in city within state sequence? The answer is simple. That's how the IBM i on Power Systemss designed.

Of course it is poor design. Try to add a record to the file and maintain this sequencing. Suppose you want to add a new employee in Scranton, for example. Let's say you want to add the next sequential employee #, employee 12, to Scranton and the data must be maintained in EMPNO sequence. What happens to the report sequencing?

Employee 12's Scranton PA record would be in the file logically and physically after Newark. Walking down the report in Figure 4-1, you can see that long after the totals for Scranton are taken in the report, another Scranton record could be read. This just does not work.

This apparently intentional poor design did not matter in the PAREG cycle program since that environment was quite controlled and adding employees was not something that you needed to be concerned about – when you were first introduced to PAREG. But as this little report grows into a bigger application, the structure of this data needs to be discussed and understood.

One way the designer could have dictated that the charade could be continued would be to increase the employee # by one or two columns. When the EMPDPT and EMPSCD fields were added for PAREG2, this would have been an ideal time. But the designer did not change the design.

If he or she had, then it would permit employees to be inserted (added) into the proper state / city slot by assigning an appropriate employee number. For example, employees 00301 to 00399 would be Scranton slots. So, the next employee for Scranton could be employee # 00301. If you are beginning to think that the data design is not too good for this program, you are very correct. But, sometimes the data design in real life Is not too good.

You may recall that BING CROSSLEY is employee # 003. If the number were expanded by two digits, an additional 99 entries could be added to Scranton PA after CROSSLEY's number was changed to 00300.

Another way would be to change the employee numbers within the three character constraint so that CROSSLEY was employee # 030 instead of 003. In this case, without a change to the file or the programs, up to 9 additional numbers could be assigned to Scranton, PA.

Data Design Matters

In data design, there are lots of ways to get the same objective accomplished. You may have noticed that the sorting within the City and States fields was not really in any sequence – other than to assure that all "Scranton" records for example were together, and all Wilkes-Barre records were together.

But, looking at the report first presented in Chapter 4 as Figure 4-2, Wilkes-Barre (W) city comes before Scranton (S) in the report and Pennsylvania (P) comes before Alaska (A). Being a Pennsylvania boy myself, you can appreciate why the sequencing is as it is. But, the designer should have done a better job.

Because the sequencing is hand–picked and not really in ascending or descending sequence, there is no real straight forward way to maintain this sequence in a report other than to tie it to some other numbering mechanism as the designer did with EMPNO. They also could have created a new sequencing file just for the report and used it as our own index to print lines in our desired sequence.

This is a common technique and used often to assure that balance sheets and P& L statements can print properly regardless of the GL account # sequencing.

If, of course we did not want to maintain a hand-picked sequence in which Pennsylvania was the first state on the list, we could have sorted the data in city within state sequence thereby making Fairbanks Alaska the first entry in our report. If we chose to use an indexed database file approach, we could have created an alternate index on employee number within city within state. These three keys would give us the employees sequenced within city and the cities sequenced within states and the states themselves would be sequenced, giving us Alaska first.

The coding for the logical file approach would be mostly the same with the READ operation delivering data from the index in employee within city within state sequence and no logic change in the program.

Overall, this would have been a better design but it is not the design that we find for this PAREG2 program or the original PAREG program. But, it does show that Level changes do not care if the next value is in sequence. Level changes do care however, whether the next value is different from the current value. And when different, either the RPG cycle, or you as the programmer as in PAREG2 have to account for the difference and fire off the appropriate level of totals on the printout.

Matching Records Processing

Whether you use the cycle as in PAREG or you use the manual method (PAREG2), matching records processing always depends on data being in the sequence in which you wish to report. Thus, all of the considerations for sequencing which we just discussed apply.

In the PAREG2 example, there is no opportunity to place M1 next to fields that logically should be matched in a program. Therefore, there is no opportunity for the MR indication to be used to tell the program when there is a match. Likewise, there is no opportunity for the NMR indication to be used to tell the program when there is no match. Again we must do the work ourselves.

And, again the fact that we changed the EMPMAST file from a consecutive data file to an indexed data file helps us in this task.

We also changed the file type of the TIMCRD file from consecutive (sequential) to indexed and this change enables us to greatly simplify the processing of the time card file. Additionally, the same logic works for the SALFILE so as you can see in File Descriptions (Figure 23-3) it too has been designed as an indexed file.

As an aside, if the SALFILE were in the PAREG RPG cycle program, it would have had to be coded as a tertiary file in column 16. Since there is no tertiary designator for column 16, it would have had to be coded as a secondary.

To make it a tertiary file, it would be the third input file defined in File Descriptions using a P or S designation in column 16. In PAREG2, the same type of operation that brings in the matching TIMCRD record is used to bring in the SALFILE record.

Other than the different record lengths, you can see that each file, EMPMAST, TIMCRD, and SALFILE use the same basic coding to assure they are processed as indexed files, in a fully procedural fashion in the PAREG2 program.

Since these three files are "sorted" in report processing sequence through the EMPNO key field of the respective files, we could have written the PAREG2 program to fully simulate the IBM MR logic.

In other words, we could have processed all three files in an input sequential manner by using the index to deliver the records in sequence. To do this, we would have had to do all the coding and checking and "looking ahead" to see which record would be processed next.

We would have to set on an equivalent of MR when we had matches and we would have had to set off MR when there were no matches.. Though this could be done, it would have been lots more work than the key access processing method that we selected.

One advantage of processing all three files in a manual matching scenario would be that we would intrinsically know which records in each file were matched and which ones were unmatched. Line 77 of the PAREG program is where we start the action in this program by reading in the master file sequentially. Both the Salary file and the Time Card files are processed randomly using the CHAIN operation.

Each employee, whether hourly or salary, is to submit a time card each pay. Therefore, when we use the EMPNO field that the program read from the EMPMAST file to access the time card file randomly via the CHAIN operation, we expect that there will be a time card record present for the employee. If there is no time card, there is an error condition, signaled as shown below by indicator 92.

```
136 C...       HLDNO    CHAINTIMCRD...      92
137 C... 92             EXCPTNOTIME
```

In the HI indicator area of the CHAIN operation, you specify an indicator (92 in this case) that will turn on if the time card record is not found in the Time card file. If there is no time card, as you can see in statement 137, the program issues an EXCPT operation to an exception print line named NOTIME.

Using Exception Output

The EXCPT operation is how we control printing from calculations. Having received its name in RPGII from its ability to perform output that was not the norm (the RPG cycle) but was the exception, the EXCPT has all of the capabilities of PRINT operations or WRITE operations or PUT operations in other languages.

The EXCPT with an exception name (NOTIME in this case) prints the lines in output that have been coded with an "E" (exception) in column 15, rather than the H (Header) or the D (Detail). See Figure 23-5.

Moreover, it prints them immediately. Since there is only one RPG cycle in the PAREG2 program, using the D entries cannot work. The output coding for the No Time Card error message is shown below in Figure 23-5,

Note the E in column 15 (D in FMT) of the Record ID and Control statement # 223.

Note also that when the PRTLN1 exception line prints at statement # 229, that an additional "** No Time Card **' message – also conditioned by indicator 92 -- appears on the normal employee print line for the report.

While you are noting things, you may have noticed that the field names in Figure 23-5 do not begin with EMP as in EMPMAST. That's because they are not from EMPMAST. This will be explained below when we take a deep look at the control break logic.

Figure 23-5 PAREG2 Exception Output Records for Printing

```
FMTO ONamDFBAN03Excnam.........................
223  O...   E 11    NOTIME
224  O...           HLDSTA    4
225  O...           HLDCTY   29
226  O...           HLDNO    27
227  O...                    53 'No Time Card this pay'
228  O...                    71 ' period for below:'
229  O...   E 01    PRTLN1
230  O...           HLDSTA    4
FMTP ........N03Field+YBEnd+PConstant/editword+++++
231  O...           HLDCTY   29
232  O...           HLDNO    27
233  O...           HLDNM    52
234  O...     N92HLDPAY1B    77
235  O...     N92HLDHRS1B    67
236  O...           HLDRAT1   57
237  O...        92...       76 '** No Time Card **'
```

When indicator 92 is not on, that means that we have successfully chained to the TIMCRD file and there is a time card for the employee. This is the equivalent function to the MR ID turning on. Thus, N92 means MR and it means that the information from the master and the time card are in memory and ready for processing.

Salary Option

There is one more file to bring into the picture, the new SALFILE. The operations to access the SALFILE and the operations to prepare the SALARY to replace the PAY calculation are shown in Figure 23-6. Let's decode a line at time to see what this little routine actually does.

Figure 23-6 Salary Routine

```
141  C  N92      HLDNO      CHAINSALFILE                98
142  C  N98N92              Z-ADDSALYR      HLDSAL  60
143  C  N98N92   SALYR      DIV  52         HLDPAY
144  C  N98N92   HLDPAY     ADD  CTYPAY     CTYPAY  92
145  C  N98N92              Z-ADD0          HLDHRS
```

In statement 141, the employee # from the master record being processed is used to CHAIN (random read by key) to the SALFILE. The HI indicator is 98 and this comes on if there is no SALARY record. You may recall that there is an EMPSCD field that was newly added to the employee master file to contain a Y if the employee is salaried.

However, this code is not used in this program. Instead, after adding the code to the master, the designers decided to use the absence or presence of a salary record as the decision point for whether an employee is to be processed with a salary or whether hours worked are to be multiplied by rate to produce the pay.

So, if indicator 98 is on, that means we have an hourly employee. It is not an error condition by design. Following #141, you see four lines of code conditioned by the negative of indicator 98 and the negative of indicator 92. In English this says that each of the four calculations from 142 to 145 will be executed only if there is a time card record (company policy) and there is a salary record (salary routine).

So, if there is no time card, the exception output at statement 137 delivers the missing time card message and the salary computations do not take place. Inn fact, as you can see in statement 141, the CHAIN to the salary file does not even take place if there is no time card.

So what happens in the salary routine if the salary record is found – also meaning there was a time card record? At statement 142, the yearly salary is moved into the current payroll record being processed (HLDSAL).

At statement 143, the yearly salary is divided by 52 to create the weekly salary and it is stored in the PAY record for the current employee (HLDPAY). At 144, the pay is added to the CIT total for control break printing. Finally, at 145, the current employee's hours are erased so that salaried employees can be differentiated in reports by not having hours printed.

That's about all of the extra code required to process matching records function with the salary option in this program – except for one thing. Because we are reading the EMPMAST file as the driver for this program's function, we have no way of knowing through this means as to whether we may have a missing master or a time card record that possibly does not match a master record.

Missing Time Card Logic

Since we access a time card record directly by key only after first reading an EMPMAST record, we do not necessarily process each of the time card records in the file. Therefore, it is possible that we have a time card record and there is no matching master for it.

In PAREG with real MR logic and the cycle, this was not a problem. On line 43 pf PAREG, for example we printed a message that there was no matching master merely by using the NMR status and the record ID of the time card file (02). There was not routine needed to find a missing master. The RPG cycle provided this status with the NMR 02 indication. Boy, was that easy.

It is not that easy doing it manually with a random file. As noted previously, if we had read all fields sequentially, the NMR conditions would be easier to spot but the code to process all files sequentially with no MR assistance by RPG would be a lot of coding. So, we opted for the easy way.

Now, we have to solve the problem that this solution created. How do we find missing masters for our time card records? The answer actually is simple. We must read each time card record and check each master to see if it exists for that particular employee time card record. In the beginning of the program at statement 71, as shown below, we launch the subroutine that gets this job done.

```
070 C* Check to see if there is a missing master
071 C                EXSR CHKMST
```

What is a subroutine?

In chapter 14 we discussed subroutines to an extent in their role in structured operations. This explanation is better and it is appropriate for the work done in the PAREG2 program.

All computer languages have subroutines. These are little chunks of code that can be isolated from all other code without the risk of one routine bumping into another. Using subroutines as tools to attack lower-level tasks in a program is a much better approach than using straight line code with decisions and branches. In the latter there is ample opportunity for a hunk of code to be inadvertently executed merely because "it is there."

In computer science, there are all kinds of techniques for writing programs and all of them like code segregation to avoid the problems of straight-line coding. Some like bottom up programming and some like top down programming and there are many wrinkles in between such as stepwise refinement. Since this is not a computer science theory book per se, the use of subroutines in the sample programs is similar in a sense to the top-down and bottom up approaches. The question has to do with when do you write the subroutines.

In bottom up, you would write the subroutines first while in top down you would write the calls to the subroutines and then provide some pseudo code for what you expect the subroutine to perform. In RPG, one would typically place the subroutine call at the top of the program and then create the subroutine at the bottom of the program. There would typically be no pseudo code because RPG is actually a high enough language that it is not really necessary to write pseudo code.

The other thing that the use of subroutines mimics, but not strictly is the HIPO (Hierarchical Input Process Output) methodologies which promote the use of separate modules to provide the major functions of the program. In RPG/400, the tool that you have to create these modules within a program is the EXSR statement. To create modules outside of the RPG program, RPG offers the CALL statement which is not used in the PAREG2 program.

Check for Missing Master

If you examined the code at the top of the PAREG2 program that initiates the check for the missing master, you would first find the EXSR CHKMST at statement 71. It is within the RUNREG subroutine that is at statement 69. The RUNREG subroutine begins as shown on statement 69 in Figure 23-7. It is called from the top of Calculations at statement 65 as shown in Figure 23-7.

Notice immediately after this statement that there is a SETON LR statement at 66. Since the entire Payroll Register is printed within the RUNREG subroutine, there are no real straight line calculations in this program. Only two statements in the program come before the first subroutine, 65 and 66. Here is how a subroutine works in RPG.

At statement 65, RPG encounters the EXSR RUNREG and immediately branches to the subroutine beginning with statement 69, the BEGSR statement for RUNREG. The first thing that happens in this very modularized program is that RUNREG executes the CHKMST code which is shown in Figure 23-8. Eventually the RUNREG finishes all of its work and finds itself at statement 111 as shown in Figure 23-1.

When a subroutine hits its ENDSR, it is finished with its work. The ENDSR operation defines the end of an RPG/400 subroutine. It must be the last statement in the subroutine. The ENDSR operation ends the subroutine (RUNREG in this case) and its default is to causes a branch back to the statement immediately following the EXSR operation. Notice that the statement following the EXSR RUNREG in the PAREG2 program is SETON LR..

Though there are only two mainline calculations, statement 65 and 66, and because there is no second RPG cycle in this program, when the PAREG subroutine is finished, the program is finished. Actually since the mainline would have just one statement without he SETON LR being included, there would be no place for the EXSR to return. In reality it would return to the end of detail calculations (prior to the first subroutine) but it would gets stuck since there is no second cycle in a program without a primary or secondary file.

Thus, once the detail calculations are over, the program has no place to go. Moreover, since there is no primary or secondary file to force an LR condition naturally through the cycle when there are no more records to be read, IBM has made it a requirement that where there is no primary or secondary file, the programmer must set on LR to tell RPG that it is done. Statement 66 fulfills this requirement. When the RUNREG subroutine completes and branches back to the statement following the EXSR RUNREG, it is at statement 66. It then sets on the LR indicator, and it gracefully ends.

Figure 23-7 Start the Main PAREG2 Register Subroutine

```
064 C*  Run default register with no prompt input
065 C...               EXSR RUNREG
066 C...               SETON                        LR
067 C*
068 C*  Body of Code- Controls Payroll Register
069 C...    RUNREG    BEGSR
070 C*  Check to see if there is a missing master
071 C...               EXSR CHKMST
072 C*  Clear CHKMST fields to begin fresh register
073 C...               EXSR CLR
074 C...               CLOSEEMPMAST
075 C...               OPEN EMPMAST
076 C*  First read ahead to check for Level breaks
077 C...               READ EMPMAST                 91
```

The RPG/400 BEGSR operation at line 69 defines the beginning of a subroutine (RUNREG) and the ENDSR operation at statement 111 defines the end of the RUNREG subroutine. All the code in between the BEGSR and the ENDSR are considered part of the subroutine.

At statement 71 the RUNREG subroutine executes the subroutine CHKMST to see if there are any missing payroll masters. This subroutine is shown in Figure 23-8. Following the CHKMST subroutine, at statement 206 as shown in Figure 23-8, control is passed back to the executable statement following the EXSR CHKMST (statement 73) in Figure 23-7.

Because the CHKMST routine as you can see in Figure 23-8 runs through the TIMCRD file sequentially and it randomly positions the EMPAST records and it puts values in the fields, it is wise to perform some housekeeping (refresh fields).

The CLR subroutine handles this. Moreover, as a simple means of repositioning the file cursor for the first PAREG2 READ of the PAYMAST, at statements 74 and 75, the program closes the EMPMAST file and then reopens it. This has the effect of setting the file cursor at record 1.

> Note: The file cursor is a place holder for a file so that the file can remember where it is when it when it is reading sequentially. Closing and reopening the file sets it back to record 1 thereby permitting the PAREG2 program to produce the register as if the CHKMST subroutine had never altered the file cursor.

Figure 23-8 Check for Missing Payroll Master

```
197  C*
198  C*  CHKMST Read time cards for missing masters & report
199  C*
200  C         CHKMST    BEGSR
201  C         *IN93     DOUEQ*ON
202  C                   READ TIMCRD                    93
203  C         EMPNO     CHAINEMPMAST          94
204  C    94             EXSR NOMAST
205  C                   ENDDO
206  C                   ENDSR
-----------------
147  C*
148  C* Write error msg for no master to separate Ext print file
149  C*
150  C         NOMAST    BEGSR
151  C                   WRITEHDR
152  C                   WRITEDTL
153  C                   ENDSR
```

In Figure 23-8, you can see the CHKMST routine. It is basically very simple. It starts with the BEGSR in statement 200. The next step is a Do until equal at statement 201. This is covered more in Chapter 19 Structured Programming. We use it in this program because it works best. In essence it says Do the routine between the next statement and the statement before the ENDO at 205 until indicator 93 turns on.

So, how does indicator 93 turn on? Notice that in statement 202, the READ operations is coded to read the TIMCRD file one record at a time. The DOUEQ (Do until equal) will keep this loop (201 to 204) repeating until indicator 93 turns on.

Indicator 93 is coded in the EQ portion of the READ statement and if you were to go back to Tables 13-2 and Table, you would see that it turns on when all the records in the file have been processed and the READ was unable to be satisfied since the file is at end with no more records to give.

So, how do you know if you have a missing master? In statement 203, the code says to CHAIN to the EMPMAST file and if there is no hit, turn on indicator 94. We are looking for time cards with no masters.

The default is time cards with masters. So, indicator 94 tells the program that there is no master for this particular time card. When that is the case, statement 204, conditioned by indicator 94 executes an error subroutine called NOMAST.

For your convenience, the NOMAST subroutine is included at the bottom of Figure 23-8. Because the program executes the CHKMST at the beginning of the program even before it prints headings on the PAREG2 Register, it did not make sense to print error messages on the register report for missing time cards.

Therefore, the program includes a new print file called ERROR, defined at statement 10 in Figure 23-1 and repeated below:

010 FERROR O E...   PRINTER

The E in column 19 differentiates this printer file from the QPRINT file defined in Line 9. The E stands for externally described. The information provided by the print file called ERROR could have been coded using O specifications in QPRINT but this technique increases your learning of RPG/400 and RPGIV capabilities.

Statements 51 and 52 send out two formats from the external print file, HDR for the header record and DTL for the detail record.

For each error, a header and detail is written using the WRITE operation The EXCPT works only with program described files so the WRITE operation was the only choice to effect this error message.

Following the NOMAST subroutine, its ENDSR causes a return to the CHKMST subroutine as shown in Figure 23-8, statement 205. To DO or not To DO, that is the question. If indicator 93 has not yet turned on, it means that there are more time cards to check for missing masters. On the other hand, if indicator 93 is on, the CHKMST subroutine ands and control is passed to statement 73 of the RUNREG subroutine as shown in Figure 23-7.

Getting back to the NOMAST subroutine in Figure 23-8 for one more look, the externally described printer file used with this program is shown in Figure 23-9.

Figure 23-9 ERROR Externally Defined Printer File

```
FMTP   TName+RLen+TDpBLPosFunctions++++++++++++++++++++++++++++
03 A************************************************************
04 A...RHDR
05 A************************************************************
06 A************************************************************
07 A...                      SKIPB(001)
08 A...                      SPACEA(002)
09 A...               14
10 A...                  'This Error Report is a result of r-
11 A...                  eading the Time'
12 A...               14
13 A...                  'Card file completely and finding a-
14 A...                  missing employee '
15 A...                      SPACEB(001)
16 A...               14
17 A...                  'master record. The time card recor-
18 A...                  d was either    '
19 A...               SPACEB(001)
20 A...               14
21 A...                  'keyed wrong or the master has been-
22 A...                  inadvertently  '
23 A...                      SPACEB(001)
24 A...               14
25 A...                  'deleted.  Check payroll input data-
26 A...                  .               '
27 A...                      SPACEB(001)
28 A************************************************************
29 A************************************************************
30 A...RDTL
31 A************************************************************
32 A************************************************************
33 A...                      SPACEB(001)
34 A...               18
35 A...                  'Employee Number & HRS entered :'
36 A... EMPN     3S 00  +1
37 A... EMPHRS   4S 20  +3EDTCDE(1)
38 A************************************************************
```

It is not the intention in this book to teach you how to create printer files, however, having the DDS as shown in Figure 23-9 is better than half the battle. As you can see in Figure 23-9, there are two record formats called HDR (Statement 4) and DTL (Statement 30) and these are used in the NOMAST routine described above.

In the sample data for this program, there is one missing master. There is a time card record for EMPNO 6 but there is no master. When the PAREG2 program encounters this, it takes the compiled formats in the ERROR DDS shown in Figure 23-9 and it prints out a message that in the IBM i on Power Systems spool queue looks like the one shown in Figure 23-10.

Figure 23-10 ERROR Report – No Master for Time Card

```
*...+....1....+....2....+....3....+....4....+....5....+....6....+
                  This Error Report is a result of reading the Time
                  Card file completely and finding a missing employee
                  master record. The time card record was either
                  keyed wrong or the master has been inadvertently
                  deleted.  Check payroll input data.
                     Employee Number & HRS entered : 006    40.00
```

This completes our look at the code necessary to replace the matching records in the PAREG program with the manual methods using READ and CHAIN as well as the method needed to find the missing PAYMAST records.

Now, it is time to examine the last and most substantial part of the new code to support the creation of a report without the RPG cycle. The following section shows the code necessary to perform control level breaks and control level output in RPG/400 without using the RPG cycle.

Control Level Breaks – No RPG Cycle

What causes a control level break? We have answered that a few times in this book but to remind you again, a control break occurs when the next record to be processed is different from the record currently being processed.

How do you know what the next record is? Ho do you read a record and have it not be the record that you're processing? Early RPG programs often used a facility called look-ahead fields, which are less frequently used today and so they are not used in this program.

Instead, in order to simulate the notion of having two records in RPG memory at a time and always processing the lead record, we chose to use a data structure to store the record being processed.

Since we need to read the EMPMAST file, the first thing we do to assure two records in memory is to read in the first record at Statement 77 as shown in Figure 23-11. Statement 77 is executed once and only once in the program.

Since statement 77 is executed just once and there will always be more than one record in PAYMAST file, the program does not have to do any work with the end of file indicator 91 from the READ statement. Instead, since this is the first record read for the Payroll Register, the next statement at 78 performs exception output to the lines marked header in Figure 23-1.

Figure 23-11 Level Calculations

```
076  C*   First read ahead to check for Levels
077  C...              READ EMPMAST...        91
078  C...              EXCPTHEADER
079  C...              EXSR PROCES
080  C*   Run register until end of file
089  C...     *IN91    DOUEQ*ON
090  C*   SECOND READ UNTIL EOF - FOR LEVEL CHECK
091  C...              READ EMPMAST...        91
092  C...91...         LEAVE...
093  C*   Replaces L1 coding as in PAREG
094  C*   LEVEL1 TEST-- See if current city different
095  C...     EMPCTY   IFNE HLDCTY
096  C...     EMPSTA   ORNE HLDSTA
097  C...              SETON...               L1
098  C...              EXSR LEVEL1
099  C...              ENDIF...
100  C*   Level 2 test -- See if state changed
101  C...     EMPSTA   IFNE HLDSTA
102  C...              SETON...            L2
103  C...              EXSR LEVEL2
104  C...              ENDIF
105  C...              SETOF...            L1L2
106  C...              EXSR PROCES
107  C...              ENDDO
108  C...              EXSR LEVEL1
109  C...              EXSR LEVEL2
110  C...              EXCPTLROUT
111  C...              ENDSR
```

The two output lines (210 and 215) are almost identical to the header lines in the PAREG program except that there is an E instead of an H in column 15 as shown below:

210   OQPRINT   E   206   HEADER
215 O   E 3   HEADER

At statement 79 as shown in Figure 23-11, the next operation is to execute the PROCES subroutine. As you can see in Figure 23-1, the PROCES subroutine at line 79 in RUNREG executes from its BEGSR operation at line 157. It calls the following subroutines and then comes back to the RUNREG subroutine at statement 89.

✓ **MOVMS1   Statement 173**
✓ **PAYCLC   Statement 132**
✓ **PRNTLN   Statement 165**

The MOVMS1 Subroutine – First Record

The MOVMS1 subroutine as shown in Figure 23-1 starts at line 173. It sets up the program for keeping two records in memory. After this first READ statement in RUNREG and the execution of the MOVMS1 subroutine, the fields of EMPMAST exist in two locations – the EMPMAST record itself and a data structure named HLDMST as shown in Figure 23-12.

Through several Z-ADD statements and a number ov MOVE statements the individual fields in the PAYMAST record are moved to the individual fields of the HLDMST data structure. At this time in the program the contents of the current record (in process) as stored in the HLDMST data structure is exactly the same as the contents of the last EMPAST record read.

Before we continue let's examine the question, what is a data structure? Chapter 17 goes over structures in detail. For now, consider a data structure as a means of defining one record in memory that has no necessary association with a database file.

Once the MOVMS1 subroutine finishes its job and returns to the PROCES subroutine, that one record structure is populated with the data from the first PAYMAST record, and that is the data that will be processed in the subsequent subroutines in PROCES, namely, PAYCLC and PRNTLN.

Figure 23-12 HLDMST Data Structure to Hold Current Record

```
049   IHLDMST         DS
050   I...              1     30HLDNO
051   I...              1     70 HREC
052   I...              4     33 HLDNAM
053   I...              4     23 HLDNM
054   I...             34     382HLDRAT
055   I...             39     58 HLDCTY
056   I...             59     60 HLDSTA
057   I...             61     650HLDZIP
058   I...             66     66 HLDSCD
059   I...             66     66 HLDDPT
```

The PAYCLC Subroutine - First Record

The PAYCLC subroutine as shown at statement 132 in Figure 23-1 calculates the Gross Pay by multiplying the hours from the time card by the rate from the employee master unless there is a salary record.

If there is a salary record the routine uses the SALARY as the pay and stores it in the HLDPAY field which is defined within the PAYCLC routine itself. In addition to this the subroutine adds the HLDPAY amount to the City Level 1 total bucket, CITPAY. The PAYCLC routine then returns to the PROCES subroutine at line 160..

Line 160 in the PROCES subroutine is an EXSR PRNTLN statement. So, at this point control is passed to the PRNTLN routine at statement 165. The PRNTLN routine as shown in Figure 23-1 does 3 tasks. It asks that Headers be printed via the EXCPT HEADER statement at line 166 if the program senses that OVERFLOW has occurred on the printer. Additionally it sets off OF at line 167 if it is in.

If OF is not on, the routine prints a detail line via the EXCPT PRNTLN1 statement at line 168 of the PRNTLN subroutine. The PRNTLN's ENDSR is at line 168 and at this point the ENDSR causes the program to branch back to statement 161 which is the line following the EXSR PRNTLN line in the PROCES subroutine. This happens to be an ENDSR for the PROCES subroutine. From here the ENDSR causes the program to branch back to statement 89 in the RUNREG subroutine.

Caution: There are a few statement numbers that are skipped between lines 79 and 89 in the RUNREG subroutine. Do not assign any significance to this.

At this point we have (1) read the EMPAST first record, (2) stored it in HLDMST, and (3) calculated gross pay and stored that in HLDPAY, and (4) printed the headings and the first detail line. Now we are finished with the unique things that must be done with the first record read when checking for control breaks. Right now it resides in EMPMAST and HLDMST and it has been processed.

Looking back at Figure 23-11, you see that statement 89 is s DO until statement. It is waiting for indicator 91 to turn on before it will end the DO loop. From Figure 23-11, you can see that this DOUEQ loop extends to statement 107 where there is an ENDO statement.

So all of the statements from 90 to 106, if properly conditioned will execute as often as the loop permits. Indicator 91 comes on when the last EMPMAST record has been processed and the program is trying to read a record after the last record that is not there. This ends the loop. Now, let's see what else happens in this very important loop.

At line 91, there is a READ statement. This means that for every iteration of the DO loop, a record will be read from the PAYMAST file. When the end of file indicator (91) is turned on with no record returned at statement 91, (No intention of confusion with statement 91 and indicator 91 – it happens) the next line tests to see if the last loop iteration should continue.

As you can see in Figure 23-11, statement 92, if end of file has been reached and thus no record has been read into PAYMAST, the loop is over and for that matter the program is almost over. The LEAVE operation takes the program to statement 108 which causes the Level 1 subroutine, Level 2 subroutine and Last record subroutine to execute. Following this, at statement 111 shown in Figure 23-11, the ENDSR for RUNREG is encountered.

This takes the program to the statement following the EXSR RUNREG or statement 66. Here the LR is turned on and the program falls to the end of detail calculations. Since LR is on the program ends.

If there are records to process however, indicator 91 does not turn on. Therefore, the LEAVE operation is not taken and the loop in Figure 23-11 continues to line 93. The code from 93 to 97 is repeated below

```
093  C*   Replaces L1 coding as in PAREG
094  C*   LEVEL1 TEST- city different?
095  C...     EMPCTY    IFNE HLDCTY
096  C...     EMPSTA    ORNE HLDSTA
097  C...               SETON...           L1
098  C...               EXSR LEVEL1
099  C...               ENDIF...
```

Control Break Level 1 Processing

Since a state change by definition means that a City has also changed, the code in lines 95 and 96 tests to see if the current record being processed (stored in the HLDMST data structure) has a city or state change. The chances of a Wilkes-Barre, Alaska and a Wilkes-Barre Pennsylvania following each other in a payroll application are remote indeed but this code solves the problem if need be for other applications as well as this one.

What is an IF statement? Statement 95 contains an IF not equal operation (IFNE). It tests to see if the contents of the EMPCTY field which comes from the record just read but is not yet in process is not equal (different) to the contents of the HLDCTY field in the record being processed.

What is an OR statement? An OR operation extends and IF statement by adding another set of circumstances for the test to be true. So, if by chance the two cities were equal making the first condition in 95 false but the state comparison in the ORNE (or not equal) statement in line 96 was true (states are different, the result of the IF would be true and the lines between the IF and OR statements (97 to 98) would therefore be executed.

On the other hand, if both conditions are false, meaning no city change and no state change, then the operations preceding the ENDIF statement at line 99 would not be executed.

If you got comfortable with level logic while decoding the PAREG program, then this logic makes sense to you because it mimics the control break logic that RPG uses in the cycle. If you have not gotten comfortable with the L1 part of the cycle, this type of coding probably makes more sense to you.

So, if there is no control break, nothing happens in between records, but is there is a level 1 control break, statement 97 turns on the L1 indicator as a marker and then executes the L1 processing subroutine named LEVEL1 at statement 98.

The ENDIF statement at statement 99 ends the IF statement that's started with statement 95. Each IF statement that you use in a program must be end with an ENDIF. If the either, any or all conditions in an ORed IF statement are true, the statements in between execute. If none are true they do not execute. If all conditions in an ANDed IF operation are true, the statements in between execute. If any condition in an ANDed IF is not true, the statements do not execute.

Level 1 Subroutine

Before we come back for the L2 tests, let's look at the LEVEL1 subroutine that gets called when there is a control break. You can imagine what must happen. Just as with the PAREG program, the calculations done at L1 detail time would be need to be done in this LEVEL 1 subroutine.

In other words, the CITPAY would be added to STAPAY Additionally the functions done at L1 output time (lines 238 to 241 in Figure 23-1) would need to be done to print the City totals. As you can see in the code snippet below the LEVEL 1 subroutine does exactly this.

```
113   C*   Level 1 Subroutine City Control break
114   C*
115   C...     LEVEL1      BEGSR
116   C...     CTYPAY      ADD  STAPAY    STAPAY  92
117   C...                 EXCPTL1OUT
118   C...                 ENDSR
```

Control Break Level 2 Processing

So now that we have processed L1 totals without the RPG cycle, let's move on to Level 2 totals. By the way, similar logic works as you extend the number of total levels to three and four and so on. In Figure 23-11, the RUNREG code dealing with Level 2 processing is as follows:

```
100   C*   Level 2 test Has state changed?
101   C... EMPSTA      IFNE HLDSTA
102   C...             SETON...          L2
103   C...             EXSR LEVEL2
104   C...             ENDIF
```

The Level 2 test is even easier than the Level 1 test. In this case, we already know that there is an L1 break. We just don't know if it was caused by a state change or not. SO we have to test to see if the state has changed. Again, the current record is in the HLDMST data structure and the next record to be processed is the record that was just read from PAYMAST. The two state fields SMPSTA and HLDSTA are compared to see if there is a state change. If there is no state change then none of the statements get executed but if the IFNE statement is evaluated as true and the states have changed, then line 102 and 103 are executed.

Line 103 is a marker to set on the L2 indicator in case we need it someplace in the program. The L1 and L2 indicators can be used as regular indicators if you choose as in this program. Once L2 is turned on, the LEVEL 2 subroutine is executed from line 103.

Before we check out the LR2 tests, let's look at the LEVEL2 subroutine that gets called when there is a control break. You can imagine what must happen. Just as with the PAREG program, the calculations done at L2 detail time would be need to be done in this LEVEL 1 subroutine.

In other words, the STAPAY field value would be added to TOTPAY field. Additionally the functions done at L2 output time would need to be done to print the State totals from State total exception output lines (lines 242 to 245 in Figure 23-1). As you can see in the code snippet below the LEVEL 2 subroutine does exactly this.

```
120  C*   Level 2 Subroutine State break
121  C*
122  C...  LEVEL2      BEGSR
123  C...  STAPAY      ADD   TOTPAY      TOTPAY  92
124  C...              EXCPTL2OUT
125  C...              ENDSR
```

Process the Record Just Read

The last few statements in the RUNREG subroutine of PAREG2 are repeated below for convenience in referencing. These statements will be referenced in this section regarding processing the current record as well as the next section dealing with Final totals at LR time.

Staring with 105 below, you can see that the SETOF operation is turning off the L1 and L1 indicators. To repeat, we could have used any indicator number to represent the fact that it was L1 time or L2 time but since special indicators L1 and L2 are not controlled by RPG in this program, we took control of then.

At the end of the L1 and L2 routines, the indicators are set off so that they can be tested properly during the next DO loop iteration.

Earlier in this chapter when we studied the first READ EMPMAST code, we examined in detail the workings of the PROCES subroutine in line 106. From this examination, we know that it moves the record just read into the current record slot (HLDMST) and it calculates gross pay and it prints the detail line.

At statement 110 the major DUEQ loop for RUNREG finds its matching ENDO statement. As long as indicator 91, which indicates the end of file in the EMPMAST, is not on, the loop continues. But when 91 is on the Do loop ends and control is transferred to the first statement following the ENDDO. As you can see, this is statement 107 and the operations to be done are shown in statements 108 to 110 below.

```
105  C...      SETOF...          L1L2
106  C...      EXSR PROCES
107  C...      ENDDO
108  C...      EXSR LEVEL1
109  C...      EXSR LEVEL2
110  C...      EXCPTLROUT
111  C...      ENDSR
```

Final Total Processing

Just as a state change would force a city change (a Level 2 change would force a Level 1 change), so also does a last record change force a next highest level change (L2 in PAREG2).

So, when the RUNREG DO loop is completed at statement 107, the program is all over but the totals.

Since there is no record at this point that was just read, it would not help at all to compare the current record in HLDMST with the record just read. If we were clearing this record out each time prior to reading it in, then that type of code could work. However, it is unnecessary for when the program is just about done and it has had or it is about to have (Line 66) LR turned on, the record being processed is clearly the last and whether it is a single record or a group of records from the same city, when the next record is no record, there is a level change.

In fact, all of the level fields have changed. The contents logically no longer represent the last PAYMAST read because no PAYMAST was read. Logically all of the new fields are zero or blank. So if we were to compare the EMPSTA with the HLDSTA we would get a logical not. HLDSTA would contain the state from the last record actually read and EMPSTA would contain a logical blank.

SWhen LR occurs, there is no need to test the other levels. LR forces all other control breaks. So the record in HLDMST, though it has been fully processed, has not had its City and State totals for this last group written until this point in the program line 108 gets the last City total out and 109 gets the last state total out 110 prints the final totals and then it runs into the ENDSR for RUNREG at 111.

As we have noted several time since discussing the logic of PAREG2, this forces the program back to the last detail calculation at line 66, which turns on LR and then drifts quietly in to post detail calc oblivion as the program ends.

There are three more permutations of PAREG2. The version we just studied, which should be called PAREG2P, is the second longest because it is program described. The longest version is the RPGIV version (PAREG2P4) converted with the IBM CVTRPGSRC command already discussed.

Since RPGIV does not like more than one indicator on a conditioning calculations specification and it needs space for keywords on may specifications, it is always a bigger (# of lines) program than a corresponding RPG/400 version. The shortest version PAREG2E is RPG/400 externally described and the second shortest version (PAREG2E4) is the RPGIV version.

Externally Described RPG/400 PAREG2E

The externally described RPG/400 version is presented in its entirety in Figure 23-13.

Figure 23-13 Externally Described PAREG2 as PAREG2E

```
      *PAREG2P int. described PAREG - no MR, No LX totals
001 H* RPG HEADER (CONTROL) SPECIFICATION FORMS
002 H
003 F*
004 F* RPG FILE DESCRIPTION SPECIFICATION FORMS
005 F*
006 FEMPMAST IF  E           K         DISK
007 FTIMCRD  IF  E           K         DISK
008 FSALFILE IF  E           K         DISK
009 FQPRINT  O   F     77    OF        PRINTER
010 FERROR   O   E                     PRINTER
011 IHLDMST     E DSHLDMAST                   70
012 I                                1  70 HREC
013 I                                4  23 HLDNM
014 C*
015 C* RPG CALCULATION SPECIFICATION FORMS
016 C*
```

```
017 C*  Run default register with no prompt input
018 C                        EXSR RUNREG
019 C                        SETON                      LR
020 C*
021 C*  Body of Code that Controls the Payroll Register
022 C           RUNREG       BEGSR
023 C*  Check to see if there is a missing master
024 C                        EXSR CHKMST
025 C*  Clear fields from CHKMST to begin fresh register
026 C                        EXSR CLR
027 C                        CLOSEEMPMAST
028 C                        OPEN EMPMAST
029 C*  First read read ahead to be able to check Levels
030 C                        READ EMPR                  91
031 C                        EXCPTHEADER
032 C                        EXSR PROCES
033 C*  Run register until EOF is hit... NU1 end program
034 C           *IN91        DOUEQ*ON
035 C*  SECOND READ -- UNTIL EOF NEED FOR LEVEL CHECK
036 C                        READ EMPR                  91
037 C           91           LEAVE
038 C*  Replaces L1 coding as in PAREG
039 C*  LEVEL 1 TEST -- See if current city is different
040 C           EMPCTY       IFNE HLDCTY
041 C           EMPSTA       ORNE HLDSTA
042 C                        SETON                      L1
043 C                        EXSR LEVEL1
044 C                        ENDIF
045 C*  Level 2 test -- See if current state is different
046 C           EMPSTA       IFNE HLDSTA
047 C                        SETON                      L2
048 C                        EXSR LEVEL2
049 C                        ENDIF
050 C                        SETOF                      L1L2
051 C                        EXSR PROCES
052 C                        ENDDO
053 C                        EXSR LEVEL1
054 C                        EXSR LEVEL2
055 C                        EXCPTLROUT
056 C                        ENDSR
057 C*
058 C*  Level 1 Subroutine - Control break on City
059 C*
060 C           LEVEL1       BEGSR
061 C           CTYPAY       ADD  STAPAY    STAPAY  92
062 C                        EXCPTL1OUT
063 C                        ENDSR
064 C*
065 C*  Level 2 Subroutine - Control break on State
066 C*
067 C           LEVEL2       BEGSR
068 C           STAPAY       ADD  TOTPAY    TOTPAY  92
069 C                        EXCPTL2OUT
070 C                        ENDSR
071 C*
072 C*  PAYCLC  Calculates Gross PAY from HRS or Salary
073 C*  Also calculates "net pay" and updates YTD files.
074 C*  Calculate pay for HELD record
075 C*  If Salaried, do not use RATE multiplier
076 C*
077 C           PAYCLC       BEGSR
078 C                        SETOF                      9298
```

```
079 C                          Z-ADD0          HLDSAL  60
080 C* REPLACES MR CYCLE WORK
081 C            HLDNO         CHAINTIMCRD                92
082 C    92                    EXCPTNOTIME
083 C    N92     HLDRAT        MULT EMPHRS     HLDPAY  72
084 C    N92                   Z-ADDEMPHRS     HLDHRS  92
085 C    N92     HLDPAY        ADD  CTYPAY     CTYPAY  92
086 C    N92     HLDNO         CHAINSALFILE               98
087 C    N98N92                Z-ADDSALYR      HLDSAL  60
088 C    N98N92  SALYR         DIV  52         HLDPAY
089 C    N98N92  HLDPAY        ADD  CTYPAY     CTYPAY  92
090 C    N98N92                Z-ADD0          HLDHRS
091 C                          ENDSR
092 C*
093 C* Write error msg- no master to External print file
094 C*
095 C            NOMAST        BEGSR
096 C                          WRITEHDR
097 C                          WRITEDTL
098 C                          ENDSR
099 C*
100 C*  Process line item
101 C*
102 C            PROCES        BEGSR
103 C                          EXSR MOVMS1
104 C                          EXSR PAYCLC
105 C                          EXSR PRNTLN
106 C                          ENDSR
107 C*
108 C* Print Detail Line on Register
109 C*
110 C            PRNTLN        BEGSR
111 C    OF                    EXCPTHEADER
112 C    OF                    SETOF                          OF
113 C                          EXCPTPRTLN1
114 C                          ENDSR
115 C*
116 C* Move Fields to Hold Area for Level Info / Comp
117 C*
118 C            MOVMS1        BEGSR
119 C                          Z-ADDEMPNO      HLDNO
120 C                          MOVELEMPNAM     HLDNAM
121 C                          Z-ADDEMPRAT     HLDRAT
122 C                          MOVELEMPCTY     HLDCTY
123 C                          MOVELEMPSTA     HLDSTA
124 C                          Z-ADDEMPZIP     HLDZIP
125 C                          MOVELEMPSCD     HLDSCD
126 C                          MOVELEMPDPT     HLDDPT
127 C                          ENDSR
128 C*
129 C* CLR Clear fields were used in missing master test
130 C*
131 C            CLR           BEGSR
132 C                          Z-ADD0          EMPNO
133 C                          MOVE *BLANKS    EMPNAM
134 C                          Z-ADD0          EMPRAT
135 C                          MOVE *BLANKS    EMPCTY
136 C                          MOVE *BLANKS    EMPSTA
137 C                          Z-ADD0          EMPZIP
138 C                          MOVE *BLANKS    EMPSCD
139 C                          MOVE *BLANKS    EMPDPT
140 C                          Z-ADD0          EMPHRS
```

```
141 C                    ENDSR
142 C*
143 C* CHKMST Read TIMCRD look for missing masters,report
144 C*
145 C          CHKMST    BEGSR
146 C          *IN93     DOUEQ*ON
147 C                    READ TIMCRD
149 C          EMPNO     CHAINEMPMAST                94
150 C     94             EXSR NOMAST
151 C                    ENDDO
152 C                    ENDSR
153 C*
154 C*
155 C*
156 C*
157 C*
158 O*
159 O* RPG OUTPUT SPECIFICATION FORMS
160 O* 161 to 198 are the same in all PAREG2 programs
```

When you become an RPG Guru, terms like externally described and internally described will have become second nature to you. Figure 23-13 directly above shows the same PAREG2 program that we coded with program (internally) described data in Figure 23-1. This time, however, the program is coded using externally described files. Of course, because we do not like externally described printer files (though we use one in this program to show you how they work), we use program described exception output that is identical to that for the program described version of the program PAREG2 in Figure 23-1. Therefore, we skipped lines 161 to 198 of the externally described program PAREG2E. Its output specs look exactly like the output lines in Figure 23-1. No change.

PAREG2E, the externally described version in Figure 23-13 checks in at 198 lines of code. This is 50 statements less than PAREG2P, the internally described version.

Considering that a lot of code is swallowed up in output definitions, which are equal in both programs, this clearly shows, even when the number of fields in files is relatively small, that there can be great lines of coding savings by using externally described data.

What are the Differences in PAREG2 – Internal v External?

To know what has changed, you must contrast the major differences. Figure 23-14 shows the File Description Specifications of both the internal and external versions – one atop of the other.

Figure 23-14 Contrast External wit Internal File Descriptions

External Version

```
004 F* RPG FILE DESCRIPTION SPECIFICATION FORMS
005 F*
006 FEMPMAST  IF   E          K        DISK
007 FTIMCRD   IF   E          K        DISK
008 FSALFILE  IF   E          K        DISK
009 FQPRINT   O    F      77     OF    PRINTER
010 FERROR    O    E                   PRINTER
```

Internal Version

```
006 FEMPMAST  IF   F      70  3AI   1 DISK
007 FTIMCRD   IF   F       7  3AI   1 DISK
008 FSALFILE  IF   F       9  3AI   1 DISK
009 FQPRINT   O    F      77     OF    PRINTER
010 FERROR    O    E                   PRINTER
```

In Figure 23-14, it is clear to see that it takes a lot less figuring and column coding in File Descriptions to work with the external file descriptions than it does to work with the internal descriptions. Moving from left to right across the columns of the File Description specification, the first difference is in column 19.

The choices are F or E. You choose F for fixed form meaning program described if you want to describe the files within the program. You choose E when you want to use the already existing descriptions within the database. As long as the field names you use in the program are the same names as those in the external description, most of the rest of the program does not matter. If the names are different, then you have lots of work in renaming fields. The both versions of PAREG use the same field names in calculations so this is not an issue.

Moving from column 15 across the File Description specification, you can see that to define an internal file, you need to tell RPG the record length, the key length, whether it uses alphabetic keys, whether it is indexed, and where the key field begins in the record. For the external versions of database files, to process by key, the programmer merely needs to put a K in column 31 and that's that. RPG knows how to look at the file while the program is compiling to pick up the other information that is needed, including input and database output specifications.

You can see by comparing the input specifications in Figure 23-1 for the internally described version to the input specs in the external version in Figure 23-13 that there is substantially less coding in INPUT. In fact, in many programs, thee are no input specs and for database adds and updates, there are no output specs required.

Externally Defined Data Structure

One of the tricks we used in the external version PAREG2E is that we created a file on disk with the description of the HLDMST data structure, which is where the in-process record is stored. This is called an externally described data structure. Because so often there is a database file that mirrors almost or exactly a structure you would like to define in the program, the RPG/400 and RPGIV compilers permit you to point to a database file for the description of the data structure. This does not mean that the database file is going to put anything into the data structure. In fact, it is merely a code saving device.

There is no relationship with the description of the data structure and the database file from which the description is "stolen." However, in cases in which the programmer can save 100 lines of code by referencig an existing file to obtain the structure subfields, nobody really cares if the structure and the file have any relationship. Again, it is just a code saving mechanism, and quite clever at that.

The PAREG2E version uses one such structure. The line of code as written by the programmer is as follows:

```
FMT.IDsname....NODsExt-file++...OccrLen+
011 IHLDMST    E DSHLDMAST...      70
```

This line of code at line 11 of the PAREG2E program says the following to the RPG/400 compiler:

Hi Mr. Compiler. I would like you to define a data structure for me that is 70 positions in length. The subfield definitions for this data structure will come from an externally described file which just happens to have the data definition for the record that I would now like to define.

No, Mr. compiler, after you grab the description of this to be data structure from the internals of the EMPMAST database file, please do not link inany way this structure to that database file. Thank you.

That about does it for our discussion on the differences between the externally described version and internally described RPG/400 versions of PAREG2.

RPG IV Program Versions

Since none of the code conversions we are doing have anything to do with EVAL constructs, BIFS, or free form RPG. The RPGIV lines of code versions that are shown in the rest of this chapter include only those elements that are changed substantially. In other words, each statement is different because RPGIV statements are somewhat different. However, certain elements of the language have changed substantially such that DS is now on the D spec and options that are used in this program are now coded using keywords on various specification types.

RPGIV Program Described PAREG2P4

The lines of code that are the same or as you would expect are not included in Figure 23-15 (Internally Described RPGIV) nor Figure 23-17 Externally Described RPGIV.

Figure 23-15 Internally Described RPGIV Version PAREG2P4

```
      * PAREG2P4 internally described PAREG RPGIV
      * - no MR, No LX totals
001 H* RPG HEADER (CONTROL) SPECIFICATION FORMS
002 H
003 F*
004 F* RPG FILE DESCRIPTION SPECIFICATION FORMS
005 F*
006 FEMPMAST    IF    F    70       3AIDISK      KEYLOC(1)
007 FTIMCRD     IF    F    7        3AIDISK      KEYLOC(1)
008 FSALFILE    IF    F    9        3AIDISK      KEYLOC(1)
009 FQPRINT     O     F    77              PRINTER OFLIND(*INOF)
010 FERROR      O     E                    PRINTER
011 D*
012 D*
013 D HLDMST           DS
014 D  HLDNO                    1       3  0
015 D  HREC                     1      70
016 D  HLDNAM                   4      33
017 D  HLDNM                    4      23
018 D  HLDRAT                  34      38  2
019 D  HLDCTY                  39      58
020 D  HLDSTA                  59      60
021 D  HLDZIP                  61      65  0
022 D  HLDSCD                  66      66
023 D  HLDDPT                  67      70
024 I*
025 I* RPG INPUT SPECIFICATION FORMS
026 I*
027 I*
028 I*   EMPMAST is the employee master file
029 I*   Basically same as the RPG/400 version
032 IEMPMAST    AA   01
033 I                                  1    70   EREC
034 I                                  etc
043 I*
044 I*   TIMCRD File basically the same
049 ITIMCRD     AB   02
050 I                                  1     3 0EMPNO
051 I                                  4     7 2EMPHRS
052 I*
053 I*   SALCRD basically the same
057 ISALFILE    AC   03
058 I                                  1     3 0SALENO
059 I                                  4     9 0SALYR
060 I*
061 C*
062 C* RPG CALCULATION SPECIFICATION FORMS
063 C*
064 C*   Run default register with no prompt input
065 C            EXSR     RUNREG
066 C            SETON...                           LR
067 C*
068 C*   Body of Code running of the Payroll Register
069 C    RUNREG   BEGSR
070 C*   Check to see if there is a missing master
071 C            EXSR...CHKMST
072 C*   Calculations are basically the same as PAREG2P
         One conditioning ind, SETOFF and  EXCEPT below:
...
134 C  N92HLDNO...  CHAIN     SALFILE...            98
```

```
135 C   N98
136 CANN92        Z-ADD      SALYR... HLDSAL...  6 0
137 C   N98
138 CANN92SALYR   DIV        52...     HLDPAY
139 C   N98
140 CANN92HLDPAY  ADD        CTYPAY...CTYPAY    9 2
141 C   N98
142 CANN92        Z-ADD      0        HLDHRS
...
159 C*
160 C* Print Detail Line on Register
161 C*
162 C     PRNTLN  BEGSR
163 C   OF        EXCEPT     HEADER
164 C   OF        SETOFF...                       OF
165 C           EXCEPT     PRTLN1
166 C           ENDSR
167 C*
...
210 O* RPG OUTPUT SPECIFICATION FORMS
211 O* Output specifications basically same as PAREG2P
212 OQPRINT    E...      HEADER...  2 06
213 O...                            32 'THE DOWALLOBY
```

File Description

As you check out the RPGIV converted code in Figure 23-15, the first big noticeable difference comes in File Description. Of course if we had any Control SPEC (H) entries, we would have seen those come over as keywords since the RPGIV H spec has no columnar values at all.

Let's look at one H spec for an indexed file EMPMAST. It is the same as the specifications for the TIMCRD and the SALFILE so by examining it in Figure 23-16, we are in essence looking at the whole notion of fully procedural indexed files (or logical files) in RPGIV.

Figure 23-16 – Contrast RPG/400 with RPGIV File Description

RPGIV Database
```
FMT FFilename++IPEASFRlen+LKlen+AIDevice+.Keywords++
006 FEMPMAST    IF   F   70      3AIDISK     KEYLOC(1)
```

RPG/400 Database
```
FMT.FFilenameIPEAF....RlenLK1AIOvKlocEDevice+.
006 FEMPMAST IF  F       70  3AI     1 DISK
```

RPGIV Printer FIle
```
FMT FFilename++IPEASFRlen+L...Device+.Keywords++
009 FQPRINT    O    F   77... PRINTER OFLIND(*INOF)
```

RPG/400 Printer File
```
FMT.FFilenameIPEAF....RlenLK1AIOvKlocEDevice+.
009 FQPRINT  O  F       77      OF      PRINTER
```

For program described indexed files in RPGIV, IBM chose to keep the length of the key (3), the notion of alphabetic keys or packed keys (A) and the indexed file designation (I) as columnar. In the RPG/400 version, you can see the 3AI very plainly about eight spaces to the left of the DISK device. In RPGIV, the 3AI is right next to the DISK device. In RPG/400, the key field starting location is columnar, two spaces to the left of the DISK device in column 38 of the F form.

IBM left no room for the key field starting location with RPGIV so they invented a keyword (KEYLOC) to handle this entry. As you can see in the RPGIV the key starting location of 1 is accommodated with the Keyword entry KEYLOC(1).

In RPG/400, the programmer had the opportunity to place a value in the overflow indicator column to define the indicator for printer overflow. With RPGIV, this entry is no longer columnar.

It is keyword oriented and you can see in Figure 23-16 that the completed keyword specification for overflow in the PAREG2P4 program is **OFLIND(*INOF)**. It means the same. It just looks different. That sums up the PAREG2P4 File Description differences.

The "D" Spec

The next big difference starts at line 13 and goes to line 23 of the PAREG2P4 program in Figure 23-15. In the RPG/400 version, in lines 49 to 59 of the input "I" specification, the HLDMST data structure is defined.

When this was converted to RPGIV, the information was transferred to the Definition "D" specification. Several of the "D" specs from PAREG2P4 are included below for closer examination:

```
013 D HLDMST          DS
014 D  HLDNO                 1    3 0
015 D  HREC            1    70
016 D  HLDNAM               4    33
017 D  HLDNM                4    23
```

The "D" spec overall is very easy to relate to compared to defining a data structure using the convoluted RPG/400 "I" spec DS formats for definition and subfields. The first thing that you may have noticed is that you can indent your field names to make the more readable. There is extra space so that field names no longer need to be left justified.

Intuitively, you can see the data structure name in line 13 with the familiar DS designation. Also, intuitively, you can see the from and to positions of the subfields and the subfield names. Again intuitively, knowing that EMPNO is numeric with zero decimals it is easy to spot the zero in line 14 in the "current record" version of EMPNO named HLDNO.

Conditioning Indicators and Operation Names

In lines 134 to 142 of Figure 23-15, you can see that one indicator was not enough to condition several of the calculations in this block of code. Instead of the three spaces for conditioning indicators in RPG/400 which came in handy for RPG indicator lovers, IBM opted to leave space for just one. The implicit ANDing of three conditioning indicators was removed from the RPGIV "C" specification definition. Each of the statements selected need two indicators to condition their respective operations. Therefore, two lines of code are needed and the mission is accomplished by ANDing them together.

Table 14-1 in Chapter 14 shows the RPGIV operations that received name changes when IBM defined RPGIV. Two of these name changes are shown in the block of code from 159 to 167 of Figure 23-15.

The operation statements look very much like their counterparts in RPG/400 except for the change to the operation name themselves. The two operations in this block of code of course are SETOFF which grew on character from SETOF and EXCEPT, which also grew one character from EXCPT. Both of these changes as well as the other operation changes contribute to making RPGIV a more readable language.

That's about it for major changes in the PAREG2P4 program. Now, right before the chapter wrap-up, let's take a look at one more flavor of PAREG2 code known as PAREG2E4. This is the RPGIV externally described version of the PAREG2 program.

RPGIV Externally Described PAREG2E4

The PAREG2E4 is the RPGIV version of the PAREG2E program that we examined earlier in this chapter. It is very similar. In Figure 23-17, the code that you see is the code that either has some reference value in itself to make the program recognizable or it is code that is substantially different and therefore worthy of review for learning purposes.

The full versions of all this code are available on the Lets Go Publish Web site (www.letsgopublish.com/files). Type in www/letsgopublish.com/files/Programs. It will show you a directory from which you can pick the source. By the way all the program files end with .doc so make sure you include this suffix with the program name.

If you are an amateur humorist as I, you must now be singing. "Is that all there is (for RPGIV external)?" Yes, that's about it. There are no input specs needed. The calcs are the same and the output is the same.

Theoretically, we could have had no code here. File descriptions changes only in the placement of the K for the external definition of a keyed file. QPRINT changes with the OFLIND keyword but it is the same as the program described version. Additionally, the HLDMST data structure is externally described but this too is very similar to the RPG/400 version except for one thing. The external name is now a keyword, EXTNAME(HLDMAST).

Figure 23-17 Externally Described RPGIV Version PAREG2E4
```
001 H* RPG HEADER (CONTROL) SPECIFICATION FORMS
002 H
003 F*
004 F* RPG FILE DESCRIPTION SPECIFICATION FORMS
005 F*
006 FEMPMAST    IF   E           K DISK
007 FTIMCRD     IF   E           K DISK
008 FSALFILE    IF   E           K DISK
009 FQPRINT     O    F    77       PRINTER OFLIND(*INOF)
010 FERROR      O    E             PRINTER
011 D HLDMST         E DS          70     EXTNAME(HLDMAST)
013 D   HREC                   1   70
015 D   HLDNM                  4   23
```

All of this reaffirms a point that we have made several times in this book. With RPG/400 as the base line, RPGIV is not that much different. If you can code in RPG/400, there is no reason to not code in RPGIV – at least for base language functions. Later, you can have all the fun you want with the elements of RPGIV that change coding substantially: EVAL, BIFs, and free-form RPGIV.

Chapter Summary

In this chapter we made a dramatic change in programming from the PAREG program that we had been studying throughout this book. There is no RPG program cycle in this program yet the program accomplishes the mission of matching records and control level processing, The PAREG2 program is shown in internal and external versions for RPG/400 and RPGIV. The major difference between the internal and external versions is that there is substantially less coding in the external version than the internal version.

All of this reaffirms a point that we have made several times in this book. With RPG/400 as the base line, RPGIV is not that much different. If you can code in RPG/400, there is no reason to not code in RPGIV – at least for base functions. Later, you can have all the fun you want with the elements of RPGIV that change coding substantially: EVAL, BIFs, and /Free-form RPGIV.

Key Chapter Terms

BIFS	DO loop	Level 1
CHAIN operation	EVAL operation	Level 2
Code, readable	Externally defined DS	No Time Card process
Coding savings	Ext described program	OFLIND,keyword
Compiling	EXTNAME keyword	PAREG2
Conditioning Indicators	H spec	Poor design?
Control break	HLDMST	No Primary File!
Control Spec	Housekeeping	Report sequencing
CVTRPGSRC	IF statement	RPG cycle missing
D spec	Index	SALFILE
Data Design	KEYLOC keyword	Sequential reads
Database		

Review Questions

1. Does it take more or less coding to roll your won matching records and control level processing? Why?

2. Why is a program-described file version always bigger than an externally described program – RPG/400 and RPGI4?

3. Why is an RPGIV program typically larger in terms of statements than an RPG/400 program?

4. In all versions of PAREG2 in this chapters, why are is there no primary or secondary file defined?

5. How is it that the data is in employee number sequence yet the breaks are on state and city?

6. What is a tertiary file and how is it coded?

7. Does the program PAREG2 use manual matching records or did we use a random read trick?

8. When using manual control level processing, are you always one record behind? Explain? Why do we chain with the HLDNO record?

9. What changes were necessary to use EXCPT and exception output instead of the cycle?

10. What happens in this chapter if an employee has a salary record?

11. How do we check to see if there is a missing time card?

12. What is an internal subroutine?

13. How do we check for Missing Master?

14. Why is there an external print file? What is this all about? Is it coded differently than an internal print file?

15. What causes a control level break in this program?

16. What function does the MOVMS1 subroutine perform?

17. What is the purpose of the HLDMST data structure?

18. What does the PAYCLC subroutine do?

19. Why are there two tests to see if L1 is on?

20. Does the LROUT exception line get printed every time that L2 is on?

21. What is the difference between PAREG2 and PAREG2E?

22. What is an externally defined data structure?

23. Why would one choose to use an externally described data structure?

24. Which line of code in which program(s) that are displayed in this chapter use the external data structure?

25. Describe the D spec changes to accommodate the data structure in RPGIV?

26. What file description differences are there in the RPG/400 and RPGIV program described versions?

27. Summarize the changes necessary to make the RPGIV version of the PAREG2 program externally described?

28. Which programming language should you use to code RPG operations that can be performed in either RPG/400 or the RPGIV language?

Chapter 24 Case Study Part II: RPG Operations in Action

The Once and Future PAREG3

PAREG3 as shown in Figure 24-1 is the reincarnation of PAREG2 with a number of enhancements to demonstrate the power of RPG and RPGIV along with powerful database and data structure capabilities. Figure 24-1 shows the RPG/400 program described version and it is the second largest of the four versions. The largest version is the RPGIV converted program described code. To round out the offerings in this chapter we show you the salient portions of the PAREG3P program in its external version, PAREG3E, and its two RPGIV versions, PAREG3P4 (program described) and PAREG3E4 (externally described).

Figure 24-1 PAREG3 Program – With Additional Functions

```
       *PAREG3P internally described PAREG - no MR, No LX totals
       *Enhanced with States File, YTD Update, Display etc.
PAREG3PDOC
001 H* RPG HEADER (CONTROL) SPECIFICATION FORMS
002 H
003 F*
004 F* RPG FILE DESCRIPTION SPECIFICATION FORMS
005 F*
006 FPAYINPUTCF  E                      WORKSTN                    U1
007 FEMPMAST UF  F      70  3AI     1 DISK...              A
008 FTIMCRD  IF  F       7  3AI     1 DISK...
009 FSALFILE IF  F       9  3AI     1 DISK...
010 FYTDFILE UF  F     128  3AI     1 DISK...              A   UC
011 FPAYHIST UF  F     512  5AI   251 DISK...              A   UC
012 FSTATES  IT  F      22        EDISK
013 FQPRINT  O   F      77      OF   PRINTER
014 FERROR   O   E                   PRINTER
015 FQPRINT2 O   F      77      OA   PRINTER
016 E    STATES          TABABR  1  52  2    TABST  20  St table
017 E                    TABDNO  1  10  4    TABDNM 30  Dep table
0172E* Yearly Gross Pay History Array - YTDFILE
018 E                    GRP         6 11 2              Yr G Hst
019 I*
020 I* RPG INPUT SPECIFICATION FORMS
021 I*
022 I*
023 I*   EMPMAST is the employee master file
024 I*   One record per employee - contains pay rate & department
025 I*   For salaried employees, Salary is in the SALFILE file
026 I*
027 IEMPMAST AA  01
028 I                                    1  70 EREC
029 I                                    1   30EMPNO
030 I                                    4  23 EMPNM
031 I                                    4  33 EMPNAM
032 I                                   34  382EMPRAT
033 I                                   39  58 EMPCTY
034 I                                   59  60 EMPSTA
035 I                                   61  650EMPZIP
036 I                                   66  66 EMPSCD--SALCOD
037 I                                   67  70 EMPDPT--DPTCOD
038 I*
039 I*   TIMCRD is updated in an independent process.
040 I*   File provides current time records for PAYROLL process
041 I*   For salaried employees, no hrs provided but the TIME
0412I*   card must be present
042 I*   If No TIMCD on Chain - salaried person does not get paid
```

```
043 I*
044 ITIMCRD   AB  02
045 I                                        1    30EMPNO
046 I                                        4    72EMPHRS
047 I*
048 I*  SALCRD is updated in an independent process.
049 I*  File mimics an extension to the PAYMAST file
050 I*  For salaried employees, the salary is stored in this file
051 I*
052 ISALFILE  AC  03
053 I                                        1    30SALENO
054 I                                        4    90SALYR
055 I*
056 I*  PAYHIST  updated with the new master record for employee
057 I*  Serves as full history for multiple years. Also serves as
058 I*  A means of recreating a given pay period's payroll for
0582I*  verification
059 I*
060 IPAYHIST   AD  04
061 I                                        1    30HSTE#
062 I                                        4    33 HSTNAM
063 I                                       34   382HSTRAT
064 I                                       39    58 HSTCTY
065 I                                       59    60 HSTSTA
066 I                                       61   650HSTZIP
067 I                                       66    66 HSTSCD
068 I                                       67    70 HSTDPT
069 I                                       71   742HSTHRS
070 I                                       75   800HSTSAL
071 I                                       81   872HSTPAY
072 I                                       88    90 FILLH1
073 I                                       91   960HSTDAT
074 I                                       97   113 FILLH2
075 I                                      114  1222HSTFIX
076 I                                      123  1312HSTSTX
077 I                                      132  1402HSTCTX
078 I                                      141  1492HSTFCX
079 I                                      150  1582HSTDED
080 I                                      159  1652HSTNET
081 I                                      166   236 HSTYTD
082 I                                      166  1762HSTYPY
083 I                                      177  1822HSTYHR
084 I                                      183  1912HSTYFX
085 I                                      192  2002HSTYSX
086 I                                      201  2092HSTYCX
087 I                                      210  2182HSTYFC
089 I                                      219  2272HSTYDD
090 I                                      228  2362HSTYNT
091 I                                      237   302 HGP
092 I                                      303   446 FILLH3
093 I                                      447   502 FILLH4
094 I                                      503  5050HSTRNO
095 I                                      506  5070HSTYR
096 I                                      508  5090HSTPWK
097 I                                      510  5120HSTNO
098 I*
099 I*  YTDFIlE updated each payroll with the new YTD amounts
100 I*  The Tax amounts have no play in this sample program
101 I*
102 IYTDFILE   AE  05
103 I                                        1    30YTDNO
104 I                                        4    33 YTDNAM
105 I                                       34   442YTDPAY
106 I                                       45   502YTDHRS
107 I                                       51   592YTDFIX
108 I                                       60   682YTDSTX
109 I                                       69   772YTDCTX
110 I                                       78   862YTDFCX
111 I                                       87   952YTDDED
```

```
112 I                                             96 1042YTDNET
113 I                                            105  128 YTDNOT
114 I*
115 I*
116 I*
117 I*   PAYPERIOD DS-- Pay period in pos. 1 & 2 - 2 digit numeric
118 I*   Needs to be read in from data area each Payroll Run
119 I*   PAYPER= data structure which holds the current pay period
120 I*   Structure gets loaded at program start from a data area
121 I*
122 IPAYPER      EUDSPAYPERIOD
123 I*
124 I*
125 I*   EMPREC is a DS used to minimize MOVE operations
126 I*   EMPMST holds this master record - HLD holds last one
127 I*
128 IEMPREC      DS
129 I                                              1   70 EDREC
130 I                                              1   30EMPNO
131 I                                              4   70 EMPMST
132 I                                              4   23 EMPNM
133 I                                              4   33 EMPNAM
134 I                                             34  382EMPRAT
135 I                                             39   58 EMPCTY
136 I                                             59   60 EMPSTA
137 I                                             61  650EMPZIP
138 I                                             66   66 EMPSCD
139 I                                             67   70 EMPDPT
140 IYTDREC      DS
141 I                                              1  128 YTDRC1
142 I                                              1   30YTDNO
143 I                                              4   33 YTDNAM
144 I                                             34  104 YTDRC2
145 I                                             34  442YTDPAY
146 I                                             45  502YTDHRS
147 I                                             51  592YTDFIX
148 I                                             60  682YTDSTX
149 I                                             69  772YTDCTX
150 I                                             78  862YTDFCX
151 I                                             87  952YTDDED
152 I                                             96 1042YTDNET
153 I                                            105  128 YTDNOT
154 I*
155 I*   HLDMST DS holds the last master record read
156 I*   It is used to mimic level totals for state and city
157 I*   values in this structure are compared to current record
158 I*
159 I*
160 IHLDMST      DS
161 I                                              1   30HLDNO
162 I                                              1   70 HREC
163 I                                              4   33 HLDNAM
164 I                                              4   23 HLDNM
165 I                                             34  382HLDRAT
166 I                                             39   58 HLDCTY
167 I                                             59   60 HLDSTA
168 I                                             61  650HLDZIP
169 I                                             66   66 HLDSCD
170 I                                             67   70 HLDDPT
171 I*
172 I*
173 I* MLHMST Holds the updated records used for this payroll
174 I* Multiple occurrence data structure has 100 record slots
1742I* Stores entire payroll information
175 I* Before it is written to the history file.
176 I*
177 IMLHMST      DS                                100
178 I                                              1  256 MLHRC1
```

```
179 I                                      257 512 MLHRC2
180 I                                        1   30MLHE#
181 I                                        1  70 MLHRC3
182 I                                        4  33 MLHNAM
183 I                                       34  382MLHRAT
184 I                                       39  58 MLHCTY
185 I                                       59  60 MLHSTA
186 I                                       61  650MLHZIP
187 I                                       66  66 MLHSCD
188 I                                       67  70 MLHDPT
189 I                                       71  742MLHHRS
190 I                                       75  800MLHSAL
191 I                                       81  872MLHPAY
192 I                                       88  90 FILLH1
193 I                                       91  960MLHDAT
194 I                                       97 113 FILLH2
195 I                                      114 1222MLHFIX
196 I                                      123 1312MLHSTX
197 I                                      132 1402MLHCTX
198 I                                      141 1492MLHFCX
199 I                                      150 1582MLHDED
200 I                                      159 1652MLHNET
201 I                                      166 236 MLHYTD
202 I                                      166 1762MLHYPY
203 I                                      177 1822MLHYHR
204 I                                      183 1912MLHYFX
205 I                                      192 2002MLHYSX
206 I                                      201 2092MLHYCX
207 I                                      210 2182MLHYFC
208 I                                      219 2272MLHYDD
209 I                                      228 2362MLHYNT
210 I                                      237 302 MGP
211 I                                      303 446 FILLH3
212 I                                      447 502 FILLH4
213 I                                      503 5050MLHRNO
214 I                                      506 5070MLHYR
215 I                                      508 5090MLHPWK
216 I                                      510 5120MLHNO
217 IPAYHST        DS                      100
218 I                                        1 256 PAYRC1
219 I                                      257 512 PAYRC2
220 C*
221 C* RPG CALCULATION SPECIFICATION FORMS
222 C*
223 C*   Run default register with no prompt input
224 C                    ADD  1        WEEK#
225 C         *INU1      IFNE *ON
226 C                    EXSR RUNREG
227 C                    SETON                      LR
228 C                    ELSE
229 C* Promot for Options if U1 ON
230 C                    EXSR OPENFL
231 C         *INLR      DOUEQ*ON
232 C* Houekeeping for Main Program
233 C                    SETOF                    101120
234 C                    SETOF                    212297
235 C* SEND MAIN PROMPT PANEL
236 C                    EXFMTPROMPT
237 C    03              SETON                      LR
238 C* Add Employee to Master before register
239 C         *IN10      IFEQ *ON
240 C                    EXSR EMPADD
241 C                    SETOF                    10
242 C                    ENDIF
243 C* Update Employee Master before register
244 C         *IN11      IFEQ *ON
245 C                    EXSR EMPUPD
246 C                    SETOF                    11
247 C                    ENDIF
```

```
248 C*   Run Employee Register from ROMPT Menu (RUNREG is DEFAULT)
249 C              *IN20    IFEQ *ON
250 C                       EXSR RUNREG
251 C                       SETOF                   20
252 C                       ENDIF
253 C* Check out register printout without exiting - update files
254 C              *IN21    IFEQ *ON
255 C                       EXSR PAYOK
256 C                       SETOF                   21
257 C                       ENDIF
258 C* Run History Report after PAYOK.. Run before or after exit
259 C              *IN22    IFEQ *ON
260 C                       EXSR HSTRPT
261 C                       SETOF                   22
262 C                       ENDIF
263 C                       ENDDO
264 C*   MAIN PROGRAM FUNCTIONS ARE OVER - SUBROUTINES FOLLow
265 C                       ENDIF
266 C*
267 C* OPENFL    File Open Subroutine
268 C*
269 C              OPENFL   BEGSR
270 C                       OPEN YTDFILE            21
271 C                       OPEN PAYHIST            21
272 C                       ENDSR
273 C*
274 C* EMPADD   Add Employee Records prior to PAREG U1
275 C*
276 C              EMPADD   BEGSR
277 C*             *LOCK    IN   PAYPER
278 C                       Z-ADDNXTEM#    EMPNO
279 C              *IN12    DOUEQ*ON
280 C                       EXFMTADD
281 C   12                  LEAVE
282 C                       MOVE EDREC     HREC
283 C                       WRITEEMPMAST   HLDMST
284 C                       ADD  1         EMPNO
285 C                       Z-ADDEMPNO     NXTEM#
286 C                       ENDDO
287 C                       ENDSR
288 C*
289 C* EMPUPD   Update Employee Records prior to PAREG U1
290 C*
291 C              EMPUPD   BEGSR
292 C                       SETOF                   12
293 C              *IN12    DOUEQ*ON
294 C                       Z-ADDEMP#      EM#OUT
295 C*   Send Out Panel for EMP# input
296 C                       EXFMTUPDATE1
297 C                       Z-ADD0         EM#OUT
298 C   12                  LEAVE
299 C* If not found ask for another EMP#
300 C              EMP#     CHAINEMPMAST            97
301 C   97                  ITER
302 C* IF FOUND SEND OUT CURRENT INFO FOR UPDATE
303 C                       EXFMTUPDATE
304 C   12                  LEAVE
305 C                       MOVE EDREC     HREC
306 C                       UPDATEMPMAST   HLDMST
307 C                       ENDDO
308 C                       ENDSR
309 C*
310 C*   Body of Code controls the running of the Payroll Register
311 C              RUNREG   BEGSR
312 C* Check to see if there is a missing master
313 C                       EXSR CHKMST
314 C* Clear fields from CHKMST run to begin fresh register
315 C                       EXSR CLR
```

```
316 C                          CLOSEEMPMAST
317 C                          OPEN EMPMAST
318 C*  First read -- need read ahead to check for Levels
319 C                          READ EMPMAST                       91
320 C                          EXCPTHEADER
321 C                          EXSR PROCES
322 C*  Run register until end of file is hit... NU1 end program
323 C            *IN91         DOUEQ*ON
324 C*  SECOND READ -- UNTIL EPF NEED FOR LEVEL CHECK
325 C                          READ EMPMAST                       91
326 C   91                     LEAVE
327 C*  LEVEL 1 TEST -- See if current city is different
328 C            EMPCTY        IFNE HLDCTY
329 C            EMPSTA        ORNE HLDSTA
330 C                          SETON                       L1
331 C                          EXSR LEVEL1
332 C                          ENDIF
333 C*  Level 2 test -- See if current state is different
334 C            EMPSTA        IFNE HLDSTA
335 C                          SETON                       L2
336 C                          EXSR LEVEL2
337 C                          ENDIF
338 C                          SETOF                       L1L2
339 C                          EXSR PROCES
340 C                          ENDDO
341 C                          EXSR LEVEL1
342 C                          EXSR LEVEL2
343 C                          EXCPTLROUT
344 C                          ENDSR
345 C*
346 C*  CHKMST Read time cards for missing masters & report
347 C*
348 C            CHKMST        BEGSR
349 C            *IN93         DOUEQ*ON
350 C                          READ TIMCRD                        93
351 C            EMPNO         CHAINEMPMAST                 94
352 C   94                     EXSR NOMAST
353 C                          ENDDO
354 C                          ENDSR
356 C*
357 C*  Write error - "no master" to separate External print file
358 C*
359 C            NOMAST        BEGSR
360 C                          WRITEHDR
361 C                          WRITEDTL
362 C                          ENDSR
363 C*
364 C*  CLR Clear fields that were used in the missing master test
365 C*
366 C            CLR           BEGSR
367 C                          Z-ADD0           EMPNO
368 C                          MOVE *BLANKS     EMPNAM
369 C                          Z-ADD0           EMPRAT
370 C                          MOVE *BLANKS     EMPCTY
371 C                          MOVE *BLANKS     EMPSTA
372 C                          Z-ADD0           EMPZIP
373 C                          MOVE *BLANKS     EMPSCD
374 C                          MOVE *BLANKS     EMPDPT
375 C                          Z-ADD0           EMPHRS
376 C                          ENDSR
377 C*
378 C*  Process line item
379 C*
380 C            PROCES        BEGSR
381 C                          EXSR MOVMS1
382 C                          EXSR PAYCLC
383 C                          EXSR PRNTLN
384 C                          ENDSR
385 C*
```

```
386 C*
387 C*  Level 1 Subroutine - Control break on City
388 C*
389 C          LEVEL1    BEGSR
390 C          CTYPAY    ADD  STAPAY    STAPAY 92
391 C                    EXCPTL1OUT
392 C                    ENDSR
393 C*
394 C*  Level 2 Subroutine - Control break on State
395 C*
396 C          LEVEL2    BEGSR
397 C          STAPAY    ADD  TOTPAY    TOTPAY 92
398 C                    EXCPTL2OUT
399 C                    ENDSR
400 C*
401 C* MOVMS1  Move Fields to Hold Area for Level Information
402 C*  & Comparison
403 C*
404 C          MOVMS1    BEGSR
405 C                    Z-ADDEMPNO     HLDNO
406 C                    MOVELEMPNAM    HLDNAM
407 C                    Z-ADDEMPRAT    HLDRAT
408 C                    MOVELEMPCTY    HLDCTY
409 C                    MOVELEMPSTA    HLDSTA
410 C                    Z-ADDEMPZIP    HLDZIP
411 C                    MOVELEMPSCD    HLDSCD
412 C                    MOVELEMPDPT    HLDDPT
413 C                    ENDSR
414 C*
415 C*  PAYCLC  Calculates Gross PAY from HRS or Salary
416 C*  Also calculates "net pay" and updates YTD files.
417 C*  Calculate pay for HELD record
418 C*
419 C          PAYCLC    BEGSR
420 C                    SETOF              9298
421 C                    Z-ADD0         HLDSAL 60
422 C          HLDNO     CHAINTIMCRD         92
4222C* No Time Card  if 92 is on
423 C    92             EXCPTNOTIME              ERROR
424 C    N92  HLDRAT    MULT EMPHRS    HLDPAY 72
425 C    N92            Z-ADDEMPHRS    HLDHRS 92
426 C    N92  HLDPAY    ADD  CTYPAY    CTYPAY 92
427 C    N92  HLDNO     CHAINSALFILE        98
428 C    N98N92         Z-ADDSALYR     HLDSAL 60
429 C    N98N92 SALYR   DIV  52        HLDPAY
430 C    N98N92 HLDPAY  ADD  CTYPAY    CTYPAY 92
431 C    N98N92         Z-ADD0         HLDHRS
432 C                    EXSR NETPAY
433 C    U1             EXSR YTDUPD
434 C                    ENDSR
435 C*
436 C*  NETPAY
437 C*  The PAREG2 Program does not compute net pay but it does
438 C*  carry these fields in its design.  The NETPAY subroutine
439 C*  puts zeroes in all of the net pay totals from
440 C*  FIT to FICA to NET PAY itself
441 C*  It also sets the MLHMST occurrence & loads up the record
442 C*
443 C          NETPAY    BEGSR
444 C                    ADD  1         RECNO  30
445 C          RECNO     OCUR MLHMST
446 C                    Z-ADDRECNO     MLHRNO
447 C                    MOVE HREC      MLHRC3
448 C                    Z-ADDHLDHRS    MLHHRS
449 C                    Z-ADDHLDSAL    MLHSAL
450 C                    Z-ADDHLDPAY    MLHPAY
451 C                    MOVE UDATE     MLHDAT
452 C                    Z-ADDWEEK#     MLHPWK
```

```
453 C                           Z-ADDUDATE      MLHYR
454 C* Zero tax fields - no tax in this program
455 C                           Z-ADD0          MLHFIX
456 C                           Z-ADD0          MLHSTX
457 C                           Z-ADD0          MLHCTX
458 C                           Z-ADD0          MLHFCX
459 C                           Z-ADD0          MLHDED
460 C                           Z-ADD0          MLHNET
461 C                           ENDSR
462 C*
463 C*    YTDUPD -- Create TYD Record if NONE - Else UPDATE Fields
464 C*
465 C           YTDUPD          BEGSR
466 C           EMPNO           CHAINYTDFILE               89
467 C           *IN89           IFEQ *ON
468 C                           Z-ADDHLDNO      YTDNO
469 C                           MOVELHLDNAM     YTDNAM
470 C                           Z-ADDHLDPAY     YTDPAY
471 C                           Z-ADDHLDHRS     YTDHRS
472 C                           Z-ADD0          YTDFIX
473 C                           Z-ADD0          YTDSTX
474 C                           Z-ADD0          YTDCTX
475 C                           Z-ADD0          YTDFCX
476 C                           Z-ADD0          YTDDED
477 C                           Z-ADD0          YTDNET
478 C                           MOVE YTDRC2     MLHYTD
479 C                           MOVE *BLANKS    YTDNOT
480 C                           WRITEYTDFILE    YTDREC
481 C                           ELSE
482 C                           MOVELHLDNAM     YTDNAM
483 C                           ADD  MLHPAY     YTDPAY
484 C                           ADD  MLHHRS     YTDHRS
485 C                           ADD  MLHFIX     YTDFIX
486 C                           ADD  MLHSTX     YTDSTX
487 C                           ADD  MLHCTX     YTDCTX
488 C                           ADD  MLHFCX     YTDFCX
489 C                           ADD  MLHDED     YTDDED
490 C                           ADD  MLHNET     YTDNET
491 C                           MOVE YTDRC2     MLHYTD
492 C                           ADD  MLHPAY     YTDPAY
494 C                           UPDATYTDFILE    YTDREC
495 C                           ENDIF
496 C                           ENDSR
497 C*
498 C* Print Detail Line on Register
499 C*
500             PRNTLN          BEGSR
501 C   OF                      EXCPTHEADER
502 C   OF                      SETOF                      OF
503 C                           EXCPTPRTLN1
504 C                           ENDSR
505 C*
506 C*    PAYOK Subroutine reads the Multiple Master DS and
507 C*    writes out the History File  PAYHIST
508 C*
509 C           PAYOK           BEGSR
510 C                           SETON                      75
512 C           1               DO   100        RN      30
513 C                           Z-ADDRN         RNDSP   30
514 C           RN              OCUR MLHMST
515 C           MLHNAM          COMP *BLANK                3333
516 C   33                      WRITEPAYHIST    MLHMST
517 C                           ENDDO
518 C                           ENDSR
519 C*
520 C* HSTRPT  Print History Report of All Records
521 C*    Lookup States & Department Names for Printing
522 C*
523 C           HSTRPT          BEGSR
```

```
524 C                        EXCPTHEAD2
525 C           *IN86        DOUEQ*ON
526 C                        READ PAYHIST                        86
527 C    86                  SETON                          LR
528 C    86                  LEAVE
529 C           HSTSTA       LOKUPTABABR   TABST               87
530 C    87                  MOVELTABST    SMSTAT 15
531 C           HSTDPT       LOKUPTABDNO   TABDNM              88
532 C    88                  MOVELTABDNM   SMDEPT  8
533 C                        MOVELHSTNAM   HSTNM  15
534 C                        EXCPTHSTLIN
535 C    OA                  EXCPTHEAD2
536 C                        ENDDO
537 C                        ENDSR
538 O*
539 O* RPG OUTPUT SPECIFICATION FORMS
540 O*
541 OQPRINT  E  206          HEADER
542 O                                      32 'THE DOWALLOBY COMPANY
543 O                                      55 'GROSS PAY REGISTER BY
544 O                                      60 'STATE'
545 O                        UDATE Y       77
546 OQPRINT  E  3            HEADER
547 O                                       4 'ST'
548 O                                      13 'CITY'
549 O                                      27 'EMP#'
550 O                                      45 'EMPLOYEE NAME'
551 O                                      57 'RATE'
552 O                                      67 'HOURS'
553 O                                      77 'CHECK'
554 OQPRINT  E  11           NOTIME
555 O                        HLDSTA         4
556 O                        HLDCTY        29
557 O                        HLDNO         27
558 O                                      53 'No Time Card this pay
559 O                                      71 ' period for below:'
560 OQPRINT  E  01           PRTLN1
561 O                        HLDSTA         4
562 O                        HLDCTY        29
563 O                        HLDNO         27
564 O                        HLDNM         52
565 O              N92       HLDPAY1B      77
566 O              N92       HLDHRS1B      67
567 O                        HLDRAT1       57
568 O              92                      76 '** No Time Card **'
569 OQPRINT  E  22           L1OUT
570 O                                      51 'TOTAL CITY  PAY FOR'
571 O                        HLDCTY        72
572 O                        CTYPAY1B      77
573 OQPRINT  E  02           L2OUT
574 O                                      51 'TOTAL STATE PAY FOR'
575 O                        HLDSTA        54
576 O                        STAPAY1B      77
577 OQPRINT  E  2            LROUT
578 O                        TOTPAY1       77
579 O                                      50 'FINAL TOTAL PAY'
580 OQPRINT2 E  206          HEAD2
581 O                                      32 'THE DOWALLOBY COMPANY
582 O                                      56 'Select PAY History Li
583 O                        UDATE Y       77
584 OQPRINT2 E  3            HEAD2
585 O                                      10 'STATE NAME'
586 O                                      18 'CITY'
587 O                                      31 'EMP#'
588 O                                      45 'EMPLOYEE NAME'
589 O                                      56 'DEP NAME'
590 O                                      65 'Y GROSS'
591 O                                      72 '>HRS'
```

```
592 O                                  77 'SAL?'
593 OQPRINT2 E 01          HSTLIN
594 O                      SMSTAT    15
595 O                      HSTCTY    34
596 O                      HSTNM     47
597 O                      HSTE#     30
598 O                      HSTYPY1   65
599 O                      HSTYHR1   72
600 O                      SMDEPT    56
601 O                      HSTSCD    76
**
MILLMILLING
PIGPINGING
GRNDGRINDING
SANDSANDING
```

This chapter does not cover the enhancements made to PAREG as PAREG2 since they were explained in the prior chapter. There are enough substantial enhancements to this program as PAREG3 to make this a long chapter without rehashing Chapter 23. For example, if we included all of the code (available on the LETSGOPUBLISH.COM Website) in this chapter for the three other versions of PAREG3, without one line of explanatory text, the chapter would be over fifty pages in length. The full example programs are available at www.letsgopublish.com/files.

Three More Versions of PAREG3

There are three more permutations of PAREG3. The version we just studied, which should be called PAREG3P, is the second longest because it is program described. The longest version is the RPGIV version (PAREG3P4) which was converted with the IBM CVTRPGSRC command already discussed.

Since RPGIV does not like more than one indicator on a conditioning calculations specification and it needs space for keywords on many specifications, it is always a bigger (# of lines) program than a corresponding RPG/400 version. The shortest version PAREG3E in Figure 24-6 is RPG/400 externally described and it is the second shortest version. PAREG3E4) is the RPGIV external version.

Externally Described PAREG3E

There are no unexpected changes in PAREG3E from what we have already discovered in PAREG2E in chapter 23.. The program is shorted because tons of input specs have been removed since the external version does not require them. Additionally, the data structures that had been fully described in PAREG3P are now externally described and thus, there are far less lines of code in this area also.

Calculations are basically identical other than the UPDAT and WRITE statements that no longer need data structure names. The salient lines of code for this external version are shown in Figure 24-6.

Figure 24-6 Externally Described PAREG3 as PAREG3E

```
       *PAREG3E
001 H* RPG HEADER (CONTROL) SPECIFICATION FORMS
002 H
003 F*
004 F* RPG FILE DESCRIPTION SPECIFICATION FORMS
005 F*
006 FPAYINPUTCF  E                    WORKSTN...            U1
007 FEMPMAST UF  E          K         DISK...        A
008 FTIMCRD  IF  E          K         DISK
009 FSALFILE IF  E          K         DISK
010 FYTDFILE UF  E          K         DISK...        A   UC
011 FPAYHIST UF  E          K         DISK...        A   UC
012 FSTATES  IT  F    22              EDISK
013 FQPRINT  O   F    77    OF        PRINTER
014 FERROR   O   E                    PRINTER
015 FQPRINT2 O   F    77    OA        PRINTER
016 E     STATES         TABABR  1  52  2    TABST  20
016 E* Above is the State abbreviation and state name table.
017 E                    TABDNO  1  10  4    TABDNM 30
017 E* Above is Department # Name Table
018 E                    GRP         6 11 2
018 E* Above is array for yearly Gross Pay Hist
019 I*
020 I* RPG INPUT SPECIFICATION FORMS
021 I*
022 I*
023 I*   PAYPERIOD DS contains Pay period in 1&2- 2 digit numeric
024 I*   Needs to be read in from data area each Payroll Run
025 I*   PAYPER is a DS which holds the current pay period
026 I*   Structure gets loaded at program start from a data area
027 I*
028 IPAYPER    EUDSPAYPERIOD
029 I*
030 I*
031 I*   EMPREC is a DS used to minimize MOVE operations
032 I*   EMPMST holds this master record - HLD holds last one
033 I*
034 IEMPREC    E DSEMPMAST                 70
035 I                              1  70 EDREC
036 I                              4  70 EMPMST
037 IYTDREC    E DSYTDFILE                128
038 I                             34 104 YTDRC2
039 I*
040 I*   HLDMST DS holds the last master record read
041 I*   It is used to mimic level totals for state and city
042 I*   values in this structure are compared to current record
043 I*
044 I*
045 IHLDMST    E DSHLDMAST                 70
046 I                              1  70 HREC
047 I                              4  23 HLDNM
048 I*
049 I* MLHMST Holds the updated rerords used for this payroll
050 I* This multiple occurence data structure has 100 record slots to
051 I*    Before it is written to the history file.
052 I*
053 IMLHMST    E DSMLHMAST            100 512
054 I                              1 256 MLHRC1
055 I                            257 512 MLHRC2
056 I                              1  70 MLHRC3
057 I                            166 236 MLHYTD
058 IPAYHST    E DSPAYHIST               512
059 I                              1 256 PAYRC1
060 I                            257 512 PAYRC2
062 C* RPG CALCULATION SPECIFICATION FORMS
063 C*
```

```
064 C*   Run default register with no prompt input
065 C                         ADD  1         WEEK#
066 C             *INU1       IFNE *ON
067 C                         EXSR RUNREG
068 C                         SETON                    LR
069 C                         ELSE
070 C*   Promot for Options if U1 ON
071 C                         EXSR OPENFL
072 C             '*INU1'     DSPLY          *INU1
073 C             *INLR       DOUEQ*ON
074 C*   Houekeeping for Main Program
075 C                         SETOF                    101120
076 C                         SETOF                    212297
077 C*   SEND MAIN PROMPT PANEL
450 **
451 MILLMILLING
452 PINGPINGING
453 GRNDGRINDING
454 SANDSANDING
159 O* RPG OUTPUT SPECIFICATION FORMS
160 O* 161 to 198 are the same in all PAREG2 programs
```

RPG IV Program Versions

Since none of the code conversions we are doing have anything to do with EVAL constructs, BIFS, or free form RPG. The RPGIV lines of code versions that are shown in the rest of this chapter include only those elements that are changed substantially. In other words, each statement is different because RPGIV statements are somewhat different.

However, certain elements of the language have changed substantially such that DS is now on the D spec and options that are used in this program are now coded using keywords on various specification types.

RPGIV Program Described PAREG3P4

The lines of code that are the same as you would expect are not included in Figure 24-15 (Internally Described RPGIV) nor Figure 24-17 Externally Described RPGIV. Looking at File Descriptions, you can see two new keywords being deployed as lines 006, 011, and 013. At line 6, the EXTIND(*INU1) defines indicator U1 as the control for whether the workstation file opens.

Likewise, the keyword USROPN at 011 and 013 tell the compiler that the TDFILE and the PAYHIST files are both to be opened under user (programmer control) Looking through the program, you will find an OPEN statement for these two files just as you did in the RPG/400 versions.

Line 32 shows the use of keywords for the externally described data area data structure. EMPREC and YTDREC are internally described data structures. Since these were displayed shown in PAREG2 in the same fashion, not all lines only a few lines are retained in this version.

Figure 24-7 Internally Described RPGIV Version PAREG2P4

```
        * PAREG3PP4 internally described PAREG RPGIV
001 H* RPG HEADER (CONTROL) SPECIFICATION FORMS
002 H
003 F*
004 F* RPG FILE DESCRIPTION SPECIFICATION FORMS
005 F*
006 FPAYINPUT   CF   E                WORKSTN EXTIND(*INU1)
007 FEMPMAST    UF A F    70      3AIDISK    KEYLOC(1)
008 FTIMCRD     IF   F     7      3AIDISK    KEYLOC(1)
009 FSALFILE    IF   F     9      3AIDISK    KEYLOC(1)
010 FYTDFILE    UF A F   128      3AIDISK    KEYLOC(1)
011 F                                USROPN
012 FPAYHIST    UF A F   512      5AIDISK    KEYLOC(251)
013 F                                USROPN
014 FSTATES     IT   F    22       DISK
015 QPRINT      O    F    77        PRINTER OFLIND(*INOF)
016 FERROR      O    E             PRINTER
017 FQPRINT2    O    F    77        PRINTER OFLIND(*INOA)
018 D TABABR... S    2    DIM(52) FROMFILE(STATES) PERRCD(1)
019 D TABST     S   20    DIM(52) ALT(TABABR)
020 D TABDNO    S    4    DIM(10) CTDATA PERRCD(1)
021 D TABDNM    S   30    DIM(10) ALT(TABDNO)
023 D GRP       S   11  2 DIM(6)
024 D*
025 D*
032 D PAYPER        EUDS                 EXTNAME(PAYPERIOD)
033 D*
034 D*
035 D*  EMPREC is a DS used to minimize MOVE operations
036 D*  EMPMST holds this master record - HLD holds last one
037 D*
038 D EMPREC        DS
039 D  EDREC               1      70
040 D  EMPNO               1       3 0
...
050 D YTDREC        DS
051 D  YTDRC1              1     128
...
070 D HLDMST        DS
071 D  HLDNO               1       3 0
072 D  HREC                1      70
...
224 C*
225 C* RPG CALCULATION SPECIFICATION FORMS
226 C*
227 C*  Run default register with no prompt input
228 C                    ADD      1             WEEK#
229 C     *INU1          IFNE     *ON
230 C                    EXSR     RUNREG
231 C                    SETON                        LR
232 C                    ELSE
233 C* Promot for Options if U1 ON
234 C                    EXSR     OPENFL
235 C     *INLR          DOUEQ    *ON
236 C*  Houekeeping for Main Program
...
545 O*
546 O* RPG OUTPUT SPECIFICATION FORMS
547 O*
548 OQPRINT    E         HEADER        2 06
...
587 OQPRINT2   E         HEAD2         2 06
...
608 O                    HSTSCD            76
**
MILLMILLING
PINGPINGING
GRNDGRINDING
SANDSANDING
```

The next major changes occur in the table / array area

```
018 D TABABR... S      2    DIM(52)  FROMFILE(STATES) PERRCD(1)
019 D TABST...  S     20    DIM(52)  ALT(TABABR)
020 D TABDNO... S      4    DIM(10)  CTDATA PERRCD(1)
021 D TABDNM...       30    DIM(10)  ALT(TABDNO)
023 D GRP...    S     11  2 DIM(6)
```

There is no longer an E spec in RPGIV so the table and arrays are now defined on the RPGIV D specification. The "Fromfile" column for the execution time array defined in line 018 is replaced with the keyword (FROMFILE). The # of entries per table is replaced by the DIM keyword. DIM refers to the computer science term dimension. The # of entries per record column is replaced by the PERRCD keyword. The alternate table array that was once able to be defined on the second half of the E spec is now handled by a separate line (Line # 019).

The compile time alternating table also uses two lines of D specs and it introduces a new keyword in Line # 20, CTDATA. The CTDATA keyword means that the program itself contains data as you can see by lagging all the way to the end of the program. You will see the same department table that was used in the program described and external described versions of PAREG3.

RPGIV Externally Described PAREG3E4

The PAREG3E4 is the RPGIV version of the PAREG3E program that we examined earlier in this chapter. It is very similar. In Figure 24-8, the code that you see is the code that either has some reference value in itself to make the program recognizable or it is code that is substantially different and therefore worthy of review for learning purposes. The full versions of all this code are available on the Lets Go Publish Web site (www.letsgopublish.com/file. Check out the Kelly Consulting Web site if for whatever reason you cannot find them. (www.kellyconsulting.com).

Figure 24-8 Externally Described RPGIV Version PAREG3E4

```
    *PAREG3E4
001 H* RPG HEADER (CONTROL) SPECIFICATION FORMS
002 H
003 F*
004 F* RPG FILE DESCRIPTION SPECIFICATION FORMS
005 F*
006 FPAYINPUT  CF   E              WORKSTN EXTIND(*INU1)
007 FEMPMAST   UF A E           K DISK
008 FTIMCRD    IF   E           K DISK
009 FSALFILE   IF   E           K DISK
010 FYTDFILE   UF A E           K DISK     USROPN
011 FPAYHIST   UF A E           K DISK     USROPN
012 FSTATES    IT   F    22       DISK
013 FQPRINT    O    F    77       PRINTER OFLIND(*INOF)
014 FERROR     O    E            PRINTER
015 FQPRINT2   O    F    77       PRINTER OFLIND(*INOA)
016 D TABABR... S... 2   DIM(52)  FROMFILE(STATES)
016 D                            PERRCD(1)
017 D TABST...  S   20   DIM(52)  ALT(TABABR)
018 D TABDNO... S    4   DIM(10)  CTDATA PERRCD(1)
019 D TABDNM... S            30   DIM(10) ALT(TABDNO)
020 D GRP...    S            11  2 DIM(6)
021 D*
022 D* RPG INPUT SPECIFICATION FORMS
023 D*
...
029 D*
030 D PAYPER        EUDS               EXTNAME(PAYPERIO
031 D*
032 D*
...
036 D EMPREC        E DS          70   EXTNAME(EMPMAST)
```

```
037 D   EDREC                      1     70
038 D   EMPMST                     4     70
039 D   YTDREC        E DS              128        EXTNAME(YTDFILE)
040 D   YTDRC2                    34    104
041 D*
047 D   HLDMST        E DS               70        EXTNAME(HLDMAST)
048 D   HREC                       1     70
049 D   HLDNM                      4     23
050 D*
055 D   MLHMST        E DS              512        OCCURS(100)
055                                                EXTNAME(MLHMAST)
056 D   MLHRC1                     1    256
057 D   MLHRC2                   257    512
058 D   MLHRC3                     1     70
059 D   MLHYTD                   166    236
060 D   PAYHST        E DS              512        EXTNAME(PAYHIST)
061 D   PAYRC1                     1    256
062 D   PAYRC2                   257    512
...
063 C*
064 C* RPG CALCULATION SPECIFICATION FORMS
065 C*
066 C*  Run default register with no prompt input
067 C                     ADD     1              WEEK#
068 C       *INU1         IFNE    *ON
069 C                     EXSR    RUNREG
070 C                     SETON                   ... LR
071 C                     ELSE
072 C* Promot for Options if U1 ON
073 C                     EXSR    OPENFL
074 C       '*INU1'       DSPLY                   *INU1
075 C       *INLR         DOUEQ   *ON
076 C* Houekeeping for Main Program
077 C                     SETOFF          ...     101120
...
391 O*
392 O* RPG OUTPUT SPECIFICATION FORMS
393 O*
394 OQPRINT     E        HEADER          2 06
...
454 O                    HSTSCD                  76
**
MILLMILLING
PINGPINGING
GRNDGRINDING
SANDSANDING
```

Chapter Summary

In this chapter we made another dramatic change in programming from the PAREG program that we had been studying throughout this book. In PAREG3 just as in PAREG2, there is no RPG program cycle yet the program accomplishes the mission of matching records and control level processing, The PAREG3 program is shown in internal and external versions for RPG/400 and RPGIV.

The major differences between the internal and external versions is that there is substantially less coding in the external version than the internal version.

A number of RPG innovations were fortified with examples in this chapter. The PAREG3 program uses conditional file descriptions with the PAYINPUT workstation file being in the program only if the external switch U1 is on. Additionally, two new files were introduced: an YTD file and a History file. The YTD file shows how databases get updated and the History file shows how databases have large records added.

Additionally, this program introduces the use of interactive programming to add and update records to the employee file based on separate options from a menu panel within the workstation file. Two alternating tables were also introduced for lookup operations for state names and department names.

The one table is pre-execution, loading from a database file and the other is compile time, loading from the back of the program source code. We also introduced an execution time array for the future for holding up to six years of yearly gross pay information in the record.

This program also uses a data area data structure that automatically gets loaded at program startup and gets written back at program end. The next pay period # and the next employee # fields are maintained in this data structure by PAREG3.

A multiple occurrence data structure is introduced that holds the current payroll information for up to 100 employees in its current form. When the register is finished, this gets used as the basis for building the history records in the PAYHIST file and. As a final option in this program the entire PAYHIST file gets printed in a report that uses a third printer file to keep the three reports produced by PAREG3 separated.

Key Chapter Terms

Alternating table	EXTNAME keyword	QPRINT2 file
Array	File Description	SALFILE DB
BIFS	FROMFILE keyword	State abbreviation
CHGJOB	HLDMST	SWS(10000000)
COMP	Input specifications	Tax calculations
CTDATA keyword	Interactive programming	U1 to U8
Data structure names	PAREG3 versions	UPDAT operation
Databases	PAYINPUT	USROPN keyword
DIM keyword	Pre-execution table	WORKSTN file
EXTIND keyword	PROMPT file	WRITE operation

Review Questions

1. What are the new files introduced to PAREG3 and what purpose do they serve?

2. What is the difference between the U1 controlled files and the UC controlled files?

3. What purpose does the PAYINPUT file serve?

4. Under what purposes is the PAYINPUT file used in this program and what happens in the program if it is not used?

5. What is the YTD file and why is it necessary?

6. What is the PAYHIST file and what is its dual purpose?

7. What is the purpose of the state table that is brought in at pre-execution time?

8. Contrast the coding for the state table file in RPG/400 and RPGIV?

9. For which report is the state name required?

10. Did this report have to be printed using a separate printer file?

11. What are the four records following the double ** at the end of the source program? How do they have play in this program?

12. Where are the records defined in question ** above defined in RPG/400, RPGIV?

13. How does the pay period and week # information get into this program?

14. Besides the PROMPT format which provides a menu service, what other actions does the PAYINPIT display file formats enable?

15. How are the functions of the PROMPT format menu enabled? Are numbers keyed and the Enter key pressed?

16. Describe the major differences between PAREG and PAREGE?

17. What is the big change in moving the code to the RPGIV internal and external versions?

Chapter 25   ILE & Static Binding.

Integrated Language Environment

One of the major plusses of RPG from the System/3 to the Systems/32 /34 /36, and /38 is that once you compiled a program, you were done – even if that program were to be called by another.

With System/38, its RPGIII brought a **dynamic call** capability. In many ways, the System/38's RPGIII language perfected the unplanned call. In other words, one RPG program could call another RPG program without doing anything special. Of course if parameters were passed, the parameters all had to line up.

Dynamic program calls unfortunately are not very efficient and when used extensively, they have a tendency to create performance problems with applications. Additionally, as hard as it is for me to accept, RPG is not the only language on the IBM i on Power Systems. As good as it was for RPGIII , that's about as bad as the inter-program environment was for C and C++ and other programming language implementations. It was tough going for non RPG or COBOL programmers on the older AS/400s. Block structured languages, which were such a natural in Unix and Windows, were discouraged from participation. .

So, in 1994, IBM changed all that with the introduction of the Integrated Language Environment or ILE. This environment was to be as good for other languages as it was for RPG, and still is.

IBM created a default set of parameters and commands for the language so that if you chose not to learn the environment, you could still use the new RPGIV language with all of its new capabilities (also 1994) with all defaults. You still can and that's what we have been doing for most of this book..

Since ILE was built to accommodate any programming environment, IBM decided not to use the one size fits all approach of its former programming environment, which eventually was dubbed the Original Programming Environment or OPM. ILE introduced a ton of new terms to the RPG programmer and became a field of study unto itself in the AS/400 arena.

Many programmers who like the syntax of the RPGIV language a.k.a. ILE RPG don't like very much about ILE itself and the majority of small-shop IBM i on Power Systems developers have avoided it.

The fact is that when you really get into it, ILE tends to be difficult for many AS/400 shops who had been accustomed to IBM taking the pain out of programming. As you learn the concepts of ILE with linkage and binding and modules etc., depending on your level of grayness, it may bring back memories of the linkage editor, EXTRNS, WXTRNS, etc. and all kinds of crazy machinations that were needed even on the System/3 to create executable COBOL programs. But, that nasty old linkage editor was never needed for RPG… at least not until ILE arrived.

Today, there are a number of solid experts in the ILE field and most of them are also RPG experts. The better versed the expert, the more they favor both RPGIV syntax and advanced ILE, not just the defaults. However, there are others who suggest that you approach ILE with caution using modular programming only when necessary such as when a major benefit can be gained.

Migrating to RPGIV & ILE

The chapters in this book first introduced you to RPG/400 and then to RPGIV. Those learning ILE typically started as we did by converting their old RPG/400 (often RPG-III and some RPG-II code) to RPGIV via the CVTRPGSRC converter that IBM provides with the compiler package. Conversions continue to occur without incident and most often the whole job is done on a weekend. Thousands of programs are set up to compile automatically and when they are placed in operation, in case after case, they ran without incident.

The programs are compiled after conversion using the Create Bound RPG Program (CRTBNDRPG) command, which compiles and binds the RPG source code to create an ILE program object (*PGM). It is as automatic as CRTRPGPGM in OPM. In essence IBM created a command and a set of defaults to emulate the characteristics of the OPM so that programming staffs could be comfortable with their minimally changed code in a new environment.

Few real changes other than the RPGIV language syntax were evident. Yet, after the migration, it could not be denied that the shop was running ILE – though in a muted form.

IBM did a good job with its converter. The user needs only to create new source files (QRPGLESRC) with the proper record length (120), set up the CL and let it fly. Some say it's a no-brainer but at the time ILE came out, there were other issues. First of all, there were benchmarks that showed that the OPM code ran faster in OPM than in ILE. Even without any subprogram calls, compiled objects are about double size than RPG400 programs.

When disk was a zillion dollars per megabyte back in the 1990's that was a much bigger issue than it is today. Twice the amount of code for the same function could also explain the sluggishness of ILE in its infancy. The problems were addressed and they were resolved release by release. But, even though the performance issues are long gone, the inherent complexity of ILE still remains.

What is ILE?

What is ILE? We know it is a new programming environment and that the ILE RPG compiler is the tool that an RPG programmer uses to take advantage of its capabilities. There is also an ILE C compiler and an ILE COBOL compiler as well as an ILE CL compiler. But, just what is ILE?

In a nutshell, ILE is an operating system structure that enables modular programming to perform well on IBM i on Power Systems. It provides static binding in an "any to any" fashion. This helps modular application designs and those designs that use multiple programming languages. ILE also provides better application control using a facility called activation groups.

Because all languages use the same environment, major advantages accrue in that there is a level of consistency across all IBM i on Power Systems languages as to how they "speak" with one another. . Moreover, with its accent on coexistence, the new ILE RPG does not require that anything be broken in order to use it effectively. In other words, all existing RPG code continued to work when moving to ILE and, more importantly, it continues to work.

Let's look at some of these major innovations that differentiate ILE from the original programming model (OPM).

Dynamic Binding

Prior to ILE, as noted above, the natural method for having one program talk to another was to use the notion of dynamic binding, sometimes called late binding. This approach still works in ILE. However, the IBM ILE developers have created a better way to run modular programs than doing all the work at execution time.

Dynamic binding is the linking of a routine or object at runtime based on the conditions at that moment. In a IBM i on Power Systems context therefore, dynamic binding means that neither program knows about the other until the RPG call takes place. Dynamic binding had relieved the programmer from requiring any of the knowledge necessary to run a multiple phase program object creation. As the rotisserie guy says, the RPG programmer merely had to "set it and forget it." That's why business programmers (working for the "man" love it. They got things done quickly and the system made it work.

Unfortunately, resolving all of the objects at program startup takes quite a bit of processor resources whenever a CALL operation is processed. So, as good as "quick and dirty" is for development, in practice, it can create performance issues that are difficult to overcome. It would be fair to conclude that dynamic binding does not support the notion of modular programming *at a high performance level.* Additionally, the linkage used to resolve parameters in the OPM environment was not very compatible with other popular languages, such as C that IBM also knew needed to execute on the AS/400 box. ILE introduced a much new way of bringing programs together that better fits the notion of modular programming and along with that ILE introduced static binding for AS/400 programmers for all languages.

Static Binding

Whereas dynamic binding works only with reference to real established objects, with ILE, the binding of programs was enhanced to support the computer science notions of bind by copy and also bind by copy/ reference.. In this context, there are new facilities and thus a number of new terms that RPG programmers now need to understand. Among these terms are procedures, modules, programs, and service programs.

Static binding was introduced to the Systesm i environment with ILE. This binding mechanism occurs before runtime in such a way that the module or program calling a module has all of the necessary parameters resolved prior to runtime, thereby requiring less runtime resources for multi-module programs. On IBM i on Power Systems, the compiler does the work.

To further explain, static binding is the term used in ILE parmance to describe the method used to "bind" two objects together well before they ever use each other. The objects are bound together and the relationship between those bound objects remains consistent until one of the objects is changed. At that point, with no other options taken, the whole program needs to be statically bound again.

Static Binding by Copy

The big advantage of static binding is that the compiled program has already resolved all the procedure calls. In other words, it has located subroutines that were independently compiled and it has copied them into the program object and it treats them as if they were built with the original source.

When statically bound, procedure calls create roughly the same overhead as a subroutine call – i.e. very little overhead. This performance comes at a bit of a cost, however. The most noticeable cost is that the executable program is larger than it once needed to be since all of the modules are "copied" into and exist within the executable program when it is run. In addition to the space taken up by a copied procedure module in a "bound program," the module object itself takes up space under its own name in a IBM i on Power Systems library.

Moreover, if the procedure module is used in multiple programs, using the binding by copy approach, a separate copy of each module exists in each program in which it is used. It's really a good thing that disk storage has become so inexpensive.

With disk being cheap, you can argue that the cost of this performance is low and this would make a good case. However, the way ILE modules are put together leads to the main drawback of static binding. If and when the procedure module needs to be changed (for a small enhancement or a bug fix for example), *all programs* that use that module must be re-created – since the only reference to the module is the copy that has just been invalidated by the change. So, a recompile is in order.

Static Binding by Reference

The notion of a static bind by reference has a number of advantages over the bind by copy. The size of the programs is just one of the advantages. The fact that the program only exists in one place is a big advantage. The same module is not scattered by COPY in many programs. It exists just once.

In ILE, there is a hybrid type of program that can have both the properties of a bind by copy and a number fo the advantages of call by reference. This type of object is called a service program. Service programs are described soon in this chapter.

Tools of the Trade

When programmers write code in RPG/400, they use the PDM to key and modify source and then they select option 14 to do the compile with nothing much more fancy. For a cursory conversion to RPGIV, they use the approach with the converted code as well as for new RPGIV programming. Most shops do not typically go right into ILE in a heavy way. But just about all shops type option 14 to compile their programs. In ILE RPG, the program that is called is CRTBNDRPG, however, not CRTRPG PGM. When you add a few procedures to the game, binder language or the CRTPGM command may be needed. But, that's a topic for the next chapter.

The fact is that when you make the move big time to ILE, it is no longer OK to compile programs blindly just because they will work. To use static binding, you have to give ILE more thought than knowing that the command under option 14 of PDM has changed but seems to behave the same. Knowing the pros and cons of static binding and modular programming will help you understand better when to use ILE to help you solve your application demands.

When you really want toi learn ILE, there are some new tools and some new object types that serve as the building blocks for ILE and static binding. You must learn these. To really use ILE, you have to understand these and you have to understand how they all fit together. Let's look at each of the objects and major components:

Program (*PGM object)

A program is still just a set of instructions to get a job done but with ILE it is a little more complicated. Only a *PGM object can be called from a command line. The other objects in this list as (explained below) cannot be called directly and therefore are dependent on the *PGM object. There are four program types of which the program object (*PGM) is just one. Program objects are the main cahunas and even with ILE are similar to programs in OPM. They are executable and require no other programs for their existence or support. When you call a compiled *PGM object, it runs.

Both the CRTBNDRPG and the CRTPGM commands can be used to create RPGIV *PGM type objects. Each command allows you to statically bind two or more modules together to form a program object. Program objects still call and can be called from other program objects under ILE using the dynamic CALL operation. Additionally, statically bound modules can call and be called within program objects. Either a bound call (CALLB) or a prototyped call (CALLP) can be used in the calling or called RPG program. Both of these CALL options are explained further in this chapter.

Module (*MODULE object)

Modules are considered the basic building blocks of static binding. Modules allow you to design your applications into related tasks that can result in smaller units of code, rather than doing it all in one program. These smaller tasks or modules can then be bound together into programs (static binding by copy) or service programs (static binding by reference). Modules cannot be called using the dynamic CALL operation but instead may use either the bound call or the prototyped call methods to achieve similar function. You create RPGIV modules with the CRTRPGMOD command.

A module must contain at least one or more procedures. Modules without a Main procedure (NOMAIN modules) cannot be called directly. Subprocedures contained inside the module can be called however, using the prototyped call (CALLP in RPG). When you type your module, unless it is the main module, remember that the source member for the module needs to have a keyword called NOMAIN in the H spec. This tells the on compiler not to include the RPG cycle in the object code.

So, like any other "program," a module is an object that contains compiled procedural code. Though it is compiled, however and it is translated, it is not "runnable" code. It must first be bound into a program to run. Unlike a program therefore, you cannot directly execute a module with a CALL command. Instead, the routines within a module must be invoked from other procedures.

Service Program (*SRVPGM object)

Any time you place a modifier in front of a word, it reduces the value of the word. A program is more than a subprogram. True. Therefore a program is more than a service program. The fact is that a service program is a *SRVPGM object and a program is a *PGM object. A *SRVPGM object is more like a kluge of modules and it is not a real program object and therefore it cannot be called directly.

So what is a service program? It is a collection of commonly used modules in the fashion of a subroutine library. All of the modules are wadded together to form this big service module. Service programs "modules" are bound by reference to the program module/ procedure in which they are used. The first time a service program is called, it has the overhead of a dynamic call but on the second and subsequent calls it has the performance of a module bound by copy.

Procedures that are built in service programs may be shared by many different programs that reference the service program – without having to be copied. To repeat, the completion of the bind occurs on the first call to the program object using the service program. Once loaded, all bound calls (CALLB or CALLP) to the service program operate as static.

The CRTSRVPGM command is used to create a service program. A service program object is built with a bind by reference and thus is inherently smaller than a *PGM object. The modules are not copied in but are referenced so that only one copy of a module is necessary. The service module is basically a whole bunch of subroutines / subprocedures / modules that are packaged together so that they can be used by the world outside the service program. When you load a service program it grabs all of the subprocedures that you exported during the creation of your service program and it loads them into memory and it shares them with other programs and service programs that need them. It is a powerful facility in ILE and because it is implemented with a bind by reference, it does not have the limitations of a regular bound ILE program.

Procedures (not objects)

Procedures are the smallest building block for static binding. Also known as subprocedures, these components are self-contained high-level-language statements used to perform a specific task. Procedures are coded together in the same source RPGIV program to create a *MODULE. The individual subprocedures are not compiled. The module, including one or more of these subprocedures is then compiled into a program or service program.

Though not a real AS/400 object (contained within a *module object when compiled), procedures do provide an entry vehicle for a subprogram so that it can be called. The code of course is contained nicely in a source file capable of having more than one procedure. In RPGIV, you can have many of these entry points per compilation and they map to procedure definitions. However, you can have just one external entry point.

The procedure building block is established as an RPG routine that is called using a bound call. In many ways, you can begin to write procedures in programs where you once would have used subroutines. In fact, in Chapter 26, we convert a subroutine into a procedure to demonstrate how this is done.

There are two kinds of procedures in RPG that you can create: a main procedure and a subprocedure. A main procedure uses the RPG cycle. It is specified in the main source section of your program. You do not need to code anything special to define the main procedure; it just happens. It consists of everything before the first procedure specification. The parameters for the main procedure can be coded using a prototype and procedure interface in the global definition ("D") specifications, or using an *ENTRY type PLIST in the main procedure's calculations. For now, let's just say that there are advantages to using the global D specs and prototyping your procedures.

There are four ILE source languages: RPGIV, COBOL, CL, and C. Reading from top to bottom, the chart in Figure 26-1 shows how these items come into being and how they get bound together into a program (*PGM) object:

Figure 26-1 Creating ILE Programs: Bind By Copy

SOURCE	RPG	COBOL	CL	C
Create Module	CRTRPGMOD	CRTCBLMOD	CRTCLMOD	CRTCMOD
Created Module	ModuleRP Proc A	ModuleCB Proc B	ModuleCL Proc C	ModuleC Proc D
Bind by Copy	CRTPGM MOD (RP,CB,CL,C)	CRTPGM MOD (RP,CB,CL,C)	CRTPGM MOD (RP,CB,CL,C)	CRTPGM MOD (RP,CB,CL,C)
Created program	PROG01 Proc A, Proc B Proc C, Proc D	PROG01 Proc A, Proc B Proc C, Proc D	PROG01 Proc A, Proc B Proc C, Proc D	PROG01 Proc A, Proc B Proc C, Proc D

The New CALL Statement

Along with the whole idea of ILE, modules, and procedures, comes a new CALL statement known as CALLB or CALL Bound. The ILE CALLB runs a procedure that was bound by copy or reference. It is at least 4 times faster than a dynamic program call and that's one of the main reason for its favor. There is also a new CALLP which is also a bound call but it is a call with prototype. The use of these calls in procedures is the topic of the next chapter.

Activation Groups

There is another term that is always associated with ILE that has nothing to do with the four building blocks discussed above. The term is activation group. An activation group is a job structure, similar but not necessarily as big as a program access group or PAG as was used in the OPM environment.

When you cut through all of the facts on activation groups, you find that there are two major purposes to their being:

✓ Protection of shared resources from other applications
✓ Cleanup of storage used by ILE programs

Static binding is a key concept in ILE and it has play in the notion of an activation group. Statically bound programs expect to be calling subprocedures and they also expect to be called. Calling external procedures which are not compiled in the same module or program object extend the notion. Considering that each program runs in the activation group for which it was compiled (See CRTPGM examples below), if you want all of the programs in a logical execution group to be managed by the system as a group, you can set them up to run in their own activation group.

So, instead of just defining an activation group as a container for lots of open resources, which it is also, it helps to consider that the grouping of programs to be activated and deactivated together is called an "activation group". See the simple CRTPGM statements below:

```
CRTPGM X ... actgrp(QILE)
CRTPGM PGM(Y) ... ACTGRP(*CALLER)
CRTPGM Z ... ActGrp(BRIAN)
CRTPGM A ... ACTGRP(*NEW)
```

Activation groups are also containers for resources needed for running programs. Some ILE experts may alternately say that these are things that an activation group owns as part of its own set of resources:

- ✓ File overrides
- ✓ Shared file open data paths
- ✓ Commitment control transactions

In addition to these "owned" items, an activation group also provides the following for the job:

- ✓ Run-time data structures to support the running of
- ✓ Addressing protection
- ✓ A logical boundary for message creation
- ✓ A logical boundary for application cleanup process

During creation as shown above with CRTPGM, ILE programs are set to run in a specific activation group. The activation group you would choose would typically be at an application boundary. There are a number of options that you have when you create the ILE object with regard to which activation group to use. The choices with CRTPGM are as follows:

*ENTMOD

With this specification, the program entry procedure (PEP – discussed later in chapter) is examined. If it is an RPGLE module, then an activation group named QILE is used. If the module attribute is not RPGLE, CBLLE, or CLLE, then ACTGRP(*NEW) is used.

*NEW

If this activation group parameter is used, when this program gets called, a new activation group is created. This called program is then associated with the newly created activation group.

*CALLER

If this activation group parameter is used, when this program gets called, the program is activated into the caller's activation group.

name

If this activation group parameter is used, you specify the name of the activation group to be used when this program is called.

Default Activation Groups

The system supplies two default activation groups for each job when it is started. In most treatments and explanations of the default activation group, both groups that are part of every job are referred to as the default activation group. In reality, there are two default applications groups refereed to by IBM as the following

1. System Activation Group

Most system functions run in the system activation group, and it is of no concern in your design.

2. Default Activation Group

The default activation group is the place where all OPM programs run. OPM programs do not have a choice about where they run. If you use the default for the CRTBNDRPG program (Option 14 of PDM for RPGIV) the program, by default runs in the default application group.

When you specify DFTACTGRP(*YES) on the CRTBNDRPG command, the resulting program behaves like an OPM program in the areas of scoping open data paths, scoping overrides, and using RCLRSC. This high degree of compatibility is due in part to its running in the same activation group as OPM programs, namely, in the default activation group.

However, with this high compatibility, you lose some of the facility for which ILE was built. It's easy to emulate OPM in ILE using the default but you lose the ability to have static binding. Static binding refers to the ability to call procedures (in other modules or service programs) and to use procedure pointers.

In other words, if you specify DFTACTGRP(*YES) on CRTBNDRPG, you cannot use the CALLB operation in your source. Nor can you bind to other modules during program creation. Similarly, you cannot use CALLPRC in a module created by CRTBNDCL (CL compiler for ILE) with the default value DFTACTGRP(*YES).

If you specify DFTACTGRP(*NO) on the CRTBNDRPG command, the resulting program has ILE characteristics such as static binding. At program-creation time, therefore, you can specify the activation group the program is to run in and any modules for static binding. You can call a service program or any other procedure if you specify a binding directory (a container for the names of modules to be bound) on the BNDDIR parameter of the command. In addition, you can use CALLB in your source.

The CRTBNDRPG DFTACTGRG(*YES) parameter specifies whether the created program is intended to always run in the default activation group. A *YES response means that when this program is called it will always run in the default activation group. Again, specifying DFTACTGRP(*YES) allows ILE RPG programs to behave like OPM programs in the areas of file sharing, file scoping, and RCLRSC. In many ways, this defeats the purposes for which ILE was built.

Named activation groups are very useful when attempting to move an application on a program-by-program basis to ILE RPG (RPGIV). Throughout this book, we have suggested using the CVTRPGSRC command to as the simplest way to start up with RPGIV and ILE. As a next step after going live on your default converted programs, you need to look at moving to something other than the default activation group.

The CRTBNDRPG alternative is DFTACTGRP(*NO). Using this option, the program is associated with the activation group specified by the ACTGRP parameter of the command. In this scenario, the ILE benefits accrue. Static binding is allowed when *NO is specified.

If ACTGRP(*CALLER) is specified and this program is called by a program running in the default activation group, then this program will behave according to ILE semantics in the areas of file sharing, file scoping and RCLRSC.

The parameter value DFTACTGRP(*NO) is useful when you intend to take advantage of concepts, for example, running in a named activation group or binding to a service program.

Activation groups have lots of specific purposes in making jobs run efficiently on the IBM i on Power Systems. For example, they can protect resources for use by different applications or enable them to be shared by many. They can guard against unwanted interference from applications and yet they also can provide cooperation. They permit software packages to run more independently of things that are currently running on a client's system and there is lot less dependence on the invocation stack which formerly was a major determinant.

In addition to protecting resources, activation groups are also used to help clean up resources when the group is no longer needed. Activation groups can be d-activated by group in much the same way as an expanded, humungous giant LR. Free at last.

Persistent Activation Groups

Programmer-named activation groups are persistent in that they remain in the job until they are explicitly destroyed. There are a number of ways that they can be destroyed such as the following:

- ✓ RCLACTGRP
- ✓ Non-RPG Hard Leave operations such as COBOL's STOP RUN or C's exit() from main.
- ✓ Call to ILE API CEETREC is used for languages such as RPG and CL that do not have hard leave op codes.

What is an ILE Signature? A signature is a construct that provides an interface similar to a "level check." between programs and service programs. It is intended to insure that the interface has not changed from when the programs were originally created. The signature values in the program are compared to the service program at startup to assure they are the same. If they are not, there is the equivalent of a system level check. This helps ensure that the program and service program can interact correctly.

Why would an ILE signature change? The value of a signature is computed based on the data names that are exported from the service program. Changing the number or size or type of these values changes the signature. When a signature changes, the programs need to be re-bound and then the new signature is copied into the program and the program works fine – just as before. However, if the programs are not rebound, the programs will fail with the level check violation unless the programmer "manages" signatures.

You can manage signatures using the binder language. Using binder language as we demonstrated above, you can specify which symbols are to be exported and included in generating the signature. A symbol in this instance is the name of a procedure or data item. Only those items, which have been made available for export outside the module in which they are defined, are considered to be symbols of the service program. Therefore, symbol can be added, changed, or subtracted, and unless they are in the binder language, they do not affect the signature.

Chapter Summary

In this Chapter you were introduced to the original program model and the default settings for running converted RPGIV code under ILE. We learned how dynamic binding of programs was one of the hallmarks of OPM and that this has been carried through to ILE. Static binding by copy or by reference is what separates ILE from OPM along with the idea of work segregation via activation groups. There are lots of other advantages to the ILE environment including the following:

- ✓ Source view debugging
- ✓ Better code optimization
- ✓ Hidden data and procedures
- ✓ Signatures for safe binding
- ✓ ILE error handling

ILE was built to accommodate any programming environment instead of the one size fits all approach of its former programming environment, which eventually was dubbed the Original Programming Environment or OPM.

ILE is a new programming environment and the ILE RPG compiler is also known as RPGIV. ILE is built to make modular programming perform well on IBM i on Power Systems by providing static binding.

The four object types and/or components that make up the ILE constructs are as follows:

- ✓ Program (*PGM object)
- ✓ Module (*MODULE object)
- ✓ Service Program (*SRVPGM object)
- ✓ Procedures (not objects)

With the first iteration of ILE capabilities, IBM introduced the CALLB (call bound) procedure. In the second iteration, IBM announced the CALLP (call with prototype – covered in next chapter). In addition to the call facilities, IBM also introduced activation groups.

Among other things, activation groups serve as containers for containers for resources needed for running programs.

Key Chapter Terms

*ENTMOD	Dynamic binding, 4	PDM
*NEW	Dynamic call	PEP
*SRVPGM	Executable program, 6	Performance problems
ACTGRP	Export	PLIST
Activation groups	External entry point	Procedure calls
Addressing protection	EXTRNS	Procedure definitions
Binder language	File overrides	Procedure specification
Bind by call	Global definition	Procedures
Bind by reference	H spec considerations	Programming languages
Binding directory	ILE	Program objects
BNDDIR keyword	ILE C	Protection
Bound call	ILE CL	Prototyping
CALLB	ILE signature	QILE
Called program	Job structure	QRPGLESRC
Caller	Linkage	RCLACTGRP
CALLP	Linkage editor	RPGIII
CBLLE	Main procedure	RPGIV modules
Cleanup	Migrating to RPGIV	RPGIV syntax
CLLE	Modular programming	Service program
CRTBNDCL	Modular programs	Source file, 11
CRTBNDRPG	Modules	Source member
CRTPGM	Multi-module pgms	Static binding
CRTRPGMOD	NOMAIN keyword	Subprocedures
CRTRPGPGM	Open data paths	Subprogram
CRTSRVPGM	OPM	System/38
CVTRPGSRC	Overrides	Unplanned call
Default activation group	PAG	WXTRNS

Review Questions

1. What is ILE?

2. What is a dynamic call vs. a static call?

3. If Dynamic binding makes a programmers life so easy, why would anyone want to use static binding?

4. What is call by copy?

5. What is call by reference?

6. What type of call is provided by a service program?

7. Do languages other than RPG play in the ILE game? If so, what role do they play?

8. Why do some developers view ILE as a return to days of old?

9. What are the four ILE tools of the trade? Explain each?

10. What is an activation group and why are they needed?

11. How is an activation group selected?

12. How do you create an ILE RPG program?

13. Describe the two ILE CALL statements.

14. When taken together, what is the one name for the System Activation group and the Default Activation Group?

15. Why is it not wise to run everything in the default activation group?

16. How can the *CALLER activation group sometimes be the default activation group?

17. Describe the notion of persistent activation groups?

18. What is an ILE Signature?

19. Why would a signature change?

20. What is the means by which signatures are managed?

Chapter 26 RPGIV Procedures and Functions

Big Changes to RPGIV

There were a number of big changes introduced to RPG in 1994. Subprocedures was not one of them. They came a little later – about 1995. The most welcome change was the syntax of the RPG language, which was enhanced in many ways with the introduction of the RPGIV version.

We have covered most of these changes extensively in this book. In addition to the syntactical changes to the language, built-in-functions were introduced and more and more of these powerful functions are introduced with every new RPGIV release.

In the last chapter we covered the building blocks to ILE applications and as you may recall, the subprocedure was the only item on the list that was not a bona fide IBM i on Power Systems object. In this chapter, we discuss the ins and outs of subprocedures and we show you how to build your own. Unlike most parts of RPG, ILE notwithstanding, subprocedures need a few doses before they sink into commonplace for most RPG programmers.

They are difficult to understand without a fully attentive mind and they are difficult to code first time out and when you make a mistake, it is difficult to understand the nature of the mistake without having a bona fide expert to whom you can ask some specific questions when it just doesn't add up.

In my case, when I got stuck putting my first couple procedure programs together, I went to the Internet for help. There are literally tons of articles that will help you in learning this powerful facility. I enjoyed reading a number of the FAQs and the RPG forums that are out there for our benefit. A number of times as I was reading the excellent dialogue in these forums, when the experts appeared to be stumped, there seemed to be this person coming from nowhere injecting the light of understanding to help solve the ILE / procedure issue du jour.

So, when I got stuck, I went right to Barbara Morris from IBM's Toronto Labs – where RPGIV is built and maintained. She is not only a powerhouse of knowledge, she is patient and she is very articulate in explaining how things work. Thank you Barbara for your willing assistance to all who have needed you -- including yours truly.

It took us a lot of chapters to get to this point where we are about to unfold the many and multiple mysteries of subprocedures in light of the ILE environment. According to Jon Paris, another major RPG Guru living among mortals, "Subprocedures are probably the biggest single change ever in the history of RPG. They open up whole new ways of building your applications." Jon and his company Partner400 that he shares with his partner Susan Gantner have helped thousands unlock the beauty of RPGIV and the mystery of ILE and subprocedures.

What is a Procedure?

In RPGIV, a procedure is a routine that is called using a bound call. (RPG operations CALLB or CALLP) You can create two kinds of procedures in RPG: a main procedure and a subprocedure. A main procedure uses the RPG cycle. It is specified in the main source section, which is the first source section in an ILE procedure-oriented program. Unless you take overt action, all RPG programs are main programs.

In other words, you do not need to code anything special to define the main procedure. It consists of everything before the first procedure specification. The parameters for the main procedure can be coded using a prototype (described below) and a procedure interface (described below) in the global definition (D)

530   The IBM i on Power Systems Pocket RPG & RPGIV Guide

specifications. You can also use the notion of the *ENTRY PLIST in the main procedure's calculations as you may be accustomed to do in RPG/400. However, once you decide to learn procedures and subprocedures, it's better to leave the *ENTRY PLIST someplace other than in your code.

All RPGIV programs have at least one procedure – whether you know it or not – the main procedure. The name of the main procedure must be the same as the name of the module being created. If you do not specify any, it takes on the name of the program.

There is also another type of procedure that is not invoked with a CALL statement. This is similar to RPGIV's built-in functions that we studied in Chapter 15. BIFs are designed to take zero or more parameters and to return a result. T

his type of procedure creates the equivalent of a function, thereby giving you the ability to write your own "built-in functions" that you think are necessary but may still be missing from RPG. The only real difference between your functions and the IBM-built built-ins is that yours cannot begin with the % sign. In this chapter, you will learn to create both the subprocedure variety and the function variety of RPG procedures.

So, what is the difference between a subprocedure and a function? We just studied the topic above so this is as good as anytime to test your skills. In a nutshell, if it returns a value it is a function and it operates in much the same way as an IBM Built-In Function (BIF) set. If it does not return a value it is a subprocedure It is simply called with a CALLP operation and then it performs the operations you request.

In a learn-by example book, you would expect that the next step is to show an example. The sample code in Figure 26-1 represents a program that we will morph many time in this chapter to demonstrate the subject matter at hand. In the first round, the program is built using subroutines, not subprograms, so that we can all relate to this code as our beginning step.

The program is compiled using option 14 on the PDM menu with RPGLE as the type or you can use the following command:

CRTBNDRPG PGM(KELLY/SUB01) SRCFILE(RPGBOOK/QRPGLESRC)

There are two subroutines in the program on the next page-- AddNumbers1 and AddNumbers2. A quick look at the code and you know you that this example does not attempt to teach anything other than how to use procedures ince the add commands in the subroutines and procedures are quite basic. In this way, you can concentrate on learning just the new material.

The subroutines and the procedures do nothing more than add a few numbers and then display the answers using the DSPLY operation.

In this ILE RPG program SUB01, the mainline routine calls inline subroutine # 1 AddNumbers1 using the EXSR shown at line 13. After adding some numbers and passing the answers to the variables used in AddNumbers2, at line # 27, AddNumbers1 calls AddNumbers2 using the RPG EXSR operation.

Ans3 is calculated and displayed in AddNumbers2 and then it is passed back to the AddNumbers1 subroutine where it is also displayed using DSPLY. Actually, there is no real variable passing with subroutines and that is one of the major differentiators of subroutines and subprocedures.

Figure 26-1 Program SUB01 – Subroutine Based

```
01.00 H  dftactgrp(*no) actgrp('QILE')
02.00 D
03.00 D Numb1          S              3 0 inz(1)
04.00 D Numb2          S              3 0 inz(2)
05.00 D Numb3          S              3 0 inz(3)
06.00 D Numb4          S              3 0 inz(4)
07.00 D Ans1           S              5 0
08.00 D Ans2           S              5 0
09.00 D Ans3           S              5 0
10.00 D N#1            S              5 0
11.00 D N#2            S              5 0
12.00 D Global         S             20   inz('Global 12.00 D
Variable')
13.00 C                    Exsr      AddNumbers1
14.00 C        'P1ANS1'    DSPLY                   Ans1
15.00 C        'P1ANS2'    DSPLY                   Ans2
16.00 C        'P1ANS3'    DSPLY                   Ans3
17.00 C                    Eval      *inLR = *ON
18.00 C*
19.00 C*   AddNumbers1 Subroutine
20.00 C*
21.00 C        AddNumbers1 BEGSR
22.00 C                    Eval      Ans1 = Ans1 + 1
23.00 C                    Eval      Ans2 = Ans1 + Numb1 + 24.00 C
Numb2 + Numb3 + Numb4
25.00 C                    Eval      N#1 = Ans1
26.00 C                    Eval      N#2 = Ans2
27.00 C                    EXSR      Addnumbers2
28.00 C        'P2ANS1'    DSPLY                   Ans1
29.00 C        'P2ANS2'    DSPLY                   Ans2
30.00 C        'P2ANS3'    DSPLY                   Ans3
31.00 C                    ENDSR
32.00 C*
33.00 C*   AddNumbers2 Subroutine
34.00 C*
35.00 C        AddNumbers2 BEGSR
36.00 C                    Eval      Ans1 = 96
37.00 C                    Eval      Ans3 = N#1 + N#2
38.00 C        'P3N#1 '    DSPLY                   N#1
39.00 C        'P3N#2 '    DSPLY                   N#2
40.00 C        'P3ANS1'    DSPLY                   ANS1
41.00 C        'P3ANS3'    DSPLY                   ANS3
42.00 C        'P3GLOBAL'  DSPLY                   GLOBAL
43.00 C                    ENDSR
```

Subprocedures vs. Subroutines

A subprocedure is similar to a subroutine, except that a subprocedure offers the following improvements:

1. You can pass parameters to a subprocedure, even passing by value.

This means that the parameters used to communicate with subprocedures do not have to be modifiable. Parameters that are passed by reference, as they are with programs, must be modifiable, and so may be less reliable.

2. The parameters passed to a subprocedure and those received by it are checked at compile time for consistency. This helps to reduce run-time errors, which can be more costly.

3. You can use a subprocedure like a built-in function in an expression. When used in this way, it returns a value to the caller. This allows you to custom-define any operators you might need in an expression.

4. Names defined in a subprocedure are not visible outside the subprocedure. This means that there is less chance of the procedure inadvertently changing an item that is shared by other procedures. Furthermore, the caller of the procedure does not need to know as much about the items used inside the subprocedure.

5. You can call the subprocedure from outside the module, if it is exported.

6. You can call subprocedures recursively. Procedures are defined on a different specification type, namely, procedure specifications. This different type helps you to immediately recognize that you are dealing with a separate unit.

If you do not require the improvements offered by subprocedures, you may want to use a subroutine because an EXSR operation is usually faster, though by a very small percentage, than a call to a subprocedure.

Local and Global Variables

The topic of RPG subprocedures has borrowed much of its terminology from other languages such as C and C++. These block structured languages, as they are called, have notions for variable scoping that had never been necessary or even desirable in RPG prior to subprocedures. In RPGIV, the subprocedure defines a block of code that is treated differently and separately from all other blocks of code in a program.

Local variables can be defined in these blocks of code (subprocedures). A variable declared as *local* is visible only within the block of code (RPGIV procedure) in which it appears. It thus has local "scope". In a function, a *local variable* has meaning only within that function block.

Quite the contrary, a global variable has full program scope. It is visible in all blocks of code built within the same source member and compiled as a program. A global variable then is a variable that does not belong to any subprocedure or subroutine and can be accessed from anywhere in a program, including from any subprocedure or subroutine. Subroutines of course can use only global variables in RPG.

In computer science, one of the major advantages of facilities such as subprocedures is the ability to hide information that exists within the internals of a procedure or a function thereby enabling the subprocedure to be treated as a black box.

These black boxes have major value in programming in that they function the same every time they are used because they are unaffected by values from the outside world. Thus, they can be deployed from one program to another with the same results.

As noted, the values from the outside world are known as global variables, meaning that the same variable name is usable everywhere in the program, globally pointing to the same storage location. Since a subroutine uses global variables, its interface cannot be pure. A change to the global variable anyplace else in the program can have an effect on the result of the subroutine. For example, if the value Numb1 were set to 50 someplace in the program, there results of the subroutines in Figure 26-1 would be computed.

Information Hiding

Information hiding subprocedures want the interface to the subprocedure to be well defined and they want there to be no other way to alter the values of the subprocedure. Thus, global variables are not recommended because they can be altered elsewhere.

The subprocedure examples that follow are not completely pure in this respect (to keep this program simple and easy to relate), but the notion of information hiding is inherent in the protected interface as long as global variables are not used. So, when you see explanations of how to export global variables across external procedures as there are in the examples, remember that this is not recommended. But it is possible to do.

Prototyoing Subprocedures

RPG IV subprocedures are built using a mechanism called a prototype. These mimic the interfaces used in the real procedures but they are not functional procedures themselves. Prototypes use RPGIV definition "D" specs to provide a means of defining the interface for the program or procedure so that during compilation, the compiler can verify that both the calling and the called side of operations are compatible.

RPGIV programs and subprocedures can call non-RPG programs and subprocedures using the same prototype interface. The prototype interface is a very common technique in other languages and with ILE it gives RPGIV far more compatibility than in the past. Thus, once you learn how to prototype procedures for RPGIV, you will be in a better position to access System APIs and C functions since they demand the same prototype-writing skills.

Before V3R2 (CISC) and V3R7 (RISC), procedures existed but a program object could contain just one procedure. With the "newer" compilers that were released in 1995, IBM introduced prototyping and the use of multiple procedures (subprocedures) in one program.

CALLP Operation

The major operation to accomplish a subprocedure call in RPG that returns or does not return a value is CALLP. One could readily conclude at first blush that the CALLP operation stands for Call Procedure. However, it does not. It stands for Call with Prototype. In almost all cases, a subprocedure is built to return a value, as is common with functions, but sometimes you will build the procedure to perform tasks that do not need to report back to the calling program or procedure.

For example, you might want to log errors that have been detected or send email messages or create a small report. In these instances, you may choose not to have the subprocedure report back with a return value to say that it has done the job

Just like all programs, procedures are packaged inside of source members when written by the RPG programmer. A source member for this purpose can be defined as all of the RPG IV source statements that are processed by the RPG compiler in any one compilation. This would include any source members, such as the prototypes that were /COPY'd into the main source. When dealing with procedures, there is no longer a necessary one to one relationship with a program and a source member.

Throughout this book in RPG/400 programming (non-procedure), a source member has meant that one source was compiled and this always resulted in a program (*PGM) object being created. This is not always the case with RPG IV source is always compiled into a module (*MODULE object), or a number of modules as a first step to combining one or more modules into a single program object.

Recursive Calls

W. C. Fields once described a difficult task as "tougher than trying to tie a hair ribbon on a bolt of lightening." Understanding the full nature and the issues that can be brought forth by recursive calls is akin to the difficulties which Fields chronicled. First of all with RPGIV, recursive calls are only allowed for subprocedures so this is another of the muddy areas introduced along with this important ILE notion.

A recursive call is one in which procedure A calls itself or calls procedure B which then calls procedure A again. Each recursive call causes a new invocation of the procedure to be placed on the call stack.

The new invocation has new storage for all data items in automatic storage, and that storage is unavailable to other invocations because it is local. (A data item that is defined in a subprocedure uses automatic storage unless the STATIC keyword is specified for the definition.). Note also that the automatic storage that is associated with earlier invocations is unaffected by later invocations.

A main procedure that is on the call stack cannot be called until it returns to its caller. Therefore, with recursive calls, one must be very careful not to call a procedure that might call an already active main procedure. In all programming languages, programmers are cautioned to avoid situations that might inadvertently lead to recursive calls. For example, you might get into the situation that IBM describes in its reference manual as shown in Figure 26-2.

Figure 26-2 Recursive Calls

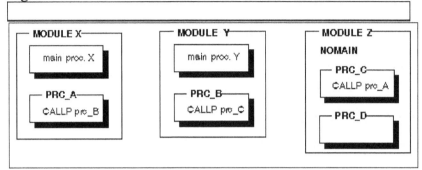

Suppose there are three modules as shown in Figure 26-2. Assume that you are running a program where procedure A in module X calls procedure B in module. You may not be aware of what procedure B does except that it processes some data. Procedure B in turn calls procedure C, which in turn calls procedure A. Once procedure C calls procedure A, a recursive call has been made. The call stack sequence is shown in Figure 26-3. Note that the most recent call stack entry is at the bottom.

As you can see, subprocedures can be called recursively. However, if you are not aware that recursion is occurring, you may exhaust your system resources. If you exhaust system resources, you can bet you will have gained the attention of management in most layers of the organization, including IT.

The fact is that unconditional recursive calls can lead to infinite recursion which leads to excessive use of system resources. It is not hopeless if you plan and program properly for infinite recursion can be avoided with proper programming. In general, a proper recursive procedure begins with a test to determine if the desired result has been obtained. If it has been obtained, then the recursive procedure returns to the most recent caller.

Figure 26-3 Recursive Call Stack

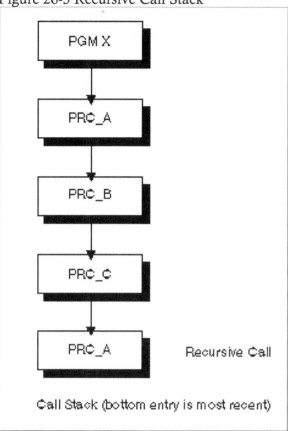

Just as the subroutine program, since this program is contained within one source member, the program can be compiled using option 14 on the PDM menu with RPGLE as the type or you can use the following command:

CRTBNDRPG PGM(RPGBOOK/PROT1) SRCFILE(RPGBOOK/QRPGLESRC)

If you are scoring at home folks, the first thing you notice is that the subroutine method takes substantially less lines of code (43 vs. 74) than the subprocedure method. The moral of the story is that if subroutines really fit your application, please continue to use them.

They work fine and because they do not take up as much resources, they are just a bit faster then subprocedures.

Decoding the Subprocedure

Right after the H specification at line 01, the program immediately looks different from any that you have ever written – if you are new to subprocedures. Lines 02 to 09 define the prototype for the AddNumbers1 subprocedure. The function of this subprocedure is exactly that of the subroutine with the same name in program SUB01. Whether you are calling a procedure or the procedure is being called, you need to specify the prototype so the compiler can check everything out and make sure all parms are compatible.

Because the number of times you need a prototype is at least n + 1 the number of procedures, the standard for prototypes is to place them in their own source modules and coy them into the programs at compile time through the /COPY compiler directive. To teach prototypes, however, we must show you the code. We use this /COPY technique in program PROT2 later in the chapter so you can see how to accomplish the /COPY source in a real example.

What do you see in Lines 02 to 09? You see the name of the subprocedure that is being prototyped in line 02 and next to it, where the DS symbol would be if this were a data structure, you see PR for prototype. Place your prototypes at the beginning of the program or module that you are creating. The subprocedures which they prototype are defined later in the program. After the prototype definition you see the fields that are part of the procedure interface. Think of these as the parms in a PLIST for they eliminate the need for you to have a PLIST when you use prototyped procedures. There are six fields at the call interface here and one blank statement at line 09.

These Are Not Standalone Fields

Lines 10 to 14 define the prototype for the AddNumbers2 procedure. Though you have not learned enough yet to be comfortable, the fact that this second procedure prototype has the same general shape as the first is probably providing some warm fuzzies about this time in the subprocedure description process.

When you are coding the fields for the prototype, resist the urge to place the standalone field S marker in column 24 of the definition spec. The compiler diagnostic routines will not like this. The prototype does not define fields for the program, just like the PARM statement does not define fields. The fields in the prototype are there to compare against the procedure interface code to be sure the correct size and attributes parameters are being provided to the procedure. As a learning exercise, maybe you should try compiling with the S in 24 and see the nasty compiler message that you get.

In lines 15 through 22, the global variables for the program are defined. Actually, these are the variables for the main module. Since this program does not have a NOMAIN keyword in the header specification (H) it is a Main module and it thus has the ILE facilities PEP and the UEP that are necessary to initiate a program.

The default or mainline procedure continues to line 37 at which point the mainline code is done. At line 38, the first procedure begins. The prototype and the procedure, which both must exist are united by name. Thus at line 38 to line 55, the name AddNumbers1 means that the compiler will verify the data parms with the AddNumbers1 procedure prototype described in lines 02 to 09.

Procedure Interface

This section of code (38 to 74) contain two procedure definitions. These are also called procedure interfaces. The procedure definition is analogous to all the code in a subroutine from the BEGSR through the ENDSR. Though shaped very much like the "D" spec, the procedure definition has its own specification called the procedure specification or "P" spec.

Only one of thse exists in a subprocedure. When you first try to figure out why the shape of the procedure is as it is, it is often confusing and it is hard to remember the next time. It may help to remember that when internal procedures are used, there will be at least three statements in the program that have the name of the procedure. They are as follows:

1. The Prototype statement   **02 DAddNumbers1   PR**
2. The Procedure beginning   **38 PAddNumbers1   B**
3. The Procedure end   **55 PAddNumbers1   E**

The procedure begin and procedure end (38 & 55) are coded on "P" specs. Sandwiched in between the procedure begin point (B in column 24) and the procedure end point (E in column24) is the heart of the procedure. Of course the line of code known as the procedure interface is always the second line of code within the subprocedure as in the following line for AddNumbers1:

```
39 D                    PI
```

Looking at the code from 40 to 54, you can see that it is like a mini program. In a procedure, after the "P" spec, you can have D specifications and C specifications. When a field is defined in a subprocedure, it is a local variable to the subprocedure. It is not global and thus it is not seen by the rest of the program

The procedure parameters are specified in the procedure immediately following the PI line. Notice that these are exactly the same as the prototype and that is not by accident. Following the parameters are the standalone fields with the "S" designation. Any standalone field that is defined in a subprocedure is a local variable.

At line 50 notice that the AddNumbers1 procedure is calling the AddNumbers2 procedure. Of course, this subprocedure could have been called from the main module if that was the objective.

Proving It Works

Lines 51 to 53 display the results so that you can see what is happening in this program with local and global variables. At line 57 to the end of the program source, subprocedure AddNumbers2 is defined. Looking at the code, you can see that Ans1 is a local variable and it is displayed in Addnumbers2 line 70. It is also displayed at lines 51 but with a different value because of the local nature of the variable. ANS3 is defined as a global variable as is GLOBAL at lines 21 and 22 respectively. Notice in the DSPLY results that these values are available in all of the subprocedures – because they are global. The results of the DSPLY operations appear in the workstation job log which for the PROT1 program run is shown immediately below:

```
Call Prot1
DSPLY   P3N#1          1
DSPLY   P3N#2          11
DSPLY   P3ANS1         96
DSPLY   P3ANS3         12
DSPLY   P3GLOBAL       Global Variable
DSPLY   P2ANS1         1
DSPLY   P2ANS2         11
DSPLY   P2ANS3         12
DSPLY   P1ANS1         1
DSPLY   P1ANS2         11
DSPLY   P1ANS3         12
```

The job log from SUB01 can be contrasted with these results as shown below:

```
Call Sub01
DSPLY   P3N#1          1
DSPLY   P3N#2          11
DSPLY   P3ANS1         96
DSPLY   P3ANS3         12
DSPLY   P3GLOBAL       Global Variable
DSPLY   P2ANS1         96
DSPLY   P2ANS2         11
DSPLY   P2ANS3         12
```

```
DSPLY   P1ANS1          96
DSPLY   P1ANS2          11
DSPLY   P1ANS3          12
```

The only difference is with field name Ans1, Since this field is defined locally in AddNumbers2, when it is displayed in AddNumbers1 or Main, it has its original value, not the value 96 as it was set in AddNumbers2.

External Programs / RPG Modules

The PROT1 program is over thirty statements longer than the SUB01 program and it is nicely enclosed in one source module, making it really easy to deal with at all levels. The subprocedure technique in PROT1 is a better technique for hiding information, preserving data, inhibiting interference and blocking access to subroutine code than the subroutine approach. However, sometimes the absolute best approach for modular is to use independent external modules and link them together as needed. This is the approach that we are about to explore. To get the code for this example we took the SUB01 program which had been modified for subprocedures and rebuilt as PROT1 and we split it into three different subprocedure modules, each separately compiled.

The three modules are shown in Figure 26-5 with a separator between each. Their module names are PROT1E1, PROT1E2, and PROT1E3, respectively. As you are about to see, PROTE1 contains all of the Mainline RPG code along with the PEP and the UEP and the cycle.

Because it is a main procedure, it is always the program that gets called first to launch the application. Independent NOMAIN procedure modules cannot serve as the starting module. PROT1E2 holds the AddNumbers1 procedure and PROT1E3 holds the AddNumbers3 procedure.

To make Figure 26-5 easier to read, lines 17 and 18 are condensed. The first thing that you may notice in the main procedure is that there are no keywords for ILE on the H spec. These are not allowed.

The AddNumbers1 prototype is next and it looks the same as in PROT1. However, there is no prototype for AdddNumbers2 because it does not get called in this module. The variable GLOBAL, which was intentionally global in PROT1 behaves differently when external program are linked.

IBM and all of the gurus in the land will tell you not to pass parameters via global values and I concur. It is a bad idea for lots of reasons. However, you may come across code that does it so I show you how. Look at lines 17 and 18 in PROT1E1 below: Notice that inline 18 I have placed the keyword EXPORT. That means that this variable can be seen by any module that is bound with it – as long as that module imports it.

The only module that needs to display the variable GLOBAL is PROT1E3. So, if you move down Figure 26-5 to line 05 of that module, you will see the IMPORT keyword. Thus, the PROT1E3 module gets to see the global variable named GLOBAL in the external procedure AddNumbers2 in module PROT1E3.

Figure 26-5 External Procedures
```
Source = PROT1E1  Module = PROT1E1
01 H
02 DAddNumbers1        PR
03 D NUMB1                          3   0
04 D NUMB2                          3   0
05 D NUMB3                          3   0
06 D NUMB4                          3   0
07 D ANS1                           5   0
08 D ANS2                           5   0
09 D
```

```
10 D N1              S              3  0 inz(1)
11 D N2              S              3  0 inz(2)
12 D N3              S              3  0 inz(3)
13 D N4              S              3  0 inz(4)
14 D A1              S              5  0
15 D A2              S              5  0
16 D ANS3            S              5  0
17 D GLOBAL          S ... 20         inz('Global Variable')
18 D...                        EXPORT
   *
19 C                 callp     AddNumbers1
20 C                           (N1:
21 C                            N2:
22 C                            N3:
23 C                            N4:
24 C                            A1:
25 C                            A2)
26 C    'P1ANS1'     DSPLY                     A1
27 C    'P1ANS2'     DSPLY                     A2
28 C    'P1ANS3'     DSPLY                     ANS3
29 C                 Eval      *inLR = *ON
```

Source = PROT1E2 Module = PROT1E2

```
01 H NOMAIN
02 D*
03 D*  AddNumbers1 SubProcedure
04 D*
05 D
06 DAddNumbers1      PR
07 D NUMB1                       3  0
08 D NUMB2                       3  0
09 D NUMB3                       3  0
10 D NUMB4                       3  0
11 D ANS1                        5  0
12 D ANS2                        5  0
13 D
14 DAddNumbers2      PR
15 D*ddNumbers2      PR          5  0
16 D N#1                         5  0
17 D N#2                         5  0
18 D ANS3                        5  0
19 D
20 PAddNumbers1      B              EXPORT
21 D                 PI
22 D Numb1                       3  0
23 D Numb2                       3  0
24 D Numb3                       3  0
25 D Numb4                       3  0
26 D Ans1                        5  0
27 D Ans2                        5  0
28 D*  Local variable below
29 D Ans3            S           5  0
30 C...              Eval      Ans1 = Ans1 + 1
31 C...              Eval      Ans2 = Ans1 +
32 C...                        Numb1 + Numb2 +
33 C...                        Numb3 + Numb4
35 C...              CALLP     Addnumbers2(ANS1: ANS2: ANS3)
40 C...'S1ANS1'      DSPLY                 ANS1
41 C...'S1ANS2'      DSPLY                 ANS2
42 C...'S1ANS3'      DSPLY                 ANS3
```

```
43 C...                 Return
44.00 PAddNumbers1      E
45.00 C*
```

Source = PROT1E3 Module = PROT1E3

```
01 H NOMAIN
02 D*
03 DC*  AddNumbers2 SubProcedure
04 D*
05 D GLOBAL           S             20      IMPORT
06 D
07 D
08 DAddNumbers2       PR
09 D*ddNumbers2       PR            5  0
10 D N#1                            5  0
11 D N#2                            5  0
12 D ANS3                           5  0
13 PAddNumbers2       B                     EXPORT
14 D                  PI
15 D N#1                            5  0
16 D N#2                            5  0
17 D ANS3                           5  0
18 D* Local variable below
19 D ANS1             S             5  0
20 C* Prime local variable for display- show local/ global
21 C                  Eval      ANS1 = 96
22 C                  Eval      ANS3 = N#1 + N#2
23 C    'S2N#1 '      DSPLY                 N#1
24 C    'S2N#2 '      DSPLY                 N#2
25 C    'S2ANS1'      DSPLY                 ANS1
26 C    'S2GLOBAL'    DSPLY                 GLOBAL
27 C                  RETURN
28 PAddNumbers2       E
```

Making GLOBAL Work

Notice the placement of the GLOBAL field definition within the PROT1E3 module. It is not within the procedure. It is in a global area prior to the start of the first procedure in the module. Because it is defined and imported globally within that module any procedure in that module can see the field. In our case, just the AddNumbers2 procedure has the need and no other procedure is defined in the module.

Why could this variable not have fit nicely within the definitions (Standalone fields) of the procedure AddNumbers2 itself? Why did it have to be in a module "global area?" Any field defined in a procedure is local to the procedure. Therefore, by being defined in the external module before the procedure it still behaved as a global variable. So, the global export of field GLOBAL is imported by the module global import within the PROT1E3 module and thus it can be printed. Now that you learned how to do this, the suggestion is do not.

What happens when the field is defined in the main program as global and there is also a procedure field with the same name? In languages like C, there are ways for you to be able to talk to both fields. In RPGIV, the local variable in the procedure has precedence over the global variable and thus the procedure with the variable defined can see only the local version. The rest of the program can see the global version.

Many RPG gurus have offered cards and letters to IBM to make this more like C but it has not yet happened.

There is a notion in ILE called a binder language which we discussed in the last chapter. With this language, you can selectively permit or disallow various items to be shared when a program is compiled.

Looking further at Figure 26-5, you can see that there are a number of other EXPORTS. In fact, on the begin specification (B) for each procedure, I coded the EXPORT keyword. This is done so that the procedures are visible to all of the code in the program – including the mainline. Without this, the calls would fail.

As you can see, the code is basically the same but it is segregated into modules. Additionally, the two modules PROT1E2 and PROT1E3 have a NOMAIN clause on the H specification. These two modules have no reason to want any part of the RPG cycle to be included and they do not need to be the first procedure called (PEP and UEP) in the program object.

Creating the Program from Modules

So, now we see the source code in these three separate modules. How do we make a program out of them? Well, first of all they must become *MODULE objects before they can be combined into program objects. The PDM command to do this is option 15 which invokes the CRTRPGMOD command and will create *MODULE objects for you in your library of choice. The CRTPGM then needs to be invoked to combine the modules into an executable program. The name of the program on the CRTPGM command is the name under which you call the program. The command to get all this working is as follws:

```
===> CRTPGM PGM(PROT1E1) MODULE(RPGBOOK/PROT1E2 KELLY/PROT1E3)
ENTMOD(RPGBOOK/PROT1E1) ACTGRP(QILE)
```

Creating RPGIV Functions

Earlier in this chapter we discussed the makeup of the procedure interface (PI) as a required statement for a subprocedure. The PI line defines the data type and size of the procedure when it is used as a function. The procedure can then be used anywhere that a field of the same type and size can be used. It will return a value that works the same as a field. We also learned that the subsequent lines define any parameters that are passed to the procedure so in essence these lines provide the *ENTRY PLIST for the procedure.

Return Value for Functions

One area that we have not discussed regarding how to construct a procedure is that the data item defined on the same line as the PI is the actual return value if requested. A subprocedure can return, at most, one value. To repeat for effect, the data item(s) following the PI with nothing specified in the column where the PI (in this example, the Numb1, Numb2 etc. fields) would be are the input parameters into the subprocedure. The last data items such as those following Ans3 in PROT1E3 are all local standalone (S) fields to the subprocedure. You can tell the end of the procedure interface by the appearance of something (in this example, an "S") in the same columns where the PI had been specified above.

To demonstrate the transition of a procedure to a function, I have created a new program called PROT2 from PROT1. It is just about the same other than AddNumbers2 is now a function rather than a procedure. The code that is germane to the explanation is provided below:

```
Source = PROT2  Program = PROT2
01.00 H  dftactgrp(*no) actgrp('QILE')
02.00  * AddNumbers2 subroutine operates as a function
       * Prototypes are copied into the program
03.00  /COPY RPGBOOK/QPROTYPSRC,ADDNUMBER1
12.00  /COPY RPGBOOK/QPROTYPSRC,ADDNUMBER2
23.00 D ANS3            S            5 0
24.00 D GLOBAL          S           20      inz('Global
25.00 C   ...    callp    AddNumbers1
26.00 C   ...             (N1: etc.
37.00 C*  AddNumbers1 SubProcedure
39.00 PAddNumbers1     B
40.00 D                PI
41.00 D Numb1                        3 0
49.00 C...       Eval      Ans3 = AddNumbers2(ANS1: ANS2)
54.00 PAddNumbers1     E
55.00 C*
56.00 C*  AddNumbers2 SubProcedure
57.00 C*
```

542 The IBM i on Power Systems Pocket RPG & RPGIV Guide

```
58.00 PAddNumbers2          B
59.00 D                     PI              5   0
60.00 D N#1                                 5   0
63.00 D*  Local variable below
64.00 D ANS1                S               5   0
65.00 C ...       Eval      ANS1 = 96
71.00 C* Very efficient RPGIV subprocedure function code
72.00 C...        Return    (N#1 + N#2)
73.00 PAddNumbers2          E
```

Starting right at the top, the first change here is that since we have been showing prototype after prototype, I felt it would be oK to show how to copy the prototypes into the source code with compiler directives at compile time. The /COPY lines at 03 and 12 above do the trick for the prototype copy. This is the recommended approach.

```
13 DAddNumbers2    PR        5 0
49 C... Eval    Ans3 = AddNumbers2(ANS1: ANS2
58 PAddNumbers2    B
59 D          PI       5 0
72 C...       Return   (N#1 + N#2
```

The above motley assortment of lines is the essence to the change from procedure to function. The copied prototype for AddNumbers 2 now has a numeric data definition of five places with no decimals as shown in line 13. That's one of the changes. That matches the unnamed PI interface at line 51. Instead of a passed value bringing back the changed value in the AddNumbers2 procedure, the procedure will behave as a function and return a value to the expression on the right side of the Eval at line 49. At that point ANS3 is set equal to the returned value of the function which is the same value of ANS3 in PROT1. Using this technique, you too can make your own BIFs,

Creating Service Programs

With minimal changes I was able to create a service program from the two modules PROT1E2 and PROT1E3. Since I wanted the service program name to be PROTSRV, and I wanted to demonstrate s simple creation, I copied the pROT1E2 module and renamed the copy PROTSRV. Then, I compiled it with option 15 and ran the CRTSRVPGM against it. There was one problem. The value GLOBAL used in Addnumbers2 needed to be in the module. Once I added it the service program created like a charm.

===> CRTSRVPGM SRVPGM(RPGBOOK/PROTSRV) MODULE(RPGBOOK/PROTSRV KELLY/PROT1E3) EXPORT (*ALL)

Service program PROTSRV created in library RPGBOOK

So, when the service program is created, the rest is all cake. Well, not exactly but maybe. It all depends on how much you are binding. Anyway, now that we have the service program created, how do we make it work with anything? I bet your glad I asked that question. A service program cannot be called from the command line because it is really not a whole program. It may be lots more than a whole program but it is non executable in much the same way as a module. So, sneaking up on what we need for service programs to compile and execute like one of our programs (*PGM object), we should first review why we may have the issue.

Dynamic vs. Static Calls

What do you think a procedure needs when it makes a call? It needs the address of the code it is calling, and it needs to provide the addresses of the parameters it is passing. The PR and the PI help establish that in each module. When we take the easiest route and choose a dynamic call approach, it means that all of these addresses are calculated each time the call is made. A static call means as we have presented in the last chapter works with addresses that are calculated just once -- each time the program is created.

So, if you have your favorite RPGIV program with one or several subprocedures coded at the end of the main source, you have learned what happens when you create the program? The CRTPGM generates a pointer with the address of the subprocedure since it is right there for the compiler to work with at compile time. That is why subprocedure calls are so fast. The main program has a direct pointer to where the procedure loaded in memory.

But what about service programs? They are separate objects just like the PROT1EX examples that we just worked through. All calls are static with a service program but there is one dynamic call involved – the initial loading of the service program. There are some other attributes about service programs which make them even more desirable. For example, you can change a service program -- which can then change the addresses of procedures – without having to recompile the linked programs.

To get it going, remember that you have a service program named PROTSRV that exports two procedures (AddNumbers1 and AddNumbers2). You saw that it was created using the binding source shown below:

The STRPGMEXP instruction identifies that this is the current export list and that 'FIRST' is a supported signature. The EXPORT instructions identify the "callable" procedures in the service program. There may be other procedures in the service program that can be called only from procedures within the service program.

As long as you have a reasonably simple linkage, you don't need binder source. But, you have to specify things properly. For example, in order for the main module to access the two other modules that are now in service program PROTSRV, everything needs to be done correctly. Since a service program cannot be called, it must be linked to a program that can be called. The following command in our example gets this done and permits us to have a program module to call that then calls the service module, which in turn calls its two procedures, AddNumbers1, and AddNUmbers2.

```
===> CRTPGM PGM(RPGBOOK/PROT3) ENTMOD(RPGBOOK/PROT3)
BNDSRVPGM(KELLY/PROTSRV) ACTGP(QILE)
```

Chapter Summary

Big changes came to the RPG language in 1994 and again in 1995. The latter changes included the notion of multiple procedures in a module and procedure prototyping.

In RPGIV, a procedure is a routine that is called using a bound call. (RPG operations CALLB or CALLP) You can create two kinds of procedures in RPG: a main procedure and a subprocedure. A main procedure uses the RPG cycle. Unless you take overt action, all RPG programs are main programs. Moreover, all RPGIV programs have at least one procedure. Procedures that can send and return one or many parameters are called subprocedures. The function type procedure is very similar to RPG BIFs in that they are not invoked with a CALL statement and they return just one return variable.

A subprocedure is similar to a subroutine, except that a subroutine is always part of the main program and thus among other things, it always uses global variables

Subrocedures permit the following:

- ✓ Pass parameters to a subprocedure, even passing by value.
- ✓ You can use a subprocedure like a built-in function in an expression.
- ✓ Names defined in a subprocedure are not visible outside the subprocedure. (Local * global variables)
- ✓ Subrpvedure can be called outside the module.
- ✓ Subprocedures can be called recursively

RPG IV subprocedures are built using a mechanism called a prototype. Prototypes provide a means of defining the interface for the program or procedure so that during compilation, the compiler can verify that both the calling and the called side of operations are compatible.

The major operation to accomplish a subprocedure call in RPG that returns a value is CALLP meaning call with prototype. Using prototypes, the program has a section at the top in which the prototype is defined and within the subprocedure itself it has a procedure interface (PI) that is coded very similar to the prototype.

With minimal changes a subprocedure module can be transferred into a service program. Once in service program state, it must be compiled using the CRTSRVPGM command and linked with calling modules with the CRTPGM command. Sometimes, depending on how complex the environment is, a binder language is necessary to describe what is exported and what is imported from/to procedures.

Key Chapter Terms

*ENTRY PLIST	External program	Procedure definition
/COPY	Fields, W. C.	Procedure end
ACTGRP compile kwords	Function type	Procedure interface
AddNumbers1 mod/proc	Gantner, Susan	Procedure Spec
AddNumbers2, mod/proc	Global variable	Procedures
Binder language	H spec	Programming languages
Bound call	ILE	Protected interface
Built-in function,	Information hiding	Prototyping subprocs
Call interface	Local variable	Prototypes
Call stack – recursion	Main procedure	QILE
Call with prototype	Modules	QRPGLESRC
Calling program	Morris, Barbara	Recursive calls
CALLP	NOMAIN Keyword	RETURN operation
Command line	P Spec	Return value
Compiler directives	Paris, Jon	Scope
Compiling	PARM	Service program
CRTBNDRPG	Partner400	Source member
CRTPGM	PDM	Standalone fields
CRTRPGMOD	PEP	STRPGMEXP
CRTSRVPGM	PI	Subprocedure
D spec in proc	PLIST operation	Subroutine
Dynamic call	PR definition	System resources
Export	Procedure begin	UEP
External module		

Chapter Review Questions

1. What is a procedure?

2. What is a subprocedure?

3. What is a BIF?

4. What is a function?

5. What makes a function different from a BIF?

6. What is the difference between a subroutine and a subprocedure?

7. What is a local variable?

8. What is a global variable?

9. Under what circumstances would you need an export with a global variable?

10. Why would you write a function instead of a subprocedure?

11. What is information hiding?

12. Why are procedures prototyped in RPGIV?

13. What does the CALLP do? What do you typically send along with a CALLP?

14. Do functions use CALLP or CALLB – explain?

15. What is a module?

16. How many procedures are in a module?

17. Is a module a program?

18. What is a recursive call?

19. Why might they create issues for your program during execution?

20. What happened when we split the PROT program into two?

21. What did we do to make a service program from the second and third module?

22. How did we make global work?

23. What is the coding change to create functions instead of subprcedures?

24. What do you think a procedure needs when it makes a call?

25. What is STRPGMEXP?

Chapter 27   Free Format RPG /FREE

Free At Last!

"Set me free, why don't you babe…"

There is another option for coding RPG. A number of the extended IIE RPG operations have been enabled for the free form version of RPG which has been available since early 2000. The basic notion is that once the compiler directives are given, the code in between does not have to pay attention to the RPG columns. It's not quite as good as the license I gave myself in making RPG functional code bigger while not preserving the exact spacing in my examples. But, for those who do not want the regimen and discipline of a fixed format columnar language, IBM has answered your prayers – to a large extent.

The RPGIV compiler directive statements /FREE… /END-FREE thereby denote a free-form calculation specification block. Whatever you place in between these directives can be free-form.

Figure 27-1 Eligible RPG Free Form Operations

ACQ	ACQ{(E)} *device-name workstn-file*
BEGSR	BEGSR *subroutine-name*
CALLP	{CALLP{(EMR)}} *name({parm1{:parm2…}})*
CHAIN	CHAIN{(EN)} *search-arg name {ds-name}*
CLEAR	CLEAR {*NOKEY} {*ALL} *name*
CLOSE	CLOSE{(E)} *file-name*
COMMIT	COMMIT{(E)} *{boundary}*
DEALLOC	DEALLOC{(EN)} *pointer-name*
DELETE	DELETE{(E)} *{search-arg} name*
DOU	DOU{(MR)} *indicator-expression*
DOW	DOW{(MR)} *indicator-expression*
DSPLY	DSPLY{(E)} *{message {output-queue {response}}}*
DUMP	DUMP{(A)} *{identifier}*
ELSE	ELSE
ELSEIF	ELSEIF{(MR)} *indicator-expression*
ENDDO	ENDDO
ENDFOR	ENDFOR
ENDIF	ENDIF
ENDMON	ENDMON
ENDSL	ENDSL
ENDSR	ENDSR *{return-point}*
EVAL	{EVAL{(HMR)}} *result = expression*
EVALR	EVALR{(MR)} *result = expression*
EXCEPT	EXCEPT *{except-name}*
EXFMT	EXFMT{(E)} *format-name*
EXSR	EXSR *subroutine-name*
FEOD	FEOD{(E)} *file-name*
FOR	FOR{(MR)} *index {= start} {BY increment}* *{TO|DOWNTO limit}*

FORCE	FORCE *file-name*
IF	IF{(MR)} *indicator-expression*
IN	IN{(E)} {*LOCK} *data-area-name*
ITER	ITER
LEAVE	LEAVE
LEAVESR	LEAVESR
MONITOR	MONITOR
NEXT	NEXT{(E)} *program-device file-name*
ON-ERROR	ON-ERROR {*exc-id* {:*exc-id...*}}
OPEN	OPEN{(E)} *file-name*
OTHER	OTHER
OUT	OUT{(E)} {*LOCK} *data-area-name*
POST	POST{(E)} {*program-device*} *file-name*
READ	READ{(EN)} *name* {*data-structure*}
READC	READC{(E)} *record-name*
READE	READE{(EN)} *search-arg*|*KEY *name* {*data-structure*}
READP	READP{(EN)} *name* {*data-structure*}
READPE	READPE{(EN)} *search-arg*|*KEY *name* {*data-structure*}
REL	REL{(E)} *program-device file-name*
RESET	RESET{(E)} {*NOKEY} {*ALL} *name*
RETURN	RETURN{(HMR)} *expression*
ROLBK	ROLBK{(E)}
SELECT	SELECT
SETGT	SETGT{(E)} *search-arg name*
SETLL	SETLL{(E)} *search-arg name*
SORTA	SORTA *array-name*
TEST	TEST{(EDTZ)} {*dtz-format*} *field-name*
UNLOCK	UNLOCK{(E)} *name*
UPDATE	UPDATE{(E)} *name* {*data-structure*}
WHEN	WHEN{(MR)} *indicator-expression*
WRITE	WRITE{(E)} *name* {*data-structure*}

For all of its 50 + years, RPG was known for its rigid, columnar format. It is a format that has been heralded by most and mocked by others. Meanwhile every other language was more or less free-form. RPG imposed a writing style on programmers that could not be compromised and thus no programmer could violate the standard columnar style. To maintain code in the freer format languages, programmer first had to learn the style of the original writer. since these languages permitted many different styles and enforced no style.

There are a number of books out on the notion of writing in /Free format RPG. These books devote a substantial number of pages to style and examples of good and bad style. This one chapter is not intended to be all things for /Free format RPGIV programmers. However, it will give you enough to get started and throughout the Internet, there are many examples of /FREE format code to begin to adopt in your programming if you so desire.

The Free Lunch Is a Sandwich

/FREE is a calculation specification operation specified in position 7 to 11 that enables you to sandwich free-format RPG operations and built-in functions within columns 8 to 80 of a coding line. The block of /Free format code ends with a /END-FREE statement in positions 7 to 15. In newer versions of RPG, the /Free is not needed.

In a free-form statement, you decide where to put the operation code. Unlike regular RPG and RPGIV, it does not need to begin in any specific position within columns 8–80. Any operation extenders must appear immediately after the operation code on the same line, within the normal parentheses convention. There must be no embedded blanks between the operation code and its extenders.

Working through the rules, following the operation code and extenders, you specify the Factor 1, Factor 2, and the Result Field operands separated by blanks. If any of these are not required by the operation, you may leave them out. You can freely use blanks and continuation lines in the remainder of the statement. Like other free format languages, the new RPG /FREE requires that each statement must end with a semicolon. The remainder of the record after the semicolon must be blank or contain an end-of-line comment. End of line comments begin with two slashes.

Before the /FREE format version of RPG as you know, the extended Factor 2 gave RPG a substantially more free look and feel using the EVAL operation and a few other statements. With /FREE, you can omit the EVAL operation code completely. The following example straight from IBM's RPGIV reference manual shows this capability in action. The following two RPG statements are equivalent:

```
eval pos = %scan (',': name);
pos = %scan (',': name);
```

More Rules

For each record within a /Free format calculation block, positions 6 and 7 must be blank. You can specify compiler directives within a free-format calculation block, with the following restrictions:

✓ The compiler directive must be the first item on the line. Code the directive starting anywhere from column 7 onward. It cannot continue to the next line.

✓ Compiler directives are not allowed within a statement. The directive must appear on a new line after one statement ends and before the next statement begins.

✓ Any statements that are included by a /COPY or /INCLUDE directive are considered fixed syntax calculations.

✓ Any free-form statements in a /COPY member must be delimited by the /FREE and /END-FREE directives.

✓ Free-form operands can be longer than 14 characters.

The following are not supported in /FREE format RPGIV:

✓ Continuation of numeric literals

✓ Defining field names

✓ Resulting indicators. (In most cases where you need to use operation codes with resulting indicators, you can use an equivalent built-in function instead.)

Control Level Calculations (L1 etc.)

To indicate the start of total calculations, you must end the /Free format group and code a fixed-form calculation specification as you would typically do for level calculations. This statement would have the appropriate control level specified in positions 7-8. Once you have performed this compiler requirement, you code is in the total calculations cycle time. From here on in, you may specify your total calculations using the free-form calculation syntax with some restrictions. Recognizing that the /FREE-form calculation specification does not include a control-level entry, calculations to be performed on specific level breaks should be conditioned using the statement " IF *INLx;"

Because of the /FREE and the /END-FREE sandwich effect for free format RPG, you can mix free-form and traditional calculation specifications in the same program, as shown in several examples below:

To get your /Free format operations going, in positions 8-80 enter an operation that is supported in free-form syntax. See Table 27-6. Code an operation code. It is up to you as to whether you want to continue using EVAL. Follow this by the operands or expressions for the /Free format operation.

/Free format operations may optionally span multiple lines. It is really easy to do since there is nothing to remember. The semicolon is what determines whether the statement is finished so use as many lines as you wish. You have no new continuation characters to learn. Of course, RPG's existing continuation rules still apply. To get a good sense as to all that you can do, see Table 27-1 for a list of the operation codes that can use /Free format syntax. Remember that BIFS are welcome anyplace in /Free format operations in which they were welcome in RPGIV. This greatly expands the /FREE-format capabilities of the language.

The following samples are derived from IBM's RPGIV Reference manual.

```
*..1....+....2....+....3....+....4...
/free
 read file; // Get next record
 dow not %eof(file);
 // Keep looping while we have
 // a record
 if %error;
    dsply 'The read failed';
    leave;
 else;
    chain(n) name database data;
    time = hours * num_employees
        + overtime_saved;
    pos = %scan (',': name);
    name = %xlate(upper:lower:name);
    exsr handle_record;
    read file;
 endif;
 enddo;
 begsr handle_record;
    eval(h) time = time +
    total_hours_array (empno);
    temp_hours = total_hours -
       excess_hours;
    record_transaction();
 endsr;
/end-free
```

This next example combines traditional and /Free format calculation specifications in regular anf free-form syntax. The following code snippets show a simple RPG calculation and its equivalent in /Free format RPGIV.

```
C testb OPEN_ALL flags 10
```

```
/free
 if *in10;
    openAllFiles();
 endif;
/end-free
```

Linoma Modernization Example

The Linoma RPG toolbox is very popular in RPG shops and for good reason. It is done quite well. Among a host of other valuable tools for your shop, Linoma offers an RPG III (We've been calling it RPG/400 in this book) to RPGIV semi-fixed format with EVALS etc. as well as a full /Free format version. In the following examples, courtesy of Linoma Software, http://www.linomasoftware.com, an RPGIII program is converted first to a much more functional RPGIV fixed format than the CVTRPGSRC command. Then, it is converted to /Free format RPG. The RPG PAREG examples are shown in Linoma form as converted by Bob Luebbe on the Lets Go Publis Website. www.letsgopublish.com/files.

Linoma Fixed-format Example 1 demonstrates how Linoma's RPGWIZ can convert RPG III source into fixed format RPG IV. In this example, notice how the subroutines were also converted to sub-procedures.

```
RPGIII Before:
I...        DS
I...                    1  7 FIRST6
I...                    4  6 PREFIX
I...                    1  3 AREACD
I...                    1 10 PHONE
C...    *LIKE   DEFN    AREACD   WAREA
C* Retrieve customer record
C...    CNBR    CHAINCUSTMAS...              99
C* Prepare values
C...            MOVE    *ZEROS   XX
C...N99         MOVE AREACD      WAREA
C N99           EXSR PROCESS
C* Calculate
C...    PROCESS BEGSR
C...            ADD  1           XX    30
C...    WAREA   IFNE *BLANK
C...    XX      MULT 100         NUMBER
C...            SETON                   61
C...            END
C...            ENDSR
```

After Fixed Format RPGIV Conversion with Linoma:

```
D...                  DS
D PHONE...                10
D FIRST6                   7...  OVERLAY(PHONE)
D AREACD                   3...  OVERLAY(FIRST6)
D PREFIX                   3...  OVERLAY(FIRST6:4)
* Work fields
D WAREA          S          LIKE(AREACD)
D XX             S    3 0
* Prototypes
D PROCESS        PR
* Retrieve customer record
C... CNBR    CHAIN   CUSTMAS
C...         EVAL    *IN99 = NOT%FOUND(CUSTMAS)
* Prepare values
C...         EVAL XX = *ZEROS
C...         IF *IN99 = *OFF
C...         EVAL WAREA = AREACD
C...         CALLP PROCESS
C...         ENDIF
* Calculate
P PROCESS        B
C...         EVAL XX = XX + 1
C...         IF WAREA <> *BLANK
C...         EVAL NUMBER = XX * 100
C...         EVAL *IN61 = *ON
C...         ENDIF
P PROCESS        E
```

Linoma's RPG Toolbox Free-format Example 2

The follow example demonstrates how RPGWIZ
can convert RPG III source into free-format RPG IV. Before RPGIII is the
same as above:

After /Free format RPGIV:

```
D...                  DS
D PHONE...                10
D FIRST6                   7...  OVERLAY(PHONE)
D AREACD                   3...  OVERLAY(FIRST6)
D PREFIX                   3...  OVERLAY(FIRST6:4)
* Work fields
D WAREA          S          LIKE(AREACD)
D XX             S    3 0
* Prototypes (not provided in this version)
D                DS
D PHONE                10
D FIRST6               7    OVERLAY(PHONE)
D AREACD               3    OVERLAY(FIRST6)
D PREFIX               3    OVERLAY(FIRST6:4)
//
D WAREA          S          LIKE(AREACD)
D XX             S    3 0
```

```
/FREE
 // Retrieve customer record
 CHAIN CNBR CUSTMAS;
 *IN99 = NOT%FOUND(CUSTMAS);
 // Prepare values
 XX = *ZEROS;
 IF *IN99 = *OFF;
     WAREA = AREACD;
     EXSR PROCESS;
 ENDIF;
 // Calculate
 BEGSR PROCESS;
     XX = XX + 1;
     IF WAREA <> *BLANK;
         NUMBER = XX * 100;
         *IN61 = *ON;
     ENDIF;
 ENDSR;
/END-FREE
```

The Linoma Toolbox is seen by most in the industry as the Cadillac in conversion to RPGIV and to /Free format. To be fair, if you are just going to RPGIV and you want it to look like RPG/400, IBM's tool is fine. Additionally, Brad Stone has a nice little command called CVTILEFMT that you can search out on the Web.

It is a piece of shareware that Brad wrote several years ago that he makes available for free download with a $25.00 registration fee payable when you find out that you like it.

Chapter Summary

There are many /Free format RPG examples in both IBM ILE RPG Reference Manual and the User Manual Combined with the syntax table shown in Figure 27-6, you can get a jump start on your way to exploiting /Free format RPGIV.

Also, as you explore the Web and IBM's manuals, a number of relevant pages are linked to the V5R4 ILE RPG Reference manual. When you follow the links, there are examples of how you would code the /Free format equivalent of the supported and unsupported operations. When an operation is not supported, there are examples of how to perform the function with supported operations.

And, of course it goes without saying that you should be able to find lots of other examples and general discussion topics on /Free format RPG by searching in Google and other Web search engines.

Key Chapter Terms

/END-FREE	ILE	READC operation
/FREE	Index	READE operation
/Free format operations	Internet	READP operation
/Free format syntax	Linoma RPG toolbox	READPE operation
Compiler directives	MULT operaton	RESET operation
CVTILEFMT	Operation extenders, 5	RETURN operation
CVTRPGSRC	PR	Stone, Brad
Free Format RPG	Procedures	Total calculations
Free-form operand	Prototypes	

Review Questions

1. What is the basic idea of /Free format RPGIV?

2. How do you begin and end a free –format segment in an RPG program?

3. Where do you put the op-code in /Free format RPG?

4. What are the /free format rules for formulating an operation?

5. What role is given to the semicolon in /Free Format RPG?

6. Does /Free Format RPG require the extended Factor 2? Why Why not?

7. Is the EVAL operation required wne coding /Free Format RPG?

8. Can /Free Format calculations be brought into the program with /COPY or /INCLUDE directives?

9. What is the max length of a /Free format operand?

10. How do you handle Level calculations with /Free format RPG?

11. Write a valid /Free format RPGIV statement assuming that no /Freee Format code precedes this statement.

12. Are /Free format statements limited to one line? Explain?

Chapter 28   Using Embedded SQL in RPG Programs

SQL Works with IBM i Languages

The capability of SQL that is always taught first is its ability to be used interactively as a programmer vehicle – for quick queries as well as for mass database changes. This is referred to as dynamic SQL. In other words, we place an SQL statement in ISQL or QM or RUNSQLSTM source files and without any preparation, the statements are immediately translated and executed with no need for compilation. This paradigm changes within the context of using SQL in programming languages such as RPG and RPGIV.

In this Chapter we introduce the notion of using the RPG programming language without the normal DB operations. Instead SQL statements are embedded within the RPG program to provide read, update, add, and delete capabilities.

After showing a simple program in RPG, we move to a more complex program that uses the notion of file cursors to walk through records returned to the program in internal SQL operations. In this program, the cursors are declared and the data from selected records is fetched into the program fields.

Create SQL Program Commands

The pre-compiler RPG commands to read the SQL statements along with the program code written in the specific IBM i language for the pre-compiler are listed below along with an explanation of each command:

CRTSQLRPG

The Create SQL RPG Program (CRTSQLRPG) command calls the Structured Query Language (SQL) pre-compiler which pre-compiles RPG source containing SQL statements, produces a temporary source member, and then optionally calls the RPG compiler to compile the program.

If the relational database (RDB) parameter is specified and a program is created, an SQL package will be created at the specified relational database.

CRTSQLRPGI

The Create SQL ILE RPG Object (CRTSQLRPGI) command calls the Structured Query Language (SQL) precompiler which precompiles RPG source containing SQL statements, produces a temporary source member, and then optionally calls the ILE RPG compiler to create a module, create a program, or create a service program.

Writing SQL Code in RPG Programs

Since in Chapter 4, you have already learned how to create RPG programs and it is the SQL part that is new to us. So, now let's write s simple RPG program in Figure 28-1 that creates a file called VENDORP file using embedded SQL. Then we will create another RPG program in Figure 28-2.

In the RPG program shown in Figure 28-1 take notice to the following:

1. The example is a complete RPG program that can be compiled
2. There are no "F" Specs or I Specs etc. required
3. If we were to remove the first and last two statements, the command could be pasted to run interactively with STRSQL or it would work with RUNSQLSTM if the code were first placed in a source file.

Figure 28-1 RPG SQL Code to Create a Table Vendorp

```
C/EXEC SQL
C+    CREATE  TABLE  RPGBOOK/VENDORP
C+        (VNDNBR      DEC(5,0),
C+        NAME         CHAR(25),
C+        ADDR1        CHAR(25),
C+        CITY         CHAR(15),
C+        STATE        CHAR(2),
C+        ZIPCD        DEC(5,0),
C+        VNDCLS       DEC(2,0),
C+        VNDSTS       CHAR(1),
C+        BALOWE       DEC(9,2),
C+        SRVRTG       CHAR(1))
C/END-EXEC
C                      SETON            ... LR
```

So, all you need to do is compile this code with either RPG compiler and you have a functioning program that creates a table in the RPGBOOK library. Now let's create an RPG program that does a simple select as shown in Figure 28-2.

You can see the RPG/400 code here as it defines four fields VNDNBR. NAME, CLASS, and BAL that will be used to store input in the program from the embedded SQL SELECT statement.

Then, a search argument is primed to look up the vendor number. Vendor # 20 is in the file and this is moved with a Z-ADD operation into the field called VNDNBR that is already defined in the input specifications.

The SELECT statement reads in the four fields from the Vendorp file and using the INTO clause of the SELECT statement places the values into the corresponding program defined fields. When program fields are used in SQLRPG, they are prefixed by a colon. Notice the WHERE clause criteria is where the value from the program (:VNDNBR primed with 20) is equal to the value from the database (VNDNBR).

Figure 28-2 Select Single Row From a Table - RPG

```
I*        This is a complete RPG / SQL program:
I    DS
I                              1   50VNDNBR
I                              6  30 NAME
I                             30  31 CLASS
I                             32  402BAL
C*
C                 Z-ADD20      VNDNBR
C/EXEC SQL
C+    SELECT  VNDNBR, NAME, VNDCLS, BALOWE
C+      INTO  :VNDNBR, :NAME, :CLASS, :BAL
C+      FROM  VENDORP
C+     WHERE VNDNBR = :VNDNBR
C/END-EXEC
C   ... 'NAME '  DSPLY      NAME
C   ... 'CLASS'  DSPLY      CLASS
C   ... 'BALOWE' DSPLY      BAL
C               SETON               ... LR
```

When the SELECT Statement is executed the four fields are in the input fields shown at the top of the program. To prove that this RPG/400 code works, I have chosen to use a DSPLY operation which takes the values and sends them out to the user of the terminal session to view.

The values retrieved from this record are as follows as shown in the display of the job log in Figure 28-3 below.

Figure 28-3 Results of Simple Select Program

```
Display Program Messages
DSPLY NAME   PHONDUS CORPORAT  2
DSPLY CLASS  20
DSPLY BALOWE 45000

Type reply, press Enter.
Reply_____
 F3=Exit    F12=Cancel
```

Chapter Summary

Once you get your SQL code verified with RUNSQLSTM or ISQL, it is time to place it in a program and give it a whirl. The SQL code in both COBOL and RPG and RPGIV is basically the same and it is learning how to deal with the host compiler's variables and nuances that make the difference.

There are a host of compiler commands available for whatever language you choose and the editors from PDM to WDSC Eclipse have the necessary formats for SQL language derivatives.

The code to process a set of data is at first annoying but as you learn what it is doing, it is no more annoying than OPNQRYF and quite frankly, the code is easier to read. When you open the cursor, the SQL statement is executed and the result set is in your program. Then, you cursor through the result set (memory file) and process one record at a time just like in subfile programming.

One of the first things that everybody notices when looking at the RPG code to create the table is that there really is no RPG code. And, there would not be any COBOL code if the program was in COBOL. There are no F specs or I specs. The only thing needed is the C specs for the SQL precompiler directives.

The same applies to the bigger programs in RPG and RPG IV. Though the RPG program is reading a file and writing a file, there are no F specs in the program and there is no RPG I/O involved. There is so little RPG code that it is easy to consider the language in this instance as merely a place for SQL to execute.

There is nothing better than getting your feet wet just to find out whether it is miserable out or not. Though there is not much RPG in this code, there is no C and no Java either – just RPG and SQL. That's not really a bad combination.

Key Chapter Terms

/END-EXEC	INTO	Result table
/EXEC SQL	ISQL	RPG compiler w SQL
CHAR, data type	Like definition	RPG program w SQL
CL program	Memory file	RUNSQLSTM
Create SQL Program	Memory subfile	Select, Data
CRTSQLRPG	Memory table	Service program
CRTSQLRPGI	Multiple records	Set option
Cursor	NOT operation	Set processing
Cursor	OPEN operation	Source file
CVTRPGSRC	OPNQRYF	Source member
DDS	ORDER BY	SQL cursor
Declaration	PDM	SQL programming
DECLARE	Precompiler	SQL query
DML	Programming lang SQL	SQL statement
DSPLY	Pseudo code	Stored Procedure
Eclipse	Query	Structured Query Lang.
Embedded SQL	Record	VENDORP
F specs	Record at a time	WDSC
Fetch	Relational	WHENEVER
Input specifications, 4	Result set	WHERE clause

Exercises

Use this chapter or look up information on the Web to answer the following:

1. When creating a table through RPG, why is there no File Description specification required for the table being created?

2. Are there any SQL statements that you can think of that are not permitted within an RPG program?

3. What re the two compile commands to run the RPG SQL and RPG ILE SQL compilers?

4. What is a cursor?

5. Why is a cursor necessary in some programs and not in others?

6. What would have to change in the last RPG programs if we wanted to process only the records in the Vendorp file that are in VNDCLS 20?

Chapter Appendix A Download Instructions

There is no CD and no real files per se. The source programs can be copied from the Kindle version of the book or they can be typed into source files from the hard copy by clerical personnel. Since I retired from Marywood University, I no longer had a skunk works AS/400 or IBM I system with which to experiment. However, all of the examples will still work as they once did and should work on your system. I do have three save file libraries that are downloadable as-is for V5.4 and V6.1. I was able to retreive those from the Marywood system while I had rights.

You may download these save files by going to www.letsgopublish.com and on the left menu, click downloads. You can also get the source code by going to www.letsgipublish.com/files The save files were designed for the RPG Lab Exercises book which is a better option for hands-on course work but some have found them of use for this book also. Thank you for picking this book. As you can see, it is very comprehensive. When it was pocket sized, it was over 900 pages. I wish you the best in your RPG endeavors.

Chapter 29 Last Chapter -- Latest & Greatest in RPG IV

What was new in V 6.1?

Here are some of the major changes to keywords in V 6.1.

- ✓ **THREAD(*CONCURRENT)** When THREAD(*CONCURRENT) is specified on the Control specification of a module, it provides ability to run concurrently in multiple threads
- ✓ Multiple threads can run in the module at the same time.
- ✓ By default, static variables will be defined so that each thread will have its own copy of the static variable.
- ✓ Individual variables can be defined to be shared by all threads using **STATIC(*ALLTHREAD).**
- ✓ Individual procedures can be serialized so that only one thread can run them at one time, by specifying SERIALIZE on the Procedure-Begin specification.

Main procedure without RPG cycle

Using the MAIN keyword on the Control specification, a subprocedure can be identified as the program entry procedure. This allows an RPG application to be developed where none of the modules uses the RPG cycle.

Files defined in subprocedures
Files can be defined locally in subprocedures. I/O to local files can only be done with data structures; I and O specifications are not allowed in subprocedures, and the compiler does not generate I and O specifications for externally described files. By default, the storage associated with local files is automatic; the file is closed when the subprocedure returns.

The STATIC keyword can now be used to indicate that the storage associated with the file is static, so that all invocations of the subprocedure will use the same file, and if the file is open when the subprocedure returns, it will remain open for the next call to the subprocedure.

Qualified record formats
When a file is defined with the QUALIFIED keyword, the record formats must be qualified by the file name, MYFILE.MYFMT. Qualified files do not have I and O specifications generated by the compiler; I/O can only be done through data structures.

Files defined like other files
Using the LIKEFILE keyword, a file can be defined to use the same settings as another File specification, which is important when passing a file as a parameter. If the file is externally-described, the QUALIFIED keyword is implied. I/O to the new file can only be done through data structures.

Files passed as parameters
A prototyped parameter can be defined as a File parameter using the LIKEFILE keyword. Any file related through the same LIKEFILE definition may be passed as a parameter to the procedure.

Within the called procedure or program, all supported operations can be done on the file; I/O can only be done through data structures.

EXTDESC keyword and EXTFILE(*EXTDESC)
The EXTDESC keyword identifies the file to be used by the compiler at compile time to obtain the external decription of the file; the filename is specified as a literal in one of the forms 'LIBNAME/FILENAME' or 'FILENAME'. This removes the need to provide a compile-time override for the file.

The EXTFILE keyword is enhanced to allow the special value *EXTDESC, indicating that the file specified by EXTDESC is also to be used at runtime.

EXTNAME to specify the library for the externally-described data structure
The EXTNAME keyword is enhanced to allow a literal to specify the library for the external file. EXTNAME('LIBNAME/FILENAME') or EXTNAME('FILENAME') are supported. This removes the need to provide a compile-time override for the file.

EXFMT allows a result data structure
The EXFMT operation is enhanced to allow a data structure to be specified in the result field. The data structure must be defined with usage type *ALL, either as an externally-described data structure for the record format (EXTNAME(file:fmt:*ALL), or using LIKEREC of the record format (LIKEREC(fmt:*ALL).

Larger limits for data structures, and character, UCS-2 and graphic variables
Data structures can have a size up to 16,773,104.
Character definitions can have a length up to 16,773,104. (The limit is 4 less for variable length character definitions). UCS-2 definitions can have a length up to 8,386,552 UCS-2 characters. (The limit is 2 less for variable length UCS-2 definitions.)

Graphic definitions can have a length up to 8,386,552 DBCS characters. (The limit is 2 less for variable length graphic definitions.)

The VARYING keyword allows a parameter of either 2 or 4 indicating the number of bytes used to hold the length prefix.
%ADDR(varying : *DATA)

The %ADDR built-in function is enhanced to allow *DATA as the second parameter to obtain the address of the data part of a variable length field.

Larger limit for DIM and OCCURS
An array or multiple-occurrence data structure can have up to 16,773,104 elements, provided that the total size is not greater than 16,773,104.

Larger limits for character, UCS-2 and DBCS literals
Character literals can now have a length up to 16380 characters.
UCS-2 literals can now have a length up to 8190 UCS-2 characters.
Graphic literals can now have a length up to 16379 DBCS characters.

TEMPLATE keyword for files and definitions
The TEMPLATE keyword can be coded for file and variable definitions to indicate that the name will only be used with the LIKEFILE, LIKE, or LIKEDS keyword to define other files or variables.

Template definitions are useful when defining types for prototyped calls, since the compiler only uses them at compile time to help define other files and variables, and does not generate any code related to them.

Template data structures can have the INZ keyword coded for the data structure and its subfields, which will ease the use of INZ(*LIKEDS).

Relaxation of some UCS-2 rules
The compiler will perform some implicit conversion between character, UCS-2 and graphic values, making it unnecessary to code %CHAR, %UCS2 or %GRAPH in many cases. This enhancement is also available through PTFs for V5R3 and V5R4. Implicit conversion is now supported for

- ✓ Assignment using EVAL and EVALR.
- ✓ Comparison operations in expressions.
- ✓ Comparison using fixed form operations IFxx, DOUxx,
- ✓ DOWxx, WHxx, CASxx, CABxx, COMP.

Note that implicit conversion was already supported for the conversion operations MOVE and MOVEL.

UCS-2 variables can now be initialized with character or graphic literals without using the %UCS2 built-in function.

Eliminate unused variables from the compiled object
New values *UNREF and *NOUNREF are added to the OPTION keyword for the CRTBNDRPG and CRTRPGMOD commands, and for the OPTION keyword on the Control specification. The default is *UNREF. *NOUNREF indicates that unreferenced variables should not be generated into the RPG module. This can reduce program size, and if imported variables are not referenced, it can reduce the time taken to bind a module to a program or service program.

PCML can now be stored in the module
Program Call Markup Language (PCML) can now be stored in the module as well as in a stream file. By using combinations of the PGMINFO command parameter and/or the new PGMINFO keyword for the Control specification, the RPG programmer can choose where the PCML information should go. If the PCML information is placed in the module, it can later be retrieved using the QBNRPII API. This enhancement is also available through PTFs for V5R4, but only through the Control specification keyword.

IBM Table 1. Changed Language Elements Since V5R4

Language Unit	Element	Description
Control specification keywords	OPTION(*UNREF | *NOUNREF)	Specifies that unused variables should not be generated into the module.
	THREAD(*CONCURRENT)	New parameter *CONCURRENT allows running concurrently in multiple threads.
File specification keywords	EXTFILE(*EXTDESC)	Specifies that the value of the EXTDESC keyword is also to be used for the EXTFILE keyword.
Built-in functions	%ADDR(varying-field : *DATA)	Can now be used to obtain the address of the data portion of a varying-length variable.
Definition specification keywords	DIM(16773104)	An array can have up to 16773104 elements.
	EXTNAME('LIB/FILE')	Allows a literal for the file name. The literal can include the library for the file.
	OCCURS(16773104)	A multiple-occurrence data structure can have up to 16773104 elements.
	VARYING{(2|4)}	Can now take a parameter indicating the number of bytes for the length prefix.
Definition specifications	Length entry	Can be up to 9999999 for Data Structures, and definitions of type A, C or G. (To define a longer item, the LEN keyword must be used.)
Input specifications	Length entry	Can be up to 99999 for alphanumeric fields, and up to 99998 for UCS-2 and Graphic fields.
Calculation specifications	Length entry	Can be up to 99999 for alphanumeric fields.
Operation codes	EXFMT format { result-ds }	Can have a data structure in the result entry.

IBM Table 2. New Language Elements Since V5R4

Language Unit	Element	Description
Control specification keywords	MAIN(subprocedure-name)	Specifies the program-entry procedure for the program.
	PGMINFO(*NO | *PCML { : *MODULE })	Indicates whether Program Information is to be placed directly in the module.
File specification keywords	STATIC	Indicates that a local file retains its program state across calls to a subprocedure.
	QUALIFIED	Indicates that the record format names of the file are qualified by the file name, FILE.FMT.
	LIKEFILE(filename)	Indicates that the file is defined the same as another file.
	TEMPLATE	Indicates that the file is only to be used for later LIKEFILE definitions.
	EXTDESC(constant-filename)	Specifies the external file used at compile time for the external definitions.
Definition specification keywords	STATIC(*ALLTHREAD)	Indicates that the same instance of the static variable is used by all threads running in the module.

IBM Table 2. New Language Elements Since V5R4

Language Unit	Element	Description
	LIKEFILE(filename)	Indicates that the parameter is a file.
	TEMPLATE	Indicates that the definition is only to be used for LIKE or LIKEDS definitions.
	LEN(length)	Specifies the length of a data structure, or a definition of type A, C or G.
Procedure specification keywords	SERIALIZE	Indicates that the procedure can be run by only one thread at a time.

i 7.1 TR 7 - Free-form H, F, D and P statements for RPG

Updated January 28, 2014 by barbara_morris | Tags:

As part of IBM i 7.1 Technology Refresh 7, a major enhancement to RPG IV is being announced: Free-form control, file-declaration, data-declaration, and procedure statements.

Please note: The RPG support is not physically part of TR7. You need RPG compiler PTF SIBM I1094, or its latest supersede.

Examples:
Here's an example that illustrates each of the new free-form statement types. Enjoy

```
ctl-opt dftactgrp(*no);

dcl-pi *n;
   caller_name char(10) const;
end-pi;

dcl-c RECORD_LEN 80;

dcl-f qprint printer(RECORD_LEN);

dcl-ds prtDs len(RECORD_LEN) qualified;
   *n char(6) inz('Hello');
   name char(50);
end-ds;

prtDs.name = transform(caller_name);
write qprint prtDs;

*inlr = '1';

dcl-proc transform;
   dcl-pi *n varchar(50);
      name varchar(10) const options(*trim);
   end-pi;

   return '*** ' + name + ' ***';
end-proc;
```

A few things to notice about the example:

Each statement (except for parameter and subfield declarations) starts with an opcode, either CTL-OPT for control statements, or DCL-x for declarations, and ends with a semicolon. Subfield and parameter declarations also start with an opcode, DCL-SUBF or DCL-PARM, but just like the EVAL and CALLP opcodes, you can omit the opcode for subfields and parameters.

The parameter for the "transform" procedure is defined as VARCHAR(10). The VARYING keyword isn't used in free-form. When you look at the full list of data-type keywords, you'll notice that several of them combine the fixed-form data-type value of A, C, D, O, T etc with a fixed-form keyword like VARYING, DATFMT, CLASS, TIMFMT etc.

A named constant is used for the record length of the printer file and the length of the data structure.

There's no /FREE at the beginning of the code. /FREE and /END-FREE are no longer needed. The compiler will just ignore them.

The procedure interface (PI) is coded before the file declaration in the main procedure. You can mix F and D specs even in fixed form.

Unfortunately, while RPG is a lot freer, it still isn't completely free. There are still some restrictions:

Free-form code still has to be coded between columns 8 - 80
I and O specs are still only fixed-form.
There is no target-release support - it is only for TGTRLS(*CURRENT) on 7.1.

Full documentation on the new free-form support

It's not possible to explain all the details here. You can read all about the new syntax in an extra PDF, that has been added to the 7.1 Info Center.
http://pic.dhe.ibm.com/infocenter/IBM i/v7r1m0/topic/books/sc092508a.pdf

IBM recommends that you start with the "What's New Since 7.1" section. From there you can navigate to the detailed information about all the new features.
Some frequently asked questions:

Q: Can I still code fixed form code mixed with the free-form code?
A: Yes, but now you don't need /FREE and /END-FREE if you want to do that.

Q: Will the RPG PTF be part of a PTF group?
A: No, it will be a separate PTF.

Q: What about the SQL precompiler?
A: TheSQL precompiler will have full support for the new free-form
syntax. DB2 for i TR7 timed enhancements

Q: Do I just need to get TR7 to get this support?
A: No, you need to get an RPG compiler PTF and the DB2 Group PTF. See "PTF Information" above.

What's New in 7.2?

This describes the enhancements made to ILE RPG in 7.2.

Free-form Control, File, Definition, and Procedure statements

Free-form Control statements begin with CTL-OPT and end with a semicolon. S

```
CTL-OPT OPTION(*SRCSTMT : *NODEBUGIO)
        ALWNULL(*USRCTL);
```

Free-form File definition statements begin with DCL-F and end with a semicolon.

The following statements define three files
An externally-described DISK file opened for input and update.
An externally-described WORKSTN file opened for input and output.
A program-described PRINTER file with record-length 132.

```
DCL-F custFile usage(*update) extfile(custFilename);
DCL-F screen workstn;
DCL-F qprint printer(132) oflind(qprintOflow);
```

Free-form data definition statements begin with DCL-C, DCL-DS, DCL-PI, DCL-PR, or DCL-S, and end with a semicolon.

The following statements define several items

- ✓ A named constant *MAX_ELEMS*.
- ✓ A standalone varying length character field *fullName*.
- ✓ A qualified data structure with an integer subfield *num* and a UCS-2 subfield *address*.
- ✓ A prototype for the procedure 'Qp0lRenameUnlink'.

```
DCL-C MAX_ELEMS 1000;
DCL-S fullName VARCHAR(50)
              INZ('Unknown name');
DCL-DS ds1 QUALIFIED;
  num INT(10);
  address UCS2(100);
END-DS;
DCL-PR Qp0lRenameUnlink INT(10) EXTPROC(*DCLCASE);
   oldName POINTER VALUE OPTIONS(*STRING);
   newName POINTER VALUE OPTIONS(*STRING);
END-PR;
```

Free-form Procedure definition statements begin with DCL-PROC and end with a semicolon. The END-PROC statement is used to end a procedure.

The following example shows a free-form subprocedure definition.
```
DCL-PROC getCurrentUserName EXPORT;
   DCL-PI *n CHAR(10) END-PI;
   DCL-S curUser CHAR(10) INZ(*USER);

   RETURN curUser;
END-PROC;
```

The /FREE and /END-FREE directives are no longer required. The compiler will ignore them. Olus ++++ Free-form statements and fixed-form statements may be intermixed.

```
         IF endDate < beginDate;
C                 GOTO        internalError
         ENDIF;
         duration = %DIFF(endDate : beginDate : *days);
         . . .
C     internalError TAG
```

New XML-INTO options

XML namespaces are supported by the "ns" and "nsprefix" options. XML names with characters that are not supported by RPG for subfield names are supported by the "case=convert" option.

VALIDATE(*NODATETIME) to allow the RPG compiler to skip the validation step when working with date, time and timestamp data

Use Control-specification keyword VALIDATE(*NODATETIME) to allow the RPG compiler to treat date, time, and timestamp data as character data, without performing the checks for validity.

This may improve the performance of some date, time, and timestamp operations.

What's New since 7.2?

Support for fully free-form source

- ✓ RPG source with the special directive **FREE in the first line contains only free-form code. The code can begin in column 1 and extend to the end of the line.
- ✓ There is no practical limit on the length of a source line in fully free-form source.
- ✓ Fixed-form code is not allowed in fully free-form source, but column-limited source which uses only columns 6-80 can be included by using the /COPY or /INCLUDE directive.

Extended ALIAS support for files
The ALIAS keyword can now be specified for any externally-described file.

If the ALIAS keyword is specified for a global file that is not qualified, the alternate names of the fields will be available for use in the RPG program.

In the following example, the field *REQALC* in the file **MYFILE** has the alternate name *REQUIRED_ALLOCATION*. The ALIAS keyword indicates that the name for this field within the RPG program will be REQUIRED_ALLOCATION.

```
dcl-f myfile ALIAS;
```

```
read myfile;
if required_allocation <> 0
and size > 0;
   ...
```

An externally-described data structure or LIKEREC data structure defined with type *ALL can be used as the result data structure for any I/O operation. See File Operations

```
dcl-f myfile usage(*input : *output : *update);
dcl-ds ds extname('MYFILE' : *ALL);

read myfile ds;
update myfmt ds;
write myfmt ds;
```

When a data structure is defined for a record format of a DISK file using LIKEREC without the second parameter, and the output buffer layout is identical to the input buffer layout, the data structure can be used as the result data structure for any I/O operation.

```
dcl-f myfile usage(*input : *output : *update);
dcl-ds ds likerec(fmt);

read myfile ds;
update myfmt ds;
write myfmt ds;
```

Summary of RPG Enhancements

As you can see, the RPG compiler team in IBM has been very busy adding to what I would call the most esoteric parts of the language. Whereas RPG and RPG/400 were and are in some cases very simple languages, RPGIV may very well now be the most complex language in existence. Of course, to be good in your business, thankfully you don't need to know it all-all at once.

Unfortunately, the added complexity of RPGIV, as much as its esoteric portions make it appealing to just the best programmers in the world.Not everybody is in that class. Some are simply separated from that class by time and experience. Some never will get it all. Some never will get it at all.

Nonetheless, with such capabilities, RPGIV code that has a combination of this and that and the other high level functions of the new language will appear in shops with normal attrition. Programmers who replace programmers will have the toughest times if they have ignored the new functions and their predecessors have used the most esoteric functions of them all. Shop standards for home-grown code are vital. Packed code may be more difficult to change.

Perhaps one day, some RPG programmers will long for the days when BAL and AutoCoder and SPS ruled the days. At least their scope was limited. God bless you all and enjoy RPG to the fullest! Despite its new found complexity, it can be the easist programming language and the most productive that can be found anywhere. Final Thoughts or Sour grapes?

If you need stuff in this chapter, I would be surprised. What I have asked IBM for—for many years is a natural way with a device like WORKSTN to talk to a Web browser. Since all IBM programmers are great programmers in C, C++, C#, Pascal, etc. their goal has been to make RPGIV more like other languages and abandon the ease of use nature of the language, which was at its peak with System/34 and System/38. George Farr, IBM's Chief person on RPG/ RPGIV for many years, a brilliant man who should be the head of Java development is responsible for the RPG Fiasco. George is a #10 programmer and so he does not appreciate how on IBM midrange systems, lowly #1's actually can produce some nice applications when they do not have to worry about the esoteric "crap" that George and his cohorts built into the RPGIV language.

C'est La Vie

Lets Go Publish! Books by Brian Kelly

(Sold at www.bookhawkers.com; Amazon.com, and Kindle.).

LETS GO PUBLISH! is proud to announce that more AS/400 and Power i books are becoming available to help you inexpensively address your AS/400 and Power i education and training needs: Our general titles precede specific AS/400 and other technology books. Check out these great patriotic books which precede the tech books in the list.

IBM i Technical Books

I had a Dream IBM Could be #1 Again
The title is self-explanatory

Whatever Happened to the IBM AS /400?
The question is answered in this new book.

The All Everything Operating System:
Story about IBM's finest operating system; its facilities; how it came to be.

The All-Everything Machine
Story about IBM's finest computer server.

Chip Wars
The story of ongoing wars between Intel and AMD and upcoming wars between Intel and IBM. Book may cause you to buy / sell somebody's stock.

Can the AS/400 Survive IBM?
Exciting book about the AS/400 in a IBM i World.

The AS/400 & IBM i Pocket SQL Guide.
Complete Pocket Guide to SQL as implemented on IBM i. A must have for SQL developers new to IBM i. It is very compact yet very comprehensive and it is example driven. Written in a part tutorial and part reference style, Tons of SQL coding samples, from the simple to the sublime.

The AS/400 & IBM i Pocket Query Guide.
If you have been spending money for years educating your Query users, and you find you are still spending, or you've given up, this book is right for you. This one QuikCourse covers all Query options.

The AS/400 & IBM I RPG & RPG IV Developers Guide.
Comprehensive RPG & RPGIV Textbook -- Over 900 pages. This is the one RPG book to have if you are not having more than one. All areas of the language covered smartly in a convenient sized book Annotated PowerPoint's available for self-study (extra fee for self-study package)

The IBM I RPG Tutorial and Lab Guide
Your guide to a hands-on Lab experience. Contains CD with Lab exercises and PowerPoint's. Great companion to the above textbook or can be used as a standalone for student Labs or tutorial purposes

The AS/400 & IBM i Pocket Developers' Guide.
Comprehensive Pocket Guide to all of the AS/400 and IBM i development tools - DFU, SDA, etc. You'll also get a big bonus with chapters on Architecture, Work Management, and Subfile Coding. This book was updated in 2016..

The AS/400 & IBM i Pocket Database Guide.
Complete Pocket Guide to IBM i integrated relational database (DB2/400) – physical and logical files and DB operations - Union, Projection, Join, etc. Written in a part tutorial and part reference style. Tons of DDS coding samples.

Getting Started with The WebSphere Development Studio Client for IBM i (WDSc).
Focus is on client server and the Web. Includes CODE/400, VisualAge RPG, CGI, WebFacing, and WebSphere Studio. Case study continues from the Interactive Book.

The IBM i Pocket WebFacing Primer.
This book gets you started immediately with WebFacing. A sample case study is used as the basis for a conversion to WebFacing. Interactive 5250 application is WebFaced in a case study form before your eyes.

Getting Started with WebSphere Express Server for IBM i
Step-by-Step Guide for Setting up Express Servers
A comprehensive guide to setting up and using WebSphere Express. It is filled with examples, and structured in a tutorial fashion for easy learning.

The WebFacing Application Design & Development Guide:
Step by Step Guide to designing green screen IBM i apps for the Web. Both a systems design guide and a developers guide. Book helps you understand how to design and develop Web applications using regular RPG or COBOL programs.

The IBM i Express Web Implementer's Guide. Your one stop guide to ordering, installing, fixing, configuring, and using WebSphere Express, Apache, WebFacing, IBM i Access for Web, and HATS/LE.

Seniors, Social Security & the Minimum Wage
The impact of the minimum wage on Social Security Beneficiaries

How to Write Your First Book and Publish It With CreateSpace
This books teaches how to create a book with MSWord and then publish it with CreateSpace. No need to find a traditional publisher.

Healthcare & Welfare Accountability The Trump Way
Why should somebody win the Lottery & not pay back welfare?

The Trump Plan Solves Student Debt Crisis. .
This is the Trump solution for new student debt and the existing $1.3 Trillion student debt accumulation.

Take the Train to Myrtle Beach The Trump Way.
Tells all about the Donald Trump Plan to restart private passenger railway systems in America while it tells you how to get to Myrtle Beach by Train.